The 72nd
New York Infantry
in the Civil War

The 72nd New York Infantry in the Civil War

A History and Roster

RICK BARRAM

McFarland & Company, Inc., Publishers
Jefferson, North Carolina

LIBRARY OF CONGRESS CATALOGUING-IN-PUBLICATION DATA

Barram, Rick, 1959–
The 72nd New York Infantry in the Civil War : a history and roster / Rick Barram.
    p.   cm.
Includes bibliographical references and index.

ISBN 978-0-7864-7644-2 (softcover : acid free paper) ∞
ISBN 978-1-4766-1419-9 (ebook)

1. United States. Army. New York Infantry Regiment, 72nd (1861–1864)
2. United States—History—Civil War, 1861–1865—Regimental histories.
3. New York (State)—History—Civil War, 1861–1865—Regimental histories.
4. United States—History—Civil War, 1861–1865—Campaigns.   I. Title.
E523.572nd.B37 2014   973.7'447—dc23   2013050520

BRITISH LIBRARY CATALOGUING DATA ARE AVAILABLE

© 2014 Rick Barram. All rights reserved

No part of this book may be reproduced or transmitted in any form or by any means, electronic or mechanical, including photocopying or recording, or by any information storage and retrieval system, without permission in writing from the publisher.

On the cover: artwork *Union Soldiers Charging at Gettysburg*, 1881, Paul Philippoteaux © 2014 PicturesNOW

Manufactured in the United States of America

McFarland & Company, Inc., Publishers
Box 611, Jefferson, North Carolina 28640
www.mcfarlandpub.com

Table of Contents

Acknowledgments vii
Introduction 1

Epoch I: Beginnings
1—Becoming Third Excelsior 3
2—Defense of Washington 15
3—Pacifying Southern Maryland 28

Epoch II: The Seat of War
4—Journey to Williamsburg 49
5—Seven Pines and on to Richmond 63
6—Going Backwards 75

Epoch III: Agony in Northern Virginia
7—Serving Under Pope 85
8—On to Fredericksburg 100

Epoch IV: The Bloody Season
9—Hooker in Command 113
10—Gettysburg 131

Epoch V: A Hard Conclusion
11—In Pursuit of Lee 151
12—The Struggle to Petersburg 174
13—End of the Seventy-Second 200

Regimental Roster by Company 207

Chapter Notes 283
Bibliography 299
Index 303

Acknowledgments

Among those who deserve thanks for getting this book to completion is one of the old boys, an original member of company B, Henri LeFevre-Brown, whose drive helped to establish the 72nd's veterans' association, leading to the creation of the first comprehensive regimental history within all of the Excelsior Brigade regiments. *The 72nd New York Infantry in the Civil War: A History and Roster* was conceived under the mandate that unless it could go substantially beyond his work in scope, it wasn't worth pursuing. Thank you, Henri, for giving us a place to start.

Going beyond Brown's work would not have been possible without the four major letter collections that made this story possible. So I offer my deepest and profound thanks to Diana Firth, who way back in 1999 sent me her collection of letters written by James Dean. James Dean joined the 72nd just before the fight at Fredericksburg, and his 70 or so letters provided the first look into the regiment at a level deeper than what Brown had provided. The letters of Emerson F. Merrell, which allowed us a look at the more cynical side of soldiering, were used with the permission of Samuel Sandoli, to whom I am very grateful. The letters published in the *Fredonia Censor* written by Arthur McKinstry, which offered such an intimate look at the early stages of the war, were provided by the Barker Historical Museum, and I wish to especially thank Douglas Sheppard, a volunteer with the museum, for his personal efforts to locate and send me the McKinstry articles. Next, my fellow historian Phil Palin, who for the past 15 years has been sending me any number of bits and pieces of 72nd lore from the Gowanda Historical Society along with pieces from other historical societies throughout western New York. Phil provided the collection of Hiram Stoddard letters, which presented such tender and poignant insight into the life of a Civil War soldier.

My good friend Mark Richardson probably read more versions of this book than anyone; without his encouragement this project probably would not have been undertaken. His knowledge of the regiment and of Civil War history was critical in shaping this book. Mark also brought an engineer's sensibility to his editing of the piece, pointing out any inconsistencies in movements, directions, terrain, and troop dispositions or speaking up when things weren't quite as clear as they should be.

A huge thank-you to another friend, Ginger Geiger, district librarian for Gateway Unified School District, for her time spent on this work. Ginger brought a valuable blend of grammar knowledge, understanding of nonfiction writing, love of history, and patience to this project, which stretched over years. Her input helped keep the tone and voice of this piece on track during the long process of writing, editing, and rewriting.

Elizabeth Fannin came to this project late; I came to know her after she joined our reenacting group and after much of the early writing on this book was finished. Her passion for history along with her deep and critical knowledge of editing and the citation process has allowed this book to move forward in a way that otherwise might have taken months longer.

There are two important others for whom I owe my thanks and whose creativity can be seen in these pages. My son, Kyle Barram, helped me to see the potential of the chapters' scenes, keeping this work the "action-adventure" story I intended and not merely a staid recounting of events. And here's to my father, Bob Barram, who read my pages with enthusiasm, despite only a general knowledge of the subject matter. Though less concerned about the great movements of armies and their generals, he championed those parts of the work that focused on the little guys, the private soldiers, whose blood and heartache formed the tragic cornerstone of this war and the 72nd's story. His input served as a check when the writing became too loaded with jargon or obscure military references, keeping the piece more accessible to the average reader.

On the technical side of things, my thanks go out to my friend Patrick Parsons, whose computer and map making skills helped to create the maps for this work. Maps are especially critical to the success of most historical works and especially to military histories when mere words cannot do the scope of the action justice.

Another deep thanks to two of my student assistants at Central Valley High School. Robert and Shyla both did yeoman service in compiling and editing the roster portion of this work, a job that was both demanding and tedious. Thanks, guys.

Next I'd like to acknowledge four writers whose work, although not all in the field of Civil War history, inspired me to find this work's voice. James Hornfischer's books about World War II naval action paint vivid accounts of individuals set against momentous events. The exciting writing contained within his books set a kind of de facto standard for many of the battle scenes in this work. By asking whether it was "Hornfischeresque" enough, my readers and I knew what was expected. The vivid and action driven work of Rick Atkinson, another World War II writer, contained a number of literary conventions that helped to draw me in as reader by giving the story a personal and often humorous flair. I hope I prove a worthy disciple of these conventions in my writing. Among Civil War writers is Gordon Rhea, whose four-piece work on the Overland Campaign demonstrated how to flawlessly flow the action between all levels of command, from company, through brigade and divisional and beyond. Finally, John Ferling's work on the American Revolutionary War helped to unlock a problem within my journalist's mind: the question of dealing with an incomplete historical record. Ferling's work demonstrated for me how, despite small gaps in direct accounts, the writer could seamlessly move the story along using reasonable speculation or references from other common occurrences of the era. Using techniques learned from all of these authors, I hope this book reads more like a novel than a history text.

Finally, my thanks to all my friends within the hobby of Civil War reenacting and the modern recreation of the 72nd New York, whose interest and enthusiasm for history proved an inexhaustible source of energy and inspiration. By embracing the past and keeping alive the spirits of the Old Boys of '61, they helped bring the sights, sounds, and smells of the campaign to life and provided me a palpable context for the story of the 72nd.

Introduction

By the summer of '65 practically all who had served with the 72nd New York Infantry were back home. A few had been promoted to positions that kept them away, a few more still lingered in northern hospitals, but for those who had survived, the war was now memory. Most carried some kind of mark indicating their service: scars from a cut or burn, a missing chunk of flesh, a twisted finger, a limp, something. For others the scars were unseen. Returning veterans sometimes slept on floors for months, unused to the comfort of a bed; others kept shoes positioned in every room for fear of being without; still others woke screaming in the dead of night. For all it was a time they would never forget.

Four years earlier, towns across the country had been frantically gathering men to fight. In the north, the war was called the "Great Rebellion." In eleven Southern states, men joined to fight in the "War of Northern Aggression." Men joined the fight for any number of reasons: for country, for friends, or for an inspirational idea or leader. In the state of New York 5,000 men were inspired to join a brigade being formed by Daniel Edgar Sickles. Dan Sickles was a former congressman, lifelong politician, rogue, philanderer, and acquitted murderer. He was many things, and men were drawn to him. His brigade would be called the Excelsior Brigade, after the state's motto, meaning "Ever Upward," and it promised to represent all of New York. Excitedly, men from New York City all the way west to the smallest villages along Lake Erie's shore joined companies that would eventually serve under Sickles.

Sickles' Excelsior Brigade consisted of five regiments. All five drew men from across the state, but one, his Third Regiment, exemplified the trans-state inspiration of Sickles. With companies drawn from New York City, upstate and western counties, and even New Jersey, the regiment eventually designated the 72nd New York would compile a fighting record few other regiments would rival. Four of the five Excelsior regiments would be listed among Colonel Fox's 300 fighting regiments, but the 72nd would lead the five in total casualties. In three separate engagements, Williamsburg, Chancellorsville, and Gettysburg, the 72nd would take losses equivalent to one-fourth or more. Few regiments in all of New York would surpass the 72nd's record of sacrifice.

This is the story of these fighting men told in part in their own words. Using letters written from the field only moments after their hottest actions, officers' reports, and memoirs laid down after a lifetime of thoughtful reflection, the full picture of their service is brought to light. Here is the excitement of a new recruit, anxious for blood; the despair of veterans, unable to foresee a campaign's successful end; and the cool, analytical dispassion of the colonels and generals. This is a "brogans-up" view of the war, looking at all aspects: the camping, the marching, the fighting, and the dying.

The Excelsior Brigade was with the Army of the Potomac's III Corps from the beginning. Few brigades embodied the history of the III Corps more than the Excelsior Brigade, and no other regiment within the brigade saw more action than the 72nd New York. Unlike some unit histories that draw narrowly from the perspectives of one or only a few men, *The 72nd New York Infantry in the Civil War: A History and Roster* draws from numerous collections of letters, diary entries, officers' reports, veterans' remembrances, and newspaper articles to paint the most complete picture of the 72nd's service from its inception in 1861 to its discharge in summer of '64. The entire strategic picture of their movements and engagements is examined so the reader will always know the role this regiment played. While focused on the 72nd, this work also examines the struggles of the Excelsior Brigade as it fought both the Confederates and within itself as officers bickered over questions of command and competency.

With the men's three-year enlistments up, the 72nd didn't finish the war, but during its service over 1,200 men filled and refilled its ranks, with over half becoming casualties. During their service the 72nd never single-handedly won a battle or defended a flank against overwhelming odds, and sometimes they retreated in disorder. But they did their duty and slugged it out when prudence may have dictated withdrawal, bringing honor to themselves and the state they represented. These men deserve to be remembered, and this is their story.

A Note About the Sources

This work was assembled from a wide range of source materials, from letters and accounts not previously published to iconic pieces of Civil War literature. To the extent possible, this history of the 72nd New York is told using the words and recollections of men in the regiment who lived and experienced these events. Some events depicted have been recounted by only one individual while other events are found in many sources. When only one source is available, the citation will of course reflect this source, but when multiple sources describe the same event, the source most immediate to the regiment will be noted in the citation. Primary sources will always take priority over secondary sources, but in cases when large events or periods of time must be compressed for the sake of space and to advance the story, reliable secondary sources are used and cited. Every care has been made to report the history of the regiment as truthfully as possible while rendering the context within which it served.

Epoch I : Beginnings

1. Becoming Third Excelsior

It was well after two in the morning, and it didn't take the old man long to fall asleep. The trip had been long and he was in frail health. Unable to sleep for their excitement, the two boys crept out of the room, being sure not to wake David's father. The two had several miles ahead of them and now was not the time to sleep, this being the first morning of their greatest adventure.

Only weeks before, Southern rebels had shelled Fort Sumter, and with President Lincoln's call for troops, companies of volunteers were forming all over New York. David Parker and his friend Martin Boyden had hoped to join "Captain" James Brown's company gathering in Jamestown, not far from David's home at Ellery Center in western New York; both towns were mere dots on the map. Eager to get things started, David rode into Jamestown the day after learning Captain Brown was forming a company. Upon arriving in Jamestown young Parker was informed by Captain Brown that he was too late; the company was full and all uniforms had been distributed.

David was only 18 yet considered himself an ardent Republican, so when Lincoln's call for enlistment came he was ready. At Sunday services in Jamestown, Brown's newly formed company attended en masse, and young Parker was there, listening intently to the sermon. The day's sermon was intended for the men of the company. While sermons in the past certainly would have called for support of Lincoln and restoration of the Union, this would have been different. With a company of future soldiers seated in the pews, war was no longer an abstract notion about duty, patriotism, and sacrifice. Men were going off to fight and some wouldn't return, although on this day it is doubtful anyone imagined just how many of these men would not come back.

As the family returned home from services, David announced to his father his desire to enlist, and to do so immediately. Charles, his father, was opposed to the idea of his son going to war; after all, he was young, and there were recruits enough, he reasoned; better to wait awhile. Grandson of a New Hampshire soldier of the Revolution, David argued with his reluctant father. David described those men he thought best suited to go to war: the young, the single with no responsibilities, in short, men just like him. David continued to explain to his father that Captain William Stevens was forming a company up in Dunkirk, destined for the same regiment as Brown's. Once enrolled, David might be able to transfer back to the Jamestown company. The elder Parker gave in and agreed to take David and his friend Martin Boyden that night the two dozen or so miles to meet with Stevens.

The three started off at nightfall. They reached Cassadaga by two o'clock in the morning, leaving them eight miles outside of Dunkirk. After finding a hotel and resting, the three planned to continue on in the morning, but the boys had other ideas. With the senior Parker now asleep, the boys snuck out, telling the hosteler they were leaving and to bid David's father that he should follow in the morning at his leisure.

Upon reaching Dunkirk, the boys found most of the town was still asleep. Finding Stevens' home, the boys waited on his porch until the captain rose. When Stevens finally met with the two, he told them he had considered his company full just the night before. However, he noted that there might still be hope as he believed there were several men whose parents were trying to induce them away and another few he doubted would pass the doctor's inspection. Stevens mentioned misgivings about David's friend Martin, though. Martin Boyden was somewhat undersized and had poor front teeth, which would make the tearing of cartridges and clinching of bullets a problem. But Stevens did like their pluck, complimenting both on their grit, saying, "You may go in, and if the doctor passes you, I will take you."[1]

Stevens' unit was part of the long-serving 68th New York Militia under Colonel David Forbes, centered in Chautauqua County, and was one of two companies based in Dunkirk. Early on there was an attempt to have the entirety of the 68th accepted for active service, but "Secretary Cameron could give no encouragement to the project."[2] Impressed with Stevens' "energy and military spirit," Secretary of War Simon Cameron subsequently invited the two Dunkirk companies, one under Stevens and the other under Patrick Barrett, to prepare for active service.[3]

Later that day, both boys passed the doctor's inspection and were told to report to the town's armory yard to commence drilling. Soon both were subject to a rain of curses in both English and German from a diminutive sergeant, Daniel Loeb. Loeb was the local tavern keeper and sergeant of Stevens' militia unit, which had recently taken second place in a national drill competition. Loeb's militiamen formed the foundation of the new company, and no one took more pride in marching than Sgt. Loeb. David and Martin were now unmistakably in the army.

Across the state of New York, men were joining their nearby companies. Some saw it as their duty to restore the Union and subdue the Rebellion; others joined for the excitement or to avoid being labeled "cowards." Among those who enlisted were nineteen-year-old Emerson Merrell and 18-year-old Lorey Wilder, neither of whom intended to join. Emerson in fact had no more thought of joining than he did of "murdering myself," he later confessed. Yet in nearly an instant after their conversation turned to joining up, they did. Motivated by what Emerson described to his mother as a "good cause" and an effort to "execute it," the two were now volunteers.[4]

Emerson was the oldest of ten children living on his family's farm near the small hamlet of Coventry, Chenango County, in the central part of New York, not far from the border with Pennsylvania. Unlike David Parker, Emerson was not an ardent Republican and often found the motives of Lincoln suspicious. Whatever the reason, the two found themselves in Delhi, the hub of recruiting activity for the area. There, Captain Robert T. Johnson was putting together a company of men, intent on being part of a brigade being assembled by former United States Congressman Daniel Sickles.

The two pairs of boys were separated by half a state but had signed their names only a week apart. Both companies were being raised with the intent of falling in with Dan Sickles' brigade. Though their respective captains didn't yet know it, both companies would find themselves belonging to the Third Regiment of Sickles' soon to be renowned Excelsior Brigade.

To say Daniel Edgar Sickles was a man of action was an understatement. By the time war broke out he was already well known both inside and outside of New York. As a young man, he had been active in Democratic Party politics and in the political machinery of New York City, unashamed to use intimidation or dirty tricks to advance his candidate's objectives. Sickles was as ambitious in politics as he was fond of female companionship, be the ladies unmarried or otherwise.

But eventually the roguish Sickles' career took a fateful turn. In 1857 Sickles had arrived in Washington as a first term congressman from New York's Third District accompanied by his wife of five years, Teresa. Teresa, who was only 16 when they married, was a lovely and charming hostess who carried on her husband's expectations to maintain hearth and home while he carried on various other indulgences. In February of '59 it came as a shock to Dan to discover that his supposedly faithful wife had carried on an affair of her own with family friend Phillip Barton Key, U.S. attorney for the District of Columbia and grandson of Francis Scott Key, author of the "Star Spangled Banner."

Dan confronted Teresa on the night of February 26 with evidence of her shame and obtained a signed confession. The next day, the still distraught Sickles looked out his window only to see the unsuspecting Key attempting to signal Teresa. Overcome with rage, Sickles collected up two derringers and a revolver, then stormed out of the house toward Key. Raging forward, Sickles fired one of the revolvers. Key vainly attempted to flee through Lafayette Park, just across from the White House. Sickles kept firing, hitting Key multiple times and killing him.[5]

The trial that followed was a sensation, covered by newspapers nationwide. Sickles' defense team included many of the finest legal minds of the day, including among other bright legal lights Edwin Stanton, Lincoln's future secretary of war, as well as Francis Thomas Meagher, Irish nationalist and future commander of the famed Irish Brigade. Sickles' defense was simple yet brilliant: temporary insanity brought on by Key's vile seducing of Dan's formerly fair and virtuous wife. Most papers supported Sickles, and when the verdict of "not guilty" was read, the jury stood and cheered. Sickles was riding a wave of popularity thanks to his decisive and manly action, but when the congressman kindly allowed the soiled Teresa back into his home, the press and public turned on him. With critics still reeling in disbelief over the acquittal of this admitted murderer, former supporters were shocked that he allowed his unfaithful wife's act of betrayal to go unpunished; Sickles found himself standing alone.[6]

Sickles' support had sunk so far he didn't seek reelection in 1860. For several months he was a man without purpose. Then a new opportunity began to reveal itself: the United States was heading into civil war.

On April 14, 1861, Fort Sumter was shelled and taken by the Rebels. On that day Daniel Sickles became a rare breed of man, a war–Democrat. With many laying blame for the war at the feet of the Republican president, any Democrat who favored war against the South, especially a Democrat with the level of notoriety Sickles enjoyed, was a potential asset to the new Lincoln administration.

Soon after Fort Sumter, Sickles and some friends were enjoying drinks at fashionable Delmonico's Restaurant in lower Manhattan. As Dan lamented his present circumstance of practicing law with his father and professed how he longed to join the Union cause, the conversation naturally turned towards war. As talk progressed, Sickles suggested to long-time friend Captain William Wiley that if Wiley would raise a company or regiment, Sickles would happily join it as a private. But after more discussion and more drinks, Wiley came to realize it was Sickles who possessed the leadership qualities, political ties, and drive for

Organization and Leadership

III Corps

S.P. Heintzelman, Brig. Gen.	Mar. 13, 1862 - Oct. 30, 1862
Geo. Stoneman, Brig. Gen.	Oct. 30, 1862 - Feb. 5, 1863
D.E. Sickles, Maj. Gen.	Feb. 5, 1863 - July 2, 1863
W.H. French, Maj. Gen.	July 7, 1863 - Mar. 24, 1864

First Division

Fitz John Porter, Brig. Gen.	Mar. 13, 1862 - May 18, 1862
Division transferred to 5th Provisional Corps May 18, 1862	
Reorganized from Third Division, III Corps, Aug. 5, 1862	
Philip Kearny, Brig. Gen.	Aug. 5, 1862 - Sept. 1, 1862
D. B. Birney, Brig. Gen.	Sept. 1, 1862 - Sept. 13, 1862
Geo. Stoneman, Brig. Gen.	Sept. 13, 1862 - Oct. 30, 1862
D.B. Birney, Maj. Gen.	Oct. 30, 1862 - Mar. 24, 1864

Second Division

Joseph Hooker, Brig. Gen.	Mar. 13, 1862 - Sept. 5, 1862
D. E. Sickles, Brig. Gen.	Sept. 5, 1862 - Jan. 12, 1863
J.B. Carr, Brig. Gen.	Jan. 12, 1863 - Feb. 8, 1863
H.G. Berry, Brig. Gen.	Feb. 8, 1863 - May 3, 1863
J.B. Carr, Brig. Gen.	May 3, 1863 - May 23, 1863
A.A. Humphrey, Maj. Gen.	May 28, 1863 - July 9, 1863
Henry Prince, Brig. Gen.	July 10, 1863 - Mar. 24, 1864

Third Division

C.S. Hamilton, Brig. Gen.	Mar. 13, 1862- Apr. 30, 1862
Philip Kearny, Brig. Gen.	Apr. 30, 1862- Aug. 5, 1862
Designation changed to First Division.	
Reorganized Nov. 8, 1862	
A.W. Whipple, Brig. Gen.	Nov. 8, 1862 - May 3, 1863
C.K. Graham, Brig. Gen.	May 3, 1863 - June 20, 1863
W.L. Elliott, Brig. Gen.	July, 10, 1863 - Oct. 5, 1863
J.B. Carr, Brig. Gen.	Oct. 5, 1863 - Mar. 24, 1864

First Brigade, Second Division
Old Hooker Brigade

H.M. Naglee, Brig. Gen.	Mar. 13, 1862 - Apr. 27, 1862
C. Grover, Brig. Gen.	Apr. 27, 1862 - Sept. 16, 1862
J.B. Carr, Brig. Gen.	Sept. 16, 1862 - Jan. 12, 1863
Wm. Blaisdell, Col. 11th Mass. Inf	Jan. 12, 1863 - Feb. 8, 1863
J.B. Carr, Brig. Gen.	Feb. 8, 1863 - May 3, 1863
Wm. Blaisdell, Col. 11th Mass. Inf	May 3, 1863 - May 23, 1863
J.B. Carr, Brig. Gen.	May 23, 1863 – Oct. 5, 1863
R. McAllister, Col. 11th N.J. Inf.	Oct. 5, 1863 - Dec. 1863
Wm. Blaisdell, Col. 11th Mass. Inf.	Dec. 1864 - Mar. 24, 1864

1st Michigan Inf.	Mar., 1862 - Mar., 1862
1st Mass. Inf.	Mar., 1862 - Mar., 1864
11th Mass. Inf.	Mar., 1862 - Mar., 1864
2nd New Hampshire Inf.	Mar., 1862 - Feb., 1863
26th Penn. Inf.	Mar., 1862 - Mar., 1864
16th Mass. Inf.	June, 1862 - Mar., 1864
120th New York Inf.	Oct., 1862 - Dec., 1862
11th New Jersey Inf	Nov., 1862 - Mar., 1864
84th Penna. Inf.	June, 1863 - Mar., 1864
12th New Hampshire Inf.	June, 1863 - July, 1863

Second Brigade, Second Division
Excelsior Brigade

N. Taylor, Col. 72nd N.Y. Inf.	Mar. 13, 1862 - May 11, 1862
J. J. Abercrombie, Brig. Gen.	May 11, 1862 - May 24, 1862
D. E. Sickles, Brig. Gen.	May 24, 1862 - July 16, 1862
N. Taylor, Col. 72nd N.Y. Inf.	July 16, 1862 - Sept. 5, 1862
Geo. B. Hall, Col. 71st N.Y. Inf.	Sept. 5, 1862 - Dec. 24, 1862
J.W. Revere, Brig. Gen.	Dec. 24, 1862 - Feb., 1863
J.E. Farnum, Lt.-Col. 70th N.Y. Inf.	Feb., 1863 - Feb., 1863
C. K. Graham, Brig. Gen.	Mar., 1863 - May 3, 1863
J.W. Revere, Brig. Gen.	May 3, 1863 - May, 1863
J.E. Farnum, Col. 70th N.Y. Inf.	May, 1863 - July 11, 1863
W. R. Brewster, Col. 73rd N.Y. Inf.	July 11, 1863 - July 23, 1863
F. B. Spinola, Brig. Gen.	July 23, 1863 - July 24, 1863
Thos. Rafferty, Maj. 71st N.Y. Inf.	July 24, 1863 - Aug. 10, 1863
J.E. Farnum, Col. 70th N.Y. Inf.	Aug. 10, 1863 - Jan., 1864
W. R. Brewster, Col. 73rd N.Y. Inf.	Jan., 1864 - Feb., 1864
John Leonard, Lt.-Col. 72nd N.Y. Inf.	Feb., 1864 - Mar. 24, 1864
W. R. Brewster, Col. 73rd N.Y. Inf.	

70th New York Inf.	Mar., 1862 - Mar., 1864
71st New York Inf.	Mar., 1862 - Mar., 1864
72nd New York Inf.	Mar., 1862 - Mar., 1864
73rd New York Inf.	Mar., 1862 - Mar., 1864
74th New York Inf.	Mar., 1862 - Mar., 1864
120th New York Inf.	Dec., 1862 - Mar., 1864

Third Brigade, Second Division
New Jersey Blues

S. H. Starr, Col. 5th N. J. Inf.	Mar. 13, 1862 - May 3, 1862
F. E. Patterson, Brig. Gen.	May 3, 1862 - May 31, 1862
S. H. Starr, Col. 5th N.J. Inf.	May 31, 1862 - June 1, 1862
J. B. Carr, Col. 2nd N.Y. Inf.	June 1, 1862 - June 6, 1862
F. E. Patterson, Brig. Gen.	June 6, 1862 - Nov. 22, 1862
J.W. Revere, Col. 7th N.J. Inf.	Nov. 22, 1862 - Dec. 25, 1862
Gershom Mott, Brig. Gen.	Dec. 25, 1862 - May 3, 1863
W.J. Sewell, Col. 5th N.J. Inf.	May 3, 1863 - June, 1863
G. C. Burling, Col. 6th N.J. Inf.	June, 1863 - Aug. 29, 1863
Gershom Mott, Brig. Gen.	Aug. 29, 1863 - Feb. 16, 1864
G. C. Burling, Col. 6th N.J. Inf.	Feb. 16, 1864 - ——, 1864*
Gershom Mott, Brig. Gen.	——, 1864 - Mar. 24, 1864*

*as indicated in *Dyer's Compendium*

5th New Jersey Inf.	Mar. 1862- Mar., 1864
6th New Jersey Inf.	Mar., 1862 - Mar., 1864
7th New Jersey Inf.	Mar., 1862 - Mar., 1864
8th New Jersey Inf.	Mar., 1862 - Mar., 1864
2nd New York Inf.	June, 1862 - Mar., 1863
115th Penna Inf.	July, 1862 - Mar., 1863
2nd New Hampshire Inf.	June, 1863 - July, 1863

III Corps disbanded in March, 1864
72nd New York to II Corps

the raising of a regiment. Soon a counterproposal was completed: if Sickles would lead a regiment, Wiley would help raise, arm, and equip it. Enthusiastically, the two men quickly received authorization from Governor Edwin Morgan to raise a regiment and obtained $500 from a local Union Defense Committee to get started. After two weeks of handbill postings and speech making, which they ensured were generously covered by the local papers, Sickles and Wiley had their regiment of eight companies.[7]

About this same time, Lincoln issued a proclamation on May 3 calling for volunteers to serve three-year enlistments. Sickles had certainly been successful in raising his regiment; now Governor Morgan asked him to go further, to raise a brigade of five regiments. Sickles, for whom rank was not unimportant, leapt at the notion of wearing the single star of a brigadier general rather than the eagle of a colonel; the creation of his Excelsior Brigade was underway.[8]

Driven by patriotism, duty, war fever or whatever it might be called, men were attracted to Sickles' sense of purpose and determination. Four hundred workers from the Navy Yards of New York joined, while a former colleague, Dennis Meehan, from the state assembly, brought another 100 men.[9] Sickles even accepted men who traded jail terms for enlistment. By the middle of the month the man who had seemed alone in the world could now claim 3,000 men as his followers and comrades.[10] Dan had his brigade.

Sickles had christened his congregation the Excelsior Brigade in deference to the state's motto, meaning "ever upward." The Excelsior title also had a secondary meaning beyond just reflecting the motto. By using the state's motto, Sickles laid claim that this brigade, unlike regiments and brigades raised only from certain cities or counties, would represent all of New York State. While he did indeed have plenty of men hailing just from New York City, there were whole companies from the upper and western parts of the Empire State. There were also several entire companies of men from New Jersey, Michigan, Massachusetts and Pennsylvania, demonstrating that Sickles' appeal extended not only to New York but to hundreds of men from outside the state, all anxious to get a crack at the Rebels.[11]

With forty companies either in hand or committed, and seemingly at the peak of his recruiting success, Sickles received a telegram from New York governor Morgan ordering him to disband all but eight of his companies. It would seem Sickles' efforts were so successful in New York City that there was growing dissatisfaction from the interior counties. Some had to go: 2,000 men by Dan's count. Soon word filtered out that the brigade had been disbanded, only independent regiments remained, and Dan was reduced back to colonel. But Sickles was sure he smelled the unmistakable stench of politics and was sure that Republican governor Morgan was looking to derail Democrat Sickles' appointment to brigadier general. Figuring that two could play at politics, Sickles took the next train to Washington and arranged a meeting with Lincoln himself.

Dan proposed his brigade be accepted directly into Federal service as United States Volunteers, not state troops. Lincoln liked the idea but worried about what states might say in protest. Yet in the end, after consulting with Secretary of War Simon Cameron, the president instructed Sickles to hold his men in readiness and promised they would be accepted. On May 18, 1861, Lincoln granted special authority to Sickles to form his brigade of U.S. Volunteers.[12] Sickles had managed to outmaneuver Governor Morgan. He still had his brigade and most importantly, had his provisional appointment to brigadier general.[13]

Back in New York things were not going so well. Wiley, acting as quartermaster for the brigade, was having difficulties handling the large number of men. Using the upscale Delmonico's as his headquarters, Wiley had hired two cooks from the restaurant to feed his men. But the gourmet chefs were unskilled at meeting the needs of 3,000 hungry customers. To complicate matters, the cost of feeding the multitudes was enormous: $12,000 in the first two weeks alone, with the cost growing as more and more recruits filed in. Sanitation was also a growing problem as the brigade quickly outgrew the state barracks they were using for housing. The excess men were packed into rented lofts and apartments, many barren and unheated. Many men arrived with only the clothes on their backs. Lacking the basics such as soap and razors, they roamed the streets in an unshaven, disheveled manner, frightening the local ladies. Threatened with eviction by the health department, Sickles struck a deal with a local bath house and a Crosby Street barber to bathe, shave, and shear the entire brigade. The mass purification staved off the health department for a while, but many of the men were growing bored and disgusted.[14] This was not the war they'd signed up for; they wanted at the Rebels.

With no disbanding of the brigade in sight, Governor Morgan started to fume over being both defied and outmaneuvered by Sickles. Given the deplorable state of Sickles' men, Morgan easily justified expelling the Excelsiors from the state barracks. Sickles, knowing morale was suffering and his mob badly required a metamorphosis into real soldiers, needed to act quickly. First getting permission to camp his men at the Fashion Race Track on Long Island, Dan shortly after obtained consent from the Federal government to use some land on Staten Island until the brigade was sworn in.[15]

The nascent Excelsior Brigade moved to Staten Island near the middle of May. Here were the wide open spaces a general would need to build a command. Dan christened the place Camp Scott in honor of the revered Union general of the army, but still problems persisted. Few of the requested tents had arrived, forcing most of the men to sleep in open fields, subject to attack from millions of bloodthirsty mosquitoes. Dan partially remedied the situation with the purchase, on credit of course, of some circus tents from his old friend P.T. Barnum. But other shortages remained. The brigade had borrowed a mere 300 muskets, which necessitated their being shuttled among companies on drill. Food was in short supply, and fresh stocks soon spoiled due to lack of refrigeration. Needless to say, among Sickles' recruits, many were becoming disillusioned with army life.[16] There was also the great uncertainty of being neither U.S. nor state troops; plus, they were suffering a miserable existence with few supplies, little shelter, and even worse food. Some men tried to get out of the whole trying ordeal by claiming that the delays had voided the terms of their enlistments and as such were free to walk away. Malcontents who took flight soon found themselves under arrest. Sickles begged Lincoln for action but was told to hang on a few more days until a time recruiting officers would come "and take you all in out of the cold."[17]

Within the brigade itself, the business of organizing the various regiments was underway, when the issue of soldier dissatisfaction came to a head. Enticed by bounties and the promise of early action, an entire company of 90 men attempted to desert in order to join another regiment forming across the bay in New York City. Arriving in the nick of time, Sickles ordered a detachment of men to head off the deserters. The detachment intercepted the would-be deserters at the points of rifle barrels before their ferry was able to depart Staten Island. A few hours later, when a captain and two lieutenants who had attempted to lure Dan's men away came to Camp Scott inquiring about the 90, Sickles had the provocateurs arrested. A drumhead court martial was held for all officers involved; their sentence was execution at midnight. At the appointed hour just as the firing squad was taking position, sealed orders arrived, reprieving the men until the court's findings could be submitted to Lincoln for approval.[18] Similar incidents no doubt curtailed further defections, whether of groups or individuals. But just how much of this scene was real and how much was theater cooked up by Sickles to discourage dissent may never be known.

By the beginning of June nearly all of the elements were in place for forming a brigade. City men had endured the greatest upheaval throughout April and May, enduring cold barracks, lice and nights on Staten Island without tents. Men from upstate and western New York who belonged to established families with good community support arrived at the end of May or early June and spent their time waiting either at home or in hotels as the companies reached full strength.[19] These groups of men, formed from local militias, arrived fully outfitted with uniforms and rifles while metropolitan men scrounged for nearly everything. But slowly the regiments were coming together.

Johnson's company of men left Delaware County to join Sickles on June 4, and their departure was both emotional and exciting. The *Bloomville Mirror* recorded the scene, which was no doubt repeated hundreds of times across the North:

> The Company were escorted through the village by the Delhi Fire Companies, preceded by the Brass Band and Martial Music. In front of Edgerton's Hotel, they were addressed by Hon. S. Gordon, who concluded by presenting the volunteers with 100 Havelocks, the generous offering of the ladies of Delhi. [A havelock is a cloth covering that fits over a cap to protect the neck from sun.] Remarks were also made by Hon. J.A. Hughston and Capt. R.T. Johnson, after which prayer was offered by Rev. A.D. Benedict. Teams were then driven up to convey them to the Railroad at Hancock, the parting scene enacted, and amid loud cheers by a large assemblage, the volunteers left the village. All along the route, the citizens cheered them on their way and in return received the cheers of the "bold soger boys." When near Walton, they were met by the Walton Band and Fire companies, who led the procession into the village under the direction of Gen. Bassett and Maj. Mead. The citizens furnished dinner for the company at the Hotels of E. Launt and S.W. Smith. The Band and Firemen escorted the company out of the village, and we left amid the cheers and congratulations of those assembled.
>
> We arrived at Hancock about dark, and took supper at Judson's and Hunter's Hotels. Several persons enlisted at Hamden, Walton and Hancock. We believe only two that had joined the company could not be found when the roll was called before taking the cars.
>
> In the evening, a meeting was held in the public hall, which most of the volunteers attended. Remarks were made by Judge Palmer B.F. Gerowe, F. Jacobs Jr., Rev. Mr. Carl J.P. Sanford and "Champ." Great enthusiasm was manifested to defend the Government and sustain the honor of the Stars and Stripes.
>
> About 2½ o'clock Wednesday morning we embarked for New York on board of the cars. We numbered about 115. By an arrangement between the State and the Railroad Company, no fare was charged the volunteers. During the journey, the company gave vent to their patriotic feeling, by frequent cheers and singing National songs. We reached New York about 9 o'clock meeting many Delaware county people at the depot. After taking a "smile" at the Libby House, we reported ourselves at the City Hall. Here we waited some time, for acceptance, after which (about 10 o'clock) we marched to the Rainbow Hotel and took breakfast. We showed the proprietor a specimen of tall eating and if marched to battle the company hoped to show some tall fighting. Justice being done to the edibles, we marched about the Park to see and be seen, and then started for the ferry boat at Pier No. 2 and crossed to Vanderbilt's Landing, on board the *Josephine*. After a brisk march some two miles, we entered Camp Scott.[20]

Sickles' brigade comprised five regiments, and they bore the designations of First through Fifth Excelsior. On June 3, 1861, the new Third Regiment, Excelsior Brigade, issued its first general order. Nelson Taylor was appointed colonel of the new Third Excelsior, and his first order was a simple one. It established the daily schedule: reveille, meals, drills and finally the drummer's call to turn-in, Tattoo. It also designated there to be eight companies, lettered A through H, and named the captains commanding each.[21]

Taylor was not new to the army or to administration. The 39-year-old Connecticut native had served as a captain with First New York Infantry during the war with Mexico but had been stationed in California the entire time. After the war he mustered out and stayed in California, settling in Stockton. In 1849 he was elected to the state senate and later, in 1855, became sheriff of San Joaquin County. Shortly afterwards, he returned to New York and graduated from Harvard Law School in 1860, the same year he unsuccessfully ran for congress as a Democrat.[22] When regimental colonelcies were being handed out, his prominence and Democratic leanings made it likely he was well known to Sickles. "Col. Nelson Taylor, our commanding officer, is a tall, dark complexioned man of fine military appearance, and pleasant and affable, though dignified, in address," wrote one private, adding, "He has served in Mexico and California, and will, therefore, be just the man for a campaign in a low latitude."[23]

Mid-June the supply problem was starting to work itself out. Arthur McKinstry was part of Steven's company and son of the local newspaperman. Beginning immediately after departure for Staten Island, young Arthur wrote frequent, homey letters, which were then published in the *Fredonia Censor*, all beginning, "Dear Uncles." Among his first letters was his take on living conditions at Camp Scott:

> Our domicils [sic] are about ten feet square and lodge 8 men each. There is quite a little village here, with regular, streets and a population of about 2,500, as near as I make out. We are supplied with rubber blankets, got up to be used as shawls in wet weather and we spread them on the ground under us and then esconce [sic] ourselves in a pair of woolen blankets, and this with our boots for a pillow, constitutes a bed.[24]

For the boys coming from out West, the gulf between their companies and the companies raised from the city could not have been wider. While cheering crowds saw the well-uniformed and educated Chautauqua boys off to war, the city companies seemed to have filled their ranks from the local bars, brothels, and back alleys.[25] McKinstry, writing to his "uncles" near mid-month, reported:

> Those who were not uniformed when they left home are not yet any better off in that respect than when they started. We are of course in excellent trim, which we owe to the liberality of our friends and the active exertion of the ladies.
>
> Our boys, the Jamestown boys, and the few other companies, occupy the northern part of the ground, and the rest is occupied by, the Lord only knows who. They are the very dregs of humanity, and are raked up from the Points and other places of similar repute. Some are coatless, more hatless, and not a few have blankets girt around them to cover the deficiency of pantaloons. All are outrageously filthy, but as no object in nature is without its use, so they furnish an inexhaustible fund of merriment, more especially when one of them is drummed out with shaven poll to the tune of the "Rogue's March," for some precious piece of rascality.[26]

During that early summer of '61, both the regiment and entire brigade were unsettled. Whole companies of men were added here and there in an attempt to get each regiment close to its full recommended strength of one thousand men. Many companies were started from scratch thanks to the exertions of motivated men while others formed around existing militia units. Some companies "failed to retain their organization" for whatever reason and were either disbanded or incorporated into other regiments. Those "failed" company letter designations would be reassigned later. Of Third Excelsior's original eight companies, C, G and H failed to retain their organization.²⁷ In July, the local Fredonia paper reported Colonel Forbes of the 68th Militia resisted allowing Company C, another one of his companies, to join Taylor. The article gave no explanation for Forbes' resistance to the company joining Third Excelsior. And while it was true the other regiments in Sickles' brigade were primarily composed of men from New York City, the same couldn't be said about Taylor's boys. Of the ten companies eventually composing the third regiment, only three, A, the new C, and K, were from the city. Company F was from Newark, New Jersey; I from Delhi in the middle part of the state; and the remaining five all from western counties.²⁸ Third Excelsior certainly lived up to Sickles' pledge of representing the entire state. During the third week in June, two regular army officers finally arrived at Camp Scott to muster Sickles' weary troops directly into Federal service as United States Volunteers.

Companies D and E were mustered in on June 20. William O. Stevens, the Dunkirk district attorney and efficient militia captain, commanded Company D, which had always been the sharpest and best organized of the companies, having won the privilege of traveling into the city to participate in the procession sending the famous Seventh New York off to war.²⁹ So it was no surprise that the honor of being the first mustered went there. The 33-

This early war picture shows the command staff of Company A. Left to right are Captain George Grecheneck, First Lieutenant Charles Grossinger and Second Lieutenant Edward B. Harnett. Grecheneck would die of wounds received at Williamsburg, Grossinger resigned in June of '62, and Harnett would survive the war. By July of 1864 only a few of the officers who started with the regiment remained (Third Excelsior Association).

year-old Caspar K. Abell served as the company's first lieutenant, and 29-year-old Hugh Hinman enrolled as second lieutenant. Keeping the western feel of this first day of mustering was company E, the other batch of 68th militiamen from Dunkirk. Twenty-nine-year-old Patrick Barrett enrolled as E's captain while William O'Neal and William Toomey enrolled as first and second lieutenants, respectively.[30]

A few days earlier the Dunkirk paper had recorded the departure of the two companies from the local depot:

> Yesterday was an eventful day in our village. It opened bright and balmy, the first really comfortable day for weeks.... The flag was presented in a neat and appropriate speech by H.A. Risley Esq. to Capt. Barrett who replied, but very briefly, overcome by his own emotions. The boquets [sic] were presented, and the procession formed.... Arrived at the Depot there was no time for the farewell address, and the soldiers immediately filed into the cars. The Depot and the walk leading to it for some distance was filled long before the procession reached it. The scene there was exceedingly touching, but passes description; warm grasps were given, parents parted from children, wives from husbands, brothers from sisters, lovers from each other. In tender sympathy, tears poured in torrents from hundreds of eyes. The boys carried away with them the warm wishes of the whole community.[31]

The next day the remainder of the regiment mustered in. Company A was a German company, reflecting the nation's largest ethnic minority. Though the company was organized in New York, men from all over the north joined. Its captain, 36-year-old George Grecheneck, was a Hungarian engineer who had participated as an officer in the failed Hungarian Revolution of the 1840s. Exiled from Hungary, he settled in Iowa, where he worked as a surveyor and land agent before finding his way to Taylor's regiment.[32] Charles Grossinger, who was nearly Grecheneck's age at 35, served as the company's first lieutenant, with Edward Harnett serving as second lieutenant.[33] Captain James M. Brown's company from Jamestown was also mustered in this day and was designated as Company B. Brown was 36 at the time and had served as an army surgeon during the Mexican War; he had shared a tent with then–Lt. Ulysses Grant for nearly 18 months. Soon after war with Mexico, Brown left medicine to pursue a career in law and was member of a prominent law firm in Jamestown when Lincoln called for volunteers.[34] The 34-year-old Dawin Willard enrolled as the company's first lieutenant, and was one of the few men with any real army experience beyond local militias, having served for two years in the U.S. Mounted Rifles as a young man. Thirty-two-year-old Alfred Mason enrolled as the company's junior lieutenant. Company F formed around a militia company located in Newark, New Jersey, that was under the command of John Leonard. The Irish-born Leonard had served in the Ninth U.S. Infantry for five years. As a sergeant, he commanded a small outpost in Washington State for two years.[35] Upon expiration of his term of service in 1860, Leonard returned to Newark and was made captain of the militia. He was only 24 when F was sworn into service. Thirty-one-year-old Henry McConnell and 32-year-old John Holmes served Leonard as his senior and junior lieutenants. Finally, the boys from Delhi in central New York were mustered in as Company I, 29-year-old Robert Johnson as captain, with John Sandford and Hugh Winters serving as first and second lieutenants respectively.[36]

The experience of the Company I men was no doubt typical for thousands of men across the state. After assembling in Delhi, the center of recruiting efforts, men boarded the train for a two-day trip into New York City. Following a hearty breakfast at 11 a.m., the men moved immediately the four miles to Staten Island. Farmer Charles W. Gould wrote his sister the Sunday after arriving about his physical surroundings:

Accommodations here for some are not so good as they expected, but I have it a little easier. Shortly after I came here I became servant for the first lieutenant John P. Sanford. I have just been out on parade. It is very hot and the excitement is very intense. The captain Robert T. Johnson has just left his tent in my hands and has gone to the seashore to bath....

For breakfast we have three large crackers and some beef. For dinner it is bread with coffee or soup. For supper we have the same again....

There are about six hundred tents made of white canvas and properly arranged, presenting a handsome appearance.[37]

But however handsome he may have found the layout of the tents, his thoughts about the moral conditions were something else:

It is Sunday, but Sunday in not regarded here. The drums are beating all day and firing off muskets with reports of pistols continually elate the ear....

The men here are of the roughest kind. Gambling, fighting, and swearing seem to be the principal amusement. Little thinking that a vast number will never see home again. There are two rows of guards. Men attempting to go by them occasionally get stabbed.[38]

These Third Excelsior Regiment colors were issued to the regiment before it was given its numerical designation in the spring of 1862. The regiment would be issued two more sets of colors before being dissolved (Brown, *History of the Third Regiment*).

Almost immediately, two of those companies that failed to retain organization were reassigned to new, fresh bodies of men. Isaac L. Chadwick, a machinist from New York City, by his own account spent $2,000 of his own money raising a company. On July 21, 1861, he and his mostly New York City boys mustered into Third Excelsior as the new company C, with the 27-year-old Chadwick as captain. Chadwick had a direct connection to regimental command; his second wife was related to Colonel Nelson Taylor. Three days later a new company G was mustered in. This was another batch of boys from western New York, where brothers Harmon and Collins Bliss had been active recruiting around Westfield. Many of the men were members of the same militia company earlier rebuffed by Colonel Forbes.[39] The Bliss brothers now served as captain and first lieutenant, respectively, with the elder Harmon in command. As for a new Company H, that would have to wait until later.

With the vast bulk of the brigade mustered in, uproarious shouts of "On to Richmond!" filled the air around Camp Scott; the men were sure they would soon be on the move. But move they didn't. Two weeks later, on July 4, Sickles' men were still in camp. Celebrating the nation's birthday, the Excelsior Brigade heard a reading of the Declaration of Independence then passed in review of their patron Sickles, who afterwards offered them a patriotic address.[40]

Taylor continued to organize, drill and prepare his men of the Third Excelsior throughout June and the early part of July for what 18-year-old Company B private Henri LeFevre-Brown would later call "the sterner duties of war." William Stevens, the dashing captain from Dunkirk, came to prominence immediately and was offered the position of major. But not until a vote was taken of his company, granting their approval, did he accept. Stevens was promoted on June 25 with Lt. Abell promoted to replace him that same day. David Parker, the energetic boy who'd walked all night to join Company B, had now come to the notice of his officers, so when Taylor needed someone who could "write plainly" in order to maintain regimental record keeping, David's name was submitted.[41] He wasn't excused from all drill and fatigue duties, but this meant he'd be spending a fair amount of time in the relative ease of headquarters. On the 9th of July, Second Lieutenant Alfred Mason was sent back to western New York on a three-fold mission: to find more men to fill the ranks of existing companies, to recruit an entire company if possible, and to recruit men for a regimental band.[42]

Two weeks after Mason left, Taylor had a start to his band. Eight members of the Jamestown Cornet Band came to Staten Island, with several more musicians from Dunkirk and Fredonia arriving a few days later. Alexander Peters, who had intended to serve as a private with Company C, was now made principal musician and charged with overseeing the 23-man band.[43]

As military organization within the brigade and regiments were coming together, Sickles and Captain Wiley struggled with yet another problem, creditors. The two founders of the Excelsior Brigade were deep in debt for food, rent, supplies, horses, forage, fuel, tents, and a thousand other items needed to maintain a brigade; in just two months, the bill had run up to nearly $400,000. Sickles sought to delay creditors' claims on the assumption that the bills would eventually be paid by Federal authorities, yet the creditors were adamant about receiving payment before Sickles was called to the front. The creditors wanted their payments now, and they wanted them in cash.

Even as some Excelsiors were being mustered in on July 21, with Sickles and Wiley cajoling merchants and landlords, the Union army was meeting with disaster at Bull Run. Though it was a grievous defeat for the nation, for Sickles and his brigade it was a curiously fortuitous event. Following the defeat, Secretary of War Cameron sent an urgent order for the Excelsior Brigade to report to Washington for defense of the capital. Eagerly the Excelsiors began to stir into action. It seemed the creditors would have to wait.[44]

2. Defense of Washington

Officers began making preparations before the day was over. News of the Bull Run loss shocked the regiment and country. What everyone believed would be a short, easy defeat of the Rebels by a superior Federal army had gone horribly wrong; the army was in shambles and the defense of Washington in question. David Parker, Martin Boyden, and indeed the entire regiment were getting ready for the move they had been awaiting. Every tool, axe, shovel, and cooking pot was marked with regimental number and company letter. Tents were labeled on their outsides, indicating regiment and company, so when folded they could be easily identified. Personal gear such as cartridge boxes, haversacks and back packs were stenciled with each soldier's name, number and company letter. Officers, who always tended toward having a few extra luxuries, would reduce gear to the minimum. Company officers such as Johnson, Chadwick and the Bliss brothers were to ensure each man had proper gear in anticipation of a move. Tin cups, plates, knives, forks and spoons were issued to those who somehow didn't have them or had lost them. Though it was the middle of summer, rain was frequent, so heavy overcoats, called greatcoats, were issued along with woolen and rubber blankets that doubled as ground cloths and rain-proof ponchos. Finally the order to move came.

Two days after Bull Run, Colonel Taylor issued the orders all had expected: "The regiment will hold itself in readiness to march at 2 p.m. precisely."[1] Amongst the chaos of the regiment's preparations to move out, Emerson Merrell, Lorey Wilder, and six other raw recruits arrived. They couldn't have been greener; yet here they were, part of Johnson's Company I. A quartermaster was summoned to issue them gear. They would need everything: coat, trousers, belt, hat and all the remaining gear. They would also need a meal and eventually a place to sleep. Perhaps the other men of Company I were envious of the new recruits; they had only one day on Staten Island and were fortunate to miss the stinking barracks, mosquitoes, and the copious amount of uncertainty. It must have been a welcomed relief for Sickles' men when they were finally ordered to Washington on July 24.

The loss at Bull Run was not just a setback; it was a disaster. The Federal army had been sent reeling back in panic. Since the army intended to stop the enemy was now in tatters, citizens worried about Rebel soldiers sweeping into Washington. Excelsior men speculated about the outcome of the battle had they participated; firebrands among the boys no doubt felt they could have single-handedly sent the Rebels scampering back. Others, the more circumspect among the companies, may have recognized that while many within their ranks looked and acted like soldiers, especially those in seasoned militia units such as Stevens' Company D, most were still raw and unfit for battle. Most had never even shot target practice, let alone learned skirmish drill or exercised with bayonet.[2] Had they been at Bull Run, they too might have been among those sent "ske-daddling." There would be plenty of war to come; better to fight when ready, many no doubt concluded. Among those anxious to defeat the Rebels and confident in the brigade's abilities was Dan Sickles. Writing of the army's disaster, he speculated about the battle had his Excelsiors been there: "It is not for me to say how the fortunes of that day might have been influenced by the presence of five thousand well-drilled troops, officers and men, all well known to each other, and animated by a strong esprit de corps."[3]

Moving to Washington was a welcome change to most in Third Excelsior. David Parker, the strong Lincoln-man, was glad to be heading for the "seat of war" and ultimate restoration of the Union, a cause for which he was determined to fight. "For we do not expect to bring back our banners untorn and unsoiled, but we expect that they will be discolored by smoke, and rent by bullets," echoed Arthur McKinstry of Company D, adding, "Not a man of us is not eager to join in the strife."[4] But certainly not all within the regiment felt the same as David and Arthur.

In Sickles' zeal to fill up the ranks of his five regiments, he mustered nearly anyone who could meet the minimum standards, and in some cases those who couldn't. In

Nelson Taylor commanded the regiment from the beginning to just before Fredericksburg in December of 1862. During his tenure, Taylor also commanded the Excelsior Brigade during Sickles' frequent absences. Before the war, Taylor had gone west during the war with Mexico and remained in California, where he served in various governmental positions in the fledgling state. Taylor would eventually rise to rank of brigadier general, but he resigned early in 1863. A Harvard educated lawyer, after the war Taylor served one term in the United States House of Representatives (courtesy the U.S. Army Heritage and Education Center).

and around New York City, unsavory characters, gutter-sweeps, and genuine convicts were accepted into the ranks. Judges often allowed men freedom from jail in exchange for enlistment with Sickles. For the anxious boys from near Lake Erie, the cramped, smelly, and unmilitary conditions of the barracks and the sparse living of Camp Scott would have seemed like purgatory if not outright hell. But for those who faced prison and whose motives were somewhat less patriotic, the mosquitoes of Staten Island were likely preferable to the bullets of Bull Run. For the sweeps, waiting would be just fine.

By the time the regiment was set to move, all field and staff positions, officers, non-commissioned officers and others serving at the regimental, not company level, had been filled. Taylor was the colonel and Stevens served as major. Prominent New York doctor Israel Moses was the lieutenant colonel; he had served with the army for some time and had invented an ambulance in 1855 that bore his name. At the end of the Mexican War, and in poor health, Moses left the army to join the staff of the newly formed Jews Hospital (later renamed Mt. Sinai Hospital). At the outbreak of the war, the soft spoken Dr. Moses was arguably among the most prominent Jews in New York. But upon joining Third Excelsior, he left his scalpel home, enrolling instead as a line officer.[5] Serving as surgeon of Third Excelsior was Dr. Charles K. Irwin. Irwin had practiced dentistry in Canada for several years before graduating from the medical college in Albany in 1856. Settling in Dunkirk, he practiced medicine until mustering into the regiment.[6] Chaplain Levi Warren Norton oversaw the spiritual well-being of the regiment. Norton was a 41-year-old Episcopalian when he enrolled in the regiment. He served as rector in New Jersey before eventually settling in Jamestown, where he was rector prior to the war.[7]

At 2 p.m. on July 24 the officers and men, except for the usual stragglers, were assembled and ready to move. Sickles' First Regiment had left the day before, and now it was time for Taylor's boys and Second Regiment. David Parker and Martin Boyden still hadn't moved an hour later, but after seven weeks in the army, they had learned to wait. Finally by early evening a boat arrived to take them the dozen or so miles to South Amboy, New Jersey, where they boarded railroad cars of the Camden and Amboy Railroad for the next leg of their trip to the threatened capital, Washington, D.C. An enthusiastic reception greeted the regiments all along the route. "The stridulous notes of small boys mingling with the deeper shouts of men who knew wherefore they hailed us. The women especially favored us with clouds of fluttering handkerchiefs at every station," wrote the Second Regiment's 22-year-old, Yale-educated chaplain, Joseph H. Twichell.[8] Arriving in Camden, New Jersey, early the next morning, the boys took the steamer across the Delaware River to Philadelphia, marching the last bit to the Cooper Shop Volunteer Refreshment Saloon on Otsego Street. The Cooper Shop was only a short distance from the Philadelphia Naval Yard, and there everyone enjoyed a fine breakfast hosted by local citizens. Arthur McKinstry observed:

> In the morning we arrived just about in season for breakfast in the city of "Brotherly Love," which we found to be no misnomer, for, almost the first thing which met our eyes was a mammoth sign reading "Coffee and refreshments free for Union Volunteers." Along in front was a roof or awning under which was a long range of wash basins, where we were overjoyed to perform our abolutions [sic]. Then we adjourned to the spacious saloon and partook of a bounteous repast which had the merit of a neatness which we who had dwelt so long in camp, knew full well how to appreciate.[9]

To ensure the soldiers remained sober, guards were posted at the door of every "rum hole" in the neighborhood.[10] And though a few bottles did make it into circulation, serious problems among the men were avoided. The Cooper's Shop had only opened a couple of months before and was one of two such refreshment saloons in the city where volunteer citizens, without state or city funds, provided thousands of soldiers with free meals as they passed through.

After enjoying a wonderful breakfast, good enough, as one soldier wrote, "for a first class hotel,"[11] and a short rest, the two regiments once again boarded railroad cars for the next leg of the trip, amid the encouragements of a thousand cheering citizens. Arriving in Baltimore on the evening of the 25th, Taylor marched his men through the city. The reception received in Baltimore was in stark contrast to their sendoff in Camden. Many Marylanders favored secession, and though it remained in the Union, there had already been serious problems between Federal troops and disloyal agitators. There was no cheering or waving crowd, no flying of the American flag. Third Excelsior marched in silence. The only encouragement came from the few slaves they passed in the fields, which served to remind them the realities of war were close. There were other signs of war along the way. Pickets, Massachusetts men mostly, posted every half-mile or so and at every bridge, kept watch.[12] Merrell, Parker, and the rest reached Washington at 5 a.m. the next morning. After unloading their baggage and eating breakfast, the brigade marched about two miles northeast of the capitol to Brentwood, where, on a hill overlooking Washington and the surrounding countryside, they established Camp Marsh.[13] Soon after arriving, Emerson Merrell wrote home:

> We occupy as splendid a position as there is in the United States. We can see the whole city of Washington, Fairfax, Washington Heights and Georgetown Heights. We have a splendid view of the Capitol and the White House, also the patent office. I have seen plenty of niggers but never have I seen a cecession flag not with standing. We are encamped on a cecessionista farm stocked with thirty nigroes [*sic*]. He has got about 20 acres of corn that stands 12 feet high average and may be we can have an ear of roasted corn now and then and once in a while a few new potatoes and cucumbers and apples.[14]

Excelsior Brigade's arrival in Washington helped somewhat to calm fears among the locals. Less than a week after Bull Run, many units that had fought and then skedaddled were still in no shape to fight again, and the presence of 3,000 or so troops in a large, cohesive body went some ways to reassure the citizens. The Excelsior Brigade contained among the first batches of three-year men to reach the capital. Lincoln's initial call had been for 90-day volunteers, so confident were the nation and government of a quick victory. These New Yorkers represented the new reality; the war would be a much longer, more costly affair. Sickles' men had enlisted for three years or until the end of hostilities, whichever came first. Men could always re-enlist if the war went longer, but most believed and certainly hoped that three years was more than enough.

The five regiments of Sickles' Brigade were a cultural cross-section of the northeast. Of the 50 companies that eventually made up the brigade, 14 came from outside of New York State. Two were from Massachusetts, one from Michigan, five from Pennsylvania and six from New Jersey. The 36 companies from New York represented the nine counties of Cattaraugus, Chautauqua, Delaware, Kings, New York, Orange, Queens, Suffolk and Ulster. The brigade represented a variety of ethnic, social, and military backgrounds. The Fifth Regiment took 400 men from the New York Naval Yard. The tough, rowdy demeanor of these dock workers kept a company of boys from the Michigan countryside nervous and at a distance. And while the Third Regiment had enough Germans to warrant their own company, there were Irish enough in the brigade to merit a Catholic Priest, Father Joseph B. O'Hagan. The Fourth Regiment was recruited primarily from the New York City Fire Department. They wore Zouave uniforms modeled after French colonial troops of northern Africa, and carried the nickname Second Fire Zouaves. While most men in the brigade wore the standard issue Federal coat and trousers, there were variations, both large and small, as companies formed around local militia units. The Third's, B and D, for example, arrived in uniforms provided them by their local citizenry. Except for the scattered Zouave companies, and the entire Fourth Regiment, the brigade was blue. Differences in social and moral fiber between troops were broad and distinct. There were seasoned, patriotic pillars of their communities, such as Stevens and Brown; there were those such as Parker and Merrell who seemed called by both a sense of duty and adventure; and then there were the hard men:

dock workers, gang toughs, and down-and-outs for whom joining Sickles made some sort of sense, be it patriotic or more practical, release from jail.

These toughs and their accompanying wickedness were the kind of men from whom 23-year-old Hiram Stoddard of Co. B prayed for deliverance: "I am where gambling is going on all of the time and profanity is used at evry [sic] breath and there is no getting out of the sound of it. I try to pray evry [sic] day that God would in his goodness keep me from sin."[15] Charles Gould of Company I echoed Stoddard's sentiments about the regiment:

> We left Staten Island two weeks ago in good spirits. I however was never so disgusted before at the effects of rum. All the officers were drunk. Half of the companies were lying around like a bunch of brutes.
>
> Many a mother bade her son adieu. Sorry to expose him to the temptations that he must meet in the Army. While they are praying for them their sons are playing a game of cards or lying around drunk on the ground. I sincerely thank god for giving me parents who taught me, by Godlike example, to shun all vice. Their prayer I believe will not go unanswered.[16]

Certainly such coarse behavior was not only limited to the Third Regiment. Father O'Hagan summed up his initial thoughts about other Excelsior men in a letter:

> Such a collection of men was never before united in one body since the flood. Most of them were the scum of New York society, reeking with vice and spreading a moral malaria around them. Some had been serving terms of penal servitude on Blackwell's Island at the outbreak of the war, but were released on condition of enlisting in the army of the Union, and they gladly accepted the alternative.[17]

Social divides between the men remained, especially in the more diverse regiments such as Taylor's. While company pride and a sense of western superiority still existed, by August the regiment was slowly coming together. "When we first came, we had few companies upon the ground which it would do to associate with," wrote McKinstry, "but now no man need remain behind on that account, for he can mingle with his peers, be they of whatever class."[18]

Arriving in Washington, Taylor reported his men to be using the Model 1842 musket, though some in the ranks wrote about using an 1833 model. Both weapons started life as .69 caliber smoothbores, designed to fire a buck-and-ball load: one large .69 ball and at least two smaller .30 ones. The 1842s the regiment now used had been altered, and were among the 10,000 or so retooled into rifles with grooves cut into the inside wall of the barrel, imparting a spin to the ball. By eliminating the buckshot portion of the load, the amount of lead fired with each shot was reduced, and in theory this would greatly improve range and accuracy. However, at least one man in the regiment reported that both expert and novice shots were equally, and wildly, inaccurate with the weapon. By the end of July, Taylor reported seven of his companies had been issued the weapon and hadn't begun either target or bayonet practice. Taylor now considered his remaining companies that had just joined Third Excelsior as nearly raw recruits. It is unclear by Taylor's report if these raw men had even been issued weapons by the time of their arrival in Washington.[19]

Despite deficiencies, Taylor now reported most units within the regiment to be nearly ready for the field. The commissary, quartermaster, and medical departments would all be "sufficiently complete in three days for campaigning except for wagons and ambulances, of which there were none."[20]

Fourth and Fifth Excelsior for the time being were still in New York, adding men to reach the recommended full strength of between 800 and 1,000 men. Without all five Excelsior regiments present, an interim provisional brigade was established, composed of Sickles' three regiments already in Washington and the 69th New York State Militia.[21]

Since their arrival and the establishment of Camp Marsh, the boys of the regiment kept busy with continuous drill, target practice and dress parades. The nation was still reeling from the defeat at Bull Run and the shaky state of the army. More than ever, Washington was a city on edge. The air was hot and muggy, which only helped fuel the rampant rumor mill. Almost daily there were new reports of imminent Rebel attacks or other military or political intrigues. Frequently the boys were rousted from sleep by false alarms in the night. The accompanying odd rifle shot only served to heighten the tension and drama. Washington was turning into an armed camp with the enemy just across the river.

Sickles issued orders on August 8 to curtail evening parade and make ready for a review at the Executive Mansion before himself and none other than Abraham Lincoln.[22] Since arriving in Washington, Sickles had been a frequent visitor to the White House, where his wit and sparkling personality won the friendship of the president and first lady. In times like these, Lincoln liked any man who could get things done and wanted to fight, and Sickles, it seemed, was just that sort of man for, despite the critics, the Excelsiors were shaping up into fine soldiers.[23] For an hour, Emerson Merrell, Lorey Wilder, and the rest paraded in front of the president, first lady, and others. "We arrived there about sun down, and drew up before the White House," wrote one Company B man. "Abraham soon came out, dressed in a linen coat and plug hat, both the worse for wear."[24] While the rank and file were proud, there certainly was no one prouder than Sickles. Of the parade before Lincoln and the rest, N.P. Willis of the *Home Journal* wrote, "I have seldom seen a finer military show. Sickles is a soldier and a brave one." In less than four months, Dan had gone from unhappy lawyer to rising star.

While Sickles enjoyed a certain celebrity in Washington, not everyone shared the enthusiasm. Captain William Wiley had been left behind in New York to clean up the messy birth of the Excelsior Brigade, facing angry merchants and demanding creditors alone. He felt abandoned and was now determined to dispel the myth of Sickles' alleged hero status, eventually putting his feelings to paper:

> So he marched off with three regiments, and paraded them before Lincoln, and said he had done all this out of his own pocket. There were piles of judgments against him in the offices. He had no more to do with the brigade than the receiving of the recruits.... It was fifteen months before I could get a settlement. He left me in the lurch.... I left him on account of it; denounced him then, and have done so since.[25]

The day after parading in front of Lincoln, the brigade received orders to move to a position on the outskirts of the capital. They moved across the eastern branch of the Potomac River, also known as the Anacostia, to Good Hope Heights in Maryland. Here they established Camp Caldwell, "about four miles south of Washington on a hill very beautifully situated about ¼ of a mile from the first regt,"[26] described Merrell. The heat and previous night's parade played havoc among the men, wrote McKinstry:

> We struck our tent and started under a burning sun for a march of six miles, but we took a wrong road and made ten of it.... After getting well over [the Anacostia], we took a good rest, and gave the stragglers who had given out a chance to close up. The men were in poor condition to travel, for they had been to the White House the night before to be inspected by President Lincoln, and the heat was so great that about forty gave out; completely exhausted.[27]

With Camp Caldwell established, new duties were added to the routine of drill and camp life. Individual companies from the various regiments were sent out on picket duty tours lasting five days. Those from Third Excelsior were stationed across from Alexandria, Virginia, and charged with guarding the roads leading to Washington.[28] This would serve not only to protect the capital but also to cut off communications between Maryland secessionists and Virginia rebels.

There was no doubt among the boys of Third Excelsior that they had arrived at the seat of war. The regiments of the brigade were spread out along the slopes of Good Hope Heights. They camped on land belonging to owners with secessionist leanings. Some landowners even had kin serving in the Rebel army. Locals gave the Yankee occupiers only cold, blank stares. "In the country about us I think a good many secessionists may be found," wrote Arthur. "Our sentries now load their guns, and any man who attempts to escape, or to enter after dark without permission, will be fired on. Ten round of ball cartridge are served out to each man."[29] Locals wanted nothing to do with the invaders. Occasionally, only the most mercenary of merchants would sell fresh produce to the blue-coated Yankees. A local Union man tried to help. "He had been attempting to supply our soldiers with milk," reported McKinstry, "but gave it up because the planters would rather feed it to their hogs than to sell it for 40 cents per gallon to Union volunteers."[30] To Arthur, it seemed only the slaves were happy to have him there.

Summer rain was common for Maryland, and the soldiers dealt with it best they could. Branches, twigs, and other foliage made improvised floors for tents, but most remained slick, muddy messes. Often rain fell for two or three days without letup. Emerson Merrell found during these wet times that his oiled cloth blanket worked well to keep him dry. The boys stood sentry for one day and one night in every eight, in shifts of two hours on and four hours off. Emerson and his mates thought the routine "not very hard if it does not rain."[31] But of course it did.

During those brief times when it wasn't raining and they weren't drilling or busy with fatigue duties, men across the army wrote letters home. Letters allowed the boys to keep in touch with far off friends and family, who were even farther now that Third Excelsior was in Washington. The boys wrote often, sometimes three or more times a week, and were even more anxious to receive correspondence from home, complaining to loved ones if expected allotments of letters did not arrive. Sometimes the desire for a letter, any letter, was more important than who wrote it. The following was posted in the local Jamestown paper by some enterprising Third Excelsior men:

ATTENTION LADIES.—We, the undersigned officers, non-commissioned officers, musicians, or privates, valiant, gay, and gallant Chautauqua County bark-peelers, having faithfully served our country since the formation of the grand Army of the Potomac, do hereby advertise, through the columns of the local press, as the last resort by which to obtain the much coveted correspondence of those some of those noble daughters of Chautauqua, who have so kindly assisted us thus far in our efforts to crush this cruel and unnatural rebellion.... If any of the above said Ladies, of that noble and patriotic County, "which we have the honor in part to represent," should choose to write, they will receive a hearty response from the subscribers.
LONELY.[32]

David Parker continued in service to Colonel Taylor, his duties expanding to include daily runs into the city to fetch the regiment's mail. Because of the controversial beginning of the brigade, many within the regiment had not been paid since mustering and hence had no money for postage. To help remedy this postage problem, David took the un-stamped mail to the offices of his Chautauqua County congressman, Reuben E. Fenton. Fenton then sent the boys' letters on for free using his congressional franking privilege. After a short period of these daily visits to the congressman's office, Fenton authorized David to write his name and mark the letters, "Free. R.E. Fenton, M.C." This saved time and money and served to popularize the congressman throughout the regiment and state, helping him to upset Horatio Seymour in the 1864 governor's election.[33]

On August 20, the regiment formed up and marched the mile or so over to the Naval Yard. Emerson and the rest marveled at the amount of stores: muskets by the tens of thousands, hundreds of cannon, everything an army would need to win a war. Here were even a few Southron prisoners bearing an expected sour look as the regiment paraded by. The purpose of the regiment's trip had been to exchange weapons. They were giving up their old muskets for newer "Harper's Ferry Muskets," and though there is some historical confusion over exactly which weapons they received, it is clear the change was met with frustration. "There we exchanged our guns for Harper's Ferry muskets. Though these are a decided improvement on the old guns, we were bitterly disappointed that we did not receive rifles,"[34] wrote McKinstry, who added:

> There were muskets enough to supply an army, but I did not see rifle enough to arm a single company.... I also visited the cartridge manufactory, and admired the expeditious manner in which powder and ball were got ready for our hands. It was a significant fact, that to the bullet which is commonly put up was added there buck shot—and four of us loaded on one of our wagons 30,000 of these cartridges, with 5,000 of ball only, for target use. We have fired at target a little and find that our guns are a hard hitting arm, *at which ever end the mark may be.* They are very inaccurate, but shoot with great force, and the fire of buck and ball by a battalion must prove terribly destructive.[35]

A shipment of uniforms arrived for the regiment around this same time. Until now the men had been equipped with a variety of outfits provided by their respective militia companies or Federal issue. Taylor's men would now start looking like a regiment rather than a mere collection of companies. Arthur McKinstry described the new allocation:

> Our new State jackets have come, and they are really a first class article. They are of dark blue, and are far more tasty than gay. Pants of the same have come, but only a few have been served round, and I do not think there are enough as yet to uniform the regiment. While at Camp Scott we did not supposed ourselves recognized as State Militia, but the uniforms and other things seem to indicate that we are.... We have no new caps as yet, but many have bought the saucy little fez caps, which the French Zouaves wear. They are of a deep crimson color with heavy dark blue tassel. I think the company will obtain them, if not the regiment. They contrast strongly with the dark blue jacket; and a body of men so uniformed look both soldierly and picturesque.[36]

By this time the Fourth and Fifth Excelsior had resolved their recruiting issues and had rejoined the brigade. For the past several weeks internal issues had been tearing at Fourth Excelsior, and it was hoped these issues were now resolved.

Initial recruiting was unexpectedly slow and erratic. From its inception there had been uneasiness about the regiment's colonel, James Fairman. A newspaper article speculated, "It is a question if the regiment will be much of a success; several of the men thus far enlisted would have to be rejected by an inspecting officer. Cannot they get hold of some spirited wide-awake well-known military officers to take a hand in the organization?"[37] Fairman had been the presumptive leader of the regiment, having given early support for Sickles' brigade. But soon there were repeated clashes with Sickles, and eventually Dan worked to rid himself of the unruly colonel. Fairman believed Sickles to be unworthy of command and felt his regiment was trapped in a brigade with an unfit general. Fairman also believed Sickles intended to strip the regiment of all vestiges of fireman origins by eliminating its "Second Fire Zouaves" designation. In August the *New York Times* reported this scene:

> While the regiment was on the dock, Col. Fairman, wearing no sword, made his appearance. "Where is your excellent march down Broadway, and your hand of music?" he asked. "There he is; that's our Colonel!" was immediately the cry; and the men who had a moment before appeared listless and jaded, brightened up, becoming all life and animation. Making his way to a pile of coal bags, Col. Fairman mounted them, and, as his soldiers pressed eagerly around him, told them of the trouble he had had in preventing that regiment of which they were the members from losing its name and organization as the "Second Fire Zouaves;" and that Sickles, who was no more of a Brigadier-General than any of them, had done his best to rob the regiment of its name and identity, and have it attached to the Excelsior Brigade and depose him as Colonel. During the above recital Col. Fairman was often interrupted with "Three cheers for Col. Fairman!" "Three groans for Dan Sickles!" "To h–11 with Dan Sickles!" "D—n Sickles!" and exclamations of a like nature not at all complimentary to Mr. Sickles. Col. Fairman then read to the men the following orders from the War Department, showing indubitably that he was their legitimate Colonel.[38]

Initially there seemed to be early sympathy for Fairman among the enlisted men and in the press: "There appears to be no inconsiderable difficulty in regard to affairs in this regiment. A number of interested parties, actuated by political feelings, have determined upon removing Colonel Fairman. Out of the ten companies, seven are decidedly in his favor, and will leave the regiment if he is removed."[39]

Eventually recruitment into the Second Fire Zouaves exceeded 800, and the regiment prepared to board ships to join the brigade near Washington. Fed up with Fairman, Sickles instructed Major John Moriarity to arrest the colonel should he try to enter camp. Moriarity disregarded the arrest order, but as Fairman attempted to board the transports the colonel was relieved of his position. Sickles placed Moriarity in command until the regiment reached the outskirts of Washington. There, an election for colonel was held. Prior to the vote, officers reflected on Fairman's shortcomings. Embracing previous agreements among the regiment's officers, Fairman believed he would be elected to the post, but instead William R. Brewster won by a landslide.

Fairman's ouster caused some excitement among the rank and file, but shortly thereafter, the men accepted Brewster. One Fire Zouave recounted in the newspaper:

> The disputed Colonelcy still excites considerable attention. The heart and soul of the regiment was once for Fairman. But when the deception practiced by him was fully exposed, the sentiment underwent an entire change. The unjust interference of New York politicians' is depriving us of our pay, which many that have families are sadly in need of. Should Fairman be forced on us, we will never fulfill the dearest hopes of our friends. When Colonel Brewster took command there was scarcely any to bid him welcome, as we then believed that Colonel Fairman had been unjustly deprived of the command. But his cool, deliberate action daily tends to increase our confidence in him as commanding officer. The same can also be said of Gen. Sickles. When the regiment left New York, the cry was, "We will never serve under Gen. Sickles!" On last Saturday, at brigade review, I can assure the readers of your paper that Gen. Sickles was never more heartily cheered in his life than he was by the Second Regiment of Fire Zouaves.[40]

Because the entire brigade was mostly untrained, they spent much of each day drilling and perfecting the skills needed on campaign. About two miles from Camp Caldwell was a large field on which the regiment often marched, conducting battalion drill "with plenty of room for the various necessary movements."[41] Nineteen-year-old musician Frank G. Stevens from Fredonia described the scene in an October letter home:

Our camp is situated about 2½ or 3 miles from Washington, but our drill grounds are about 2 miles from here, in the State of Maryland. The Regiment goes over there every day, right after dinner, and the Band go anywhere from 3 o'clock to 5, and escort the Regiment into camp. We take it easy going over, and gathering chestnuts which are in great quantities and very large. I like it first rate, and would not come home if I could. We have large wall tents with a flyleaf over the top which covers the whole top, making it a double top and perfectly water tight.

This week, Tuesday, the whole Brigade was reviewed by Gen. Sickles and staff, on our drill grounds. It was the greatest military display that I ever saw. Our regiment had the position of honor in the Brigade, (the right of the Brigade,) as it is the best drilled. We are the only regiment that has got a Band and that sets us up a peg or so.[42]

Men from the western companies enjoyed the reflected glory of their former captain's prominence within the regiment. "At battalion maneuvers, whenever Col. Taylor is absent, Major Stevens takes the lead," commented a Company D man, "for however good an executive officer Lieut. Col. Israel Moses may be, his voice is so deficient in power that he is utterly unable to take any effective command."[43] Many took great pride in drill and in their preparations for the sterner duties that waited, but Henry B. Taylor of Company B held another opinion:

Take a man from his work-shop or farm, he is running over with patriotism, and is ready to shed the last drop of blood in defence [sic] of his country's honor; let him enlist, and put him under strict military discipline, and in less than three months he will be a mere machine, which must work perfect in all its parts, he does his work mechanically, his patriotism drilled and starved out of him. We gain nothing by drilling; while we are drilling and perfecting our army, the enemy are not idle, they can drill as long as we can. The best fighting that has been done was done by undisciplined troops, who had no chance to drill.[44]

Following the defeat at Bull Run, Washington had turned into the most fortified city in the Western world, with troops arriving every day and defensive works being built at every possible approach. So in addition to daily drill, the boys of the regiment were detailed in the construction of two forts. Fort Wagner and Fort Baker sat on the heights opposite the Navy Yard and commanded the city's approaches from the Potomac's east side. Major Stevens was put in charge of the building effort, using men from throughout the brigade.[45]

But building forts was only one part of the defense of Washington. On September 8, the boys of the regiment joined an expedition into the counties of lower Maryland to root out enemy spies, scouts, and provocateurs. Fearing Rebel infiltrators might use the Southern-sympathizing region as a base of operation within the Union, the president wanted potential troublemakers off of his side of the river or in jail. The Excelsiors had orders to stop any flow of information or war materials to the Rebels. To fulfill those orders, a special detachment was formed from companies throughout the brigade. Lt. Col. H.L. Potter of the Second Regiment would lead it. Third Excelsiors' contribution to the expedition would be Stevens' old Company D, now under Captain Abell. For the next two weeks Potter's battalion stormed about Maryland looking for enemy agents. Arthur McKinstry was part of the expedition and wrote a lengthy and detailed account of the adventure:

Last Sunday, Sept. 8th, we received orders to prepare to leave with one day's rations in our haversacks. Every man was all astir with excitement, the sick, who could walk, suddenly got well, and the biggest company was turned out that had ever been seen since pay day.[46]

Arriving after a short ways at Good Hope Tavern, Abell and his band joined two more companies, one of Fire Zouaves from the Second Regiment and another of Zouaves from

2. Defense of Washington 25

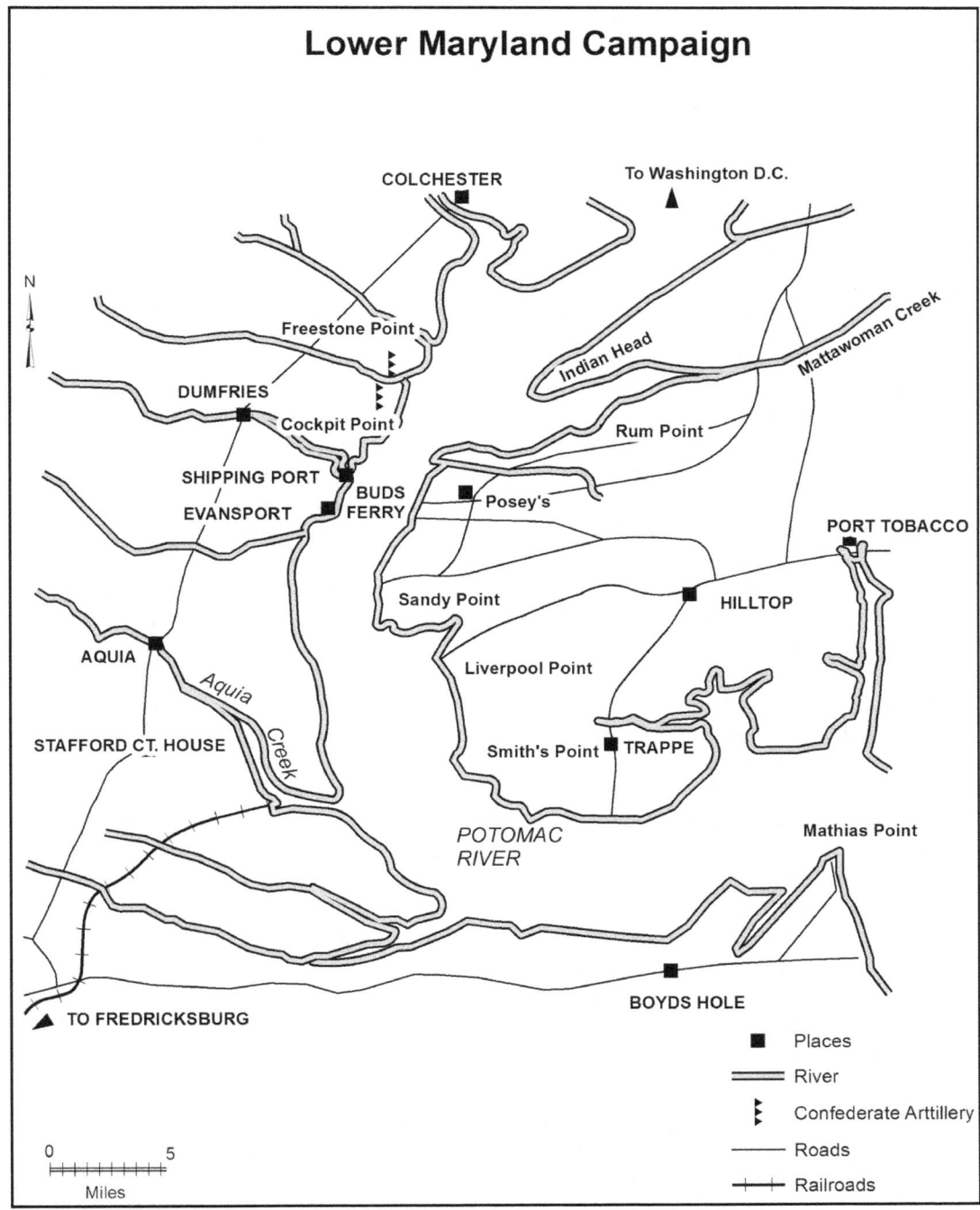

the Fifth. Heading southeast, the expedition loaded their pieces about three miles out after passing pickets from First Excelsior. A company of cavalry soon took the lead as scouts. Within the first few days Potter's force had trudged through Cedarville and on to Upper Marlborough, collecting suspicious weapons of sometimes dubious importance as they went, a fine double barred shotgun and ancient flintlock among the haul.

The column eventually arrived at Butler's Tavern late one night, eleven miles or so from Annapolis. While the men slept, Potter roused an "army of niggers" to cook hoe-cakes and boil meat. "A number of persons were brought in here," reported Arthur. "One had in his house a Southern captain's uniform, and Col. Potter desired the pleasure of his company back at headquarters. This invitation was unhesitatingly complied with."[47] Next they forded the main branch of the Patuxent River on their way to Queen Anne. Here Arthur recorded a welcome sight:

> On entering the village we passed a neat house, in the doorway of which, a lady stood, waving a small Union flag. This was the only hearty Union sign that we saw in the place, and was greeted by our boys with round of applause. As the lady kept somewhat within her dwelling, I concluded she desired to escape the observation of the neighbors.[48]

Encountering mostly contempt, Potter's band continued to scour the countryside for signs of trouble as they worked their way further south, marching as many as 14 miles a day in an unusually roundabout manner. Operationally the expedition resembled a wagon wheel, with marches frequently radiating out from Potter's headquarters near Good Hope Tavern. Other times the men merely marched from place to place, overnighting in the field. While on the march McKinstry reported that he felt unwell and stayed behind as the rest went on without him. Feeling better, he then plodded along the roads by himself, eventually hitching a ride in a wagon with a transplanted Connecticut man who took McKinstry home with him. "Here we were received by his wife and two children, who were quite refreshing to behold, from their neatness and evident intelligence, as contrasted with the ignorance and almost beastial [*sic*] degradation of some of their neighbors."[49]

The expedition marched as far south as Allen's Fresh, a small creek east of where the Potomac winds south again after rounding Mathias Point. After a few days of combing the countryside for rebel activities the Excelsiors moved north from Allen's Fresh to Port Tobacco, the supposed "grand centre of treason for Southern Maryland."[50] Here Sickles joined the expedition, bringing with him a squadron of cavalry. The general now conducted his own reconnaissance for 30 miles in each direction. From Port Tobacco the Excelsiors moved 16 miles north to their next stopping place, Piscataway. Piscataway, while only several miles from Washington, was another supposed nest of treason. Though home to a "rebel recruiting office,"[51] here shone one of the few glimmers of Union patriotism of the trip; a small flag, the Stars and Stripes, was displayed in the window of a local home.

For the boys of Company D, searching farms, questioning disagreeable locals and camping in the field, while unpleasant, was still better than swinging pick and shovel back at forts Wagner and Baker. For McKinstry, the adversities of the adventure had served to further bond the company:

> While upon our march, Capt. Abell was found to be good and jovial company, and the unbending rules which he enforces in camp were relaxed. Indeed a common sense of duty and of danger kept every man in his place ready to attack the foe or defend our expedition. The men all bore up bravely, while toward the last the Zouaves dropped behind us by the dozen. The baggage wagon was loaded, but by other men.[52]

When it was all over, commanders reported that a large number of Rebel agents had been caught and their job was done. Though it is uncertain just how successful the Excelsiors were in clearing the land of traitors, it was doubtless they were in hostile territory. A *New York Times* writer traveling with the expedition summed it up this way:

The inhabitants are intensely treasonable in their sentiments, and the soldiers of the Union were very much of an eye-sore to them. The men were silent, but the women gave free vent to their feelings of hatred. But this mattered little. The Negroes were true to the Union and to us, and the most valuable information was gained.[53]

But while "valuable information" may have been gained in Maryland, it would not be enough. The Potomac River was critical to the North and had to be kept safe for Union ships. As long as Rebels occupied its banks, there was a threat. Two-week expeditions into Maryland would not be enough to secure the river; Sickles' men would soon be leaving Washington.

3. Pacifying Southern Maryland

Oct. 21, 1861
Dear Parents,
I will write a few lines to let you know I am—first place, I do not know the name of the place but we are about 50 mile from Camp Caldwell. We started on friday and traveled in a southerly direction. We have stoped [sic] for now—while I write I do not know where we are going but I think we are gowing [sic] to take a rebel battery of 25 guns— We are now within about 5 miles from it—our boys are in fine spirits anxious for a fight we shall get it this time. You had better direct your letter to camp Caldwell for it will come to me—I shall write again soon for I think you will be glad to here how the scale turns—I do not know when we shall go back to camp but I cant spend time to write any more at present.[1]

—Emerson F. Merrell

Washington was still vulnerable, and the Rebels could not be allowed to make gains in Maryland. Expeditions by the Excelsiors and other Federal troops had already gone into southern Maryland to apprehend enemy agents and to disrupt anti-administration activities. But occasionally charging about the Charles County countryside was not enough to secure Maryland, nor was it enough for the eager New Yorkers. With Rebel cannons on the Virginia side of the Potomac shooting at Union boats headed for the capital, there was much more to be done.

After much anticipation, the regiment was formed up on October 18 and began the march from Camp Caldwell, moving from the outskirts of Washington south into the heart of southern Maryland. Captain R.S. Williamson of the engineers accompanied the regiment. Williamson's job would be multifold. First was to pinpoint the exact location of several Rebel cannon posted along the river near Budd's Ferry, 40 miles or so from Washington. Secondly, it was to measure the width of the river at the points in question, with this information then leading to the positioning of Federal batteries.[2]

Budd's Ferry was just one location among many Rebel batteries. Ranged all along the Potomac, Southern guns regularly took shots at Union craft. Till then, Rebel gunners had been poor shots and few craft were hit, but there was uncertainty about the extent of enemy strength and it was vital the Potomac remain open to Union shipping. The army around Washington was growing, and as it did, fear of enemy attack declined. Troops could now be spared for other operations. So it fell to the Excelsior Brigade and the other regiments of General Joseph Hooker's newly formed division to make the river safe.

Joe Hooker's star was rising fast as high command sorted out the organization of a growing army. A West Point graduate, young Hooker had been dazzling in various staff posi-

Schooners dodging Rebel fire near Budd's Ferry. Confederate batteries near Budd's Ferry and elsewhere along the Virginia side of the Potomac fired on Federal ships making their way to Washington. Third Excelsior and others units within the brigade crossed the river, making frequent raids into this area in order to disrupt enemy activity (*The Illustrated London News*).

tions during the Mexican War but resigned in 1853 after a two year leave of absence. Hooker came to regret his decision as he eked out a living in northern California and Oregon. By 1858 he was sending out feelers regarding rejoining the army. When nothing came of his solicitations, Hooker struggled until war with the South broke out; he then traveled to Washington in search of a colonel's commission. Fate and timing were kind to the 37-year-old Hooker; he quickly made general and was offered a brigade, with placement on the general's list two slots ahead of Ulysses Grant.[3]

Hooker originally had been assigned only a brigade. Unlike the Excelsiors, his original brigade had not been covering the approaches to the capital, but rather had been held behind Washington in good supporting distance should Confederates attack. Hooker's brigade comprised five volunteer regiments. Though the First Massachusetts was present at Bull Run and performed creditably it hadn't seen heavy action; it was one of several regiments adding to the general confusion by wearing gray uniforms. The 11th Massachusetts was recruited from Boston and performed miserably at Bull Run when officers couldn't prevail upon their men to fight. The Second New Hampshire fought hard in the early stages of the battle, doing as well as most before the tide began to turn. The First Michigan had seen some action at Bull Run but was undistinguished, while Hooker's fifth regiment, the 26th Pennsylvania, had missed the battle altogether.[4] These five regiments would be known as the "Hooker Brigade" or "Old Hooker Brigade" and composed the First Brigade of his new division, with the Excelsiors designated as Second Brigade. Adding to these ten regiments of infantry, Hooker received eight companies of Third Indiana Cavalry and one battery from the First United States Artillery. In just a few weeks, Joe Hooker had gone from a colonel in search of a 1,000-man regimental command to general of a 10,000-man division—one-third more troops than Winfield Scott had commanded at Mexico City two decades before.[5]

Third Excelsior welcomed the move south. They had joined the army to fight, not stand guard or build forts. The boys often saw General McClellan tearing around as if some great action were imminent, yet nothing ever came of it, adding to the notion that he was reluctant to fight or worse, was a Rebel sympathizer.[6] Yet, here they were; the boys stepped off at 10 p.m. on the night of the 18th. With 20 pioneers and two companies of cavalry, the column stopped frequently for the building of bridges and road repair. Nearly constant rain created ankle-deep mud the entire march. The regiment marched two-and-one-half days to get to Budd's Ferry. The countryside was as pitiful as had been seen during the previous expeditions. Henry Taylor of Company B related the scene to newspaper readers back in Fredonia:

Federal batteries stationed near Budd's Ferry on the Potomac shore in southern Maryland fire across the river at Confederate artillery installations that harassed Union shipping plying the river. Third Excelsior was deployed during the early part of 1862 to southern Maryland to keep the river open and suppress secessionist activity (*The Illustrated London News*).

> We passed through the village of Piscataway, and I must say that I never saw its *equal* in any of the Northern States. Its appearance would indicate that it was built some time during the Revolution. The roofs of the houses are covered with moss, and the whole village presents a decayed appearance. Two thirds of the houses, a Northern farmer would not allow to disgrace his farm.[7]

The march was somewhat uneventful for Taylor's men, which couldn't be said for other Excelsior regiments. Much of Second Regiment started the march without enough rations for even one day. "The result can be imagined," as Chaplain Joseph Twichell described it; "they had to get something to eat as best they could. At one time not more than two hundred men were in line, the rest being scattered over at least five miles of the road cooking pigs, turkeys and geese etc. which they had shot."[8] Second Regiment's Colonel Hall was soon arrested on neglect charges over the ration debacle. But the march even caused friction between strong willed Sickles and Hooker. Hooker had intended the move into Maryland to serve as an infantry exercise and had ordered each regiment to take only one ambulance, the rest being left in Washington. While the First Brigade complied, Sickles' men gathered all the ambulances they could find. Hooker reported they were used for "lazy soldiers, officers' and women's trunks and knapsacks to such an extent as to lead one to fear that if they reached camp at all, it would be with crippled horse and broken down ambulances."[9] While there were no charges filed, Sickles protested the accusation to McClellan, serving only to deepen the rift between the brigadier and his divisional commander.[10]

Meanwhile in Dunkirk efforts were underway to recruit the still missing Company H. A small article in the October 9 *Fredonia Censor* reported:

> Adjutant S.M. Doyle, of Dunkirk has returned to that village for the purpose of raising a new company of Chautauqua men for the 3rd Regiment Excelsior Brigade. It is designed to create a Chautauqua battalion and raise the strength of the Regiment to 1,600 men. The Dunkirk *Journal* states the Adjutant Doyle's company "H" is already nearly filled and the uniforms have been received.[11]

Opposite: **Since the summer of 1861, regimental officers had been back in western New York in search of men to form a new company, fill out existing companies, and join the regimental band. By October these efforts were complete and successful with Company H being mustered in on November 1, 1861, and a band in place (courtesy the *Union Drummer Boy*, Gettysburg, Pennsylvania).**

EXCELSIOR BRIGADE!
3D REGIMENT
COL. TAYLOR!

50 ABLE BODIED MEN WANTED!

For the above Regiment, to go immediately into active service for the term of 3 years, or during the war.

PAY FROM 13 TO 24 DOLLARS PER MONTH!
FROM THE DAY OF ENLISTMENT, AND ALSO
A Bounty of $100 & 160 Acres of Land
AT THE EXPIRATION OF SERVICE.

This Regiment is composed principally of men from Chautauqua Co., and is encamped near Washington, D. C. Good men capable and willing to serve their country, can be enrolled, by applying immediately to the undersigned at Sinclearville.

Oct. 10, 1861.

Lieut. SAMUEL T. ALLEN,
Recruiting Officer.

Dunkirk was in the heart of western New York's fertile recruiting territory, the stomping grounds of Captain Stevens and young David Parker. Young Lucius Jones, Jr., was among the first to join the reconstituted Company H. Denied enlistment in another regiment two months earlier because of his age and size, the smallish Jones was nonetheless accepted into Doyle's legion and pronounced fit for duty. With his new uniform in hand, Lucius returned home seeking his father's consent and to have his picture taken at the local Monroe's photography rooms. It took Doyle nearly three weeks to raise his company, as many boys waited in Dunkirk's Eastern Hotel, headquarters for the endeavor. Stephen Doyle, who had originally enrolled to serve as Taylor's adjutant, was made captain of the new H, and Dan Loeb, the German speaking, bar-keeping sergeant from Stevens' old militia unit, became second lieutenant. With his company filled by a generous helping of "big, stout fellows"[12] employed at Brook's car shop, Doyle's Company H was ready for the trip east.

The company complete, Doyle, Loeb, and the rest boarded the train for the trip to Baltimore. Arriving in Maryland, more than just a few of his men were "soaked with whiskey,"[13] sick and played out. The next day Company H arrived in Washington and were promptly taken across the Potomac to Maryland where they camped a couple days while being issued muskets and their remaining gear. The 40-mile march down to Camp Wool and the rest of the regiment was not easy for these new men, who were unaccustomed to life in the field, but eventually they made it, many sick and spent. Despite the sorry condition of some, Arthur McKinstry was happy to see them:

> Yesterday our hearts were made glad by the sight of the new Dunkirk Company, headed by Adj. Doyle and our old friend Charlie Loeb, who looks as jolly and rotund as ever. The new company are a pretty promising set, and they seem to be of a far different material from those recruits which are picked up in our crowded cities.[14]

With the march from Washington over, the regiment settled into camp just across the river from the Rebel batteries they had been sent to investigate. The main shipping channel was near the Virginia shore, forcing large vessels to avoid the river altogether while smaller craft escaped Rebel shot and shell by hugging the Maryland side. An exciting pastime of the boys was watching enemy gunners blaze away in vain at passing boats. "The river here is three miles across," wrote Henry Taylor. "They fire at most every boat that goes by, but seldom do any execution, and the balls come over this side. Several have struck in a field and passed through a house close by the camp."[15] Soon after their arrival sometime on the 21st, a large, errant Rebel shell landed on the river bank near camp. The unexploded shell was collected by a guard and brought in. Officers inspected the missile, removed the cap, poured out a substantial amount of powder, doused it with water and set it aside. The shell soon fell into the hands of some bored, young enlisted men who used it as a plaything. The next day Private John Rouse of Company E took his turn with the shell. As he and his other Dunkirk mates played with it, the idea of pushing a smoldering ember or lit cigar into the fuse hole gained popularity. As Rouse shoved the ember in with his foot the bomb instantly exploded. Men were thrown about camp, peppered with fragments while others dove for cover. Rouse was killed almost immediately. A company sergeant, Michael Daly, was badly hurt and eventually transported to the hospital in Washington where his leg was amputated. Daly lay in Union Hospital for a month before dying on November 24. In all, ten Company E men were hurt playing with the Rebel shell. Martin Boyden was hit in the wrist but was soon seen "carrying his musket as defiantly as ever."[16]

It was difficult for Colonel Taylor to discern the exact nature of the enemy batteries situated across the river. There was plenty of speculation as to the location and types of guns being used by the enemy but not much hard evidence. The area directly across the river from the Third Regiment was a five-mile or so stretch of shoreline between Neabsco Creek to the north and Chopawamsic Creek, located further south. Two other creeks flowed into the Potomac along this stretch, creating a number of points upon which the Rebels had actually or in some cases only reportedly placed guns. Earthen redoubts could be seen easily, but the cannons they contained could not. Often times the only evidence of a Confederate cannon's location was a plume of smoke rising from the trees. When guns were seen, either with the naked eye or with field glasses, they were of the smaller, horse drawn, "field battery"[17] type, not the large coastal guns that had the size and range to do real damage. After a few days Taylor reported that the Rebel guns seemed to be concentrated along a one-mile length of shore, ranging north from the Chopawamsic to Quantico Creek. Reporting to Sickles, Taylor pointed out that the batteries north of Quantico Creek at Freestone Point had been abandoned with the establishment of new ones further south. Where troops supporting these guns were camped was also a matter of some speculation. They couldn't be seen directly, and only from the constant smoke rising above the timber could Taylor estimate their location. Any estimate of the size of the force supporting the guns was of course supposition.[18] McKinstry, writing his "uncles," said:

> We noticed the numerous columns of smoke which ascended from their camp-fires, and heard the measured beat of their drums. But few tents were seen, and it seems pretty evident that the most of them have none, I think by the smoke of the camps, that their numbers are exaggerated, and their force immediately upon the river does not exceed our own. What force may be behind the hills it is of course impossible to conjecture.[19]

Over and above assisting engineer Williamson with his river survey, the boys of the regiment were kept busy rooting out enemies of the Union among the local citizenry, seizing suspicious property, and administering loyalty oaths just as they had done earlier during Potter's expedition. Knowing who was a Rebel, who had Rebel sympathies or the exact depth of those sympathies often depended on who was asked. Third Excelsior was camped about one mile south of the home of Timothy Posey and his family, whose house lay about one mile inland from the river. Just days after arrival on Tuesday the 22nd, Taylor welcomed the master of a small navy steamer bringing word that his commodore wished Mr. Posey and others to be arrested, as Taylor saw it, "for no other reason that I could understand, than that they were suspected of entertaining secession sentiments." The colonel declined to make the arrest.[20] But while Taylor may have felt no pressing need to arrest the Poseys, a short time later the entire family was arrested under orders from Hooker himself and the whole lot were carted off to Washington.[21]

The following day, a detail of men disguised as civilians were working with Capt. Williamson along the shore at Budd's Ferry as they had regularly done. Throughout the day Rebel gunners lobbed shells at the group and by late afternoon had decided to take further action. Around 4 p.m. a steamer loaded with soldiers set out across the Potomac toward Maryland, heading for a bayou just above Budd's Ferry, their target being Williamson and his work party. As they approached, the alarm was sounded and the entire regiment formed a line of battle along a bluff on Posey's plantation. Company E was deployed as skirmishers down by the water's edge. Not one to miss their first real action, Martin Boyden, still nursing a wounded wrist, turned out and, using an aiming technique of his own contrivance, gamely fired. The exchange of musketry between the skirmishers and the shipboard Rebels was heated as Company E's buck and ball churned the water and peppered the tug. Thinking better of the endeavor, the steamer reversed course, chugging back to Virginia.[22]

A week passed with Taylor's regiment and the entire Excelsior Brigade held in a state of readiness. Hooker had been anxious for a significant move south against the enemy and was anticipating the go-ahead from McClellan at any time. But with the recent retirement of army head General Winfield Scott, and McClellan's subsequent rise to army chief, there were now too many distractions for Little Mac to entertain a move by Hooker.[23] With no signals, and with no move imminent, the division began preparing winter quarters. Camping on the Posey farm had one big disadvantage for Emerson Merrell, David Parker and the rest: it was close enough to Reb batteries to receive daily shellings from across the river and the occasional enemy steamer. This spot would never do as semi-permanent, winter quarters. By early November, winter quarters were established further inland, away from annoying artillery, closer to Liverpool Point, at a place they'd call Camp Wool.

At Camp Wool the boys commenced to cut down trees for their winter huts. These were fairly large structures, capable of housing upwards of ten men. They were circular log cabins on the bottom with the regiment's Sibley tents serving as the top portion. Henri LeFevre-Brown of Co. B described their quarters thus: "log houses containing good fireplaces, and covered with tents, were erected and everything made as comfortable as possible for the winter."[24] Arthur McKinstry took particular pride in the work of western companies:

> Fire-places of all imaginable patterns, with stick and stone chimneys, are all in full blast, and Co. D is now pretty comfortable, and the rest of the regiment is rapidly taking pattern. If it had not been for the patterns which companies B and D set, I believe the whole parcel of Gothamites would have frozen to death.[25]

Indeed, so advanced was the design of the quarters in which Arthur dwelt that he said, "Our company officers wisely excused us from a good deal of drill that we might complete these arrangements." So once the model was perfected, others might steal their design and build them in "like style."[26]

November was cold. No one reported snow, but they did write home of frost every morning. Emerson Merrell spent nearly the whole month of November sick with measles, eventually landing in the hospital. Writing home, Emerson explained how it was no wonder a soldier would stay sick in the army:

> Now you want to know how I fared when I had the Measles. It was not very good fair.... I was taken to the hospital, a tent about 11 ft. square and there was 10 of us in there sick and nothing but straw to lay on and it was raging sour weather and no fire. So you can judge how sojers [sic] have the measles.[27]

For the sick, relief was on the way. A hospital built of logs was under construction, intended to improve the lot of the infirmed. Also underway was the construction of a regimental bakery whose fresh bread would help fortify sick and healthy alike.

With the regiment encamped out of range of Rebel artillery at Camp Wool, companies now rotated through picket duty at the various points on the river. This put them in better position to observe Confederate activity, interdict bellicose communications and get shot. "You can hardly form an idea how efficiently the river is guarded," wrote McKinstry. "In addition to the pickets which are of themselves impassable, the whole river is alive with boats as soon as darkness falls."[28] The Potomac Flotilla kept a close watch on gun emplacements on the Virginia shore. Some new batteries drew a quick response from one or two Union gunboats while others received attention from nearly the entire fleet: "If the rebels undertake to start fortifications upon the forbidden ground, one or two gun-boats slide gracefully into the bay, and down comes a perfect hail of eight inch shell and fixed ammunition, which operation is the precursor of a very active stampede inland."²⁹ Sometimes Rebel gunners would hold their ground, resulting in a pitched duel between the Virginia batteries, Federal gunboats, and Yankee cannon posted on the Maryland side. These contests prompted cheers from the various sides depending on the success or failure of each round. George Shelly describes his first experience at one such session:

> It was our turn to cheer now, and we did it right lustily. The rebel ire had been kindled now, and "take care boys," was the next word from the officer in charge. I had not thought of this before. What he meant by taking care, I did not know ... but as they had seen the thing before, I determined to do as they did, which was to throw themselves on the ground, and crawl under an old hovel which stood near ... scarcely had I got my position before the death dealing missile came roaring, whizzing through the air. It passed directly over us, and exploded some 60 rods from our position. We came out of our hiding place ... and suddenly recollecting that I had business in camp, I took double quick for home, or any other place of safety.³⁰

Nothing recommended the location of Camp Wool except its distance from enemy batteries, for the ground was sandy and poor for cultivation and there were few inhabitants. Because of the poor roads, Hooker immediately decided his division would be supplied by boat rather than overland by wagon. Traveling the forty miles from Washington to his command over such tracks would only serve to wear out wagons and men alike. Small steamers could bring supplies right to his division, saving men and equipment. Any subsequent trips to Washington would be done on horseback, a trip not without its own hazards.³¹

David Parker became the man in charge of fetching the regiment's mail even before settling into winter quarters. Starting at Camp Caldwell and now at Camp Wool, Parker rode daily to Washington, often accompanied by the courier from the First Regiment. Eventually mail would be carried by steamer to camp, but until then David rode the 70 miles roundtrip every day. Secessionists frequently came down from Baltimore to this stretch of Maryland to cross into Virginia and join the Confederate army. Parker had been warned repeatedly about traveling after dark because of possible encounters with men eager to harm a lone Yankee rider. One night Parker returned late and was close enough to see the lights of camp less than two miles off. As the road passed through an undergrowth of bushes on both sides, a band of three men jumped out, guns in hand, commanding the 18-year-old to stop. With no intention of surrendering, David touched his mount with his heels, springing the mare forward. One marauder grabbed at the horse's bridle but couldn't find purchase. He lunged next at David's foot in equal futility as the mare lurched away. With one Rebel reeling, the others leveled their weapons. Shotgun blasts ripped the night as Parker sped off. Alerted by the commotion, a detachment of cavalry hurried to the scene, but after some time combing the brush, failed to find Parker's assailants.³²

Winter had yet to begin by early November, and already the boys were getting sick and bored. One brigade colonel, tired of waiting for McClellan and Hooker, decided to take matters into his own hands. Colonel Charles Graham of Fifth Excelsior rounded up a cutter from the Potomac Flotilla and with 400 hand-picked men crossed the river on November 9 into Virginia. In dead of night the expedition sailed to Mathias Point. Meeting no resistance, Graham's men burned some forage, scouted enemy emplacements, shot at some pickets and returned with two secessionist prisoners. Sickles was pleased with the initiative, Hooker far less so. But since the operation had come off without incident, Hooker forgave the breach in discipline. McClellan, however, was furious a subordinate would undertake such a mission without approval and promptly placed Graham under arrest,³³ which only served to confirm many men's suspicions that McClellan was all bluster and no fight.³⁴

The day after Graham's foray, Thaddeus Lowe, the Yankee aeronaut, arrived on a naval tug, putting in at the mouth of Mattawoman Creek, about five miles north of Budd's Ferry. The arrival of Lowe and his balloon at Hooker's camp was exciting and temporarily relieved the boredom. Hooker dismissed the value in balloons, yet Sickles was intrigued and was among the first to go up. The brigadier eventually made several 1,000-foot ascents with Lowe in his little three-man basket. "We have balloon reconnaissances, and it seems to tantalize the rebels not a little to see the aeronauts so coolly and securely overlooking their operations," described one Company D private. Despite coming under frequent Rebel artillery fire, "too distant to stand any chance of hitting it,"[35] Lowe continued to fly, pinpointing the location and disposition of enemy troops well inland of the Potomac shore. Once presented with detailed maps produced from the sketches of balloon-borne artists, even the reluctant Hooker came to appreciate the new technology.[36]

Deficiencies in government-issued gear were becoming more evident as winter drew near. For Arthur McKinstry and his fellow westerners, used to being swaddled by caring kin and kind, Federal issue was a big step down:

> The weather here is milder than at Camp Caldwell, but it is pretty cold, and the Chautauqua people would do well to find out whether their friends are supplied with flannel underclothes, for we need something better than the government shirts and drawers, which are not fit to be worn, and which are not at all comfortable. They are made of cotton and wool (I mean dog's hair) and are very harsh. The government socks are a very poor thing, and the shoes, however good for summer, are not at all suited for the deep mud we must pass through whenever we move. Every man ought to have a pair of stout calfboots, reaching about to the knee. We have each a pair of thin blankets, (one good wide blanket with a good nap, is worth a dozen of them) and that is all we can very well carry.[37]

Though the regiment was well established and already in the field, there were still plenty of men eager to join the fight, specifically with the Excelsior Brigade. By late fall there were enough men, mostly from New York City with sprinklings from around the state, to form an eleventh company within Third Excelsior. So on November 14, officers were selected and Company L was added to the ranks. There was no captain at first, but rather two first lieutenants, James Cormack and John Graham. David Jones would serve as second lieutenant.

By the end of November there were big changes in the division. Hooker's division was the smallest in the army, and on the 28th a third brigade was added. The "Jersey Blues" consisted of the Fifth through Eighth New Jersey Volunteers and were under the command of Colonel Samuel H. Starr. These four regiments arrived in camp during the first week in December along with some artillery, which was a welcome addition. The strengthening of the division did not mean a move was imminent, however. On the contrary, McClellan had already decided that nothing could be accomplished in the face of winter's rain and mud. So Hooker would stay put.[38]

There were other changes, too, that would affect the Excelsiors. During the fall, the Federal government called upon the loyal states to meet their quota of troops. This again raised the question of who might claim Sickles' brigade. With this new call for troops looming, Governor Morgan, apparently reconciled his being out-maneuvered by Sickles, claimed the Excelsior Brigade for New York. Thus on December 5, the secretary of war issued orders that went into effect on December 11, re-designating Sickles' regiments as New York State Volunteers, no longer United States Volunteers. From now on, the five regiments of the Excelsior Brigade would officially be designated the 70th thru 74th New York State Volunteers. Col. Taylor and his boys, being the third regiment, were thenceforth the 72nd New

York. "It is now a certain fact that we are recognized as the 72nd N.Y. Volunteers. This is substantially a triumph to Gov. Morgan, and an embarrassment to Gen. Sickles," viewed Arthur McKinstry. "In their personal quarrel I can sympathize but little," Arthur added, "but the result of it is evidently beneficial to us. If we were classed U.S. Volunteers, we should in all probability be retained to garrison disaffected localities," and not sent home until all volunteers had been discharged and "the very last drudgery of warfare accomplished."[39] Aside from the change of designation, there was also a big change within the regiment. Captain James Brown, responsible for recruiting Company B, resigned on November 5 to become the colonel of a regiment still forming, the 100th New York. Filling Brown's spot, 34-year-old first lieutenant Darwin Willard was promoted to captain that same day.

Defending lower Maryland from Confederate invasion and rounding up dissident troublemakers wasn't the only task undertaken by the newly renamed 72nd New York. Lincoln had ordered Hooker's men to assist in any way possible to ensure that the upcoming Maryland state elections were conducted fairly. Leading up to the balloting, certain candidates were arrested for secessionist leanings, while in another incident, a troop of Indiana cavalry broke up a political barbecue held by Southern sympathizers. Federal troops were also posted at various polling places around the state. The election's result: a heavier than expected pro–Union turnout, with a surprisingly small anti-administration vote.[40]

After months in the disaffected locality of southern Maryland, many of the men's beliefs about the institution of slavery were changing, especially among those who had never seen a Negro until joining the army. The popular image of "the Southern planter with his smiling family of domestics around him, over whom he exercises so mild and benevolent a sway," as Arthur McKinstry writes, was merely an illusion. "This picture, so charming in the perspective, upon nearer approach, fades away into a dirty-looking farmer, in a coarse suit of clothes ... and a ragged parcel of chattels, who look eagerly to us for one ray of hope for their delivery."[41] During earlier contacts, many slaves saw the Excelsiors as their emancipators and flocked to them, only to be disappointed when, under orders, the New Yorkers sent them away. As the months wore on, an uneasy status quo was maintained. Slaves were increasingly an issue that required attention, one that caused yet more friction between Sickles and Hooker. McClellan had issued strict orders allowing slave-owners to enter camps in search of their human property and retrieve the slaves if found, an order Hooker obeyed. This order's observance in the regimental camps was a different story, however. New England and New York men were particularly unwelcoming of slave hunters, frequently barring them access to camp; Sickles even went so far as to countermand Hooker's decree and ordered slave hunters out.[42] One Third Excelsior man stated flatly, "It is not our business to return slaves,"[43] and men of the regiment took a measured approach:

> Citizens, whether black or white, are generally allowed pass our lines in the day time, and the slave owner has precisely the same privilege as the darky. We suffer, but we never aid in the capture of fugitives. We are more passive spectators, though sometimes, when a "Chiv," is scampering hot foot after a contraband, it has occurred that the sentry didn't see the latter until he had got past the lines, while the owner was discovered just in time to bring him up at the point of the bayonet, and send him around to No. 1 post, where he could get out and dash after his property, which had got about a half mile into the woods.[44]

Hooker increasingly found himself in a no-win situation, pulled three ways between the orders of McClellan, the reality of the camps, and the edicts of radical Senate Republicans who wanted to make it a crime for Federal officers to return runaways. An anecdote told in the camps illustrates Hooker's eventual, less than wholehearted cooperation with the slave-owners. It would seem a group of slave-hunters came to Hooker demanding access per McClellan's orders to the camp of a Massachusetts regiment where their slaves reportedly hid. "Yes I have seen the order," Hooker supposedly replied, "and if your slaves are there and wish to go with you, and the Massachusetts boys are content, I have no objections. But if they refuse and a row occurs over there, I fear you will get into the guardhouse—the same as any other marauders."[45] But when the hunters asked if Hooker would not apprehend the slaves for them, Hooker responded, "I am Brigadier General United States Volunteers, and no nigger catcher. I was born and bred in New England."[46]

Not every anti–Union man in southern Maryland was necessarily a slave owner, and the line between secessionist sympathizer and an outright rebel was often a fuzzy one. Oaths of loyalty were frequently administered throughout the population. Though these oaths were readily recited, both soldiers and citizens alike knew mere words weren't usually enough to change a person's politics. "The people here are all secessionist, and it is only the presence of an overpowering Union force which cause them to feign loyalty," confided a local Union man. "They are all ready to take the oath of allegiance; that doesn't hurt them a bit; but just so soon as they think they can help Jeff Davis, so soon their dispatches will be sent on."[47] Among the oath takers were the Posey family, who were allowed to return home after a stint in a Washington prison and recitation of appropriate pledges. Hooker made amends with the family, whose land he occupied, paid them a handsome stipend for use of their parlor, and even wrote a letter to Washington on their behalf requesting the return of some personal papers. While Mr. Posey had seemingly ceased any dubious activities, his wife and daughter continued their unmannerly habit of secretly signaling to unknown accomplices across the river with looking glass by day and lantern at night.

As the wet and muddy winter wore on, the men of the 72nd N.Y. went about their routine duties as best they could. Not all was well within the regiment or the brigade. Men continued to get sick, and many were not as lucky as Emerson Merrell. "More die from disease than from battle,"[48] wrote Charles Gould. By the end of the year several within Company I had died; Robert Maxwell lasted four months after enlisting while Robert Penny died after only two months of service. While all companies within the regiment suffered, these early deaths by disease hit the rural western companies of B, I, and the like harder than city-raised companies C and K. Perhaps the close quarters of city dwelling served to vulcanize these men to the rigors of army life more than the wide-open spaces enjoyed by Chautauqua and Chenango county farmers. Arthur McKinstry, who frequently updated his hometown readers on the condition of convalescing western men, offered his thoughts about the disparity: "The health of the Metropolitan companies is still better than ours, for the fellows who used to sleep on coal boxes, and who never owned a decent suit in their lives, are better fed and clothed, and in some instances, better lodged than when at home."[49] The frequent passing of comrades set against the dispassionate routine of army life struck Company B man James Hall:

> One by one passes away, and still the regular routine of duty and business goes on as ever, never stopping for the death of one or of twenty. The drummer's call at daylight; the reveille beat around the whole camp some ten minutes later; the hurrying out from the log-houses to fall in for roll-call, morning ablutions, and street cleaning; the call to fall in for rations; the rush for cup and plate; the breakfast; guard-mounting at eight, when the guards are inspected, and pass in review before the officer of the day, led by the band playing sweet music for those less accustomed to hear it, but tunes that are becoming old and worn-out with us.
> Then men are detailed for various duties, such as bringing water and wood; then comes

Jesse L. Walker enlisted with Company E and is shown here wearing the New York State jacket, the typical uniform of New York troops. Walker was wounded at Chancellorsville and mustered out with the regiment in July of 1864 (courtesy the U.S. Army Heritage and Education Center).

dinner at twelve, of beans, hominy and meat; then, if the day be pleasant, battalion drill, and beating of retreat at sunset; then supper; and at eight, tattoo and roll-call, when all hands prepare for going to bed. This is our daily round, never stopping if one is taken sick, or goes to the hospital, or breathes his last, and is borne by a few to his final resting-place, and the three volleys are fired over his grave.[50]

Emerson described a typical funeral in a letter to his parents:

> It is a sight worthy of note to witness the funeral of a soldier—the music forms the head of the column followed by 8 men with guns—the next is the coffin with a gard [sic] of 6 men on each side and behind follows the rest of the company without guns. The paul [sic] cloth consists of the stars and stripes spread over the coffin. After the company is formed in this manner the music commences playing a death march and in this manner proceeds to the grave. After the coffin is lowered into the grave the escort marches to the grave and fires 3 rounds of blank cartridges and then the grave is filled up and the band strikes up a lively tune and the company returns to camp.[51]

City companies were losing men too, not to disease but to desertions, especially Company K. Desertions were occurring throughout the regiment, to be sure, but before the end of 1861, fully eleven men had deserted Company K. Some Company K deserters such as Thomas Carroll and Humphrey Fisher left only two weeks after enlisting. Whether these two enlisted for the bonus money or to avoid prison, they probably never intended to see the thing out. Whatever the reasons, K's losses represented more than ten percent of the company's numbers, and they had yet to see combat.

Sickles was frequently absent from camp throughout the winter. Congress had yet to approve his appointment to brigadier, and there was cause for worry. A bloc of radical Republican senators had serious doubts about the aspiring "General" Sickles. Before the war, Congressman Sickles had been an outspoken, uncompromising Democrat, and these radical Republican questioned the advisability of entrusting such a large command to such an "otherwise-minded" man. Unscrupulous partisans and some newspapers feared "troops raised by Sickles or other Democrats would march over to Jeff Davis in the first battle in which they were engaged."[52] So Dan worked the halls of Congress prospecting for votes he'd need later to win confirmation.[53]

With Sickles gone there was growing dissatisfaction in the 72nd New York's winter camp with their absentee brigadier. Like Hooker, who was suspicious of political generals, some of Taylor's officers were also apprehensive, while men such as Arthur McKinstry took a more practical view:

> I opine that the Excelsior Brigade has never been so well managed as when during the absence of Gen. Sickles, Col. Taylor has been acting brigadier. Sickles displayed great energy and patriotism in the raising and equipment of the brigade. He has governed it however in a civilian manner, and whatever talent and administrative ability he may have, he is evidently incompetent to personally maneuver the brigade.... I think that we might have played some other role than that of special policemen, and labored up on a Maryland highway, if we had been headed by an experienced soldier.[54]

A petition was eventually circulated within Third Excelsior asking the regiment be transferred to a brigade commanded by a more experienced officer. While the names of the signatories or who initiated it are lost to history, reportedly almost every line officer in the regiment signed the document. Certainly the veteran men among the field and staff officers, along with the senior captains, may have found Sickles' absenteeism, personal style, and dearth of military knowledge wanting and may have sought a commander with more martial fortitude. Perhaps with a large portion of the 72nd N.Y. coming from the substantially Republican-leaning western counties, the notion of a deficient Sickles may have found a fonder reception there compared with regiments raised from Dan's New York City bastion. Had there been any Sickles loyalists within the 72nd, they would have surely been the Gothamites. Captain Isaac Chadwick was a New York City machinist prior to the war and raised Company C, while Captain John Austin had been a clerk at Washington Market and recruited Company K. Presumably both Chadwick and Austin knew Sickles or knew of him and may have declined to sign any petitions viewed as damaging. No matter who actually signed the petition, the men appreciated Sickles' energy in forming the brigade, and there is no evidence the petition's authors schemed to derail Dan's appointment to general. These men had come to fight, and if Sickles was only capable of "policing a Maryland highway,"[55] then they wanted out. Sickles was aware of dissension within the 72nd but felt "everywhere in the Brigade—except for a fraction of the 3rd Regt—there is the sharpest possible solicitude for my confirmation."[56]

Sickles wasn't just having problems with Third Excelsior that winter; the 71st New York (Second Excelsior) seemed on the verge of open war with itself. Following Col. Hall's arrest for his neglect of rations during their October march from Washington, Lt. Col. H.L. Potter took command of the regiment; most assumed Hall would be cashiered and Potter made permanent commander. During Hall's absence, many officers voiced support of Colonel Hall and their displeasure with Lieutenant Colonel Potter; some even resigning over the issue. Choosing sides between "Hall sympathizers" and "Potter men" grew more contentious when at the end of November Hall was released and returned to command. By the time of his return, battle lines had been drawn, with most of the regiment evenly split. Hall and Potter bickered furiously throughout the winter while officers on both sides preferred a variety of charges against each other. Events reached a head following an afternoon parade witnessed and applauded by General Hooker. It was now that men of the 71st N.Y. decided it was a good time for a spree. Drinking started early in Potter's tent and picked up steam as hours passed, unhindered even by the presence of several ladies. As revelers left Potter's tent, they stopped by Hall's quarters long enough to hurl insults, which brought forth a group of Hall supporters, starting a free-for-all fight involving nearly the entire camp. In the end several men were badly injured, with both Hall and Potter having new charges pending and awaiting courts-martial. Disgusted, Sickles recommended Hooker bar both men from camp. He further requested the regiment be reduced to battalion status under command of its major and combined with the 70th New York (First Excelsior). Ultimately the regiment kept its integrity, and Hall and Potter kept their posts, with animosity between the two continuing.[57]

While Second Excelsior tore itself apart, Taylor and his officers found workable solutions to discipline issues. Drunk and marauding soldiers from throughout the division were the bane of the local citizenry; the depredations fell upon secessionist and loyalist alike. Taylor had taken a firm stand early on against drunkenness and other vices, and now here in Maryland the restraint instilled in the regiment began to tell. "Some of our officers have been sent to Piscataway to examine the claims of many people who have been injured by the robberies committed by our soldiers when they passed through," wrote McKinstry home, adding, "about $1,400 had been demanded, *not one of which had been charged to the 3d Regt....* Our own regiment had won the good opinion of all on account of its sobriety, good order, and neatness."[58] Indeed Taylor had turned Third Excelsior into the class of the brigade if not the entire division, winning accolades from Hooker as to appearance and precision of drill. Arthur elaborated further on Taylor's handling of the regiment in a December 3 letter:

> Col. Taylor is a very prudent man, so far as the health and comfort of his men are concerned, and few men could enforce such strict discipline, and exact so severe a drill as he has done until lately, and yet retain so thoroughly the love and confidence of the men. He is very severe upon gaming, and in this he is ably seconded by Cpt. Abell, who gave out the word that if any of his men were caught playing for money they would get lodging at the guard house forthwith, and that if the offender was a non-commissioned officer, he should be degraded to the ranks. As regards punishment of ordinary offences, our officers have pursued a very wise course. Instead of sending a culprit to the guard-house, he is required to pack his knapsack and walk to and fro with one of the sentries down in the woods. This punishment, while more severe than imprisonment, is more private, and in proportion less prejudicial to self-respect. Drunkenness also is an offence which Col. Taylor has little leniency for. At present it is almost impossible to procure liquor, and the man who returns home an inebriate must indeed be lost to all sense of honor and self. As a whole, I think that the effects of military life upon the minds of young men will be generally good, and certainly, habits of idleness are not apt to be acquired under Col. Nelson Taylor.[59]

Of all the deficiencies hitherto endured, on December 7 the lack of decent weaponry was finally resolved. "The French rifles have come this evening, and now we have a really serviceable arm," wrote 34-year-old George Shelly of Company D, adding, "we shall feel disposed to take better care of it than we have done heretofore. These Harper Ferry guns are a miserable thing, and I would not have one about me unless for shooting pigeons."[60] Though the record of this rifle's issuance is lost, given the men's enthusiasm for the piece, it is likely they received a Belgian-made copy of the French Model 1859. This .61-caliber piece accepted the Minié ball and was considered on a par with the '61 Springfield; it was widely imported for the use of Federal troops. Rifle being in hand, a notice was soon posted on the regimental bulletin board announcing a shooting competition scheduled for Christmas Day. Sponsored by the three senior officers, the prize would be a $50 gold medal. The target was specified as being six feet high by 22 inches wide at a range of 300 yards. The ten best men of each company would compete. With no private practice allowed, the captains immediately set their companies to work. Many were able to register hits at 100 yards, but only the top marksmen did "much execution"[61] at 250. Christmas arrived, but the shooting match had to be postponed until New Year's. Without the excitement of the big match, the boys settled into their cabins for a more somber holiday. The men enjoyed a holiday pudding or oyster stew. Many within the regiment appreciated a supply of new uniform jackets, which were a big improvement over previous shoddy ones. Despite receiving a batch of good shirts, there was still a problem. "Now we get very nice summer shirts and drawers of white cotton," wrote Arthur McKinstry. "They are very good, but I must say they are very unseasonable and by no means the thing for a winter campaign."[62]

Expectantly on New Year's Day the regiment assembled for the shooting contest with the representatives of each company "marched out to compete for the golden prize. There was a good deal of excitement, and bets ran high,"[63] recorded Arthur McKinstry. Delaware County's Company I seemed most confident that one of their numbers would wear the "yellow metal."[64] Arthur relates the scene:

> The day was clear but rather cold, though overcoats were not exactly indispensable, and the wind pretty strong. The target was at full 300 yards and, though the sun shone fair upon it, the wind crossed our line of shot in such a manner as to make it very difficult to take aim.

Markers were established near the target, and also men to pass the numbers of the shots between the umpires and the markers. The umpires were Captains Doyle, Willard and Chadwick.

The marksmen were drawn up in line, and numbers written upon bits of paper were handed round in a cap. Each man drew one, and, when the number upon his ticket was called, stepped forth to shoot.[65]

Each man fired three shots from whatever position he wished. Smoke, bullets, and the sound of judging filled the air for three hours before a winner was declared. At evening parade, Sergeant William Post of Company D was called out and presented the trophy by Colonel Taylor; it bore the inscription "Presented by the Field Officers of the 3d Reg. Excelsior Brigade, U.S. Volunteers, to _____ the best marksman. Dec. 25th 1861." The medal had the likeness of Washington on the reverse. Almost immediately, Post became the subject of good-natured taunts from disappointed competitors, "who have all along been of the opinion that 'the Chautauqua element was the ruination of the 3d Reg.' and are now more convinced of it than ever."[66]

By January the routines of army life had become ingrained into former farmers, shop keepers, craftsmen and coal-box sleepers. While some complained, they came to view drill as part of army life and accepted it with a certain amount of stoic pride. "We used to think two or three hours drill with knapsacks a pretty tough exercise," reflected Arthur. "Now we consider it a mere bagatelle, not worth mention. If any of your readers have any curiosity to try that drill, let them fasten a bushel of wheat upon their shoulders, a half-gallon jug of water and a day's provision at their side, and shoulder a crowbar of medium weight, for a walk of about three hours duration."[67]

Men were becoming inured to army life, and without the immediate dangers of combat, some saw it as little different from civilian life. But for many the most disheartening part of the military was the chronic and wanton disrespect for the Sabbath. For men raised in the bosom of the church who strove to lead a moral and Christian life, to work, drill, or march on the Lord's day of rest was inexcusable. Letters home bristled with complaints about the irreverence they were forced to endure. Owen Street described what his friend James Hall suffered while corporal:

> He had heard that "war knows no Sabbath," and now he was to learn what this means. It became necessary to open a practicable road to Liverpool Point, as nearly all their provision and forage must reach them in that way, and the ordinary road had become so bad, that an empty wagon could scarcely be drawn upon it. To meet this necessity, his company and two others were obliged to work the whole of one Sabbath in building a "corduroy road." This was revolting to his feelings, and to those of "the other boys...." However, he says, he "did his duty in overseeing and directing the men" on that day. He had on a former occasion deplored the disadvantages of the Sabbath as passed in camp; contrasting it with the peaceful Sabbath at home. Now he assures us, that a Sabbath in camp, with no such work to be done, and with one of Mr. Beecher's sermons in the Independent to read, is a privilege which he greatly enjoys.[68]

James Hall described his moral plight of having no Sabbath while at the same time being surrounded by wickedness:

> But how great is the change—no church, no Sabbath school, no prayer-meeting, no religious instructions to attend, no religious influences whatever, thrown around me! On the contrary, there are many and great temptations for me to fight against. I can hardly hear a conversation but what is intermixed with oaths and profanity of the direst kind, and the most vicious language that the hearts of men can devise, is used by those in the same tent with me, as well as

in every other tent. And not only this, but books of the basest description, written by the basest of men, are scattered through the camp for the soldiers to read. Gambling, drinking and smoking, are vices that meet us at every turn. But my trust is still in God. I have not forgotten to pray, and the good influences that were thrown around me in Lowell, are still fresh in my memory. I do not yet smoke, drink, or swear, neither do I read these vile books, nor indulge with others in base conversation, and, with the help of God, I never intend to. I am fighting hard against these temptations: other boys say I will get into these habits before long; but so long as my trust is in my heavenly Father, and I continue to rest on Him for help and support, and pray often to Him, I know that He will help me, and I shall at last be victorious.[69]

Others enjoyed more wholesome pursuits while in winter camp. Among these less base amusements were dominoes, chess, checkers and cards, which served to "help the days to drag their slow length along."[70] Newspaper reading and letter writing of course served to "guile away the evening hours."[71] On the street of Company D, participation in the Pioneer Debating Club took hold. Covering topics of general interest, the group made every effort to keep things friendly. "The strictest rule of parliamentary debate are enforced, and owing to the exclusion of politics, and other subjects which are likely to awaken latent prejudice, the most marked courtesy and absence of personality prevails,"[72] explained McKinstry. Subjects for debate included these: "Is military service necessarily demoralizing.... Resolved, That the Pulpit exercises a greater influence than the Press,"[73] and "Resolved, That man is the architect of his own fortunes."[74] Disputants were chosen without regard to their personal preference on a subject, causing some contestants, as Arthur observed, "to take up a train of argument, and follow it so keenly as to cause a material change in their own opinions."[75]

Liquor, of course, was another avenue many sought to entertain themselves. Officers went after not only intemperate soldiers but also local peddlers who found ready customers at $1 per bottle. Locals moving goods by boat were a common sight on the Potomac and its small tributaries. It was unsafe to be caught with whiskey, so secret stashes were hidden during the day and then trotted out at night. Regimental scouting parties combed likely hiding places, hoping to find such stashes, smashing as many as eight dozen bottles in a single cache. One January day Lieutenant Hugh Hinman of Company D and his party of six apprehended one such peddler with only four bottles on hand. Arthur McKinstry picks up the story:

> Hinman applied his nose to the bottle, but his air of expectation gave way to one of great disgust, as he exclaimed: "Boys, that will kill at forty rods!" Solemnly the bottle passed from nose to nose, and all were unanimous in the opinion that a man whose stomach was not lined with copper sheathing, or boiler plate iron, had no business with whiskey of that quality.[76]

As winter moved into early spring, the pace of life in camp picked up. Many of the men anticipated momentous things, and an end to the rebellion come campaigning season. Charles Gould wrote of his expectations in a letter home:

> The war is getting to be a desperate one. Immense armies are being raised. Lincoln has now the service of over 600,000 men and talks of enlisting 200,000 more.... I do not see how the war can last any longer than this spring. If it does I shall be content to stay until it is over and see the government rule.[77]

George Shelly echoed Gould's anticipation. "There are now 15,000 men on this side of the river, swearing, scolding, praying, and in every way showing much impatience to cross over, and wipe out the rebels. This feeling assumes a very malignant form, when the boom of the rebel's guns is followed by the hissing sound of the shell intended for the destruction of some unarmed trader."[78] This malignant form was increasingly laid at the feet of Sickles. As the months rolled by, news of fights and Union victories elsewhere brought men to the conclusion that they were serving in a military backwater, a second-rate theater of operation that would never see any serious action. For men eager to fight, Sickles' lack of military experience was the undoubted cause for their plight; the troops serving under him seemed doomed to while away their enlistments in some unheralded corner of the war.

Hooker, however, continued pestering McClellan for the go-ahead for a serious offensive across the river into Virginia. With Lincoln's growing impatience over McClellan's lack of movement, it was looking like Hooker might get his wish. McClellan told Hooker to put his plan in writing, a clear sign McClellan was warming to the idea. But when submitted a few days later the proposal proved far too ambitious, requiring a second division and complicated multiple amphibious landings. There was uncertainty about the shoreline chosen, and the plan likely needed McClellan himself to supervise. After some delays the plan was shelved. Despite the cancellation, throughout the late winter and very early spring, there were a number of small scouting missions across the Potomac giving commanders a truer picture of what lay ahead. When time came for a move, they'd be ready.[79]

As the 72nd emerged from winter quarters, it was clear that the addition of an eleventh company would not be permanent. On December 15, the same day John Graham was promoted to captain, eleven men of Company L deserted; the reason, whether because of or in spite of Graham's promotion, is unknown. Company L added a few men after the mass desertion, but enrollment never reached much above 80 men. On February 7 the officers were dismissed from service and allowed to do as they pleased, while enlisted men were transferred throughout the remaining ten companies. As of February 25, Company L ceased to exist.

The following day, Lieutenant John Sanford of Company I, for whom Charles Gould was servant, performed the sad task of composing a letter to Hanna Thomas, Charles' sister:

> Dear Madam,
> Although an entire stranger, I trust you will pardon the liberty that I take of addressing you upon this occasion. I would that the circumstance that calls me at this time to an unwelcome task.... Your brother Charles was taken sick about two weeks since, which proved fatal. He died on Saturday night last and was buried on Monday following the honors of war. His disease was typhoid fever....
> While the life of a soldier is not calculated to improve his morals, I can, with pleasure, say that the vices and immoralities of camp had no influence upon Charles.... Always maintaining his rectitude of principals that were the basis of his actions.[80]

Indeed, the frequent and seemingly random deaths from camp disease, about which Charles Gould had often written home, had now claimed him.

In early March the Rebels actively kept huge fires burning day and night. By March 9 it was clear the Confederates were evacuating their positions across from Budd's Ferry and were destroying everything that could not be moved. Parties from the regiments conducted missions across the river to determine the extent of Rebel withdrawal and to curtail the activities of Rebels still remaining.[81] On March 19 it was the 72nd's turn to cross the river.

The mission fell to Captain Robert Johnson's Company I and would take 50 men, Emerson Merrell among them. Fifty left camp near 11 p.m. marching down to Liverpool Point, where they boarded a small steamer. Their mission was to track down and capture a rebel spy who had been running mail across the river. This spy was reportedly a lieutenant in the Confederate army, and there was a $5,000 reward for his apprehension. The steamer cruised downriver about 15 miles before landing Johnson and his men on Virginia soil. As Company I "scoured the country"[82] for the spy, three Reb cavalrymen appeared; after discovering Yankee infantry, they turned back. Johnson's men fired on the mounted men but missed. Unable to locate the spy, they returned unmolested to the steamer and the short voyage home. Their take for the night according to Emerson: "2 niggers and 20 turkeys, 1 revolver and a 15 inch bowie knife."[83]

The next night Captain Darwin Willard took 100 men from companies A and B over for a reconnaissance near Aquia Creek, where there were reported to be two pieces of artillery and about 200 Reb soldiers. Marching through the dark and rain to Liverpool Point, Willard's men embarked near 9 p.m. on the gunboat *Satellite*, eventually pulling away from the dock two hours later. *Satellite* was a small side-wheeler that was part of the Potomac Flotilla and a common sight on the river. The night was exceedingly dark and foggy, compelling the ship's master to stop, set anchor, and wait for it to lighten. After a two-hour wait, *Satellite* continued on to near Boyd's Hole, where the 100 men transferred to small boats and finally went ashore near 3 a.m. The first boat landed near a small picket of enemy cavalry. Moving toward the pickets, the uninitiated men of Company B felt a rush of excitement as bullets whizzed through the air and splintered a nearby fence. With Willard's men returning fire, the Reb horsemen fell back half a mile. With his entire force now on Virginia soil, Willard took his men forward. The 72nd men continued to advance in the face of light resistance from Reb pickets and followed the enemy into the woods.[84] With the New Yorkers about a mile inland, Willard's skirmishers could see the enemy camps in full alert, while straight ahead a full regiment of Confederate infantry had formed into a line of battle. In the face of such a large force, Willard called for withdrawal back to the boats. It was a mile back to the river, and the boys engaged in some foraging along the way. When the 100 reached the river and the safety of *Satellite*, it was daylight. The boys reached home around noon with no further incident and no injuries, with "everybody thoroughly tired but well satisfied with the trip,"[85] declared Co. B man Henri LeFevre-Brown.

These encounters improved the regiment's spirits after a wet, cold winter. "Our troops are raising hell with the rebels and we are all anxious to lock arms with them,"[86] Emerson wrote home. While the boys were certainly learning to become soldiers, such small and easy encounters with the enemy may have given them a false sense of confidence regarding the rigors of a bigger, truly pitched battle.

But the battle for Sickles' generalship was not going well. On March 17 the Senate had voted to disapprove Dan's nomination to brigadier. Despite the trips to Washington, the lobbying, and the courting of votes, it seemed radical Republicans in the Senate as well as Governor Morgan back in New York had had the last laugh. Hooker acted quickly, issuing Special Order 132, which removed Sickles and placed Nelson Taylor in command of the brigade. Dan was livid; he had come too far and worked too hard to be denied now. Claiming the order was illegal based on his seniority within the brigade, Sickles refused to obey and fired off letters to both McClellan and Lincoln. Pending a verdict from higher authorities, Dan was allowed to remain at his post, creating more than just a little uncertainty. McKinstry reflected on Sickles' plight:

> We have had some more brigade drills lately, and Gen. Sickles has done much better than his former management would have justified our expecting. I cannot but admire his indomitable resolution, and have no mean opinion of his talent. If the time spent at Washington in intriguing for the confirmation of the Generalship had been employed as at present, I believe

that his nomination would have been more favorably received.... If Sickles is to be our General why not confirm him and let him apply himself to his business? If he is not to be, why not at once appoint his successor and let him assume his harness as promptly as possible. It should be to us a source of humiliation, that military experience and signal ability have weighted so lightly when opposed to political trickery and partisan prejudices.[87]

By April 1 activity in camp was reaching a climax. Orders had been received to evacuate the sick and wounded to Washington and prepare to break camp.[88] A big move was imminent, but the forays into Virginia would continue.

A detachment of 250 men prepared to move on the 2nd under the direction of Lieutenant Colonel Moses, with similar sized details being readied from each Excelsior regiment. In all about 1,500 men were crossing the river. Lieutenant Colonel Charles Burtis of the 74th N.Y. would command the men, while Sickles went to command the operation.[89] Stafford Court House was the objective. The various detachments boarded boats that night for the long ride down-river. Upon landing, the Excelsiors formed a line of march and proceeded inland. Within a mile of the town, Sickles' men encountered enemy pickets, which were quickly routed. With the New Yorkers approaching, Confederate troops set fire to their camp and stores, burning anything of value ahead of the invading Yankees. Soon a number of enemy cavalry drew up in line of battle on a hill just beyond town. As the bulk of Sickles' force advanced slowly forward, a company of Zouaves (most likely from the 73rd N.Y.) was sent around the hill. Private Talmon Bookhout, another Delhi man with Company I, described the rest of the fight in a letter home:

> We sent a French Co. of Zouaves around the hill, to take them in the rear, which was done in instant by the nimble-footed French; they were deployed as skirmishers and came up in the rear of the cavalry unobserved, they then poured in a volley of musketry scattering them in all directions. We were then ordered on by the General in double quick time to charge on the rebels which we had nearly surrounded. With yells of triumph we made for them; they might have thought that all the fiends of the lower regions were after them, as the yells seemed to increase every moment. On we went after them, but soon we had to give up the chase, for we came upon a regiment of infantry and another cavalry.[90]

Hooker's orders were to only scout enemy positions, so Sickles called off the fight and withdrew back towards the river. Withdrawing through town, men vented their aggressions on the "secessia"[91] there, destroying, among other things, a large piano, which was "smashed in a thousand pieces."[92] The expedition's loot included seven prisoners, 15 horses, some pistols, sabers and some "valuable"[93] papers. The men considered the night's work a success, coming out of it in good shape with only three men wounded.

Sickles and his 1,500 made it back to camp on the 5th. Within hours orders arrived that all had been expecting: instructions to leave Camp Wool and begin packing onto transport steamers waiting for them at Liverpool Point.[94] Sickles was satisfied; his men were turning into real soldiers. He'd just completed three successful missions into Virginia and faced an upcoming campaign season sure to cover all with glory; perhaps there was still hope for Sickles' generalship. But another letter had arrived, one whose contents were devastating: Sickles was officially relieved of command of Excelsior Brigade.

All of the appeals had been exhausted, and Hooker needed to put Sickles behind him and move on. Hooker believed Sickles was unfit for command and, with plenty of unseemly intrigues to Dan's credit; any higher-ups were reluctant to rescue him. The April 5 note from Hooker's headquarters left no doubt, Dan was to immediately depart the brigade and turn command over to Taylor. Crushed, Dan retired to a cabin aboard the steamer *Elm City*, which he had used as his headquarters, and on April 6 penned a defiant yet hopeful farewell to his brigade just as the men of Taylor's 72nd N.Y. loaded themselves onboard:

> Headquarters, Excelsior Brigade
> Second Hooker's Brigade On Board Transport "Elm City,"
>
> April 6, 1862
>
> General Orders, No. 6
>
> Soldiers: Special Orders No. 132 will announce to you that I am relieved from further duty in the Brigade, by order of the Brigadier General commanding this division.
>
> My last act of duty is to bid you farewell. After a year of service with you, it is hard to yield to the necessity which separates me from so many brave and devoted companions-in-arms, endeared to me by more than ordinary ties.
>
> While protesting that it is unlawful and unjust, I obey this command, because obedience to superior authority is the first duty of a soldier.
>
> It is my earnest hope that a prompt appeal for redress, to the General commanding the army, will permit me to share with you the honors of the campaign now so auspiciously begun.
>
> Whether we are separated for a day or forever, the fervent wishes of my heart will follow your fortunes on every field. You have waited patiently for the hour now at hand, when the Army of the Potomac will move upon the stronghold of the enemy.
>
> Your discipline, courage and bearing will place you among the foremost of our legions. The glory which surely awaits you will help to reconcile me to the pain it costs me to say again— Farewell![95]

In the confusion of loading, many men were unaware of the news, and fewer still were in attendance for Dan's farewell address. Sickles left the ship and headed for Washington. He loved being general, so it was off to the capital to find what strings were left to pull in order to reclaim his stars. As for the men he left behind, those who cared were disheartened but had little time to dwell on it. Colonel Graham of the 70th N.Y., and Sickles' longtime friend, resigned in protest, leaving the regiment in the hands of Lt. Col. Burtis. But most of the men believed Sickles could take care of himself; they could sense something big was awaiting them at the end of this steamer voyage, and they looked forward, bursting with anticipation. "I think we will soon find ourselves in business...," wrote Pvt. Bookhout, "... and that is just what we want, if we have got to fight we may as well do it first as last. I would like to wade in secession blood for one week, then I think I would be satisfied."[96]

Epoch II: The Seat of War

4. Journey to Williamsburg

Nelson Taylor chafed at inaction. With orders in hand to load the Excelsior Brigade on ships bound for Virginia, the newly appointed commander was stymied by the lack of suitable ships. Chadwick's Company C and the rest of Third Excelsior packed aboard the *Elm City* beginning Saturday, April 5, but by Tuesday the other regiments were still stranded without transport. While waiting, they received an additional two days of rations on *Elm City,* but Taylor's patience was growing thin. Insistent the entire brigade move as one, Taylor took matters into his own hands. "By Col. Taylor's orders, the next two steamers passing up were brought to by a gunboat, and taken *nolens volens* to transport our brigade,"[1] wrote Arthur McKinstry. Despite Taylor's dubious legal authority to commandeer the vessels, he could now move his men.

The men's uncertainty over the destination, Port Royal or Fortress Monroe, was removed at 4 p.m. on Wednesday, when Taylor's impressed flotilla cast off for Fortress Monroe at the tip of the Virginia peninsula, a peninsula that ran straight up to the Confederate capital of Richmond. At the beginning of the war, while other Federal forts and installations along the southern coast were falling into Rebel hands, war planners in Washington recognized Fortress Monroe's value and fought to keep it a Union possession. This was the starting point for McClellan's long-awaited offensive to end the war by taking Richmond. By starting at Fortress Monroe instead of Washington, he could avoid crossing countless rivers and streams, any of which the rebels could build into a defensive nightmare for the advancing Federals. So here they were. Since mid–March the Army of the Potomac had been gathering and preparing for the great shove that would lead to Richmond's capture and the end of the war.

But for the boys of Third Excelsior the trip onboard the *Elm City* was not going well. Soon after loading, a snow storm set in. The *Elm City* now rode at anchor near the mouth of Port Tobacco awaiting navigable weather. McKinstry wrote of the trip:

> We at last got off and steamed down as far as the mouth of Port Tobacco creek, where we dropped anchor for the night. We had two barges and two schooners in tow, and the *Elm City* kept their hawsers as taut as fiddle strings. On Thursday morning we steamed down as far as Point Lookout, at the mouth of the Potomac. As the seas were running high in the bay, we lay at anchor until they should subside, fearing that the tow lines would part.[2]

Planners expected the time on *Elm City* to be short, only two days, so the regiment had been crowded aboard in conditions unsuitable for a longer voyage. As conditions conspired to make men sick, the men accustomed to the water, the Lake Erie and Chesapeake Bay fishermen, fared better in warding off the collywobbles than the upstate farmers and Chadwick's New York City men.[3] There was a sense of confidence among the regiment. This campaign would be a quick one with glory enough for everyone, assuming it wasn't over before they reached Virginia. Those who managed to avoid sickness surely pondered their role in the upcoming crusade. Nelson Taylor too must have had time to wonder as he waited out the storm from his brigade commander's cabin. Had the petition signed weeks before gone too far? Certainly no one had wanted to have the general removed from command when they signed; no one had schemed to have Taylor run the entire brigade; but despite their intentions, both had come to pass, and in the eyes of the other regiments Third Excelsior was to blame.

It is unknown whether Third Excelsior's petition carried any weight back in the Senate. Dan Sickles carried enough political impedimenta of his own to be rejected regardless of an officers' petition. But back at the front, McKinstry felt compelled to explain the regiment's position to folks in Fredonia:

> I presume that the final rejection of Sickles has created some surprise among your readers. The other regiments of the brigade accuse us of being the cause of his rejection. I have no doubt that they are correct in their opinion, though the movement which caused his downfall was not initiated with any intention of creating that result. It was a petition, signed almost unanimously by our line officers, requesting that the regiment might be transferred to the command of an experienced officer; which, instead of affecting the desired transfer, defeated Sickles' confirmation....
>
> When this brigade was organized, our feeling were strongly enlisted in favor of Gen. Sickles, and Governor Morgan's double dealing with him, created against the latter a feeling of distrust and prejudice, which still holds good as originally. We gave Sickles the credit of great energy and patriotism, and we do not yet see cause to deny him those attributes. But Bull Run and Big Bethel forced upon us the reflection that something more than mere civilian talent and shrewdness were necessary in a military commander. Gen. Sickles was not a soldier, and you might as well suppose the babe an hour old to perform the labors and duties of experienced manhood, as for a peaceful citizen to assume the responsibilities of a grade which a lifetime of service most frequently fails to attain. His labors and responsibilities deserved a high reward, but are the lives and fortunes of five thousand men to be risked on that account?[4]

McClellan started his move toward Richmond the day before the 72nd boarded *Elm City*, and Chadwick's Gothamites didn't need to worry that the war would pass them by. Upon moving up the peninsula, Union troops immediately discovered their maps were faulty. Bad roads combined with foul weather turned their advance into a wet and muddy ordeal. Despite the poor conditions, McClellan moved north and was drawn up in front of Yorktown before the Warwick River. Confederates fooled McClellan into stalling by making their positions and troop strength look more formidable than they actually were. Calling up ever more troops, McClellan, "Little Mac," started siege operations against Yorktown while he massed his forces for a great push across the Warwick.[5]

Back on *Elm City* things were beginning to look up. The weather cleared, allowing the steamer to leave Maryland waters on the night of the 10th from Fortress Monroe. *Elm City* arrived at Hampton Roads early the next morning. Dawn's light revealed the ship to be anchored next to the ironclad USS *Monitor*,[6] which famously had fought the CSS *Virginia*, formerly the USS *Merrimac*, in these very waters a month earlier. James Hall describes what happened next:

> While I was on the hurricane deck of the *Elm City*, looking at the *Monitor*, I noticed that the watch on the top of the turret was looking very anxiously with a spy-glass towards Craney Island, near Norfolk. On looking that way myself, I saw four large vessels approaching. These,

on coming nearer, proved to be the *Merrimac*, with the rebel flag floating over her, accompanied by the *Jamestown*, *Yorktown*, and another vessel.

The crew of the *Monitor* were soon clearing her deck and greasing it. Her smoke-stack was lowered, and the American flag hoisted in the twinkling of an eye. A signal gun was fired, and she was ready for action.... We were anxious to see a fight, but none occurred.[7]

Arriving in Virginia, rumors abounded among the Excelsior's ranks that Yorktown had already fallen and they'd missed the real action of the campaign. But the Confederate works were still occupied, even if lightly. McClellan, always with an eye to the butcher's bill of an upcoming clash, chose to lay siege to Yorktown rather than take it by direct assault. While the men under him who would do the actual fighting and dying very much appreciated the general's thrift, McClellan often missed opportunities to exploit enemy weaknesses. This slowness caused Lincoln great consternation; he wanted swifter execution of the campaign and an end to the war.

Disembarking *Elm City*, the boys of Third Excelsior were astonished by what they saw. Though the port was not much more than a collection of a few wooden docks used to service the fort, the amount of men and material collected there was mind-boggling. Everywhere were stacked crates of food, ammunition, and other supplies an army of 100,000 men would need. And the artillery! It was said there were 100 batteries present, each with four to six guns.[8] With artillery like this, the New Yorkers assured themselves, Yorktown and the other towns on the road to Richmond would soon fall.

Now on dry land, George Grecheneck's company of Germans and the rest of the Excelsior Brigade began its march away from Fort Monroe. They were headed towards Yorktown and the front, which was teeming with activity every bit as frenzied as back at the dock. McClellan was digging in his army, sinking earthen redoubts that would protect the heavy artillery from enemy counter-battery fire and excavating parallel lines of trenches for the infantry. These infantry trenches were as old as siege warfare itself and allowed attackers to move very close to the defenders while remaining safe behind mounds of earth or other moveable protection such as a log or earth-filled cylindrical basket. When diggings were close enough and the time was right, attacking infantry would enter the protection of the trench, rush forward and overwhelm the defenders. Taylor's men wanted to fight, but for now they toiled with the pick and shovel.

All five Excelsior regiments settled into camps about two miles from the enemy's works. Camping on the property of Confederate general John Magruder, they enjoyed a plantation of nearly 100 acres of fruit trees and wheat fields, all in full blossom. Despite the idyllic surrounding of the Virginia Peninsula, life in camp was anything but. The constant digging, frequent rain, and Rebel bullets made some men long for the relative ease of Southern Maryland. One Company I man, who signed off his letter only as "F," described his ordeal this way:

> I have just finished my dinner, such it may be called. We had a tin cup of poor bean soup, not more than two beans to a cup and a chunk of fat bacon and hard crackers.... We have had pretty hard fare since we left camp Wool. I thought it was hard there, but we lived like kings to what we do now. We have to sleep on the ground, with a rubber blanket and our overcoats under, and two pieces of canvass, about 6 feet square, buttoned together for a shelter over our heads, with both ends open.... Some would find a better shelter for their hogs, but we are willing to put up with this for the sake of our glorious country! But I think if I was home I would not enlist, but there is not use of grumbling here. All we have to do is obey orders.[9]

By the time the regiment set up camp near Yorktown, many duties had become routine, and some procedures in place back on Staten Island had long since been abandoned as overly

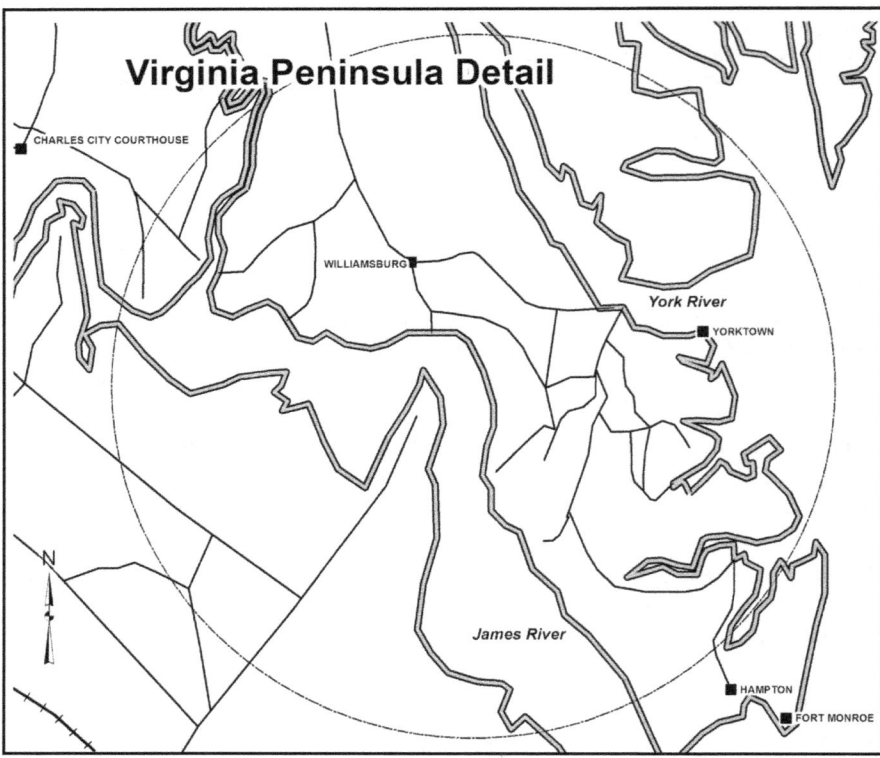

controlling. One such rule was regarding the selection of tent mates. In the beginning, men were assigned tents alphabetically based on last names, so men such as David Parker initially tented with those whose last names all started with P. But that had changed, and company men tented with whom they pleased.[10] Therefore by the time they reached Yorktown, Parker's tent mate was one of the more interesting characters of the regiment, Claus Wriborg.

Wriborg had come from Holland but spoke English well. He was considered "merry, jolly,"[11] but unused to the ways of America. Additionally, he was almost totally deaf. Though Wriborg soon became the subject of ridicule and jokes, he showed no resentment over his treatment, and young Parker took pity on the Dutchman. When a vacancy became available David invited "Carl" to tent with him. Immediately David discovered Carl wasn't the bumbler others imagined. The only child of a high ranking officer in the Dutch navy, Carl had come to America to seek his fortune when his father died. Well-educated and fluent in several languages, Wriborg secured a position with the Chautauqua county clerk's office in Mayville. When war broke out, the 28-year-old enlisted to fight for his adopted country. When offered the position of Company D's clerk because of his exquisite handwriting, Carl turned down the post, insisting he could be a clerk anytime, choosing instead to serve as a regular soldier. Despite the early mocking, Claus eventually became popular with the men of the regiment, remaining zealous in his soldierly duties and always the gentleman.[12]

Routines and organization within the regiment continued to evolve and change, and so had those of the Federal army. Before leaving southern Maryland, Hooker's division folded in with two others to form the new III Corps, one of several corps now composing the Army of the Potomac. Command of III Corps fell to Major General Samuel P. Heintzelman, a 57-year-old West Point graduate. After serving in the quartermaster service during the Mexican

War, Heintzelman saw enough action in the Southwest to earn a brevet promotion to brigadier general in May of '61 when rebellious storm clouds gathered.[13] The new corps consisted of three divisions: Fitz John Porter commanded the First Division and Hooker commanded the Second Division. In the beginning, Charles S. Hamilton commanded the corps' Third Division. But that soon changed when on April 30, 1862, Hamilton was replaced by Philip Kearny. On April 30, the new III Corps counted on paper 39,710 men with 64 pieces of artillery, although fewer than 35,000 were actually listed as "present for duty."[14] Ultimately the lives of David Parker, Martin Boyden, Lorey Wilder, and the rest would rely upon the skills of generals such as McClellan, Heintzelman and Hooker.

Taylor still commanded the brigade, but by the end of April there was growing frustration that neither had Taylor been promoted nor had another brigadier been brought in to take his place. This frustration only heightened when word arrived that President Lincoln was set to resubmit Sickles' nomination to the senate. Editors at the *Fredonia Censor* felt that politics was taking precedence over the lives of their boys and that the Excelsior Brigade would be condemned to second-rate generalship:

> We see it announced that the President has re-nominated Gen. Sickles as a Brigadier General. By what maneuvering he was induced to do this is the face of the unanimous rejection of Sickles' previous nomination by the Senate, is a mystery which the people would like to have unraveled. Sickles, friends pretend that this rejection was brought by the misapprehension of facts, which has been explained away. But no explanation can do away with the damaging fact that Sickles has not the confidence of his men, and that his best officers signed a petition to be transferred from his command. In time of war no one ought to be appointed to a military position unless fully competent for the discharge of its duties. The lives of 5,000 men are of too much value to be hazarded recklessly, for the purpose of rewarding politicians ambitious of military glory. We believe President Lincoln has been bamboozled, in making this re-appointment, and trust that the Senate will again save the country from the disgrace, and the army from the hazard which must result from investing Sickles with such a responsible position.[15]

Below Yorktown, 72nd men anticipated a big fight to take the town against an enemy pulling out all the stops. "We will lose more than we have in any other battle that has been fought," wrote one Company I man. "This is their last hope, if they lose this, all is gone. They have drafted every man that can bear arms, even boys not over 16, and some not more than 15 years old."[16] Still the digging went on, every day bringing the Federals that much closer to the Rebel lines and ultimate victory.

Siege warfare was more like hard labor and less like the adventure many of the boys had been expecting. Companies rotated between the trenches, picket duty, and recuperation in camp. Even the dangers of picket duty were seen as preferable to the digging. After a couple of weeks in the trenches, Emerson Merrell wrote his brother:

> I have been on picket duty for the last 36 hours and had a bully time too—we were close enough to the rebels pickets so we could hear them talk—they are industrious cusses for they work all the night on their breastworks and make their niggers work days—they fired at us several times through the day from their batteries and were constantly sending messengers in the shape of a piece of lead weighing about an ounce at us when they could get a fair chance.[17]

Arthur McKinstry penned a letter to readers back home on April 29 relating his experience on recent picket duty:

> At 4 p.m. Co. D fell in and relieved Capt. Bliss' men, who had been in the advance all day. We were now in plain view of the enemy, and could see them by looking over the wall beyond

the trench. Great care was necessary, however, that the observer did not get hit by the enemy's sharp shooters. On the right, Burdan's [sic] sharp-shooters had tormented the enemy very much, and when darkness fell, their artillery began to play at our woods, to disturb the men who were working upon our batteries. Another object was probably to draw our fire, and thus discover the situation of our principal works, which are still masked by trees but can be unmasked at very short notice, when all is ready. Growing tired of this fruitless business, they began to depress their guns until they bore directly upon the rifle pit where our pickets lay. Their aim was perfect, but so too was our shelter. A few men were thrown out in advance of the pit as lookouts. Averill and Babcock were sent out from the squad I was in, and as they lay close to the ground, a shell with blazing fuze rolled within a few feet and stopped. The boys lay low as possible, and the shell, exploding, scattered its fragments near them, but left them unharmed.[18]

Israel Moses was a prominent Jewish doctor in New York City with army experience before the war who set down his scalpel to accept the lieutenant colonelcy of the 72nd N.Y. A few months after commanding the regiment at Williamsburg, Moses resigned from the regiment to accept the duties of regimental surgeon with another unit (courtesy the U.S. Army Heritage and Education Center).

By May 1 Rebels inside the Yorktown works had maintained ten days of steady musket and cannon fire against besieging Yankee troops. "The rebels are getting very impatient, supposing that we are erecting formidable works to reduce their batteries and have been pouring their shot and shell pretty thick upon us," wrote James Hall, "and though they fire at us night and day, very few have yet been seriously injured."[19] Two days later, men of the 72nd under command of Lt. Colonel Israel Moses received a half-hearted enemy push designed to drive in their pickets. Seventy-Second men fought all day in the rain, and in addition to being soaked through had had nearly nothing to eat. Eventually the poor weather and the regiment's

4. Journey to Williamsburg

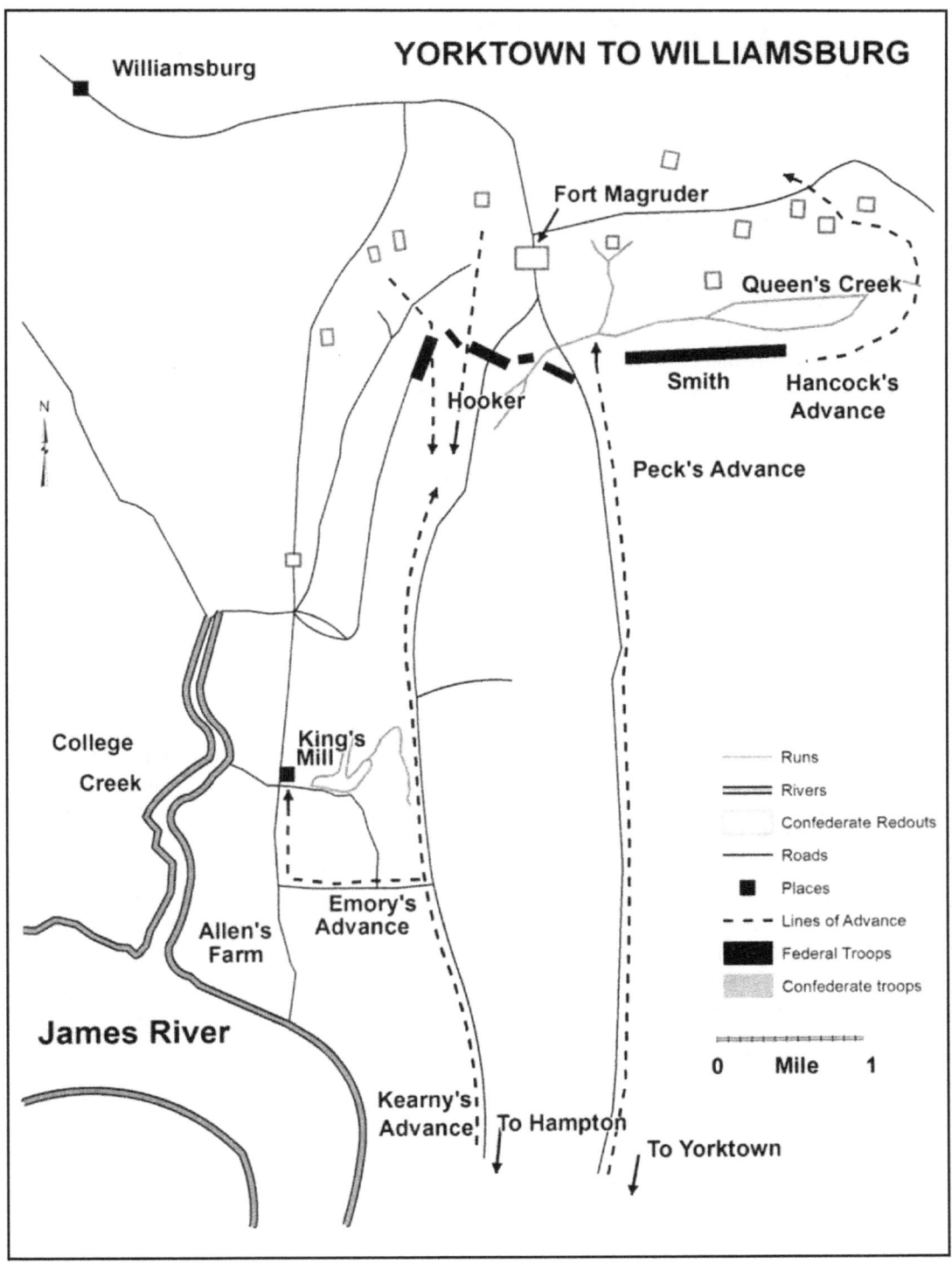

resolve combined to repel the attack. Confederate defenses at Yorktown could not resist the mighty siege guns of the Union, and the Southern commander Joseph Johnston knew it. That night, under the covering noise of his cannons, Johnston withdrew from Yorktown, one day before McClellan had planned to attack.

In the early morning darkness, while Rebel artillery shot and shell flew overhead, pickets from the various Federal commands crept forward to the furthest reaches of the trenches. As men peered toward Rebel lines it soon became clear the enemy had vacated their works. Officers went forth to confirm the news, and even before a final verdict was rendered, regiments began packing wagons for the anticipated move forward. With the 72nd and the rest of Hooker's division in advanced positions, they would be among the first to mobilize in pursuit of the enemy.

The morning of May 4 was hectic for the Excelsiors and the other elements leading the pursuit of Johnston's retreating Rebel army. Excelsiors who only hours before had been on picket duty fell in and readied themselves for a march. Some units, mostly cavalry under Brigadier General George Stoneman, moved out ahead of the Excelsiors and engaged in a day-long, running battle with the Confederate rear guard.

Two main roads ran up the peninsula from Yorktown to Williamsburg and beyond: the Yorktown Road and the Hampton Road. Of the two, the Yorktown Road serviced the more northerly, right side of the peninsula, while the Hampton Road traveled the southerly, left side. These roads first diverged then joined at Williamsburg, 12 miles distant from Yorktown.

By noon the regiment and the rest of Hooker's division was on the march along the Hampton Road. Commanding the division's First Brigade was Curvier Grover. Born in Maine in 1828, Grover graduated fourth in his class at West Point in 1850. After receiving his commission, he served in a number of western posts including the Mormon Expedition. When civil war broke out, Grover was serving as a captain with the 10th Infantry, stationed at Fort Union, New Mexico. Taking leave from his captain's post in the regular army, Grover received a temporary appointment to brigadier general of volunteers and command of the First Brigade.[20] Riding ahead of Third Brigade was Francis Patterson, who had taken over command of the brigade only two weeks earlier from Starr. Born in 1821 in Philadelphia, Patterson had served in the Mexican War as a second lieutenant on the artillery. After the war he remained in the service and rose to captain in the Ninth Infantry only to resign his commission in 1857. When war against the Confederacy broke out, Patterson was made colonel of a 90-day militia unit. Once this unit was mustered out, he was eventually made brigadier general and given Third Brigade.[21]

Passing through Yorktown, the men gazed at the once dangerous defenses, now abandoned and harmless, which only a few hours before they'd been preparing to assault. Nineteen-year-old Hartwell Dickenson, a musician in the regiment, described what he saw: "We passed through the fortifications at Yorktown, and all were surprised that the enemy should have such works. To me they appeared impregnable."[22] Initially marching was good, and with the First Brigade in the lead, the thousands of tramping feet of Hooker's division quickly turned the dirt road to a fine dust. It was a humid day, and the men began to throw away equipment they deemed unnecessary. Blankets and overcoats littered the road. Pushing ahead, Rebel bullets weren't the only hazard. As the New Yorkers continued toward Williamsburg they encountered improvised land-mines, known as torpedoes, placed by the retreating Rebs. The young musician Hartwell wrote:

We had to pick our way very carefully, on account of torpedoes being placed in every place the army would likely pass. For miles the road was strewn with articles of clothing, cast off by the flying rebels and occasionally would be found a rope or chain with one end buried in the ground, attached doubtless, to a shell that would explode upon pulling the rope or chain, but happily no accident occurred.[23]

Cavalrymen heading for the rear near 3:00 p.m. told the Excelsiors there was a skirmish ahead. With troops from another division blocking the road, Hooker's pursuit ground to a halt. After a near five-hour delay the brigade continued their march as the rain and dark set it. Rain mixed with the pulverized dirt, turning the road into a nearly impassable morass. "The roads, which up to this time were splendid," explained young Hartwell, "had become so cut up and muddy that it was almost impossible to advance."[24] With mud knee deep in places, Hartwell's shoes became completely filled. Realizing they could not reach the skirmish that day, Hooker's men camped for the night around 1 a.m., still three miles from the fight. By the time the Excelsiors fell out, their uniforms were soaked through to the skin—"wringing wet"[25] as one man described it. Though the ground was wet, the men rested as best they could. At 5 a.m. the New Yorkers fell in, ready to go, but stood in the rain another 90 minutes as they waited for horse-drawn artillery to pass.

As Colonel Taylor's men marched, General Stoneman pursued the enemy to behind the protection of their refuge, Fort Magruder: the culminating defensive position at the junction of the Yorktown and Hampton roads. Surrounding the fort was a series of trenchworks, rifle pits, and lesser redoubts carefully planned and built. Enhancing these positions were cleared parcels of land designed to rob attackers of usable cover; in other places trees had been felled to create a maddening tangle of branches and timber called "slashings"[26] by the men. All of these were designed to offer Johnston's defenders the best possible fields of fire and the Federals the worst possible ground for a swift, orderly attack.[27]

General William Smith, commanding the Second Division of IV Corps, arrived near Fort Magruder early on the morning of the 5th. Smith had at first moved his troops along the Yorktown Road during the pursuit of May 4 but blocked Hooker's advance when he shifted to the Hampton Road. Smith now awaited orders from Gen. Edwin Sumner, McClellan's second-in-command, who was in charge of the pursuit. With no orders forthcoming, Smith waited.[28]

Moving up Hampton Road, less than a mile south of where Smith stopped, Hooker's division prepared to attack. Confident in the knowledge that more than 30,000 Federal troops were within a few hours' march of his position, the aggressive Hooker didn't waste time engaging a force he estimated to be three times his number. Hooker was on Smith's left and didn't wait for orders before sending in his First Brigade at 7:30 a.m. under cover of a massive artillery barrage.[29]

First Brigade's attack was led by General Cuvier Grover. Initially Federal fortunes went well: Grover's men drove the enemy from the first lines of rifle-pits as day broke. Second Brigade struggled against persistent rain and the deplorably slow condition of Hampton Road and finally arrived around 9 a.m. Taylor had only four of his five regiments available to fight, since the 71st N.Y. had remained behind unloading ships back in Yorktown. Musician Dickinson described the scene as they approached: "We were now in dense pine woods, and the [artillery] firing continued to increase, accompanied by volleys of musketry, but still we thought it was nothing but a skirmish."[30] After waiting about half an hour for stragglers to come up, the regiment were directed to load their weapons and members of the regimental band ordered to report to the surgeon for service as litter bearers.[31]

Taylor now ordered his own regiment into the fray to relieve the 1st and 11th Massachusetts along with the 26th Pennsylvania of Grover's brigade. Acting commander Moses received some last minute instructions from the withdrawing Grover upon moving the 72nd into line: "Repress any advance, destroy the horses and gunners of a section of a rebel battery on the left, and to protect a section of our own on the right, and in case of an opportunity presenting, to take the [Rebel] section."[32] The typical artillery battery consisted of six guns and was divided into sections of two guns each. With both enemy and Federal guns nearby, it was clear Moses' boys and the rest of the regiment had their work cut out for them.

As the deployed regiment advanced, the magnitude of the obstacle presented by the fallen trees became apparent. Luther Howard of Company B described it as "a slashing of about forty acres, skirted by dense woods on three sides, and the Rebel works in the front of Williamsburg on the other."[33] The position of the felled trees served to limit use of Federal artillery and prevented the New Yorkers from charging the enemy to "capture or put to flight the whole lot."[34] Howard summarized the effect of the slashing in a letter:

> This "slashing" was fallen for the very purpose which it was used for—that is to slaughter Union troops in. The woods were full of Rebel Infantry, and as our Brigade deployed in this "slashing" as skirmishers, they poured a murderous fire of musketry onto our heads. And beside all this, when they could they poured in the grape and canister to match. It was a terrible place for men to fight in, for nothing could be used but our Infantry, and the trees were felled so that a man could not advance or retreat without exposing himself to a deadly fire of musketry.[35]

The battle was shaping up to be much more than a protracted rearguard action, as the enemy showed no signs of withdrawal. Hooker sent a message at 11:20 a.m. to Sumner requesting help. The tone of the note reflected both his offensive spirit and his expectations:

> I have had a hard contest all the morning, but do not despair of success. My men are hard at work, but a good deal exhausted. It is reported to me that my communication with you by the Yorktown road is clear of the enemy. Batteries, cavalry, and infantry can take post by the side of mine to whip the enemy.[36]

Despite pleas from Hooker, Sumner failed to act, leaving Smith's division wide to the right of the main fighting, effectively out of the action and leaving Hooker to fight unsupported.[37] Whether or not Hooker knew, the only relief headed his way was from his own corps commander, Heintzelman. First Division had been detailed elsewhere and was unavailable, so Phil Kearney's Third Division was headed to Hooker's aid by way of Hampton Road.

Around the same time Hooker was sending his note to Sumner, Confederate commander Johnston had ordered Major General James Longstreet to about-face and countermarch back to relieve Fort Magruder. Soon these additional troops would change the complexion of the fight, as Longstreet counterattacked around noon with eight brigades. It was about this time that heavy firing developed to the left of the 72nd. It was Gen. Francis Patterson and his four regiments, the New Jersey Brigade (5th through 8th N.J.), moving against the enemy at that point. With the New Jersey men now engaged, the battle began to seesaw as Longstreet's regiments forced in the pickets of the 72nd, while Col. Moses reported the enemy advancing in strength on his position. Helped by the 70th N.Y. under Col. William Dwight, along with four companies of his own under Major Stevens, Moses initially stymied the Rebel advance. But Longstreet's reinforcements were determined and launched at least three separate attacks along the Federal front.[38]

New Yorkers now buckled under the weight of the Confederate assault. Squads of men were swept away under the roar of massed volley fire. Captain Willard of Company B, fighting desperately with a rifle, was killed instantly when a bullet pierced his skull. Skirmishers Jerome Sprague, Elias Rowe, and Arthur McKinstry were amongst the first killed in Company D as Rebel lead shattered all in its path. Stevens, fighting at the center of the action, narrowly escaped death as a Southern bullet grazed the major's chin while another claimed the tip of his sword. A treacherous Rebel colonel advanced his regiment under a flag of truce only to order his men to fire, cutting a swath through the 72nd's line. But upon the regiment's returning fire, the "black hearted Colonel"[39] was among the first to fall.[40]

As the fighting continued, the greater number of Confederates began to have a telling effect. Soon both the 70th and 72nd began to run dangerously low on ammunition, forcing the two regiments to fall back.

The fallen trees intended to hinder the Union advance now played havoc with the Rebel counter-attack. Pvt. Edmund Patterson of the 9th Alabama described the assault:

> We continued advancing as fast as we could under the circumstances, though it was impossible to preserve anything like a well-formed line and the Yankees being stationed and posted behind the logs had much the advantage of us, for we had to expose ourselves continually in getting over the logs, while we could but seldom get a shot at them.[41]

One Yankee who used his advantage against advancing Rebels was David Parker's tentmate, Claus Wriborg. Badly wounded in the leg and unable to retreat with the rest of the regiment, he lay among the fallen timber. As Confederates moved past him, a Rebel clubbed him with a musket. Still conscious, the Dutchman grabbed up another rifle and fired into the back of his attacker. Feigning death to avoid discovery, Carl continued his fight even after the Confederates were forced to retire. Pvt. Wriborg eventually claimed five dead Rebels for his day's work.[42]

As the regiment slowly withdrew, Moses sent quartermaster Thomas Fry to request additional support. After forwarding this request on to Hooker, Col. Taylor took the remainder of the Excelsiors into action. Moving Col. William Brewster's 73rd and the 74th under Lt. Col. Charles Burtis, Taylor marched these last two regiments into action at around 1 p.m. arranging them to the right of the two already engaged. Once they were in place, Taylor advanced them at an angle, putting the attacking Rebels in a cross fire, with the 70th and 72nd on the Confederate front and right, and the 73rd and 74th on their left. With the enemy receiving steady volleys from his regiments, "the enemy now began to fall back slowly, but desperately contending for every foot of ground forced from," Taylor related.[43]

With the field a maddening tangle of fallen trees and stumps, units were unable to maintain their normal alignments. Since effective communication was impossible, company commanders were allowed extra latitude to "advance and retire under cover of the fallen timber as well as circumstances would permit,"[44] Lt. Col. Burtis later reported. Corporal Henry Ford of Company I experienced a similar situation within Moses' command. He wrote, "We were compelled to retreat slowly at time and would again gain ground."[45] Over in Company B, Luther Howard became separated from his command and wandered too close to the enemy position. When a group of Rebs demanded his surrender, he ran for the rear and upon hearing the enemy's order to fire, Howard dropped to the ground as a volley flew over his head. Clambering back to his feet, the 18-year-old skedaddled back to his own lines to carry on the fight. Howard survived the battle but was wounded before it was over.[46]

Here, during the heavier fighting, two New Yorkers earned the Medal of Honor. Sgt. John Coyne of the 70th N.Y. garnered his for his capture of an enemy flag during hand-to-hand fighting, while 22-year-old Corporal John Haight of the 72nd's Company G was recognized for carrying a wounded comrade from the field before being wounded himself and taken prisoner.[47]

As the battle raged into the afternoon, the lack of ammunition played havoc among the Excelsior Brigade regiments, forcing men to scrounge cartridges from the dead and dying. The 72nd was out of ammunition and placed in reserve, while the 70th teetered on the verge of collapse. "This state of affairs endured for some time, the enemy's fire increasing, mine diminishing,"[48] wrote Col. Dwight of the 70th. With the situation deteriorating and the enemy pressing in on his right, Dwight began to pull back, fearing a charge by the Rebels. While moving, Dwight was wounded twice, the second injury rendering him unconscious. In the withdrawal's confusion Dwight was left behind and was eventually captured.[49]

With two of his regiments effectively out of ammunition, Taylor could not keep up the pressure on the enemy, and he withdrew the entire brigade. Under cover of Federal artillery, Taylor worked to reform his broken regiments as officers sorted out mixed and disorganized companies. Fresh supplies of ammunition finally made it to the Excelsiors, allowing the regiments to hold on until General Philip Kearney's Third Division arrived on the scene near 4 p.m. Once deployed, Kearney's men gradually forced back the Rebels, retaking all the lost ground and pushing the enemy back to the doorstep of Fort Magruder.[50] A lieutenant in the Excelsior Brigade set out the scene:

> Terrible was the roar of musketry, and dreadful the enemy's fire; but suddenly came two terrific reports, louder than all.—Our artillery ... was pouring [heavy fire] into the rebels. It checked the enemy, they were driven back, and then loud cheers, ringing through the woods, announced the arrival of Gen. Kearny, who appeared at the head of fresh troops. Oh what a relief. They passed us on the double quick, soon formed, attacked the enemy, and then the roar of musketry was louder than before. But fresh troops kept coming, and it was after dark before the firing ceased.[51]

With a fresh division in the fight, Hooker withdrew his badly mangled regiments. Three of Taylor's four Excelsior regiments were pulled out of the line, retired to a stand of timber, and under the continuing rain, made camp for the night. Only the 73rd N.Y., those New York City firemen clad in their bright Zouave uniforms, stayed forward, posted in support of an artillery battery.[52]

While Hooker's Division was bearing the brunt of the battle, Gen. Winfield S. Hancock, commanding two brigades of Smith's division, found some unoccupied Rebel redoubts at the extreme right of the Union line. Recognizing their importance, Hancock seized the fortifications and requested permission to launch a flank attack, which he was sure would break the Confederate line. Sumner, realizing the pounding taken by Hooker's men, became unsure of the overall situation and refused Hancock's request for an attack. Seeing an opportunity slipping away, Hancock devised a plan. He hid much of his infantry behind the crest of a hill, then baited the Confederates with an artillery barrage. The gambit worked. The provoked enemy advanced on what they took to be unsupported batteries, only to be mowed down by musketry when the order to rise and fire was given at the murderous range of 30 paces. Scores of Confederates fell, including Gen. Jubal Early, who led the attack. Hancock's men surged forward.[53] Though the enemy was falling back in a rout, Sumner, still worrying about the overall flow of the battle, ordered the pursuit halted.

As Hancock's men stopped their pursuit, the battle of Williamsburg drew to a close.

McClellan was jubilant with the "superb"[54] job done by Hancock and readied himself for an attack on Fort Magruder the following morning.

That night David Parker, Lorey Wilder, and the rest camped in the rain with no tents or shelter. In the wet camp of the 72nd, men reflected on their first taste of battle. Had they performed under fire as they imagined they would? Did they do their duty? Perhaps Emerson Merrell's reflections on the fight were common. He'd been anxious prior to battle, probably frightened if the truth were told, but once the fighting started, he did the task before him. He was too busy to be afraid and did his duty, his hands never failing as "every fear seemed to leave me."[55] The fight had been furious; they had expected that. But how this fight played out was certainly unexpected. Of course there was the weather; a steady rain all day had served to soak friend and foe alike. Artillerymen serving their pieces were nearly knee deep in mud, while the guns were effectively immovable. Dead men, buried in the mud, were trampled on by infantry and driven over by wagons. Then there were the slashings, the felled timbers. For an army practiced in close order drills, movements and evolutions by companies, battalions and regiments, the broken ground forced commanders to throw away the drill manual and improvise. In between the logs, down low, men were safe in their private little Gibraltars, but try to move and they became instant targets, slow and exposed. The fight here proved a deadly one, due in part to the high percentage of head wounds directly attributable to the slashings. And while the day's work was over and their numbers thinned from the night before, most must have taken some measure of pride in having done their duty that day. While it was unpleasant, dirty and deadly, most knew this was the soldier's lot and there would be other battles to fight. Many had never imagined it would be like this, those many months ago back in Jamestown, Dunkirk, or New York City. The eloquent speeches made no mention of the mud and rain. Certainly the screams of the dying could never have been heard over the sound of the brass bands and cheering crowds in those village squares back in Westfield and Delhi. One Chautauqua man later described his experience following the battle:

> The different Regiments now came in, but were scattered everywhere. The men had all thrown off their knapsacks, and had to sleep in the rain, without any covering, and expecting to commence the fight at an early hour the next day: but when the day broke, the enemy was gone. They had been out all night rifling the dead and wounded, and taking all prisoners that could walk. They treated the wounded kindly, giving them water, and in some instances covering them with blankets. I went out with a party early in the morning to look for the wounded of our Regiment, but did not find any, and so I took a tramp over the battlefield. The fight was all in the woods, and the rebels had felled trees so that it was impossible to make a bayonet charge. The dead lay thickly scattered around, and the sight was horrible. Nearly all the rebels killed were shot through the head, and their faces were covered with clotted blood. I soon became accustomed to the sight, and cooly turned the dead secesh over to find some trophy, but every one had been rifled. I managed to get three buttons, a canteen and a ten cent postage stamp, but could find nothing of any value. I have not time to write much more, for my candle is most gone.[56]

During the night, the commanding general planned his assault on Fort Magruder, but as dawn broke, McClellan discovered the Confederates had once again evacuated their strong point, denying him the smashing victory he sought.[57] So while McClellan concentrated on moving beyond Williamsburg and pursuing the fleeing Rebels, the men of the 72nd recovered the wounded who had lain in the field all night, among them Carl Wriborg. While resting among the other injured, Wriborg told comrades about his lonely fight. When the surgeon examined him and said his leg must be operated on, Wriborg insisted three or four others be cared for ahead of him, but by the time the others had been treated, the kind-hearted Wriborg had lost too much blood, and he died before his surgery could begin.[58]

That night, the men knew many of their own to be either dead or dying, but the real scope of the butcher's bill wasn't fully realized till the next day. When the counting was done, 72nd's loss for the half-day battle was 195. Sixty-one men were killed outright, and another 23 died later from their wounds. There were 67 men wounded, some of whom would recover and return to the ranks; another 44 men listed as missing, most captured, but whose fate would never really be known; and some who eventually found their way back into the ranks. The officers, the captains and lieutenants who fought side by side with the men, died too. Captain Darwin Willard, who had led the night-time reconnaissance to Boyd's Hole, was dead on the field. Dunkirk man Patrick Barrett of Company E, whose company was among the first to enlist back on Staten Island, died on May 6 from his wounds. George Grecheneck, the Hungarian émigré and captain of the "German" Company A, lingered on for ten days but eventually died of his wounds on May 17. With numbers like these, everyone experienced a loss. But David Parker, who survived, must have felt doubly vexed, because not only did tent-mate Wriborg succumb to his wounds in the surgeon's tent, but Martin Boyden, the man he'd traveled with to see Major Stevens back in Jamestown, was also dead; he was among those 61 killed on the field.

In all, the four regiments of the Excelsior brigade suffered a loss of 772 men—the size of an entire regiment. Though these numbers were chilling for the 72nd, theirs wasn't the greatest loss within the brigade. The 70th N.Y. lost 330 men, nearly half the regiment, and suffered the capture of its commander, Col. Dwight.[59]

While McClellan heaped much of the official praise for repulsing the enemy on Hancock, the toll of the fighting tells a much different story.[60] Hancock's men suffered the loss of at most 97 men killed, wounded, captured or missing, while Hooker's three brigades and the Excelsiors reported combined losses of 1,575. The New Jersey Brigade lost four senior officers, who were either killed or wounded, included in its loss of 526. Nearly half of all the divisional losses came from Taylor's Excelsior Brigade.[61] Such numbers demonstrated the lack of ability of Gen. Sumner to manage the attack and bring other units to bear upon the enemy, given that total Federal losses at Williamsburg amounted to 2,239. Commentary on the conduct of the battle came from III Corps commander Brigadier General S.P. Heintzelman, who lamented "the disheartening circumstances that our troops knew we had three divisions idle on their right, within hearing of their musketry."[62]

The staggering sacrifice experienced by his division was not lost on Hooker, who wrote in his official report:

> History will not be believed when it is told that the noble officers and men of my division were permitted to carry on this unequal struggle from morning until night unaided in the presence of more than 30,000 of their comrades with arms in their hands. Nevertheless, it is true. If we failed to capture the rebel army on the plains of Williamsburg, it surely will not be ascribed to the want of conduct and courage in my command.[63]

5. Seven Pines and on to Richmond

Camp started to look more organized by Wednesday, May 7. The chaos immediately following Monday's battle before Fort Magruder was over, and Col. Nelson Taylor's men began sorting things out. Privates, corporals, and sergeants seemed to do better, and many were close to being their old selves. Able to put the loss of a friend or two behind them, many laughed and joked. After all, this was a soldier's lot. But the officers were still in shock. Men whom they had asked to join them a few months before now lay dead, wounded, or counted among the missing. Some companies had lost but a few men, while others were down nearly half their number. Yet the routine of army life, the parades, the fatigue details, the roll calls, went on.

As early as 3:00 a.m. the morning after battle, Tuesday the 6th, forward scouts began reporting the Rebel works abandoned. Johnston had withdrawn his army through Williamsburg and further toward Richmond, but McClellan did not pursue pell-mell. His Army of the Potomac was widely scattered and needed to consolidate in Williamsburg first before an orderly and deliberate advance. But while the rest of the McClellan's force made preparations to move, Hooker's division did not.

Losses in Hooker's division were staggering; the Excelsior Brigade was down the equivalent of an entire regiment. The New Jersey Blues were down almost as much, with Grover's First Brigade slightly fewer. Among the officers, the division reported 19 killed and 67 wounded with two missing. Hooker's men had to take time to recover so they stayed behind[1]—at least for now. General Cuvier Grover was made military governor of Williamsburg and his brigade assigned to provost marshal duties, while the rest of the division set about the grim task of cleaning up.[2] In the Confederates' haste to retreat they left an appalling number of dead and wounded strewn everywhere about the field. As cleanup continued, the strain on medical care increased; more and more wounded were discovered hidden among the slashings, brush, and small ravines that characterized the battlefield. Men of the regiment were kept busy all of Tuesday collecting the wounded. Emerson Merrell and a few others found time to dash off a quick letter home with sparse information; there had been a great fight and he'd survived it. Others later wrote longer letters home, full of details, but for now, those would have to wait.

The Excelsiors fought at Williamsburg with only four regiments, the 71st N.Y. having been detailed to move stores back in Yorktown. All of May 5, Second Excelsior men heard the sound of the cannons and anticipated the order to form up and advance to join the fight, an order that never came. Two days after the fight, with the 71st still in Yorktown, Chaplain Twichell rode forward to inspect the battlefield for himself:

The signs began to appear a full two miles from the scene of the conflict. Huge piles of knapsacks thrown off in the rush for the field—and guarded by sentinels left behind for the purpose ... a rod or two further on, and our horses shied at a rebel corpse, lying stark and stiff, the hand clutched above the head, while the open bosom showed a ghastly wound—then another and another.... They were all Confederate, the work of burying our own dead being nearly finished. They lay in heaps almost—a half dozen together. Wounds of every description were open to view, some horribly disfiguring, some scarcely perceptible leaving the slain with a look of sleep upon them.[3]

The scores of casualties endured by Hooker's regiments were due in great part to the lack of timely support from other commands, many within just miles of Hooker's location. Despite Hooker's losses, McClellan praised Hancock and his late-day attack on Williamsburg's Redoubt #11, though both III Corps commander Pete Heintzelman and his Confederate counterpart General James Longstreet concurred in their respective reports that Hancock's role had been a "very small matter."[4] McClellan's description of Hancock's performance as "magnificent"[5] was greatly resented by the men and officers throughout Hooker's division; Hooker himself even quipped to the 5th New Jersey's commander, "I say Mott, it seems to me that you and I, and your Jersey Blues and the Excelsior brigade were not at Williamsburg at all. Hancock did the business."[6] Such slights further damaged Hooker's opinion of McClellan, but eventually newspaper reports of Williamsburg painted a more accurate picture of the battle, conferring upon the division the recognition they rightly deserved.

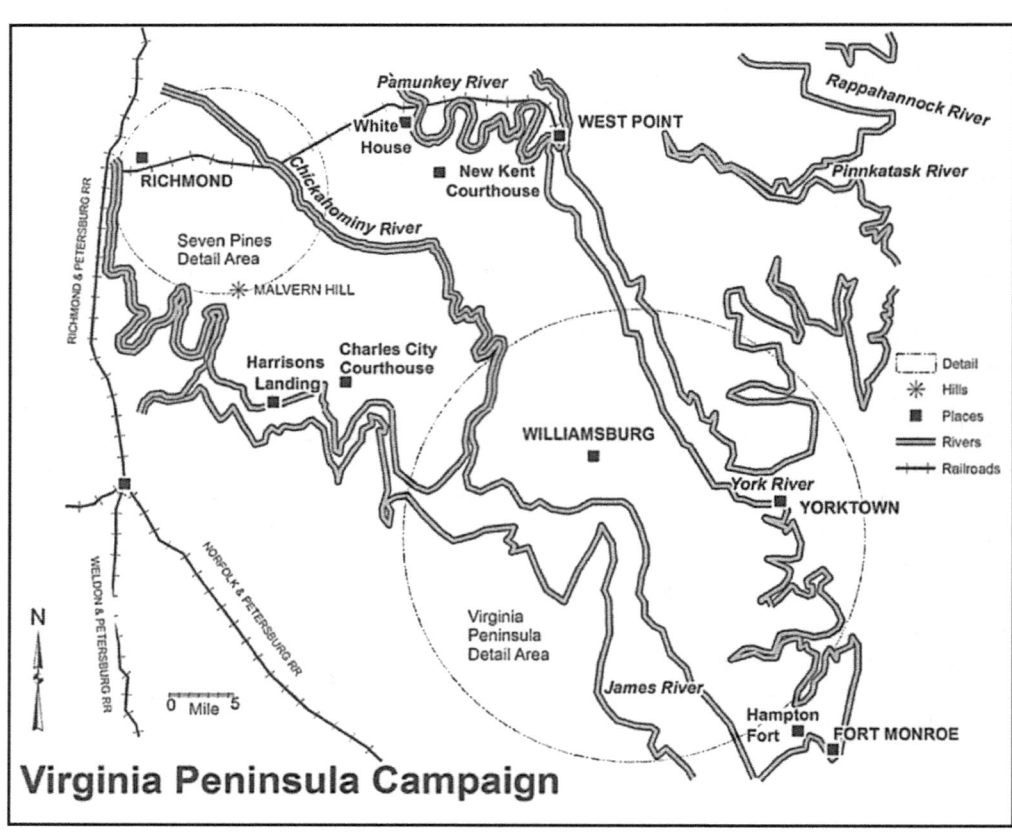

Dan Sickles was beside himself when news of the battle arrived back in Washington. For his brigade, the brigade he'd labored so hard to build, to fight and suffer 25 percent casualties, and not yield the field, was indeed a remarkable achievement, and his not being there was almost more than he could bear. But while his men had been digging around Yorktown, the defrocked general had been hard at work, pulling strings at both the Capitol and the White House. He had managed to get Lincoln to re-nominate his commission to the Senate, which was a big step. Sickles hoped the laurels won on the field by the Excelsiors might be worth a vote or two on the way to getting his stars back. He'd know for certain on May 13.

Seventy-First New York moved up from Yorktown by week's end and camped with the rest of the Excelsiors. McClellan had taken the army and pursued Joseph Johnston's Confederates up the Virginia Peninsula toward the gates of Richmond. The Federal army's fortunes had seldom looked brighter. With the Rebels in retreat, McClellan received news that Lincoln had authorized nearly 38,000 troops under Irwin McDowell to begin moving south from northern Virginia and toward Richmond. The joining of these two powerful Yankee forces was believed to be irresistible, and panic swept Richmond. In anticipation, the Southern legislature voted to burn the city rather than let it fall into Northern hands.[7]

For David Parker it was also an important week. Around this time General Hooker had expressed dissatisfaction with the division's mail service and wished to make improvements. After Colonel Taylor told Hooker the 72nd was getting its mail satisfactorily, Hooker requested Parker to be detailed to his personal staff so that Parker might improve the entire division's mail service. David would still be listed on the rolls of the 72nd New York, but attached to Hooker's staff, he was free from the tedium of fatigue duty, drill, and most importantly, fighting with the regular line infantry. Unless something extraordinary happened, David could be reasonably sure he would survive the war.[8]

Since leaving Maryland, the regiment had been handled by Lt. Col. Moses while Taylor ran the brigade. It was time to get Taylor back to the 72nd and put a real general at head of the Excelsiors. John J. Abercrombie was that man.[9] Already in his early 60s when the war broke out, Abercrombie had had a long career starting with graduation from West Point in 1822. He had served well in many posts throughout the South and Northwest and was promoted to full colonel when war broke out. Abercrombie was made brigadier general of volunteers in August '61, fought in the ill-fated Shenandoah Valley campaign early in the war, and was named commander of the Excelsior Brigade on May 11.

For Dan Sickles, May 13 couldn't come fast enough. He'd seen anyone and everyone who could help, and now it was up to the Senate. Dan waited for results in a D.C. restaurant he knew well from his days in Congress. The owner escorted Dan to the rear, where a man of his prominence could wait in peace. Dan had sent a young man to wait at the Senate and return with news as soon as it broke, and now he was coming through the door. Sickles rose from his chair, but before he could even ask, the messenger blurted out, "Confirmed!"[10] The vote was 19–18. By one vote Sickles was a general again. Charles Graham, who'd resigned in protest over the Sickles' demotion, was also waiting for the results. Dan immediately sent his messenger to track him down. Together they could return in triumph, Sickles leading the brigade, Graham back at head of the 70th. It appeared Abercrombie would need a new job.

Back on the Peninsula, Hooker finally received orders to move toward New Kent Court House. On May 15 they continued along the Williamsburg Road, the same road they had marched up from Yorktown. The Williamsburg Road ran north-west, following the contour of the peninsula, and then headed almost due west within ten miles or so of Richmond. As they moved out, Abercrombie rode at head of the Second Brigade while Taylor rode in front of the 72nd.

There were many changes that took place within the regiment. Williamsburg was a baptism of fire, and the past two weeks had served to winnow out the weak and undedicated, especially among the company officers, who unlike their enlisted counterparts could resign and go home when the going got too rough. Most prominent to go was Chaplain Levi Norton. Continued ill-health had forced the 41-year-old to resign and return home. First Lieutenant William P. Holl had resigned his post in Company K back in mid–April just after arriving in Virginia, while 31-year-old First Lt. Alfred S. Mason of Co. B quit only three days before Williamsburg. Of the two Bliss brothers, Warren, the first lt. of Co. G, left on May 16, leaving his brother Harmon, captain of Co. G, to carry on without him. With the death of some officers and the resignation of others, company commands and lieutenancies were being shuffled about, each promotion bringing with it a transfer to a new company. As new officers were needed, vacancies were satisfied by promotion from the ranks, usually from the top enlisted position, regimental sergeant-major. Since April 17, three newly minted second lieutenants joined the officer corps: James Fogarty to Co. I on April 17, Thomas Clark to Co. C on May 6, and John S. Mann to Co. A on May 17. Prior to becoming sergeant-major, each man had been an outstanding first sergeant in his particular company. As each campaign season drew on and the need for officers continued, some men experienced only brief tenures as sergeant-major; in Mann's case, only eleven days before sewing on the lieutenant's straps.[11]

Details of the great fight at Williamsburg had now reached home. There had been rumors and fragments of news of the big battle but by May 14 most was known, including the list of the dead and wounded. "The friends of the Chautauqua Companies in the Sickles Brigade, have waited with the most anxious solicitude for the list of the killed and wounded in the engagement," read the lead sentence of the *Fredonia Censor* above its listing of the killed and wounded in Companies D, E, H, and B. "Up to this date but a partial report has been received.... It is likely that many names of the wounded, and perhaps some of the killed, remain as yet unreported."[12] Ironically, listed among the dead was the name of Arthur McKinstry, whose "Dear Uncle" letter from April 29 laid only two columns away. In another part of the paper the battle itself was described, as was Third Excelsior's role in it:

> Sickles' brigade, in Gen. Hooker's division, bore the great brunt of the battle, and fought most gallantly, though greatly overpowered by the numbers, superior position, and earthworks of the enemy. The approaches to their works were a series of ravines and swamps, whilst rain fell in torrents all day. The men had also been lying on their arms all the night previous, and were soaked with rain and chilled with cold. The battle raged from early in the morning till 3 o'clock P.M., when McClellan arrived with fresh troops, relieving Hooker's division, who were nearly prostrated with fatigue and exposure, while the third regiment of Sickles' brigade had its ranks badly thinned by the balls of the enemy. They are represented as having fought with such imprudent bravery that not less than 200 were killed and wounded.[13]

A week later the lists of the dead and wounded were complete, and hopes for loved ones serving were either answered or dashed. Obituaries of prominent Chautauqua men and officers killed ran among the columns of the *Fredonia Censor* and other papers across the state. "The funeral took place on Wednesday afternoon last," ran the report on the death of Jamestown native Captain Darwin Willard. "Business of all kinds was suspended and the emblems of grief everywhere exhibited. In accordance with the wishes of the friends of the deceased, only civic honors were paid to the remains."[14] For Company E's Captain Patrick Barrett of Dunkirk, the services were even grander:

The body was brought to Dunkirk for interment, and the funeral obsequies took place on Thursday last. An immense assemblage, by some estimated as high as 5,000 persons, was present, many of whom came from a distance, to testify their respect for the memory of the deceased soldier.... The procession from the church to the grave in the Catholic Cemetery was very imposing. The Fredonia Zouaves headed the procession with arms reversed, and the 68th Regimental Band, the members of the old D. Co. in uniform, the Firemen, and a long train of Civic societies and Citizens followed in the column.[15]

Even for readers of the *Fredonia Censor* who had no loved one campaigning, the loss of Arthur McKinstry touched a nerve, because his letters had brought the war home in a very personal way. His death brought an outpouring of compassion to his uncle, the editor of the *Censor*. "You have my warmest and most heartfelt sympathies for the terrible sacrifice you have laid upon the altar of our bleeding country. Alas! How much woe has been brought upon this peaceful land by this unhallowed rebellion,"[16] wrote one reader. The sacrifice had indeed been terrible, but for the men of the regiment, regrettably, there would be more.

Marching to rejoin the rest of the army was miserable and wet, and kept the 72nd's newest sergeant-major William McGinnes busy moving the men forward. The foul weather induced McClellan to order extra whiskey rations to fortify the men on the advice of army doctors.[17] Despite conditions, morale among the Excelsiors was fairly good, with many confident they would be within sight of Richmond in just a few days. Able to leave many of the sick and infirm back in Williamsburg, the regiment traveled unencumbered and was satisfied knowing their comrades were well taken care of. On the march, Captain I.L. Chadwick and the rest saw the war-ravaged countryside. The absence of men to work the fields struck Emerson Merrell:

Corn is up almost big enough to hoe, but a divil [sic] a man is there left to hoe it. A few nigger wenches constitutes the inhabitance here at present, for all the whites are all soldiers and most of the niggers have been taken along by the rebels to build fortifications for them to hide behind.[18]

Despite Hooker's division's late start, they caught up with the army on May 23 near Bottom's Bridge on the banks of the Chickahominy[19] where the road turned near due west toward Richmond. McClellan concentrated his army here on the north side of the river. The true prizes, Richmond and Johnston's army, lay on the river's south side. For the past few days after news of his confirmation, Excelsior men, with exception of those few remaining petitioners in the 72nd, anticipated the return of their beloved General Sickles. Finally he arrived at Bottoms Bridge astride his favorite white horse. The *New York Times* described the scene:

About noon the General made his appearance. The lucky individual who first espied him made it known with a "There comes our General." His words had not died away ere a thousand voices took up the refrain.... The camp guard vainly essayed to keep the men inside the lines. They broke through every barrier and met him on the road. In a moment he was in the midst of the excited crowd. Shouting at the top of their voices, throwing their caps high in air, they tumbled over one another in their scramble to get to his side.[20]

Sickles first visited camp of the 74th along with every other regiment and ended with the 70th. While greetings were lusty in each camp, there was more reserve among those officers of the 72nd who had signed the petition back in Maryland and perhaps thought old Abercrombie a better brigadier. Regardless, the scene was full of jubilation, and even the normally reserved Sickles, clad in a new uniform, was taken aback and unprepared for the overwhelming show of affection. Col. Graham was also welcomed back heartily as he resumed his position at the head of the 70th.[21]

Sickles took official command of the brigade the next day, but time for celebrating was past for the army was on the move. McClellan moved a portion of his army to take Mechanicsville, a mere six miles north of Richmond, while other elements struck south across the river. This southward move dislodged the enemy from Seven Pines, a village sitting astride the Williamsburg Road only eight miles east of Richmond. Taylor's men and the rest of Hooker's division crossed the river to support the advance toward Seven Pines. While artillery crews established their forward positions, the regiment occupied nearby rifle pits in case of Reb attack. Every man in the regiment knew the danger of being south of the river, because they were isolated from the bulk of the army should Johnston attack. Even though the bridges across the Chickahominy were sound, there was relief when Hooker's division was recalled back north of the river that evening.

That night, word came that a worried Lincoln had postponed McDowell's move south because of his concern that Stonewall Jackson might move boldly in the Shenandoah Valley should McDowell head toward Richmond. Despite not having McDowell's large force bearing in on Richmond from the north, McClellan moved all the same. He decided to move two of his five corps south of the river for the advance on Richmond, while leaving the remaining three on the north side for the eventual link-up with McDowell. The III and IV Corps were chosen for the move south.[22]

Hooker moved his First and Third brigades on Sunday, May 25, about a mile forward, crossing the river onto Poplar Hill where they composed part of the army's extreme left wing. Sickles and his Excelsiors remained north of the river at Bottom's Bridge for the time being.

The division was now split. Grover's First Brigade and Patterson's Third Brigade were camped at Poplar Hill, which provided fairly high ground, surrounded by the Chickahominy River on one side and swamp along the others, while Sickles remained north of the river. The welfare of the men was of great concern. These were the swampy, low lands of the peninsula, and quinine mixed with water was issued regularly in hopes of warding off disease. Around the camps, the forested land was lush with wild berries and other ripe fruit ready for picking, but good conditions for berries were often ill-suited for soldiers. Heavy, continuous rains pounded the division for a week. With his men in deteriorating health, Hooker might expect to muster roughly 7,000 men at any time.[23]

McClellan had moved most of his massive army into positions of his choosing by the last week of May. Two corps, the III Corps under Heintzelman and the IV Corps under Keyes, were on the south side of the river where lead elements of this force held positions along the Williamsburg road near the small crossroads hamlet of Seven Pines. The other three corps were not far away, on the Chickahominy's north side. Little Mac was confident of his move; should an emergency arise there were many usable bridges troops could cross.[24]

With the Union army split and McDowell delayed, Johnston divined an opportunity to defeat at least part of the invading Yankee army. He quickly conjured a plan to hit the Yankee IV Corps around Seven Pines with a three-pronged, three-division attack under James Longstreet; many of these boys were the same who had tangled with the Excelsiors back at Williamsburg. Under Johnston's plan, the main body of Confederate troops under R.H. Anderson would move from the north, down Nine Mile Road, which intersected Williamsburg Road at Seven Pines. Anderson would be supported by a division under W.H.C. Whiting. This combined force would then hit the Union right flank as it sat facing west along the Williamsburg Road. Troops under D.H. Hill representing the middle force

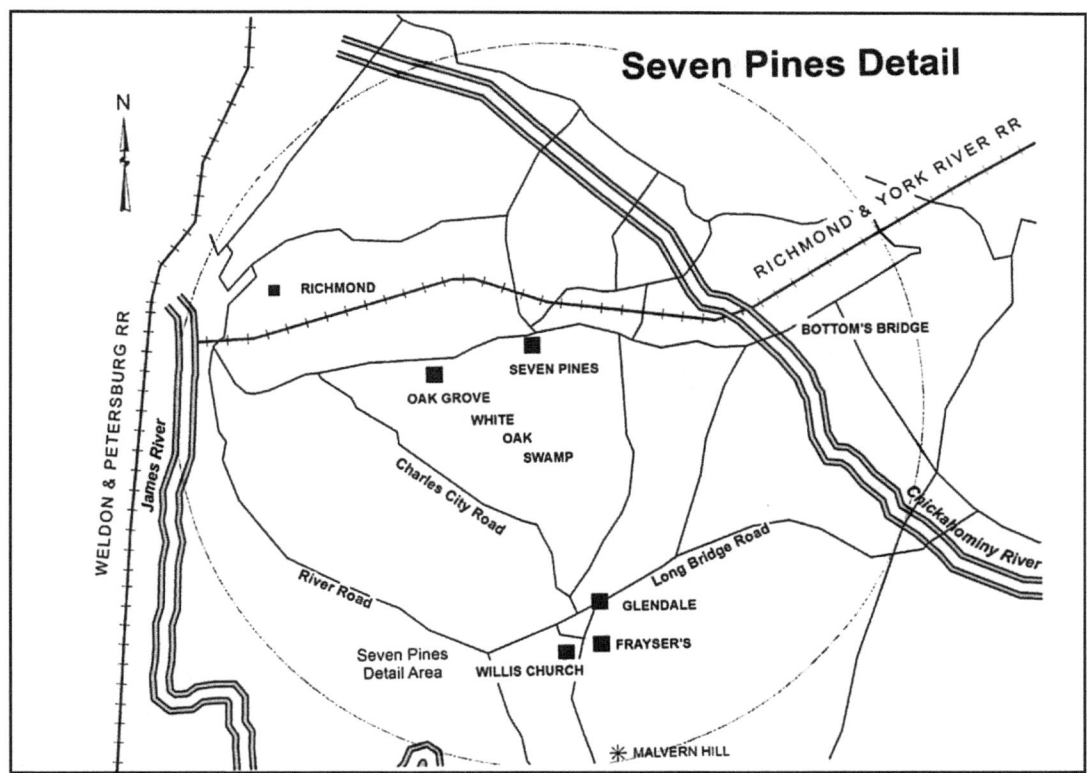

were to move east along the Williamsburg Road and hit the Yankee front. A third force of two brigades under Benjamin Huger would swing south using the Charles City Road, then use lesser roads to move back north, attacking the Union left. When Huger was in position on the Confederate right, he would signal Hill to start the attack. Upon hearing the sound of the cannons, Anderson, on the Rebel left, would launch his attack. Johnston planned on hitting the Yankees early on the morning of May 31.[25]

The night before the attack, Confederate fortunes looked even brighter as a severe rain storm raised the river's level, swamping several bridges McClellan had planned to use should problems arise, and further isolating III and IV Corps. But with time approaching to launch the attacks, luck seemed to turn against Johnston as miscues plagued the Confederates. Normally reliable Longstreet sent Anderson down the wrong road into position along the Williamsburg Road and blocking the movements of Hill and Huger's brigades. All of Longstreet's brigades were on Williamsburg Road, with only Whiting's Division remaining to attack from the north along Nine Mile Road. With Huger blocked, there would be no attack from the south, effectively turning the affair into only a two-pronged attack. To sort things out, Johnston pushed back the start of the attack from 8 a.m. till 1 p.m. as Hill's men got into proper position.[26]

Finally in place and deployed in thick woods and undergrowth, Hill's center force went forward with the attack, shattering the advanced positions of Silas Casey's IV Corps. Despite the protection of prepared positions, the Rebel advance slowed only slightly as Casey's Federals fell back en masse, clogging the Williamsburg Road as they made for the rear.

Troops from the III Corps, Third Division, under Phil Kearny made their way to the front, reinforcing the shaky Union lines. Around 4 p.m. Johnston realized his plan was in serious trouble as Yankee resistance stiffened with some of his units' failing to attack. Taking personal command of Whiting's Division, Johnston moved to the attack south down Nine Mile Road.

Back at Bottom's Bridge, the Excelsiors stirred with the sound of distant artillery. Chadwick, Bliss, Leonard and the other captains roused their men into columns for the cross-river march and a link-up with the rest of the division. Merrell and Stoddard fell in with their respective companies, ready to move quickly in light marching order, leaving all garrison equipage and knapsacks behind.[27]

As Johnston moved south along Nine Mile Road to hit the Federals, a lone Union battery made its way across a single rickety bridge and began hurling shot into his ranks. The Federal guns were located near Fair Oaks Station, about a mile north of Seven Pines. As the confederate commander turned left to deal with this pesky artillery, Union infantry from the II Corps under Edwin Sumner arrived from across the river in support, turning this from a distracting skirmish to a stand-up fight and derailing Johnston's notion of a multipronged attack.[28]

Back along the Williamsburg Road, the Confederates overcame lines of abatis and had pushed the Federals nearly a mile. Yet with no further support to give weight to their attacks and with Yankee regiments arriving from the rear, the southern attack stalled. By nightfall Union lines held about a mile east of Casey's original positions.

The companies of the 72nd along with other Excelsior regiments had been on the road since before 4 p.m. and were now near the Richmond and New Kent Old Stage Road. The regiment made bivouac at 8 p.m. lying on their arms, only eight miles from Richmond and only a couple of miles east of Seven Pines.[29]

Federal positions reorganized during the night as additional troops came up. Hooker's division now straddled the Williamsburg Road just east of where the fighting had stopped the day before. On the other side of the line, as Johnston rode among his lines inspecting their dispositions, a Yankee musket ball hit him in the shoulder and was soon followed by a shell fragment that slammed into his chest. Unhorsed and unconscious, the Rebel commander was carried from the field and eventually to a Richmond hospital.[30]

Confederate command now devolved to Major General Gustavus W. Smith, who after pondering his options, ordered Longstreet to continue the attacks in the morning by striking north from the Williamsburg Road toward the Federals beyond the railroad and around Fair Oaks. On Sunday morning the planned attacks toward the railroad went forward. Union lines had been reinforced in the night, and advancing Rebels faced a swelling maelstrom of Yankee lead. Unable to weather the storm, the Southern attack gave out.

Heintzelman readied his Second Division for an advance along the Williamsburg Road east of Seven Pines. Hooker had only two regiments of New Jersey men from the First Brigade and Sickles' Excelsiors available to him. Forming around 7 a.m., Sickles and his brigade stepped off and went forward. Moving only a few hundred yards, they met Heintzelman, who issued Sickles new orders. Hooker continued forward with the two New Jersey regiments and encountered stiff resistance in a patch of woods north of the Williamsburg Road near the Richmond and York River Railway tracks, but Sickles was not to follow. Sickles instead marched his brigade farther to the left of Hooker, staying astride the road.[31]

"General Hooker gallantly led the Fifth and Sixth New Jersey Regiments forward near the railroad. General Sickles' brigade followed, but finding the enemy in force to the left of the Williamsburg road, turned, by my direction, a portion of the brigade to the left of this road," reported Heintzelman.³² The enemy force concerning Heintzelman was mainly some Alabamans from Wilcox's brigade who had found a good position in a small wood.

Sickles issued orders to deploy his regiments. Taylor positioned the 72nd left of the road and sent forward two companies as skirmishers.³³ The regiment was in line with Col. George Hall's 71st New York, whose men were initially on the right of the road, but orders from Heintzelman moved both regiments to the left of the road. With the 72nd on the extreme left and the 71st between it and the road, the brigade was ready to advance. The 73rd, 70th and 74th New Yorks formed on the road's right.³⁴ "These dispositions were made under an annoying fire from the enemy's skirmishers and sharpshooters, who were in the woods and undergrowth in front. Their fire seemed directed almost entirely upon mounted officers,"³⁵ wrote Sickles.

"A rebel sharpshooter posted in a tree near a house on the right of the pike had been making some good shots, with Gen. Sickles and his staff as his target.... My attention was called to the lively and adventurous youth. Instantly the right of Co. F, including some 20 rifles, aimed for that tree, which unloaded its dead fruit as food for worms almost immediately,"³⁶ reported Captain Walter A. Donaldson of the 71st New York.

Skirmishers went forward to flush the trees and bushes of remaining Confederate snipers and laggards as the Excelsiors moved forward. Taylor's men conspicuously advanced at the right shoulder shift as if "on parade."³⁷ Being closest to the road and in the most exposed positions, the 71st and 73rd New York bore the brunt of "a severe fire from the enemy, consisting of about four regiments, concealed in the woods directly in our front,"³⁸ wrote Col. Hall. Responding with one or two volleys, Hall ordered a charge of his 71st N.Y.

Firing continually, the 71st, flanked closely by the 73rd on its right and the 72nd on its left, rushed forward at the double quick. "With a vigorous shout and cheer we broke with headlong speed toward the edge of the woods sheltering the enemy, whose volleys had been making things uncomfortable for the welfare and good health of the Sickles' Brigade,"³⁹ wrote Donaldson. Enduring continuous fire and with the weight of the entire Excelsior brigade bearing in upon them at fixed bayonets, the concealed Rebels broke and fled, littering the field with equipment and wounded.⁴⁰

Advancing into the wood, thick brush and timber prevented the Excelsiors from maintaining perfect alignment. Each regiment pursued best they could. On the left, Taylor's companies slowed to a halt while on the right, the 70th and 74th moved through the wood under instructions from Sickles to "proceed cautiously, observe the enemy, and to engage him if this could be done with advantage."⁴¹

With the enemy flushed from the wood but his brigade disorganized, Sickles ordered a consolidation of his position just as orders arrived from Heintzelman to detach two regiments to support II Corps. The 70th N.Y. and 74th N.Y. were dispatched toward the railroad tracks, where they offered timely service. After driving the Rebs from the field, they returned to further bolster Sickles' new line. Around noon a Confederate battery began shelling the woods held by the Excelsiors, "evidently trying to ascertain or drive us from our position,"⁴² reported Taylor. But the firing was only intermittent and ceased entirely after an hour.⁴³

Their attacks now spent and requested reinforcements still absent, Confederate General Hill saw little hope in stopping the overwhelming number of blue-coated Yankees. As the last major command engaged, Hill finally ordered a general withdrawal around 1 p.m. effectively ending the Battle of Seven Pines, leaving the field and all positions originally held by the Federals back in Union hands.⁴⁴

In their new advanced positions, Union commanders summoned ambulances to care for both Northern and Southern wounded, as McClellan unexpectedly ordered a general halt. Attacks by Sickles and the rest of Hooker's division had gone well, with the Excelsiors suffering only eight men killed, 58 wounded, and six missing.[45] Indeed, with news of no more offensive action, both Hooker and Kearney complained bitterly to each other over McClellan's reluctance to press the attack, both men believing the Rebs to be on the verge of complete collapse.[46]

For the remainder of the day and through the night, Taylor's boys and the rest of the Excelsiors held the ground captured that morning. Skirmishers from the various commands were sent out in case of Rebel counter-moves, with two companies from the 72nd deployed for this purpose. With the men of the regiment lying on their arms, there was no firing that night, only a distant drum roll and sound of troops moving across the regiment's front.[47] Young Lucius Jones of Company H was one of those keeping watch:

> Night put a stop to the fighting. Soon as it was dark pickets were called for, and I was one of them. We were taken out in front in a strip woods; it was a swamp. We were posted along a line about ten feet apart, with orders not to talk, but to keep a sharp lookout. James P. Knox was next to me; we had to stand in the water up over our shoes. We took turns standing on a big root of a tree to keep out of the water—only room enough for one at a time. We were glad when morning came.[48]

With the enemy close by, Pvt. Stoddard and the rest of the regiment remained under standing orders against building fires despite the frequent rain. With everyone under arms and on constant vigil, the dead men and horses went unburied. This added to the already unhealthy conditions as the bodies began to fester and rot in the heat and wet. The stench of death filled the air. Survivors of the fight often fared no better. The injured, some with their wounds crawling with maggots, were loaded like cordwood onto stifling boxcars heading for hospitals at the rear. Many died en route.

Despite the hardships endured by the regiment, the day did have at least one moment of levity. It seemed some patriotic Richmond gentlemen sought to render aid to the soldiers fighting on their behalf. Procuring a four-horse omnibus from the American House hotel, they filled it with various food delicacies and other supplies intended for the Southern wounded. Four or five of them then boarded the coach and started for the front. Traveling on corduroy roads near Seven Pines, the group encountered many fleeing Confederate soldiers streaming toward Richmond. The omnibus began to pick up speed, bouncing the occupants about. Calling for the driver to slow down, the riders discovered the coachman was not in his seat. The black coachman, lying on the floor, raced the bus and its forlorn passengers toward the Federal lines. As they bounced around the inside, the Good Samaritans struggled to open the door, which had been tied shut with a leather strap. Firing their pistols at the driver proved fruitless. The passengers eventually cut through the leather strap and flung open the door. Disgruntled, they piled onto the road as the driver made good his escape toward Union lines.[49]

The wayward carriage made it to the lines of the 72nd New York and to one of its officers, probably First Lt. Michael McDonald of Company E. A New York City omnibus driver on Broadway before the war, MacDonald took the possession of the coach and headed for brigade headquarters. With the colored driver seated beside him, McDonald swung the coach in front of General Sickles and asked, "Bus for the Battery?"[50] Sickles replied he would wait for the next one. McDonald turned the omnibus and team over to the quartermaster.[51]

Not satisfied to let the joke die there, Sickles ordered the coach sent to corps commander

5. Seven Pines and on to Richmond

Peter Heintzelman, suggesting the commanding general might wish to patronize the hotel. Heintzelman reportedly quipped upon receiving the omnibus, "It seems that those damned fellows of Sickles' have got into Richmond already and are keeping the hotel."[52]

Taylor received orders at daylight on Monday the 2nd to move his regiment forward with the rest of the brigade. At 8 a.m. the New Yorkers followed a battery of artillery to Casey's old camp. The boys remained in trenches around the cannons until 3 p.m. when they moved to the rear of the guns and a camp previously occupied by Couch's division.[53] Around five in the afternoon, Hooker reported he had traveled a considerable distance up two roads advancing away from these forward positions and found them clear of the enemy. The overly cautious McClellan discouraged reconnaissance like this, only adding to Hooker's frustration over Little Mac's failure to advance.[54]

The regiment was assigned picket duty that night in front of the entire III Corps. At 9:30, Major William O. Stevens took six companies comprising 260 men and moved forward. One hundred men from the Fifth New Jersey under Major Ramsey reported to Taylor, who then directed Ramsey to take charge of his men along with the four remaining companies of the 72nd. Ramsey was to support Stevens' right flank while keeping some men in reserve. During the night a light was seen in the distance and there was more drumming, but except for a drenching rain and the constant threat of a nearby enemy, the night was uneventful.[55] That night men had time to reflect on the past few days. They had performed well, pushing the enemy from the woods; only one man had been wounded and another listed as missing. Despite the light losses of this battle, the companies were getting worn out and the regiment with it. "Company B which left Jamestown with one hundred and ten men, and was afterwards recruited by the addition of twenty more, has now not more than thirty-five or forty men capable of service,"[56] wrote James Hall. But the hearts of the Company B men may have been a little heavier, as news of the loss of their beloved Captain Brown reached them. The man who formed the company, the young doctor who left the 72nd to colonel the 100th New York, had died leading a charge at the head of his men. Though some thought the attack to be suicidal, he led the assault "with a smile and a hurrah."[57] Brown had left Company B some weeks before, yet many held his memory with affection and felt his loss.

Taylor received welcomed orders in the morning for his regiment to go into camp. Withdrawing pickets, he moved about a half mile to the rear, yet within 20 minutes Taylor received new orders to report back to the front. Near Couch's old camp, Taylor formed his regiment right of the 71st N.Y., standing in line under arms until 4 p.m. Remaining in the area under arms through the night, they suffered through another violent rainstorm. The next morning, June 4, the regiment moved forward to near Casey's old works. Along the way some Rebel soldiers and an officer were discovered in one of the local houses. Taylor ordered surgeon Charles Irwin to attend to the wounded men. Irwin discovered that while none of the wounds were mortal, the Southern men lacked proper care. Taylor referred the matter to the brigade staff, recommending an ambulance take the prisoners to the rear for more thorough treatment.[58]

Two companies under Maj. Stevens were sent near 5 p.m. to relieve some companies of the Sixth New Jersey as pickets. About the same time, the 11th Massachusetts relieved the balance of Taylor's regiment. Taylor's men returned to Couch's old camp, finally setting up a camp of their own—the first time since leaving Bottom's Bridge, five days before.[59] Hooker was now confident in his ability to repulse any unexpected Rebel attack and relaxed precautions by allowing the men to cremate dead horses and bury the many bodies that still littered the field. Emerson Merrell wrote:

> The ground was covered with the killed and wounded and some of the dead lay till yesterday before they were buried. It has been very hot all of the time till night last when it began to rain and the ground was covered with magets [*sic*] and blood and a sight too horrible to mention.[60]

Camp offered relief for the men of Third Excelsior from the strain of the past several days, but conditions still took a huge toll. Picket lines were too close for comfort, and skirmishing and other forays continued constantly. Rain and enemy shelling added to the men's stress. Duties rotated through the division: two brigades manned the forward trenches and picket lines, while the third rested in camp. Unfortunately, unhealthful conditions continued to swell the sick call rolls to alarming proportions.[61] One soldier detailed, "We could not get a breath of fresh air, a drink of good water, or a sound night's rest."[62] David Parker described what he saw:

> Both horses and men lay about in every direction, and the heat was intense. The horses would quickly swell up so that they would all be lying on their backs with their legs extended in the air, and the poor dead soldiers, on both sides, were in the same condition, swollen so full that their clothes would burst. As soon as possible men were detailed to bury the dead, but in most cases this was done by simply shoveling earth upon them as they lay, and the earth was in clods so that the covering was not complete. The stench was intolerable. No good water could be obtained. A little well was dug and a barrel sunk in the ground, which speedily filled with surface water, and this after being boiled was the water the soldiers drank. Strict orders were issued that all the water should be boiled. Sickness immediately affected nearly every man. Barrels of whiskey were issued. The open barrel was given a large amount of quinine, and soldiers stood by with a stick to stir it when the men were marched up with their cups, given a ration, and told to drink it then and there.[63]

Fighting at Seven Pines moved General McClellan to within sight of the spires of Richmond, requiring only one last Yankee push. But perhaps the most portentous result of the past ten days of movement and fighting wasn't that the Federal army lay within a half-day's march of the Confederate capital, but rather that the Rebel army had a new commander to replace the wounded Joseph Johnston. That commander was Robert E. Lee.[64]

6. Going Backwards

For Emerson Merrell it must have seemed the digging would go on forever. Every day for two weeks he and the rest of Company I worked to improve their defensive works near the Williamsburg and Richmond Stage Road. The site was only six miles or so from Richmond, and on good days they could hear church bells from the Rebel capital.

Federal forces had settled into strong positions in front of Richmond following their victory at Seven Pines and Fair Oaks. The III Corps was stationed on the army's left flank, and General Joe Hooker's Second Division followed a routine that served them well. Each day, one of the division's three brigades occupied the forwardmost trenches, while the other two enjoyed the relative comforts of camp. Camp life was preferable to the forward trenches, but many Excelsior Brigade men complained that while they rested, the other brigades allowed the enemy to advance upon their line and thus, as one Excelsior man wrote, "entail upon us the work of driving them (the enemy) back."[1] Of course the other brigades didn't necessarily see it this way, and some concluded that the Excelsiors were overly aggressive and eager to start a fight where none was warranted.

Men worked at improving the forward defensive works every day, and they grew increasingly confident in the earthworks. Conditions, however, upon Richmond's doorstep were poor. Swampy ground, intolerable heat, frequent rain, and constant threat of enemy attack made life in the forward trenches miserable. Life in the rear was only slightly better. The stench of unburied men and horses hung in the air, while the lack of good water kept the men wanting.[2] "The water is scarce here.... I have not seen a bit of pure water since we left Yorktown. I had drank water here that I would not wash my hands in at home,"[3] lamented Emerson Merrell.

Hooker's men had built fine defensive works, so fine that they discouraged any real attempts by the under-strength Confederate Army to dislodge them. Good as the works were, McClellan's troops remained too far from Richmond to employ the heavy siege guns Little Mac hoped to use in pounding Richmond and, by extension, the Confederacy, into surrender.[4] The New Yorkers maintained their position for nearly two weeks. Though there had been many rumors of an impending push, orders finally did come. Heintzelman's III Corps was to advance west to clear a section of woods lying mostly south of the Williamsburg and Richmond Stage Road. This preliminary attack was part of a general offensive designed to move the Army of the Potomac close enough to Richmond to employ those big guns of which McClellan was fond. Chaplain Joseph Twichell described the situation in a June 25 letter home:

> Hitherto the hostile pickets have met about midway in a swampy wood affording cover to each alike and leaving to each the open ground beyond, both sides, to operate in as they

pleased. If I understand it, it was regarded necessary to clear those woods of the enemy and establish our outposts in the further edge, thus giving us some jurisdiction over a wide plain beyond.[5]

The III Corp's First Division had previously been detached, so Hooker's Second Division would form the right wing of the advance while Third Division, under Phil Kearney, formed the left. Hooker had arranged his division with Sickles' Excelsior Brigade sitting astride the Williamsburg Road. Sickles now positioned two regiments right of the road and the remaining three on its left. Colonel Taylor's 72nd N.Y. formed the left-most regiment of the brigade, contacting Brigadier General Cuvier Grover's First Brigade, which formed to its south. Third Brigade, temporarily under Col. Joseph Carr, comprised the reserve. Kearney's division was then aligned south of Grover. Heintzelman's III Corps, two divisions strong, now held a front nearly a mile-and-a-half long.[6]

"For half a mile to the front of our line of battle, heavy forest covered the ground and running through the middle of this was a belt of swampy soil, on each side of which was an almost impenetrable undergrowth," wrote Hooker as he described the ground before him. The swamp was waist deep in places and had "tacitly become the dividing section between the advanced pickets of the two armies."[7] Any attempt by either side to cross the swamp would be met with a swift and strong response.[8] Movement through the swamp would be slow, becoming a potential death trap for any attacking force.

Captain Chadwick stepped off with his New York City men on June 25 at 8 a.m. Enemy troops were close; almost at once the whole division was engaged with the Rebel pickets. But for Sickles' men the situation was worse. Regiments advancing left of the road faced the worst of the swamp and with the going slow, had a hard time keeping up and maintaining the line of advance. Company officers encouraged the men, but poor terrain and hidden enemy pickets slowed the advance; nevertheless, advance they did. Despite maintaining a steady hail of fire on the enemy, the Excelsiors soon found themselves lagging behind Grover's brigade to their left.[9] Hooker's men outnumbered the enemy pickets initially, but with the fight on, Confederate commanders busily sent reinforcements to the point of the attack. With Federal and Confederate troops slugging it out at close quarters in the woods, Union artillery held their fire for fear of striking friendly troops.

With Excelsiors advancing, increasing musketry on their right alerted those in command that Sickles' men were outnumbered and the flank was in danger. But before reinforcements could be brought up, a serious demonstration threatened to turn the brigade's right. Sickles and 71st's Colonel George Hall surveyed the situation, but panic gripped the regiment when someone yelled, "We are flanked, retreat."[10] As men stampeded to the rear even the color company was swept up as nearly the entire left wing of the regiment broke "in disgraceful confusion." Only the exertions of Sickles, officers from the adjacent regiment, and members of Hooker's staff were able to restore order and reform the wing. The episode was even more "mortifying," wrote the narcissistic Sickles, "as it happened in the immediate presence of the brigadier-general commanding the division, who was in front throughout the day."[11]

Order to the line was restored by 10 a.m. Sickles' right was now supported by the addition of 7th New Jersey from the reserve brigade, and the advance continued "in the face of a galling fire and an obstinate resistance on the part of the enemy."[12] Taylor's men continued to make steady progress on the brigade's left, supported by regiments from adjoining commands.

With the fight progressing, the first of the brigade's wounded were treated under some nearby trees and in two houses in back of the entrenchments. Eventually a hospital was established half a mile to the rear near the railroad. "Each regiment furnished its quota [of wounded] and it was not long before ambulances were in great demand," wrote Chaplain Twichell, adding, "As before, wounds of every description were to be found, from those that were mortal in an hour to those that were a slim apology for leaving the ranks."[13]

Although the fighting was heavy, by mid-morning the division and entire corps had gained ground. Despite the progress, around 11:00 orders came from McClellan to suspend operations. Sickles was in a state of disbelief and questioned the orders, but Hooker assured him further protests would be in vain and the advance would stop.[14] McClellan, directing the battle from his headquarters far to the rear, had only now received messages about the panic amongst the 71st N.Y. Concluding the attack was faltering, McClellan ordered a halt, though in reality the situation at the front had already been remedied.

Pickets were reluctantly thrown out as commanders waited. The Excelsiors moved back to where they'd formed earlier that morning. Finally McClellan himself arrived on the scene around 1 p.m. and finding the situation well in hand, he ordered the attacks renewed.[15]

As Taylor's men moved forward Rebels kept up their fire, especially on the right of the brigade where men had earlier broken and run. A brigade from IV Corps along with a battery of Napoleons soon arrived to lead the attack. Helped by "well directed and rapid fire"[16] from the cannons, the enemy began to fall back as IV Corps men pressed the attack. On the Excelsior's left the volume of noise increased dramatically as Kearney's men came to close grips with the enemy.[17] With pressure all along their front, around 4:30 Confederate defenders abandoned the woods Hooker had been ordered to take. Having taken his objective and stopped, Hooker's men, especially on the right, were exposed to enemy artillery fire. Strong pickets were thrown out and as night fell, the day's fighting drew to a close. Men from the IV Corps relieved Hooker's division, allowing his men to return to camp. Fighting at Oak Grove had cost Hooker's division 28 killed, 262 wounded, and 19 missing.[18] Sickles' Excelsior Brigade, already thinned to about 1,500 men, suffered 8 killed, 116 wounded, and 11 missing.[19] Taylor's New Yorkers entered the fight with near 300 men and lost 23 wounded, with 5 missing.[20]

Chadwick and the rest of the Excelsiors remained in their forward camps for the next two days. The III Corps had done well, but other events along the front convinced the seemingly reluctant McClellan that his position was untenable and a redeployment of his forces toward the rear was in order. When news of the withdrawal reached Hooker, the aggressive divisional commander was livid over what he believed amounted to a retreat. Orders received by Sickles on the night of the 28th directed him to prepare to move at daylight. These instructions called for the men to have three days cooked rations in their haversacks and "employ all available means of transportation"[21] to bring away entrenching tools, ammunition, food, hospital stores and other equipment. Once loaded, the supply wagons would be sent to the rear. Any gear that could not be removed was to be destroyed.[22] Lucius Jones of Company H later reflected on the situation:

> Following Fair Oaks was Seven Pines, a mile or more in the rear of Fair Oaks. Our forces urged the battle, in fact it was a mere continuation of the same battle, while we were masters of the situation, and probably could, by an energetic movement, have captured Richmond. Gen. McClellan, terrified by the unknown, hesitated, trembled, and, when Dame Rumor whispered the untold thousands that were pouring forth to meet him, he began the retrograde movement. The unknown element is one of the mightiest factors in all problems. McClellan was forever magnifying this element, until it was more terrible than the armies of his enemies; it unquestionably proved the ruin of the otherwise able General.[23]

Excelsiors broke camp early the next morning. Pioneers from the various regiments assembled under the command of Lieutenant Van Buren Bates of 70th N.Y. As the rest of the brigade marched to the forward defenses to screen the withdrawal from any Rebel interference, Bates and his men set about destroying gear that couldn't be moved.[24]

With the valuable artillery safely to the rear, Hooker's division pulled back, with Sickles forming on the left. As they moved, Lt. Bates followed as rear guard, felling timber and placing obstacles as he went.[25] Captain John Leonard's Company F from Newark deployed as pickets between the old camp and the brigade's new position. Both Heintzelman's III Corps and II Corps under General Edwin Sumner were assigned to protect the withdrawal of the entire army. The plan was to first move east back toward Williamsburg, then turn south on roads near Savage Station and proceed towards Harrison's Landing, which rested on the James River.

Hoping to engage the Yankees while moving and exposed, Rebel troops wasted no time in attacking. By nine that morning of the withdrawal, Confederates under John B. Magruder hit Sumner's rear guard around Allen's Farm, just west of Fair Oaks. When the Southern men attacked, Heintzelman was positioned south of Sumner and south of the Richmond and York River Railroad; thus only Grover's brigade was slightly engaged in the morning's fight. With the Excelsiors posted south of Grover, Sickles reported only the annoyance of an occasional artillery burst, which nonetheless killed two and wounded five.[26]

Sickles received orders at 4:00 to deploy his brigade and move in line of battle the roughly two miles east to Savage Station. Approaching the station, Heintzelman directed the Excelsiors to countermarch and move briskly south toward the Charles City Road, across Brackett's Ford and over White Oak Swamp.[27] Rebel pursuers pressed on to the east, engaging Sumner's II Corps and William Franklin's VI Corps at Savage Station. Heintzelman had been in a good position to support this fight, but owing to a misunderstanding, withdrew III Corps south across White Oak swamp, leaving Sumner and Franklin to fight alone. In his haste to withdraw across the swamp and amidst the general confusion that gripped the army, Heintzelman ordered a trainload of ammunition and other stores destroyed and abandoned more than 2,000 of his wounded.[28]

Flankers were deployed along the line of march as Sickles crossed the swamp at sunset. The march was a trying affair for the New Yorkers, as columns were frequently harassed by Confederate troops and the boys had to share the road with an endless line of wagons that crossed White Oak Swamp at a rate of over 100 per hour.[29] The Excelsiors reached the Charles City Road soon after dark. There, Sickles reported to Hooker and bivouacked with the rest of the division near Glendale.[30] Chadwick, Merrell, and the rest of the regiment were now about six miles south of Savage Station and less than ten miles north of Harrison's Landing.

Franklin and Sumner moved their men south across White Oak swamp early the next morning, destroying bridges as they passed. The destruction of the White Oak bridges frustrated Confederate pursuit from the north. But enemy troops under James Longstreet and A.P. Hill were already south of the White Oak and marching hard to intercept the Yankees from the west.

It was critical for McClellan's men to keep the roads around Glendale open long enough for the long lines of supply wagons to continue moving south. The V Corps was located west of Glendale in position to defend against Rebel attack. Hooker's division was sent to support the V Corps and took up positions on the left of these men. The morning of June 30, Hooker directed Sickles to reconnoiter the country in front of the Quaker Road, south toward the James River. After riding about three miles to Malvern Hill, Sickles returned to the sound of artillery fire and discovered that the Excelsiors were on the move under the command of Colonel Taylor.[31]

After some uncertainty about how the troops should be aligned, Sickles settled his brigade on the division's left at 9:00 a.m. in what he considered to be a good defensible position. Two 72nd men, Private Patrick Connell of Company E and Corporal James Bowen of Co. D, were detailed to Sickles to serve as lookouts, being posted in a tall tree with a commanding view of the field.[32]

Following some early confusion, Confederate attacks finally got on line by afternoon. The Rebel push concentrated on the right of the Federal line against George McCall's division of the V Corps. The Federal troops here represented a rough collection of divisions from various corps, with no one in overall command. With no well-coordinated defense, McCall fought superior numbers almost alone. Around 5:00, a strong Confederate attack pierced McCall's lines, and his left brigade retreated in disorder.[33] The Excelsior Brigade then moved to help restore the Federal line, only to be mistaken for Southern troops. Sickles reported that McCall's men, "mistaking us for the enemy, poured several volleys into us. Our colors were promptly displayed along the line,"[34] and only through the exertions of various officers, Maj. Stevens among them, and a company of Berdan's Sharpshooters, did it happen that "these fugitives were driven back to their line."[35] Units from Sedgwick's division and Hooker's 16th Massachusetts helped stem the Rebel momentum and redirected their push toward Kearney's Division, which finally stopped the Southern advance.[36]

Later during the battle (known also as Frayser's Farm), Sickles sent word that his left flank was in jeopardy of being turned. As commanders in the rear decided upon what action to take, it became clear the threat had passed when a fresh message arrived from Sickles requesting permission to advance. Observing the enemy advancing nearly perpendicular to his front, Sickles requested a battery be brought forward to support the advance of his left regiments "so as to assail the enemy in the rear and on his right flank."[37] But when orders came directing him to detach the 71st New York to support General Sumner, Sickles abandoned his notion of a general advance, satisfied instead to throw forward skirmishers from Taylor's 72nd N.Y., the 2nd N.Y., and the 11th Massachusetts, capturing at least 150 enemy men and officers.[38]

The heaviest of the action for Hooker's division was over by early evening, except for some regiments of Grover's brigade who were ordered to clear away some remaining Rebels in their front. This situation became alarming when First Massachusetts worked themselves into a pocket of enemy troops. Grover had advanced with them, and only through his skill were they able to save themselves. Second Division's actions were not considered crucial to the battle's outcome, but Hooker nonetheless lost 192 men.[39] Col. Taylor reported three of his men captured and two wounded on the day, among them Private Connell, who injured himself severely by falling from a tree while in the service of General Sickles.[40]

That night, Hooker's division held its position around Glendale as the rest of the army continued south toward Harrison's Landing, collecting at Malvern Hill, where McClellan had decided to make his next stand in resisting the Rebel pursuit. The cries of those wounded earlier in the day burdened the air, making for a restless night. Men of the regiment and brigade rested on their arms as the enemy prowled unseen in the darkness. Twice messages came reporting that the Confederates had formed a battle line extending far beyond Sickles' left, but the expected attacks never came.[41]

When word came that the wagons were safely out of reach of the enemy, the regiment moved again. In the pre-dawn darkness of July 1, Hooker's men marched down Quaker Road. Arriving near Malvern Hill, the Excelsior Brigade halted and stood in columns of battalions, exposed to enemy artillery, which they weathered without harm for several hours. Eventually the entirety of Hooker's division was directed to the right center of the defensive line. Kearney's men, now re-designated as First Division of the III Corps, were on Hooker's left, while VI Corps occupied Hooker's right and rear. Hooker deployed his division with Grover's First Brigade on the right and Carr's Third on the left, with the Excelsiors placed in reserve behind Grover. All dispositions, including the placement of some artillery, were complete by 10 a.m. despite sporadic Rebel artillery fire into Grover's ranks. Sickles placed his New Yorkers in a nearby ravine where they were protected from the cannon fire yet close enough to provide immediate support when needed.[42] Despite the incredible noise and flurry of activity around them, many boys not actively engaged within the brigade, exhausted from the days of near constant marching and fighting, obeyed their bodies' commands and slept.

But sleep would have to wait for some. To cover his position Sickles picketed two regiments, the 70th and 73rd New Yorks. Company G under Captain Bliss was deployed as scouts. Bliss soon captured two Reb soldiers, whom he sent to divisional headquarters. Both prisoners confirmed previous intelligence predicting an imminent Confederate attack on the Federal front.[43]

Confederate advanced guards appeared in some woods by late morning along the Quaker Road. Bringing some artillery to bear, the enemy fired several rounds that were too close for comfort. Hooker's battery of the Second New Jersey then wheeled into position and fired on the unwelcome foe, sending them scurrying back to the protection of the woods. Other enemy guns soon appeared, and a brisk artillery duel commenced while infantrymen took turns piling undergrowth to form breastworks.[44]

Confederate infantry attacks finally began around five o'clock. Assaults came on the Federal left and center, where Rebels had concentrated much of their day's cannon fire. On the other side of the line, massed Union cannons formed a slaughter pen for Lee's men pressing up the hill. Odds were slim the enemy would pierce the defensive line, yet some Federal regiments reported being low on ammunition, so V Corps' General Fitz-John Porter called for reinforcements on the Federal left just the same. Sickles now received orders for the Excelsiors to support this weakened part of the line with less than an hour till sunset.[45]

The New Yorkers moved to a field left of where Porter's headquarters was located. Upon Sickles' arrival, Porter was away at the front lines, leaving no one to direct the placement of Second Brigade. After some discussion with other officers present, Sickles moved to Porter's right "at a brisk pace to that part of the field where the firing was most vigorous and sustained."[46] Still unable to find an officer to report to, Sickles halted the Excelsiors in a shallow depression that provided partial cover as he and Maj. Stevens rode off to find Porter. Within minutes, Porter arrived and directed Sickles to support two batteries of artillery positioned just right of the Quaker Road, which bisected the Federal line. But just as the Excelsiors were forming, a staff officer arrived to announce that the brigade was instead to report to General Couch, whose division held much of the center of the Union line.[47]

The Excelsiors were already in close proximity to Couch's line. Sickles had difficulty at first finding General Couch, though lesser officers bearing messages requesting support soon found Dan and his men. Couch's regiments were running out of ammunition, and they urgently needed relief.[48]

Colonel Taylor described the situation in his official report: "Soon several officers, representing themselves to be of General Couch's staff, appeared, and in answer to my inquiry where to place my regiment, commenced to give a variety of directions, which were confused and conflicting."⁴⁹ Taylor eventually found an aide to General Couch who directed the regiment forward up a narrow road past a small wood and to an open field. Following orders, Taylor's men found a portion of J.J. Abercrombie's Brigade hotly engaged; this was the same General Abercrombie who had briefly commanded the Excelsiors six weeks earlier near Williamsburg. Captain Bliss and the rest of the regiment formed a battle line behind the 31st Pennsylvania. As the 31st Penn. moved off by the left flank, each company began firing by files as they became unmasked from right to left. With the Pennsylvanians clearing the field, Taylor moved the entire regiment forward to the ground previously held by the Keystoners, all the while maintaining a heavy fire. Taylor now saw Confederates posted on the edge of a wood to his front and right. Throwing back his two right-most companies, he formed them at an oblique angle with instructions to silence Rebel fire on his right, which was actually closer than that to his front.⁵⁰ In the furious exchange of volleys, enemy bullets whipped through the ranks of Company H. Captain Doyle, at the head of his company, already hit in the arm, received a ball through his right leg, shattering the bone. He refused to be carried from the field, and another ball clipped his skull. There he died "on the field of battle, mourned by the soldiers who loved him and whom he loved."⁵¹ With the sun low, James Hall, firing from the front rank of his Company B, was hit by a shell fragment that sent him staggering back behind the line. As Co. B continued its desperate fight, James was struck again in the head and killed. His death went unseen by any of those dearest to him, and the place of his last breath unmarked.⁵² With the arrival of dusk, Rebels became discernible only by the discharges of their rifles. In the fading light, Taylor yelled for his men to watch for the flashes and aim low.⁵³

Taylor's men were in a fight to be sure, but something was wrong—too many men on the right were going down. Taylor soon recognized the deadly problem; their own men were killing them. In the heat of the fight, Federal cannon had grown careless and were now firing their deadly canister rounds too low. It was these rounds wreaking havoc on his line. Two men were already dead and one wounded, probably more. Taylor threw his four right-most companies to the rear and in column and waited till the battery ceased firing. With the situation at least safe from Union artillery fire, the companies returned into line.⁵⁴

Both sides fired briskly for about 45 minutes. Running low on ammunition, Taylor's men scrounged 15 rounds each from the boxes of the 70th N.Y. in reserve nearby. The regiments in this part of the line were so low on ammunition that Sickles ordered up an additional 20,000 cartridges. Merrell and the rest used a new "patent cartridge"⁵⁵ with an ignitable paper wrap. This allowed soldiers to ram the entire round down the barrel without first tearing the bullet from the powder. By skipping this time-consuming step, the New Yorkers fired more rapidly. But while early use of the patent cartridge proved successful, they were never used extensively again.⁵⁶

Dead men lay where they fell, while the wounded were placed just to the rear of the line by file closers.⁵⁷ Around 8 p.m. Captain Chadwick was hit and led to the rear for treatment, with his left leg and hand peppered with lead or iron fragments.⁵⁸

As evening settled in, the battle wound down as Rebel fire slackened, giving Taylor and his men the impression the enemy had withdrawn. Taylor ordered his men to cease fire but to remain loaded. This order sent up a cheer from the regiment, which seemed to provoke the enemy, who in turn sent up a loud cheer and, advancing out of the woods near enough to be seen, fired a volley into the ranks of the regiment. Taylor's men responded with a volley of their own and then a rapid steady fire, which sent the Southern men beating a hasty retreat.

As the enemy retreated further into the woods, the New Yorkers were directed to fire slightly higher to reach their increasingly distant foes. Afterwards, "nothing more was heard of the enemy that night, except the slight noise of men collecting their dead and wounded,"[59] reported Taylor.

The piecemeal Confederate attacks had been totally repulsed by nightfall. The Army of the Potomac still held the top of Malvern Hill, with Lee and his Army of Northern Virginia left to sort out a costly defeat. The 72nd N.Y. held its position with pickets deployed and the men lying on their arms until they were ordered to withdraw near 2 a.m.

Though Malvern Hill was a victory, many in the Army of the Potomac had grown disillusioned with its commander, George McClellan, for both his lack of offensive spirit and his battlefield management. Private Robert Knox Sneden, a map maker on Heintzelman's staff, described the situation this way:

> General McClellan was not on the ground (as usual) until the battle [Malvern Hill] was over.... McClellan had first placed the troops in position this morning before leaving.... And as there was no headquarters staff, every general did as he pleased in changing battle lines during the day. But the Army of the Potomac has fought so many battles without General McClellan's supervision or assistance, that he is not missed when the fighting commences! His cautionary measures are so well known that the corps commanders win battles, and move troops to ensure the enemy's defeat, and are not hampered with McClellan's orders or presence, though McClellan gets all the credit. The fighting generals, such as Heintzelman, Sumner, Kearny, Hooker, Sedgwick, Richardson, and the others, have a profound contempt for General McClellan's fighting qualities, and several officers high in command denounce him without stint.[60]

Nearly all of the dead and wounded in Hooker's entire division came from Taylor's ranks. The regiment had taken about one-fifth casualties, with 14 killed and 47 wounded from a force of about 300.[61] Captain Steven Doyle of Company H was dead, being replaced the next day by John Holmes. Death visited the companies somewhat evenly; Company E got the worst of it with four killed, yet none were killed in C, I, or K.[62] The 74th New York had eight men wounded.[63] This was the extent of the divisional loss, since neither First nor Third brigades were engaged. Hooker would write in his battle report of the brilliant conduct of 72nd New York by summing it up thus: "the loss sustained by that regiment is the truest index of its services."[64]

James Hall's death wasn't confirmed to his company-mates until the next day's light. Within days Hall's friends and family received contradictory reports, first stating James to be dead, then safe, and then, sadly, dead. Folks back in Lowell clambered for details about their Jimmy. "It was a mile from our camp, and beyond our cavalry pickets,"[65] wrote Captain Bliss of Company D, who had visited the battlefield the night of the action, in a letter to Hall's family anxious for information about his death:

> I had no trouble in finding the field and in tracing out our different positions. On the night of the battle, Sergeant Brooks of my company from Panama, saw a corpse he thought to be his. Owing to the blood on the face, and darkness, he could not be positive. He took the things from his pockets, and when light came, from the letters, there was no longer any doubt. This is all we can ever know about his death. We could have buried our dead and marked their graves, if we could have found a spade or shovel. It was painful for us to leave them as we did, and until now we feared they were still unburied. But I found they had been decently interred by the rebels.... The position of Company "D" in line, would partly designate which of the four graves Jimmy was buried in, but it would be impossible to identify his body. He sleeps with his comrades on the field of his glory. There he must rest.[66]

Though his victory was clear, McClellan insisted on further movement south, eight miles to Harrison's Landing on the James River, where supplies and the protection of Navy gunboats awaited. Excelsior Brigade began its march to Harrison's Landing during the pre-dawn darkness of July 2; the now delirious Captain Chadwick and other wounded were carried along the way. Heavy rains made the march even more miserable, and the move was a clear admission that McClellan had given up the campaign despite recent victories at Malvern Hill and Glendale. Upon reaching Harrison's Landing, the brigade reported to Hooker that late afternoon. The entire Second Division was placed on the left-center of the Union line, the most likely point of a Rebel attack should they see fit to repeat the carnage of Malvern Hill.[67]

Hooker's men finally moved into permanent camp several days after arriving at Harrison's Landing. Defensive lines had been finished, and the duties required of the regiment's men were light. Men throughout the regiment caught up on their correspondence and tended to the other small tasks soldiers do while in camp. The season was painfully hot, and the sand, lack of trees, and annoying flies conspired to sap both the nerve and the strength of man and beast alike.[68] Men endured constant bites from infested trousers and tunics. While the more pious men like Hiram Stoddard may have prayed for relief while picking off nits, some of the harder men from Companies C and K no doubt cursed the Almighty. A nearby pond and a few wells dug for fresh drinking and cooking water offered only the slimmest relief. It was a land full of berries and wheat ready for harvest, but with most able-bodied Southern men gone for soldiers, the crop went uncollected or fell prey to opportunistic Yankee foragers such as Emerson Merrell and his mates. The various regiments and brigades eventually resumed the routine of camp life with morning parade and volleyed salutes. The men were back on normal whiskey rations, which helped buoy sagging spirits, as did the airs from the various regimental bands. Earlier McClellan had banned the playing of music during the campaign so as to not give away the position of his troops, but now music was a daily part of camp life appreciated greatly by enlisted men and officers alike. At least now Stoddard and the rest could enjoy a rollicking tune as they boiled six-legged guests from their uniforms.

The Federal lines were well entrenched, and both flanks rested on creeks. It was an excellent defensive position—too excellent in fact to be attacked, so Lee sent most of his army back to Richmond, leaving only cavalry patrols to watch the Yankee army.[69]

The army was at relative rest during July as Hooker contemplated his only real organizational problem: the poor condition of the Excelsior Brigade. The brigade was worn from the heavy fight at Williamsburg back in May and near-constant campaigning since, and brigade strength more closely resembled the 1,500 to 2,000 men of two regiments. Hooker recommended and received approval from Heintzelman to consolidate the brigade. McClellan concurred but felt Sickles, who was gone on recruiting duty, should be consulted. When finally asked, Sickles requested such action be postponed, certain he could raise the necessary manpower.[70]

Reports that Richmond was being evacuated came from Washington by month's end. McClellan immediately chose Hooker's division to check out such reports. "Fighting Joe" was eager for action and, sure the lightly defended Malvern Hill could be retaken, he submitted a plan to higher-ups. With the plan approved, Hooker set about regaining the offensive.[71]

Reinforced with a squadron of cavalry and some additional artillery, Hooker's division set out on August 2. With the guides proving particularly incompetent and progress slow, all hope of surprise was lost, provoking Hooker to cancel the endeavor and return to camp.[72] The project was tried again two days later on August 4, this time on a larger scale with a division from Sedgwick's corps added for good measure. Sickles was still gone recruiting, so command of the Excelsiors once again fell to Colonel Taylor. With Taylor in command of the Second Brigade, 72nd New York was back in the hands of Lt. Col. Moses.

Second Division left camp near eleven that morning. The approach was a 12-mile march past the Willis Church. Merrell, Stoddard, and the rest foraged liberally on green corn, tomatoes, potatoes, and even fresh pork available along the way.[73] At 11 p.m. Hooker called a halt to rest, but when Brigadier General Francis Patterson of the Third Brigade blew his bugle to halt his line, all secrecy was lost.[74] The march continued just before sunrise, moving past the site of the Glendale fight of June 30. Eventually the division arrived at the rear of Malvern Hill. With complete surprise lost, Confederate pickets stirred into action as Rebel artillery became more active than hoped.[75]

The plan called for the First and Second brigades to make a frontal assault while the Third Brigade swung far to the right, attempting to cut off the fleeing Rebs. During the assault, the First Brigade came under heavy artillery fire from a Confederate battery directly in front of the two brigades, while Taylor's Excelsiors contended with mounted enemy scouts on their left. Eventually the hill was taken, with fleeing Rebs leaving behind a caisson and implements for one gun.[76]

The attacks went forward but the ultimate prize of capturing the enemy was missed due partly to the intoxicated state of Third Brigade's General Patterson. Despite the failure of the Third Brigade, the hill was captured, and the men of the division busied themselves building breastworks should the enemy attempt to retake the position. McClellan and his staff visited the hill around noon as guests of Hooker. Satisfied with the course of action, McClellan prepared to move more divisions out of Harrison's Landing toward Malvern Hill. Near 6 p.m. the division formed into lines and threw out pickets to the front and right for several hundred yards. Upon hearing reports of these moves, Lee sent three divisions to check this potentially dangerous development.[77]

On August 6 Lee's divisions drove in Hooker's pickets, setting the stage for a second battle of Malvern Hill. But it was not to be. Hooker withdrew his command that night under orders from McClellan; the Excelsiors made it back to camp about daylight on the 7th. This time McClellan's reluctance to fight was because two days earlier he had received orders from Washington to withdraw his army from the Peninsula. And though McClellan protested vigorously,[78] the general had been given his chance and the War Department refused to reconsider; by the next week the great withdrawal would be underway. For Emerson Merrell, David Parker, Harmon Bliss, and the rest of the regiment, the Peninsula Campaign would soon be over.

Since its first real battle at the beginning of May, the Excelsior Brigade had been worn down to less than half its original strength; Taylor's 72nd now counted well under 300 men. In letters home only two months before, Emerson Merrell wrote of his excited anticipation to see the spires of Richmond. Now he wrote of his disgust over this "grand skedaddle."[79] Some officers felt the brigade had been fought too hard and allowed to be used up. Indeed, for whatever the official reasons, the resignations continued. Since the beginning of June, first lieutenants Hugh J. Winters (Co. K), Wakeman Holburton (Co. C), Michael McDonald (Co. G), and second lieutenant George W. Wallace of Company E had all quit.[80] Chaplain Twichell summed up the thoughts of many other New Yorkers when he wrote, "When I think of how grand our army was last winter, and of how much it has since cost in men and money, and how little it has been made to accomplish, and of its present condition.... I am persuaded that something or somebody is all wrong."[81]

Epoch III: Agony in Northern Virginia

7. Serving Under Pope

Food may have been the best part of life at Harrison's Landing for many of the men. The local Virginia countryside offered much: tomatoes, fresh corn, potatoes, and an occasional piece of pork. Emerson Merrell and his mates took full advantage of the bounty lying just beyond the edge of camp.[1] Fresh corn was a welcomed supplement to the less savory army rations that were now in abundance. Whiskey rations had been restored, and all but the most temperate men enjoyed the return of hard drink. Days were often hot, wet and miserable, but the men had fashioned a tolerable camp, complete with daily parades, cannon salutes and music played by the different regimental bands. Aside from morning and afternoon drill, the men were pretty well on their own. The health and morale of the boys was better than it had been in weeks.

Harrison's Landing's strong defenses were virtually unassailable, so the enemy did the only rational thing — they ignored McClellan's army. Robert E. Lee ordered only a few cavalry units to monitor the situation while he redirected the bulk of his army elsewhere. Without threat of enemy action, commanders such as Nelson Taylor could breathe and sort things out. Arriving in early July after the near constant fighting of the so-called Seven Days Battle, many men had only the uniforms on their backs and a rifle. Since then, the regiment had been able to resupply and began looking like proper soldiers once again.

Within some of the companies, the command structure had been something of a game of musical chairs, with officers coming and going due to transfers, resignations, wounding or death. Six companies had served the same captain since the Staten Island days, but in other companies there had been changes. Company C's Chadwick was gone, leaving the 23-year-old first lieutenant, Berend Huttmann, to run things. Huttmann began as first sergeant with the Germans over in Company A and in less than a year he moved up to first lieutenant.[2] Chadwick was sent back to New York, bypassing the normal regimen of army hospitals and doctors thanks to Taylor's largess (partially due to the fact that Chadwick's wife was a member of Taylor's family) and recuperating from his wounding at Malvern Hill and subsequent high fever. Company B was on its third captain since the beginning, with John Sanford running things after Williamsburg's fight, and both Company H and E were on their second captain. The Germans in Company A must have thought their captaincy cursed that summer of '62. After Hungarian engineer George Grecheneck, their original captain, had been killed at Williamsburg, his replacement, Charles Grossinger, resigned after only five weeks on the job, and Horatio Pennock, who came over from Co. C to command on June 23, died of disease just six weeks later on August 2. Now, Edward B. Harnett, Company A's original second lieutenant, was the Germans' fourth captain in three months.[3]

For Dan Sickles this was a critical time in his career. He had won the battle with Congress to keep his stars, to be sure, but now he was fighting to keep the command he had so painstakingly built. Excelsior Brigade was nearly worn out, and divisional commander Joe Hooker threatened consolidation. Unless Sickles could find enough new men to bring his five regiments back to strength, he'd be a general without a command. Sickles confidently assured Hooker he could find the men, and by mid–July, Dan was back home in New York drumming up badly needed levies. Dan's itinerary included much more than recruitment rallies and speeches at county fairs—there were serious political fires that needed tending. With the success of the Excelsior Brigade, some in New York felt Sickles' stock had risen high enough that consideration for a run for Congress was in order. Dan Sickles was nearing an important crossroads: continue as the heroic military figure, triumphant at the head of his legion, or give it up for a possible return to the halls of Congress and the accompanying power that he desperately craved.[4] All of this meant Dan would be gone for weeks or months, leaving Nelson Taylor to run the brigade just as the colonel had done frequently since leaving Maryland.

Back in Washington with his army holed up at Harrison's Landing, President Lincoln faced some tough decisions. Lincoln wasn't ready to sack McClellan for his inactivity, but he would allow units to be taken away from him and given to a general who might use them to better advantage. Major General John Pope had recently been given command of Federal troops within the Army of Virginia and talked a good fight. Pope had been moderately successful in the west, and he vowed a vigorous campaign to smash the Confederate army on his way to taking Richmond by gathering the Federal units that his predecessor Irwin McDowell had left ineffectually scattered about northern Virginia. The frustrated Lincoln had concluded it was the aggressive sounding Pope who would be the recipient of McClellan's idle veterans.

Third Excelsior, along with all of III Corps, received orders on August 11 to break camp and move back down the Peninsula. In Yorktown they would board steamers and sail for an eventual rendezvous with Pope. For three days everyone in the regiment organized company gear and stenciled identifying names and numbers on haversacks, backpacks and tents. Finally, on the 14th, the 72nd and the rest of the Excelsiors were on the march.

For many men, the march back down the Peninsula was a clear admission of McClellan's failure. Others saw it as a grand redeployment that would eventually take them far onto the enemy's flank, in position for the true final offensive. Yet for others, just being on the move somewhere—anywhere—was better than sitting swatting sand fleas at Harrison's Landing. Moving south was a slow affair; the corps moved only about six miles per day, less than half of what could really be accomplished, "but McClellan is taking things easy though Pope is badly in want of reinforcements,"[5] wrote Private Sneden, of the III Corps staff. The men plodded along many of the same roads on which they had fought and many of their comrades had died just months earlier. Excelsior Brigade chaplain Joseph Twichell wrote:

> Here we are, retracing, retracing, retracing steps that cost blood and glorious young life. It almost broke my heart to go by Williamsburg again. I seemed to hear the gallant fellows calling from the woods to hail us on our way. So you see the splendid "change of base" was all poppycock.... I can't think of the 30,000 corpses we leave behind without a bitter thought. The 30,000 corpses stand for a million sighs and tears which will not be stopped for a score of years.[6]

(Official losses at Williamsburg are put at around 3,200 but perhaps Twichell was referring to the entire Peninsula campaign—ed.)

Southern civilians, women and old men mostly, were happy to see the defeated Yankee

Catlett Station was a point along the Orange and Alexandria Railroad that was the focus of attack by raiding Confederate cavalry, especially during the weeks leading up to Second Bull Run (Third Excelsior Association).

invaders going home and shouted insults from their front porches, doorways and windows. Good Christian men such as Hiram Stoddard probably just endured the taunts as they passed, while other blue-coats no doubt hurled biting replies of their own. Nearing Williamsburg, many of the officers rode over to Fort Magruder, the former Confederate defensive strong point south of the city. Corps commander Peter Heintzelman, First Division commander Phil Kearney, Second Division commander Hooker and others were among the party. The fort's trenches, which once had held Rebel marksmen, now brimmed with stagnant water. Thick bushes and vines mingled with graves and faded wooden markers, the names of the dead nearly obliterated by the pernicious Virginia rain and sun. Piles of the partially burned bones of horses and mules killed in the early May battle lay nearby; the previous pyres having failed to completely consume the carcasses.

III Corps began boarding ships at Yorktown on August 21 for the trip north to Pope, a week after leaving Harrison's Landing. The boys of the 72nd's companies packed aboard the large ocean steamer *Vanderbilt* while other Excelsior men boarded different ships. The regiment left Yorktown the next day for the trip up the Chesapeake, and almost immediately the *Vanderbilt* ran aground. She languished there nearly all day before getting herself off and resuming the trip. The steamer was scheduled to land at Aquia Creek, but a change of orders had her landing 30 miles farther up the Potomac, just south of Washington at Alexandria. She arrived at noon on the 24th. The next morning Taylor's boys and the rest of Hooker's division marched three miles west of town and made camp at Shuter's Hill. Here they waited to board rail cars for the rendezvous with Pope at his headquarters 40 miles or so down the line at Warrenton Junction.[7]

With most of McClellan's army still encamped at Harrison's Landing and another part being removed to bolster Pope, Confederate army commander Robert E. Lee recognized an opportunity. He now felt free to shift forces away from the Peninsula to meet Pope's threat from north of Richmond. Pope had established a strong position on the north side of the Rapidan River, which ran west-east from the Blue Ridge Mountains to Fredericksburg. And now Pope grew even stronger with the addition of the Peninsula veterans. Lee needed to force Pope out of his prepared defensive line were he to have any chance of defeating him and pushing the Yankees out of northern Virginia. The Confederate commander decided upon a risky plan, one he hoped would pull Pope's army northeast and away from the Rapidan. By sending Stonewall Jackson's I Corps on a wide march around the Federal right, Jackson might then strike at the Yankee rear, forcing Pope to react. Lee knew James Longstreet's II Corps remained opposing the Federals south of the Rapidan and would be in danger should Pope choose to attack rather than pull back as hoped. Jackson recognized the risk that either he or Longstreet could face the entirety of Pope's army alone, but Jackson also understood such a sweep into Pope's rear presented great possibilities for defeating small, isolated Federal commands, burning stores and bridges, and in general, creating havoc.

With corps commander Heintzelman and the rest of his blue-coated veterans now firmly established on the solid ground of northern Virginia, there was a problem: many of his senior regimental commanders were absent on leave. With little opportunity these past few months to spend their pay and even fewer opportunities for furlough, most of the corps' colonels, majors and many captains were gone to nearby Washington or parts north, leaving junior officers in charge. Sickles was still away recruiting, and Col. Taylor commanded the Excelsiors. Taylor faced the hard fact that of his five regiments, only two were commanded by men above the rank of captain. With Lieutenant Colonel Moses and Major Stevens away, his own regiment, the 72nd New York, was now under the temporary command of 30-year-old Captain Harmon J. Bliss of Company G. Harmon didn't know it yet, but his ability to lead would be tested like never before.

Bliss and his men would be traveling along a 40-mile or so stretch of the Orange and Alexandria Railroad that reached west and south from Alexandria to the center of Pope's operations at Warrenton Junction. This important supply line crossed over Bull Run and through Manassas Junction, near the old battlefield and over other small creeks including Broad Run and Kettle Run. The last 10 miles of the trip, the track passed through Bristoe Station and Catlett's Station before arriving at Warrenton Junction.

Striking camp at Shuter's Hill, the train leaving Alexandria was eventually packed and on its way. Many aboard had an actual seat but others rode atop baggage cars fully exposed to the weather. Still more were crammed inside cattle cars, faring only slightly better than their comrades, protected from the elements by slim slatted sides. When the last of Hooker's men arrived at their destination late into the evening of the 26th, many had endured what one Excelsior man described as a "protracted shiver." As the New Yorkers reached Warrenton

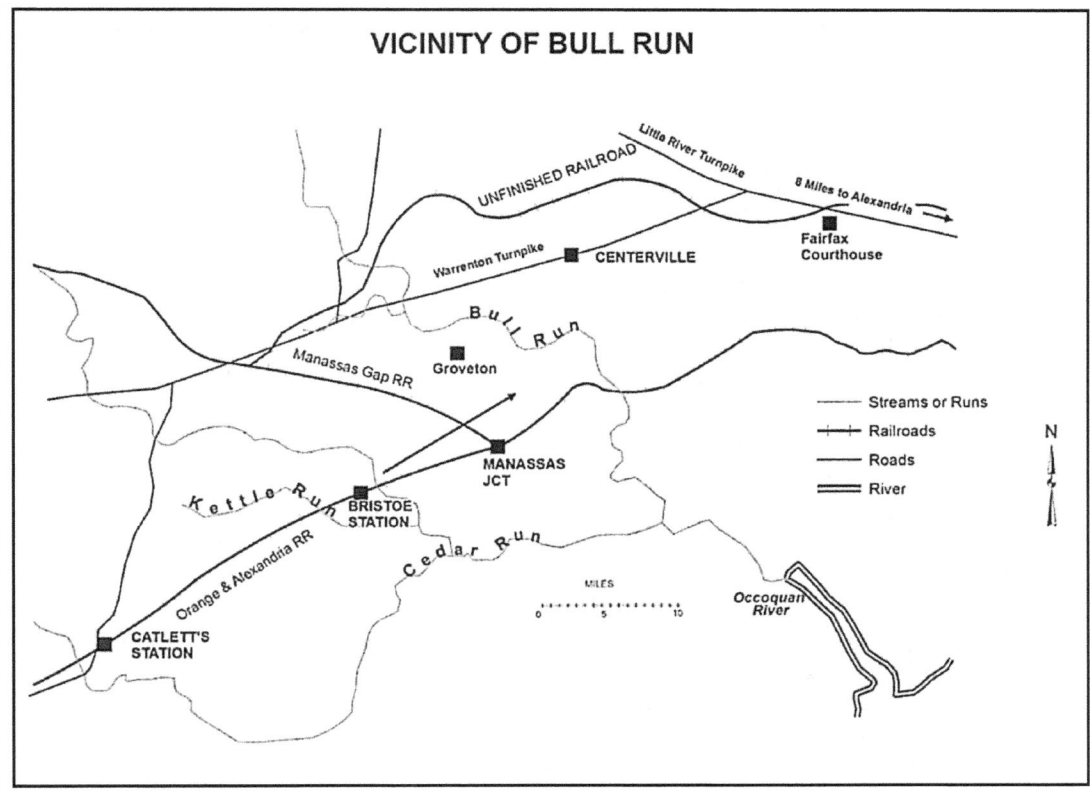

Junction, Hooker arrived back from Washington. During their trip these Peninsula veterans saw Pope's men preparing defenses for an expected Rebel attack. Though Pope's troops worked diligently, it was clear they were oblivious as to the direction the attack might come. These disorganized preparations were disheartening to the III Corps veterans, signaling Pope had no real plan and no real idea the location of Jackson's Confederates.

Serving only to maximize Yankee bafflement, Jackson's men cut the rail line at Bristoe Station only hours after Hooker's Third Brigade passed through. Striking here was critical to Jackson's run around Pope's flanks and onto the Federal rear. Southern troops quickly overpowered the small garrison at Bristoe Station and began to feast upon the rich hoard of supplies. Many Rebs ate or gathered those supplies that could be carried off, while others set about the task of burning storehouses, rail cars and locomotives. Soon fires burned brilliant enough for III Corps men to see the glow from over ten miles away. Equal acts of pillage and destruction occurred further up the line at Manassas Junction as more of Jackson's units descended there.

At Bristoe Station, Confederate troops worked to disrupt Yankee rail traffic. After building barricades across the tracks, a Yankee train bound for Alexandria soon came upon the station. Either unable or unwilling to stop, the train smashed the obstacles, scattering timbers as it pressed on through a hail of Rebel curses and musketry. Arriving at Manassas Junction and the safety of Federal troops, the shaken engineer showed off his bullet riddled locomotive, *Secretary*, and told his harrowing tale. Union troops telegraphed Alexandria, reporting the incident to commanders there. Little did they know this would be among the last messages sent before Jackson's men arrived. Back at Bristoe Station, frustrated Confederate troops resolved to do better at catching trains. After reinforcing their obstacles they had soon derailed two unsuspecting locomotives. As a third northbound train approached, its sharp-eyed engineer spotted the previous wrecks, and after stopping in time, he returned to Warrenton Junction. Because of earlier sporadic raids by marauding Rebel cavalry, initial reaction to moves against Bristoe Station garnered only mild concern from senior Union commanders at both Alexandria and Warrenton Junction.

This stretch of the railroad had been subject to the attentions of Confederate raiders before, and Pope needed to know the full magnitude of the attack. After all, a commanding general wouldn't base the movements of his great army solely on the testimony of a rattled railroad man. Only four days earlier, a large force of Rebel cavalry under Jeb Stuart had fallen upon the small garrison at Catlett's Station. There, they helped themselves to what supplies could be carried, including one of Pope's dress uniforms. The looting complete, enemy horsemen set fire to anything flammable, including a railroad bridge. Fortunately for the Federals, just as the Confederates began their work a heavy rain set in, extinguishing the flames and saving the vital bridge.

Well before the last of Hooker's division arrived at Warrenton Junction and before the entirety of the Excelsior Brigade had arrived, the 72nd was on the move. Needing more information about events back up the rail line, Hooker ordered Taylor to dispatch a regiment to investigate. This chore fell to Captain Bliss and his 300 men.

Finding no rail transportation immediately available, Bliss marched the boys on the 26th around 10 p.m. along a wagon road that paralleled the tracks. Soon after their departure, though, a small train was detailed to move the regiment. Bliss countermarched his men and returned. Loaded back on the cars, Bliss and his men finally left Warrenton Junction around 2 a.m. Eventually the regiment arrived at Catlett Station, the buildings scarred by frequent skirmishes with Rebel horsemen. Here Bliss requested a detail of cavalry be assigned to join him, presumably to serve as scouts and pickets as they moved in this dark and uncertain land. He was told a group of horsemen were already in position awaiting him near the stream of Kettle Run, which lay about a mile this side of Bristoe. Bliss accepted this and moved forward.[8]

Bliss deployed flankers and skirmishers for the last mile of his advance, but upon crossing Kettle Run found no Federal cavalry awaiting him. Despite the lack of mounted support, Bliss pushed on, bringing his men to within half a mile of Bristoe Station. Moving forward, his troops were greeted by destroyed telegraph lines, the wires cut or ripped from their insulators, and burned rail cars, some of which were reduced to a pair of trucks sitting amidst smoldering wreckage. Discovering the station still in enemy hands, he placed the regiment into line of battle, threw out skirmishers and crept forward for a better look. It was still before dawn, but in the glow of burning cars Bliss could see and hear all "Southron" activity. Presently the Rebels became alerted to the presence of Yankee troops. Major General Richard Ewell hastily formed his three Confederate brigades, which held the station, to move against Bliss' New Yorkers. "I saw one column file to the left, and had no doubt their purpose was to flank us and cut off my train at the Kettle Run Bridge," reported the Chautauqua captain.[9]

Outnumbered by three brigades of infantry and with Reb cavalry moving on his right to block his line of withdrawal, the veteran captain paused to weigh his options. "I called Adjutant Hinman to my position to confirm my opinion and to profit by his judgment,"[10] remembered Bliss, mindful of his own lack of experience in commanding such a large body as a regiment. While anxious to launch a heroic attack into the still-forming Rebel troops,

Bliss thought better of it. "My pride urged me to accept the honor leading the gallant Third into battle, but my judgment rebelled against this desire ... and I reluctantly gave the order to embark again."[11]

Retreating back across Kettle Run, Bliss deployed pickets to cover all lines of possible enemy advance. He ordered the telegraph operator to establish contact with Warrenton Junction and soon the telegraph wires were tapped and the operator, using his small, portable key, sent the following message addressed to Pope's aide-de-camp, Col. T.C.H. Smith:

> Have proceeded to near Bristoe Station. Find a train of cars burning and telegraph wires broken and enemy in very heavy force. Do not deem it prudent to go on without further orders. Have conductor of burned train with me, who reports there being a large force of the enemy. Have returned to this side of the Kettle Run Bridge.[12]

Bliss deployed three companies, ordering them to hold the bridge at all hazards, but he recognized that "it had no natural advantages for defense, in fact, they were all against us."[13] With the situation worsening and no word from headquarters other than to "wait a little," men anxiously looked to Bliss for a decision. For 45 minutes he had watched Southern troops advance on both flanks, followed by a larger body to his front. Unable to "consent to the useless sacrifice of my brave 300 men,"[14] Bliss ordered his three companies back from the bridge while the rest of the regiment loaded on the train. Rebel bullets buzzed through the air as Emerson and the rest clambered aboard the cars. Enemy skirmishers nipped at the heels of Union stragglers. With everyone aboard, Bliss ordered the engineer to move back. Ewell's men now unmasked a cannon previously hidden behind the Confederate column and wheeled it near the bridge. With the locomotive gathering steam, the Rebel artillery opened up; its first two shots ricocheted within 30 yards of the engine. As the train collected speed and chugged into the darkness, other cannon shots flew wildly into the night. Despite the exhilaration of their narrow escape, some men found time and room enough to sleep while returning to Warrenton Junction. Bliss was finally back near 5 a.m. and reported to Taylor the night's ordeal.[15]

Pope, realizing this enemy force was much more than a raiding party, saw an opportunity. Hoping to cut off Jackson, the general ordered most of III Corps to concentrate near Gainesville, about seven miles northwest of Manassas Junction. Flushing the Confederates out of Bristoe Station and restoring the railroad was assigned to Hooker's division of three brigades with help from two and one-half regiments from Kearney's First Division.

Lee's bold gamble had worked. Pope abandoned his positions along the Rapidan and set out for Jackson believing he could trap and destroy this wing of the Confederate army. Pope failed to realize that by leaving his positions along the river, Longstreet would be free to move and join Jackson. In reality it was now Pope who was being stalked.

Captain Bliss and his weary New Yorkers were now back in Warrenton Junction, bringing Hooker's division back to full strength and allowing him to move against the unwelcome foe. Hooker set out near 7 a.m. toward Bristoe and Manassas. Little in the way of supplies had arrived, and the division moved without wagons or its customary artillery. There was only ammunition enough for each man to pack about 40 rounds into his cartridge box and pockets. Pope accompanied the Second Division, and while he and Hooker rode horseback, nearly every other officer walked for lack of mounts. The day was hot as Hooker's division marched along the same road Third Excelsior had hiked earlier. Overtaken by heat and fatigue, men throughout the division fell out. Despite conditions, the brigades made good progress. Upon reaching Catlett's Station, two batteries of cannon joined Hooker's force as

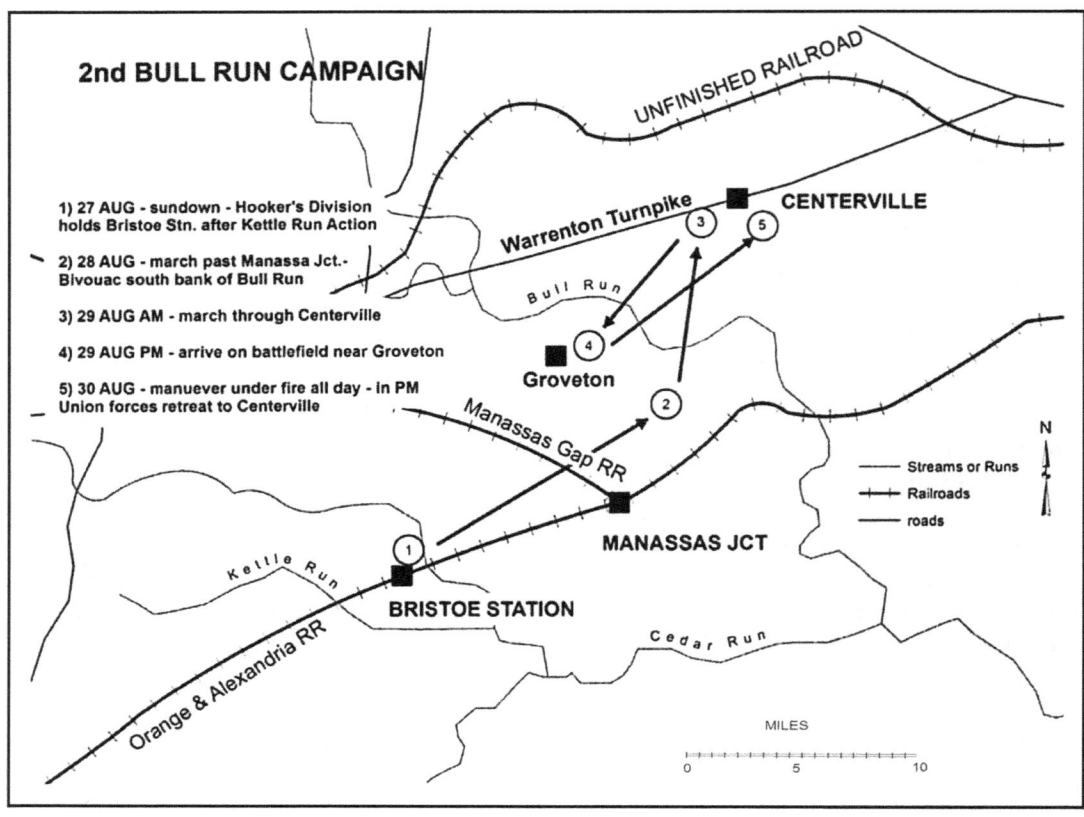

it moved northeast.[16] Near noon, the men encountered an enemy outpost and a section of Rebel artillery. Skirmishers went forward and easily brushed aside the enemy nuisance. Two hours' march later, the division came upon Kettle Run, which ran nearly perpendicular to the tracks and their line of march. Here the Confederates were in force beyond the creek and beyond a formidable stand of woods and some other uncertain ground. Hooker ordered the division into line of battle, placing Grover's First Brigade right of the tracks. Four regiments of Third Brigade, under temporary command of Colonel Joseph Carr, formed somewhat astride and to the left of the tracks. Carr's other two regiments, the 6th and 7th New Jersey, went with Hooker, who advanced them and Kearney's loaner regiments to a slight rise on the left, offering a good vantage point. Colonel Taylor and his Excelsior Brigade lined up to the left and slightly behind Carr's main body to protect his flanks.[17]

As the Federals advanced into the woods, Grover's First Brigade, moving on the right, became bogged down, while the other two brigades managed to press forward. Dismounted officers effectively pushed their men through the thick trees and undergrowth. Carr's Third Brigade continued toward the bridge, and the Second New York were sent ahead as skirmishers. To hinder Carr's progress, two regiments of Louisiana skirmishers deployed to the Yankee side of Kettle Run. Around 2:30 p.m. and within one-half mile of Bristoe Station, the enemy engaged Carr's men. As one enemy regiment poured an effective fire into the struggling ranks of Third Brigade, the other set fire to the bridge. "I formed line of battle with the Second New York Volunteers and the Fifth and Eighth New Jersey Volunteers and advanced through a dense wood, when the enemy made a stand," Carr recalled.[18] As Yankees pressed the attack, the Louisiana men fell back across the stream in the face of Carr's superior force and went into line several hundred yards ahead of Ewell's main body.

Carr continued across Kettle Run with his brigade straddling the tracks. Advancing through a clover field mixed with brambles and blackberry vines, the Yankees pulled against the vegetation, which clung and tugged at their trousers.[19] Carr maneuvered the Second N.Y. and Eighth N.J. left of the tracks while the Fifth N.J. remained on the right. Gen. Hooker took over command of both the Sixth and Seventh N.J. and stayed on the far left. Emerging from the woods, Carr's exhausted men again came under heavy musket fire. Previously hidden artillery batteries were now unmasked and began pouring solid shot and canister into Third Brigade. Yankee soldiers clung to the ground as sheets of iron flew overhead. The few officers and aides on horseback galloped about the field despite the maelstrom, relaying orders and reassuring the men.[20]

Carr shouted orders to regimental commanders to organize and align his three regiments. Meanwhile, company officers scuttled amongst their lines, which were crouched under the terrible storm of Rebel lead. Hooker took two regiments under his command wide to the left in an effort to flank the enemy. Moving forward, color bearers uncased their regimental standards as "the Second New York Volunteers and Eighth New Jersey Volunteers advanced through the woods and charged the enemy, driving him about 200 yards into a thick woods, where they again made a stand and gave battle," reported Carr.[21] With Third Brigade now butted up against the bulk of the Confederate force, Col. Taylor brought up the Excelsiors. Finding no enemy on the extreme left of the battlefield, Taylor recognized how hotly Third Brigade was engaged and "at once brought forward the Second, Fourth, and Fifth Regiments of the brigade, and placed them in position on the left of the line formed by Colonel Carr."[22]

Stalled in heavy woods, Grover's First Brigade was unable to support Carr's right as Confederates moved to threaten this exposed flank. "I observed a column of the enemy's infantry file down the hill in front and take position parallel to and on the right of the railroad and to the rear of the line formed by a portion of the Third Brigade," recalled Col. Taylor.[23] Enfilading fire from the 60th Georgia Infantry ripped through the companies of Carr's line. Responding to this danger, Taylor ordered the 70th N.Y. under Captain Charles Young and Capt. Bliss' 72nd N.Y. to change front and advance toward the enemy. The two Excelsior regiments formed a second line behind Carr's line and moved from the left side of the battlefield toward the right, as Southern lead tore into the New Yorkers. "Musketry from the front, artillery from the left, played furiously upon us, soon followed by a murderous fire on our right flank from behind the railway embankment,"[24] reported Capt. Young, adding, "Under this terrible triple fire the First and Third Regiments were ordered forward."[25] Despite the hellish conditions these Peninsula veterans responded coolly and precisely to the orders as they moved right. Halting his two regiments within a short range of his enemy, Taylor ordered fire on his foe, who now scrambled for the protection of the track's roadbed. Pouring round after precious round into the Georgians, the Excelsiors stood their ground, as the two regiments came under the concentrated fire of two sections of enemy cannon. The regiments were getting cut up as Rebel lead and iron ruthlessly cast about. Chaplain Twichell worked to bring off the wounded and thought it astounding he was not killed. "For a space of fifteen minutes I expected every minute to be hit. The sound of the bullets was like the humming of bees, while the roaring, crackling, shells plunged and burst on every side."[26] A cannonball cut through one of the few Yankee mounts, taking the rider's leg with it.[27] Enemy artillery played havoc on the brigades as Taylor rode off to the rear seeking "to bring forward one of our own batteries" to silence the Rebel guns.[28]

After finding General Grover and explaining the situation, Taylor persuaded the reluctant commander of an unengaged battery to come to the aid of his brigade. The battery moved so slowly, however, that by the time they arrived at the fight, "the necessity of his services had ceased."[29] Capt. Young described the action during Taylor's absence: "At this time the fight raged fearfully, each contestant holding well his ground. Our comrades fell thick and fast."[30] With men dying and cartridges running low, Lt. William J. Kay of First Excelsior proposed a charge. Young and Bliss conferred, and a hearty cheer was thoughtfully substituted, though the effect on the Rebels seemed the same. "Hardly had that glorious cheer mingled with the whistling bullets ere the Rebels began to fall back before the eyes of our eager men,"[31] remembered Young. With ammunition at a premium and their men already anxious to attack, both captains saw an opportunity and ordered their two regiments to advance. New York men surged forward, scattering the Georgians. Soon the regimental colors of the 70th N.Y. flew above the track. "I never have seen a handsomer sight than Sickles' brigade charging on the car track behind which the rebels lay firing at them. One of Sickles' regiments got their colors planted on the track and soon Johnny Rebel was skedaddling across the hill,"[32] observed one of Carr's Seventh New Jersey men. Some suggested continued pursuit, "but fearing to disarrange plans, we thought best to remain in our present position,"[33] concluded Young.

Hooker deployed other artillery that began to silence Rebel guns, forcing some to limber up and retire to the far side of Broad Run, which lay about two miles beyond Kettle Run. Jackson allowed Ewell's division to conduct a fighting retreat in face of this superior Yankee force, yet both Confederate flanks seriously faltered as they began falling back. Capt. Young wrote, "General Hooker had placed a battery in position on the left, which under his personal supervision quickly silenced the guns of the enemy. His [the enemy's] right and left broken, we found no difficulty in piercing his center and gaining possession of the field."[34]

Third and First brigades both continued their pursuit of the retreating enemy. As Taylor's Excelsiors reformed, General Grover ordered them to hold in reserve, right of the tracks. The New York men remained here a short time but then were ordered forward a short distance and to the left of the tracks. Here, Taylor's brigade bivouacked for the night behind a strong picket line.[35]

Losses among the Excelsiors were heavy, nearly one-third of Taylor's men having been either killed or wounded. Captain William Burns of the 73rd New York reported 12 killed, 44 wounded and 3 missing out of his already weakened regiment of 99 men. The three regiments who remained on Carr's left all suffered nominally higher casualties than the two fighting to take the tracks. Capt. Bliss reported over 20 casualties among his 72nd, with Captain John P. Sanford of Company B counted among the wounded. Losses in Capt. Young's 70th N.Y. were only about half that number.

Bristoe Station was in Federal hands as the last of Ewell's division retreated just before sundown across Broad Run on their way to Manassas Junction. Hooker made little attempt to follow, because each man was down to just a few cartridges. During their retreat, Confederate troops successfully burned the wooden bridge over the stream, further complicating any notion of a Federal pursuit. Total losses for the attacking Federals exceeded 400, while Ewell's Confederates suffered around 150.[36]

By driving the Confederates from the field, Pope believed he had won an important victory despite the losses and ordered his forces to continue movement toward Manassas Junction. Pope's maneuvers played right into the hands of the Confederates, who sought to divert attention away from Thoroughfare Gap, 20 miles to the west, where Longstreet would soon be marching to unite with Jackson.

Emerson Merrell, the Germans of Company A, and the rest of the regiment made camp that night the best they could. With most of their gear either lost in transit from the Peninsula, back at Warrenton Junction, or worse, having been burned for fear it might fall into enemy hands, some no doubt remembered the Seven Days fight, with its constant movement, lack of rest and short supplies. But these were veteran troops who took pride in accomplishments past and future. So with confidence in their pickets, they did what all true veterans did at a time like this—they slept.

Morning broke near Bristoe Station as Captain Bliss assembled the men and prepared to march. Following the rail line, they would continue northeast toward Manassas Junction, where a larger body of Jackson's army had earlier destroyed Union interests. From here Bliss would head west toward Centerville, where Pope was summoning his legions to concentrate.

For several days, Pope had received varied and often conflicting reports regarding the exact location of the Confederate Army. Pope was exhilarated by Hooker's victory at Bristoe Station and desperately wanted to press his advantage, but Pope was unsure of the enemy's location and had sent Union forces marching and countermarching in an effort to make meaningful contact. The enemy was close, but Pope was making only slightly more than an educated guess when he ordered his army to concentrate near Centerville. But before Pope could fully assemble his army, Jackson himself established contact with his Yankee foe late that afternoon.

A portion of Jackson's corps had taken up positions in a railroad cut near the Warrenton Turnpike and near 6 p.m. launched a flank attack into Rufus King's division of green troops from Indiana and Wisconsin as they moved north toward Centerville. A fierce fight followed, lasting into the night and costing both sides a combined 2,300 men, but the weakened King broke off the action come morning, gathered his division and continued toward Centerville.[37]

When word of the fighting reached Pope, the commanding general issued new orders. Instead of marshaling all available units at Centerville, the new orders called for Union troops to collect farther south, near the site of King's fight with Jackson, close to Groveton on the old Bull Run battlefield.

All of the 28th, Colonel Taylor marched his Excelsior Brigade north, past Manassas Junction, eventually halting to bivouac on the south bank of Bull Run Creek. The following morning with new orders in hand, the New Yorkers continued their march, moving through Centerville, then southwest, reaching Pope's new assembly point around 2 p.m. Here Captain Bliss and the rest discovered the battle against Jackson's Confederates well under way.

Still deployed in the natural defensive position of the unfinished railroad cut, Jackson's brigades stretched their battle line for over two miles. Jackson fully intended to make his fight in the cut, but Pope was convinced the Confederate general was attempting a withdrawal. Pope planned to launch attacks at both of Jackson's flanks, turn those flanks and bag the entire Confederate I Corps.

During late morning, troops of Franz Sigel's corps launched their attacks. In sometimes desperate fighting, the Rebels held their ground, but Jackson worried he might not have men enough to persevere in the ever-escalating battle. At 10 a.m. some of Jackson's worries were eased. He learned the leading division of Longstreet's II Corps was taking up positions on his extreme right, though Longstreet still refused to commit his troops to Jackson's fight.

Pope was focused on Jackson's troops while remaining ignorant that Longstreet's Rebel troops were moving onto his left flank. Pope committed fresh troops to the fight by relieving Sigel's Corps at 3 p.m. and beginning new attacks using men from Heintzelman's III Corps and Reno's IX Corps. Among III Corps men, Hooker's First Brigade under Grover was in lead position. Carr's Third Brigade and Taylor's Excelsiors supported Grover. Hooker would aim his attack near the center of Jackson's line.

Grover's men advanced over ground upon which earlier Federal attacks had failed. Unlike these earlier attacks, Grover avoided open ground and struck the Confederates from the cover of a patch of woods adjoining Jackson's railroad cut. First Brigade quickly came to grips with the enemy. A well-directed musket volley staggered the Confederate line as Grover's men used the bayonet to secure the breach. "We rapidly and firmly pressed upon the embankment, and here occurred a short, sharp and obstinate hand-to-hand conflict with bayonets and clubbed muskets," Grover reported. "Many of the enemy were bayoneted in their tracks, others struck down with the butts of pieces, and onward pressed our line."[38] Fighting through the enemy's first line, Grover's men then defeated the full weight of the Reb second line. But with their lines now seriously thinned, Grover's men could not overcome the closed ranks of a third Confederate line and though fighting furiously, First Brigade was forced to retire.[39]

As Grover brawled with three lines of Confederates, Carr advanced Third Brigade toward the railroad cut just southwest of Grover. Carr's New Jersey men fought hard for two hours after relieving troops under Gen. Sigel, but with their ammunition exhausted, Third Brigade withdrew without gaining appreciable ground.

Now relieved, Carr conferred briefly with Taylor, who began positioning his Second Brigade. Bliss, Merrell, Stoddard and the rest were posted on the extreme right of the line. Captain Young's 70th New York was posted just to the left of the 72nd. Moving to within 15 paces of the line formerly occupied by Carr's men, Taylor halted and dressed his line of battle and sent skirmishers forward: "Having everything in readiness, I gave the order to advance."[40] It was then that disaster struck.

A Federal brigade under Colonel James Nagle, already heavily engaged on Taylor's front-left, was surprised by a sudden Rebel charge. Unable to hold, Nagle's line collapsed. Fleeing Yankees and Confederate pursuers crashed squarely into the left side of Excelsior Brigade, carrying most of the 71st New York away with them. The brigade crumbled from left to right as the human wave obliterated Taylor's ordered ranks. "We had fairly time to reach the point designated when the rebels, with a murderous shout, accompanied by a sharp fire, broke through the brigade in front, forcing them pell-mell on our line of battle,"[41] recalled Capt. Young.

Located on the far right, the 72nd boys were able to hold firm as Taylor galloped immediately to the brigade's left, where men fought in a desperate, whirling, hand-to-hand contest. "Seeing the confusion, I rode hastily to this part of the line, accompanied by my two aides, lieutenants Tremain [Henry Tremain, 73rd N.Y.] and Dwight [Charles Dwight, 70th N.Y.], and endeavored to stay this disgraceful retreat, but it was in vain; the tide could not be stemmed."[42]

The attack came from Colonel Bradley T. Johnson's brigade of Virginians, who had been lying down, concealed, and completely unexpected. "I ordered a charge, and with a yell the Second Brigade went through them, shattering, breaking, and routing them,"[43] remembered Col. Johnson. As surging Confederates completely caved in the Excelsior's left, so transfixed were the charging men of 42nd Virginia that they neglected to pick up the prize of the fallen New York regimental colors.[44]

Taylor worked to salvage his position and issued orders to units still cohesive enough to comply. The 72nd turned its muskets towards the brigade's faltering left and the Confederate attackers, but with the mixing of friend and foe, Bliss' regiment was "powerless by the influence and presence of the disorganized troops"[45] to fire upon the enemy. Rebels and broken remains of the other Federal regiments were soon amongst Bliss' boys and in "overpowering numbers."[46] The fight was mob warfare of the worst kind. Regiments in once ordered ranks were now reduced to countless acts of single combat. Rocks and rifle butts served as clubs, the bayonet used freely as men gouged, slashed and stabbed. Opponents fired at one another from less than an arm's length. Mounted officers were pulled from their horses as hand-to-hand fighting churned beneath their stirrups. Regimental color bearers seemed to be the particular targets of trophy-seeking Southerners. Men in the 70th N.Y. fought off repeated enemy attempts to seize their flags. Nearby, as the 71st's color bearer was shot, his mates gathered the banner and evacuated it safely. As Rebels pressed in on the flag of the 74thNew York, the color sergeant tore it from the staff, and fighting a swirling, 360-degree battle, saved it. Aides Tremain and Dwight were soon both captured while attempting to bring order to the situation. With all organization and cohesion lost and attempts to hold position futile, Taylor called for the brigade to fall back.[47]

As the Federals pulled back, the Confederates continued to press forward, bolstered by the arrival of another brigade under Gen. William E. Starke. "The enemy now broke and ran, and we pursued, firing as fast as we could,"[48] described Private John Worsham of the 21st Virginia. "We followed them into the woods, and drove them out on the other side, where we halted and were ordered back to the railroad."[49]

Falling back 60 paces or so, the Excelsiors stopped to fire upon their Confederate foes. Rebel regiments and companies were jumbled, with men mixed, one in front of another, with no formed firing lines. For fear of hitting each other, the Confederates could not return an effective fire. Despite the Yankees' brief stand, the Rebels continued to swarm after the retreating New Yorkers, all the while threatening Taylor's flank and rear. The Excelsiors eventually rallied in a small wood nearly 300 yards from their original line. "After extricating the brigade from its entanglement I reformed the line," wrote Taylor.[50]

After deploying skirmishers, the Excelsiors awaited the advance of the enemy. Taylor rode among the regiments, aligning formations and encouraging men just as he had done all day. Surprisingly, the expected attack failed to materialize. "The enemy had also fallen back, and seemed unwilling to improve his temporary advantage,"[51] Bliss wrote later.

Returning to their original positions, the Confederates took with them two captured Federal cannons that had supported the now failed attacks. As Rebs dragged the captured guns, another Federal battery fired upon their retiring enemy. "As we returned, a Yankee battery of eight guns had full play on us in the field,"[52] wrote Virginian Worsham, adding, "Our line became a little confused; we halted, every man instantly turned and faced the battery. As we did so, I heard a thud on my right, as if one had been struck with a heavy fist. Looking around I saw a man at my side standing erect, with his head off, a stream of blood spurting a foot or more from his neck."[53] The decapitated man was a captain in the 42nd V.A., one of four men killed by that single round.

With Rebels pulling back to the railroad cut, Taylor and his men held their position until the arrival of General Phil Kearney's division, which promptly went into formation and engaged the enemy. After Kearney's advance, and with his brigade out of immediate danger, Taylor called in the skirmishers. With Kearney committed and Taylor's brigade safe for the moment, Hooker ordered the battered Excelsiors to an open field farther to the rear.

Here the men of the five regiments bivouacked for the night. Bliss had lost six men wounded and four captured in the day's fight. The combined brigade losses were 63 killed, wounded or missing; nearly half this number came from the 71st N.Y., who had borne the brunt of the Confederate charge and ensuing melee.[54]

Come the morning of the 30th, Pope still believed he could "bag" the entirety of Jackson's Corps. Recognizing that the previous day's attacks had gone forward in a piecemeal fashion, the offensively minded Pope ordered large, coordinated and well-supported assaults. Attacks would press along the whole enemy line, eventually breaking what surely must be a weakened enemy. Whether Pope fully understood the danger or just chose to ignore it is uncertain, but nearly all of Longstreet's II Corps was now positioned on his left flank and an attack solely against Jackson would present a tempting target.

Hooker's Division would be held in reserve on this day. The emaciated regiments that made up the three brigades of this smallish division would best be used in support. By afternoon, Bliss' men and the rest of the brigade had broken camp and were under arms. Hiram Stoddard and the rest of his mates of Company I, and indeed the entire brigade, had repacked their backpacks with the little gear they had. Cleaning their muskets, the sound of popping caps filled the air as they readied weapons and themselves for battle. With orders in hand, the Excelsiors stood prepared to march in pursuit of an enemy Pope was sure would soon be in rout.

After some preliminary probes into Jackson's line, Pope launched his grand attack at around 3 p.m. sure that the weight of numbers alone would smash his stubborn opponent. Jackson recognized the danger and urgently asked Lee to send him more men. Lee passed the request along to Longstreet, who, instead of sending men, answered with an artillery barrage directed into the left flank of the advancing Yankees. Within ten minutes the Federal troops were retiring, their packed ranks suffering heavily from well-aimed Confederate cannon fire.

His attack thrown into some confusion by the artillery bombardment, Pope doggedly sought the initiative and pressed forward. When Confederate infantry from Longstreet's Corps were discovered moving to assist Jackson, Pope ordered John Reynolds' division to move in to counter this threat. Reynolds had been guarding much of the Federal left, and this was the opportunity the patient Longstreet had been awaiting. With Reynolds out of position, Longstreet launched a general attack into the whole of the Federal left. Without men enough to counter an assault into his flank, Pope's entire attack broke down and quickly turned into a full-fledged retreat.

Federal units frantically moved about the field, desperate to establish a defensive line that would hold, but the Rebel counterattack seemed unstoppable. Bliss and the other Excelsiors were ordered here and there in preparation for meeting the enemy, sent to support this battery or that. As Bliss' companies moved about the field, men flinched and ducked under a leaden sky screeching with the sound of solid shot and bursting shell. In each new position the regiment prepared itself, but neither orders to advance nor enemy infantry ever materialized. Though Stoddard and the rest had stood under a nearly constant hail of lead and iron, the regiment suffered no losses for the day.[55]

With their army in total retreat toward the protection of Centerville, the Yankees had to get across the Bull Run Creek at the Stone Bridge (the same bridge Union troops had been sent scampering across 13 months before, in the first battle here). Holding the crest of Henry Hill near the bridge was critical to covering the retreat, and by 7 p.m. the Confederate onslaught began to run out of steam. Confederates had threatened both Federal flanks, but their energies were sapped by a day of hard fighting and effective Yankee artillery fire that helped discourage two assaults against Henry Hill. Before a third attack could be made, night fell, leaving the hill in Federal hands. Under the cover of darkness, the remainder of Pope's army made good its escape.

Private Emerson Merrell summarized the fight this way in a letter home:

> We cornered old Stonewall and his crew and haunted him about a day ½ until he was reinforced by the whole of the rebel army in Virginia. The rebels threw railroad track instead of balls, the pieces would come through the air over our heads, a screeching like a jackass in a fit of nightmare. The Yankees gave them a warm reception till about 4 o'clock in the afternoon when they succeeded in turning our left flank.[56]

The endeavor had cost the Federal Army dearly. Pope's offensive campaign resulted in losses of over 16,000 men against nearly 9,200 of the enemy. The Excelsior Brigade had lost 329 men since its hard fight at Kettle Run and was practically useless as a fighting force. Hooker's entire division was a mere shell of its former self, prompting Fighting Joe to pen this report from Centerville to his III Corps commander, Peter Heintzelman, on August 31:

> It is my duty to report for the information of the major-general commanding the corps that my division is in no condition to meet the enemy. This was communicated to me yesterday by my brigade commanders, and on inquiry I find their *morale* to be such as to warrant me in entertaining the most serious apprehension of their conduct in their present state. I ascribe this great demoralization in the men to the severe losses they have sustained in battle, both here and on the Peninsula. They are in no condition to go in to battle at this time.
> Very respectfully,
> Joseph Hooker[57]

8. On to Fredericksburg

Centerville was supposed to be far enough. By yielding the field at Bull Run and retreating to Centerville, General Pope had expected his army to be safe. But a Rebel force under Stonewall Jackson was moving around his right flank, moving to block the Warrenton Turnpike, Pope's route to Washington and safety.

It didn't take Emerson Merrell, Hiram Stoddard and the rest of the regiment long to prepare for the march. Since arriving in northern Virginia they had been without much of their gear: tents, backpacks, blankets and the like had all been lost since leaving the Peninsula. Now they were veterans and experienced in overcoming such hardships; plus the lack of gear made preparations inadvertently quicker.[1] Sometime after noon on September 1, they began their move toward Fairfax Court House and eventually Washington.[2]

The Warrenton Turnpike was Pope's main line of retreat from Bull Run. From Centerville it ran nearly due east to Germantown, which was only about six miles beyond Centerville. At Germantown the Warrenton Turnpike terminated into the Little River Turnpike, which came down from the northwest, and ran another mile east to Fairfax Court House and then onto Washington. After marching only a little while, Stoddard, Merrell and the rest of Hooker's division could hear firing off to their left. About a mile north, a Union division had slammed into Jackson's Confederates moving south past a little town called Chantilly. As the fight to the north unfolded, word came that the Federal division needed help. III Corps' position in the line of march placed them closest to the fighting, and reinforcements were ordered in. Kearney's First Division would lead the attack, with Second Division providing support. With Hooker detailed to organize a defense at Germantown, command of Second Division temporarily fell to General Grover.[3] By 5 p.m. Kearney had formed most of his men, who were aligned along the turnpike and ready to advance north. While Kearney prepared to move north, Captain Harmon Bliss and the rest of Second Division had continued to move beyond Kearney and on to Germantown. By 5:30 they had turned northwest onto the Little River Turnpike. Orders were relayed; companies went forward into line, then the column of companies formed the regimental lines of battle, and the brigades formed their formations. As Emerson and his Company I mates took their place in line, they could see the other brigades, indeed the whole division, readying for battle. Second division wasn't what it once was, being down to less than half the number they'd started with at Yorktown. The division looked more like a fresh brigade, but 4,000 veteran troops still presented a respectable force. Facing west, Emerson could easily hear the sounds of battle before them. Their rifles at the ready, Bliss and the rest were poised either to support Kearney's assault or threaten the Confederate left flank with an attack of their own.

As the battle progressed, most of the fighting was on the Union left, away from Bliss and the Second Division. Yet knowing how the tides of battle could change at any moment, everyone remained under arms with lines formed. Around 8 p.m. General Kearney was killed as he rode too close to the enemy lines, and by ten the battle was over; both sides were too tired and too low on ammunition to continue.[4]

Eventually the Rebels moved off to the north and east, and at 2:30 a.m. the regiment resumed its march toward Fairfax Court House, arriving around eight that morning. Persistent rumors about the location and intentions of the enemy kept officers debating the best dispositions for the regiments, but after a short rest, Bliss and his men resumed the march. Moving only a few miles, they stopped and camped for the night.[5] The following morning, September 3, the division continued its march. Nine miles later, upon reaching Fort Lyon on the outskirts of Alexandria and within sight of Washington, they halted. For the next few weeks at least, the regiment would call Fort Lyon home.[6]

While the regiment was settling in to life at Fort Lyon, back in New York, Dan Sickles' recruiting campaign was still in full swing. Since leaving Harrison's Landing at the beginning of August, Sickles had stormed around the state, speaking at this rally and that, drumming up badly needed replacements for his beloved Excelsior Brigade. Many of Sickles' old Tammany Hall cronies were now confirmed Copperheads who sought peace at any price and were angry at Dan for his unwavering advocacy for continuing the war and his avid support of Lincoln. "Every man ... can put implicit reliance in the good faith, the integrity, the intelligence, the patriotism, and the nerve of Abraham Lincoln," Dan told an audience at the Produce Exchange, continuing, "I did not vote for him, but I will fight under his orders, and I will trust him everywhere, and pray for him night and day."[7] These were strong words for a confirmed Democrat, but for Dan victory was the only option, and at his rallies he argued for a greater commitment to bring the war to a successful end. "A man may pass through New York, and unless he is told of it, he would not know that this country was at war.... In God's name, let the State of New York have it to say hereafter that she furnished her quota to the army without conscription—without resorting to a draft."[8] For Dan, the fact that his brigade was a volunteer unit was one of special pride. He railed against those who would wait to be drafted and especially against those who would hire a substitute to go in their places if conscripted. "Would you wait for the drafting and be dragged to the battlefield by the Collar?! I want no conscripts! I have none! I have all volunteers and I know they will fight."[9] For Dan Sickles, leading his men to the war's glorious conclusion was his first and only priority; any intentions he may have harbored about returning to Congress would have to wait.

Captain Chadwick had been in New York recuperating from his wounding at Malvern Hill but was well enough by mid–September to join the general on the recruiting circuit both in New York City and throughout the state. Familial connections allowed Chadwick to bypass the normal procedure of stays at army hospitals along with its accompanying bureaucracy and go straight home to the care of his own doctor. Other officers and men from the brigade who received time away from their regiments joined Chadwick with recruiting, and though Sickles was clearly the star of the show, they did what they could.[10]

III Corps had been assigned to defenses in and around Washington. With a Rebel threat to the capital slim, regiments throughout the corps were afforded a chance to rest, recuperate and recruit. But Robert E. Lee was not a man to rest. Seizing upon Pope's retreat to Washington, he positioned his army for a move into Maryland. The defeated Pope was through as head of the army, and Lincoln reluctantly restored command to George McClellan. But the normally plodding McClellan recognized the danger and at the start of September was moving 70,000 troops northwest from Washington to meet Lee's threat. Joe Hooker was too valuable an asset to be sitting around the defenses of Washington, and on September 5 was given command of I Corps. Eventually the two great armies clashed on the 9th near Sharpsburg, Maryland, while all of III Corps and the Excelsiors remained in Washington. The fighting around Antietam Creek was the bloodiest one-day affair of the war. Lee ultimately withdrew back to Virginia, leaving the Army of the Potomac to claim the field but denying the numerically superior North another superb chance to crush his Rebel army.

In Alexandria, change was in the air. Three days after establishing camp, Nelson Taylor was promoted to brigadier general and moved from the regiment to command a brigade within I Corps. Temporary command of the Excelsiors fell to Colonel George Hall of the 71st New York. Sickles' position within the army was changing too. With Hooker out, Second Division was in need of a new commander and, despite missing all of the August fighting, Dan enjoyed the reflected glory of his Excelsior Brigade and a reputation as an aggressive fighter. And so, on September 5, Sickles was given Second Division.[11]

Sickles' time spent recruiting had been a success. Perhaps the numbers weren't quite the 1,200 recruits that had been rumored, but there were certainly enough new men to keep the brigade in business and avoid consolidation. Among the newly added was an entire company of New York City firemen ready to join the 73rd, while in the 72nd, 112 new men helped to restore depleted companies.[12] Replacements for Third Excelsior came from across the whole state, but recruiting in New York City had gone especially well. Thirty of the new men fell in with Company C and First Lt. Berend Huttmann, who had been keeping shop since Chadwick's wounding. The influx established C as the largest company within the regiment.[13] George Russell, Tom Roper, and a young Scotsman from Astoria named James Dean were among the new men. Dean had missed joining up back in '61 but wanted to serve. He was a gardener, just like his father, and felt a life of tending flowers could wait.[14] Even with the new men, the regiments remained small compared to newly minted organizations. To ensure the brigade could fight on more or less equal terms, a whole new regiment was added. The 120th New York, a brand new outfit from Kingston in upstate New York, became the brigade's sixth regiment.[15]

As new enlisted men were filling the depleted ranks of the 72nd, there were other changes in the regiment's officer corps. Lieutenant Colonel Israel Moses, the regiment's fighting doctor, had grown tired of command or perhaps felt his talents were best used elsewhere. Whatever the reason, he left the 72nd on October 4 and picked up his scalpel as surgeon with a different regiment. With both Nelson and Moses out, Major William O. Stevens was now the regiment's senior officer and was promoted to colonel on October 25. By the end of October other field positions were sorted out with John S. Austin, captain of Company K, becoming lt. colonel and the Indian fighter from out west, John Leonard of Co. F, named major.[16] Up at III Corps headquarters, Heintzelman was out as corps commander, and George Stoneman, who led the pursuit of the Rebs back at Yorktown, was in.[17]

The weather around Alexandria had been fairly good through the first part of October, but occasional heavy rainstorms played havoc with some men. "Had fine weather till Friday night when the rain came down in torrents, running through some tents in a regular stream and when the boys woke up they were in a regular puddle,"[18] wrote Private Dean in a letter home, adding, "but I have a comfortable bed made of young trees and covered over with rushes and it is about a foot off the ground ... our tent was as dry as if there had been no rain owing to the trench we dug around it."[19] With October's changing weather and winter on the way, the boys were issued tall, circular Sibley tents.[20] These large Sibleys held as many as 12 men, and their conical shape offered room enough to stand upright. The tent was designed around a central stove that vented out through a hole at the roof's apex. This kept the men warm; each man could put his feet or head, depending on preference, close to the fire. The men soon learned that the feature that made the Sibley comfortable was also its biggest liability. With it circular design and only one door, nearly every man had to step over a tent mate to get out when either nature or the corporal of the guard called.

On the morning of October 22 the call sounded through camp for the companies to fall in, each man's leathers fully blackened, all brass polished and every hand donning a white glove; the division was being reviewed by Lincoln. It was a brilliant day, "all that could be wished for," described one Excelsior man.[21] As they stood at attention, Sickles and the president engaged in a pithy exchange that perhaps harkened back to the early days and the brigade's uncertain beginnings. As the commander-in-chief reviewed the troops, many of the men gazed upon him for their first and possibly only time. Private Dean described the affair this way in a letter home:

> We had a grand review last week, we were reviewed by President Lincoln, Secretary Stanton, Major General Banks and Heintzelman and two hundred generals and staff officers. There must have been 40 thousand troops present consisting of infantry, Cavalry and artillery and [it] was a splendid affair to see the Cavalry dashing up and down with their sabers drawn, the artillery flying and occasionally stopping and give a salute and off again. The infantry on a double quik [*sic*] with fixed bayonets and on a charge and yelling and it seemed impossible for any rebel army to defeat us.[22]

While the boys may have been getting used to life at Fort Lyon, high command had other ideas. Under its new commander, Dan Sickles, Second Division on November 1 began a reconnaissance along the Orange and Alexandria Railroad. With the notion of being able to support any offensive moves the army might make into northern Virginia, they would rebuild bridges and repair track.[23] Excelsior Brigade struck camp and stepped off for Manassas Junction at four that afternoon. By eight that evening, after a march of eight miles, the boys stopped for the night. With weather mild and dry, few likely even pitched a tent. Before dawn the regiment was on the move again, moving through land it had travelled only weeks before. Eighteen miles later, four miles from Centerville, and on the same ground they had camped on the eve of the Second Bull Run fight, privates Merrell and Dean, with their new colonel William Stevens in the lead, stopped for the night. At daybreak on November 3 the boys continued on, eventually stopping around eight that morning to make camp about ½ mile from the junction.[24] While the Excelsiors established their base at Manassas Junction, Third Brigade under General Francis Patterson—the same General Patterson who back on the Peninsula had revealed the division's location by blowing his bugle—made camp further down the line at Warrenton Junction. Near Manassas Junction there was little enemy activity, but rumors abounded of a sizeable enemy force just south of Patterson's New Jersey Blues. Soon the rumors of a large enemy cavalry force were too much for Patterson and, acting upon the belief his position was too isolated, he retreated.[25] "My position is untenable. The whistles of cars are going freely, indicating the arrival of troops. I am returning to my old camp,"[26] wired the shaken Patterson. Whether due to drunkenness as rumored or simply a loss of nerve, Patterson's retreat was the last straw in a list of failings, and Sickles immediately relieved him from command. With Third Brigade out of position, the enraged Sickles ordered Patterson detained and the Excelsiors to move south to restore order. "Friday night [Nov. 7th] the Brigade, in the midst of a cold, driving sleet, was again on the march for Warrenton Junction,"[27] wrote the Excelsior's Chaplain Twichell. When the New Yorkers arrived, the phantom enemy had gone, purportedly withdrawn to below the Rappahannock. With the Excelsiors now in Warrenton Junction, redeployment was decided upon. The 71st, 73rd and 120th New Yorks returned all the way back to Manassas Junction, while the 70th and 74th moved back to Bristoe Station. Colonel Stevens and the boys of the 72nd N.Y. would stay in Warrenton Junction with two Massachusetts regiments, "thus giving about 15 miles of the Rail Road into our (Excelsior Brigade's) keeping,"[28] observed Twichell.

The arrest of their general created hard feelings against Sickles among the New Jersey boys. They liked Patterson in spite of his shortcomings—be it his absence from important battles or his drunkenness. The Blues had always been suspicious of Sickles and did little to hide their ambivalence, even going so far as to recite the homemade ditty, "Johnny stole a ham and Sickles killed a man," within earshot of the Excelsiors.[29] For two weeks following his arrest, Patterson awaited investigation; then he was discovered dead in his tent. Although he was judged to have been killed by an accidental discharge of his pistol, many instead believed he had committed suicide rather than face the shame of an inquiry. The increasingly bitter boys of the Jersey Brigade believed their beloved Patterson was now the second man murdered by Dan Sickles.[30]

Camp near Warrenton Junction was less hospitable than in Alexandria. Rations were frequently short, as men of Third Excelsior carried on through frost and the occasional snow. "The weather is pretty cold and every night we have ice from a quarter to half an inch thick, last week we had snow over 4 inches deep,"[31] wrote James Dean in a November 13 letter home. Dean and his fellow New Yorkers camped and patrolled on much of the same ground over which they had fought the previous August. The countryside was littered with razed buildings, burned hulks of locomotives and destroyed rail cars. Sickles' division was spread out over a sizeable area of northern Virginia and charged with protecting a considerable amount of track. "Posts are established at all stations, bridges, causeways, culverts and high embankments along the line and the interval between the posts are vigilantly patrolled day and night,"[32] Sickles reported. With the Confederate Army close and Rebel cavalry still a menace, the capture of enemy horsemen was worthy of mention by Dean: "Three nights ago we captured forty 3 calvary [sic] and horses. They were dressed all kind of suits and them and their horses looked pretty hard."[33] Aside from contending with enemy cavalry, the boys kept busy tracking down errant enemy soldiers, sympathizers, agents and spies. On Saturday night the 15th, Emerson Merrell and his newly minted corporal, Edgar Hyatt, were out of camp foraging for chickens. Coming upon a house about three miles from camp, they told the residents, who viewed the two with considerable suspicion, that they had been in pursuit of some Rebels. The story went that they had followed the Southern men there and had now lost them. As the pair continued their explanation, they happened upon some unexpected information. "I took one of the niggers aside," described Emerson, "talked with him awhile and he told me that thire [sic] was a rebel spy courting one of the girls."[34] According to the servant, the spy was in the habit of staying at the home all night and observing the camp all day, adding that "he had been there that day and was comeing [sic] again that night to take the girl away with him."[35] Excited at the prospect of catching a spy, Merrell, Hyatt and another returned to the home later that evening. In the dark of the Virginia night, the three crept toward the house, muskets at the ready. Once within 50 feet of the house, "his horse commenced snorting and blowing which gave him the hint and before we could get to the road ... he was on his horse and a gowing [sic] with the velocity of lightning,"[36] leaving Emerson and his frustrated mates behind with nothing to show for their late night sortie.

While Merrell, Dean and the rest of their regiment camped at Warrenton, critical events were unfolding in Washington. General George McClellan was relieved of command of the Army of the Potomac for failing to adequately pursue the retreating Confederate Army after his strategic victory at Antietam. His replacement was Maj. Gen. Ambrose Burnside; the date was November 7, 1862. Burnside felt himself inadequate to the task of such a large command, but he reluctantly accepted President Abraham Lincoln's offer. This was Burnside's third offer of army command, and he feared a third refusal might mean the post falling to his rival, Gen. Joseph Hooker. Burnside had risen to leadership of the IX Corps by performing well at Bull Run and in other campaigns to secure coastal waterways in North Carolina. His poor showing at Antietam caused his standing among many senior officers to fall several notches.[37] Despite all this, he tackled his new job with vigor and on November 9 sent Washington a new plan for taking the Rebel capital.

The plan was a simple eastward sidestepping of the Confederate army: cross the Rappahannock River at the town of Fredericksburg and then plunge south to Richmond. Once across the Rappahannock, Burnside would be in a position to block any attempts by Robert E. Lee's pursuing Confederate Army to stop him. The plan relied on the Union army's ability to move speedily through Fredericksburg, and speed was something this army had yet to demonstrate. President Lincoln hesitantly agreed to the plan, commenting, it "will succeed, if you move rapidly; otherwise not."[38] For William O. Stevens and his men, their time tending the track of the Orange and Alexandria was coming to an end.

With speed the primary condition for Lincoln's permission to pursue his campaign, Burnside quickly set his large army in motion. He divided the army into three large "Grand Divisions," each containing two corps and commanded respectively by Generals Joseph Hooker, Edwin Sumner and William Franklin. Sumner's grand division, comprising II and IX Corps, left its camps on November 15 and marched south. Franklin's grand division, made up of I and VI Corps, along with Hooker's command consisting of III and V Corps, left the following day. The army had orders to concentrate at Falmouth, and Stevens and his 72nd boys stepped off from Warrenton Junction on the 18th. Poor weather with nearly constant rain turned the roads thick with mud. Since leaving Alexandria two weeks before, the supply situation had been rather shaky, with men going on short rations much of the time and replacement gear almost unheard of. Wet blankets, "heavy as lead,"[39] only served to compound an already difficult march. Many veterans wore shoes and uniforms that were worn out, while the new October-recruits no doubt enjoyed fresher equipment. Men who wore shoes and boots sent to them from loved ones back home were likely the envy of their companies. Second Division's route had been a long backtracking, but after reaching Fairfax Station, the regiment finally turned south toward Fredericksburg on the 21st. For four days the regiment camped at Wolf Run Shoals along the Occoquan Creek. Eventually Col. Stevens and the rest completed the remaining 20 or so miles to Falmouth, arriving there on the 28th.[40]

With unprecedented speed, lead elements of the Yankee army moved the forty miles to Falmouth in only two and a half days. This positioned the army only a mile from the critical Rappahannock River town of Fredericksburg and a skeleton Confederate force that held the town. As Burnside planned his next move, things began to go awry. Those same heavy rains that Merrell and the rest had slogged through had caused the river to rise. This threatened important fords, while the resultant mud brought all troop and supply movements to a crawl. But the worst blow was yet to follow: the pontoon bridges critical to the river crossing had failed to arrive. Despite chief-of-staff Halleck's assurances that the pontoons would be there, the situation's urgency was not realized, and the bridges did not begin their move south from Washington until November 19. Encountering washed-out bridges and endless mud, movement of the bridging supplies was painfully slow until at last the material arrived on November 27. Burnside's Army of the Potomac meanwhile sat idle for a full ten days.[41]

During these delays, Robert E. Lee and his Confederate Army were anything but idle. Though unsure of Burnside's intentions, Lee was certain the Yankees were on the move. As Sumner's Yankee troops moved toward Falmouth, the Confederates began moving two divisions of James Longstreet's I Corps in the direction of Fredericksburg. Once the objectives of the balance of the Union Army became clear, Lee ordered the remainder of Longstreet's and all of Stonewall Jackson's corps to the heights above Fredericksburg. By the 29th of November the bulk of the Rebel Army was taking defensive positions in and around the town.[42]

With the regiment stopped and camped at Falmouth with the rest of the army, James Dean busied himself with letter writing and seeking out friends belonging to other units. During one walk along the banks of the river, a Rebel soldier from the far side hailed him. The curious Confederate asked him to which regiment Dean belonged. After an exchange, the Southron then complimented the Excelsiors as one of the North's best fighting brigades.[43]

Company C's Captain Chadwick, wounded on July 1 at Malvern Hill and recuperating in New York while on recruiting detail, had requested to be released from that duty and allowed to return to his men. By December 1, he had rejoined the company at Falmouth and in command in time for the coming campaign. The miserable weather and rigors of the campaign, however, would prove the undoing for Chadwick's now-fragile health.

Despite having taken a beating the previous months on the Peninsula with McClellan and under Pope, many of the 72nd men remained hopeful. "We have soldiered 1 year ½ and have not gained ground enough for our winter quarters ... but it is impossible for the tide to be out always,"[44] wrote Pvt. Merrell. The Harvard educated chaplain Twichell echoed some of the private's melancholy but was perhaps a bit more philosophical:

> The army cannot be called disheartened, but dull. Its pulse beats, not feebly, but very moderately. The prospect at best is not charming.... If we are held here in readiness, yet do not advance, we shall attain a condition which while it cannot be called discomfort, will yet be far from comfort—a kind of uneasy ease.[45]

But as the fall turned to winter and with the regiment camped just across the river from Fredericksburg, the cold, boredom, and political changes—particularly the pending Emancipation Proclamation—caused Merrell to question Lincoln's motives. In a December 7 letter to his parents, Emerson offered his views:

> Write and let me know what the peoples' opinion is of the Presidents Message—my opinion is the same as the majority of the soldiers and that is, he is bound to do away slavery at all hazards and has been working into it by degrees until he has finally come to the spot. President Lincoln is bound to die with the party which it is very evident is short lived.[46]

Attitudes about slavery and the plight of the negro ran the gamut throughout the entire army, and the 72nd reflected this diversity. Men such as Emerson Merrell were ambivalent about slavery and saw emancipation as a distraction for Lincoln, drawing his attention away from the war effort. Others, such as George Bailey of Company H, had none of Merrell's doubt and viewed freedom for slaves as a great double-cross. "When I enlisted, I laid my politics aside until such time as the war should be over and the Union restored which was the cry of all Loyal people ... then Politics was again brought up, the interests of the country were thrown aside, the Allmighty nigger [is now] the question."[47] But many men on the other side of the question, such as Charles Gould, saw the issue of slavery as intertwined with winning the war. "I think that the rebellion must, and will be crushed. I hope slavery will be crushed with it."[48]

Drawing three days' cooked rations, the regiment and the rest of III Corps began preparations to move on Tuesday, December 9. The boys had since fashioned comfortable winter quarters for themselves from logs, sod and whatever else kept out the elements, and each man regretted leaving such accommodations behind. During the afternoon of the 10th, Sickles accompanied General Stoneman forward to plan the corps' dispositions and the best routes to the bridges over the Rappahannock. At 4 a.m. on Thursday morning the boys were rousted from their sleep, and four hours later Sickles' Second Division had left Falmouth and marched to the rear of the Lacy House: General Sumner's headquarters. Colonel George B. Hall of the 71st New York was in temporary command of the Excelsior Brigade (Second Brigade), while Brig. Gen. Joseph Carr commanded the New Jersey men of the First Brigade and Brig. Gen. Joseph W. Revere, grandson of the Revolutionary War hero Paul Revere, commanded the Third Brigade.[49] Chaplain Twichell described the scene behind Lacy House.

> There we met the other regiments of our Brigade and Division, in fact, of the Corps and Grand Division with the Cavalry and Artillery thereto belonging. It was a magnificent morning, several degrees warmer than it had been for the week past, yet cool and bracing. The air was humid and the rising sun showed a face of blood, presaging, as it were, the terrible scenes about to be enacted. I have never witnessed so splendid a military display as that morning furnished. The long dark columns of infantry with fifty thousand gleaming bayonets and waving ensigns; the numerous trains of Artillery with guns of shining brass or black steel, heavily rumbling over the frozen ground; the quick moving bodies of cavalry with resounding hoofs and the jingling of the sabres, combined with the music of the bands, the blare of bugles, the shouts of command, the galloping of aides and the tramp of multitudes; made up a spectacle not easily forgotten.[50]

Burnside's army of 118,000 Federal troops stood on the east side of the Rappahannock River. Directly on the other side lay the town of Fredericksburg, which hugged the river's bank for about a mile. West of town, the hills gently rose for nearly one and one-half miles, most of that distance an expanse of treeless fields, perfect for a parade but offering no cover whatsoever for an attack. Just beyond the treeless plain a fine Virginia forest began. Here, in the cover of the woods, 78,000 Rebels would eventually be dug into positions that commanded every possible approach.

With Rebel strength increasing, Burnside sought alternatives to a direct assault through Fredericksburg. Finding none to be satisfactory, the commanding general convinced himself that Lee had split his army and that an attack across the river, through the town and up the heights would be successful. No other Union officers shared their general's confidence. A IX Corps brigade commander, Col. Rush C. Hawkins, said to attack would "be the greatest slaughter of the war; there isn't infantry enough in our whole army to carry those heights if they are well defended."[51] Lt. Col. Joseph H. Taylor told Burnside more pointedly, "The carrying out of your plan will be murder, not warfare."[52]

Beset by delays and doubt, the Federal Army finally began their attack in the pre-dawn darkness of December 11. The 50th New York Engineers began bridging operations just as the Excelsiors were readying for their march from Falmouth. Confederate marksmen were stationed among the buildings on the river's far side, and the exposed engineers took heavy losses as progress on the bridges slowed. Finally, around 2:30 p.m. the next day, the Federals succeeded in spanning the river. Only after a building-leveling barrage from 150 cannons and an amphibious assault did Union troops manage to clear the opposite bank of Rebels. Yankee engineers eventually placed a total of six bridges across the Rappahannock: two at the northern end of town, another at its southern edge, and three more about two miles south of the town.[53]

Rebel skirmishers gave up the town and retreated to the safety of the heights as Federal troops poured across the bridges. All night long, troops moved across the six bridges and before dawn on Saturday the 13th, the bulk of Burnside's force was on the Confederates' side of the river. In and around Fredericksburg were II and V Corps, with IX Corps positioned in reserve. Near the lower crossings slightly to the east lay men of the I, VI and III Corps, with Sickles' division composing the bulk of the reserve, which remained on the east side of the river. Opposing these Federal troops near the lower crossing were four divisions of Stonewall Jackson's corps.[54]

"The 13th of December opened with a dense fog enveloping the whole field,"[55] wrote Pvt. George Shreve of Henry's Battery, part of the Confederate artillery facing Franklin's oncoming troops:

> Beyond the hedge, we could hear the Federal Infantry maneuvering; distinguishing a medley of voices, but could not see them. Evidently they were only a few hundred yards distant. The fog commenced to lift between nine and ten o'clock, and exposed to our view as we peered through, the hedge, a grand spectacle of marshalled soldiery, in readiness for the fray, spread out in vast proportions, on the level plain, in our immediate front.[56]

Burnside's written orders contained critical errors that seemed to contradict earlier verbal instructions, yet Federal corps commanders began launching their attacks around 8:30 that morning. Nearest Fredericksburg, divisions comprising the Federal right took a horrible beating as they attacked the entrenched Confederates at Marye's Heights. Rebel infantry and cannon, positioned in the protection of the Sunken Road and the Stone Wall, decimated advancing Union regiments. Two major attacks were launched here over the course of the day, the first by the II Corps and the second by the IX Corps. Shortly after 5 p.m. the fighting on this side of the line was over; Gen. Hooker called an end to the disaster, declaring he had "lost as many men as my orders required."[57] When the day's attacks were finished, 7,000 Yankees were either killed or wounded in the futile endeavor, and it was said no Federal soldier advanced closer than 25 feet to the fortified Rebels.

Below the town, on the Union left, the day began slightly better for Franklin's men. With the 72nd and the rest of the Excelsior Brigade still on the far side of the river, General George Meade's division had inadvertently found a weak spot in the Confederate line and by 1 p.m. was making nice progress. Franklin inexplicably refused to offer sufficient support to Meade's advance, and despite this early success, effective counterattacks by Jackson's Confederates sent the northern men reeling.[58]

During this phase of the battle, the Second and Third brigades of Sickles' division were ordered across the bridges. Earlier that morning Carr's First Brigade went across to secure the bridge's approaches. By the time it was Col. Hall's Excelsiors' turn to cross, the brigade had been severely depleted. Seventy-Fourth New York was missing, having been detailed to support the First and Fifth New York Artillery, still on the east side of the river, two miles below the three bridges of "Franklin's Crossing." Hall's largest regiment, the 120th N.Y., had only about 100 men present during the crossing, the remainder sent earlier to assist General Woodbury of the engineers.[59]

Across the bridges the regiments continued south for another mile. The division formed two lines in support on the left of Ward's Second Brigade of Birney's First Division. Excelsior Brigade formed their line of battle to the right of the Carr's men, while Revere's Third Brigade formed a second line in support. Sickles' men were in position by 3 p.m. and, almost at once, skirmishers were deployed who took up a heavy exchange with the Confederates.[60] Col. Hall's reports described the intensity of the exchange:

> Upon arriving in line of battle, skirmishers were immediately thrown out. We were exposed to the enemy upon open ground, with but a slight rise between us, at a distance of about 400 paces. The skirmishers were immediately engaged, and their ammunition (60 rounds) was entirely expended shortly after being posted, owing to the heavy and continued firing of the enemy's sharpshooters, stationed in the trees in front, but the men were promptly relieved from their own commands, until dark put an end to the fire on each side.[61]

Worried about a Rebel counterattack, Col. Stevens ordered his men to fix bayonets. Circulating about the regiment as best he could, Stevens urged his boys to make every shot tell.[62] But their enemy was well concealed; the men of the regiment had little to shoot at, flashes from Reb muskets being the only hint of their enemy's position. Confederate riflemen enjoyed the protection of the trees and the occasional wall, but the New Yorkers struggled on a bare field. James Dean remembered that he and his comrades were exposed to fire with "not as much as a straw to cover us."[63] To present as small a target as possible, Dean and the rest attempted to fire as they lay on their bellies. In awkward convolutions, the boys struggled against the cold and gravity as they attempted to place powder and bullets down the barrels of their Springfields. But struggle they did, Dean being sure any man who rose up would become the target of at least 30 or 40 Rebs.[64] Even with the New Yorkers lying low, Confederate infantry kept up a blistering fire. Dean wrote that the enemy musketry "put one in the mind of a swarm of bees which had just hived," and recalled, "I came off very lucky although the bullets came as close to me as they could come without hurting me; one burnt my hair and I got one in the pants below the knee and one in the coat tail."[65] The Excelsiors held their ground throughout the afternoon waiting for orders to advance. Chaplain Twichell had not initially moved forward with the regiments but now rode across the river to see his boys:

> They were standing in the field, waiting to be sent, with a coolness and quietude that became veterans. Several of the officers remarked to me, "Chaplain, if we have to go into the woods, you will never see many of us alive after it."[66]

The din of battle began to quiet as night settled over Fredericksburg. The Excelsior men were relieved that the order to advance never came. It was now that the men of the regiment were subject to the agonized groans of the wounded and dying. Moving about in the freezing dark, Dean and his fellows tended as best they could to those around them:

> The wounded commenced to get cold [and] it would melt a heart of stone to hear the cries and mones [sic]. There were about a dozen of them within 10 yds of me and as soon as it got dark I went and gave them water and covered them up with blankets.... One orderly sergeant asked me my name that I gave water and covered during the night and he commenced calling my name and some of the others commenced to and it was awful to hear the moans and asking for us to carry them off the field.[67]

While his men held their positions throughout the night, Gen. Burnside held a council of war with his subordinates. Initially, the despondent Burnside contemplated renewing the attacks in the morning, leading the troops himself. But officers eventually convinced Burnside that further attacks would be fruitless and the campaign had failed. The Army of the Potomac must now be withdrawn.[68]

As dawn broke on Sunday the 14th, firing resumed between the Excelsiors and an enemy that had been reinforced during the night, much of it taking place between Rebel skirmishers and Col. George Sharpe's 120th New York. During the afternoon of the previous day, the detached portions of Sharpe's regiment had rejoined the brigade and the full 120th was held in reserve. Now, as morning came, the full ranks of the previously un-bloodied 120th found themselves on the brigade's right and "briskly" engaged. In a show of bravado never seen among veteran troops, some 120th man proposed three cheers for the first shot that "sternly saluted" the regiment. Just as the untimely outburst was beginning, it was checked for fear of attracting further notice of the enemy.[69]

As the morning dragged on, it became clear to both sides that the anticipated attacks each expected were not materializing. Frontline commanders, colonels and majors began to strike their own informal cease-fire agreements with their opposite number. By noon, most firing died away and ambulance crews with other medical teams circulated among the Federal dead and wounded. Col. Hall described the situation, "Sharp skirmish firing was commenced ... and continued till toward afternoon, when they followed the example of this brigade by an agreement with the enemy's skirmishers to stop the desultory firing along the line."[70] Sickles in his official report witnessed, "by a tacit, though informal, understanding, no more picket firing occurred along my lines. The ambulance men, frequently assisted by the enemy in pointing out our wounded and placing them on stretchers, brought off all of our men who had been left on the field along my front."[71]

That night and early the following Monday night, the rebels continually improved their positions, still anticipating a renewed Federal attack. "The enemy resumed their industrious efforts to strengthen their position in front. Without ceasing, their axes and other implements were heard at work from the base to the crest of the heights,"[72] reported Sickles. Throughout Monday, 72nd N.Y. men and the whole of the Excelsior Brigade held their positions. When First Brigade came to relieve Hall's men at 5 p.m. the New Yorkers had been under arms for 50 hours.[73] Sickles received orders at 9:30 that night from corps commander Stoneman to withdraw his division. Under a driving rainstorm, Hall's brigade was moving to the rear by 10:00 and a short time later re-crossed the very bridges they had marched across two days earlier. After marching for another two miles or so, the New Yorkers laid down and slept.[74]

When the Rebel defenders awoke the next morning, they were amazed to find that the entirety of the Union Army had disappeared silently during the night. Burnside and his generals had withdrawn the army under cover of rain and darkness, going so far as to lay straw and dirt on the pontoon bridges to muffle the noise of caissons, hooves and brogans. So complete was the retreat that it was said not one living Federal soldier was left on the far side of the Rappahannock.[75]

News of the Yankee retreat was hailed in the South as a "stunning defeat to the invader, a splendid victory to the defender of the sacred soil."[76] When the gloom of defeat fell upon the North, President Lincoln, upon hearing reports of the battle, commented, "If there is a worse place than hell, I am in it."[77]

Losses had been very light for Steven's regiment with only four men slightly wounded, and losses throughout the brigade were equally light. But losses for the rest of the army were another matter. Federal casualties topped 12,500 while Confederate losses were well below half that number.[78]

With the failure at Fredericksburg, disgust among the ranks could no longer be contained, as Emerson Merrell expressed soon after the battle:

> Old abe is bound to save the niggers and let the union go to hell—The papers say that we are in the best condition that we were ever in and all eager for a fight—but it is all humbug this army has been growing more and more demoralized since the 2d battle of Bull run and this battle (or rather this slaughter) has put on the finish—we have always wrote to our friends the best side of the story but it is played out—I will not hesitate at all to telling the truth any longer—for the last two years people have not been allowed to express his opinion and the Editors of the papers have not been allowed to print the truth and there by the people of the north have been mesmarised [*sic*] and their pockets picked.[79]

Epoch IV: The Bloody Season

9. Hooker in Command

Christmas 1862 came and went with little notice by most of the regiment. Defeat at Fredericksburg had put many boys in a reflective mood. "Christmas was a lonesome day to me,"[1] wrote Company B's Hiram Stoddard. "I staid [sic] in my tent the most of the day and thought of the dear ones at home, but let us as the New Year is about to merge in upon us try to pray that it may bring with it glad tidings and the voice of freedom."[2]

The regiment and brigade camped near Falmouth, Virginia, for the winter, their same camp prior to the mess at Fredericksburg. The boys endured as best they could the cold and inactivity. The men also endured the recent capture of the regimental sutler, which meant that small personal luxuries such as tobacco and writing paper were in short supply.[3] Setbacks of the earlier campaign season had some beginning to question if it was all worth it. None questioned their ability to fight—they had casualties enough to prove it—but some wondered if their generals were up to the task or if the political winds were changing too much for their taste. Men had volunteered to defeat the traitors and restore the Union, but now it seemed the conflict was being turned into a war to free the slaves. Emerson Merrell described his feeling this way:

> Soldiering is an old story—I am tired of the drum and fife and everything else pertaining to the soldiers life—we are not fighting for the union any more—it is merely a political strife, nigger or no nigger—but I hope that it will soon end for I consider the time that I serve a dead letter, lost to me intirely [sic], [I] shall forget all that I ever knew about civilized life. I can stand it another year if necessary but I had rather not.[4]

Others such as Pvt. Stoddard took the defeats in stride and tried to count his blessings as best he could:

> Seeing it is the last Sabbath in the year 1862 & still I am a Soldier for Country ... when I think what the Lord has brought me through for the past year I have to ask my self why is it I trust it is for some good purpass [sic]. Sometimes I get tired & impatient & almost discouraged but when I take second thought I feel as though I had no cause to complain as long as the Lord has been & still is so good to me. Oh when I think how many families the past year has left desolate of sons & fathers & yet your Children in the army are spared.[5]

But the work of war went on, despite how many families were left desolate. The Excelsiors had been without a proper commander since Sickles' promotion. Colonel George Hall of the 71st N.Y. had been in temporary command since then and had led the boys at Fredericksburg. Now on Christmas Eve, General Joseph Warren Revere took over, though most of the boys probably didn't notice. Chaplain Twichell wrote his father:

> Gen. Revere has been assigned to this brigade. He took command yesterday relieving Col Hall who had been acting ever since we left Alexandria. The Col. started immediately for

Washington and New York on leave of absence, for the purpose, it is supposed, of entering the list for a Brigadiership. I sincerely trust he will not succeed for he is not worthy of promotion.... I am sorry to say this but it is true.[6]

Revere was the 50-year-old grandson of Revolutionary war hero Paul Revere. He entered the navy at age 16 and served till resigning at age 38. Living in California for a time, he also served in the Mexican army as a colonel charged with organizing the artillery arm until returning to New Jersey in 1852. With war's outbreak, Revere entered service as colonel of the Seventh New Jersey, part of Third Brigade, the New Jersey Blues. Revere rose to command of the Blues after the death of the ill-fated Francis Patterson.[7]

Christmas for many men was uneventful and melancholy, though it was a different story among the officers come New Year's Day. Twichell related the evening's festivities in a letter to his father:

> At 3 o'clock the officers of the brigade met at the camp of the 1st Regt., and from thence, headed by Gen. Revere, proceeded to Headquarters of Division to visit Gen. Sickles. We found everything in real gala-day order. The wide street lying between the staff tents, which face each other, was spanned by arches of evergreens, adorned with appropriate devices, and all the place was gaily attired. At a short distance stands a small house. This was used as the eating and drinking rendezvous. On its piazza, a band of two violins, two flutes, an accordion, and a man who chirruped like a bird, discoursed sweet music and drowned the noise of mastication.... The programme was to first salute the General, then salute his victuals and drink.[8]

Soon the cheer of New Year's was forgotten and the routines of camp life resumed. By January 13 Emerson Merrell had been made cook of Company I. Claiming no culinary abilities for the feeding of 50 men, the primary benefit of Emerson's new post seemed to be that it excused him "from all other duty."[9]

The attack at Fredericksburg a month earlier was an unqualified disaster for the Federal army, but Burnside wasn't done; he still believed there was an opportunity to flank Lee and turn the tide of the war. Excelsior Brigade received orders on January 20 to move toward Bank's Ford. Bank's Ford was about four miles west of Falmouth and was in the left-rear flank of Lee's army. The brigade moved only about two miles before stopping to let Franklin's Grand Division pass. Instead of proceeding, the New Yorkers returned to their old camp in a heavy rain that continued all night. The next day the brigade moved again, going only about eight miles before camping for the night in the woods.[10] While the Excelsior marched and countermarched, the army fared no better as it sat idle on the banks of the Rappahannock, waiting for pontoons that had been delayed by sluggish roads.

Trying to unstick themselves and the army, the Excelsiors were turned into road-gangs. All afternoon on the 22nd and next morning, the Excelsiors cut and laid logs, cobbling together corduroy roads that would enable artillery and wagon trains to pass.[11] Burnside realized the endeavor was futile and returned his army to camp. Emerson Merrell summed up the rainy adventure this way: "Although we made an attempt to cross about five miles above Falmouth but it came on and rained for three days and we got stuck fast in the mud and wallered for two or three days and then backed out and gave up the chase."[12]

Soon the three days of "wallering" became known as the "Mud March." But even before this ordeal, some within the regiment had had enough of soldiering. Privates Thomas Roper and George W. Russell, both among those 112 recruits brought into the regiment who helped swell the ranks of Company C, were gone, deserted.[13] Others deserted as well, but some, the officers, left for reasons of their own, and the complexion of the regiment had changed since those early days back in summer of '61. Company C's captain, Issac Chadwick, was out. Supposedly recovered from his wounding, the cold and strain of the campaign together with his recurring carditis and rheumatism rendered him "entirely unfit for duty."[14] He resigned on January 16. John Howard, who had led Company F since September, left the regiment on January 7, leaving the Newark Company in command of a Dunkirk man, William Post. Two second lieutenants, Warren Stanton (Co. H) and William McGinnis (Co. I), rounded out the wave of January resignations, both having received their commissions earlier that summer.[15] Lt. Col. Austin was on leave again, home to recuperate from one of his varied chronic ailments, which affected his bladder and prostate among others.[16] One man gone from the regiment but not from the army was David Parker. Before Fredericksburg, with the army's reorganization, Parker remained detached to Hooker's staff, working to improve mail service to the Center Grand Division.[17] But the army's biggest change was still to come.

There was no question Burnside was to be sacked after his short but disastrous tenure as army commander. But who would follow Burnside was not clear. Finally, after much debate within his inner circle, Lincoln decided to give command of the Army of the Potomac to Joseph Hooker. Hooker was a hard choice. A harsh critic of Burnside's handling of matters, his name headed a list of generals whom Burnside wished removed from command, both for their criticism and for their hindering of operations by failing to fully carry out orders. Burnside presented his list to Lincoln with an ultimatum: either they go or he would. With no thought by Lincoln of retaining Burnside, the next question was who would replace him. Hooker's name quickly percolated to the fore of potential replacements. He was a fighter, to be sure, and he had demonstrated abilities to command large bodies of troops, but the real question was whether his massive ego would get in the way. Lincoln and others knew this was not the kind of man expected to take orders from Washington, but they also recognized Hooker's public appeal. Hooker disliked the "Fighting Joe" label, which nonetheless rang a true chord with the nation. "Hooker does talk badly; but the trouble is, he is stronger with the country today than any other man,"[18] Lincoln conceded. Despite reservations, Lincoln gave Hooker command of the Army of the Potomac on January 26, penning perhaps the most reluctant presidential appointment letter in history. Lincoln penned:

> There are some things in regard to which, I am not quite satisfied with you.... I think that during Gen. Burnside's command of the Army, you have taken counsel of your ambition, and thwarted him as much as you could, in which you did a great wrong to the country, and to a most meritorious and honorable brother officer. I have heard, in such way as to believe it, of your recently saying that both the Army and the Government needed a Dictator. Of course it was not for this, but in spite of it, that I have given you command.[19]

The men of the 72nd trusted Hooker; he was a fighter and had led them to hard-earned glory at Williamsburg and elsewhere on the Peninsula. Many boys believed if earlier matters had been left to the likes of Hooker and Sickles, the army would be in Richmond with the war over. It was the higher-ups, Burnside and the rest back in Washington, who were the guilty ones. Some even pined for George McClellan. Certainly there was plenty of blame to heap on George McClellan, but many 72nd men were fond of their old general, and many held on to the notion of a Republican conspiracy, rather than inept generalship, behind his departure.

Back in Falmouth men hunkered down for winter. Stoddard, Merrell and the rest of the regiment, the brigade, and the whole army for that matter, built winter quarters. These were both of vital necessity and a point of personal pride. Messes of four or more men often combined their efforts toward the construction of dwellings that were water tight and spacious with a functioning fireplace-stove. Many were combination of log hut on bottom and tent canvas on top. All had chimneys, and those with stoves that could draw properly were particularly envied; their builder's design services were sought by other messes. "I have got me a log house built with a fireplace in it. My bed is made out of pole with a little brush on them. I have three men with me now. The Col. told me I had got the best house yet,"[20] boasted Hiram Stoddard. James Dean, who'd only been with Company C since the end of August, noted that the chore of building the quarters was made frustrating by the lack of proper tools. "We had been building little old shanties for 2 or three days which has kept us busy as we had only 4 or 6 axes to the company. I have a hatchet that I pulled out of a dead man's knapsack on the battlefield and I would not part with it for any amount."[21]

Winter quarters meant a time of routine. As the army settled in, Hooker immediately began granting furloughs to help build morale and curb desertions. The New Yorkers waited and wondered when their turn for some time home would come. Picket duty broke up the routine and the waiting while providing relief from the various fatigue duties of camp. Veteran troops like the Excelsiors looked forward to picket duty and the small amount of freedom it offered. The 72nd boys knew what the regulations forbade and also knew just how far they could push things. Conversations and even trade with their Rebel counterparts were outlawed but commonplace, as long as there were no officers about. Dean discovered that many of the Rebels bivouacked across the river were some of the same they'd leveled rifles at back on the Peninsula. Over the weeks they compared stories of the different battles and concluded the whole war could be resolved quicker if the privates and corporals could be left to settle the matter, leaving the generals out of it.[22]

On January 18 the paymaster arrived in camp, long anticipated. It had been months since the boys had been paid, and the paymaster's coming was a welcomed sight. "We were paid 2 months pay yesterday and I have sent 25 dollars home by the express,"[23] wrote James Dean to his parents, adding that collectively his company had sent more than $600 home. Emerson Merrell also sent money home, along with his picture: "There is an artist putting up a tent in our camp and I will have my likeness taken and send it to you." He had been punished by the captain for disobeying orders, he added, "so I am no longer cook ... but that don't trouble me much for I can get along any way."[24]

Winter camp's boredom was broken on February 5 when the division packed up to support a cavalry reconnaissance up the Rappahannock. For three days the boys marched and camped in the snow and rain. After burning a bridge they returned to camp late in the afternoon on the 7th. Later that month, after days of cold and wet, on the night of the 21st orders came that the regiment would be deployed again. This time the brigade was going out on a heavy picket up the river. The next morning, with the regiments formed up behind rows of stacked muskets, men stomped their feet and rubbed numb hands in an effort to maintain circulation amidst the falling snow. Officers meandered through the ranks as men grumbled with wry dissatisfaction but little true anger. Captains and lieutenants no doubt felt the same but kept their comments private lest decorum not be maintained. Eventually the Excelsiors formed a long line of outposts along the Rappahannock. Fires were not permitted, and Colonel Stevens' men endured eight inches of snow overnight, as they camped in small shelter tents, away from the comfort of their winter cabins.[25] While on picket, both Yankee and Reb made concessions to the cold. "By mutual consent on both sides, the pickets do not fire on each other," wrote Private Dean, adding, "The other morning when the relief came around, the Rebels presented arms to us and you would laugh to see them snowballing each other."[26] The expedition had left Sunday morning and by Wednesday had returned to camp with all now persuaded that "camp was a luxurious place."[27]

Emerson Merrell's patience with the war was growing thin. Despite two months' pay, the war's slow progress, the shifting political situation, and the camping in snow, all came to a frustrating conjunction in a February 21 letter to his parents:

> We have some of the d d weather since I wrote last—it comes on and snowed last Tuesday all day and night and rained 24 hours without cessation so you can judge something near what kind of going we are blest with at present. All we have to do is cut wood enough to keep warm and a little camp dutys [sic].... There is two men from the company absent on furloughs and their time is about up and when they get back two more will go and it may be such a thing as I shall be lucky enough to get one—old Joe is doing his best to gain the confidence of the soldiers which he will accomplish to some considerable extint [sic]—but he can never make them what they were when McClellan left them.... Old Abes proclaimation [sic] and Burnside together has made the army a regular gang of dead beasts.... There is 116,000 deserters from the army and a good many more that would cut the same paper if they dared—the people north are taught to believe that we are anxious to fight but it is a d d lie.[28]

One Company A man, George Bailey, saw Lincoln's proclamation as a national double cross and took an almost sadistic glee in the plight of local blacks and what it might bode for the president:

> Uncle Abes free Niggers are catching the very Devil this cold stormy weather. There are thousands of he and she niggers laying out on the ground without any thing to eat. Many of them are sick with the small pox and measles, dying by hundreds. Im glad of it dam em. They might stay with their masters but no, *ise a free niggah sah, ise tastin de sweets ob liberty.* These are dark days for old Virginia, the darkest She ever saw, and who knows how long it is going to last. My christian friend I can arise and say for one it will last as long as Abe Lincoln is president. The old fellow promised when he was on his Electioneering tour, that he would give us all a job, and well has he kept his word. Hes rightly called honest Abe for that if nothing else. But I am afraid the contract will run out before the job is finished.[29]

The camps had always been notorious for spreading disease. Men throughout the regiment continued to die; Charles Hoffman and Anthony

William O. Stevens was the district attorney for Chautauqua County and a militia company commander at the outbreak of the war. Immediately recognized for his competency, Stevens was soon made the regiment's major as the unit coalesced at Staten Island. Stevens eventually rose to the rank of colonel and was mortally wounded at Chancellorsville while maneuvering the regiment to face an enemy threat (courtesy the U.S. Army Heritage and Education Center).

Gardner, both of Company C, were among the more recent. But some sought to exploit their ailments and avoid the trials Emerson and the rest were enduring. "Dick [Richard Lindsey, Co. E] and I have made up our minds to *dead beat* it until warm weather comes and then we are ready to go to the regt.,"[30] wrote George Bailey from his hospital bed in Washington:

> Dick looks quite well now ... but I don't think they will ask him to do any more duty at the regt. if he goes back to it.... I could get mine [a discharge] but I am not able to do anything and I may as well stay here and do nothing for twelve Dollars a month as to come home and do nothing and have it cost me twelve Dollars a month.[31]

Early in March, Stevens sponsored a regimental shooting match. For a month prior, enlisted men of the 72nd engaged in the unusual practice of honing their marksmanship skills. With conventional army wisdom holding that target practice by men more accustomed to firing in massed ranks was a waste of ammunition, this was odd indeed. The competition was held on March 5. Regimental Chaplain Eastman, along with visiting chaplains O'Hagan and Twichell from the 74th and 71st N.Y., respectively, rounded out the umpiring corps. At 10 a.m. they began. Each man came to the line and fired three shots. The target was man-sized, six feet high by 22 inches wide, and was 200 yards distant. After each man fired, the judges took measure. As the competition wore on even General Sickles stopped by to take a shot, though there is no record of his particular results. By the time the 98 competitors had fired their combined 296 shots, only 76 bullets had struck the target and of those, only 22 were within ten inches of center. With judging complete, 23-year-old Pvt. John Bourne of Co. D was declared the winner. His shots averaged about 15 inches from center, earning him the $25 first place prize. Thirty-seven-year-old Pvt. Horace Wilcox of company E took the $15 second prize, while Emerson Merrell got $10 for third place, averaging 17 inches from center with his three shots.[32] As for Stevens' part in the contest, to Private Merrell's satisfaction, "the colonel forked over the money as soon as it was desided."[33]

Hooker had been charged by Lincoln to "go forward and give us victories," and he planned to do just that, but the first thing needed was reorganizing the army in his own image. Among the changes, the most enduring Fighting Joe introduced was the instituting of identifying corps badges. Identification of troops in the field had always been a problem, especially when small units became separated from their brigades or divisions. Merely knowing your side from the enemy wasn't good enough, and Hooker's new system went a long way toward identifying the larger organizations and eliminating confusion. Each corps was assigned a particular shape, unique to them. The I Corps used a sphere, II Corps a trefoil, and the III Corps a lozenge (diamond) and so on. The badge color would denote a particular division: red First, white Second, blue Third and orange Fourth. These colored shapes were incorporated into flags and other unit insignia.[34] Soldiers wore these distinctive badges on their uniforms, and soon the corps badges became a source of pride within the army. Shortly the Excelsiors were proudly wearing their white diamonds indicative of III Corps, Second Division. "Diamonds are trump"[35] was soon a common phrase among these New Yorkers, adorning diaries and letters home.

To keep in touch with friends and family back home, soldiers relied on the mail. Anytime the army stopped for more than just a few hours or was hunkered down in camp, letter writing mushroomed. During the winter of '62–'63, James Dean wrote home frequently. On March 11, James wrote home to two of his younger siblings, David and Agnes, and gave his soldier's perspective about camp routines:

> I received your kind letter and am surprised to see the improvement in your letter writing, you have wrote me a better letter than I expected.... David how would you liked to be raised every morning at sunrise at the beating of the drum to answer at roll call. You then fold up your blanket and go down to the brook and take a wash. Come up and get your cup, go up to the cook house and get your coffee and 4 hard crackers and a piece of fat pork for your breakfast. You then go out on company drill from ten to eleven. You come in then you then have from then till dinner time to yourself then at three you go out on Battalion drill. Then we have evening Parade. Then we have to get our supper then we have to wait till Roll call at 9 o'clock P.M. You then go to bed as I would call it, liable to be called up at any moments. But I have got so used to it that every thing goes on like a well regulated clock.[36]

Emerson Merrill was of course a committed letter writer, but despite his placing in the shooting contest and the improving weather, his view of the national condition continued to be skeptical. By mid–March his tone to his mother reached sarcastic proportions:

> I am well as usual and I am getting to be almost a sececk [psychic]. One glimpse at the past and the prospects of the future and what have we to encourage us [?] The prospects are now that Old Abe will issue a proclamation suspending the law of gravitation as that is the only law now left to us. In the mean time I will introduce a bill into Congress granting straight hair and white skin to all the negroes who take the Oath of Allegiance and Hickman has under contemplating, an act to provide for straight legs and shortning [sic] the heels of free Americans of African descents in order that they may line better in the ranks to soldiers.... In the mean time Senator Sumner will also introduce a measure that will astound the hole [sic] world. He has discovered that every rebel yet taken has been a white man and he has finaly [sic] come to the conclusion that white men and not slavery is the cause of the Rebellion. He proposes, therefore to pass an act declaring that black is the only loyal color and that no man can be an unconditional union man unless he adopts the loyal standard and blacks himself with ink and water. Evry [sic] man refusing this test of loyalty is to be arrested and fined $500 in greenback, to be laid out in Spelling books, Bibles and Black board for the contrabinds [sic]. If he is unrule [sic] and insists upon sticking the rebel color he is to be sent to Fort Lafauette and put on ration of salt junk and Pollywog water.[37]

Spring's onset found Hooker and his men readying for a new offensive. Hooker's basic plan was to bring Robert E. Lee to heel by maintaining a force in front of Fredericksburg while the bulk of his army moved northwest onto Lee's left flank. There the army would cross the Rappahannock River and pass through the small Virginia crossroads known as Chancellorsville and ultimately on to Richmond. Private Dean made an uncanny prediction about the upcoming campaign in a March 30 letter home:

> I do not think that we will attack the Heights of Fredrickburg [sic]. I think that we will cross in three places, he will cross on the right and left of their forces and flank them while he keeps a vigorous attack on their center, but there is no knowing what he will do.[38]

Hooker's plan was set in motion during the last week of April 1863. By the 30th, the Army of the Potomac was on the move, with the various corps converging on Chancellorsville. Major John Leonard of the 72nd New York reported, "On April 28, in pursuance of orders, my command was marched to a point near the river, 3 or 4 miles below Fredericksburg."[39] The regiment continued moving throughout the next two days and by April 30 was encamped in the "immediate vicinity of the United States Ford."[40]

Early on May 1 most of the army was across the river with XI Corps under Gen. Oliver O. Howard making up the Federal right, XII in the middle, V Corps and II Corps on the left, and III Corps in reserve still on the far side. Seventy-Second New York and the rest of the Excelsior Brigade finally crossed the United States Ford sometime around 11 a.m. "We crossed the river above Fredricksburg [*sic*], took the Hights [*sic*] & advanced some eight miles, we crossed the River on the first day of May, one of the prettiest days that ever shone," wrote Hiram Stoddard.[41]

Hooker's plan of attack had been working well. Federal forces had surprised Lee and enjoyed a sizeable numerical advantage as Confederate commanders groped for a solution. Both XII and V Corps had expanded their bridgeheads nicely and were in possession of advantageous ground. But when an expected counterattack by a Confederate division momentarily rocked part of V Corps, Hooker suddenly called a halt to the advance. He ordered corps commanders to assume a defensive posture by pulling back and consolidating positions. Corps commanders protested the order as unwarranted, given their good progress. Hooker now believed his road-bound troops would become isolated, unable to deploy properly if needed and subject to defeat in detail. Hooker told commanders not to worry, preferring to fight Lee on ground of his choosing and entice the Rebels to attack him.[42] Years later, an aide would declare this was the moment the battle was lost.[43]

After crossing the river Colonel Stevens took his regiment and accompanied the rest of the brigade going south. About a mile later they stopped. Halted, many men made coffee and washed their faces and feet to seek relief from the overpowering heat. They resumed marching south, and by late afternoon the 72nd and the rest of III Corps were positioned to support the right of XII Corps engaged with Jackson's Confederates.[44]

Both armies exchanged cannon shots throughout the evening and into the night. Seventy-Second men fired occasional volleys toward the enemy but to no real effect. In the darkness the regiment changed position and eventually the firing subsided, allowing those men in the regiment who could, to sleep. James Dean recalled the days' events:

> We then resumed our line of march till about 3 o'clock when we fired into some woods and the boys had begun to make themselves comfortable for the night when bang bang went the muskets of the pickets and the firing became hotter and hotter till whole volleys were given and then we lay on the ground and the artillery opened and whistled like a good fellow. Then came the word fall in boys, fall in, fall in quick we then marched up the road and then filed into the woods and some of the boys light fires without leave. And as soon as the rebs seen the smoke they commenced the throw shot and shell and you would laugh to see the boys kick out the fires one of the solid shot went clean through the haversack of the man on the left of the company next ours but did no more damage only to spill his coffee and sugar. Our guns then opened on the battery that kept annoying us and the third shot burst one of their caisons [*sic*] that is the box attached to the gun that holds the ammunition they then left us alone for a time.[45]

While Stevens' men slept, Confederate General Lee held a counsel of war with his most trusted lieutenant, Thomas "Stonewall" Jackson. Lee knew he was badly outnumbered and in a difficult position. Only a bold, hard hit against the Yankees could turn things around, so he and Jackson set about formulating such a plan.

With dawn the next day, James Dean, Hiram Stoddard, and the rest of the regiment began building breastworks and cutting slashings in front of their lines. They were now positioned in reserve just south of Hooker's headquarters.

Hooker knew the Confederate army to be mainly on his left, but throughout the morning of May 2 he received sporadic reports of enemy movements across his front and on toward his right. Hooker sent messages warning the XI Corps of the enemy movements. But what Howard did to prepare his corps for an attack remained unclear. Following a request by Sickles, Hooker now allowed two divisions from III Corps, the First under David Birney and

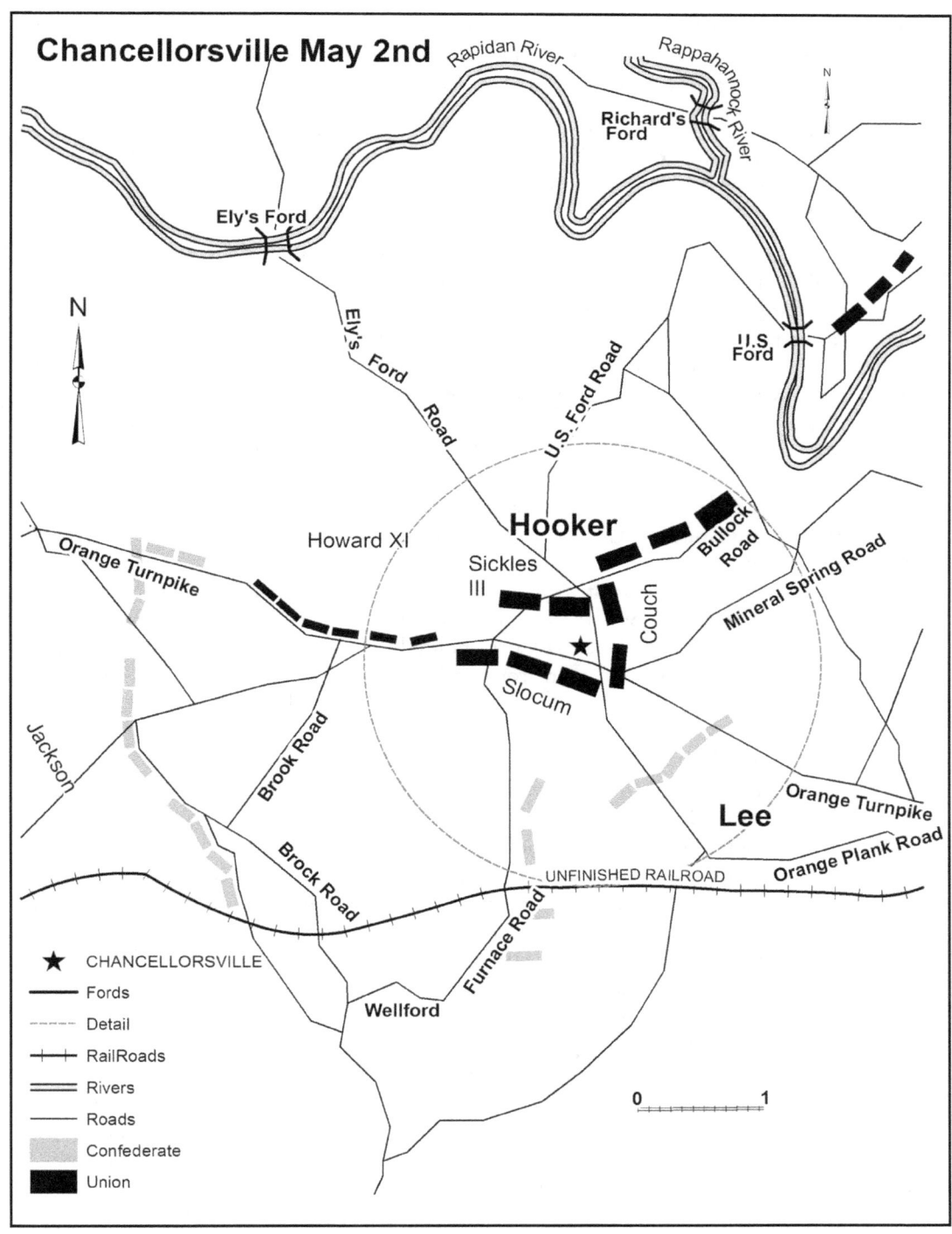

the Third under Amiel Whipple, to move cautiously forward from the corps' central position to see about intercepting some of those traversing enemy troops. This move now effectively extended the Federal line south. Sickles observed:

> This continuous column—infantry, artillery, trains and ambulances—was observed for three hours moving apparently in a southerly direction.... The movement indicated a retreat on Gordonsville or an attack upon our right flank—or perhaps both.... The unbroken mass of forest on our right favored the concealment of the enemy's real design.[46]

With Sickles' First and Third divisions moved south, only the three brigades of the Second Division remained in reserve. Second Division had been commanded by Hiram G. Berry since late November. The 38-year-old Berry was a Maine native with a pedigree that included veterans of both the Revolutionary War and the War of 1812. Before the war Berry had been a bank president, politician and head of the local militia. As colonel of the Fourth Maine Volunteer Infantry, he soon came to the attention of his superiors and eventually rose to major general and divisional command.[47] The three brigades that answered to Berry included the First Brigade, commanded by Brig. Gen. Joseph Carr, composed of the 1st, 11th and 16th Massachusetts, the 11th New Jersey, and the 26th Pennsylvania regiments; the Second Brigade, the Excelsiors, commanded by Revere; and the Third Brigade, or "New Jersey Blues," commanded by Gersham Mott, composed of the 5th through 8th New Jersey, the 2nd New York, and 115th Pennsylvania.[48]

By 5:00 p.m. the Confederate troops, which had been moving all day, were in position. Fifteen minutes later, with only three hours of daylight remaining, Gen. Jackson gave the order. Soldiers of the Confederate II Corps poured through the rough, forested ground, driving wildlife of all kinds before them, routing the wholly unprepared Yankees of XI Corps. As the XI fell back in a panic, word reached Hooker, who called upon his closest troops to stem the flood.

Camped near Hooker's headquarters, Berry's Second Division was ordered to the aid of XI Corps. Hooker had commanded these boys and was confident they would not fail him. The men of the 72nd and the rest of the Excelsiors were rousted from camp and ordered to march at the double quick, leaving their backpacks behind, never to be reclaimed. "Then came the words 'fall in' and we were ordered to leave the knapsacks behind us, some even left their haversack behind them. We went on a double quick for about a mile up the plank road and during that time the eleventh army chore [sic], part of it was giving way,"[49] remembered James Dean. Dean and the whole division were now at the double-quick going west on the Orange Plank Road, straight towards Jackson's Rebel corps.

A short march later, Col. Stevens and his men discovered the whole of the XI Corps retiring in bad order. Jackson's surprise attack had found them cooking supper, completely unprepared for battle, their only hint of the impending storm the bounding deer and scurrying rabbits racing through camp. "We were ordered to proceed up the Fredericksburg and Gordonsville Plank road [also known as the Orange Plank Road], to take a position in rear of the Eleventh Army Corps, which had been repulsed and broken, for the purpose of checking the enemy at that point,"[50] recalled Major John Leonard.

The brigade moved a mile up the road. There, Stevens' boys deployed to the right with 73rd New York going left, forming at right angles to the road. As other regiments arrived they were hastily "dispersed in the thick woods and undergrowth on the right of the Plank Road in a short time, no two regiments joining together,"[51] reported Revere.

"We then filed into the woods and formed into line of battle," remembered Private

Dean. "We had hardly got into the woods and the line formed when we heard the rebs coming on us, we thought, but it was the eleventh army corps flying in every direction ... like a lot of sheep."[52] As XI Corps men stampeded through the lines, Dean and others tried to stop them by using bayonet and saber as needed: "They thought to get through our line but we pricked them with the bayonets and then you would see them run up our lines till they got to the end of it."[53] One XI Corps man said he would stay and fight but ran at his first chance, remembered Dean. "I hollowed for him to come back and I raised my gun on him when our lieutenant [sic] saw him.... He made for him and laid his head open with his sword and took his ear off with the second cut."[54] By early evening the new Federal line was taking shape, comprising the III Corps' Second Division, a few thousand unpanicked stragglers from XI Corps and a single brigade from the II Corps that had also been in reserve. When leading Confederate elements hit the line, their advance stopped. Nightfall and Rebel ransacking of the abandoned XI Corps' camps combined to drain the energy from Jackson's advance. With no immediate threat of attack, the former Chautauqua district attorney Stephens directed his boys to the business of building breastworks. As men readied for a new attack by scrapping together a line using rocks, logs, dirt, anything that would stop a bullet, officers began the business of sorting through the day's events.

With his Excelsior regiments scattered and misaligned, Revere and his staff worked to restore order. "The whole line was moved several times, and the movement of our own regiment confused by contradictory orders.... Finally, late in the evening, the connection of lines was perfected,"[55] reported Lt. Col. Cornelius Westbrook of the 120th New York. Excelsior Brigade now formed a rough semicircle. The First Massachusetts, having been detached from the First Brigade and temporarily attached to the Excelsiors, now rested on the Plank Road. Forming to the right of the First Massachusetts were in order the 74th, 120th, 71st, 70th, and 72nd New Yorks, with the 26th Pennsylvania, also detached from First Brigade, on the extreme right, and the 73rd New York in reserve.[56]

Later, at 2 a.m. on the morning of May 3, Mott's Third Brigade arrived from reserve and was placed south of Plank Road. Second Division was now in place. Revere's Second Brigade composed the front line with its left resting on the road, in contact with Third Maryland, the right end of Williams' division of the XII Corps, which was positioned wholly south of Plank Road. Third Brigade under Mott and First Brigade under Carr formed the second line. Mott was formed on the left of the road and in the rear of the XII Corps men, while Carr was placed 150 paces to the rear of the Excelsiors. Sickles was on the scene and stated complete satisfaction with the division's arrangement.[57]

Night was not easy for Stevens and his New Yorkers. Captain Caspar Abell's Company D was deployed as skirmishers, while the rest of the regiment continued to build up their breastworks of logs, sticks and earth. Frequent alarms drove the pickets in a number of times. The capture of a Confederate captain and 20 enlisted men confirmed to General Revere that "A.P. Hill was in our front, with a large force."[58] It was a brigade of Hill's division, William Pender's North Carolinians, that opposed the Excelsior Brigade. To gain a better understanding of the enemy arrayed before him, Stevens sent forward pickets and a small patrol led by Lieutenant Michael Cooke of E Company.[59]

Confederates also probed the darkness for signs of the enemy. General Jackson himself, while scouting positions in woods opposite the Excelsior's line, was mistakenly fired upon by his own troops. Severely wounded, Jackson was carried from the field, dying a few days after the fight which followed, costing General Lee the man he considered his right hand.

Sporadic fire continued throughout the night and gained strength with the coming of daylight. "We lay in line of battle all night and as the Sabbath morn came in, the pickets in front of our line commenced firing,"⁶⁰ described Pvt. Stoddard. By 6 a.m. the expected Confederate attack was underway. James Dean wrote:

> As the last stick was laid on the works, the pickets began firing and I was out cutting down brush when they came, when the bullets came too thick. For when I got over the works the fighting and the musketry was terrific and the cannon, the sound of shell schreching [sic] and bursting was truly magnificent and sublime although some poor fellows was sent to his long home by every shell.⁶¹

With their pickets driven in and collected behind the line, the battle-hardened veterans of the Excelsior Brigade anticipated the enemy's advance on their prepared positions. With

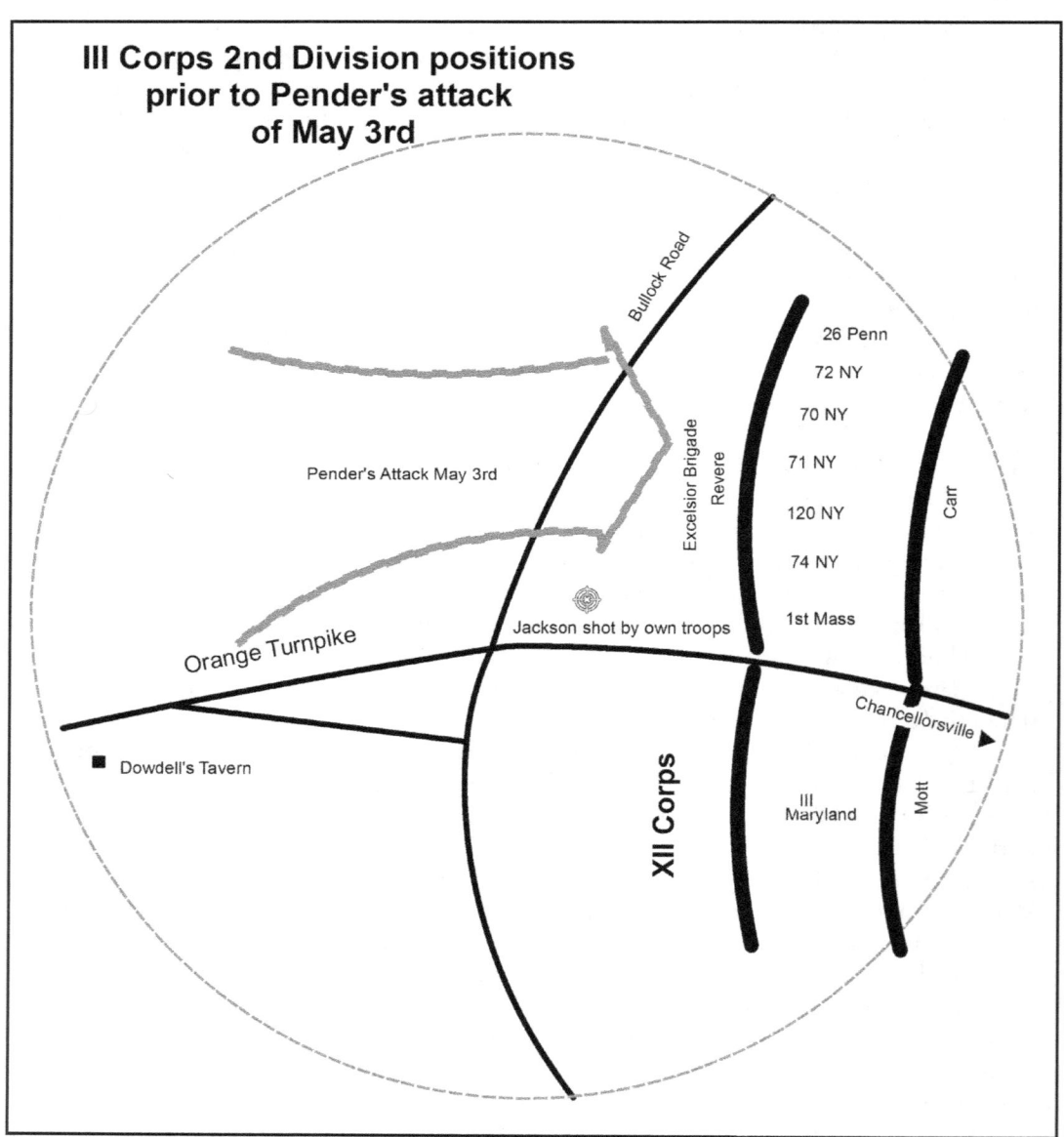

low breastworks and dense forest serving as concealment, the Excelsiors allowed the enemy to move to within 80 paces of their hidden positions. When the order to fire was finally given, Northern bullets ripped into Rebel's troops, first staggering then stopping the enemy advance.[62]

Berry's line was holding well as the fight eventually developed along the whole of the Federal front. Earthworks built by Stoddard, Merrell and others served their purpose well. Excelsior men reloaded under cover, exposing themselves only to shoot on one side while the other absorbed deadly Southern lead. Stevens' men kept up a heavy fire on the Rebels, but for some in or around Company C, the fight was too much and they broke for the rear. Intent on maintaining order, Lt. Charles Hydorn, a Pennsylvanian who'd joined C in the early days as a sergeant and since had worked his way through the ranks, moved after the cowards. Catching the men, he employed his sword. Cutting at least one shirker, he persuaded the others to return to the line. Back on the line a Rebel ball found the lieutenant. Reeling onto his back, Hydorn threw away his pistol and frantically unbuttoned his coat and pants searching for the wound's location, knowing gut wounds were usually fatal. Finding the mortal gash, Hydorn pressed his hands upon his stomach and died, "as brave an officer as was in the service,"[63] remembered Pvt. Dean.

Revere's brigade held the line for better than 45 minutes. As Union men used the shelter of the breastworks to advantage, Rebel troops sought protection among the battlefield's scattered trees and broken ground. Eventually Pender's Carolinians mustered a push that came straight into the face of Third Maryland, XII Corps' right-most regiment. Third Maryland was a veteran outfit, but a number of raw and innocent recruits were fully unprepared for the rush of screaming Rebels. The unnerved journeymen broke first, leaving holes in their company's firing lines.[64] With their line thinned, disgusted Maryland veterans motivated by self-preservation abandoned their posts, setting off a "premature and precipitate withdrawal."[65] Through the resulting gap Pender's men poured. The 115th Pennsylvania was hurried forward from Third Brigade to plug the line, but it was in vain. All the while, General Berry directed the fight from the road. But in the chaos of Pender's attack, an enemy bullet found the division's chief and he fell mortally wounded. As aides rushed to Berry, chief of staff Captain John Poland dispatched a messenger to General Carr "with notice that the command devolved upon him."[66]

Rout of the Marylanders now threatened Revere's left. Sickles' report reflected the desperate situation: "The vigor and tenacity of the enemy's attack seemed to concentrate more and more upon my lines near the Plank road and on my left flank. As fast as their lines were broken by the terrible fire of artillery and musketry, fresh columns were deployed."[67] Enemy troops gushed through the breach, as Excelsiors found increasing numbers of Rebels both on their flank and rear. One by one the regiments began to give way as the brigade's battle line lost integrity. His colonel and major both wounded, Captain Francis E. Tyler now was senior captain and in command of the 74th New York, left-most of the New York regiments. Tyler recalled the critical moment when "the left of the line gave way, entirely exposing our left flank, which rested near the road, and rendering the position we held untenable. It was with great reluctance that I then gave the order to fall back."[68] For many of Tyler's men the fight had been going well, with the enemy kept at bay in their front. They were unaware of the breach on the left, so only reluctantly did they withdraw from their protected positions. Now that the Yankees were in the open, Confederate bullets that before had struck only intervening breastworks hit flesh and bone. General Revere wrote:

> Our gallant soldiers, however, undauntedly returned their fire from behind their low defenses, and defiantly answered their savage yells by hearty cheering, and for several hours maintained their position, when, the enemy having turned our left flank and enfiladed the breastworks, the brigade broke off gradually, regiment after regiment, from the left, and reluctantly yielded their ground to a vastly superior force, which was, however, well punished by our men.[69]

Near the far end of the line, the 72nd continued their desperate fight, somewhat romantically described in the *Jamestown Journal*:

> Early in the morning the enemy attacked a slight breastwork of logs that our boys had erected during the night, had driven back part of the brigade and were rushing over the works and pouring a raking storm of death on the brave 72d. They were also gaining their rear. Col. Stevens, cool, unappalled, fearless, was arranging his men to meet the new exigencies of this enfilading fire along the whole of his regiment in the midst of a perfect hell of fire and death, waving his sword and cheering his men to face the tempest of bullets.[70]

To meet the increasingly dangerous threat on his left, Stevens began to change the facing of the regiment. He ordered, "Change front to the rear on the first company! Boys follow me!"[71] Stevens then turned partially around to lead his men and was struck through the chest by an enemy ball. Pressing his hand to his breast, Stevens exclaimed, "O, God!" and fell. Lieutenant Henry Yates of Co. D immediately attended to Stevens, who lay unconscious under the lethal Confederate cross fire. Captain Samuel Bailey of Co. I and Captain Harmon Bliss of Co. G struggled to bear their beloved colonel to safety, but the situation was too far gone. With the enemy swarming over their position, Bliss, who had led the regiment at Kettle Run, was struck and severely wounded as he attended his colonel. As Stevens lay wounded with the other officers, command devolved to Major John Leonard, who struggled to keep the regiment together. As the 72nd line continued to recede before the Rebel tide, Stevens, Bliss and the other wounded or disabled men were reluctantly left to the enemy. Becoming prisoners, they were at once removed to the Confederate rear.[72]

With enemy troops swarming over the regiment's position and the fighting now hand to hand, Confederate trophy-hunters became intent on seizing the regimental colors. Thomas Auldridge was the color sergeant this day. Auldridge had started the war with the 73rd New York, comprising mainly New York City firemen, but had transferred to the 72nd's Company K.[73] In the swirling fight, four Rebs in succession made grabs for the flags and each was cut down in the process. The situation was too hot and Auldridge knew it. Tearing the colors from their staff, he stuffed them inside his coat and made his way to the rear. Sgt. James Anderson of Co. F, posted behind the colors, recognized the situation, gathered up the staff and followed the colors out. Beyond the reach of the enemy, staff and colors were reunited and Third Excelsior's flag flew again.[74]

"They threw a very heavy force on the left of our Brigade and broke through the line and got on our flank and in that way our Regt. suffered a cross fire. But we hung on to them till our little Col. Stevens was killed and the orders came for us to fall back out of the woods,"[75] remembered Pvt. Stoddard.

Over in Company H the situation for Lucius Jones and his mates was no less desperate. "It seemed all over with us, and our prospects for Rebel prison was very flattering,"[76] remember Lucius. With New Yorkers and Carolinians completely mixed, Rebels demanded Yankee surrender. In a desperate moment of democracy, the choice being surrender or potential death, H's Captain John W. Holmes asked his men what they intended to do. When word came back that all would stick with their captain and make a run for it, "we took leg bail and started—the Rebels after us."[77] Running pell-mell through the woods, two of Jones'

Company were overtaken and made prisoner, but speed and Yankee cannon worked to save the rest. "As we came to the open field we could see our artillery on the other side. When we got almost across we were signaled to lie down,"[78] recalled Jones. "In a moment we were flat on our faces. Hell seemed to let loose over our heads, and the ranks of the pursuers seemed fairly to vanish. We were saved, but not the battle."[79]

Retreating, the men supported a battery of Federal cannon that fired upon the advancing Confederate ranks. As the enemy continued to follow, the artillery played upon their ranks, halting their advance. The fighting was among dried leaves and brush, and embers from the exploding shot and shell soon set the woods on fire, burning both corpses and the immobile wounded alike. James Dean described what he saw:

> The troops on our left then gave way when we cheered them to their works and they fired a few more volleys but the rebels marched up in coloms [sic] 4 or 5 deep and got over the works on our left and the first thing we knew was we were receiving a fire on our flank. We then had to run and it was then we lost a good many men. We fell back to our old breast works and as soon as they drove out of site [sic], our artillery open on them and must have mowed them down by the hundreds. The woods was set on fire by the artillery and all the wounded must have been burnt to ashes that could not get out.[80]

With Berry dead, Carr continued to fight the Rebel advance, though both ammunition and his men's nerves were giving out. Seventh New Jersey, part of Mott's Brigade, took itself out of the line, marching their 400 men far to the rear. To Carr, the timing could not have been worse; he wrote, "At this critical period of the engagement, he [commander Col. Louis Francine] could illy be spared, and the loss of his men was severely felt."[81]

Severely outnumbered, the various brigades began falling back. Revere, thinking he was now the division's senior officer, took matters into his own hands. The brigade was becoming more disorganized, so around 8 a.m. Revere took the 73rd New York and nearly 600 stragglers from "almost every regiment in the division"[82] under tow. He then sought instruction from General William French, commanding a division of II Corps, as to the best place to employ his small force. Directed to a line of abatis and breastworks, Revere found the position full of troops and reasoned any additional would be "superfluous." The area was covered with troops, and Revere noticed a constant stream of men heading to the rear. He "decided to intercept them by striking a straight course by compass through the woods from that point toward the ford."[83]

Men couldn't understand why they were being pulled out and moved to the rear while the fight was here, the popular view holding that the Excelsiors had never run from a fight. Subordinate officers quietly questioned the wisdom of marching to the rear,[84] while others recognized they could better intercept the fleeing men from a position further in the rear and that they "had an opportunity for rest and a meal."[85]

When in position nearly three miles in the rear, Revere sent out officers from all the regiments present to collect up stragglers. By noon his command numbered barely 1,700 men, representing nine separate regiments. With Lt. Col. Austin still absent, Major Leonard was in charge and could account for only 204 of the more than four hundred 72nd men who had taken the field. This number slowly increased as they were resupplied with ammunition, rested and refreshed, getting them ready to again "take the field," though only about half the brigade was present.[86]

With Revere's pull-out, the entire division began to crumble. Facing "galling fire from the enemy's artillery,"[87] Carr moved his division back. Locating Sickles, Carr was directed to position his men in support of Whipple's Third Division.

Overall the battle was going poorly for the Army of the Potomac. Enemy attacks and the collapse of the XI Corps had shaken Hooker's offensive spirit, and he now saw the battle strictly in defensive terms. Early in the day's battle, Sickles' First and Third divisions found themselves defending the only real piece of high ground on the battlefield, a place called Hazel Grove, south of Plank Road. The Hazel Grove position was effectively dividing the Rebel assault, preventing the enemy from presenting a unified front against Hooker's right flank. Sickles argued in favor of holding this ground, but Hooker ordered him to withdraw, worried the position would become isolated and cut off from the rest of the army. As Sickles reluctantly removed his two divisions, Confederates scrambled to occupy the newly vacated high ground. Soon several batteries of Southern cannon were firing down on surrounding Union positions, positions occupied primarily by Sickles' men, who only minutes before had held the grove. Not long after the order came to vacate Hazel Grove, Union efforts were dealt another heavy blow. A well-placed Rebel cannon ball shattered a porch column of the house used by Hooker as headquarters. The ball struck near where Hooker was standing, having just receiving a message from an aide. Flying timber struck the commanding general, dazing him severely. Essentially incapacitated and unable to command effectively, he nonetheless refused to transfer command to subordinates. While some of his corps commanders urged him to counterattack with the several unengaged divisions at his disposal, Hooker instead ordered withdrawal.[88]

Both the right flank and center of the Union lines fell back under strong pressure from the Confederates. But despite the lack of decisive leadership from Hooker, Union defensive positions gradually improved. Good defensive ground combined with a consolidation of men and artillery to help stall the Rebel advance. By mid-afternoon Federal lines were holding. At 2:30, with the heaviest of the fighting over, Revere brought his brigade, now 2,000 men strong, back to the front. Upon reporting to his corps commander, the wayward brigadier was promptly relieved of duty by the livid Sickles. Colonel J. Egbert Farnum of the 70th New York then took command of Second Brigade.[89] Revere felt justified in his action and claimed the support of at least a few of his officers. Yet Sickles would still conclude, "Brigadier-General Revere, ... heedless of their murmurs, shamefully led to the rear the whole of the Second Brigade and portions of two others, ... thus subjecting these proud soldiers for the first time to the humiliation of being marched to the rear while their comrades were under fire."[90] Colonel Farnum recalled, "At about 3 p.m. the same day, I was officially informed that General Revere was relieved from duty, and then the command of the brigade devolved upon me, whereupon I assumed command, and Lieutenant-Colonel Holt took command of the regiment."[91]

Sometime that afternoon, Corporal George Tate of Company D woke up to find himself a prisoner. Wounded and rendered unconscious during the heaviest of the morning's fight, Tate and others were at Dowdall's Tavern, now about one mile in the Confederate rear. Among the Union wounded and captured was Colonel Stevens. Recognizing the colonel's condition as mortal, Tate, and the others who could, worked to comfort their chief. Throughout the remainder of Sunday and into the next day the men did what they could for Stevens. Finally, around 8 p.m. on Monday the 4th, Stevens slipped away. Grief stricken, Tate and others from the regiment dutifully buried their beloved colonel near Old Wilderness Church, taking special care to mark the grave for future identification should a later opportunity come to move him.[92]

By the end of the 4th, fighting around Chancellorsville was mostly over. "We laid the next day at the breast works and were not disturbed only by an occasional shell,"[93] recalled

James Dean. By 3 a.m. on the morning of the 5th, the remaining men of the regiment began marching north. Heavy rains turned the roads into an "awful condition,"[94] but by five o'clock that afternoon they reached the camp they had left only a week earlier.[95]

Major John Leonard later reported that of the 29 officers and 411 enlisted men of the 72nd New York who had gone into action at Chancellorsville, 104 were either, killed, wounded or listed as missing, one-fourth of the entire command. Among them were their commander, Colonel Stevens, and the highly respected Captain Bliss. Bliss, an integral fixture within the regiment, was held by the enemy until the 13th, when he was released and placed in the III Corps hospital.[96] The fight cost three lieutenants including Hydorn, William Brooks of Co. F, and Harrison Ellis of Co. K. Of the three winners of the March shooting contest, only John Bourne survived unscathed. Horace Wilcox was captured in the battle. Once paroled, Wilcox deserted six weeks later. Emerson Merrell, the oldest of ten children from upstate New York, was among the dead. His body was never identified, and Emerson was eventually interred in one of the mass graves used to bury the large number of unidentified dead.[97]

The Army of the Potomac was once again repulsed. The various regiments began to look toward their own well-being. A detachment from the 72nd New York was formed on May 13 to search for the missing and wounded under agreement with the Confederates. It was headed by surgeon Charles Irwin and regimental chaplain William Eastman. While searching the battlefield they learned the details of the death of their beloved Col. Stevens and his burial place. Men throughout the regiment wept at the news. Stevens' body was removed from its Wilderness Church grave and brought across the United States Ford by ambulance. There, the Colonel's father, Judge William Stevens met it. On May 14, Stevens' body was taken under regimental escort to Stoneman's Switch, where it then proceeded home to Dunkirk and final burial a few days later at nearby Fredonia.[98]

Hooker's army eventually retreated back to the north side of the United States Ford. Their offensive, intended to end the war, had lasted less than two weeks. The Excelsior Brigade suffered over 300 killed, wounded, and missing during the Chancellorsville campaign. This number was far less, however, than either of the other two brigades within III Corps' Second Division, whose losses exceeded 500 each. Of the six regiments under Revere, 72nd New York's losses were heaviest.[99]

With his corps safely back north, Dan Sickles turned his attention to Gen. Joseph W. Revere. Not satisfied to relieve Revere of his command, Sickles leveled charges and instituted court-martial proceedings. The charges centered on Revere's acting without orders and subjecting Sickles' former brigade, the Excelsiors, to the "humiliation" of being marched to the rear. Revere argued that his command had become scattered and disorganized. He said he intended to withdraw the command, rebuild its numbers, feed, rest, and rearm them, and then return to the field as a potent fighting force. Because he had done this without orders, the court-martial board found him guilty, sentencing him to a disgraceful dismissal from the service. Hooker was quick to endorse the dismissal order, lest there be too few scapegoats.[100] But soon after the court-martial, Revere campaigned to regain some shred of his reputation. Eventually none other than President Abraham Lincoln interceded on the defrocked general's behalf. Though it is unclear what motivated the decision—perhaps interest in minimizing the political damage from the Chancellorsville debacle—Lincoln revoked the dismissal in exchange for the general's resignation, which was accepted on August 10, 1863. So sure was Revere of the rightness of his action that before the year was out he published a 50-page pamphlet complete with maps and transcripts from the court-martial in a further attempt at self-exoneration.[101]

With Revere out and his reputation in tatters, command of Excelsior Brigade devolved to Colonel William Brewster of the 73rd New York. Brewster had been with the brigade since the beginning and would be there during some of its most desperate hours.

Back in camp a meeting of the regiment was held on May 18. Chaired by Col. Brewster, a letter of praise for Col. Stevens and condolence to his family was drafted. Expressing their grief over his loss and the heroic nature of his leadership, the letter was submitted to various newspapers throughout New York state and elsewhere, a symbol of the regiment's sense of loss and devotion to their fallen comrade:

> In the loss of Colonel William O. Stevens, the regiment and the army has been deprived of the services of a most gallant and efficient officer, an accomplished gentleman and true patriot, who has sealed with his life his devotion to his country, and our highest aspirations for the future shall be to emulate the noble example of fidelity to trust that he has bequeathed to us…. To the afflicted family, in their bereavement, words of condolence and sympathy are all we can bestow; our loss has been great, theirs has been greater … realizing that though he sleeps, his memory will not be forgotten, but will descend to posterity with names of the illustrious dead, which a grateful country will render immortal.[102]

Newspapers throughout New York reported the death of Stevens, but the loss was especially deep-felt in Dunkirk and Jamestown, where he and Captain Bliss were looked upon as a home-town heroes. The *Jamestown Journal* invoked the words of Shakespeare's *Julius Caesar* in reporting on the life of Stevens and of his funeral attended by 5,000 mourners:

> Brave soldier! Noble man! Glorious martyr! Pride of thy country! We will weep over his grave and cherish his memory when stone and "enduring brass" moulder…. His character, combining all the nobility of nature with the accomplishments of culture … so mixed in him, that Nature might stand up and say to all the world—THIS WAS A MAN![103]

With their colonel now dead, the officers of the 72nd looked to the regiment's founder as its next commander. At a regimental meeting, it was decided Nelson Taylor, the now retired, original commander of the 72nd, should be asked to come back and assume the role of colonel. In a letter dated May 26, the men of the Third Regiment and the Excelsior Brigade did "earnestly request," that Taylor "assume the duties and become our commander." The letter was signed by Lt. Col. John Austin, Major Leonard, and captains Caspar Abell and John Sandford.[104]

Taylor wrote on May 29 that while he was flattered by the offer and gratified to be so favorably remembered, circumstances were such that he must "forego the acceptance of your generous offices."[105] He thus declined to again command the 72nd, trusting the position would be more ably filled by an officer still with the regiment. That officer was Lt. Col. John Austin, who was promoted to full colonel and to command of the 72nd, backdated to May 4, the day of Stevens' death. As for Captain Harmon Bliss, he would linger for a month, finally succumbing to his wounds on June 6.[106]

Within days of the first shots at Chancellorsville, Hooker's defeated army was back in camp at Falmouth. The campaign to end the war that had looked so good on paper and had prompted the over-confident Hooker to crow that the Confederate Army was now his "legitimate property"[107] was over. Hooker was shaken and unsure, uncertain of the army's next move. But despite his army's losses, Robert E. Lee was sure and confident and now cast a covetous eye north, away from war-ravaged Virginia and to the rich, unspoiled farmlands of Pennsylvania.

10. Gettysburg

The march back to Falmouth only took a few hours. There was a great relief that the Confederates had not pursued or shelled the river crossings as the Union corps jammed the approaches. No one had expected to return to Falmouth, so most camps had been razed before they left; now they had to be built again. The new camps were located a short distance from the old sites. Wood supplies had long been worn out, and fresh sinks were imperative. The Excelsiors welcomed their new site atop a small hill that caught refreshing, cool breezes. With spring's warmer weather settling in, men wouldn't need the elaborate winter-proof cabins they had built before; the lighter canvas tents would be just fine.[1]

James Dean and the rest were anxious to let parents know they had made it through the big Chancellorsville fight. A fourth of the regiment had been killed or become missing or wounded since just a few days before. Within ten days of the battle, Dean had already sent three letters home and was restless to get a reply. With many of Third Excelsior's officers either killed or wounded, there commenced the great shuffling and promoting of company lieutenants and captains that had always followed other bad fights. Twenty-four-year-old Charles Foss, first sergeant of Company D, was now promoted to second lt. of Company C. New Jersey man Luke Healy, who was top sergeant with Company F, was now made second lt. of Company G. Sergeant Major John McKinley was promoted to second lt. and assigned to Company K. William E. Wheeler was promoted to captain and moved to Company D following the promotion of Casper Abell to major. With the death of Colonel Stevens, Lt. Col. John Austin was moved up to full colonel, with Major John Leonard being promoted to lieutenant colonel.[2] Much of the day-to-day running of the regiment fell to Leonard, and he commanded with the common touch that Austin lacked. Immediately after their return to Falmouth, Leonard kept the drilling to a minimum, which was deeply appreciated by the men.[3]

For Dean, the men of Company C, and the others on the various company streets, newspaper reports of the battle had been sketchy at best. They knew they had taken a beating, as had the entire III Corps. Only Sedgwick's VI Corps, which attacked independently from the east through Fredericksburg, had gotten it worse, but then only barely.[4] Two of the III Corps' three divisional commanders, Hiram Berry and Amiel Whipple, were dead. Most men hadn't seen the papers but heard the conduct of the Excelsiors was reported as exemplary. "We have not seen the *New York Herald* since the battle, they say it runs down Hooker terrible and gives Sickles great praise,"[5] commented Dean. Indeed the *Herald* article would go on to describe the "Valor of the Excelsior Brigade," which "fought like tigers wherever placed,"[6] clearly distinguishing the high conduct of the troops from the cowardly performance of General Revere.

Unlike Revere, the New Yorkers liked Hooker; after all, he was their old divisional commander who had led them well back on the Peninsula. Plus, he reportedly wore the white diamond corps badge of his old outfit.[7] But if the Excelsiors had fully appreciated the extent of his recent failings, their opinion might have changed. The unsupported fight along Chancellorsville's Plank Road and resulting retreat by Revere smacked of a second Williamsburg. Again, thousands of Federal troops had rested and waited without orders, within striking range of the enemy, while the Excelsiors bled. Unlike Williamsburg, where Hooker had begged superiors for help, this time it was Fighting Joe who, despite urging from his top generals, ordered withdrawal and consolidation rather than advance and exploitation. After the fight even Hooker admitted he had "lost confidence in Joe Hooker,"[8] but once safely across the river it didn't take Fighting Joe long to regain much of his old bravado. Hooker circulated a flier extolling the quality of the army's performance and how it had "inflicted heavier blows than we have received"; he added, "We lost no honor at Chancellorsville."[9] The flier even questioned whether events of May 2 through 6 could be called a full-fledged battle at all. This blusterous tone had many who experienced the fight pondering where Hooker had been the past few days.[10]

Hooker's reputation was in ruins with both the government and senior commanders. His position as head of the Army of the Potomac was on the shakiest of ground. Rumors circulated that Hooker would soon be arrested, and even Secretary Stanton had resigned over the fiasco. But for now, Hooker kept his job while the army sorted itself, especially the ravaged III Corps.

Revere had been sacked, and command of the Excelsior Brigade devolved to Colonel William R. Brewster of the 73rd New York. Brewster had been born in Connecticut and was 35 when the war broke out, working as a revenue agent in New York City. With no formal military training, he initially served with a three-month regiment, guarding bridges over the Potomac River at the time of Bull Run. Eventually he was named colonel of the 73rd New York, one of the original Excelsior Brigade units. Brewster led Fourth Excelsior in battle at Williamsburg back in May of 1862, but for reasons unexplained, he was not with the regiment later that month at the Fair Oaks battle and was still absent while the Seven Days' Battles raged in late June and early July. Brewster was again absent for his regiment's tribulations during Second Bull Run; the official report cryptically mentioned he "had been left in Alexandria."[11] But he rejoined it immediately after the fighting. The Connecticut colonel was present for Fredericksburg, but his regiment did not participate in any fighting, and during the recent fighting at Chancellorsville, Brewster had once again been absent. A disturbing and unflattering pattern of absenteeism was emerging.[12]

While the Excelsiors got used to the familiar Brewster in his new role as brigade commander, the Second Division was getting a commander entirely new to the corps. Andrew A. Humphreys was a lifelong soldier, demanding, profane and professional. After finishing in the middle of his 1831 class at West Point, Humphreys eventually made a name for himself in the Topographical Engineers, writing an important treatise about the Mississippi River. In 1861 he was assigned to McClellan's staff, where he served until just before Antietam, when he was given command of a division in the new V Corps. Though held in reserve at Antietam, his division saw heavy action at Fredericksburg, where Humphreys grew his reputation as someone who pushed his troops hard yet always led from the front. After Chancellorsville, Humphreys' division, made up mostly of ninety-day enlistments, disbanded. The hard-swearing general was then moved to Sickles' III Corps and given Second Division on May 23, becoming the only West Pointer in the corps.[13]

> *Received from the Committee on National Affairs of the Common Council of the City of New York, the Stand of Colors for the 72nd Regiment, N. Y. S. Volunteers, forwarded to me per Adam's Express, by said Committee.*
>
> *Dated Camp Nelson Taylor*
> *Falmouth Va June 5th 1863.*
>
> *John S. Austin Colonel,*
> *72nd Reg't, N. Y. S. Vol.*

Colonel Austin received via Adam's Express a replacement stand of regimental colors just before the march north to counter Confederate moves into Pennsylvania and the resulting fight at Gettysburg (Third Excelsior Association).

In camp the men continued their routine duties. Many caught up on both reading and writing letters home. James Dean had recently received a letter containing a photograph of his beloved little sister, Maggie:

> I received your kind and welcomed letter containing the stamps and likeness of little Maggie and she looks so sweet and natural that I have had the card out 50 times since I received it, I hope you will send me another.... I carry them in ... the pocket of my cartridge box and never lose sight of them.[14]

By the end of May, regimental life around Falmouth had returned to normal. Both Yankees and Rebs stared at each other across the intervening Rappahanock. Men resumed picket duty and enjoyed both the cooling breezes of their hilltop camp and Leonard's light drill schedule. Some did more than just stare at their enemies, however. "We have been out on picket," wrote Dean, "and I suppose you will hardly believe that I was over and took dinner with them and they came over and took dinner with us. I had dinner with a capt. of the 9th Ala. Regiment. They are a bully lot of boys, they seem to want the war at an end."[15] While camp life and their current arrangements with the Rebels were quite satisfactory, many of the boys anticipated another movement soon, but where was a guess.

Lincoln always placed a priority on the defense of Washington and required his commanding general do the same. This rationale was sound; if the capital were to fall, how could the government then claim legitimacy? Whatever movement the Army of the Potomac undertook, it must always maintain itself in position, ready to defend the capital. The current position of the army at Falmouth provided for this part of the strategic equation. This was a good base from which to launch a move toward Richmond. It also allowed the army to move north to interpose itself between an enemy advance and Washington. Hooker pondered the many reports that Lee was planning some sort of invasion of the north. Fighting Joe was sure the expected enemy movement would be up the Shenandoah Valley and out of the defenses they now occupied. Hooker saw this as a great opportunity to cross the river and move against Richmond. War planners back in Washington, however, were cool to such a notion for fear of leaving the capital open to attack. Hooker had other problems besides the movement of Lee. The size of his army would soon be greatly reduced through the expiration of thousands of enlistments. He now faced the prospect of fighting a major action with even less of a numerical advantage than he had had when he was whipped at Chancellorsville.[16] Additionally, Hooker was in great peril for his job. Senior generals and some prominent newspapers were pounding the drum for Hooker's head. Criticisms that Hooker had earlier heaped upon McClellan and Burnside were now being leveled back at him. Among Hookers' many detractors was the *Herald* of New York. While at the same time it called for the sacking of Hooker, it praised Sickles as the only man with enough offensive spirit to lead the army.[17]

On June 4 the situation along the Rappahannock became clearer. Hooker had learned from observers in balloons that some of the enemy camps around Fredericksburg had been abandoned. Hooker proposed to promptly attack those Confederate troops left behind. The plan was thwarted, however, within an hour of its being telegraphed to Washington. Lincoln wired Hooker warning of the perils of an attack against a fortified enemy on the far side of the river while another enemy force of an unknown strength operated on the near side. The president concluded that such a move could result in the army's being "entangled upon the river, like an ox jumped half over a fence and liable to be torn by dogs front and rear, without a fair chance to gore one way or kick the other."[18]

Frustrated and confused as to his next course of action, Hooker received information that the Confederate cavalry under Jeb Stuart was concentrating near Culpepper, about 20 miles northwest of Falmouth. Hooker sent his cavalry, now under the command of Alfred Pleasonton, to investigate. The resulting battle on June 9 near Brandy Station was the biggest cavalry battle fought in North America and helped provide another clue to Robert E. Lee's intentions. Hooker now ordered his army to prepare to march, but the direction of that march, either south toward Richmond or north toward Washington, was yet unknown. In a letter to his brother, James Dean speculated:

> We are now under marching orders and have 3 days rations in our haversack ready to move at a moments notice. We have been called upon three times and stack arms but the orders were countermanded. The Bulldog were barking the other eveing [*sic*] and I thought the ball had opened. I think the rebels are going to make a raid on a large scale into Maryland. I do think Hooker does not know which way to move. I hope he does not try to take the heights of Fredericksburg again.[19]

By the tenth, the War Department was making preparations for a possible Confederate raid into Pennsylvania by alerting outposts in northern Virginia and Maryland. Hooker was still unconvinced Lee intended to take his whole army north and believed the real Union opportunity lay in an attack against Richmond, a city that Federal commanders now believed was defended by as few as 1,500 men. Hooker reasoned that once Richmond was captured he could reverse course and march north to deal with the rest of Lee's army, sure the defenses of Washington could hold until then. Lincoln quickly ordered Hooker not to go to Richmond, insisting the destruction of Lee's army was to be the general's objective. On the 11th the picture of a northward movement grew even clearer as reports came in of more and more

Rebel units concentrating near Culpepper. Hooker had to act. That afternoon the Excelsiors were in the last hours of preparations to move. "We are on the wing," wrote Chaplain Twichell, "our tents are struck, the baggage with three days rations is packed, we are only waiting for the men who went on picket this morning to return; then we will start."[20] By three the next morning the men of the 72nd and all the Excelsiors were roused. For two hours the camps were abuzz with activity as men sorted and packed gear, rolled tents, and put on leathers. By five, Captain Mann had formed his Company C and was moving it to the color line. There, they joined the other captains and companies of the regiment. William Wheeler had commanded Company D for only a month now, since Caspar Abell's promotion to major. Over in Company G, Patrick Anderson stood with his boys, transferred there just a few days earlier after the death of Harmon Bliss.[21] After the usual commotion, at 7 a.m. on the 12th, the men stepped off in pursuit of Robert E. Lee's Army of Northern Virginia.

A stand of new colors flew at the head of the regiment, recently arrived from New York, a gift from the Common Council of the City of New York. They had arrived a few days earlier, on the sixth, via Adam's Express, signed for by Colonel Austin, who now proudly rode at the front of the regiment.[22] Austin came to Third Excelsior as captain of Company K, one of three companies from New York City. Employed as a clerk prior to the war, Austin was active in the rough and tumble world of New York City politics, namely as a prominent member of the Empire Club. Though never seeking office himself, Austin wasn't above getting his hands dirty in support of his favorite candidate or fellow Empire Club member. Throughout the 1840s and '50s Austin earned the reputation as a man at ease using either a knife or pistol, ready to produce both should circumstances warrant. For his part in disrupting a Tammany Hall meeting, the local authorities granted him a three-month stay at the penitentiary on Blackwell Island. And in 1848 Austin stood trial for murder, though he was ultimately found innocent in the death of one Timothy O'Shea.[23]

At 44, Austin was among the oldest men to enroll in the regiment, and his time with Third Excelsior was far from exemplary. From December of 1861 to June of 1862 Austin served double duty as brigade quartermaster and as captain of Company K, presiding over a company that led the regiment in desertions.[24] Whether the desertions were Austin's fault or due to the nature of his New York City recruits is unclear, but his problems didn't stop there. Austin's record of attendance with the regiment had been spotty at best. He was away from the regiment recruiting in August of '62 and then listed as sick from January to April of '63, suffering from a long history of bladder and prostate problems. Additionally, there is no mention of him in the after-action report from Chancellorsville written by Leonard, a strong indication he was absent from this action too. Just days before the army left Falmouth to pursue the Rebels, on June 7, Austin was summoned by Brig. Gen. Joseph Carr. Austin was to stand at court-martial the following day "for the purpose of examining into the alleged absence of leave of Lieut. Col. John S. Austin."[25] But given the hectic state of affairs, it is likely the whole issue was forgotten or dismissed since there is no record of the trial's outcome or if it was even held. Right now Austin needed to move his men; the worries of a court-martial would have to wait.

Austin and the rest covered 12 miles that day as the army sorted itself out on its race north. Camped northwest of Falmouth, the regiment was moving again by 4:30 the next morning. The trek was hot and dirty as Dean and his mates breathed the rising clouds of fine dust churned up by a thousand marching feet. As the dust settled it clung to the men's countless rivulets of sweat and penetrated their throats and lungs. The New Yorkers traveled well into the night, finally coming to a halt near Rappahannock Station on the Orange and

Alexandria Railroad. Men dropped where they stood, utterly spent from their 21-mile march. The next morning the boys were rousted early as the regiment marched out several miles and placed into picket where they spent the day. Around 7:30 that evening the regiment was called in, rejoining the division to continue a night march north.[26]

The regiment followed the tracks of the Orange and Alexandria R.R., the same line that had formed the axis of the fighting back in the summer of '62 when the boys fought under Pope, chased the Rebels at Kettle Run, and then suffered defeat at Second Bull Run. It was Monday morning, June 15, around seven o'clock, when the Excelsiors finally stopped after marching ten miles to Cedar Run. The morning sun was already broiling as the men slept and ate. The rest was short lived. At 1:30 p.m. the order to fall in was given and the regiment was moving again. The march went deep into the night and men fell out all along the route. "The poor fellows lay stretched all along the road choked [sic] and panting, and many a one was sun-struck,"[27] observed chaplain Twichell. So struck was Twichell by the scene of suffering that he thought it immoral to ride while so many trudged along in agony, indeed offering his mount to others, "most of the way I yielded him to some one of my parishioners feebler than myself."[28] By eleven that evening, the column finally halted at Manassas for the night. As the brigade slept, stragglers trickled into camp, so by morning there were surprisingly few still unaccounted for.

Foss, Healy, and the other new officers pushed their companies throughout the day of the 17th toward Centerville, the focal point of the Federal retreat after the Second Bull Run battle the previous August. Rain showers had been frequent, but this day had been dry and proceeding troops had "thoroughly pulverized"[29] the dirt road to a depth of two or three inches. The resulting clouds of dust once again enveloped the men as they marched. A hot sun beat down heavily on the men as they panted in the choking dust. Men were covered in dust; it penetrated every seam and flap, filled their shoes and coated the contents of haversacks and backpacks. All along the route men fell out of the clanking columns and sank onto the arid field, completely spent. That night they reached Centerville and stopped. All through the night and into the next day stragglers made their way into the camps, restoring the already shrunken companies. When word came that the brigade would remain a second night, a wave of relief swept the ranks. "We rested at Centerville two nights and never was rest more grateful,"[30] wrote one Excelsior man.

On June 19 the regiment and the rest of the brigade marched over to Gum Springs, about ten miles west of Centerville. Here they camped for several days as the regiments rotated through picket duties. Eventually on the morning of the 25th the division was on the move again. Six companies of the 72nd were now detailed to act as guard for the slow moving divisional wagon train, while another two were assigned elsewhere.[31] By four that afternoon the brigade had covered the 13 miles north to Edward's Ferry, which lay on the Potomac. The day's march was going well as the men moved easily in welcome coolness. At the ferry, they trundled across a pontoon bridge, crossing into Maryland. Along this stretch of the Potomac ran the Chesapeake and Ohio Canal, which paralleled the Potomac for nearly 200 miles, from Washington into central Maryland. On the north side of the river, men followed a narrow tow path that ran between the two waterways. Around five a summer shower set in, soaking man and beast. The tow path used to pull canal boats was mostly clay, slippery under dry conditions, but now the rain only served to heighten the march's difficulty. Reaching the mouth of the Monocacy River at 11 p.m. the division went into camp. But the wagon train was lagging far behind and hadn't even reached Edward's Ferry until 5:30 p.m. At the ferry crossing, the tardy column was then cut off from the division by the passage of the I Corps.

By the time other corps had passed it was three the next morning. Eventually the wagon train made it to Point of Rocks where the six companies were relieved from guard duty and reunited with the rest of the regiment. Newly minted lieutenant Foss and the rest continued north with the column throughout the 27th, stopping about two miles south of Middletown, where they camped for the night.[32]

While III Corps was moving north there were great changes within the army command. Hooker, who had so disappointed planners in Washington, had been feeling particularly unsupported by Halleck, Stanton and the rest over their refusal to place certain troops in the area of operation under his direct command. In what may have been an attempt to bluff Washington into seeing things his way, on June 27 Hooker asked to be relieved of command. His bluff was called, and before the day was out, Lincoln had landed upon George Meade as his new choice to lead the army. The following morning it was made official. For Hooker, the man so beloved by the Excelsiors, the news came almost as a relief when he received word of the change and then met with Meade to discuss the transition. In contrast, to Dan Sickles, who had returned from leave in New York the same day Meade took command, the news came as a blow. Describing the change to a friend as a "misfortune to the army," Sickles regarded it as a personal misfortune as well. Gone now were the days of amiable familiarity with the commanding general, ripened over the months from a shared offensive spirit, a mutual respect for fine liquor, cigars, and a common love for female companionship. Dan now had to deal with stuffy old Meade, a man with whom he shared little and who in turn harbored his own reservations about Sickles. Perhaps Chaplain Twichell summed up the thoughts of the average Excelsior man this way: "Poor Gen. Hooker, it seems, has finished his reign. I'm sorry for it, for I had faith in him. Gen. Meade has an excellent name among soldiers. God guide him."[33]

By 3 p.m. on the 28th, Captain John Mann and his Company C were marching through Frederick. Excelsiors marched with a bounce in their step as citizens turned out to greet them with cheers, sandwiches and coffee.[34] Many marched with a new sense of urgency as they neared Pennsylvania. Though they belonged to New York regiments, many men came from outside New York, many from the Keystone State of Pennsylvania. For these soldiers this was a chance to defend their home state.[35] Frederick was north and slightly east of where they had camped, and before the day was out they had gone another seven miles to Walkerville where they stopped at nine that night. The next day they continued on to Taneytown. On the 30th, they moved a few miles more onto Bridgeport, near Hagerstown, just a few miles from the Pennsylvania border. The reception among the citizens here was a great change compared to their reception 18 months earlier in southern Maryland. Chaplain Twichell described the greeting of the locals in a letter to his mother:

> One circumstance has operated greatly to mitigate our discomfort and revive our drooping spirits, and that is our meeting friends and receiving friendly greetings. The set Virginia sneer and frown are left behind. Here another mood prevails. The farmers as we passed had pails and tubs of fresh, clear water at their gates and the loyal kitchens of their wives yielded abundance of good bread—but better still are the smiles, and waving flags and cheers with which they meet us. At one place a bevy of country girls sang Union songs as we passed—Bless their dear hearts! It was better than their mother's biscuits.[36]

The next day the regiment resumed their march north towards Emmitsburg. As III Corps marched its final leg on July 1, opposing forces already fighting in and around Gettysburg were shaping the battle and the Excelsiors' coming role in it. The fighting of July 1 was determining the various positions to be held by the two armies come the fighting of

July 2. Of utmost importance to the Federal Army would be their holding of critical high ground south of town. Though the town of Gettysburg was already lost to the Confederates, Culp's Hill and Cemetery Hill were still in Union hands and Meade intended to extend his line south along the high ground of Cemetery Ridge. It was here, on this ground, that Meade hoped Lee would attack him.

The men of III Corps were on the move by 8 a.m. the morning of July 1. Though serious fighting was taking place in and around Gettysburg, General Humphreys still did not have clear instructions for the movement of his command. But this was soon to change. Humphreys reported, "On July 1, marched through Emmitsburg, and halted 1 mile out of the town, on the Waynesborough pike. While I was engaged in a careful examination of the ground in front of Emmitsburg, the division was ordered at 3 p.m. to move up to Gettysburg, 12 miles distant, where an engagement had taken place between the two corps of Generals Reynolds and Howard (the First and Eleventh Corps) and the enemy."[37]

Humphreys had orders to detach his third brigade under Col. George C. Burling along with a battery of artillery to protect the Hagerstown Road. With his two remaining brigades he moved northeast towards Gettysburg. The road they used paralleled the main road but lay about two miles west of it. Unknown to Humphreys, this was some of the same country being traveled by the enemy as they rushed north to consolidate their forces. "When halfway to Gettysburg, a dispatch from General Howard to General Sickles, commanding the Third Corps, was delivered to me ... which the latter general was warned to look out for his left in coming up to Gettysburg,"[38] Humphreys reported. He learned at this same time that no Federal forces occupied ground west of the Emmitsburg Road. But this was the precise route Humphreys intended to take to comply with earlier orders that he form his division on the west side of Gettysburg once he arrived. With night fully upon him, the general now thought better of his situation and decided to move his men east towards the main road north. After a march of a mile and one-half, they reached the main road. Here the general relied on the instructions of a guide sent to him from Sickles, and they moved north by way of Black Horse Tavern. In this country Humphreys fully appreciated his proximity to the enemy:

> Upon approaching the Black Horse Tavern, I found myself in the immediate vicinity of the enemy, who occupied that road in strong force. He was not aware of my presence, and I might have attacked him at daylight with the certainty of at least temporary success; but I was 3 mile distant from the remainder of the army, and I believed such a course would have been inconsistent with the general plan of operations of the commanding general.[39]

The division managed to stop only 200 yards from enemy pickets. In the darkness Humphreys quietly retraced his steps away from Black Horse Tavern. But while Humphreys groped his way at the head of the column, stragglers from the Excelsior Brigade were having their own close call. Drawn to the light from a farmhouse, a few enterprising New York men approached, anticipating a home cooked meal for their efforts. As they peered through the window, they were surprised to discover a number a Confederate artillerymen enjoying themselves. Not wishing to be made prisoners or betray their presence, the Union men skulked back in the darkness to the protection of their regiment while the Rebels made merry.[40]

The division finally located Federal positions around 1 a.m. James Dean and his mates bivouacked, throwing gear and themselves to the ground for a welcome rest. The division was about one mile south of Gettysburg, but more importantly, well east of Emmitsburg Road and away from the enemy.

The next morning the whole of the regiment awoke to find itself located in the middle of the lush green fields and the rolling hills of central Pennsylvania farm country. It was a beehive of activity as the various regiments and brigades positioned and then repositioned themselves along the face of a gently rising ridge. Facing west, Captain Mann could see Emmitsburg Road a few hundred yards in the distance and some woods beyond that concealed the Confederate army. The division was situated on a local landmark called Cemetery Ridge, with Gettysburg off to the north and two prominent hills, Little Round Top and Big Round Top, to the south. General Meade's orders to the III Corps were to form with II Corps on its right while its left flank rested on Little Round Top, the northernmost of the two hills.

Burling's Third Brigade rejoined Humphreys' division at 9 a.m. and at noon the division was ordered into line of battle. Final adjustments were made to the entirety of the Federal line, which stretched along Cemetery Ridge from Culp's Hill at the north to the Round Top hills at the south. Humphreys found David B. Birney's First Division of the III Corps on his left. The right of Humphreys' division touched the left of the II Corps' First Division under General John C. Caldwell.[41]

Active in New York City politics prior to the war, John S. Austin raised Company K of the 72nd N.Y. and served as its captain until his promotion to lieutenant colonel following the resignation of Taylor and Moses. Following the death of Col. Wm. O. Stevens at Chancellorsville, Austin took command of the regiment (Brown, *History of the Third Regiment*).

From its assigned position in line, Sickles' corps faced a low, tree-covered ridge. A few hundred yards beyond these woods was another ridge. Upon this ridge ran the Emmitsburg Road. On the far side of the road sat another large clump of woods where the Rebels gathered in force. Enemy troops in these far woods and others farther south worried Sickles. As the morning dragged on he received reports from probing units, which included the First United States Sharpshooters, that large bodies of Rebel troops were forming in his distant front and left.[42] Lacking confidence in the defensive opportunities of his position should the enemy attack, Sickles now looked for other ground his corps might occupy. Vexing Sickles most was the area in front of his First Division, near the intersection of the Emmitsburg Road and a lane that ran east toward the Round Tops (now called Wheat Field Road). This small plot of land contained a small peach orchard and was perched on some slightly higher ground, ground Sickles was sure might soon contain Confederate artillery hurling shot and shell into his inferior position. Two months earlier at Chancellorsville, Sickles had learned firsthand what evil enemy cannons placed on high ground could wreak. Reluctantly he had obeyed orders and withdrawn from Hazel Grove's high ground, only to have the place soon dotted with Confederate guns that proceeded to rain down shot and shell onto his corps.[43] Sickles also remembered the fate of Oliver Howard's XI Corps, which was taken by a surprise flank attack at Chancellorsville. He now fretted about how other poor ground on his left might afford the Rebels the same kind of opportunity.[44]

So sure was Dan of the inferiority of his position that he spent most of the morning seeking clarification and interpretation of his orders regarding what leeway he might be granted as to the dispositions of his corps. Throughout the morning, Sickles and his staff officers traveled to Meade's headquarters, with officers from Meade's staff in turn, including Meade's own son, coming south to inspect the questioned ground. So frustrated was Sickles that he finally asked the chief of artillery, Brigadier General Henry Hunt, for outright permission to move his corps. Hunt acknowledged the potential threat, but he respectfully declined to grant such permission, leaving Dan to his own devices.

West of the Emmitsburg Road, the Sharpshooters' probe to the III Corps' left was proving successful, as they soon found the enemy in overwhelming numbers. Near noon, after a heated skirmish, the First U.S.S.S. was thrown back towards Birney's line with losses of about 60 men.[45] This threat on the left was the last straw for Dan.

"Communicating this important information to Major-General Sickles," Birney later reported, "I was ordered by that officer to change my front to meet the attack. I did this by advancing my left 500 yards, and swinging around the right so as to rest on the Emmitsburg Road at the peach orchard."[46]

First Division was now almost perpendicular to the rest of the army, with both flanks in the air, unsupported by any other units. Birney's division ran from roughly near the base of Sugar Loaf Hill (Little Round Top) west along the Wheatfield Road to the peach orchard and then north along the Emmitsburg Road. "My line was formed with Ward [Second Brig.] on the left, resting on the mountain, De Trobriand [Third Brig.] in the center, and Graham [First Brig.] on my right in the peach orchard, with his right on the Emmitsburg road,"[47] wrote Birney. Artillery batteries were scattered throughout the division's line.

Humphreys received orders from Sickles near 1 p.m. to move Second Division forward to the west side of the small woods that stood in front of Cemetery Ridge. Humphreys now formed his division. The First Brigade under Brigadier General Joseph B. Carr made up the first line of battle. The 243 men of the 71st New York were detached from the Excelsior Brigade and formed on the left of Carr's front line. Brewster's Excelsiors then formed in line of battalions 200 yards to the rear of the main line, while the New Jersey men of the Third Brigade formed similarly 200 yards farther behind.[48]

Sickles' orders called for Humphreys' men to be placed on the right of First Division along the Emmitsburg Road, his intention being to extend that line north, eventually connecting with the left of Caldwell's division of the II Corps. Humphreys reminded Sickles, however, that Caldwell had no order to advance, and if his (Humphreys') division were to move, it would leave his flank exposed with Caldwell still on Cemetery Ridge and in Humphreys' rear. Sickles ordered him forward anyway. Humphreys, sensing this to be only a temporary move, settled the division in advance of his original position on Cemetery Ridge

10. Gettysburg

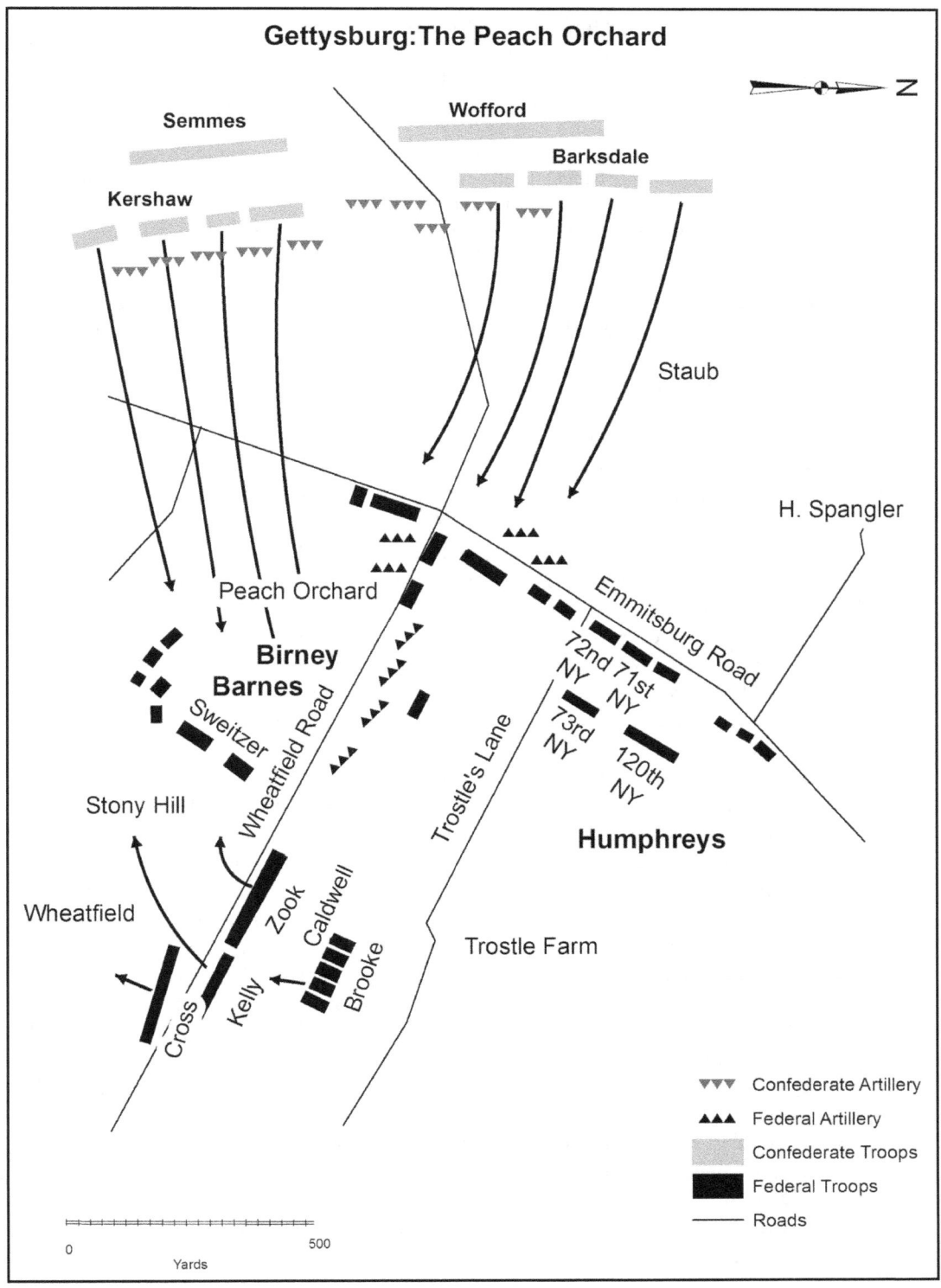

but still short of Graham's right flank on Emmitsburg Road. Second Division was now located with its front line running about 300 yards east of and parallel to the Emmitsburg Road. Second Division's left flank rested near Trostle Lane, a road that ran back east from Emmitsburg Road to the Trostle Farm. Of this position Humphreys wrote:

> The line I was directed to occupy was near the foot of the westerly slope of the ridge I have already mentioned [Cemetery Ridge], from which foot-slope the ground rose to the Emmitsburg road, which runs on the crest of a ridge nearly parallel to the Round Top ridge. This second ridge declines again immediately west of the road, at the distance of 200 or 300 yards from which the edge of a wood runs parallel to it. This wood was occupied by the enemy.[49]

In the middle of Humphreys' line, about 250 distant, on the near side of the Emmitsburg Road, stood a house belonging to local shoemaker Daniel Klingle and his family. The 73rd New York was now sent to occupy the house, one of the few landmarks along the entire position. And should the enemy try to take it, the regiment was under orders hold at all hazards.[50]

About the same time Fourth Excelsior was moving forward, Sickles ordered Humphreys to peel off Burling's third brigade to support Birney's First Division. Though not yet engaged, Humphreys could anticipate the fight to come and was angry at being deprived a third of his force and his main source of reserve troops.[51]

With Birney's First Division fully deployed facing southerly along the Wheatfield Road and Humphreys' troops in supporting position, General Meade arrived to sort things out for himself. After finding Sickles, Meade surveyed the field and told Dan this was not the ground he should be holding. Sickles argued the merits of the new position and agreed to withdraw his corps should Meade wish it. Meade pondered this for a moment and responded, "You cannot hold this position, but the enemy will not let you get away without a fight and it may as well begin now as at any time."[52] With the promise of support from II and V Corps, Meade rode off.

Sickles' order to advance was relayed by Humphreys to the two brigades now making up the division. With Carr's brigade leading, they formed into line of battle with Brewster's following arrayed in "battalions in mass." No sooner had they begun their forward movement than a messenger from Gen. Meade's staff rode up to Humphreys with new orders. General Warren had requested additional troops be sent to Little Round Top to counter the growing Confederate threat.[53] Without hesitation Meade issued orders for Humphreys to move his division there. With new orders in hand, Humphreys barked the appropriate commands, and with the "simultaneousness of a single regiment," the entire division marched by the left flank.[54] Amid incoming artillery shells of First Division's still escalating fight, Humphreys moved his force away from the Emmitsburg Road and toward the Wheatfield and Round Tops beyond. Moving away from the Emmitsburg Road, Humphreys told Meade's messenger that he was no longer in position to support Birney's division and that a large gap was developing between the III and II Corps. As the courier hurried off to find the commanding general, another staff officer galloped up to Humphreys. This courier had orders countermanding the current movement and directing V Corps to protect Little Round Top.

First Division's fight was just developing, and Second Division was much to the rear, beyond Trostle Farm. Despite much cannonading, the infantry fight was just getting started. Confederate General James Longstreet's I Corps began its move around 3:30. Not expecting any Federal troops this far forward of Cemetery Ridge, Longstreet and his commanders modified their plan of attack. A Confederate brigade under Joseph Kershaw would be among the first to encounter Sickles' men. Intending to sweep around the left flank of Birney's division, Kershaw's men headed for the Wheatfield, a movement that marched them almost parallel to Birney's battle line. When Federal artillery began to take a toll, two Southern regiments wheeled left to attack the line of guns. As the Confederate regiments closed in on overrunning the Union batteries, a misinterpretation of Kershaw's prompted the regiments to stop short of the guns. As the Confederate men then continued on toward the Wheatfield, Federal fire played upon their ranks as they moved across the Union front.[55]

Humphreys now retraced his steps back towards the Emmitsburg Road, but unlike the movement of Birney's division, the movement of Second Division was in the full view of Winfield Hancock's II Corps, still positioned on Cemetery Ridge. This advance would later come to symbolize the movement of the entire III Corps. Major St. Clair A. Mulholland of the 116th Pennsylvania later wrote:

> Soon the long lines of the Third Corps are seen advancing, and how splendidly they march. It looks like a dress parade, a review ... and the dread sound of artillery comes loud and quick, shells are seen bursting in all direction along the lines. The bright colors of the regiments are conspicuous marks, and the shells burst around them in great numbers.[56]

William F. Fox described the scene this way for New York's official account:

> The sun shone brightly on their waving colors, and flashed in scintillating rays from their burnished arms, as with well-aligned ranks and even steps they moved proudly across the field. Away to the right, along Cemetery Ridge, the soldiers of the Second Corps, leaving their coffee and their cards, crowded to the front, where they gazed with soldierly pride and quickened pulse on the stirring scene. Conspicuous among the moving columns of this division was the old Excelsior Brigade, each one of its five regiments carrying the blue flag of New York.... They march with no other music than the rattle of the rifles on the picket line; they were inspired only with the determination to acquit themselves worthy of the State motto, which the brigade had adopted as its name.[57]

Humphreys' movement back took only a few minutes, and by 4:15 he was in position. He wrote, "I moved my division forward, so that the first line ran along the Emmitsburg road a short distance behind the crest upon which that road lies."[58] As Second Division moved forward towards the Emmitsburg Road, it came under enemy artillery fire from its front and left. Though the fire had little effect, Humphreys inquired about the advisability to attack. The reply instructed him to hold his position while cannon under Lt. Seeley were brought forward, which "soon silenced the battery in our front."[59] As Carr's brigade advanced, he detailed 100 men from the 16th Massachusetts Volunteers to relieve the 73rd New York, still occupying the Klingle house.

Carr's brigade was not long enough to cover the entire front assigned to it, so Humphreys split up the Excelsiors to extend the battle line. Of the 266 men present for duty, Colonel Thomas Holt's 74th New York were placed on the extreme right of Carr's entire brigade. The two largest regiments within Excelsior Brigade, the 120th and 73rd, were placed in the rear as support, along with the 70th N.Y. The 71st New York under Colonel Potter was the smallest Excelsior regiment on the field and was placed immediately left of Carr's men. Col. John Austin's Third Excelsior was now positioned left of the 71st. The 305 men of the regiment were bordered by Second Excelsior on their right and Trostle Lane on their left.[60] On the other side of the lane stood the men of the First Division, thus making Third Excelsior the left-most regiment of the entire division. In their front, beyond the Emmitsburg Pike, Dean, Mann, Stoddard and the rest faced a Confederate division under Lafayette McLaws, lurking in the woods, waiting to attack.

Sickles now occupied the high ground he had worried about for so long. His corps of 10,000 men defended a front nearly one and one-half miles in length, double the distance had he remained on Cemetery Ridge. Sickles did have the promise of support from two other corps. But whether such support would come quickly enough and in sufficient strength was in doubt. With the Confederate attack coming at a slight oblique to Birney's front, there was soon fighting along the east–west length of the line. Messengers raced to the rear with desperate calls for reinforcements to shore up the ever-thinning Federal ranks. Reinforcing troops from other corps positioned on Cemetery Ridge responded, but they were not enough. Birney struggled to maintain his line as he shuffled regiments along the line, placing them wherever the threat was most immediate and dangerous.[61]

Moving into position, the order came almost immediately for the boys to lie down. No order was required; Henri LeFevre-Brown in Company B and Dean in Company C with the rest wasted no time in hugging the Pennsylvania soil.[62] Peering up from their place on the extreme left, Henry could see enemy cannons to their left and front as Rebel shot flew horizontally in two directions. Austin sent out pickets to cover the regiment's front, but the fire was withering and soon they were withdrawn. Dean and the rest had never seen artillery so intense, and despite the hail of iron the boys set about fortifying their position.[63] Crouching and crawling, they broke down fences, gathered up nearby rocks, sticks and logs, and scooped piles of dirt, anything to fashion a serviceable wall capable of stopping an enemy ball or shell fragment. Such works had served them well back at Chancellorsville. Barricades like these would stop a bullet, and they hoped the enemy would throw themselves against the regiment's prepared position and massed musket fire. Many remembered their retreat at Chancellorsville, and what the boys feared most was being forced, or worse, ordered from behind these works that kept Rebel iron from striking Yankee flesh and bone rather than Pennsylvania rock and dirt.

Attacking Confederate regiments did not hit the whole of the Second Division all at once. The en echelon attack rolled against them from left to right like an angry wave crashing upon the shore. Humphreys was holding his own nicely, but Graham's position on the left, in the peach orchard itself and at the apex of the whole III Corps' line, was beginning to weaken under a hard, no-nonsense attack of William Barksdale's brigade of Mississippians. By six o'clock things were starting to heat up for Humphreys' men as the fighting became more general. The situation for the III Corps was becoming desperate as the need for assistance grew dire. Humphreys received frantic messages from Sickles asking for aid, only in turn to fire off requests from other corps for help. "The demand for aid was so urgent, however, that I sent Major Burn's Fourth Excelsior [73rd N.Y.] to General Graham's brigade." Humphreys added, "At the same time dispatched one of my aides, Lieutenant Christiancy, to General Hancock, commanding Second Corps with the request that he would send a brigade, if possible, to my support."[64]

With no adequate support, the First Division began to give way around 6:30. It was about this time that one of the many hurtling cannonballs found its way into the rear of the III Corps' line. Almost inaudibly the errant ball tore off the leg of Dan Sickles, leaving his horse unscathed. The general slumped in his saddle and then down to the ground. Members of his staff immediately rushed to his side as the lower part of his right leg lay dangling in shreds. Soldiers gathered up Sickles and carried him a few yards to a nearby wall of Trostle Farm. Excelsior men and the rest of the corps saw the cluster of attendants and assumed the worst. But for a man whose leg hung in rags, Sickles remained remarkably cool. And though the exact details of the next few moments varied slightly, the core elements of events were

10. Gettysburg 145

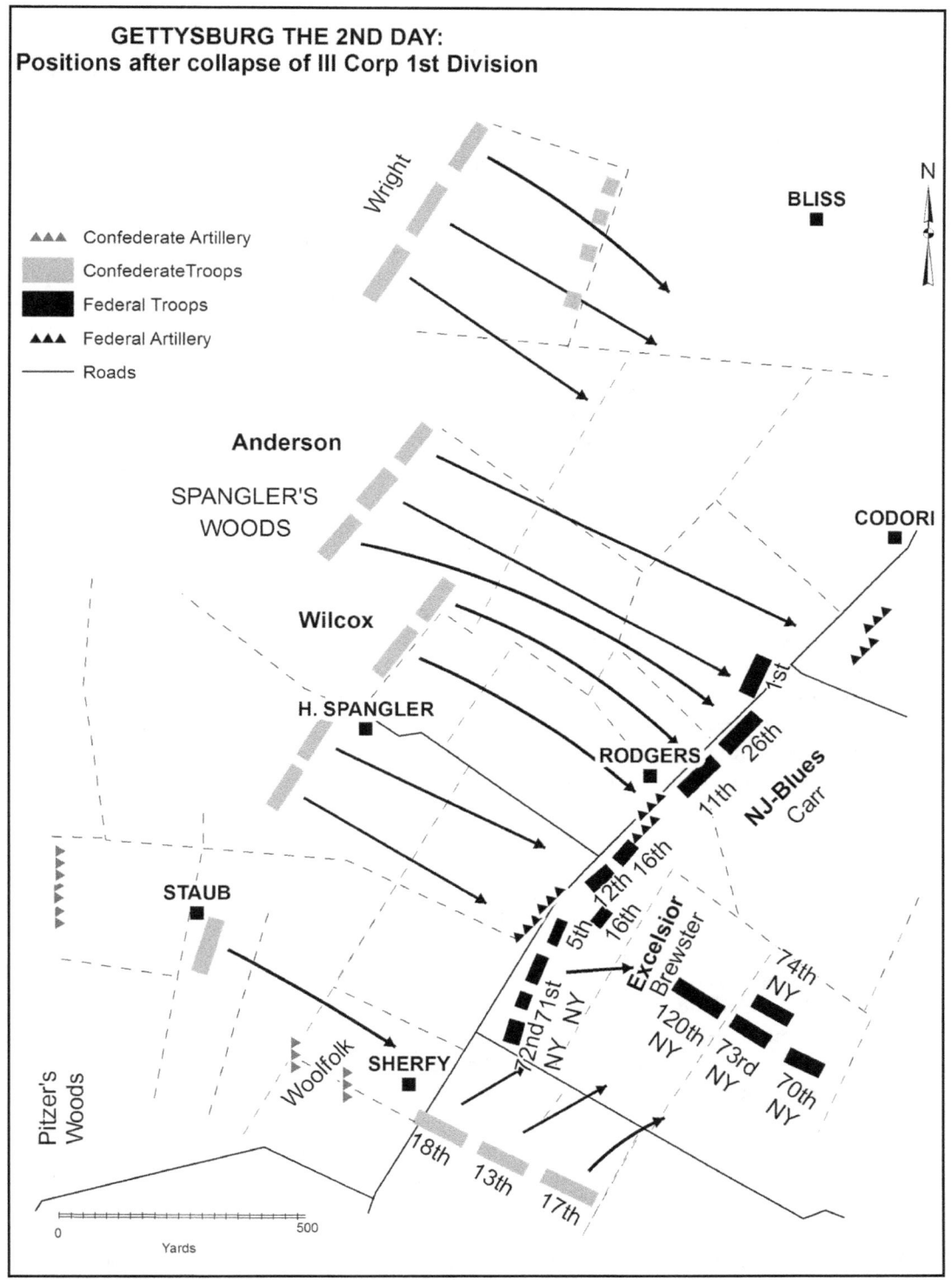

Gettysburg collapse of Second Division positions

as follows. Grasping the situation, Sickles directed those around him to use part of a saddle strap to fashion and apply an improvised tourniquet. Just then Major Tremain returned from an errand. Dan calmly instructed Tremain to notify General Birney that command of III Corps had devolved to him. Just as Sickles was to be stretchered to the corps' hospital, he was informed that a rumor of his death was sweeping through the ranks. With characteristic flair for the dramatic and an effort to bolster the spirits of his men, Dan had an aide pluck a cigar from his coat pocket. With it soon lit, Dan proceeded to nonchalantly puff as he was carried from the field.[65]

The pressure upon Graham was too much, and indeed for the entire First Division. The battle was becoming an east–west facing affair, and Birney issued orders for the corps to pull back and form a new line to better face all threats. The new line would run from the First Division's left resting at the Wheatfield, northwest to Humphreys' right on the Emmitsburg Road, effectively forming a single, more dense line of troops by connecting the two extreme ends of III Corps line. This new line would require Humphreys to swing part of his division back and away from the road. Though Humphreys was in position to execute the order, the ever-worsening condition of First Division meant this new line would never be formed, as Graham's brigade desperately fell back under Barksdale's crunching attack.[66]

Though Graham's brigade was being pushed from the field, the regiments from Brewster's Excelsior Brigade nearest this action weren't yet directly engaged by enemy infantry, suffering only from artillery fire. Pvt. Dean said, "The shells then began to come over us and they had a splendid range of us, we lay thus under the fire for 2 hours when the rebels drove in our pickets and advanced."[67] While most of the attacking Rebels continued east toward the Wheatfield, in pursuit of First Division, two of Barksdale's regiments turned north into the now unprotected flank of the Second Division and the 72nd New York. "Up to this time we had not been engaged at all, but now the troops on our left being obliged to fall back, the enemy advanced upon us in great force, pouring into us a most terrific fire of artillery and musketry, both upon our front and left flank,"[68] reported brigade commander Brewster.

"We remained in line of battle about two hours, under a most terrific fire of shot and shell, when we were pressed so hard on the left flank that we were obliged to fall back,"[69] wrote Colonel Austin. With their flank in the air, the 72nd and 71st attempted to face the new threat by refusing the line with some of their companies.[70] Amidst the shell bursts, musket fire, and screaming officers, the situation only became more confused. "The dreadful crash of battle resounded," wrote an Excelsior man, "the rattle of musketry, the bursting of shells, the roar of cannons, mingled with cries of the wounded, and with the cheers and yells of the determined foemen."[71] As the regiment tried to maneuver, Austin was hit in the arm and side. Wounded, he remained on the field, but within minutes his horse was shot out from under him. Deciding he could not go on, Austin relinquished command to Lt. Col. Leonard and retired to the rear. Officers in both regiments shouted commands through the din of bursting artillery and crackling musketry. Efforts to establish a new line were proving to be in vain, and the regiments gave ground in bad order.[72]

The 120th New York, which had been posted in reserve at this end of the line, briefly held the flanking Confederates as they poured a steady volley into onrushing Rebels. But the enemy push was too much and they now threatened to overlap the 120th's left and envelope the whole regiment. "The enemy at last broke the first line, and we advanced to meet him," wrote Captain Abram Lockwood of the 120th N.Y., adding, "The regiment soon became hotly engaged, and held its position without flinching until it was flanked."[73] Another 120th man wrote, "All at once, our line was swept by an enfilading fire, under which no troops could remain and live, and it became necessary to fall back [beyond] the range of the deadly hail. We were losing very heavily in our regiment, but fell back in good order, contesting stubbornly every inch of ground."[74] Of the Excelsior regiments posted on the left of the line, the 120th N.Y. was performing best, its sacrifice of men keeping the division's flank from collapse.[75]

Second Division's left was in peril, but both Carr and Humphreys were unhappy with Birney's orders to change facing. To do so now would mean moving from behind the breastwork and into the open just as three brigades from Confederate Richard Anderson's division of A.P. Hill's III Corps were hitting the division's front. Carr liked his position and requested permission to charge, certain the enemy would break under a counterattack. Humphreys was also confident of his position, but vetoed the notion of a charge.[76] Possibly unaware of all the events taking place around him, Humphreys felt strongly against Birney's order to change fronts, believing that at this stage of the fight, the maneuver would cause only more casualties and disorder. But change front they did. "My infantry now engaged the enemy's, but my left was in air (although I extended it as far as possible with my Second Brigade), and, being the only troops on the field, the enemy's whole attention was directed to my division, which was forced back slowly, firing as they receded,"[77] Humphreys later reported.

With First Division chased from the field, Birney's plan to form the entire corps into one long line had unraveled. With the arrival of two regiments from Hancock's II Corps sent to support his right, Humphreys received new orders. "At this time I received orders through a staff officer from General Birney to withdraw to the Round Top ridge ... this order I complied with, retiring very slowly, continuing the contest with the enemy, whose fire of artillery and infantry was destructive in the extreme."[78]

As the elements of the division moved back to the ridge, Carr was able to keep his First Brigade intact and conduct a fighting retreat, keeping the Rebels at a "respectful distance."[79] Brewster's Excelsior Brigade, however, which had been parceled out along the line, was now a mix of shattered, disorganized units, some men no doubt mixed in with Carr's regiments. Among the Excelsiors, the 120th N.Y. seemed to be in the best shape. The division withdrew in a northeasterly direction, across open fields and away from Trostle Lane, the same ones upon which they had formed earlier that morning. Austin reported afterwards that his men "were still hard pressed and obliged to fall slowly back."[80] Units were shot-up and disorganized, but the withdrawal itself was not a rout. Instead, it was a steady march to the rear with men loading on the move only to stop, turn and take steady aim before firing, and repeating the process. "We had to give way, it being too hot a place but we contested the ground inch by inch,"[81] recalled Private Dean. Brewster, known previously for his absenteeism, walked calmly among his men. Making his way to the rear, the colonel gave and received orders, keeping the brigade together as best he could while carrying his horse's bloody reins, which had been retrieved for him. Humphreys, too, circulated among the various commands. Over in the 72nd, Leonard directed his mangled regiment as best he could. Nearly a third of the command lay either dead or wounded. In Company C, Captain Mann struggled toward the rear with two wounds, one to his hip. Young Lieutenant Foss was being carried with hits to both legs. James Dean had been struck in the arm by "spent shot,"[82] which although painful, was quickly only a memory.

Shortly the division and Leonard's remaining men were back on the slopes of Cemetery Ridge, "to the crest of the hill from which the brigade started in the morning."[83] Here, on the ridge and a few hundred yards north of Trostle Lane, units of the II Corps worked to form a new line. "Upon arriving at the crest of the ridge mentioned, the remnants of my division formed on the left of General Hancock's troops, whose artillery opened upon the enemy, about 100 yards distant,"[84] wrote Humphreys.

Hancock was laboring frantically to put together a credible defense. To stymie the enemy advance he called upon the nearby First Minnesota Infantry to charge into the approaching Rebel line with orders to seize their colors. Without hesitation the Minnesotans threw themselves into the superior enemy force. Surprised, the tired and unsupported Confederates were initially rocked backwards but soon recovered. The Confederate advance now stalled as the First Minnesota withdrew. Hancock gained 15 desperately needed minutes, but the attack cost the Minnesota boys 215 of their 262-man regiment, the highest percentage loss of any Federal regiment at Gettysburg.

It was now after seven, and the thinned-down brigades of Georgians and Floridians had fought their way to the base of Cemetery Ridge, where Hancock's infantry joined the fight in earnest. Here the Confederate advance ground to a halt.

Supported by men of the II Corps, Humphreys' harried troops soon regained their composure. Among the fresh troops of II Corps was the 13th Vermont, which had yet to see battle. Hancock held reservations about allowing this untried unit to attack, but the Vermont colonel assured the general his men would fight. Hancock acquiesced, and the New Englander's charge sent the Rebels reeling back. The 13th Vermont had been posted immediately north of the rallied remains of Humphreys' division, and its success invigorated the III Corps men. "The enemy broke and was driven from the field, rapidly followed by Hancock's troops and the remnants of my two brigades,"[85] wrote Humphreys. Dean recalled that with "order restored we advanced under a murderous fire and drove the rebels off the ground that we lost."[86] Carr remembered his men "moved forward, driving the enemy and capturing many prisoners. I continued to advance until I again occupied the field I had but a few moments previous vacated."[87]

Counterattacking Federals drove the Confederates across the fields back to Emmitsburg Road. The Excelsior Brigade was still a jumble of disorganized regiments with many men still missing when Brewster gave the order to charge. He wanted to retake several cannons left on the field when the battery's horses were killed. As Brewster led the way, only a mere 150 of his brigade followed, with representatives from every regiment except the 70th.[88] The enemy gave ground as the Excelsior surged forward. "We charged on them with the bayonet 3 or four times and retook it all again," described James Dean, adding, "There was a rebel color bearer shot and I tried hard to capture the colors but I was too late, a sargeant [sic] of company E got it."[89] As men scrambled for the trophy, Thomas Horan eventually secured Eighth Florida's colors and later received the Medal of Honor for his effort.[90]

Charging across the field, Lt. Col. Leonard along with Sgt. LeFevre-Brown and Private Luther Howard, both of Company B, were the first to reach and retake the most advanced of the abandoned Union artillery. Reaching the gun, the three loosed the reins of the disabled horses and began to turn the piece when assistance arrived.[91]

Rebels retreated beyond the Emmitsburg Road, and the area between Cemetery Ridge and the road was back in Federal hands, but the Yankee generals had no desire to pursue any further and a halt was ordered. Excelsior men consolidated their gains and put their collection of Confederate prisons to use hauling the retaken cannon back to the rear.[92]

Here in these fields and further back on the ridge, Humphreys' regiments settled in for the night. Preparing his small camp, James Dean could count only 21 members of the regiment available for duty.[93] With a bivouac established, men from each of the regiments moved out onto the battlefield to search for wounded and to identify the dead. In the bright moonlight, soldiers wandered between the ridge and Emmitsburg Road amid the moans and cries of the wounded. They collected the hurt and tried to identify friends and comrades as they turned dead bodies face up into the moon's light.

Early the next morning, the entire division was moved to the rear for food and provisions. After eating and stocking up on ammunition, the various brigades moved into position to support II and V Corps. The ranks of Humphreys' regiments were now somewhat replenished as stragglers returned throughout the night and early morning. The 72nd counted near 140 present for duty.[94]

Around this time preparations were being made to transport the wounded General Sickles to Washington. His leg had been amputated well above the knee, but the leg of a major general was too valuable to be thrown away onto a pile with the countless others, so saved it was. The nearest train station was in the hands of Confederate General Ewell, so Sickles and his leg would be transported to Littlestown, about 12 miles to the southeast. The subsequent collection of stretcher-bearers, attendants, guards, and cavalry couriers transporting Sickles to the rear cost the Federal Army the equivalent of a small regiment.[95] Among the entourage was James Dean, who wrote:

> The word was who would volunteer to carry General Sickles to the cars, I at once got up and volunteered. We then marched to where the general was. He had his right leg taken off with a solid shot and had it amputated about the knee. We had to carry him on a stretcher to Littletown, he appeared quite cheerful and conversed with us and smoked a cigar and read the paper and told us it would not be long before he was soldiering again.[96]

Shells from nearly 170 Confederate cannon began peppering the Federal lines near 1 p.m. on July 3. This was the preparatory bombardment before the attack of Gen. George Pickett's division. Bluecoats on the front line hugged the ground while most of the shells flew over into the rear areas. Here in the rear was where regiments of the Excelsior Brigade had been posted, behind a portion of II Corps' Second Division and a bewildering amount of Federal artillery. Despite their position in the rear, several Excelsior men were killed in the enemy barrage.

Enemy artillery fire eventually stopped as Rebel infantry began the final stage of the attack. Pickett's graybacks pressed across the field under a hail of Federal artillery and small arms fire. By the time they hit the Union lines most of the attack's punch had been whittled away. Fierce hand-to-hand fighting broke out at points, but the integrity of the Federal line was never in serious danger and the Rebels were soon forced to retire. The battered Excelsior Brigade remained in reserve during Pickett's attack, which struck a few hundred yards north of their position. Because of this location, the brigade suffered only from the earlier errant artillery fire.[97]

The next day the worn out 72nd men acknowledged the 4th of July, Independence Day, but there was no celebrating. The day was spent instead burying the dead: in some cases men whom they had known, in most cases strangers from other units, and even a Rebel or two. For the entire day both armies did nothing but collect wounded and bury the dead. For two more days the armies waited and continued to bury the dead.[98] Most Union men believed Lee's army was ripe for destruction, but Meade chose not to attack. Finally, without interference from Meade, Lee began to move his army back toward home; there would be no continuation of the Battle of Gettysburg.

The fighting at Gettysburg had cost the men of the III Corps severely. With fewer than 12,000 troops, Sickles received the full weight of 30,000 attacking Confederates. His resulting loss was 4,211 killed, wounded, or missing. The Excelsior Brigade took nearly 1,837 men into action and lost 778.[99]

With 486 troops ready for duty, the 73rd New York was the largest of the brigade's six regiments. After occupying the Klingle House during most of July 2's early action, they were moved to support Graham's overwhelmed brigade and suffered heavily with 51 killed, 103 wounded, and 8 men missing.[100]

The next largest of Brewster's six regiments, the 120th New York, marched 383 men in to action and took losses of 204, nearly single-handedly keeping the Confederates from turning the flank of Humphreys' Second Division.[101]

The 70th New York was posted in reserve and helped to defend the division's left flank when Graham's Brigade collapsed; of its 371 men, it lost 117.[102]

At the other end of the line, the 74th New York supported the right side of Carr's Brigade during most of the battle. Fifth Excelsior reported 285 present for duty and suffered 17 killed, 69 wounded, and 3 missing.[103]

The smallest regiment within the brigade was the 71st New York under Col. Henry L. Potter. These troops had been posted immediately to the left of Carr's men and were on the right of the 72nd. Of their 243 men, Second Excelsior lost a total of 91.[104]

For the 72ndNew York, the regiment lost 7 killed, 94 wounded, and 15 missing, of the 305 who took the field. Colonel Austin was wounded but not severely, yet his future with the regiment seemed in doubt. The regiment had been reduced by a third.[105] All throughout the regiment officers commanded companies of only two dozen or so. In improvised field hospitals, wounded men waited their turn for the surgeon's table, where such visits offered only marginal hope for survival. And men such as Lt. Charles Foss, scheduled for an amputation, hoped he'd be one of the lucky ones.

After four days of waiting, the regiment moved again.

Epoch V: A Hard Conclusion

11. In Pursuit of Lee

The regiment still hadn't moved when James Dean returned from delivering General Daniel Sickles to the Littletown station. Dan was on his way to Washington to recover from the loss of his leg, but almost as importantly, to report on events surrounding his III Corps, at least as he saw them. Dan knew instinctively it was important both Lincoln and Halleck hear his versions of events firsthand, before his critics had their chance to report. Going to Washington may have been a blessing in disguise for Sickles, never mind the leg.[1] When Dean arrived back in Gettysburg, the regiment was still burying the dead. A hard rain had set in a couple of days after Picket's failed charge, making dealing with corpses even more miserable. A III Corps man in Carr's brigade described the scene of death:

> Some, with faces bloated and blackened beyond recognition, lay with glassy eyes staring up at the blazing summer sun; others, with faces downward and clenched hands filled with grass or earth, which told of the agony of the last moments.
>
> Here a headless trunk, there a severed limb; in all the grotesque positions that unbearable pain and intense suffering contorts the human form, they lay. Upon the faces of some death had frozen a smile; some showed the trembling shadow of fear, while upon others was indelibly set the grim stamp of determination.
>
> All around was the wreck the battlestorm leaves in its wake—broken caissons, dismounted guns, small arms bent and twisted by the storm or dropped and scattered by disabled hands; dead and bloated horses, torn and ragged equipments, and all the sorrowful wreck that the waves of battle leave at their ebb; and over all, hugging the earth like a fog, poisoning every breath, the pestilential stench of decaying humanity.[2]

At army headquarters George Meade was feeling pressure from Washington over the army's apparent inactivity. Meade felt the army needed time to recover from the heavy exertions of battle, reequip itself and, most of all, move cautiously against a still dangerous foe.[3] But Lincoln saw this as the perfect opportunity to pounce on Lee's crippled army and end the war. To Lincoln, Meade was hesitating just as other commanders had done before. On July 4 Meade sent congratulations to his army for a battle well fought. The circular read: "Our task is not yet accomplished, and the commanding general looks to the army for greater efforts to drive from our soil every vestige of the presence of the invader."[4] Reading the message Lincoln scowled and groaned in frustration, saying, "Drive the invader from our soil? My God! Is that all?"[5] The president was discouraged Meade didn't see Lee's destruction as his primary purpose.

While Meade wrung his hands over how best to proceed and worried over the condition of his army, Robert E. Lee recognized the danger of remaining in hostile territory and made plans to return to Virginia. An opportunity to withdraw his army from Gettysburg presented itself, and he began moving on the 4th of July, under the cover of rain and darkness.[6] The full extent of the Confederate evacuation was discovered the morning of the 5th, and immediately Meade ordered a meaningful pursuit using portions of the V Corps. Following an eight-mile march, Federals found the rear guard of Lee's army posted strongly in mountain passes, effectively checking the Union chase. On July 6, Meade decided to pursue the Confederates by way of a flank movement, keeping east through Frederick and Boonesboro, Maryland, on his way south to Williamsport, Lee's clear destination for his Potomac crossing. This was an 80-mile trip for the Yankees, while the Rebs enjoyed a more direct route that was only half that. Lee arrived at Williamsport on the 7th and found the Potomac, nearly dry a few days before, a rain-swollen torrent. Unable to cross, Lee entrenched and awaited an inevitable attack while Meade pushed the remainder of his army south.[7]

Few corps in Meade's army were more shot up than III Corps, and few brigades more mangled than the Excelsiors. On July 2, William Brewster had taken 1,837 men onto the field and by the end of the action, 778 had been killed, wounded or come up missing. The 72nd was sorting itself out; Colonel Austin was wounded and officers in half the companies had been hit. Seven men had been killed outright, but by July 8 four more had succumbed to their wounds.[8] Among them was young Charles Foss, the newly appointed second lieutenant in Company C. Foss died from complications resulting from amputation. Foss was among an ever dwindling breed, an original 72nd man who'd joined with Stevens and Company D in the beginning back in Dunkirk. As the war went on, the regiment was shrinking, now barely 200 men with fewer and fewer who remembered the likes of James Brown and the early hardships of Staten Island. Indeed of all who carried the true flame of the Excelsior Brigade, now Dan Sickles, its patron saint and founder was gone too.

Sickles' successor was not an obvious choice at first, having not even served in the recent battle. The III Corps' two divisions were ravaged and the decision was made to add a third division. This would bring the corps back to an appropriate fighting strength. There was a large division in garrison at Harpers Ferry under the command of William French. These troops would constitute the new division and French would be the new III Corps commander.[9] French was 48 and born in Baltimore. He graduated in the middle of his West Point class, which included the likes of Hooker, Sedgwick, Bragg, Early and Pemberton. After stellar service in the Seminole wars he was moved briefly to Texas at the outbreak of the rebellion. After promotion to brigadier general, French commanded a brigade within II Corps on the Peninsula and a division at Antietam. In November of '62 he was promoted to major general, and after serving at Fredericksburg and Chancellorsville, was placed in charge of the District of Harpers Ferry, thus missing the battle at Gettysburg.[10]

Andrew Humphreys, who had performed well during the battle, was now Meade's chief of staff. Humphreys in turn was replaced by Henry Prince to lead Second Division. Prince was a career West Point man and among the oldest generals in the army. Having served with distinction against both the Seminoles and Mexicans, Prince had earlier commanded a brigade, then a division in Banks' corps, and was captured at Cedar Mountain and held prisoner for four months.[11]

Commanders at all the levels were in flux. Second Division's Second Brigade, the Excelsiors, was under new command of 42-year-old New York politician, Brigadier General Francis B. Spinola, replacing the 73rd's Col. Brewster. Prior to commanding the Excelsiors, Spinola had taken part in minor operations in Southeast Virginia and North Carolina while at the head of several regiments of Pennsylvania militia.[12] While the commander of the 72nd New York was still officially the wounded Colonel Austin, effective leadership fell to Lt. Col. Leonard.

After a couple of false starts, on July 7, the regiment received orders and marched to Mechanicstown, where they camped for the night. Leaving near 6 a.m., the men marched nearly due south to Frederick, where they arrived at 10 p.m. and spent the night. The following day Dean and the rest moved west to Middletown. There they received rations for the first time in two days and encamped on the old South Mountain battlefield. By nine o'clock on the morning of the 10th Leonard and the captains had them on the move again, crossing Antietam Creek and halting for some time on a portion of the old battlefield there. They moved again around 10 p.m. re-crossed the creek, and finally halted for the night at two the next morning. With only four hours' sleep, Leonard and his men moved to a spot two miles away, where they remained in position until 4 p.m. At that time they re-crossed Antietam Creek and camped for the night. On the morning of July 12, Leonard moved his regiment about one mile and camped in a piece of woods.[13] Here, stopped for a while, James Dean penned a quick letter to his sister assuring her that he was fine and the recent letter from her and the family had buoyed his sagging spirits: "I believe if it had not been for your prayers I might not been

John Leonard began with the regiment as captain of Company F, raised from Newark, Jew Jersey. Leonard had served with the regular army in frontier postings in Washington State before the war and became the 72nd's lieutenant colonel after Chancellorsville. Leonard commanded the regiment following Austin's wounding at Gettysburg through to its dissolution in July of 1864 (Brown, *History of the Third Regiment*).

able to write you today and I hope you will continue your prayers for my safety."[14] Dean's note also reflected a confident tone that mirrored the army's: "I think we can whip the rebels if not capture nearly all Lees army and I hope we do, so the war will come to a close soon."[15]

Meade now believed his army was in position for a meaningful attack on Lee's flank. During two days of reconnoitering while the bulk of Meade's army inched itself west to Williamsport, orders were issued for an assault the morning of the 14th. When the daybreak attack went forward, Meade and his men found they were too late. Lee and his army had constructed pontoon bridges from old barns and derelict houses and had escaped across the swollen Potomac River.[16] President Lincoln, who had pushed Meade to close with Lee and finish the job, was livid at the news. "The fruit was so ripe, so ready for plucking that it was very hard to lose it."[17] The president went on to express his disappointment in terms so sharp Meade offered to resign command, a request Lincoln denied.[18]

Having made good his escape across the Potomac, Lee camped near the town of Winchester, upon some of the same ground where he had rested his army following its retreat from Antietam ten months before. With the Confederate Army locating itself on the west side of the Blue Ridge Mountains, Meade faced a choice of how best to pursue his enemy.

Choosing not to pursue directly upon Lee's rear, Meade decided to move the Army of the Potomac down the east side of the Blue Ridge Mountains. Such a move would allow the Federals to easily resupply themselves by rail, while at the same time allowing the army to constantly threaten Lee's flank. Meade reasoned Lee would be forced to retreat south while he pursued on a parallel march with both armies on their respective sides of the Blue Ridge Mountains. Meade also believed that when the opportunity presented itself, he could strike at the Confederate flank through many of the passes and gaps along the range. Meade now set upon the task of getting his Federal Army out of Maryland, across the Potomac and after Lee in Virginia.[19]

Leonard's New Yorkers briefly camped in some abandoned enemy positions near Williamsport following the fruitless morning assault of the 14th. After spending the night, the boys trudged back, countermarching south toward Sharpsburg. Stopping in early afternoon for the night, Dean and the rest were two miles beyond the town. By six the next morning the regiment was again marching south, where it stopped for the night within three miles of Harpers Ferry at the foot of the Maryland Heights. The morning of the 17th brought a small treat for the regiment: no rush to begin the march. Instead the boys were able to linger about until 4:30 that afternoon, when they finally left their bivouac. Soon they moved across a pontoon bridge that spanned the Potomac at Harpers Ferry. Next they crossed the Shenandoah River and went on to Sweet Run, where they rested for the night, settling down about three miles beyond Harpers Ferry.[20]

Both armies were now in Virginia, and the movement south quickened as Meade sought to close with Lee. Since mid-June when the Federals had left Falmouth, the army had been on nearly continuous march, stopping only to fight. As men marched there was the distinctive sound of infantry on the move. Leather cartridge boxes and straps, along with canvas haversacks, creaked and groaned as gear swayed with the rhythm of their step. Tin cups and canteens clanked against rifle butts, small skillets or other personal equipment. To lighten their loads, blankets, heavy and unnecessary in the summer's heat, were collected. They would be returned once the weather cooled. The Army of the Potomac was moving south along the west side of the Blue Ridge Mountains, paralleling the Confederates just as Meade had wished. For Hiram Stoddard the strategic situation since the battle at Gettysburg couldn't have been more clear: "We have been after them ever since. Our army went down on one side of the mountains and Lee's army on the other."[21]

The next day Leonard led the regiment south from Sweet Run. For three days the New Yorkers moved south along the eastern base of the mountains, making better than ten miles a day. Meade's supply situation was still in chaos. Most men's uniforms were a collection of rags, many soldiers marching without proper shoes. But despite these conditions, on the 20th they reached Upperville, located on the road leading to Winchester and Lee's side of the Blue Ridge. Nearly worn out, men dropped and made camp, relieved when word came they would stay for two days.

His army had ignored other mountain passes as they moved south, but Meade now learned the enemy was marching nearly opposite him. Manassas Gap was only a day's march away. This was the opportunity Meade had planned for: to throw a column through one of these gaps and fall upon the center of Lee's battered and unprepared army.

On July 22, III Corps' commander French received orders to occupy the Manassas Gap, through which ran a railroad of the same name. This east-west line connected Manassas Junction with Front Royal and Strasburg as it cut through the Blue Ridge Mountains. The plan intended III Corps to lead the attack, followed by V Corps, with II Corps held in reserve. To speed their movements, both attacking corps were ordered to leave their supply trains behind, the III's in Deplane and the V's in Rectortown. "I was ordered to move upon Manassas Gap, to hold two divisions at Piedmont, and send forward a third to re-enforce Brigadier-General Buford, who had been directed to seize the Gap,"[22] reported French. By midday the Excelsiors were well on their way from Upperville. Near 7 p.m. Leonard had gotten his boys, along with the rest of the Second and Third divisions, down to Piedmont Station, which sat on the rail line about two miles east of the gap. Here they bivouacked for the night. As for the rest of the III Corps, French reported, "The First Division, under Brigadier-General Ward, arrived at Linden Station, in the Gap, at 11 p.m. and, in conjunction with cavalry, took possession of the Gap."[23] Federals now occupied a portion of the gap, but the enemy still controlled the commanding high ground farther to the west.

In the early dark of the next morning French moved his Second and Third divisions forward. By 9 a.m. they had covered nine miles or so and reached the staging area at Linden Station. As the Excelsior Brigade arrived at the station, 120th New York was detached and sent on picket duty. This left only the five original regiments behind, reducing brigade strength to well under 1,000 rifles.[24] Anticipating the fight to come, men throughout the companies prepared. Men checked their supply of cartridges while others cleaned rifles, scraping and scouring their muskets' nipples, inside and out; this was no time for a misfire. As a finishing touch, men fired a percussion cap or two to clean out the narrow passage leading from the nipple to the barrel chamber containing the powder charge and Minié ball. Soon the sound of snapping caps floated on the air, a sure sign an attack was imminent.[25] While Dean and his fellows tended their Springfields, a small battalion of skirmishers from Ward's First Division were sent forward to "feel the enemy and to compel him to show his pickets on the heights as well as in the ravines."[26]

Moving forward Ward's skirmishers found Wright's Brigade of Georgia troops under command of Colonel E.J. Walker. The Confederate position consisted of 3rd Georgia on the right, the 48th Georgia in the center, and the 22nd Georgia protecting their left. French correctly concluded this was "a large flank guard to delay our advance,"[27] and he could see that beyond the gap were "continuous columns of Lee's cavalry, infantry, artillery and the baggage wagons moving all day from the directions of Winchester toward Strasburg, Luray and Front Royal."[28] It was the destruction of these unprepared enemy columns that Meade wanted.

By late morning Ward's First Division was in position for an assault against the first line of Confederates, which occupied a high, steep ridge; but French delayed giving the order to attack. Captain C.H. Andrews with the Third Georgia described the scene from his vantage: "About 11 a.m. the enemy appeared in the valley in our front in force—infantry, cavalry and artillery. About 2 p.m. they formed for an advance."[29] Urgent messages were sent to General Richard Ewell reporting the Georgians' situation and requesting reinforcement. But on came the Union men. "The skirmishers met the enemy at various points of its extended line, and steadily drove them until the entire line of heights had been carried,"[30] reported French. From below, troops moving forward in support of the attack could see the fighting above, providing them with "a magnificent scene."[31] On the rebel side both generals Ewell and Robert Rodes had appeared on the field carrying promises of more troops, but none arrived in time before Ward's Federals had swept the Georgians off the first and highest ridge, known locally as Wapping Heights.[32]

By 4 p.m. the steep and rocky Wapping Heights were in Federal hands. The men of the III Corps now consolidated their position, which looked down onto a second ridge where the retreating Rebels had reformed. Confederate Colonel Walker was wounded in the fighting and command of the enemy brigade devolved to a staff officer, Captain Victor Girardey. Girardey now conducted the movements on his brigade's left while Captain Andrews of the Third Georgia commanded the brigade's right. "Our line now extended about 2 miles, and was very weak, as our numbers were small,"[33] wrote Andrews. Federal officers from their side of the line could see they faced only about 600 enemy muskets flank to flank.

Despite commanding Wapping Heights, French hesitated to press the attack against the rallied but still outmanned Georgians. Advancing over the rough ground, a substantial gap had developed between his leading First Division and the supporting Second Division. Fearing an attack on his flank, French halted the advance and ordered Brigadier General Henry Prince to bring Second Division forward to close the worrisome gap between divisions. Prince took an hour to get into proper position, during which time many bored and hungry men of III Corps busied themselves picking berries and chasing sheep.[34] Finally the order came for Prince "to send a brigade to penetrate the ravine in front and cut enemy's line, and to drive them away."[35]

Prince selected Second Brigade for this move into the ravine, but it wasn't until around 5 o'clock that brigade commander Spinola received orders to move the Excelsiors forward. Marching over the crest where Ward's men had formed their line, Spinola led the Excelsiors down toward the defending Georgians. "Descending the precipitous slopes of Wapping Heights, they were directed upon the valley which separated the series of knolls in our front, behind the principal of which the enemy, perceiving the object of the movement, concentrated."[36]

Halting at the base of the heights, the New Yorkers formed a line of battle. Spinola rode along the line shouting encouragement. The order to "charge bayonets" ran through the brigade like an electric shock. "Though I never doubted their courage, the effect which this order had on the men by far surpassed my expectations,"[37] wrote Captain Lovell Purdy of the 74th New York. "We were put into line of battle and there told what we had to do. There were no use in telling us that for, we could see what we could do,"[38] wrote James Dean. "The word was given to advance."[39] General Spinola rode ahead of the boys amid the regiments' flying colors. With his sword and pistol drawn, he urged his men forward shouting, "Now boys of the Excelsior Brigade, give them Hell."[40] As the men went forward their eyes flitted between the colors, Spinola, and their enemy's positions.

Moving at the double quick, enemy bullets whizzed past the brigade as it picked its way through a cornfield and some swampy ground. Part of the 72nd soon encountered a wide ditch. As men edged their way through, progress of the regiment slowed. Once across, they clambered up the far side where they were promptly greeted by a Rebel volley. Concentrated mostly onto Company B, men fell or went to ground. Though rocked by enemy fire, the men quickly regained the initiative. And with the weight of numbers on their side, Leonard's boys surged forward into the fast-disintegrating Confederate position.[41] "With a yell that would have done credit to a band of demons, our boys sprang to their feet and rushed the foe,"[42] read the official 72nd New York report.

Organized enemy defense was collapsing as the regiment swarmed over rifle pits, driving the Southerners before them and collecting hapless prisoners. Excelsiors made liberal use of the bayonet as fleeing Rebels discarded weapons, belts, cartridge boxes and other impediments to escape. "I know that some of them was wounded with the bayonets of our men. I do not want to brag but I gave one of them an inch of steel myself,"[43] Dean remembered.

On the Confederate side, Captain Andrews related the Excelsior's attack and his own frustration: "Between 4 and 5 p.m. the enemy advanced again, and we resisted them to the utmost of human capacity; fought till our ammunition was exhausted, and, to enable us to fight at all, the ammunition was taken from the killed and wounded and distributed. Ammunition was ordered up, but failed to reach us."[44] With ammunition low and his men outnumbered, the Confederates retreated in disarray. Andrews continued, "The fight was made in open field, and at the distance of 15 paces. General Rodes sent forward a squad of 60 men ... but they failed to render any service."[45]

Confederate self-preservation was now the only priority, as Rebs scrambled for the rear ahead of Excelsior cold steel. "The rebels had hardly time to fire a shot at us and after we got them on the run, they had no chance to load,"[46] wrote Dean.

Chasing the fleeing Georgians, Dean and the rest came to another small hill lying about 200 yards beyond the enemy's original position, "behind which the enemy rose from his prone posture as thick as men can stand, opening a furious fire of musketry. At the same time a six-gun battery, still farther beyond, opened with shell,"[47] wrote General Prince. This "furious fire" came from men of O'Neal's Brigade, who had recently arrived to support the Georgians.[48]

As the Excelsiors charged toward this second hill in the face of renewed Rebel firepower, Spinola received a second, more serious wound. Shot now in both the side and heel, he was forced to relinquish command. Former brigade commander William Brewster was gone on sick leave, so command devolved to 70th New York's Colonel J. Egbert Farnum.[49]

The Excelsior's formation was becoming seriously misaligned. Having charged over three-quarters of a mile across rough ground, the unequal speed of the advancing men created gaps and malformed companies. Facing a reinforced line of Confederate infantry supported by artillery, the advance began to falter. Despite the misalignment, the Excelsiors managed to carry the second hill and scatter the enemy. "The first and second heights were carried in the face of a severe fire, when the enemy opened from the opposite hill with a four-gun battery, and the men, who were now completely exhausted, were ordered to hold the position, of which they had so gallantly taken possession,"[50] read the 72nd's official report. "Directions had been sent by me to the brigade while charging the second crest to halt upon and maintain that crest, and to restore its line there,"[51] wrote General Prince, explaining further, "a farther advance without preparation would have been irregular."[52]

Under orders to stop and consolidate his position, Farnum threw out strong pickets on either flank. The remainder of the brigade frantically built breastworks in their front, gathering available stones and nearby fence rails.[53] Hunkered down behind the improvised earthworks, Leonard's men traded shots with the Rebels. "We were ordered to fall back to the top of a hill and laid their [sic] in line of battle while the rebels amused themselves by throwing shell at us for time,"[54] wrote Dean. Of particular concern to the men of the regiment was the accurate fire of some enemy sharpshooters, the effect of which was more than mildly exaggerated by Dean: "Our brigade of 900 muskets, we lost 150 by sharpshooters and were the most fatal wounds I ever see. There were any number of legs that had to be cut off."[55] Dean added, "They must have had quite a number of sharpshooters as every shot that is made, a fatal wound and 3 legs out of every 5 had to come off."[56]

The New Yorkers settled in behind their new barricades as ineffective Rebel artillery fire flew over and around their position. Prince moved his two remaining brigades into supporting positions. The First Brigade under Brig. Gen. Joseph Carr established a second line while the Third Brigade under Col. George Burling formed his men to the right of the Excelsiors. "The enemy threw solid shot and shell at the troops of General Carr and Colonel deTrobriand [Burling] during their movements without effect,"[57] reported Prince. As the division made its final dispositions, "darkness settled down and overtook us."[58] Federal troops slept on their arms in line and prepared for another push the next day. Meanwhile, the Georgians and indeed the whole of Rodes' division began their retreat. "After dark, under orders from General Ewell, we commenced our march through Front Royal,"[59] reported Captain Andrews. After making their way across the Shenandoah River, Rodes' men pulled up the pontoon bridges behind them, finally stopping two miles beyond Front Royal, eight miles or so from Wapping Heights.

As dawn broke in the gap, the men of Prince's Second Division awoke to discover the enemy positions abandoned. Probing the enemy line, the men found only Southern corpses. Detached from the brigade, the 70th New York advanced about three miles but with the enemy gone, soon returned. With the entire brigade back together, the Excelsiors advanced all the way to Front Royal and also found it vacant of Rebels. "Here, finding the enemy had gone, we were marched back, a distance of about 5 miles, and bivouacked for the night,"[60] reported Major William Hugo of the 70th New York.

Federal high command believed the Confederate force near Front Royal was a strong line of battle protecting Lee's main force. In reality, this was only a rear guard and Lee's main column had been moving swiftly along roads further west. Having lost his chance to deliver a blow, Meade withdrew his men from Manassas Gap and as *Harper's Weekly* described, the Northerners "marched leisurely on toward the Rappahannock."[61]

The Excelsiors started marching back east on the morning of the 25th, following the railroad through the town of Salem. They stopped for the night about seven miles from Warrenton. There, the 120th New York rejoined the command after having been detached for picket duty.[62]

General Prince had had the entire Second Division at his disposal up on Wapping Heights, but it was the Excelsior Brigade that carried the heaviest burden this day. Confederate losses numbered somewhere near 170, while the Excelsiors lost a total of 75 men killed and wounded (half of James Deans' understandably inflated estimate), with the greatest amount coming from the 70th New York with 32 casualties. Leonard's command suffered only eight men wounded during the day's fight. Company B lost one man with a leg broken above the knee that later had to be amputated.[63] The twice-wounded General Spinola was sent to the rear, with his return to the brigade in serious doubt. But until a new general was found or Brewster returned, Farnum would continue to lead the New Yorkers.[64]

The Excelsior Brigade had deported themselves well as they chased the enemy nearly a mile, much of it in plain view of the rest of III Corps. "Everyone that looked on and saw the charge said there was nothing since the war that [would] compete with that,"[65] wrote Hiram Stoddard. He added, "everywhere we go, the bystanders are whispering, 'is that the old Ex company, are they the ones that made that charge?'"[66] Purdy of the 74th N.Y. summed up the movement and fight of July 23 this way: "I may justly add that none but the often-tried heroes could have passed through the fatigues of such a march and accomplish what they subsequently did."[67]

Sergeant Henri LeFevre-Brown of Company B, Stoddard, Dean, and the rest of the regiment continued their "leisurely march" south. The Excelsiors finally stopped for the night about two miles from Warrenton, on the road to Sulfur Springs, close to the Rappahannock River. It was the 26th of July, the day William H. Lovell died. Lovell was 22 years old, a Company B man, and was the last of 14 Third Excelsior men who eventually died from the Gettysburg fight.[68] Of the 14 dead, only six had been killed outright on July 2. One, Sgt. Dan Bourke of Co. E, died of his chest wound later that same day, but the rest would linger; some there in Gettysburg, others in hospitals further north. Two of the oldest men in the regiment would also die: John Hilger of Co. H and Frederick Platte of Co. E; both were 42. Company E was the same company to which Sgt. Tom Horan, who had captured the Eighth Florida's flag, belonged. With five dead, E seemed to have gotten the worst of it. Three men in B would die; George Hankin was killed outright near Emmitsburg Road, and Elliott Homer was hit in the knee and lasted till the 23rd, when he finally died in a Baltimore hospital. Last to expire was Pvt. Lovell.[69] Hiram Stoddard wrote his parents about "Willie":

> Since I wrote you last Willie Lovell of Co. B has died of a wound received at Gettysburg. He was shot through the leg and had his leg amputated his sister was with him when he died. She took his remains home and has them intered [sic] by the side of his mother. He was a good soldier one that was always at his post. He received his wound fighting and refusing to yeald [sic] one inch of ground to those traitors till he was shot through the leg and was obliged to leave the field.[70]

The army had been on the move since the beginning of June. Except for their time in Gettysburg, they had been on the march every day. But now the pace seemed to be slowing. "Since we have started on this march we have marched over 400 miles,"[71] pointed out Hiram Stoddard, with "our bedding, three days' rations, 60 rounds and cartridges and a heavy gun."[72] But time and Lee's army, it seemed, were slipping away from Meade. And the farther the pursuit went south into Virginia, the less likely the crushing blow Lincoln demanded would come. By early August the Federal Army had aligned itself along the north side of the northern arm of the Rappahannock River, positioned at its most important crossings. For the New Yorkers, the end of the constant marching was welcomed relief; camp meant a chance to rest and catch up on lice detail and important letter writing:

> Dear Father and Mother,
> I take this opportunity while it is cool to write a few lines to you to let you know that I am well and enjoying good health and fast regaining my strength for 2 months steady marching is enough to kill a horse alone men. We are now in camped near the Rappanook. The weather is verry warm and it is verry uncomfortable to move around to any extent. It is curious to see the boys with nothing on but their shirt and drawers and go down behind the woods, some stripped and busy washing them selves, some was washing their clothes others under some trees or bush with their shirts off busy looking over them to see if they can find any of the animals which bother a soldier.
>
> James Dean[73]

The men of the regiment were indeed enjoying their break from the hard marching of the past months. Camped near Beverly Ford, the Excelsior regiments rotated through the various picket and reconnaissance chores.[74] Colonel Brewster returned from sick leave on August 10 to resume command of the brigade. The men were growing weary, and the stop was doing them some good. Hiram Stoddard, who tried to stay upbeat in letters, couldn't help but cast a darker tone:

> While we were making that charge in Monnassas Gap another of our best men was shot through the leg and had to have it amputated and has since died. His name was Slaitor [Bernard P. Slater, ed.]... Mother you wanted to know how many of the Boys that were from Busti are left.... There was 11 of us at Orlandoes that night and out of 11 there is only three left, myself, Ayres and Fip. Oh dear parents this cruel war has cut down many a blooming rose. It has clothed our dear country in deep mourning and I have to ask myself why have I not fallen.[75]

The boys' enlistments weren't up for almost a year, but already there was talk about staying longer. One idea kicked around had to do with the entire brigade's reenlisting for another three years as a unit of mounted infantry. This idea included a 30-day furlough for enticement. For some the idea of riding into battle then fighting on foot was certainly appealing, but for others the notion of staying three more years was unthinkable. But for now it was just an idea.[76] There was no question the need for more men was acute, both within the brigade and the army. To ease the shortage, men and officers from the III Corps were sent back home to recruit or at the very least return with a few draftees to help replenish the severely depleted ranks. And though the reputation of draftees was, on the whole, not a good one, for Pvt. Dean, the sorry state of the regiment was more worrisome than the potential poor character of new men:

> I am in not hurry for a brush with him [Lee] for the army is not verry strong at present and we might stand a chance of getting whipped. There has been quite a number of conscripts come out for the division but none as yet for our Brigade. I wish they would send some out and get them in a state of discipline. You must know when a regiment like ours so decimated a fellow stands a poor show for his life. I saw in the Hearald that the draft had taken place in queens county. Let me know some of the fellows that have been lucky enough to draw a ticket for the ball.[77]

The regiment and the whole of the army were in a depleted state, but Lee's army was in worse shape. And Meade's strategy of pulling up behind the Rappahannock while the enemy rested, resupplied, and recuperated their numbers was a sore point in the North. In early September Lee had sent two of his divisions west to Tennessee to support hard-pressed Confederate General Braxton Bragg. This now gave the cautious Meade an opportunity. Without waiting for directions from Washington, Meade issued orders to his army on the 13th for a general move south toward Culpepper Court House.[78] That night Federal troops were on the move, but for the III Corps and the men of the Excelsior Brigade the problems were just beginning. Chaplain Twichell described what happened in a letter to his sister:

> We marched Tuesday night ... and with a vengeance. It was a march, and nothing else. Our first destination was Fox's Ford on the Rappahannock. This being neared, our course was changed, by order, toward Freemans Ford. Then commenced our tribulations. Through forests and morasses, through highways, byways, through hedges and ditches, we groped, huddled and floundered. Vain the splendor of the night, with crisp air and stars and thousand voices and blazing camps, consigned to abandonment and flames—vain indeed, the songs and quips and laughter of the merry rank and file.... Well, we marched and countermarched, and filed right and filed right, until the "noon of night" was past when, after half an hour in the thick woods to dense and dark that candles were necessary to light the column on its way, we emerged, not at the river crossing which was our quest, but upon the very field from which we set out, and lay down with mingled cursing and laughter to sleep in the old camps.[79]

The next morning division commander Prince was reportedly arrested "to account before a Court Martial for our nocturnal vagaries."[80] But evidence of any such arrest is lost to history. Despite the intrigue, the division regained its composure and set out again. With the correct route to their destination now apparently well in hand, the division set off around 7 a.m. By noon they had crossed both the Rappahannock and Hazel rivers. After stopping for their midday meal, the column continued on to Culpepper Court House, where they camped for the night. The next day LeFevre-Brown, Dean, Stoddard and the others moved three miles or so to the side of a small hill overlooking Culpepper, near the main road. Several days before, all the Rebel pickets had cleared out, allowing the movement to go on unchal-

September 1863. John Henry Ward (brigadier general), John S. Austin (colonel), John Egbert Farnum (colonel), William R. Brewster (colonel), Gershom Mott (brigadier general), Culpeper, Virginia. By September of 1863, Colonel Austin was no longer running the day-to-day operations of the 72nd N.Y. This was being done by Lt. Col. Leonard while Austin was relegated to some forgotten staff position within the division. Farnum commanded the 70th New York while Colonel Brewster commanded the Excelsior Brigade from Gettysburg onward (courtesy the U.S. Army Heritage and Education Center).

lenged and uneventful. The only hostile signs were the occasional cannon booms from down by the Rapidan, several miles off.[81]

By now some of the old doubts were creeping back. Having been marched in a circle by Prince only added to their sense of frustration. Many were feeling that the brigade was getting used up, and Stoddard gave voice to those frustrations in a letter home: "We expect to march evry [sic] minute. It seems to me some times as though the Old Ex had done her share of the fiting [sic] but I think there is no rest for us for we are always at the front."[82] In the face of this superior force, Lee withdrew his army south of the Rapidan River into strong defensive positions. This move placed the two opposing armies in roughly the same positions Union General John Pope had enjoyed a year ago, prior to his defeat at Second Bull Run in August of '62.

Soon the regiment settled into the usual camp routines. Occasionally the division would move for a few days on reconnaissance, but usually without results. One day, a few of the boys went over to V Corps to watch the execution of five deserters. Though all who witnessed it were horrified by the sight, all agreed the convicted got what they deserved.[83] Winter was approaching and the evenings were turning cool. Men sought relief by building fires and bundling up in whatever sheet, coat, or blanket could be had, but there was a problem. The supply situation was still not fully resolved. Marching down from Gettysburg, most of the blankets had been collected in order to lighten the men's loads, but for many, these blankets had yet to be returned.[84] Waiting, the men suffered at night as they huddled for warmth. "It is quite cold here at nights and a woolen blanket would feel verry [sic] comfortable but we have drawn no blankets or coats as yet,"[85] wrote one 72nd man.

It was approaching the end of September, and it was looking as if the war in the East might pass into the next year without any more real action at all. For weeks Meade and Lincoln argued over what could and couldn't be done against Lee's army. In a kind of concession that things were winding down, during the last week of September Meade sent two of his corps, the XI and XII, west to support the Union armies in Tennessee. These western troops were fighting some of those same Rebels Lee had earlier sent west.[86] Despite the departure of two corps, Meade still enjoyed a numerical advantage over Lee, though somewhat less overwhelming than before.

Lee had desired to go on the offensive for some weeks, and the reduction of Meade's army provided such an opportunity. It had taken the Confederate commander almost two weeks to confirm transfer of the two Yankee corps, but on October 9 he set his plan into motion.[87] The plan was a near reprise of Stonewall Jackson's accomplishments against Pope a year before. Lee's army would cross both the Rapidan and Rappahannock rivers, moving west and north, then sweep around the Union right flank and into their rear areas, creating havoc near places such as Manassas Junction. If all went well, Washington itself could be threatened. To carry out his plan, one corps under A.P. Hill would march a wide, circuitous route west, intent on hitting the Yankees either in their flank or rear areas. The other corps under Richard Ewell would follow Meade's inevitable route of retreat along the Orange and Alexandria Railroad.[88]

When intercepted messages indicated a major Rebel move, Meade acted quickly. Union cavalry were sent in every direction from Culpepper Court House to divine the nature of the action. The Excelsiors started marching early in the morning of October 8 in support of the reconnaissance, heading west toward James City.[89] The march was a short one, and the brigade stopped by 11 a.m. for dinner. While Leonard's 72nd N.Y. and most of the brigade established their regimental bivouacs, the 120th New York was detached from the brigade and left around 3:30. Supporting Brigadier General Judson Kilpatrick's cavalry division, the 120th established a forward picket post four miles beyond, near Mason Court House. While some harbored concerns about the fate of their fellow New Yorkers, most Excelsiors went about the business of setting up camp.[90]

The next day the New Yorkers remained under arms while they waited for the cavalrymen to figure out what was going on. The camp being situated near the foot of the Blue Ridge Mountains, some men took time to admire the range's beauty. "Next morning, at daybreak, word was brought that the enemy was crossing at a neighboring ford. The division was immediately put in order of battle and the general pulse beat quick,"[91] wrote Twichell. Artillery was rushed forward, and the sounds of heavy fighting could be heard in the distance. At least three brigades of Confederate horsemen under J.E.B. Stuart had descended upon Kilpatrick and the 120th. The fight was furious and desperate, but the Federals were overwhelmed and by 9 a.m. what was left of the 120th came dragging back into James City. One hundred men were now prisoners, including their dead and wounded, a number not easily spared by the brigade.[92] This loss by the 120th represented about one-third the entire regiment and almost one-tenth the brigade's strength.

Without proper authorization from above, Prince ordered his division back toward Culpepper near 1 p.m. Many men were anxious they'd need to form a line of battle at any moment and fight, but the cavalry protected the division's rear and near midnight they safely reached the outskirts of Culpepper.[93]

After some initial debate whether this Confederate move was an advance or a retreat, Meade concluded it to be a Rebel offensive and immediately set his army into motion. Wishing to fight on ground of his choosing, Meade began moving the army north, along the line of the Orange and Alexandria Railroad, instead of launching into Lee below the Rappahannock. Meade thus maintained his army between the Confederates and Washington.[94]

Leonard moved the regiment early the next morning, his men tired and chilled. The march was an all-day affair and went well into the night. While resting in the dark woods an alarm was raised amongst the Excelsiors and "for a few minutes the panic was fearful."[95] Men flew in every direction as the tempest descended upon them as a lone pack horse, loose from its handler, charged through the brigade. Stampeding through the forest, the horse threw off forage, saddle bags, books and other treasures belonging to none other than Chaplain Twichell. As the horse disappeared into the night, men set about recovering the good chaplain's possessions. While most were collected, some were never found and were consigned to the pursuing Rebs. As for the horse, Twichell gave up the poor beast for lost, but later in the night the nag returned to the column. A man in the 70th caught the discourteous mount and returned it to the grateful chaplain. "I received him right thankfully and almost felt as if I had had a horse given me. The rascal felt no remorse for his evil deeds, but looked perfectly lamb-like when I reproached him,"[96] recounted Twichell. With everyone's composure regained they proceeded, crossing the Rappahannock at Freeman's Ford at 10:30 and bivouacking for the night.[97]

Rear guard units of Meade's army, following behind the Excelsiors, skirmished heavily with Lee's advancing troops. By the end of the 11th the Confederates once again held Culpepper.[98]

The Excelsiors started a hard, fast march north early on the 13th. Having marched all day, that night the head of the III Corps column was hit hard by attacking Rebel cavalry and artillery. Battling units serving as the corps' headquarters guard were badly cut up, and French himself barely escaped capture or injury. The attack cost the column nearly two hours, and the New Yorkers didn't stop until three the next morning at Gainesville, almost due west of Manassas Junction.[99] The regiment rested only two hours before the order came to move again. It was another hard march, a weary march, the kind of march some men would claim they had done while asleep or in a trance-like state. The boys crossed Bull Run Creek (Union namesake and site of the war's first major battle, over two years prior) and finally stopped, groggily forming a line of battle near 3 p.m. Not far off, A.P. Hill had attacked a portion of the Union's II Corps, and the Excelsiors prepared for the worst. When the fighting with II Corps was over, Hill's troops had been badly mauled and the Excelsiors had remained unengaged. With the threat passed and darkness fully upon them, the regiment dragged itself back west to Centerville, where it spent the night. The next day they marched east again to Fairfax Station and formed a line of battle near Union Mills. Dean and the rest remained in battle array all day on the 16th.[100]

A.P. Hill's defeat at Bristoe Station allowed Meade to solidify his positions around Centerville. With the Yankees firmly entrenched, each side probed for an opening; finding it impossible to attack and worried about his exposure to a numerically superior force, Lee demurred and commenced his retreat on the 17th.[101]

For Dean and the rest, the marching and countermarching in anticipation of a battle was a terrible grind, and the cold nights provided no relief for these weary troops. Though

Lee was heading south, the danger had not passed. Meade moved only cautiously, but for the boys of the Excelsior Brigade, the 17th brought a welcomed diversion, the return of their old chief.

The boys of the III Corps had been expecting the return of Dan Sickles for two days, and no expense was spared to mark his homecoming. When word finally came that Dan was near and soon to review the troops, all were excited, especially the boys in the Excelsior Brigade who had known him from the beginning and with whom he had shared his most trying hours. The officers had their companies looking as good as was possible for under-supplied and over-marched men on active campaign, but still they were satisfied the general would be pleased. With the various companies formed, Dean and the rest moved to the road upon which Sickles would proceed. For Chaplain Twichell, Colonel Leonard and the rest it was a grand sight as two divisions, the Second and Third, took their positions (First Division being detached elsewhere). The men were of course formed by regiment with each brigade massed a regiment deep, allowing all to see Dan in his mounted eminence. There was some delay, and Stoddard and LeFevre-Brown, the real veterans, the ones there at the beginning, grew especially anxious. Finally the general appeared, atop his horse like some great emperor of old followed by a cloud of mounted officers. A great cheer was sent up from the mass of men; even those who hadn't actually seen Sickles yet cheered. As he rode down the line, his head uncovered and bowing as he went, each regiment mustered a bit more enthusiasm and volume like a great breaker rolling against the shore. Men waved and tossed their caps in the air as officers flourished their swords. Getting a full view of the general they all thought he looked well. Sickles wore his missing limb like a badge of honor, perhaps the greatest mark of devotion to country and duty a loyal soldier could give. But except for the absence of the leg, the boys thought he looked healthy and fit. Sickles' pride showed on his face as he struggled to hold back the tears that flowed freely on other men. When he reached his beloved Excelsior Brigade the excitement and jubilation exploded: "the old Brigade strained its individual and collected lung to the utmost and the results were immense."[102]

Sickles' trip to Fairfax Station was more than just a social call on his old comrades; there was the unpleasant business of asking Meade for his old job. Even before he advanced the III Corps without orders back at Gettysburg, relations with Meade had been cool; now, after all the accusations about events on that fateful day, relations with the commanding general were downright Arctic. There was a painful politeness to the meeting: a handshake, a smile and an inquiry about Sickles' leg. But as to getting the III Corps back, Meade held firm; his answer was no. He didn't come out and say he didn't trust Sickles but merely pointed out the impracticality of a one-legged general attempting to keep up with a fast-moving army while confined to carriage, unable to ride a horse except under the most sedate of conditions[103]; this, even though by this stage of the war, there were plenty of examples of active one-legged generals (Confederate generals Ewell and soon, Hood) and one-armed generals (Union generals Howard and Kearney). The men of the III Corps would have preferred Sickles over anyone else, carriage or no. But it was not up to the men, and Dan soon returned to Washington, a general in search of a job.

While Lee retreated south, much of the Federal Army pursued and harassed the Confederate's rear guard. By the 20th most of Lee's army had crossed the Rappahannock. The Bristoe Campaign, as it came to be called, had cost the Rebels nearly 1,400 men, while Meade placed his losses around 2,300.[104] As Lee withdrew across the river, the Excelsiors remained along the Orange and Alexandria. Leaving Fairfax on the 19th, they moved to Bristoe Station. The following day they advanced slowly, camping in the field for the night, only to finish their march by arriving near Catlett's Station around 11 a.m. on the 21st (the same Catlett's Station from which the regiment had begun their role in the Kettle Run and Second Manassas actions back in August of '62). Here the Excelsiors would stay to protect the rail line that Ewell's Confederates (whom the Second Division had fought against back in '62) had thoroughly mangled. Whereas the Federals had burned only a few bridges along the O&A, denying the enemy only immediate use of the line, the Rebels had destroyed much more. The 40 miles of wrecked track that lay in their wake looked to the infantry as if it would take weeks if not months to fix.[105] Unable to feed itself, Meade's army would be slow to regain the offensive in any meaningful way. On the 27th Dean wrote about what he saw and included a bit of technical explanation:

> The rebels have destroyed the Orange and Alexandria track complete. They have torn and burn the bridges of which there's quite a number from 50 to a hundred feet wide. I suppose you do not know in what manner they destroy the track, they first tear up the iron rail the cars run on then tear up the sleepers, that is the wooden rails that the rails are nailed to, they then pile up the wooden sleepers and put the iron rails on the wood being careful to lay the rails so that when the fire is started the rails will heat in the center and the weight of each end bends it double and in some instances they would drive a stake in the ground and run the rail around it so as it could not be of any use.[106]

James Dean had joined the regiment too late to have seen this part of Virginia when the Excelsiors were here a year before with Pope. After a walk to a local village named Weaverville, he was taken by the poverty of the region, especially when compared to the abundance of Pennsylvania: "I knew that they lived poorly but never thought that they were in such a destitute condition, not hardly a thing to wear. The old man has a coat patched like a bed quilt and the women the same ... some corn meal, a little coarse flour and what they do for coffee I do not know. No hogs, no fowls, cows or anything."[107] One day Dean went off into the woods in search of some wild hogs he knew were there. He soon found one and shot it. The beast was only wounded and its terrible squealing soon attracted the rest. With a bounty of targets, Dean commenced to shoot another then bayonet yet another. With three hogs, the men of Company C were soon living high on fresh pork as they kept an eye out for Rebel raiders.[108]

Since forcing Lee back from his expedition toward Centerville, Meade and Lincoln continued to exchange telegrams; the president demanded to know why more couldn't be done. Meade's force was growing in strength, yet the Confederates sat and rested below the Rappahannock, seemingly unmolested by the Yankees. From October 20 through the first week of November, Lee waited for the Bluecoat army to arrive. On November 5 the Confederate commander received the news he'd long been expecting: the Federal army had been detected probing the various fords across the Rappahannock. Meade was finally on the move.[109]

Back up the line at Catlett's Station, the captains and first sergeants of the 72nd rousted the men into line for the march south to rejoin the rest of the corps. Of the regiment's captains who had begun the war, all were either promoted, gone, or dead. The two newest company commanders had gotten their promotions since Gettysburg. Henry J. McDonough had been running the show in Company B since the end of July. He had been around since the early days and had originally enlisted as John Leonard's first sergeant in Company F out of Newark. Before making captain, Henry had served as lieutenant in both companies I and D. Over in Company F, William McConnell was now captain, having gotten his promotion on August 27. He had joined Company C as a corporal back in '61 and served as lieutenant in companies E, C and H before coming to F.[110] The captains pushed their men hard and by the end of the day had joined the rest of III Corps at Warrenton Junction.

Prince had apparently avoided any disciplinary action resulting from his star-crossed night march back in September and on November 7 had the Second Division again marching hard south.[111] They reached Kelly's Ford, a critical crossing across the Rappahannock, by 3 p.m. While on the march, III Corp's First Division had already been hard at work, with spectacular results. Two Confederate regiments assigned to guard the crossing had been taken completely by surprise when their rifle pits, which commanded the river, were suddenly flanked by First Division troops who had waded across. Nearly 400 Rebs were killed or captured and the rest went headlong for the rear. Yankee engineers quickly erected a pontoon bridge, and First Division men soon poured across the Rappahannock while Union artillery on the north bank pounded enemy positions well into the night.[112] Elsewhere, a Confederate commander had assured Lee that his two brigades were sufficient to hold their works and thus they remained on the north side of the river rather than join the main body. But when massed Union troops stormed their position, most using just the bayonet, the whole command was lost except for 600 or so Rebs who either swam the river or ran a gauntlet of musket fire as they scampered across a pontoon bridge. The swiftness and completeness of the Union attack shattered any plans Lee had for holding his line along the Rappahannock. Seventy-Second New York bivouacked that night in a cornfield where the sheaves made good beds for the men and even better forage for the horses. The next morning the brigade was roused by the sound of bugles and after a hasty breakfast pressed on. But the Confederates whom the Excelsiors had expected to encounter that day had fled, leaving only their abandoned entrenchments for inspection.[113] For the next two days the two armies marched, skirmished and countermarched in the area between the Rappahannock in the north and the Rapidan to the south. November 9 seemed like the final showdown as both armies faced off, but when Meade failed to press the issue Lee withdrew the next day across the Rapidan. The next morning, the two forces occupied essentially the same positions held a month earlier before Lee's adventure toward Bristoe Station.[114] "The battle which I prophesied with such confidence did not take place, contrary to universal expectations,"[115] wrote Twichell, who described:

> the whole army compactly arranged, toward Brandy Station where it was thought he would make a stand.... From some points of the march the whole army could be taken in at one view—the hosts of the Union advancing in combined grandeur. The 2nd, 3rd, 5th and 6th Corps stretched out across the plain—shoulder to shoulder—pressing on with equal step.... It was a magnificent spectacle. One's pulses leaped with enthusiasm, pride and hope at the sight.... The Confederates had declined the proffered challenge.... They had left at 12 o'clock—the last of them—and fled beyond the Rapidan, leaving for our use their winter quarters just finished.[116]

The three days between the rivers had been fruitful for Meade's army. Lee's losses were four times the Federal's 450, which helped to redress the balance of losses in the campaign.[117] The momentum of victory seemingly being with Meade, *Harper's Weekly* wrote, "It is difficult to understand why the signal advantage which had been gained was not followed up.... But the golden opportunity of falling with his [Meade's] whole force upon a portion of the Confederate army was lost."[118]

Meade was hesitant about any further moves. Repair of the railroad, so vital to his army's resupply, was still days if not weeks away, and to undertake a move without proper provisioning would be risky.[119] In the meantime Dean, Stoddard and the rest of the Excelsiors enjoyed camp near Brandy Station, a cozy camp built by their enemy hosts. "Meanwhile we are comfortably housed," wrote one Excelsior officer, "in the cabins reared at great expense of labor by the enemy, who must gnash his teeth at the very idea.... Our regiment is making itself at home under roofs intended for the 23rd North Carolina Vols.... I would ask no better fortune than to winter in it, although it needs a little Yankee contrivance to make it perfect."[120] The boys continued a full schedule of picket and fatigue duty, but given the rigors they had endured, their health was surprisingly good. There was still talk about reenlisting, with the notion of serving on horseback as mounted infantry. "It is all the talk among the boys and every one is making fun of the other," said Dean, "to see what a gallas [sic] fellow he will be when he gets mounted on his mule and gun and saber."[121] By November 22 James Dean was nearly positive his army was settling in to ride out the winter. "They are busy laying switches down at the station and I think the army will winter between here and Culpepper or they would not be building the switches there."[122] Across the Rapidan, Robert E. Lee had come to those same conclusions.

Lee had about 48,000 troops present for duty on November 20 but had allowed them to go into winter quarters, and to ease the difficulties of feeding his army, allowed them to be dispersed over a wide area. Meade now set to pondering. With the Confederate army dispersed as they were, a rapid advance across the river and attack into the Rebel flank less than 20 miles away seemed quite feasible. By mid-month Meade had received the reports he had been hoping for: important fords on the Confederate extreme right had been left practically unguarded. If "prompt and vigorous action"[123] was used in crossing them, a large part of the Union Army could crush Ewell's II Corps before Hill's III Corps could come to its aid. Meade quickly formulated a plan and set November 24 as the day to move. But severe rainstorms forced a two-day delay. After the rain was gone, in the early morning darkness of Thanksgiving Day, November 26, the Federal Army moved to cross the Rapidan River.[124]

The plan was fairly straightforward, and rations for eight days were issued to ensure that cumbersome supply wagons wouldn't slow the advance. The Federal II and V Corps would cross at Germanna Ford while the I, III, and VI Corps would cross a little farther west, upstream at Jacob's Ford. The five corps would then meet near Robertson's Tavern, which would place Meade's army east and south of the dispersed Confederates. Once together, the combined Federal force would roll west down the Orange Plank Road and into the Confederate rear areas, destroying Rebel units piecemeal as they were encountered.[125]

Extensive planning had gone into this advance, but delays plagued Meade's men from the start. Muddy roads made movement slow, but most frustrating of all, someone had incorrectly measured the width of the river, resulting in every pontoon bridge being one boat short. Fixes were made, but precious time was lost.[126] It was intended that French take III Corps over the river at Jacob's Ford first, thus putting them in the vanguard of the advance, with its Second Division leading the way. But delay seemed the order of the day for French and his men; even getting across the river seemed overly taxing. "The enemy were showing themselves in some small force on the opposite side.... It therefore became necessary to act with a due amount of caution,"[127] reported French. But even after the infantry was deployed and bridges were built, the steep banks on the river's far side were impossible for horse-drawn artillery to scale. French sent his artillery downstream to cross at Germanna Ford, where other Federal corps were crossing. The resulting traffic snarl created even more delays.[128]

"At 4 o'clock, however, the bridge being completed, my division crossed upon it, and advanced along the road for the purpose of giving space for the remainder of the corps and the Sixth Corps on the farther bank,"[129] wrote Prince. He attempted to make room for those Union troops following close behind. Advancing down the road, Prince halted at the first fork he encountered and reconnoitered one-half mile in both directions. Encountering "a little fusillade,"[130] Prince deployed the 26th Pennsylvania, who chased away a few Confederate horsemen. With dark fast approaching, Prince passed word back to Third Division commander General Joseph Carr that he intended to bivouac in the woods surrounding the road's fork and that proper arrangements of the divisions should be made. Orders were received from French instructing Prince to establish contact with the Second Corps and to prepare to march toward them at daybreak. Though he had cavalry at his disposal, Prince thought it impossible to establish such contact at night amid the tangle of trails and woods.[131] Regiments settled in for the night, which promised to be cold. Large warming fires were not allowed, though smaller ones sufficient to make coffee were. Although the men shared blankets and snuggled together for warmth, "every mother's son of us was chilled to the heart."[132] Pickets were positioned, and Thanksgiving night passed without major incident. But it also passed without any definite directions from General French as to the division's exact location or the location of their intended objective, the linkup with II Corps.[133]

Meade had hoped to reach Robertson's Tavern on the Orange Turnpike by the end of the first day, but poor road conditions and logistical miscues left his army far short of this goal. This delay gave Lee all the warning necessary, and he immediately sent troops to meet the advance. Rebel troops began skirmishing on the morning of the 27th with men of the Federal II Corps near Robertson's Tavern. Confederates from Jubal Early's and Robert Rodes' divisions grappled with the bluecoats, fighting a holding action until early afternoon. Another Rebel division was holding some key high ground until around 2:30, when it was pushed off by the newly arrived V Corps under General George Sykes. Meade ordered Sykes to hold his position and wait until the entire army was ready for the main advance down the Orange Turnpike.[134]

While the Federal II and V Corps had been skirmishing in and around Robertson's Tavern, the III Corps had been on an odyssey of their own. French and his generals had gotten moving at daybreak but by 8:30 had stopped when they became uncertain as to which direction to take at a fork of the Raccoon Ford Road. General Prince had sent out scouts, but "the enemy's cavalry kept them from examining the road."[135] The presence of Reb cavalry, combined with no clear instruction from corps commander French, resulted in a two-hour delay before the Second Division got moving again.[136]

French crept south around 3:00 p.m. as a Rebel division under Edward Johnson marched along the Raccoon Ford Road in search of Rode's Division, with which it was to connect. Near Payne's Farm, the two forces collided. Unaware he now faced an entire Federal corps, with another one, the VI, close by, the aggressive Johnson deployed his 5,300 Southerners and prepared to fight.

Finding a suitable open field, Prince deployed Blaisdell's First Brigade. Brewster's Second Brigade formed a second line behind Blaisdell's men, but there was still some uncertainty as to the correctness of the road, and Prince was told to "cease all operations."[137] Prince wrote, "After some time waiting in expectation of orders, Adjutant-General Hamlin came to me from the headquarters, and informed me that the major-general commanding had announced that this was the right road, and that we were all right."[138] With only two brigades at his disposal and his left flank exposed, Prince sought help from Gen. Carr's Third Division. Carr declined to deploy his division, citing orders that called for him only "to follow."[139] But after a flurry of dispatches between Prince, Carr, and French, things finally got straightened out and Carr eventually went into line of battle.[140]

Despite Carr taking pressure off the left flank, Prince and his men still faced stiff resistance in their front. As Blaisdell's brigade of Yankees advanced, pickets were thrown ahead of the formation, "and we continued our advance for short time, when the enemy showed himself in force,"[141] wrote Colonel Robert McAllister of the 11th New Jersey. As the fighting become more general, Prince sent the Excelsiors to the right of First Brigade and then fired off dispatches stating his entire reserve had been committed and he was requesting reinforcement.[142]

"On the 27th of November, about 3 p.m. I received an order to march my regiment to the support of Colonel Blaisdell's brigade. Lieutenant Lockwood, of Colonel Brewster's staff, conducted me to the right of the line, where I took position in line on the right of the Eighty-fourth Regiment Pennsylvania Volunteers,"[143] reported Lt. Col. Leonard. The 70th N.Y. and 71st N.Y. regiments fell in on the right of Leonard's men. As the fight continued, individual regiments, North and South, charged and counter-charged depending on the relative advantage of their position. Units took cover in woods and behind rail fences as the opportunities allowed.[144] "The rebels fell back and we advanced and skirmished nearly all the day till 3 p.m.,"[145] remembered Private Dean. Chaplain Twichell, riding along the rear of the 71st line, was nearly struck by a bullet that instead hit a sergeant standing nearby in the thigh. "He was immediately placed on a stretcher and I accompanied him off the field, thanking Heaven for my narrow escape."[146] And though the sergeant's wound proved not to be too serious, Twichell "felt under peculiar obligation to him"[147] for the sacrifice.

Early in the fight, the 84th Pennsylvania (posted to the left of the 72nd) broke, "leaving a large interval on my left unprotected, and through which the enemy were moving and attempting to turn our flank,"[148] recalled Leonard. The New York men concentrated their fire, but the enemy advance went unchecked. "Volley after volley given, all to no use. Then we fixed bayonets and sent up such yells and cheers and charged on them,"[149] described Dean. Facing the 72nd's wall of cold steel, the enemy advance staggered to a halt as the Rebs turned heel. Joining in the chase was at least one other Excelsior regiment, the 70th N.Y. under J. Egbert Farnum. Soon the New Yorkers had driven the enemy a half mile. Having advanced this far, Leonard believed he was exposed and beyond effective support should the tables turn. The colonel called off the pursuit and halted the regiment in an open field. A short time later he moved them back to the road.[150]

Distinguishing friend from foe in the thickness of the woods was not always easy. "We ran on a battery and the officers told us it belonged to our side. They soon found their mistake when the grape and canister came whistling through our ranks,"[151] remembered Dean. Fire from the Rebel battery was having "little effect"[152] on the regiment, but caution prevailed and the New York men fell back to the cover of a small hill.[153]

As the afternoon wore on, part of the line on the division's left was in jeopardy of being turned. As the Confederates pressed Prince's left, the division gave ground "slowly and reluctantly."[154] Noting that this movement was general, Prince did not attempt to stop it, instead allowing them to fall back until they were in line with two batteries of the Fourth U.S. Artillery. At about this same time, reinforcements from the First Division reported they were in position and awaiting orders from Prince. "At my request he marched a line of his [Ward's] brigade by the right flank across the road so as to show it in rear of the battery. This had a magical effect, as it spoke to the eye what in the noise might not be heard. All the officers of my staff and the brigade staff suddenly disseminated my orders among the troops to halt at the battery, and they did so, restoring their formation with wonderful quickness."[155] Prince went on, "The moment the battery was unmasked by our men, it opened with the utmost rapidity, deluging the rebel ranks with double charges of canister."[156] With the threat to his flank over, Prince advanced his newly reinforced line and retook all the ground previously lost.

By the end of the day Rebels fighting around Payne's Farm and Locust Grove had taken the worst of it. Despite their losses they had protected their division's flank and kept French's III Corps four miles short of a link-up with the remainder of Meade's army. Meade refused to advance piecemeal, so the action at Payne's Farm and Locust Grove had effectively halted the entire Federal offensive. Meade's army was still effectively divided; the "right road"[157] chosen by French for his III Corps was in fact the much longer of two routes to Robertson's Tavern. French's failure to link up with and unify the army had cost the Union army important time and initiative. Stalled, the bulk of the Federal Army camped on the ground they held at the end of the day's fight, far short of the hoped for objectives.[158]

James Dean stood watch during the night. "It being my turn I had to go out on picket and had to stand all night without anything but a jacket."[159] In the darkness, Dean could hear the distinct rattling of leaves to his front. "I got behind a tree and pressed my finger on the triker [*sic*] of my gun and cocked."[160] With the intruder three feet from him, he "put the bayonet to his breast and ordered him to halt." Asking the stranger what regiment he belonged to, the reply came back, the Sixth Maryland. Dean asked what corps, and he responded, "the Second."[161] Instantly knowing this was the wrong corps, Dean grabbed the intruder's musket and ordered his surrender, "or I would blow his brains out."[162] Dean then delivered his unexpected catch to Colonel Brewster. After an interrogation by the colonel it was discovered the Rebel sergeant belonged to George Dole's brigade of Georgians, some of the same boys the Excelsiors had a couple of months earlier pushed off Wapping Heights.[163] The fighting now over, doctors, orderlies, chaplains and regular soldiers collected the wounded and brought them in. With the ground picked over and unable to find any more wounded, the boys settled in for the night. In the camp of the 71st, the 72nd's chaplain, William Eastman, called on his old college classmate. Twichell was eager to host his old friend and they bedded down for the night, no doubt exchanging tales of their long and harrowing day.[164]

As morning broke on the 28th, the various wings of the Federal Army quickly established communication. During the night the Rebels had withdrawn, yielding the field to their Yankee foe. Confederate general Early's report illustrated the untenable Confederate situation: "The enemy had the whole or the greater part of his force in my front and on my flanks. I therefore determined to fall back across Mine Run, as the position I then held was very unfavorable either for attack or defense."[165] Matters were made worse for the Yankees as Lee moved troops to support Early and others along Mine Run.[166] Meade's bold plan to quickly crush the Confederate flank had failed.

Prince's division moved during the remainder of the 28th toward the eastern bank of Mine Run, which ran roughly north–south and perpendicular to the Orange Turnpike. Leonard led his men on a hard slog over wet roads churned into muddy morasses by hooves and the wheels of the artillery's guns and caissons. As guns stuck fast up to their hubs, the regiment and entire column halted until each piece was freed.[167] Some of the boys of Company B shared the duty of carrying a stretcher with the body of their beloved, respected, and recently promoted Captain McDonough, who'd been killed the day before. The boys struggled along, anxious to have his body embalmed and sent home for burial. The cold weather

11. In Pursuit of Lee 171

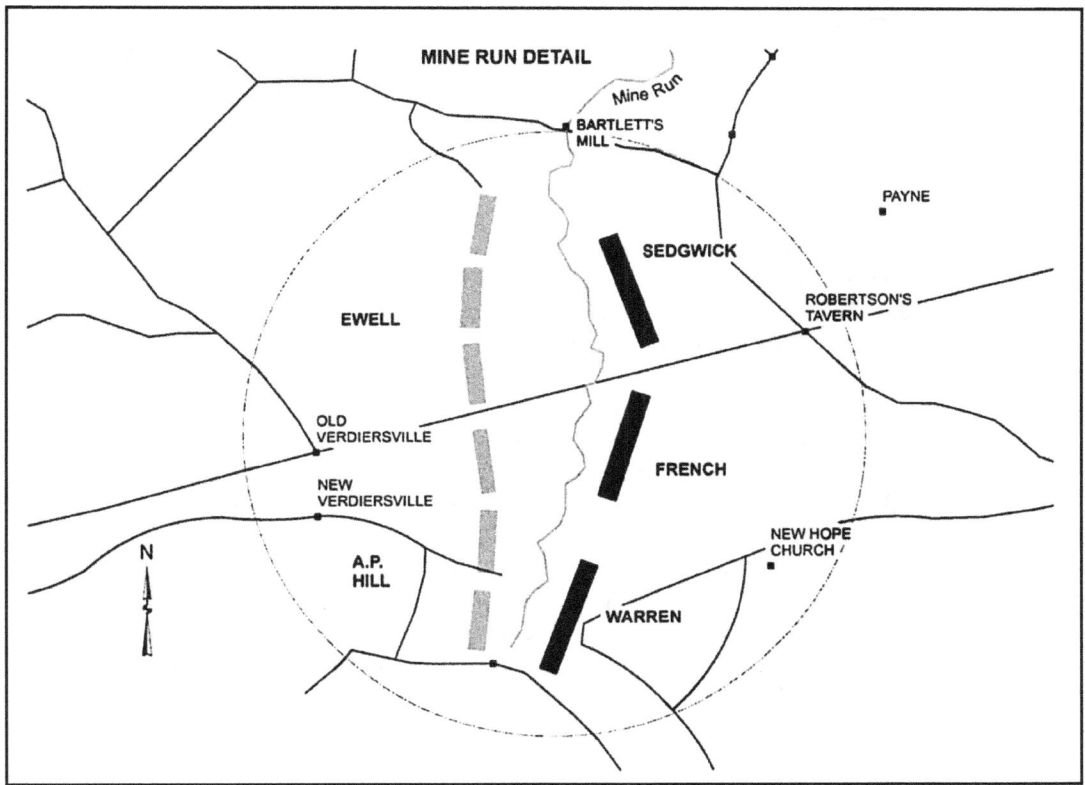

helped to preserve McDonough and thus, as one man described, aided "their loving purpose."[168] Once in position the division joined other elements of Meade's army, which had moved from near Robertson's Tavern, west to Mine Run, and settled in for the night. As things were shaping up, the two armies were massing on opposite banks of Mine Run, stretched over a six-mile front.

"On the 29th, the division received orders to be in readiness at daybreak to proceed on a reconnaissance. In the course of the day it reconnoitered the east bank of Mine Run to the plank road and drove all the pickets of the enemy,"[169] reported Prince. The Federal Army continued to maneuver and probe, settling on an alignment with General Gouverneur Warren's II Corps on the left, French's III in the middle, and General John Sedgwick's VI Corps on the right.[170]

Meade held a counsel of war during the night of the 29th. Of the three corps commanders holding the front line on Mine Run, only French, whose corps held the center, advised against attack. Both Warren and Sedgwick saw opportunity for feasible attacks on their fronts. So confident, in fact, was Warren that he assured the assemblage he would encounter little if any resistance as he rolled up the Confederate flank. It was decided that come morning both Sedgwick and Warren would launch attacks on their respective fronts. Warren's attack was to be bolstered by the Second and Third divisions of the III Corps, giving him a force of 26,000 men.[171]

By 4 a.m. the Excelsiors were on the move, placing themselves in position about two miles south of the turnpike. The divisions were massed by columns of brigades, providing for an attack along a narrower front. There was a dense fog surrounding the brigades and the boys murmured amongst themselves, sure no one could maintain proper direction or alignment in such a soup. There was a foreboding amongst the troops as men exchanged forlorn looks as if this would be the last they'd see of one another. Men collected their letters along with what little money they had and gave it for safe keeping to the chaplains and surgeons, those men most likely to live through the day.[172] After a while word came that the attack would be postponed because of the fog. A collective sense of relief swept the ranks, but most knew their stay was only temporary. To the rear, many could see General Warren riding here and there, and as the hours ticked by with still no attack the men began to wonder. By mid-afternoon the men in the ranks had their answer. There would be no attack this day. As dawn had broken, Sedgwick opened the attack as planned with a thunderous artillery bombardment. But just as he was to send in the infantry, an aid arrived with a dispatch from General Warren stating he was suspending his attack. Lee had gotten wind of the attack plan and with time to bring up additional reserves, had bolstered both flanks with formidable earthworks and fresh troops. Sedgwick reported to Meade that indeed the area in his front had also been reinforced and suspending the attack was best advised. Only David Birney, commanding the First Division of III Corps, which had started a strong demonstration in the middle, was surprised to hear that the attacks were called off.[173] To many of the men throughout the army who could see the entrenched enemy in their front and who envisioned another murderous repeat of Fredericksburg, the order to cancel the attack came as salvation. As evening set in, the Excelsiors withdrew to join the rest of the corps for the night. "We moved off with an unutterable feeling of relief," wrote Twichell, "for the men had all day been creeping to the top of a little hill in front and looking at the works they had to take, and all now felt that they had experienced a great deliverance."[174]

Warren lobbied Meade to maintain position and probe further west, attempting to turn the enemy's flank where there wouldn't be time to entrench. But with dwindling supplies and worsening weather, Meade recognized the limits of the endeavor and ordered a withdrawal.[175] The next day, the Army of the Potomac moved back across the Rapidan, returning to their former positions. "At 6 p.m. on the 1st of December, left the bivouac and marched by newly made route to the plank road, and thence to Culpeper Mine ford, where we crossed the Rapidan and bivouacked,"[176] reported Prince. The 72nd New York served as guard for the divisional ammunition train and didn't cross the river till three in the morning of the 2nd. By 6 p.m. the New Yorkers arrived at their old camp near Brandy Station, where they prepared to camp for the winter.[177] The weeklong endeavor had cost the Second Division 27 men and officers killed, 135 wounded and 26 missing; 58 of those were from the Excelsior Brigade. The 72nd New York suffered 20 men killed and wounded.

The army was done campaigning for the year, but it was not done with General William French. Meade demanded French provide "a full explanation" as to the movement of his corps and "its failure to reach the point designated for it near Robertson's Tavern."[178] On December 14, French submitted a second report of the campaign. This report was intended to be the "full explanation"[179] demanded by Meade, but also was sculpted to cast French in the best possible light. Extolling the "prowess of the corps beyond any terms which it is in my power to express,"[180] French nevertheless tried casting the blame onto bad roads, poor intelligence and the hapless Prince by referring to the great "embarrassments of the general commanding the leading division."[181]

By mid–January it was clear Meade was still unsatisfied with French's version of events. Though French wouldn't be sacked outright, his failure at Mine Run and his inability to exploit an earlier opportunity to hurt Lee at Manassas Gap meant his days as a corps commander and Prince's with Second Division were numbered.

Dean and the rest of the regiment settled into their Confederate-built camp to ride out winter. On December 13, James penned a letter home: "I am well and sitting by a comfortable fire in my log shantie ... and I am happy to tell you that we have splendid quarters and the duty is quite light, and we enjoy our selves pleasantly for since I have been transferred to company B I have had good time of it for they are all a nice lot of boys, and like a lot of brothers."[182] He ended by adding a note of confidence about the spring campaign, predicting, "We will make the Johnnies fly around livelyer than they have been accustomed to."[183]

12. The Struggle to Petersburg

The men welcomed 1864 the same as the previous New Year's. Some celebrated the passing of another hard year and looked forward to better times, while others were indifferent, both to the season and to any celebratory traditions that accompanied the new year. Camp around Brandy Station was wet and cold, typical for Virginia in winter. Most trees had long since been cut down and used up as opposing armies moved and counter-moved over this land. Mud was everywhere and the constant activity guaranteed it stayed mixed and sloppy. Despite the conditions, James Dean and the rest enjoyed the snug comfort of well-built cabins that served to keep the cold out and the heat in.[1] Cabins were trophies of war, fairly won from their Rebel foe who now resided across the river Rapidan, which separated the two armies. There was added satisfaction in the belief that the Reb builders of these fine accommodations sat shivering and damp, suffering in hastily built dwellings through which rain and cold entered at their own caprice. Army supplies were plentiful, so everyone ate well and replaced worn out horses. Among some officers whose rank was high enough to preclude question, their wives had come south to join them. This created an unusual social climate for an army camp, but despite the relative luxury of Brandy Station, the business of war continued.[2]

Every man in the fight from the lowliest private to Lincoln himself knew these days were coming, and now they were in sight, the discharge of whole regiments full of men. Back in '61 thousands of men had joined hundreds of regiments, enlisting for three-year stints. Within just a few months, those enlistments would be expiring, and the government would be helpless to compel them to stay. Just as the new campaigning season of May, June and July would be in full swing, the Federal Army would start to come apart.[3] Officers campaigned for weeks to keep each man in the ranks, lest there not be an army with which to fight. To help keep the men in the field, Congress passed a special act on December 10 allowing soldiers who had served two or more years to reenlist as veterans. Terms of service would be lengthened under this deal. In exchange they would receive a 35-day furlough and reenlistment bounties, which sometimes were as much as $700.[4]

Men throughout the Excelsior Brigade argued the merits of reenlisting. Some had long felt abused and wanted no part of the army or further fighting. Others pondered the question longer. Back in November an article had appeared in the *New York Times* with a reprinted letter purported to be from Excelsior commander Brewster. In the letter Brewster acknowledged the proud reputation of the brigade and then proceeded to extol the fact that the entire brigade had agreed to offer itself for another three years of service to the government. There were a few caveats of course, foremost of which was that they be allowed to form as a brigade of mounted infantry and then be permitted to return to New York for a period to refill their depleted ranks.[5] Soldiers within the brigade howled with laughter upon reading it and wondered out loud where they were when this "unanimous" vote was taken.[6] Others were intrigued by the idea of riding into battle, of continuing the fight as mounted infantry. Even if it really was Brewster's notion, it quickly died. "There is great talk about reenlisting for three years as mounted infantry but I do not know how it will work," wrote James Dean, "the conditions are to let the brigade come home and recruit till its ranks are filled again and each man have a furlough for 30 days to go home ... but let the men get home I do not know whether they will enlist.... I would not be responsible for them, but I think it is camp rumor."[7] Later, in a letter to his brother, Dean added, "It is all the talk among the boys and every one is making fun of the other to see what a [gallant] fellow he will be when he gets mounted on his mule and gun and saber."[8] For the men of Company H, the deal the army was offering for veteran reenlistment was slightly better, since their terms of enlistment would not expire until October anyway. For Lucius Jones the thought of going home was overpowering:

> So, on December 23rd, 1863, I re-enlisted as a veteran volunteer: took my furlough, and started for home. Was in Baltimore on New Year's day—the coldest day in many a year. Hardly any trains were running. We arrive at Elmira in due time, and there took the train for Buffalo; and finally got home. Was glad to see everybody, and had a fine visit. My mother thought there was nothing too good for me—chicken pot pie, mince pie, and in fact everything in the eating line had to suffer.[9]

The plan was simple: if regiments could reenlist a minimum of three-quarters of their men, they could keep their organization and designations; units that could not would be disbanded with men still owing time being dispersed out to other regiments.[10] For two of the Excelsior units there was no question of continuing. One Hundred and Twentieth New York, which had been mustered into service in August of '62, still had many months of service owing and would eventually receive men from the 72nd. The same was true for the 73rd New York but for different reasons. The influx of 250 or so men collected from the 163rd N.Y. upon its dissolution back in January of '63 would mean Fourth Excelsior would carry on.[11]

On December 24 everyone in the regiment intending to reenlist had done so, making it clear how matters would resolve themselves come early summer. Around 200 men from the 72nd would remain to go on, not enough to meet the three-quarters requirement. This meant the regiment would be disbanded. These 200 comprised all of the original Company H along with men who had joined after the October '61 mustering and some others. Men who joined during the few recruiting surges would have time remaining to serve.[12] Men such as James Dean who had joined just before Fredericksburg and those few others who joined later still owed time. Of course a few reenlisted, either anxious to see the thing through, with no better prospects back home, or still driven from a sense of old fashioned duty. Three other Excelsior regiments would face similar dissolutions. The remaining men from First Excelsior, the 70th New York, would be transferred to the 86th N.Y. Those left in the 71st N.Y. would go to the 120th N.Y., while men with unexpired terms in the 74th N.Y. would be sent to the 40th N.Y.[13] Thoughts of home, now even more pressing upon the minds of the men, would have to wait; there was still fighting to be done.

In early February word came for the regiment to ready itself for a move. Instinctively the men knew something wasn't right. The time of year, the weather and the ground conditions were all wrong; spring campaigning shouldn't be for months at least. But ready themselves they did. On February 3, Major General Benjamin Butler, who commanded 6,000 men holed up on the Virginia Peninsula at Bermuda Hundred, had won approval from Washington war planners for a surprise attack upon Richmond. Key to Butler's plan was a diversionary attack across the Rapidan by Meade's Army of the Potomac. Major General John Sedgwick, in temporary command of the army, strongly objected; he argued that not only were the conditions wrong for such a large attack, but also an attack now would only serve to alert Lee to weaknesses in his defenses, thus making any future attacks all the more difficult. "Uncle John," as he was affectionately called by his men, privately believed the operation was designed more to serve Butler's ego than any military requirement. Overruled by Halleck, Sedgwick reluctantly went forward with the attack set for February 6.[14]

Leading the attack at Morton's Ford was II Corps, with portions of III Corps, including Excelsior Brigade, in support. II Corps men sloshed through knee-deep mud while crossing the still ice-choked river and assaulted the Rebel positions on the far side. Initially the Federals made good progress, but as Confederates reacted to the surprise attack, the assault stalled and was eventually pushed back. The attack cost II Corps 200 men. Making matters worse, Butler had called off his attack on Richmond after only a few hours into the operation, rendering the entire effort and its accompanying sacrifices an exercise in futility.[15] One Excelsior Brigade man summed up the whole affair this way: "We was out on reconoisance [sic] to the Rapidan, our division was reserve for the Second Corps. We lay about 2 days at the river & then turned about & came back to camp. The road's was in an awfull condition, mudd over shoe tops."[16] Uncle John's worst fears had been realized. Now come spring, when the real push would come, Lee would be prepared.

Back in camp, Lieutenant Colonel Leonard was running the day-to-day operations of the regiment as necessitated by Colonel Austin's nearly continuous absence that fall. By late January the sickly Austin was back in the field and anxious to take care of unfinished matters dogging him since spring. Hanging over the colonel's head were a number of charges including embezzlement stemming from his acquisition of a horse and mule. The question was whether these animals were for his personal use or if Austin had repaid the army the cost of feeding them. Charges focused on events from late May while back in Falmouth and from September while camped near Culpepper.[17] With the army stopped and in camp, Austin pressed for a resolution to these matters, which he saw as completely unfounded. In a letter to brigade commander Brewster dated January 29, Austin asked, "that a *Court* may be called as soon as the exigences [sic] of the Services will permit."[18] The colonel continued in the letter to accuse an unnamed "*Gang* of *Conspirators*" of working their "hellish designs" against him for the past year and said that he was "determined to settle" the matter.[19] Austin left the conspirators unnamed but it is clear he considered Leonard among them. In another letter to Brewster dated the next day regarding a request from Leonard for leave, Austin stated, "He had made charges against me and it would [be] unjust to keep me awaiting his return."[20] Perhaps Austin's notion of the gang of conspirators wasn't all in his imagination. Austin was frequently absent from the regiment and had a reputation among the rank and file as a stuffed shirt.[21] Additionally, one charge against him included allegations that he had ordered a quartermaster lieutenant to falsify records surrounding the ownership and feeding of the mule in question. Taken together, Austin's actions may have cultivated such a degree of resentment within the regiment as to create fertile ground enough for his "gang of conspirators" to flourish.

Conspiracy or not, the exigencies of the service were on Austin's side, and he had his court-martial just days later on February 11. Convened in the camp of the Third Division under the supervision of Brigadier General William Morris, the court found Austin not guilty on 35 of the 37 charges and specifications leveled against him. Of the two specifications

12. The Struggle to Petersburg

assigned guilty verdicts, both were modified, removing any criminality. In accordance with the verdicts the court concluded, "Colonel Austin is released from arrest and will return to duty."[22] What Austin's duties were at this point weren't exactly obvious. Though it is clear in the Brewster letter of January 30 that he still held some sway over Leonard and presumably the entire regiment, every official report from Gettysburg onward, and at every level of command, indicates Leonard as commanding the 72nd New York, with no further mention of Austin. Perhaps the reduced size of the regiment at this stage of the war was too small to necessitate command by a full colonel, hence command devolved to a lieutenant colonel. Given Austin's sickness and frequent absences from the seat of war, it is easy to conclude he was dubbed a supernumerary and served out the rest of his service in some forgotten staff position, eventually mustering out in July of '64 for reasons of disability.

While many of the men pondered and argued over enlistments, reenlistments, and possible discharge dates, there were big moves up north. Major General Ulysses S. Grant was summoned in early March to Washington D.C. There, the hero of the West was promoted to lieutenant general and given overall command of Federal forces, leaving his old friend William T. Sherman to command the western army. Grant determined to travel with the Army of the Potomac and concentrate on the war's grand strategy, while daily running of this army would remain with George Meade.[23]

Though Meade half expected to be removed from command for failing to wrap up the war following the Confederate defeat at Gettysburg, Grant assured him his job was secure but issued succinct instructions: "Lee's army will be your objective point. Wherever Lee goes, there you will go also."[24] The destruction of the Army of Northern Virginia was the goal of Grant's new initiative, and the method of realizing this goal was equally clear and uncomplicated. Recognizing his abundant ability to replace men lost on the field and Lee's complete lack of manpower reserves, Grant would wear down the Rebels in a war of attrition by setting all the armies at his disposal in motion at once, effectively preventing him from shifting forces to wherever the threat was greatest. Believing Lee hadn't army enough to fight such a war, Grant took the strategy of denying him manpower one step further by suspending the prisoner parole system, which had effectively allowed freed prisoners to return to the fight. Prisoners North and South from now on would stay in prison and wait out the war as best they could.

Anxious to carry the war to Lee, Grant made two important adjustments prior to his first offensive as general in chief. First he would bolster the size of his army by tightening up on leaves and furloughs and by bringing previously unused units into the fight. On paper his army looked massive, but many men were absent from their units and the army had done a poor job of getting them back from leave in a timely manner; this would be fixed, yielding fuller units. Grant would also get units previously held in reserve or which had served months or even years of garrison duty back into the field. Surplus teamsters, staff, and heavy artillery units who had sat idle in the defenses of Washington now found themselves packing muskets as infantry. By the time Grant was ready to move he would have nearly 120,000 men set to oppose Lee's estimated 65,000.[25]

The second of Grant's adjustments would be the streamlining of the Army of the Potomac by disbanding the undermanned I and III Corps, their troops to be parceled out between the II and VI Corps.[26] Disbanding III Corps would serve at least two purposes. III Corps was a mere shell of its former fighting strength and its commander, William French, was seen as a liability. French was blamed for much of what had gone wrong at Mine Run, and Grant could indirectly sack the ineffective general by dissolving his command. This move would also rid Grant of the troublesome Second Division commander Henry Prince, who had marched his men in circles the previous fall back near Brandy Station. Feelings ran high among the men of the two corps slated to be disbanded. Many men made appeals to Washington, asking the corps remain intact. On March 16 the III Corps was assembled for review. All the old regiments were there. Some who had been successful in drawing in replacements looked fit and ready to fight, while still others fielded barely 200 men. Generals French and Sedgwick reviewed the men and then it was over, the last review of the III Corps.[27] Henri LeFevre-Brown of Company B would later write, "Orders were issued by the War Department March 23, 1864, disbanding the 'Old Third Army Corps,' than which there was none better; and no corps of the army had done more, or harder fighting. This fact, however, had no weight at headquarters."[28] Inevitably both the First and Second divisions of the III Corps were combined and transferred to the II Corps under General Winfield S. Hancock, comprising his new Fourth Division. Hancock reviewed the new Fourth Division for the first time on April 14. As a nod to their service, these proud men of the old III Corps were allowed to continue wearing their former corps' badges, the white and red diamonds, which they did till the war's end.[29] "We belong to the 4th Div. 2nd Corp. but wear the Diamond yet and all the power in the army could [not] take that badge from us,"[30] declared Private Dean. Another Chautauqua man offered his perspective to the readers of the *Jamestown Journal*:

> At last our glorious old 3d Corps has passed away, and is now numbered with the things of the past. This event has been expected for some time, but, notwithstanding all that, when the news came that it was no more, our feeling were those of sorrow, for we felt as though we had lost our dearest and best friend. The "Diamond" [which was the badge of the 3d Corps] has been our guiding star on many a hard-fought battle-field, and we felt that in wearing it we were wearing a badge of honor, which to-day is as pure and free from stain and defeat as when we received it. Our two old Division [Hooker's and Kearney's] are still permitted to retain it, but how long that privilege will be given us we cannot tell. Our family circle is broken—the old homestead has passed into strange hands and we have commenced a new life as a Junior member of the 2d Corps. No murmuring are heard against this order, for a true soldier never questions the acts of his leader, but a quiet and subdued sorrow has settled upon us, which nothing but an active campaign can brush away.[31]

Grant in charge was a welcome change from the uninspired leadership of before. Grant's reputation as an aggressive leader who knew how to win preceded him, although some men took his arrival with a dash of skepticism. "You've never met Bobby Lee and his boys," was a common taunt directed toward Grant, "and mind you, Lee is just over the Rapidan."[32] James Dean concluded, "The men like General Grant well enough but they think that old Lee is more than a matter for him."[33] Other soldiers decided to give the new man a chance. "He cannot be weaker or more inefficient than the generals who have wasted the lives of our comrade during the past three years," wrote one man in his diary. Another Third Excelsior man penned a sardonic view of Grant for his hometown paper:

> Lieut.-Gen. Grand arrived here yesterday, and has established his Head Quarters at Culpepper. His arrival is hailed with joy by the soldiers, although they do not expect that he will accomplish such wonders as the people of the North are looking for, and, strange as it may appear to some of your readers, it is the candid opinion of the majority of the Army that Richmond will remain in the hands of the Rebels ten days longer to say the least.[34]

Six days after Hancock's review, on April 20 the 72nd was presented with a new national flag. A gift from New York City, it was presented to the regiment by the Rev. Joseph T.

Duyrea. "We were presented today with a new flag,"[35] wrote Pvt. Hiram Stoddard of Company B in a letter home:

> It was presented to us by a minister from New York City. It is the third flag we have been presented with. We have never disonered [sic] one yet & if we must carry this Banner into the smoke of battle, may God go with it & us & may its bright collors [sic] never be trampled beneth [sic] the feet of Traitors but may it soon wave over hill & valley & throughout the whole land. And may the time not be far distant when there will not be one to say ought against its being unfurled by the breez. May they be proud to have it wave over their heads.[36]

The entirety of the revamped II Corps was held in review two days later on the 22nd. Hancock was there, of course, as corps commander, along with George Meade and U.S. Grant, plus the usual cloud of lesser nobles.[37] Something was definitely afoot, and the men could tell the long-awaited big move would soon begin. Wives who had adorned the camps were among the first ordered out, certainly a sure signal to snooping Confederates a move was coming. Chaplain Twichell, just back from a furlough in New York, wrote his mother, "The note of preparation sounds on every side. All superfluous persons and baggage have been sent away, the supply trains of food and ammunition are being loaded, the inspectors are busy searching out and remedying all deficiencies."[38]

Marching orders were received late on May 3 and by eleven that night the boys had formed on the color line. With the 72nd being detailed to guard the divisional ammunition train, the regiment and their charge finally stepped off near two on the morning of the 4th, nearly a whole day's march behind the rest of the army.[39] Grant's massive army was heading east and south from their base at Culpepper in order to skirt the Confederate pickets. The bulk of the army would cross the Rapidan River at two places: the V and VI Corps at Germanna Ford across newly built pontoon bridges, and the II Corps farther east at Ely Ford.[40]

Though Hiram Stoddard, Lucius Jones and the rest found themselves in a new corps, very little else had changed. The five original regiments were still together supplemented by the 120th N.Y. Now the brigade was bolstered by the addition of two other regiments from outside New York: the 11th Massachusetts and the 84th Pennsylvania. Both were refugees from the III Corps' First Brigade, Second Division.[41] Excelsior Brigade commander Colonel William Brewster had been with them since after Chancellorsville, having also led the Second Fire Zouaves, the 73rd N.Y. The New Yorkers did have a new division commander, one with whom they weren't totally unfamiliar: Brigadier General Gershom Mott. Mott was a 42-year-old New Jersey businessman who had been intermittent commander of the New Jersey Blues, a brigade mostly made up of New Jersey units now comprising the Third Brigade, Second Division, II Corps. This was Mott's first divisional command.[42]

All day of the 4th Stoddard and his mates marched with the plodding ammunition train. After an uneventful day, the parade finally bivouacked near Ely's Ford at midnight.[43]

Grant's plan was straightforward: cross the Rapidan, flush out Lee's army, which would be encamped on its south side, drive it into open ground and crush it with superior numbers. To do this, the Federal army would have to pass through a thick forest of trees and bushes known as the Wilderness. Grant's plan was to move through the Wilderness quickly, engaging Lee on the far side. But Lee perceived fighting in this tangle as a way to offset the Federals' superior numbers, especially in artillery.[44]

Lee moved quickly to stop Grant in the Wilderness by moving two corps east under Richard Ewell and A.P. Hill. These units would slow down the advancing Yankees until the remainder of Lee's forces could move up. On the night of May 4, after one day's march,

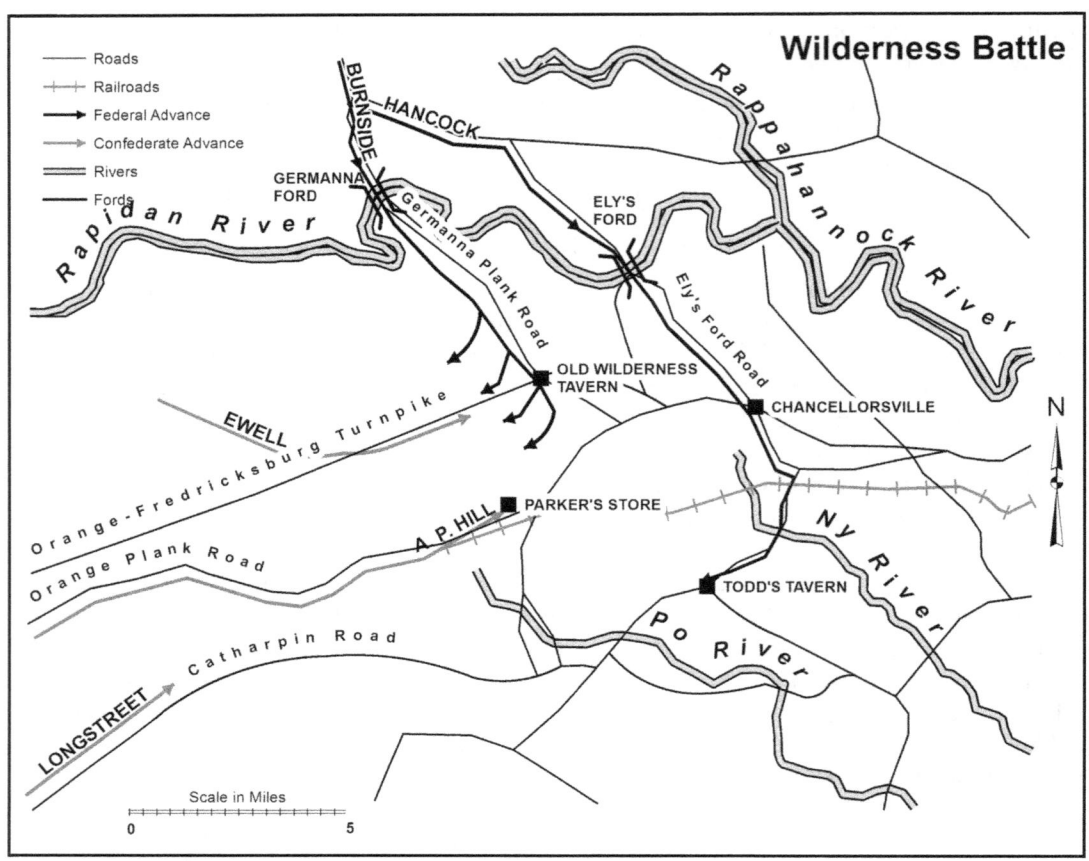

Union forces unwittingly helped Lee achieve his aims by camping in the Wilderness for the night, believing the Confederates were too far off to engage them in the waste. Near daybreak of May 5, lead elements of Ewell's Confederate II Corps clashed with Gouverneur K. Warren's V Corps on the Orange-Fredericksburg Turnpike. The battle was begun.[45]

The Wilderness was providing the confusion Lee had bargained for. Early in the fight elements of the V and VI Corps engaged the Rebels in what was developing as an east–west running affair along the Orange-Fredericksburg Turnpike. Slightly further to the east, Hancock's II Corps was not engaged as his troops followed roads south.[46] With the fight just beginning off to their west, the 72nd and the ammunition train finally moved south of the river around 9 a.m. It continued moving south until later that afternoon when it stopped to bivouac on the old Chancellorsville battlefield, the same ground they had fought over just a year before.[47]

Stopped and settled, the men now wandered around the old battlefield. Recognizing ground upon which they had fought one year earlier, the men of the regiment identified a skeleton lying by a large fallen tree as of an old comrade, 18-year-old Private Henry Heyl of Company H, his initials written in a hat and scratched on a cup still by his side. While certainly the sight of a corpse, even one reduced to a skeleton, was nothing new, some took time to remember young Henry as a fine soldier and man.[48]

May 5 saw both armies concentrating the fight in two areas: Federal corps under Sedgwick and Warren hammered at Ewell's confederates along the Orange-Fredericksburg Turnpike, while further south, Hancock began his fight against A.P. Hill's III Corps. At dawn of the second day of battle, Grant decided to concentrate his attacks against Hill by moving west along the Orange Plank Road, which somewhat paralleled the Orange-Fredericksburg Pike. Grant would reinforce Hancock's II Corps while sending Burnside's IX Corps between the two main battle areas in an attempt to hit Hill's left flank.[49]

The regiment was relieved as train guard at 2 a.m. on the morning of May 6 and ordered to the front to rejoin the brigade and the rest of II Corps. Before heading out the regiment broke ranks and made coffee. With coffee finished, Leonard led his regiment south and around 6 a.m. rejoined the brigade near the junction of the Orange Plank and Brock roads. It was at once deployed ahead of the breastworks as skirmishers. After advancing some distance into the dense undergrowth, Leonard halted the regiment and asked for five volunteers to go ahead of the regiment to locate the enemy. Sergeant-Major John M. Lyon led the detail with four privates from various companies. After advancing several hundred yards, the party crested a small rise and faced a "heavy rebel skirmish line, which was advancing, supported by two lines of battle."[50] With the enemy's first fire, the sergeant-major fell, shot through his left side. Private James Young of Company B, also among the scouting party, made it to Lyon's side, and with enemy pressing all around, was able to move the stricken Lyon through the thick brush, effecting their escape back to the regiment. Soon after their return, sparks and embers from the ensuing battle set the woods afire at the spot where Lyon had fallen. The other men of the advance party were never seen again.[51]

With the sergeant-major back in the relative safety of the regiment, the battle continued to grow as Hancock's men, with portions of other corps, worked to drive Hill's Confederates back. Seventy-Third New York and others joined the line held by Third Excelsior as the Federal attack gained momentum. With weight of numbers on their side, Federal troops began to steadily advance against the Rebels. After pushing a brigade of Georgians nearly a mile, Rebel reinforcements brought Yankee progress to a halt. With neither side strong enough to push the other, the Excelsiors stood their ground and slugged it out.

After two hours of nearly continuous skirmishing and with the remainder of Longstreet's Confederate I Corps now advancing, the Federal position could not be held. The weight of additional enemy troops moving into and through the maze of trees and underbrush and the increasingly disorganized state of the Union lines proved too much. Disorganized units were not exclusive to Federal troops, however. As Southern troops advanced, smoke and brush reduced visibility, and men shot at shadowy figures or mere outlines. Moving among his various units on horseback, Longstreet and his staff were particularly vulnerable to stray and ricocheting lead. In the confusion a Virginia unit fired at a group of riders; Longstreet slumped in the saddle as blood poured from his neck and shoulder. With his final orders being to press the enemy, the general was removed to the rear for urgent treatment.

Mott's Yankee division faced fresh enemy troops on their left and rear flanks; unable to hold, they were forced back to the line they held at daybreak. Confederates pursued Brewster's Excelsiors but were repulsed as they attacked the newly reestablished line.[52] By 4 p.m. this line of log breastworks, "formed as they were of dry logs and brush, caught fire and soon became untenable,"[53] wrote Lt. Col. Michael Burns of the 73rd New York. Flames and dwindling ammunition supplies forced the Excelsior Brigade to fall back to a second line of works. Retiring yet another 300 yards to form a second line of battle, the brigade was soon resupplied with ammunition. Using a blanket as a sling, Private Henri LeFevre-Brown resupplied the regiment by carrying packages of ammunition between the various companies. Dodging

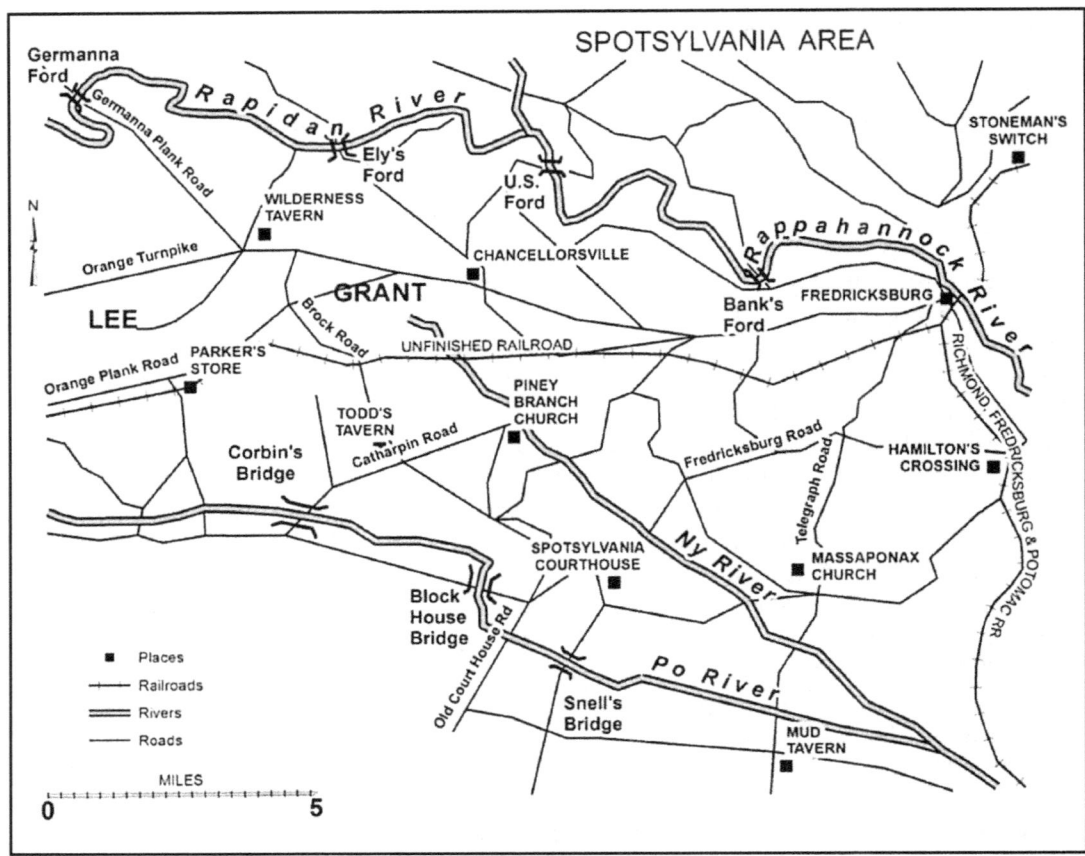

enemy fire, the brave private made three trips along the line.⁵⁴ "The enemy attempted to occupy the ground so abandoned between the two lines of breastworks, but were received with such a withering fire from the troops in the second line that they were forced to retire,"⁵⁵ wrote Burns. With the fires of the first breastworks dying down, the men of Excelsior Brigade charged the staggered Rebels. Rebels scampered for the rear as the New Yorkers retook the first line of works, along with several prisoners.⁵⁶

Fighting in the Wilderness trailed off with the coming of night. The 72nd had losses of 21 men for the day. Their actions of the day earned two of their number the Medal of Honor: Private Young for his rescue of the sergeant-major and Private LeFevre-Brown for exposing himself to enemy fire as he resupplied the regiment with ammunition.⁵⁷ General Grant realized he would be unable to drive Lee's army as he had planned, and further attacks here in this tangle would be futile; he would attempt to slide around Lee. Grant soon concluded that the town of Spotsylvania Court House would now be the objective of his army, allowing him to place his army on Lee's flank and to disrupt the enemy's already tenuous supply lines.⁵⁸

But Grant faced a problem. Never before had the Army of the Potomac continued south after such a severe setback as the Battle of the Wilderness. There were losses of well over 17,000 men during three days of fighting. Grant nonetheless decided to keep to his strategy of maintaining the pressure and wearing down the Confederate Army. Army of the Potomac corps and divisional commanders had grown cautious under the command of previous generals more committed to not losing the war than to winning it. Grant's offensive spirit went contrary to this mindset held amongst those senior officers who had, after the previous three years, expected withdrawal and regrouping following a defeat rather than attack. As for the men, though they had been in a hard fight, the rank and file knew there was a change for the better when they began moving south rather than retreating north.[59]

Grant began to disengage from the Rebels and shift his army south on May 7. Robert E. Lee understood the importance of Spotsylvania and immediately dispatched troops there. The first to arrive would have an advantage in the battle that was sure to follow. As the Federals moved south, the regiments of the Excelsior Brigade formed the rear guard of the army and occupied ground once held by V Corps.[60]

Yankee cavalry was in the vanguard as Union troops began their march, but the task of opening the way seemed too much for the Northern mounted men. Too many untried, green troopers failed to mix well with too few veterans, causing problems with command and control. This only served to exacerbate vague and conflicting orders and sometimes stubborn Rebel resistance. So the job of clearing the way was given over to Gouverneur Warren's V Corps infantry on the morning of the 8th. Warren's infantry was soon pushing aside the Confederate rear guard, but progress was still painfully slow, allowing lead elements of Lee's army to extend south first.[61]

By the time all troops, North and South, were in place, and the race over, Lee's army held the key positions. It was now up to Grant's men to dislodge them from what were fast becoming ever more formidable entrenchments north of Spotsylvania. By the morning of May 9, the Confederate position was shaped like a north-pointing V. At the apex of the V was a strong salient nicknamed the Mule Shoe, so named because of its shape. Recognizing that this prominence invited Yankee attack, Lee studded the scarcely half-mile-wide area with a formidable array of artillery. A Yankee attack here would no doubt be costly.[62]

Grant was making the rounds to the various commands all morning. Sedgwick had established his headquarters near Warren's V Corps and was helping to work out some command issues within that corps. After Grant's departure Sedgwick continued to take an active role in positioning troops, despite effective and incessant Rebel sniper fire. Noticing some infantry had moved forward of the artillery line, Uncle John moved to correct the situation. When enemy bullets splattered near his position and Yankee underlings dived for cover, Sedgwick chided them and concluded, "They can't hit an elephant at that distance." After the sergeant in question righted himself, saluted and explained an earlier near-miss, Sedgwick relented and laughed. A moment later a bullet whined through the air, hitting with an audible thud; Sedgwick fell with a small hole beneath his left eye. Blood gushed from the wound as the general's staff carried him to the rear; Uncle John was dead.

At the time Sedgwick was being shot, Winfield Hancock's II Corps was locating itself on the extreme right side of the Union position.[63] Excelsior men and the remainder of the corps built breastworks most of the day. Seventieth and 72nd New York regiments received orders around midnight to fall in with a temporary "Provisional Brigade" under Colonel John Ramsey and were on the march toward the other end of the Federal line by 3 a.m. of the 10th.[64] The rest of the Excelsior Brigade remained with Mott.

By 10 a.m. a portion of Ramsey's ad hoc brigade, including Third Excelsior, was in motion probing the strength of the Rebel defenses in front of the V and VI Corps. This "feeling party" encountered and engaged the enemy and drove in "a heavy rebel skirmish line, which retired to a strong line of works on the second ridge." Too weak to press further, the 72nd N.Y. and rest of the provisional brigade fell back, but not before colonel Leonard had gained important information about the terrain and enemy positions. Ramsey's brigade continued skirmishing until being relieved around 5 p.m. when Grant's planned main attack was scheduled to begin.[65]

Grant's design was to commence a general attack across the entire Confederate front to develop a vulnerable spot. A key to this plan, developed by Colonel Emory Upton and presented to Grant, would be a charge made by 12 veteran regiments led by Upton himself. Upton would smash into the Rebel line at the Mule Shoe on a narrow front only three regiments wide without pausing to reload. Once the breach had been made, Mott's Division would hit near the gap, exploiting the breach, and collapse Lee's line.[66]

Almost from the start things went wrong. Warren began his V Corps' attack on the right of the Federal line an hour early of the 5 p.m. start time and promptly got bogged down in front of strongly entrenched Rebels. Shortly after, he withdrew. Because of Warren's miscues, Grant postponed the entire attack until after 6. Mott, still minus the 72nd, was now positioned to the left of Upton and slightly east of the Mule Shoe's apex, but he was not informed of the change and attacked as scheduled.[67]

To prevent Confederate pickets from divining the full nature of the attack, much of the positioning of both Mott's and Upton's men was done far to the rear of the front lines. Grant's timetable had unfortunately not allowed all the planning needed by the typically sluggish Army of the Potomac. Both Upton and Mott had only the most general ideas of what enemy works might lie before them and only the basic notions of the best routes of attack. Still with an unclear picture of where the enemy was, Mott stepped off at the appointed time and easily overran a light enemy skirmish line. As the division exited the protection of the concealing woods, he discovered they were moving oblique to the Confederate front, in full view of enemy artillery. Mott's division was several hundred yards from the designated point of attack, but they would never make it. Almost immediately Rebel guns began to pour fire into Mott's advancing division. Under this hail of iron, the lead regiments soon broke for the rear, followed by most of the division, leaving officers frantically trying to urge men on and reform disintegrating companies. With enlistments of many of Mott's men's soon to expire, reforming for a new attack with these reluctant soldiers was futile.[68] Mott's debut as a divisional commander had become an utter failure.

Upton, unaware of Mott's situation, attacked at the revised, later time and met with spectacular results. His charge opened an immense hole in part of the Confederate line held by a brigade under General George Doles of Richard Ewell's corps. The narrow front offered by Upton allowed regiments in the rear to push on beyond the first and second enemy lines. But without Motts's supporting troops, the attack could not be sustained. Upton soon realized help would not be arriving, stranding him and his 12 regiments far ahead of the Union lines. Lee brought up reinforcements that were able to pour a galling fire into Upton's men, driving them to ground as Yankee objectives turned from attack to survival. Upton eventually withdrew under the cover of darkness. The miscues of the day had cost Grant a superb opportunity and Upton over 1,000 men.[69]

Despite the losses, Chaplain Twichell remained steadfast in his beliefs about the conflict.

> It seems awful to be here in the midst of this wild country with such scenes of slaughter and carnage occurring daily, but it is God's war and the Truth is being vindicated. I begin to feel, after witnessing the death of so many noble young men, that I will not keep myself back if I am in any way called on to make a sacrifice of my life....
> I wish all the North could look in here and behold how much is given freely for the

national cause. It would give a higher love and a quicker pulse to the public love of country than all the reading and thinking in the world.[70]

Leonard's men had fallen back during the night and joined the rest of II Corps. Around 3 a.m. the New Yorkers and much of the rest of the corps moved west about two miles and bivouacked there. At eleven that morning they moved again, this time back east to occupy rifle pits.[71]

Grant made plans for the next day while his men prepared breastworks throughout the 11th, anticipating the upcoming action. Hoping to seize the success that had eluded him earlier, Grant wondered, if a large brigade attacking along a narrow front could breach the enemy's defenses, why not try it at corps strength? As for Lee, he expected Grant to move away from Spotsylvania. Lee needed to be able to follow quickly, so he moved most of his artillery to more accessible roads, roads far from the Mule Shoe, the very point of the unexpected Federal attack.[72] Confederate artillery would be out of position just when it would be needed most.

Seventy-Second New York along with the rest of the provisional brigade moved still further to the left and to the front around 9 p.m. Here they continued to build breastworks near the spot where Upton had launched his failed assault.[73] The massive attack that Grant envisioned would be led by Hancock and his II Corps.[74] Ramsey's Provisional Brigade along with Leonard's men would be held in reserve.[75]

Hancock's II Corps stepped off early on the morning of the 12th, around 4:30 a.m., across some of the same ground that Upton had attacked. Within minutes his compact force of 20,000 had charged and then overwhelmed the defenders, capturing more than 3,000 Confederate soldiers including generals Edward Johnson and George Steuart. Despite the success of their attack, Hancock's men became disorganized in the crowded confines of the Mule Shoe's trenches. They had punched through a sizeable portion of the Confederate line, but the Rebel earthworks were built with breaks that ran perpendicular to the front breastwork. These breaks were placed to protect against enfilade fire should there be a breach. They now served to hinder the lateral movement of Hancock's men and provided hard points of defense for the Southerners.[76]

Lee reacted by sending in reinforcements including the previously withdrawn artillery toward the apex of his line, the point of the breach. The battle raged into ever-greater chaos and intensity as both sides poured in troops. Fighting became hand to hand in places, with troops from both sides becoming a hopeless tangle of humanity. Northern and Southern men took cover behind respective sides of the same log barricade as men reached over and fired blindly into massed enemy troops. Dead bodies hit by so much repeated cannon and musket fire were turned to unrecognizable mush.[77]

The Excelsior Brigade, minus the 70th and 72nd, were heavily engaged in the midst of the fight. Three men from the 73rd New York earned the Medal of Honor for their work this day. Irish-born Christopher Wilson earned his when he picked up his unit's flag from the wounded color-bearer and carried it as they charged the enemy works and then later captured the colors of the 56th Virginia. He carried both banners to safety.[78] Colonel Robert McAllister, commander of Mott's other brigade, later wrote, "These massed columns pressed forward to the Salient. The Stars and Stripes and the Stars and Bars nearly touched each other across these works."[79]

Grant tried to break the stalemate by sending additional troops to breach the Rebel line.[80] Three hours after the attack started, around 8 a.m., the 72nd N.Y. was sent to an open field in support of a battery of artillery near where Mott's division had attacked. Shortly afterward the battery was sent elsewhere, and Leonard's boys were sent by General David Birney to help protect another section of artillery, this one composed of captured guns.

All morning the fighting had slowly moved around to the left face of the Mule Shoe and it was here, near the Bloody Angle, where the 72nd N.Y. had been sent, some distance from the balance of Mott's Division. With the contraband guns now repositioned along a road leading into the enemy works, Yankee volunteers fired on the gun's former owners. Exposed to Rebel return fire, the guns were quickly disabled, forcing the men of Third Excelsior to fall back to better cover. From here the regiment was repositioned closer to the enemy works and continued to fight all day. The regiment was in the front lines, while Rebels made repeated attempts to retake lost portions of the Mule Shoe. Each enemy attack was repulsed as the 72nd spent the entire night on line, keeping up a steady volume of musketry until the division pulled back the next morning.[81] James Dean of Company B described the fight this way:

> The morning of the 12th the division which is now called Birney's Division charged (at their) 1st Div. 2nd Corps and took 22 cannon and 8000 prisoners. We took them by surprise and used the bayonet more than the ball that day. The hardest fighting of the whole war took place, nearly the whole army took a part of it. There were a terrible slaughter took place but we held our own we were on one side of a fence and they were on the other, or breast works I should say, there where the dead and wounded lay on the works 3 deep.[82]

Lee formed a new defensive line during the middle of the day. Giving up claim to the Mule Shoe, this new line stretched across the apex of his V-shaped lines, below the Mule Shoe and Bloody Angle. Torrents of rain were washing over piles of dead bodies when part of Ambrose Burnside's IX Corps advanced near 2 p.m. against this new line and was stopped. Federal troops continued to press in and around the Mule Shoe and Bloody Angle, but the new Confederate line was too strong, Grant's men too tired and the cost was already too high. Fighting began to trail off.[83]

By dawn's first light on the 13th, Grant had ceased most offensive actions; he'd now have to find a new way to get behind Lee. Grant needed to move quickly. Many men within his Army of the Potomac would be going home with their enlistments set to run out. Already many commands behaved timidly, as men questioned the value of assaults they saw as hopeless. Grant had green troops on the way, but they would need time to develop into seasoned, reliable troops. He believed Lee's army had been badly hurt during the fighting at the Mule Shoe. Indeed, Richard Ewell's II Corps had been nearly wrecked in the fight, but Grant also knew Lee soon would enjoy reinforcements coming from other minor fronts to make good Ewell's losses. Grant had no time to lose in exploiting this advantage, or the carnage at the Mule Shoe would truly have been in vain.

While Grant pondered his next move, both armies took advantage of better weather and a lull in the fighting to dry out, rest, eat and tend to army business.[84] With Mott's failure to properly support Upton's attack, together with his poor showing in the Wilderness, the former dry goods clerk was reduced back to brigade command and his small division consolidated into the Third Division of the II Corps under Major General David B. Birney. The Excelsiors were designated Fourth Brigade, and Brewster remained in command.[85]

Grant ordered an attack for the following day, certain there had to be a weak spot somewhere in Lee's line either at or very near the Mule Shoe. The two-pronged assault started with great hesitation by the commanders charged with leading it. The assault soon bogged down thanks to poor planning, appalling terrain conditions, and effective Confederate counterattacks. Once again, at the end of the 14th, Federals sat frustrated as both sides stared at each other from secure and ever-improving earthworks.[86]

Hancock's troops were not involved in the attacks of the 14th. But Leonard's men were up at 3 a.m. to occupy the forward line of rifle pits, where they skirmished with the Rebs all day. Foul weather ruled out any further attacks the next day by Grant, and the Union general doubted Lee would attack him given the conditions. With a break in the battle, the armies sorted themselves out. Hancock's troops still composed the right of the Federal line, and the men spent their time improving earth works and trading shots with enemy skirmishers. Hancock's men had extended their lines toward the Federal rear, in order to protect their own supply lines and to better address any enemy probing coming from the north. During this entire time the men of the regiment continued to dig trenches and reposition their lines as the terrain and officers dictated. With the army's almost constant shifting, the chores of caring for the dead were left undone. "On the 15th we were on picket along part of the works,"[87] wrote Pvt. Dean, "and some of the wounded lay there moaning yet and had not been touched yet. And the smell from the dead was sickening and it is a question if they are buried yet."[88]

Hiram Stoddard described his situation this way:

> While I am writing to you I am sitting in a rifle pit & they are skirmishing but a little ways in the front, rather a poor place to write a letter but I thought I must drop you a line to let you know that through the goodness of the Lord I am still spared. O how good the Lord is to unworthy me. I never thought that human beings could undergo what the Army of the Potomack has for the past ten days.[89]

Increasingly Grant mulled over the idea of giving up on Spotsylvania and moving south. Such a move would only lengthen the war, and there were no guarantees he could come again to grips with Lee like he was here in the mud of Spotsylvania. But a time-consuming stalemate would only enhance the Southern situation, as more Confederate reinforcements were sure to arrive, while at the same time Federal enlistments were running out and Union troops left the front.[90]

With his enemy before him Grant decided on another grand assault modeled after earlier attacks, which while proving ultimately unsuccessful, had shown spectacular initial promise. Multiple divisions, mainly from II Corps, were scheduled to crunch through the now-abandoned Mule Shoe and collapse what Grant believed was a weakened Confederate line that crossed the base of the Mule Shoe salient. Throughout the 16th and 17th troops maneuvered into position with Birney's Division on the left and in reserve. For three days the men of the 72nd shifted from one line of trenches to another, building new breastworks as needed. "Lay still on the 17th," remembered Henri LeFevre-Brown, "and it was the first day since May 5 that the regiment was not under fire."[91]

At 3 a.m. on the 18th the regiment was called up to find the rest of the II Corps in battle array. Hour later Union artillery opened a massive pounding of the Confederate line, soon followed by advancing waves of blue infantry. But stubborn Rebel works and canister brought the Union attack to a halt. By 6 a.m. messages were streaming back to Grant's headquarters requesting reinforcements or saying that the advance had stalled and brigade and divisional commanders were slugging it out best they could.[92] By noon all Yankee offensive actions had been cancelled, and the rest of the day was spent withdrawing units as safely as possible.[93]

For most of the day Leonard and his regiment occupied a line of rifle pits, and the carnage raged in front of them, but by eleven that night they returned to their bivouac from the night before.[94]

Before the sun set on the 18th Grant resolved to move south and attempt to cross the North Anna River. Crossing the North Anna would place him on the same side as Richmond and avoid more difficult river crossings further south. Several roads would provide good, usable routes for his corps. There were also enough smaller rivers and creeks to help protect these corps' flanks while moving and at their most vulnerable. As Grant mulled over this next move, he saw an opportunity to bring the Confederates out of their defenses and draw them into battle. If II Corps under Hancock could be sent ahead of the rest of the army, Lee might take the bait and move to attack it, whereby the rest of the Union hordes could descend for the kill. Grant knew there were risks to be sure, but the network of roads, together with proper use of concealment and aggressive movement, offered an opportunity the general could not decline.[95]

Orders were issued and the army was put into motion late that night with instructions to conceal movement as much as possible. Hancock's corps now held the right-most part of the Federal line north of Spotsylvania. His men would need to pull out of the line and swing far to the rear and left to clear the other corps still entrenched. Once east enough and clear of the other Federal units, Hancock would have an unimpeded march south. The 72nd N.Y. along with the rest of Birney's Division would bring up II Corps' rear while troops from other commands manned the trenches to cover the withdrawal, repelling any potential Rebel snooping and maintaining the appearance that Grant was still focused only on Spotsylvania.[96] By 2 a.m. on the 19th, the regiment and the rest of II Corps were on the move south.[97]

With arrival of daylight, Confederates were unsure of exactly what moves the Federals had made during the night. It was thought Grant was merely extending his lines to the south, but it wasn't clear which troops were involved. Lee and his generals increasingly believed the Union right had somehow changed but were uncertain as to how, since effective volleys from Yankee pickets kept peering Southern scouts at a distance. Lee became increasingly anxious about the disposition of Grant's troops and ordered Ewell to send a substantial force to investigate.[98]

Ewell's II Corps had been especially hurt during the fighting at the Mule Shoe. His brigades were thinned and in many cases served under new commanders. The Rebel advance began with some hesitation. Unsure of the roads and worried about Yankee counterattack, the probe east became increasingly disorganized. Regiments advanced without clear directions, creating a situation where mutual support might be tricky should an emergency arise.[99] As Confederates groped forward, some of the Union troops facing them on this end of the line weren't Hancock's veteran infantry at all, but heavy artillery. These were units fresh from forts around Washington pressed into service with rifles. These "heavies" were well fed, well supplied and well armed, but certainly were not seasoned infantry. Eventually Ewell's advancing troops looped east and south, running smack into some of these new troops posted at the extreme northern edge of the Yankee line around Harris Farm. Fighting with all the errors that bedevil green troops, the heavies were taking an awful pounding.[100] Alerted to the danger to his rear, Grant sent orders for Birney's men and others to counterattack. At 7 p.m. the division, along with the 72nd N.Y., was formed and moved quickly northeast. Despite heavy losses, the artillery-turned-infantrymen were able to stop the Reb advance before the meat of Birney's Division arrived. The addition of veteran blue infantry to the mix was more than the Confederates, already stalemated by the heavies, could take. Ewell now worried about being completely overwhelmed. As dusk settled, Rebel troops prepared for withdrawal and by nightfall were well on their way back to the defenses of the Mule

12. The Struggle to Petersburg 189

Shoe.[101] Some Federal troops engaged in a half-hearted pursuit but most, along with Third Excelsior, were back in their original positions by six the next morning.[102]

Leonard and the rest of his regiment rested until 11 p.m. when they began the march south. Birney's division was moving south to join up with the rest of the Union II Corps, which was dug in several miles south of Spotsylvania near Wright's Tavern. Birney's men marched all day on the 21st and crossed the Mattaponi River at dark. Third Excelsior camped there and moved into trenches with the rest of Hancock's corps around 10 a.m. on the 22nd.[103]

Hancock's II Corps was in position, but the rest of Grant's plan to trap Lee was going awry. The Confederates had countered Union movements much faster than Grant had anticipated by sending Ewell's corps south. The prospect now loomed that Hancock might be attacked beyond supportive reach of other corps. Worried about Hancock and uncertain of exact Confederate intentions, Grant modified his plan so that by mid-day on the 22nd, the remainder of the army was moving south along a variety of routes. If the Rebels could be caught making a move against Hancock all the better, but Grant's objective now was to cross south of the North Anna and catch Lee in the open. Lee was moving south too and had an advantage over Grant of several hours. Thus Lee would be in position to meet Grant at important river fords. But Lee also believed the Yankees intended to make their westward swing further south and planned accordingly.

As both armies marched south, opportunities were missed by each side to attack isolated and unsupported enemy columns. Lee's troops were in position that night with some men north, but most south, of the North Anna River. Grant too was satisfied with the position of his corps and issued orders around 10 p.m. calculated to bring battle the next day.[104] Beginning at five the next morning, the various Union corps would move on "all roads to their front leading south and ascertain, if possible, where the enemy is."[105] The road leading south from Hancock's position led to the Chesterfield Bridge, the southern-most of two crossings Grant planned to seize and exploit.

Lee was still confident early the next morning that Yankee moves would come further south. The ford near Jericho Mills, the most upstream crossing Grant sought, was virtually unprotected. The closest Rebel troops were posted nearly a mile away. At Chesterfield Bridge two regiments of South Carolina infantry and two batteries of artillery were dug into a small redoubt and nearby trenches that extended parallel to the river. Colonel John Henagan commanded this redoubt and it soon took his name. But Henagan's Redoubt was never expected to repulse the Yankee host now bearing down on it.

Warren's V Corps led the advance further upstream toward Jericho Mills. Rebel skirmishers slowed the advance, but Warren's men fought their way across and controlled the situation. By 3 p.m. construction of a pontoon bridge capable of supporting artillery was underway.[106] While Warren's men advanced on Jericho Mills, Birney's Division of the II Corps crossed Long Creek and mistakenly reported they had crossed their objective, the North Anna. Realizing their mistake, they continued another 500 yards until coming upon Henagan's Redoubt. Within two hours Birney's division was arrayed for attack. II Corps artillery fired from excellent positions that brought shot and shell directly into the redoubt. Confederate artillery responded but was outclassed by Yankee gunners, who continued to fire unhindered. Rebel defenders huddled under the barrage while Birney worked two brigades into position: the First under Colonel Thomas Egan and the Second under Colonel Byron Pierce.[107]

With 71st N.Y. and 72nd N.Y. detached from the Excelsior Brigade to support Pierce,

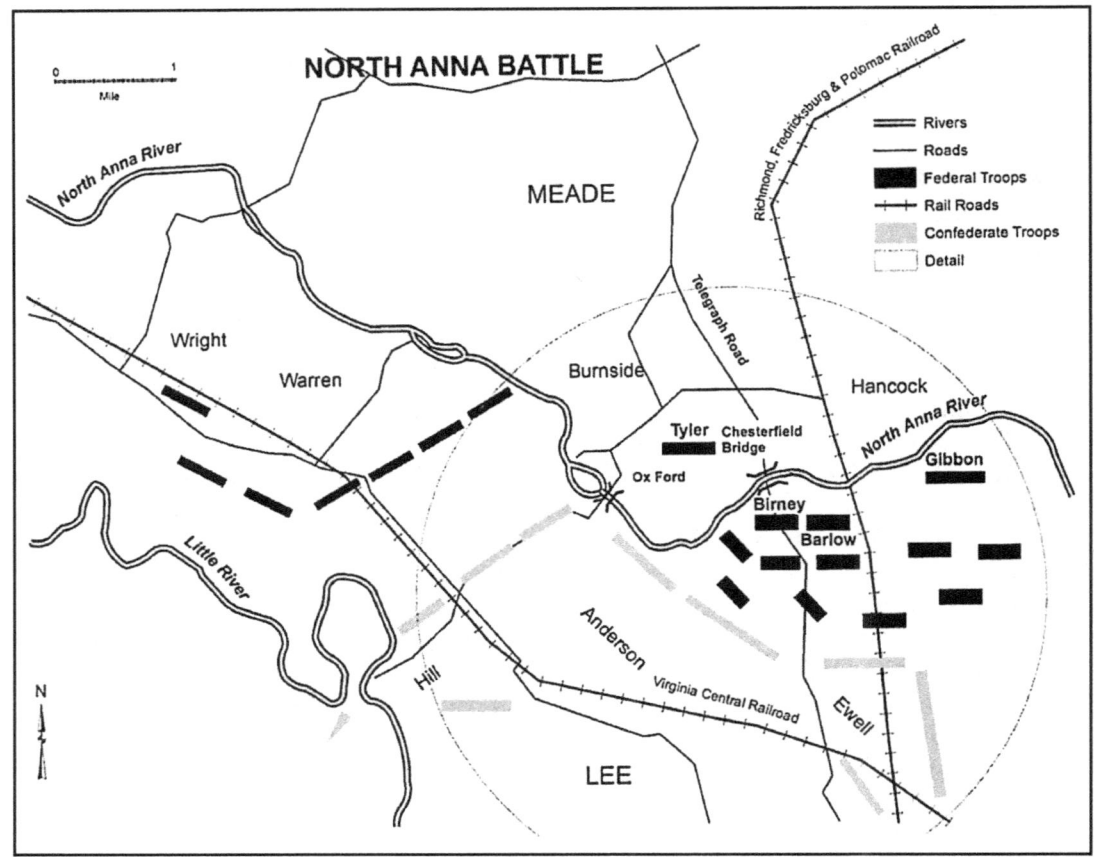

North Anna general area

they approached the redoubt on the right while Egan approached from the center and left. At 6:30 Pierce and Egan's 3,000 men charged the enemy works. Sergeant James Anderson of Company F led the way as Third Excelsior's regimental color bearer.[108] Close behind was Milton S. Bacon, a corporal in Company G. Bacon was one of those rare individuals, an original member of the regiment who'd reenlisted back in December, determined to see the thing through.[109] Pressing forward, Rebel musketry from the redoubt whistled through Union ranks. Supporting Rebel cannons shot from across the river and served to momentarily stagger the Union line, but the boys pushed on. The wave of blue was more than the Rebels could take, and shortly the 7th S.C. collapsed, its men running for the river and abandoning the supporting line of trenches. Federals swarmed the trenches and moved toward the main works. Once at the foot of the redoubt they found its walls steeper than expected. With Third Excelsior men in the van, an improvised ladder was soon fashioned using bayonets and rifles. "We had to stick our bayonets into the sides of it to climb up into it,"[110] remembered James Dean. Samuel Bailey, who had enrolled back at Staten Island as the regiment's sergeant-major, was now captain of Company I. With the fight swirling about him, Bailey shouted orders as Sergeant Anderson and the rest scrambled up the banks of the redoubt. Defenders rained hot lead down from the top of the works as Minié balls plowed the earth. In the frenzy, Corporal Bacon fell dead with a bullet through his head. Undaunted, the New Yorkers pressed forward. Soon Anderson and Third Excelsior's colors were up and over the parapet; he was the first Union soldier into the works.[111]

With Federal troops now swarming the position, defense of Henagan's Redoubt collapsed as numbers of defenders threw down their muskets and were taken prisoner. Other Rebels skedaddled headlong across the Chesterfield Bridge, chased by whizzing volleys of Yankee rifle fire. Soon the only Confederates still fighting were beyond the bridge south of the river. The next line of Lee's defenses overlooked the bridge, and Southern soldiers exchanged shots across the river with Northern troops, who quickly dug in.[112] Companies and regiments disorganized in the confusion of taking the redoubt were soon put right, as officers and sergeants collected wayward men and stragglers found their companies. Battle lines were formed near the river where Dean and the rest of the regiment remained all night.[113] "We made another charge on the enemies [sic] works on the Banks of the South Anna River," wrote Hiram Stoddard to his brother about the day's work: "They were strong works but we carried them driving the Rebs into the River."[114]

Birney's men now held the approach to the Chesterfield Bridge, and further upstream Warren's troops continued to consolidate their position on the far side of the river; Grant's plan to advance across the North Anna was shaping up nicely indeed.

Federal troops had crossed the river at one point and held an important bridge at another, but Lee was not fully convinced Grant's true objective was to cross here.[115] Certainly the holding of a bridge presented some concern for Lee, however having an entire Union corps (Warren's V Corps) on his side of the river required action.

Lee issued orders to attack Warren's Corps later that day. But as the attack went forward Confederate commanders badly bungled the advance. Uncoordinated Confederate assaults, countered by quick action by Warren's Yankees, resulted in miserable failure. The attacks cost Lee precious resources he could ill afford to squander and left Warren's men in even stronger positions, convincing the Southern chieftain further attacks here would be futile.[116]

Lee was in a bad spot. Grant was able to move across the North Anna at two locations and could bring the entirety of his army to bear, and Lee could ill afford another Spotsylvania-style brawl. The Confederate commander believed withdrawal toward Richmond would only limit his options for future maneuver and permit Grant nearer to his objective. Lee wanted an offensive opportunity to hurt "those people," to somehow isolate one or more of their corps and destroy it. Lee now cast about for ideas from his top commanders and staff.[117]

Confederate chief of engineers Martin Smith had a canny ability to read the terrain, and now he proposed a solution. Between Jericho Mills to the west, near the spot Warren's corps had crossed on pontoon bridges, and the Chesterfield Bridge to the east held by Birney, lay an inverted V-shaped ridge with its apex resting on the river. Smith proposed that each wing of this inverted V could serve to block the Yankee advance: Warren on its west wing as he moved along the southern side of the river and Hancock on its east wing once he crossed the Chesterfield Bridge. If Grant attacked against both wings, his army would be split and unable to move supporting troops between the two fronts without first recrossing the North Anna, twice. Furthermore, across the open end of this wedge-shaped alignment ran a portion of the Virginia Central Railroad, which provided Lee excellent interior lines of communication, allowing him to move troops east and west between the two flanks of his army easily as threats dictated. With Grant unable to reinforce either wing of his army quickly, engineer Smith's plan gave Lee the further option of being able to attack a Yankee corps should it become isolated with its back against the river. With little hesitation Lee ordered his army to occupy the ground proposed and then waited for Grant.[118]

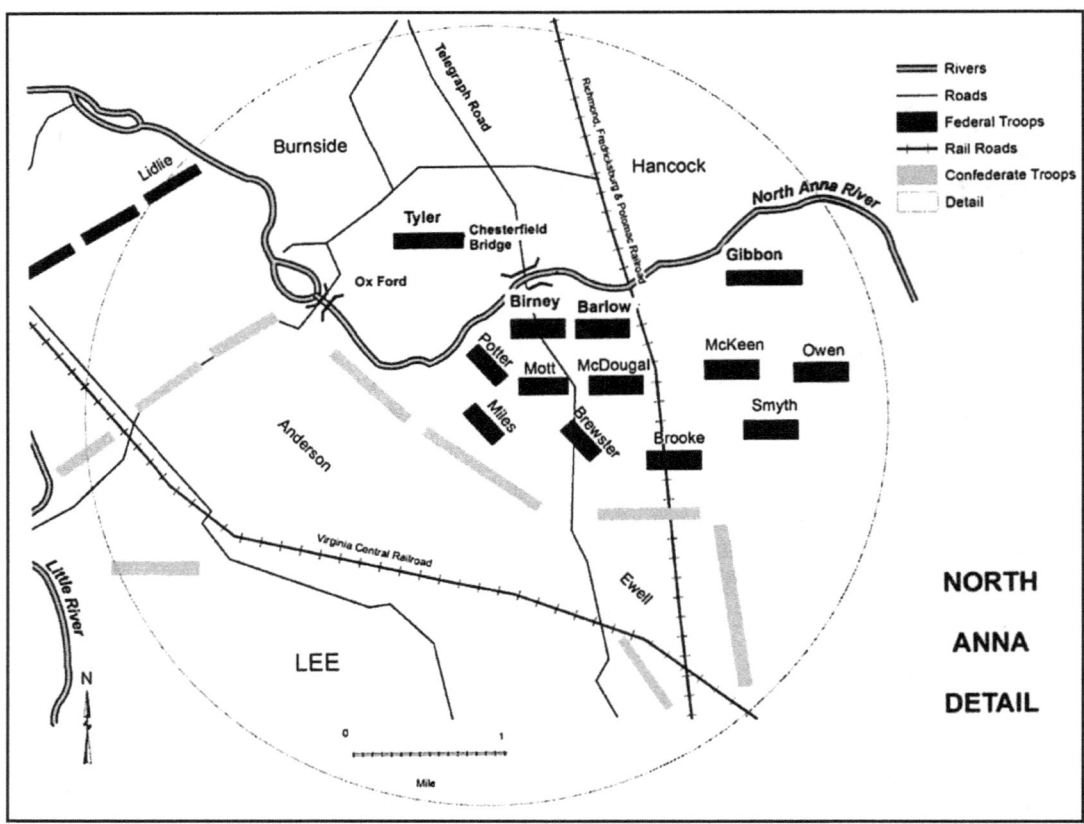

Morning broke on the 24th. Grant was anxious to continue the attacks. Unsure of Lee's true dispositions, Grant was still convinced Lee was in retreat. Warren's men moved east along the far side of the North Anna toward Hancock's troops, which were still crossing at the Chesterfield Bridge. Lead elements of Warren's V Corps soon ran into a low ridge topped with freshly excavated dirt, a sure sign of newly built Rebel earth works. The ridge ran left to the river and right to a swamp that was impassible for a large army. Sure this was just the Confederate rearguard; Warren's men attacked the ridge but were repeatedly hurled back.[119] Messages streamed back to Grant's headquarters and soon V Corps was halted.

Near Chesterfield Bridge enemy artillerymen started their work early. By 4 a.m. Hiram Stoddard and the rest were hunkered down under rain of shot and shell that peppered the brigade's lines. Birney's Division led the II Corps in starting across the bridge around 8 a.m. From prepared positions, Confederate guns showered hot iron on Yankees crossing Chesterfield Bridge. Birney's men raced across the exposed bridge and approaches to establish themselves on the river's south side.[120] Near 11 a.m. the Excelsiors moved to relieve First Brigade, which was beginning its move over the river. Two hours later the Excelsiors began to cross. As each regiment moved across the bridge, Rebel lead and iron unceasingly peppered their ranks.[121] Arriving on the south side, the New Yorkers established their line of battle behind some crude rifle pits hastily dug by previous brigades. Grant was splitting his army just as Lee had hoped.

Union forces were now bumped up against the Rebel works on both legs of Lee's inverted V. Now began the hard work of breaking through. Grant poured more troops across the river, hoping to develop a weak spot in the enemy line. Fighting was desperate as Federals hugged the earth in search of what little cover the terrain offered. The hoped-for weak spot was proving elusive. Grant's best corps, Hancock's II, was now in a vulnerable position, stalled and exposed. Hancock's men were ripe to suffer the counterattack Lee had envisioned. But Lee had been sick and resting far to the rear, unable to direct fast-developing events firsthand. Fighting in the Wilderness and Spotsylvania had taken many of his best commanders, and their replacements were proving themselves slow and tentative. Lee reluctantly concluded it was best to forgo the opportunity to descend upon Hancock rather than attempt a risky offensive maneuver, this attack perhaps being beyond the abilities of those asked to execute it.[122]

Birney's division continued to inch forward as the late afternoon dragged into evening. Near 9 p.m. on that first day the fighting wound down. Since crossing Chesterfield Bridge, the Excelsiors had advanced a mere quarter of a mile and established a new front line.[123]

Hancock had made little or no progress as the morning of the 25th gave way to afternoon. Reports received by Grant suggested enemy resistance was increasing. By early evening the situation was becoming clearer to the Federal commander. Instead of a mere Rebel rearguard, Lee's entire army arrayed against him, and Grant realized the danger of having his forces split. Grant immediately issued orders to cease offensive operations and to dig in in preparation for an enemy counterattack. Northern troops hastily threw up breastworks. As blue-coated soldiers frantically scratched the earth with their bayonets and stacked random logs and rocks, Lee's vision of delivering a crushing blow by descending on his foe faded.[124] Leonard's boys had waited all day in their improvised positions for the order to go forward, but now attentions turned to defense. Around 5 p.m. First Brigade took the front and the Excelsiors were moved to a second line, where they spent the night.[125] A member of the 120th N.Y. described the situation as he saw it:

> In line of battle across the North Anna river. We are having a rough time. I reckon the world never heard of such fighting. Since May 5th we have been under fire of the enemy nearly every day. All confidence is placed in General Grant, and all earnestly hope for success. We are working night and day building line after line of intrenchments [sic]. Although worn with fatigue, the men cheerfully obey every order.[126]

Hancock's troops were the most vulnerable to Rebel attack and spent the night digging rifle pits and erecting breastworks. With every shovelful of earth the Yankees' moved to strengthen their positions lessened Lee's prospects of success. By morning's light it was clear the two armies faced another stalemate: both sides now in positions too strong to be successfully carried.[127]

The Confederate Army had no option but to hold its ground. The Yankees were here, in their front, and for the time being at least, were no closer to Richmond. It was Grant who would dictate the next phase of the campaign. Realizing his way was blocked and an attack here had little hope of success, Grant made plans to withdraw his army back to the north side of the river. Realizing how lucky he'd been, Grant ordered his army to re-cross the North Anna. Under cover of darkness on the night of the 26th, all four Federal corps would withdraw using the Chesterfield Bridge, Ox Ford, and an assortment of temporary foot bridges. Once on the north side Grant could continue his attempts to move around Lee with moves south and west.[128]

Leonard's men had spent the entire day of the 26th in the second line of works waiting for orders. Shortly after midnight, the 72nd N.Y. with the rest of Birney's division withdrew across the North Anna using the Chesterfield Bridge. Soon after crossing they went into bivouac for the night. At noon they marched and made camp at 7 p.m. near the Pamunkey River. Out of range of Rebel cannons, the boys paused to assess the past week's action. The regiment on the whole had been lucky; despite the shelling and the desperate fight at Henagan's Redoubt, the regiment counted only nine men wounded and only young Milt Bacon killed.[129]

With the army out of immediate peril, Grant continued southward. Following the North Anna, the Federals passed where the river joined with the South Anna. From here south, the river was called the Pamunkey. Grant's men traveled using parallel routes. Burnside's and Warren's corps formed the eastern-most columns, while Hancock's and Wright's fashioned the western column, remaining closest to the river. North of Hanovertown the Federals crossed the Pamunkey and moved southwest toward Richmond. Grant's army was now 15 miles from Richmond, ten miles closer than at the North Anna crossing. On this line of march Grant's men needed only to cross two remaining water obstacles, Totopotomoy Creek and the Chickahominy River on their way to the Confederate capital.[130] Stoddard reflected on this latest move in a letter to his brother:

> We crosed [sic] the Pamunkey River & steped [sic] our feet once more on the soil of the Penninsula within 15 miles of Richmond where I am now writing to you. When we left this contry I little thought I should ever be here again but so it is. May God grant that as we leave this again that Richmond mint fall & the Cruel war ended.[131]

Third Excelsior was on the move at noon on the 27th and halted for supper near 7 p.m. They bivouacked for the night near the Pamunkey. The regiment was on the move the next morning by 8 a.m. Moving slowly all day, they eventually crossed the river near Hanovertown late in the afternoon and finally halted for the night at 7 p.m.[132]

Grant's course of action was now clear, allowing Lee to more effectively shift his troops to meet the threat. When lead elements of Grant's army reached the Totopotomoy on the 29th, they found Confederates firmly established on the far bank. Leonard's men arrived near the creek around 10 a.m. and were immediately put to task digging a line of works of their own. The situation was fast developing into another North Anna–style standoff. By seven that night the regiment advanced and began building more works. Throughout the day of the 30th the two sides skirmished and probed, while the Excelsiors remained in their rifle pits. General Francis Barlow's Federal division made an attack late in the afternoon that gained some important ground. Barlow's push went forward with the customary increase in supporting artillery fire. A battery of the small Coehorn mortars position near the 72nd worked away during the attack, holding the attention of some fascinated boys within the regiment.

Barlow followed up his success the next morning with another attack, this time supported with additional brigades, including the Excelsiors. Seventy-Second New York was again among the leading regiments as the assault went forward. "In this charge," reported Henri LeFevre-Brown, "the colors of the Third Regiment were the first to mount the enemy's works; they were gallantly borne by Corporal Ovett Burr, of Company E, who was one of the first Union soldiers to reach the breastworks, and who was helped up the parapet by those with him."[133] With the enemy works secured, Corporal Burr and the rest again dug in.

But the decision against remaining to slug it out had already been made by Grant. With a newly established supply base 15 miles south of Hanovertown at White House Landing, a shift south would put him closer to both Richmond and his supplies. Even while Corporal

Burr was scrambling up the parapet, Grant had already initiated the next move by sending cavalry ahead to clear the way and to secure the small town of Cold Harbor. Two days of fighting followed to secure the town for Grant, and lead elements of his infantry began to arrive on the evening of the 31st.[134] Lee was now certain where the Yankee army was heading. It became another race for position. Grant needed sufficient army to flank Lee and drive onto Richmond, while Lee needed enough men to stop the attacks he knew would come.

Federal designs were clear, and leading elements were pouring into their position around Cold Harbor on June 1. Lee's men were moving into position west of town, but the Federals had a big lead. Grant planned for an early morning attack the next day against what he knew would be undermanned Rebel positions.[135]

The Federal army had been moved piecemeal in order to fix in place as much of the Rebel army as possible. The last to leave their positions along the Totopotomoy were Hancock's II Corps and a group of cavalry. Grant intended to extend his battle line as far south as possible in hopes of overlapping Confederate defenses. Orders went to Hancock to move his corps to the south, to the left end of the Union line, a move that would take II Corps from one extreme end of the line to the other. At daybreak of the 1st, Leonard roused his men from their trenches and fell back to their positions of two days earlier. There they remained for the rest of the day. With nightfall, Third Excelsior, along with much of II Corps, moved three miles and bivouacked for the night.[136] Grant wanted to go forward with all five of his corps and set 4:30 on the morning of the 2nd as the time for the attack. But Hancock was still not in position at the designated time. Faulty directions had sent II Corps on a roundabout trek, and they failed to arrive until 6:30, two hours late, exhausted and certainly in no condition for an assault. Grant reasoned that moving the attack to five that afternoon would serve his purposes just as well. But as the day wore on, skirmishing along the line required extensive repositioning of troops, until finally Grant postponed the endeavor to 4:30 the next morning.[137]

Lee's men took full advantage of the delay as they dug, barricaded, positioned, and then repositioned both men and artillery. In many cases the officers worked to conceal the extent of the works, fearing the defenses might appear too formidable and thus discourage Yankee attack.[138]

When dawn broke on the 3rd, LeFevre-Brown and the rest of the II Corps were firmly positioned on the left side of the Union line. Leonard and his men had done a lot of shifting of position, but for now at least Birney's division was stationed in reserve.[139]

By the time Grant's attack was ready, the two opposing armies had managed to arrange themselves into roughly the shape of two parallel crescents. With the Federals forming the inside of the two crescents, their attacks would diverge from the center as they went forward, with each corps unwittingly forced to act independently, unsupported by the others. Grant and his commanders were unaware of this, and as the attacks went forward, corps commanders would blame each other for failures of proper support. Northern men on the front lines knew from past experience the coming attack would be bad. Men took time to pen farewells in their diaries and pin makeshift identification tags on their coats giving their name and regiment.[140]

The attack lasted only about eight minutes. Furious Rebel defense stopped the Union advance cold. Yankees gained some success in places, but quick Rebel counterattacks stopped each breach. A few local commanders attempted to regroup and try again or to shift a regiment here or a brigade there, but everyone on the line knew it was over and the expected slaughter had come true.[141] Confederate commanders, reflecting on the lightness of their casualties, found it hard to believe the battle had begun in earnest, let alone was already over.[142] Dead Yankees covered nearly five acres. The fighting of June 3 had cost Grant 7,000 men, most of them in those first terrible eight minutes; Lee's army suffered only 1,500.[143]

With his attack stopped, Grant desperately looked for an avenue to break through. Orders to corps commanders to probe the enemy for weak spots all came back the same; further attacks would be futile and the morning's losses had served to severely weaken, disorganize and demoralize Northern troops.[144]

Union men on the front lines dug in as best they could. Some were able to pull back to safer positions, while other were stranded, unable to move for fear of being shot by some unseen Southern rifleman. With the dead all around, shocked survivors were forced to endure the moans and cries of the wounded, which filled the air. But with every approach covered, the blue coats were unable to help their comrades until the arrival of nightfall.[145]

Unit commanders begged Grant to parlay for a cease fire in order to collect the wounded, but the Federal commander, not wishing to admit defeat, sparred with Lee over the exact wording of such an agreement from June 5 till the 7th. By the time Union troops were permitted to recover their comrades, most wounded had already died from exposure or thirst.[146]

While men in frontline divisions attempted to collect their dead and wounded, the Excelsiors enjoyed the relative safety of the rear. From the 3rd to the 8th the New Yorkers had been shifted along Birney's line a number of times, either relieving brigades behind existing works or building new works as needed.[147] During the several days of action, Hiram Stoddard and the boys were either on picket, anticipating an enemy counterattack, or were hunkered down behind breastworks clear of Rebel snipers and artillery.[148] Since his enrollment in Company B, Stoddard had always placed his fate into the hands of God and tried to live a life of which his parents would be proud. In letters home Hiram often praised God for seeing him through another day of battle and thanked his parents for providing him with a strict and proper Christian upbringing that allowed him to endure his many trials. On June 8 he wrote:

> Alone through the goodness & sparing mercies of almighty God am I spared to once more drop you a few hasty thoughts. Though the dangers of nearly 20 days fiting [sic] in which time thousands upon thousands of my Dear Comrads [sic] & Defenders of our Contry have fallen & here I [might] ask myself why am I spared, it is not because I am enny [sic] better than they.[149]

But if Hiram ever questioned the Lord's providential hand watching over him, the tale he relates to his parents should have removed all doubt. Behind "thin"[150] breastworks during the fighting of June 3, a Company C man had just been mortally wounded by a shell fragment to the head.[151] More aware than ever of the dangers of the bursting artillery, Hiram and the other boys squirmed a little lower for cover.

> Soon after this there was a twelve pound shell struck the works right in front of me as I was sitting down on the inside. It came through so as to just touch my arm & and it stoped. All that saved me from being blown to pieces was this ... the shell having to go through a little shirt. The dampness of the shirt put out the fuze of the shell. As I at once stepped one side for fear it [might] burst. The thought at once struck me how easy it would have been for the Lord to have let that burst. Oh I will praise his name for his goodness to us all.[152]

Since the beginning of the Overland Campaign, Grant had been losing men at the rate of about two for every one of Lee's. Now there was Cold Harbor, where losses were about

12. The Struggle to Petersburg

five to one. Grant realized his army would be wrecked beyond repair if he continued this kind of fight over this kind of ground.[153]

Grant had enough manpower and was practically at the gates of Richmond. With Lee's army in front of him, Grant began again to look for ways around and on toward the Rebel capital. Union cavalry ranged far and wide looking for a spot to exploit. General Benjamin Butler's 10,000 Federal troops had been inactive until now; at Bermuda Hundred, south of Richmond, they finally began to stir. By June 10 there were hints of opportunity for an advance, with only the time, place and method remaining for Grant to decide.[154]

From the 8th through to the 12th of June, the regiment lay in their breastworks beyond Cold Harbor. That night around seven Leonard deployed his men as advance pickets. By 3 a.m. on the morning of the 13th the regiment was recalled and began a fast march south. The decision to pull out had been made, and the 72nd was lagging behind the rest of the brigade.[155]

Grant had made his decision and was moving toward Petersburg, an important rail junction south of Richmond. Federal men moved quickly as they pulled out of the line and marched south and crossed the James River by boat. Grant's lead element was Smith's XVIII Corps. The II Corps followed later. Marching throughout the 13th, II Corps reached the James River near Wilcox Landing, where it waited out the night.[156]

Third Excelsior caught up with the rest of the brigade by 6 a.m. By three that afternoon they crossed the Chickahominy and continued south. Much of this was the same ground the veterans of the regiment had tromped back in the days of the Peninsula Campaign with McClellan. "The march part of the way led through places familiar to many of us,"[157] wrote one Excelsior Brigade man, "and in one instance I noted the very spot where my tent was pitched overnight in the Spring of '62."[158] By 10 p.m. they bivouacked for the night at Charles City Court House, only a mile or so from Wilcox Landing. Soon after arriving a picket detail was formed, Lucius Jones of Company H among them:

> We were taken down in a strip of woods where it was swampy, and was told to keep a sharp lookout. As it became dark, the officer of the picket line came along and took over half of the men from each post. We supposed they were going to lengthen out the line. As they moved off the Captain said, "Goodbye Jones." I thought it strange at the time, but it soon passed off. As it began to get light in the morning, we looked back. Some of the boys said the army was gone.... We soon found out that we were left there to be captured by the Rebels—left there for a blind.[159]

With young Lucius and the rest still in the woods, the regiment packed up and moved the short distance to Wilcox Landing, where pontoon bridges had been established. Near 11 a.m. Leonard led his men as they tromped across the James and went into bivouac near Windmill Landing with the balance of the II Corps.[160] Back in the scrub beyond the courthouse, Lucius and the rest took matters into their own hands: "We struck out and marched all day. About dark we came up with the army. When we got to the regiment the boys all came to shake hands with us and said they never expected to see us again."[161]

Luckily for Jones and the rest, the entire day of the 14th had been spent waiting for rations, allowing Lucius and his mates a chance to catch up. Not until noon of the 15th would Third Excelsior move again. The XVIII Corps had been fighting around Petersburg since the 14th and had taken the outer defenses as Lee was hurrying to reinforce his heavily outnumbered garrison.[162] "Had the Second Corps continued its advance at this time Petersburg could probably have been occupied with but little opposition,"[163] recalled Henri LeFevre-Brown. "A division of colored troops of the Eighteenth Corps had captured the main line of rebel works, next the Appomattox River on the evening of the 15th, and developed the fact that there was but a small force of rebels in Petersburg at that time."[164]

While a concerted Federal push could have taken Petersburg, no one had informed Hancock of the urgency, and II Corps moved unhurried, not arriving until almost midnight of the 15th. Once at Petersburg, II Corps men took over some of the outer works that had previously been captured by colored troops of the XVIII Corps. Hancock's men concluded that if colored troops could capture the works then the Rebel defenders must be weak indeed. And though fatigued from the march, they prepared for an attack. Hancock's men waited, yet no orders came. They settled into the captured works for the night, the second without rations. In the distance was heard the sound of pick, shovel and the axe; the enemy was improving their defenses.[165] LeFevre-Brown later remembered the blundered move against Petersburg.

> But for the misunderstandings which held a large part of the Second Corps in idleness on the bank of the James River, waiting till a late hour of the morning for rations which did not come, and even then, but for the mistake which led their march by a circuitous route, our troops might have been in position early in the afternoon to support this gallant assault, and perhaps to push it home to the capture of the city, which was but slenderly defended till after midnight.
>
> Many have thought that even at night, under the light of a full moon, a determined advance of the Second Corps would have carried them into the city. But this service was not asked of them by the general in command on that part of the field. As lines were being formed for bivouac under the shadow of the captured works, and throughout the night, the locomotive whistles and constant rumble of trains told the story of troops being hurried down from the direction of Richmond to hold the threatened position.[166]

As daylight broke on the 16th it was discovered that neither pickets nor skirmishers had been placed in front of the division, but soon the entire corps was in line of battle. Though there was no general assault, breastworks were erected under a rain of Rebel artillery fire as much of the corps engaged in "severe skirmishing all day."[167] That evening the regiment was able to make a small advance. Once it was determined the boys could go no further, another line of works was hastily build to help consolidate their gains. This pattern of skirmishing during the day and advancing at night continued for the next couple of days. "We were very close to the Rebels," remembered Lucius Jones, "not over twenty rods, and in some places not that fare distant, fighting night and day."[168] With enlistments in the 72nd expiring, it was probably a miracle Leonard and the other officers could get the boys to load a rifle, let alone fight, as most were going home in just a few days and no one wanted to be wounded or killed this late in the game. All were filthy and spent. Perhaps a few dozen men in the whole army had gotten to bathe back at the North Anna, but chances were it was none of these boys. They wore the same clothes as when they had stepped off from Brandy Station seven weeks earlier. But there was some consolation: by the 18th, the supply situation had been resolved and the men finally enjoyed fresh rations.[169] Skirmishing proceeded all day on the 19th and 20th. Stoddard wrote on the 19th to reassure his parents:

> This is the first opportunity I have had since getting your letter, for we are at work day & night creeping up under the Rebel works at night & by daylight we have up good Brest works. Last night we worked all night throwing up [works] & I am so tired & sleepy I can hardly write but I felt as though I must ansure [sic] your letter.... God is still with me in mercy, this is truly a trying time to all. The poor soldiers in the field, we are under fire day & night. There seems to be no rest for us at all but may God grant in his infinite goodness that this terable [sic] campain mint [sic] end this terable war.[170]

12. The Struggle to Petersburg

On the evening of the 20th, the 72nd was pulled out of the line and replaced by elements of the IX Corps. The New Yorkers marched nearly the entire next day, going into line of battle near the Weldon Railroad. Nothing came of the 72nd's move to the Weldon Railroad, and as it would turn out, this was the last time the 72nd would go into line.[171]

With its term of service expired, the regiment was relieved from the front on the morning of the 22nd, going to the rear to be mustered out. Men who had reenlisted back at Brandy Station or those whose term of service had not yet expired were consolidated into Companies C, G and H. The next morning these three companies were attached to the 120th New York.[172] "Then the parting came, with goodbye to all; and off the boys went, wishing us good luck, and we the same to them."[173]

From that point on the 72nd New York State Volunteers ceased to exist. All that was left was for the discharged men to be paid and get themselves home. For those left at Petersburg, Lucius Jones, James Dean, and others, the war went on.

13. End of the Seventy-Second

For the men who remained, the business of war went on uninterrupted. "Then all of us veterans were transferred to the 120th Regt. N.Y. Vol., and put into different companies," remembered Lucius Jones. "Then we wished we hadn't re-enlisted, but it was now too late, and the boys were off for home. And we veterans turned our faces to the enemy."[1] For one more day, those who were finished with their obligation lingered near the front. On the afternoon of June 25 they took their first steps towards home, beginning the eight-mile march to City Point and the James River.

Arriving near the wagon camp at 10 p.m. the homeward-bound made camp for the night. Early the next morning they were on the road again and reached the James River early in the day. Additional processing and mustering-out took place on the 27th, and the regiment boarded the steamer *Keyport* at 10:30 the morning of the 28th. Leaving City Point, the *Keyport* passed Fortress Monroe at five that afternoon and turned north for Washington. The regiment arrived near eight the next morning and found quarters at the Soldier's Rest. Being New York men, their journey was not complete; they moved on to New York City, arriving on July 1 and staying at the soldier's depot on Howard Street. Eventually, the boys were paid off on the 5th and 6th, and as Henri LeFevre-Brown put it, "at once scattered for their homes."[2]

New York City men were home within minutes of being paid off. Some, the hard men Dan Sickles had plucked from dire circumstances for a chance to serve, were no doubt back to their old ways, while others may have arrived home somehow cleansed by their three years of trial and looked forward to a better life. For the western boys of Chautauqua County, their reception was in many cases no less exuberant than their departure three years before. One Chautauqua paper captured the poignant scene:

> The remnant of old companies D and E, belonging to the 72d, N.Y. (3d Excelsior Regiment.) having received an honorable discharge at the expiration of three years term of service, arrived in Dunkirk on Thursday last. The news of their coming having preceded them, a large throng of friends and citizens from Dunkirk and the towns adjoining assembled at the Depot to greet the war-worn heroes on their arrival. The occasion was painfully suggestive of the scene witnessed at the Depot three years before, on the memorable 30th day of May 1861, when these gallant companies, with full ranks, over 200 strong, left their homes with all their pleasant associations and endearments, to peril their lives in defence of the honor of the National flag. Then, as now, a large throng assembled to witness the event. They were sorrowful, yet hopeful. Could their eyes have then pierced the veil of the future, and followed the career of the devoted band to the finale of its glorious three years of service, keenly as they felt the trial of parting, their anguish would have been yet keener. STEVENS, BARRETT, DOYLE, and a host of gallant spirits then waved their adieus as the long train swept from the

Depot to the gay music of "Girl I left behind me." Of that brave array, the first precious contribution of our County to the cause of the Union, a handful only—some 25 or 30—returned on Thursday last to receive the greetings of their friends, amid old familiar scenes. A few others remain in hospitals, unable to endure the fatigues of the homeward trip, and still another remnant have re-enlisted, animated with a determination to see the struggle through, and are now adding new laurels to the reputations won in the old "Fighting Brigade," in the trenches fronting Petersburg.[3]

While the homecoming scene in Chautauqua County was all that could have been expected for returning veterans, apparently the reception was somewhat different for the Delhi boys of Company I. With the presidential election just a few months away, it would seem that the Republican citizens of Delhi may have considered the returning men too loyal to the Democratic nominee George McClellan for their local tastes, prompting a cool welcome home. This motivated one Delhi citizen to write the local paper to complain about the injustice done to its veterans:

Mr. Mirror—The surviving "veterans" of Capt. R.T. Johnson's Company, who enlisted from this town three years ago in the "3d Excelsior Regt," Sickles Brigade, arrived home yesterday. They return few in number, still are a band of "brave bold boys." We would ask why are they permitted to return to their homes without the usual public reception? Can it be that the deeds of valor and bravery of these war worn veterans, on countless bloody battle fields for the past three years are so soon to be forgotten? We hope not. It has been suggested that their bronzed faces are not of that all sufficient dark hue to entitle them to proper regard! And then again, it is hinted that their political sentiments are not muddy enough to suit the major part of our loyal voters, be that as it may, one point no one can doubt! but what they are individually and collectively McClellan veterans, ready to battle at all times for the honor of "Little Mac," or for the cause he so nobly defended. There is a class of soldiers, or, "shoulder strappers," who may generally calculate on a warm reception, at the hands of a certain class in Delhi. They are the fine "Blue coated, and brass buttoned warriors," of recent manufacture, whose principal merit consists not in any fighting they have done "down in Dixie" but in their "chin exercise" at home trying to show up the incapacity of McClellan as a Gen. and the immediate necessity of wiping out northern traitors, and doing other things too numerous to mention, We trust that one of these days honor will be given to those who are entitled to it, and less awarded to the undeserving. Hastily, S.Q.B.[4]

Men with time still to serve remained at Petersburg with the 120th New York. Some now former 72nd men had only a few days left on their enlistments and were on their way home within weeks. The rest continued to fight alongside the 120th as they participated in the various actions around Petersburg, including the October fight at Boydton Plank Road and Hatcher's Run, which cost the regiment 8 killed, 30 wounded and 21 missing. In February of '65 the 120th lost another 6 killed, 32 wounded and 46 missing at Dabney's Mills and Hatcher's Run. That spring the 120th pursued Lee's army to Appomattox Court House and the eventual surrender, participating later in the Grand Review at Washington. When the 120th disbanded in June of '65, those men with time still to serve were moved to the 73rd New York until it was disbanded a month later.[5]

Despite whatever welcome home they may have received or whenever they eventually made it home, within a year of the war's end, Union veterans began to come together locally to share their common experiences. By April of 1866, the first of many chapters of the Grand Army of the Republic had been formed. The GAR was an organization devoted to veterans' affairs and community service. Local chapter memberships reflected the regiments drawn from each area, but as was the case with the 72nd New York, being drawn as it was from across the state, something more needed to be done should the bond they forged in battle continue into the peace; so up stepped Henri LeFevre-Brown.

Whether inspired by the highest ideals of camaraderie or by something less noble, Brown, the former sergeant and Medal of Honor winner, now became the engine driving the 72nd NYSV Veteran's Association. In 1888 the new association elected its first slate of officers with Brown as president, Henry Yates serving as vice president, Samuel Bailey acting as secretary and Ensign Jones taking on the duties of treasurer. This board of officers would serve in these respective capacities for the next eight years. While subsequent boards would change president and vice president each year, Brown remained a steadying hand at secretary. It was clear that preserving the memory of the 72nd was a high priority, especially for Brown, who wrote an extensive history of Company B which appeared in the May 1891 issue of the *Jamestown Journal*.[6] During the second half of the 1890s,

Henri Lefevre-Brown of Company B earned a Medal of Honor for his actions in the Wilderness. Thanks to his efforts, much of the history of the 72nd N.Y. was preserved (Brown, *History of the Third Regiment*).

with Brown at the center of the project, the veterans' association worked to collect firsthand accounts of the regiment's battles and movements from its membership. The objective was to preserve the most accurate collection of accounts possible so a definitive history of the regiment could eventually be written, a history Brown wrote and published in 1902 and a work frequently cited by subsequent historians. But by 1902 most of the energy of the veterans' association had long waned. And with its last official document dated 1900, it appears the association stopped operating that same year.[7]

Whether they participated in the veterans' group or not, the boys of Third Excelsior went back to their lives as best they could. Some, raked by the lingering effects of disease or wounds, would pass away within just a few years of their discharge, while others lived into their eighties and nineties. Many boys remained close to home and finished out long lives in New York while others went elsewhere.

Among those who would not last long was Colonel John Austin, who spent the last few months of his army service battling illness. He was discharged for disability on June 27, 1864, due to "nephritis and enlarged prostate with general debility," about the same time the 72nd N.Y. was disbanded because of shrinking numbers and expiring enlistments. Austin died on May 8, 1865, less than a year after his discharge. Austin's body was available for public viewing at New York's City Hall before burial at Greenwood Cemetery in Brooklyn.[8]

Israel Moses, the doctor who served as the regiment's lieutenant colonel, died at age 47 in 1870 after spending his last few years in Philadelphia as a member of the U.S. Sanitary Commission and helping to found the American Public Health Association.[9]

13. End of the Seventy-Second 203

This letterhead of the 72nd New York's Veteran's Association is designed around a white diamond representing the Second Division of the III Corps, with two sickles symbolic of its founder and the brigade (Grand Army of the Republic records, 72nd NYV, New York State Library, Preservation Unit).

John S. Mann, who joined the regiment as sergeant in Company F and rose to captain, returned to his home in Newark, New Jersey, after the war. Suffering the lingering effects of his wounding at Gettysburg, Mann, who remained in frail health, finally succumbed to a form of lung tuberculosis on April 2, 1876, leaving a wife and three children behind.[10]

Among those who would move afar was John C. Willing of Company G. Sometime after finishing out his reenlistment commitment with the 120th N.Y., Willing moved to Colusa County, not far north of Sacramento in California. There, he raised a family and worked as carpenter until at age 52 he fell off a roof, dying a rather unremarkable death the next day from internal injuries. Ironically, he had as a young man escaped the most extraordinary hazards of war.[11]

Hiram Stoddard, who put so much faith in the Lord and in the teachings of his parents, reenlisted when the regiment was phased out and fell in with the 120th. In the lines at Petersburg, Hiram wrote, "the enemy in our front are deserting fast, there is from 7 to 10 come over evry [sic] night, they all say they are tired of this cruel war."[12] Eventually the strain of the trenches began to take its toll on Stoddard as his letters' tone and handwriting reflected his fatigue. He requested transfer from the front, to hospital duty but soon after the letters home stopped; Hiram Stoddard had been captured. Languishing in Libby Prison, Hiram suffered all the hardships associated with the notorious prison: lack of food, inadequate sanitation, and poor ventilation. When finally released, Stoddard carried a "somewhat crippled condition" the rest of his days. Back in Busti, Hiram married, had a daughter and died in 1915, his home becoming a Baptist parsonage and eventually a home for runaway girls.[13]

James Dean, who joined the regiment just before Fredericksburg in the fall of 1862, finished out his enlistment with the 120th New York, as did many others once the 72nd disbanded. Upon his discharge Dean took employment in Astoria with "one of the most prominent florists of the time" and by 1877 had opened a business of his own. Four years later he moved his shop to Brooklyn, where his business grew; he became one of the most celebrated florists in New York. Dean received high awards from the various florist guilds and presided as president over numerous floral conventions held in New York, Washington and Toronto.

In addition to his professional duties, Dean served for several years as commodore of the South Shore Yacht Club. Dean was an avid collector of firearms and his "collection comprised antique arms from centuries back and was probably the most complete private one in the United States." This collection was unfortunately scattered at public auction, according to Dean family legend, by an uncaring relative who took control of the collection while James was in failing health.[14]

Another man who continued on with the 120th New York was Lucius Jones. Jones, the smallish lad who fell in with Company H, was obligated due to his reenlisting to remain in service until July of 1865 and did the last month of his service with the 73rd New York. Upon returning home, Jones found it difficult adjusting to many of the small normalcies of civilian life. "It was a long time before I could sleep in bed. Would sleep on the floor; but by degrees got used to a bed again," remembered the veteran. In 1881 Jones received a pension, backdated to his discharge, for asthma that resulted in heart disease. Jones participated in the 30th anniversary recognition of the battle of Gettysburg. In February of 1913, Jones finished his memoir of the war while residing at his home in Fredonia, New York.[15]

The man recruited out of the regiment to help organize the division's mail service, David Parker, had perhaps one of the most fascinating careers following the war. While placed in charge of mail service for the Army of the Potomac by General Hooker, this assignment continued under both Meade and Grant. After the war Parker was given the task of reestablishing mail service in Virginia, later being appointed by President Grant as U.S. Marshal for the District of Virginia. Parker then returned to the post office, where he served as chief post-office inspector from 1876 to 1883, at which time he left government service and joined the fledgling American Bell Telephone Company. Over the years that followed, Parker served the phone company in a variety of executive positions throughout New England and New York. For the last ten years of his life, Parker was a "confirmed invalid, unable to leave his bed or to assist himself in any way," but maintained a steady schedule of receiving friends and compiling his collection of reminiscences: *A Chautauqua Boy in '61 and Afterward*, which was published after his death in 1910.[16]

Another who served the regiment with great devotion ironically wasn't a man at all. Sarah Sinfield was married to Private William Sinfield (also spelled Senfield), who was among the first to join what would become Company E. With both her husband's and the company commander's blessing, Sarah joined the company at Staten Island in July 1861 a day before it moved to Washington. From that point on, she accompanied the regiment during its most harrowing engagements and "at each and every one of these battles she aided in caring for sick and wounded soldiers, carrying food and drink to those who could not help themselves, preparing bandages for wounds, and in many and various ways making herself useful, and putting up with such accommodations as were furnished soldiers."[17] With her unwavering service endearing her to many, she was considered the "mother" of the regiment; doing all without pay. After the wounding of William at Gettysburg, Sarah joined her husband as he recovered at Fort Smith Hospital in Rhode Island, where she served with distinction, earning $3 per month. Finances following the war were difficult for the Sinfields as they struggled along on William's disability pension until 1884, when a special act of Congress granted Sarah a pension for her "incalculable value to the sick and wounded soldiers" with the 72nd N.Y. in the amount of $15 per month.[18]

With the Federal defeat at Chancellorsville, the task of burying the Union dead, Emerson F. Merrell among them, was left to advancing Confederate troops. Soon after the war's end, the remains from the Chancellorsville battlefield upon which the 72nd fought were reinterred at the National Cemetery at Fredericksburg, Virginia. Here, over 15,000 Union troops are buried though fewer than 2,500 are identified. It is believed that here, in one of these smaller plots, Merrell is buried along with 34 of his comrades. At the family plot in Coventry Cemetery many years later, a small tombstone was placed alongside his parents' graves with the simple inscription, "Emerson F. Merrell, killed in action battle of Chancellorsville." One hundred and thirty-three years after his death, a bronze marker provided by the Department of Veterans Affairs was placed next to the family tombstone; it reads, "In Memory of Emerson Merrell, Pvt. Co. I. 72nd NY Inf. Civil War Feb 27 1842–May 3, 1863."[19]

For Captain Isaac L. Chadwick of Company C, the war ended in January of 1863, when he was declared "entirely unfit for duty" due to his inflammatory rheumatism and carditis following his apparent wounding at Malvern Hill. Despite there being little doubt he was wounded at Malvern Hill, Chadwick was allowed to go directly home following the battle and bypass the normal round of inspections by army doctors. After a short recovery and brief return to duty he resigned following the rigors of Fredericksburg. Nearly crippled and racked with pain, Chadwick's own conflicting recollections of events coupled with imprecise descriptions of his wounds by various doctors, resulted in a maddening bureaucratic odyssey for the former captain to claim his rightful pension. As the fight for his pension raged, Chadwick argued in vain for just benefits, describing his personal sacrifices associated with his raising of Company C. "I took over $2,000 of my own hard earned money and raised and subsisted a company of 108 men" and "never had one dollar back for it. I had a good trade blacksmith and machinist—but from my poor health I have never been able to work one day at my trade from 1863." Chadwick was now moving from job to job in order to make ends meet. Adding to his heartache, Chadwick's second wife died in 1880. Two years later he was married again, only to be sued for a separation in 1888 by this third wife, who complained that he abused her for not sharing his spiritualist beliefs. The beleaguered Chadwick died on January 4, 1896, and was buried in Hudson County, New Jersey. Ironically, his estranged third wife reappeared to claim his pension, while continuing to fight for an increase in survivor's pension benefits until her own death 22 years later.[20]

In September of 1862, Nelson Taylor had been promoted to brigadier general and eventually given command of brigade in Gibbon's division of I Corps. Despite a good showing at Fredericksburg, Taylor requested resignation from the service and after initially being rebuffed by superiors was granted his separation from the army in January of 1863. Taylor returned to his New York City law practice. He declined the 72nd's offer to return to its colonelcy following the death of Stevens in May '63, but that summer took temporary command of some troops during the Harlem draft riots. In 1864 he was elected to Congress and served only one term, having failed to be reelected. Two years later Taylor returned to his home town of South Norwalk, Connecticut, where he practiced law and served many years as the city attorney. Nelson Taylor died on January 16, 1894, and is buried in his home town at Riverside Cemetery.[21]

From the Gettysburg fight to the disbanding of the regiment, Lt. Col. John Leonard commanded the 72nd. Two months after the June 1864 dissolution, Leonard was appointed as a captain in the Veteran Reserve Corps. He served in the regular army until 1870, when he was placed on the retirement list on account of wounds. After his army service, Leonard settled back in his home town of Newark, New Jersey. Leonard was active in the 72nd N.Y. veterans' association, being elected as its president for the 1901 year. It is doubtful Leonard ever served since he died on February 26, 1902, and there is no record of the association's existence past 1900.[22]

Daniel Sickles never returned to the field after the fight at Gettysburg; George Meade saw to that. In 1864 and '65, Dan spent much of his time defending his actions of that July day. By the time the war was over, most men wanted nothing more than to get on with their lives and set the war behind them. After helping with Southern reconstruction, Sickles landed a post as minister to Spain, where he carried on a liaison with the deposed Queen Isabella II. Dan eventually ran afoul of the State Department and was withdrawn from Spain just in time to join in the groundswell of veterans' remembrances of the war back home in the U.S. With little else to keep him occupied, Sickles supported the various veterans' groups, especially those associated with the III Corps, with great vigor. The 1880s saw a new wave of books and articles that looked back on the war with a more critical eye, a perspective that placed Sickles' actions at Gettysburg in an increasingly unfavorable light. Sickles' path was now clear; restore his reputation (as he saw it at least) as the hero, not the goat, of Gettysburg. Eventually this effort would lead to a friendship with former Confederate general James Longstreet, who wrote that Sickles' actions saved the battle for the Union. Another important step towards redemption was being appointed chairman of the New York Monuments Commission for the Battlefield of Gettysburg. This position would require countless dedication speeches in front of enthusiastic veterans and their relatives; how better to rehabilitate one's image? Among many veterans Dan was indeed able to revamp his reputation. But by the early 1900s when his time at the head of commission was over, more than $20,000 came up missing, and the last several years of his life were spent trying to avoid jail over this and other accumulated debts. During one visit to Gettysburg with his good friend Chaplain Joseph Twichell, the reverend mused that of all the monuments, not one was dedicated to Sickles, after which Dan supposedly responded to the contrary that the entire park was a monument to him. This tale, whether true or not, would serve as a fitting exclamation point the old general's legend. Sickles died on May 3, 1914, after lingering for several days after suffering a cerebral hemorrhage.[23]

It may never be known when the last 72nd man died. Some veterans of the Civil War lingered well into the middle part of the 20th century and perhaps among them was one of the 1,250 men who served in the regiment. How these men have been remembered through the intervening years from July of '64 to now cannot fully be known. Certainly there are descendants who hold the memory of their 72nd veteran close with reverence and solemnity, while most others are doubtlessly unaware of the sacrifice an ancestor has made. There are only a few groups of modern-day Civil War reenactors who portray the 72nd New York. And it is among these few that some of the names of these "Boys of '61" are ever spoken aloud and acknowledged. The deeds of the 72nd New York do not immediately jump off the pages of the history books. These men did not single-handedly win a battle or hold the line against impossible odds, yet they took a measure of pride in the job they performed. For three years the men of Third Excelsior were in the thick of the most important and well known fighting of the Eastern Theater, never flinching, never breaking when the struggle was at its worst, earning them a place among Colonel Fox's "300 Fighting Regiments." It is because of this dedication to service that they deserve to be remembered and their deeds told here.

Regimental Roster by Company

This roster of men who served with the 72nd New York is organized by company but starts with officers who did not serve with a particular company. Band members and field and staff men appear in their own sections. Officers frequently moved from company to company as the needs of the regiment dictated, and the list of all officers who served within a company appears at the beginning of each company's section. The full description of each officer along with their date of commission and subsequent promotions appears with the company into which they were originally mustered. Errors regarding name spellings, ages, dates served or discharge information are regrettable but reflect the information found in the source material. This roster is based on information found primarily in the *Annual Report of the Adjutant-General of the State of New York for the Year 1901*, which provides comprehensive information for each man who served; *New York in the War of the Rebellion, 1861 to 1865*, which provides a compilation of officer assignments; and the *History of the Third Regiment Excelsior Brigade 72nd New York Volunteer Infantry, 1861–1865*, which provides a more detailed description of officer assignments within the regiment, along with a list of field and staff and band members.

OFFICERS OF THE REGIMENT

Colonels
Nelson Taylor, from July 23, 1861, to September 9, 1862.
William O. Stevens, from September 8, 1862, to May 3, 1863.
John S. Austin, from May 4, 1883, to June 27, 1864.

Lieutenant-Colonels
Israel Moses, from June 3, 1861, to October 20, 1862.
John S. Austin, from October 25, 1862, to May 4, 1863.
John Leonard, from May 4, 1863, to June 19, 1864.

Majors
William O. Stevens, from June 25, 1861, to September 8, 1862.
John Leonard, from September 8, 1862, to May 4, 1863.
Caspar K. Abell, from May 4, 1863, to June 19, 1864.

Adjutants
Stephen M. Doyle, from July 23 to November 1, 1861.
William J. O'Neil from November 1, 1861, to April 29, 1862.
Hugh C. Hinman, from July to December 26, 1862.
James A. Smith, from December 26, 1862, to June 24, 1863.
Alexander M. Clark, from June 24, 1863, to January 1, 1864.
Robert H. Savage, from January 1 to March 5, 1864.
Henry Jones Yates, from March 1 to June 19, 1864.

Quartermasters

Thomas W. G. Fry, from July 23, 1861, to April 2, 1863.

John McNeil Grant, from November 22, 1862, to June 19, 1864.

Surgeon

Charles K. Irwin, from July 24, 1861.

Assistant Surgeons

Nathaniel W. Leighton, from July 23, 1861, to October 3, 1862.

Edward T. Perkins, from October 17, 1862, to May 13, 1863.

George D. Townsend, from October 21, 1862, to October 1883.

William M. Jones, from November 3, 1862, to July 29, 1863.

Fredrick W. Simpson, from November 13, 1863, to May 9, 1864.

Chaplains

Levi W. Norton, from July 24, 1861, to April 20, 1862.

William R. Eastman, from January 1, 1863, to June 19, 1864.

Officers Who Were Commissioned or Appointed but Did Not Serve in the Grades Named

Phillips, John P., as assistant surgeon.
Clark, Thomas, as captain.

O'Neil, William J., as captain.
Kiener, John, as second lieutenant.

Medals of Honor Granted by the President

Brown, Henri Lefevre, sergeant, Company B, for great bravery at the battle of the Wilderness, Va., May 6, 1864.

Haight, John H., sergeant, Company G, for great gallantry in the battles of Williamsburg, Va., Bristoe Station, Manassas, Va., May 5, August 27 and August 29, 1862, respectively.

Horan, Thomas, sergeant, Company E, for most distinguished gallantry in action at Gettysburg, Pa., July 2, 1863.

Young, James M., private, Company B, for most distinguished gallantry in action at the Wilderness, Va., May 6, 1864.

Brevet Commissions of New York Volunteers Granted by the Governor of the State to Enlisted Men

Baker, James T., private, Company B, second lieutenant.

Hall, James, corporal, Company B, second lieutenant.

Marvin, Wm. R., private, Company B, second lieutenant.

Torrence, George S., private, Company E, second lieutenant.

Record of the Officers

Abell, Caspar K., age 33 years; enrolled May 20, 1861, at Dunkirk to serve three years; mustered in as first lieutenant, Company D, June 20, 1861; as captain, June 25, 1861; as major, May 4, 1863; mustered out with regiment, June 19, 1864, near Petersburg, Va.; not commissioned first lieutenant; commissioned captain, January 7, 1862.

BAND

Organization complete in August 1861.

Men Who Were Mustered Directly into the Band

Akan, Seaton L.—Age, 44 years. Enlisted, August 16, 1861, at New York, to serve three years; mustered in as musician, band, August 19, 1861; mustered out with band, July 22, 1862 (2nd E flat tuba).

Bailey, Hiam G.—Age, 30 years. Enlisted, August 16, 1861, at New York, to serve three years; mustered in as musician, band, August 19, 1861; mustered out July 14, 1862, at Washington, D.C. (1st E flat tuba).

Barclay, Edward M.—Age, 21 years. Enlisted, August 12, 1861, at New York City, to serve three years; mustered in as musician, band, August 10, 1861; mustered out, July 14, 1862, at Washington, D.C. (1st B flat bass).

Blakney, John H.—Age, 25 years. Enlisted, August 16, 1861, at New York, to serve three years; mustered in as musician, band, August 19, 1861; mustered out with band, July 22, 1862 (1st B flat tenor).

Boynton, Frederic B.—Age, 27 years. Enlisted, August 16, 1861, at New York, to serve three years; mustered in as musician, band, August 19, 1861; discharged by order of Major-General Heintzelman, no date or place (2nd B flat soprano).

Chase, Thomas H.B.—Age, 31 years. Enlisted, August 12, 1861, at New York, to serve three years; mustered in as musician, band, August 19, 1861; mustered out with band, July 22, 1862 (baritone).

Dickenson, H.R.—Age, 19 years. Enlisted, August 16, 1861, at New York, to serve three years; mustered in as musician in band, August 19, 1861; mustered out with band, July 22, 1862 (4th B flat soprano).

Dodge, Edwin M.—Age, 24 years. Enlisted, September 15, 1861, at New York City, to serve three years; mustered in as musician in band, October 31, 1861; discharged, June 19, 1862, by order General Heintzelman.

Gibson, William H.—Age, 24 years. Enlisted, August 12, 1861, at New York, to serve three years; mustered in as musician, band, August 19, 1861; mustered out with band July 22 1862 (bass drum).

Leathrop, John S.—Age, 23 years. Enlisted, August 16, 1861, at New York City, to serve three years; mustered in as musician, band, August 19, 1861; mustered out with baud, July 22, 1862 (4th B flat soprano).

Norris, William B.—Age, 30 years. Enlisted, August 10, 1861, at New York, to serve three years; mustered in as musician in band, August 19, 1861; appointed leader, May 16, 1862; mustered out with band, July 22, 1862 (1st E flat soprano).

Sandford, William S.—Age, 18 years. Enlisted, October 1, 1861, at Delhi, to serve three years; mustered in as musician in band, October 3, 1861; mustered out with band, July 22, 1862 (side drum).

Smith, Dewit C.—Age, 19 years. Enlisted, August 12, 1861, at Dunkirk, to serve three years; mustered in as musician in band, August 19, 1861; mustered out with band, July 22, 1862 (3rd B flat soprano).

Smith, William C.—Age, 19 years. Enlisted, August 16, 1861, at New York, to serve three years; mustered in as musician in band, August 19, 1861; no further record.

Stevens, Frank G.—Age, 19 years. Enlisted, October 1, 1861, at Fredonia, to serve three years; mustered in as musician in band, October 3, 1861; discharged with band, July 22, 1862.

Tew, Albermarle H.—Age, 38 years. Enlisted, July 16, 1861, at Dunkirk, to serve three years; mustered in as musician in band, August 31, 1861; discharged for disability, May 6, 1862, at Budds Ferry, Md. (3rd B flat soprano).

Wheeler, James W.—Age, 23 years. Enlisted, August 16, 1861, at New York City, to serve three years; mustered in as musician in band, August 19, 1861; mustered out with band, July 22, 1862 (2nd B flat soprano).

Other Men Who Served in the Band but Were Mustered Initially into Other Companies (Source: LeFevre-Brown, pp. 13–14)

A.G. Peters, Leader	1st B Flat Soprano
H.K. Willard	2nd B Flat Soprano
C.H. Warren	1st Flat Tenor
A.N. Ayers	3rd B Flat Tenor
M.F. Curtis	2nd B Flat Tenor
C. Curtis	2nd B Flat Bass
A.M. Comstock	Side Drum
D.C. Dinnin	Cymbals
M.F. Tower	Asst. Bass Drum

Company A

Organized in New York City in May 1861. Mustered into the United States service June 21, 1861.

Captains

George Grecheneck, from June 21, 1861, to May 17, 1862.
Charles Grossinger, from May 18 to June 23, 1862.
Horatio B. Pennock, from June 23 to August 4, 1862.
Edward B. Harnett, from August 5, 1862, to June 20, 1864.

First Lieutenants

Charles Grossinger, from June 21, 1861, to May 18, 1862.
Edward B. Harnett, from May 17 to August 5, 1862.
John S. Mann, from August 5 to November 1, 1862.
Henry J. McDonough, from November 1862, to October 1863.
Robert H. Savage, from October 29, 1863, to January 1, 1884.
John Kiener, from February 10 to June 16, 1864.

Second Lieutenants

Edward B. Harnett, from June 21, 1861, to May 17, 1862.
John S. Mann, from May 17 to August 5, 1862.
Warren J. Stanton, from November 1, 1862, to May 1, 1863.
John B. Hare, from May 1 to September 1, 1863.

Batz, John—Age, 19 years. Enlisted at New York City, to serve three years, and mustered in as private, Co. A, October 29, 1862; transferred to Co. B, One Hundred and Twentieth Infantry, June 23, 1864.

Baum, Hermann—Age, 23 years. Enlisted, May 24, 1861, at New York City, to serve three years; mustered in as private, Co. A, June 21, 1861; transferred to Seventy-sixth Company, Second Battalion, Veteran Reserve Corps, February 11, 1864.

Becker, Jean—Age, 25 years. Enlisted, May 29, 1861, at New York City, to serve three years; mustered in as private, Co. A, June 21, 1861; killed in action, May 5, 1862, at Williamsburg, Va.

Berend, Adam—Age, 24 years. Enlisted, May 29, 1861, at New York City, to serve three years; mustered in as private, Co. A, June 21, 1861; re-enlisted as a veteran, December 23, 1863; transferred to Co. B, One Hundred and Twentieth Infantry, June 23, 1864.

Bitsch, August—Age, 35 years. Enlisted at New York City, to serve three years, and mustered in as private, Co. A, April 6, 1864; transferred to Co. B, One Hundred and Twentieth Infantry, June 23, 1864.

Boereked, Franz—Age, 41 years. Enlisted, May 27, 1861, at New York City, to serve three years; mustered in as private, Co. A, June 21, 1861; missing in action, May 5, 1862, at Williamsburg, Va.; no further record.

Bolantz, Ernst—Age, 20 years. Enlisted, May 25, 1861, at New York City, to serve three years; mustered in as private, Co. A, June 21, 1861; promoted corporal, December 6, 1863; mustered out with company, June 20, 1864, near Petersburg, Va.

Bowers, Henry—Age, 22 years. Enrolled, May 25, 1861, at New York, to serve three years; mustered in as sergeant, Co. A, June 21, 1861; promoted first sergeant, November 5, 1861; second lieutenant, Co. IV, May 12, 1862; discharged, September 15, 1862.

Boyle, John—Age, 54 years. Enlisted at Jersey City, N.J., to serve three years, and mustered in as private, Co. A, October 30, 1861; discharged for disability, May 14, 1862, at Budd's Ferry, Md.

Brockelmann, Ernst—Age, 26 years. Enlisted, May 30, 1861, at New York City, to serve three years; mustered in as corporal, Co. A, June 21, 1861; promoted sergeant, December 6, 1863; re-enlisted as a veteran, December 23, 1863; transferred to Co. B, One Hundred and Twentieth Infantry, June 23, 1864.

Brown, James—Age, 54. Enlisted at Delhi, to serve three years, and mustered in as private, Co. A, November 16, 1861; discharged for disability, March 15, 1862, at Camp Wool, Charles County, Md.

Clausmann, Henry—Age, 39 years. Enlisted at New York City, to serve three years, and mustered in as private, Co. A, August 11, 1862; wounded in action, May 3, 1863, at Chancellorsville, Va.; discharged for disability, April 4, 1865, at David's Island, New York Harbor.

Cruel, Friederich—Age, 35 years. Enlisted, June 3, 1861, at New York City, to serve three years; mustered in as private, Co. A, June 21, 1861; transferred to Seventy-third Infantry, July 23, 1861.

Cuwine, Dennis—Age, 18 years. Enlisted at Chautauqua, to serve three years, and mustered in as private, Co. A, January 1, 1864; died of disease, February 27, 1864, in General Hospital, Elmira, N.Y.

Duncker, Frederich—Age, 40 years. Enlisted, June 3,

1861, at New York City, to serve three years; mustered in as private, Co. A, June 21, 1861; transferred to Seventy-third Infantry, July 23, 1861; also born as Dunker.

Eckel, William—Age, 37 years. Enlisted, June 20, 1861, at New York City, to serve three years; mustered in as private, Co. A, June 21, 1861; wounded, no date; mustered out with company, June 20, 1864, near Petersburg, Va.

Eckhardt, Philipp—Age, 39 years. Enlisted, June 3, 1861, at New York City, to serve three years; mustered in as private, Co. A, June 21, 1861; transferred to Seventh-third Infantry, July 23, 1861.

Engels, John—Age, 19 years. Enlisted at New York City, to serve three years, and mustered in as private, Co. A, August 26, 1862; mustered out, June 2, 1805, at Washington, D.C.

Faigel, Conrad—Age, 37 years. Enlisted, June 3, 1861, at New York City, to serve three years; mustered in as private, Co. A, June 21, 1861; transferred to Seventy-third Infantry, July 23, 1861.

Fischer, Casper—Age, 37 years. Enlisted, June 3, 1861, at New York City, to serve three years; mustered in as private, Co. A, June 21, 1861; transferred to Seventy-third Infantry, July 23, 1861.

Fitzpatrick, John—Age, 30 years. Enlisted at Staten Island, to serve three years; mustered in as private, Co. A, July 10, 1861; killed in action, August 19, 1862, at Bristoe Station, Va.

Foerstner, Charles—Age, 38 years. Enlisted, May 20, 1861, at New York City, to serve three years; mustered in as private, Co. A, June 21, 1861; died of disease, January 7, 1864, at New York City.

Fraenkel, Moses—Age, 19 years. Enlisted, May 30, 1861, at New York City, to serve three years; mustered in as private, Co. A, June 21, 1861; mustered out, July 1, 1864, at New York City.

Fridrich, Friederich—Age, 19 years. Enlisted, May 27, 1861, at New York City, to serve three years; mustered in as private, Co. A, June 21, 1861; killed in action, May 5, 1862, at Williamsburg, Va.

Gheisking, Friedrich—Private, Co. D, Seventy-third Infantry; transferred to Co. A, this regiment, July 1861; discharged for disability, January 2, 1863, at Providence, R.I.; subsequent service in Co. B, Thirteenth Artillery.

Gibbs, Thomas S.—Age __ years. Enlisted at New York City, to serve three years, and mustered in as private, Co. A, September 18, 1862; died of disease, April 29, 1863, at Falmouth, Va.

Gleason, Michael—Age, 28 years. Enlisted at Hornellsville, to serve three years, and mustered in as private, Co. A, December 4, 1861; re-enlisted as a veteran, December 23, 1863; promoted sergeant, February 10, 1864; transferred to Co. B, One Hundred and Twentieth Infantry, June 23, 1864.

Grecheneck, George—Age, 36 years. Enrolled, May 22, 1861, at New York, to serve three years; mustered in as captain, Co. A, June 21, 1861; wounded in action, May 5, 1862, and died of his wounds, May 17, 1862, at Williamsburg, Va. Commissioned captain, January 7, 1862, with rank from June 21, 1861, original.

Grossinger, Charles—Age, 35 years. Enrolled, May 22, 1861, at New York, to serve three years; mustered in as first lieutenant, Co. A, June 21, 1861; as captain, May 18, 1862; discharged, June 23, 1862. Commissioned first lieutenant, January 7, 1862, with rank from June 21, 1861, original; captain, May 30, 1862, with rank from May 17, 1862, vice G. Grecheneck deceased.

Guenthor, Valentine—Age, 18 years. Enlisted, June 3, 1861, at New York City, to serve three years; mustered in as private, Co. A, June 21, 1861; transferred to Seventy-third Infantry, July 23, 1861.

Hamburg, Lambert—Age, 34 years. Enlisted, May 29, 1861, at New York City, to serve three years; mustered in as sergeant, Co. A, June 21, 1861; returned to ranks, May 1864; mustered out with company, June 20, 1864, near Petersburg, Va.

Hampton, Joseph—Age, 35 years. Enlisted, September 26, 1862, at New York City, to serve three years; mustered in as private, Co. A, September 27, 1862; wounded in action, July 2, 1863, at Gettysburg, Pa.; transferred to Co. B, One Hundred and Twentieth Infantry, June 23, 1864.

Harnett, Edward B.—Age, 27 years. Enrolled, May 27, 1861, at New York City, to serve three years; mustered in as second lieutenant, Co. A, June 21, 1861; as first lieutenant, May 17, 1862; as captain, August 5, 1862; absent, sick, at muster-out of company. Commissioned second lieutenant, January 7, 1862, with rank from June 21, 1861, original; first lieutenant, June 30, 1862, with rank from May 5, 1862, vice J.P. Sanford, promoted; captain, December 1, 1862, with rank from September 9, 1862, vice G. Grecheneck, deceased.

Hartmann, John—Age, 38 years. Enlisted, June 12, 1861, at New York City, to serve three years; mustered in as private, Co. A, June 21, 1861; mustered out with company, June 20, 1861, near Petersburg Va.

Hauser, Andreas—Age, 21 years. Enlisted at New York City, to serve three years, and mustered in as private, Co. A, September 27, 1862; wounded in action, July 2, 1863, at Gettysburg, Pa.; discharged for disability, June 2, 1865, at Philadelphia, Pa.

Hausleiter, Conrad—Age, 24 years. Enlisted, June 1, 1861, at New York City, to serve three years; mustered in as private, Co. A, June 21, 1861; promoted sergeant, February 1, 1863; re-enlisted as a veteran,

December 23, 1863; transferred to Co. B, One Hundred and Twentieth Infantry, June 23, 1864.

Heis, John—Age, 20 years. Enlisted, June 17, 1861, at New York City, to serve three years; mustered in as private, Co. A, June 21, 1861; deserted, no date.

Herman, Rudolph—Private, Co. D, Seventy-third Infantry; transferred to Co. A, this regiment, July 1861; discharged for disability, January 25, 1862, at Baltimore, Md.

Hess, Jacob—Age, 21 years. Enlisted, May 24, 1861, at New York City, to serve three years; mustered in as private, Co. A, June 21, 1861; died of disease, December 22, 1861, at Camp Wool, Charles County, Md.

Hesslor, Martin—Age, 18 years. Enlisted, May 27, 1861, at New York City, to serve three years; mustered in as musician, Co. A, June 21, 1861; discharged for disability, July 13, 1862, at Harrison Landing, Va.

Hirshe, Gottlob—Age, 20 years. Enlisted, June 12, 1861, at New York City, to serve three years; mustered in as private, Co. A, June 21, 1861; wounded in action, July 2, 1863; died of his wounds, July 26, 1863, in hospital at Gettysburg, Pa.; also born as Hersche.

Hoechtle, Fridrich—Age, 26 years. Enlisted, June 12, 1861, at New York City, to serve three years; mustered in as sergeant, Co. A, June 21, 1861; deserted, no date.

Holderet, Williams—Private, Co. D, Seventy-third Infantry; transferred to Co. A, this regiment, July 1861; promoted corporal, May 21, 1862; discharged for disability, November 10, 1862.

Hornung, Johann—Age, 35 years. Enlisted, June 12, 1861, at New York City, to serve three years; mustered in as private, Co. A, June 21, 1861; killed in action, July 1, 1862, at Malvern Hill, Va.

Huck, Jean—Age, 34 years. Enlisted, May 29, 1861, at New York City, to serve three years; mustered in as private, Co. A, June 21, 1861; discharged for disability, April 7, 1863, at Washington, D.C.

Huttmann, Berend—Age, 23 years. Enrolled, May 25, 1861, at New York City, to serve three years; mustered in as first sergeant, Co. A, June 21, 1861; promoted sergeant-major, November 5, 1861; mustered in as second lieutenant, Co. F, January 3, 1862; as first lieutenant, Co. C, June 23, 1862; as captain, Co. K, November 1, 1862; mustered out with company, June 20, 1864, near Petersburg, Va. Commissioned second lieutenant, January 17, 1862, with rank from January 2, 1862, vice J.H. Holmes, promoted; first lieutenant, December 1, 1862, with rank from June 23, 1862, vice W.H. Post, promoted; captain, October 6, 1863, with rank from October 31, 1862, vice D. Loeb, resigned.

Ider, Philipp—Age, 20 years. Enlisted, June 12, 1861, at New York City, to serve three years; mustered in as private, Co. A, June 21, 1861; mustered out with company, June 20, 1864, near Petersburg, Va.; also born as Eder.

Janson, John—Age, 18 years. Enlisted, June 1, 1861, at New York City, to serve three years; mustered in as musician, Co. A, June 21, 1861; sent to the ranks, September 1, 1861; discharged for disability, July 23, 1862, at Harrison's Landing, Va.

John, Charles—Age, 18 years. Enlisted, May 25, 1861, at New York City, to serve three years; mustered in as private, Co. A, June 21, 1861; deserted, August 18, 1863, from hospital, Fort Schuyler, N.Y.

Kaiser, Jean—Age, 35 years. Enlisted, May 25, 1861, at New York City, to serve three years; mustered in as private, Co. A, June 21, 1861; wounded in action, May 5, 1862, at Williamsburg, Va.; discharged for wounds, October 26, 1862, at Fort Wood; also born as Keyser.

Kantreiner, Gustav—Age, 20 years. Enlisted, June 19, 1861, at New York City, to serve three years; mustered in as private, Co. A, June 21, 1861; mustered out with company, July 20, 1864, near Petersburg, Va.; also born as Kantrina.

Kellor, Anton—Age, 34 years. Enlisted, June 3, 1861, at New York City, to serve three years; mustered in as private, Co. A, June 21, 1861; transferred to Seventy-third Infantry, July 23, 1861.

Kern, Emanuel—Age, 23 years. Enlisted, June 17, 1861, at New York City, to serve three years; mustered in as private, Co. A, June 21, 1861; died of disease, November 24, 1861, at Camp Wool, Md.

Kiener, John—Age, 23 years. Enrolled, June 12, 1861, at New York, to serve three years; mustered in as private, Co. A, June 21, 1861, promoted corporal, September 19, 1861; sergeant, May 25, 1862; wounded in action, July 2; 1863, at Gettysburg, Pa.; transferred to Co. A, September 1, 1863; re-enlisted as a veteran, December 24, 1863; promoted second lieutenant, Co. F, to date February 11, 1863; mustered in as first lieutenant, February 10, 1864; killed in action, June 16, 1864, near Petersburg, Va.; also born as Keimer and Kuner. Commissioned second lieutenant, October 6, 1863, with rank from February 11, 1863, vice R. Leonard, discharged; first lieutenant, December 15, 1863, with rank from October 25, 1863, vice J. Kessler, dismissed.

Kiessling, Alexander—Age, 40 years. Enlisted, June 3, 1861, at New York City, to serve three years; mustered in as private, Co. A, June 21, 1861; transferred to Seventy-third Infantry, July 23, 1861.

Kinatt, Michael—Age, 32 years. Enlisted, June 3, 1861, at New York City, to serve three years; mustered in as private, Co. A, June 21, 1861; transferred to Seventy-third Infantry, July 23, 1861.

King, Julius—Age, 16 years. Enlisted, July 12, 1861, at New York City, to serve three years; mustered in as private, Co. A, August 8, 1861; re-enlisted as a veteran, December 24, 1863; transferred to Co. B, One Hundred and Twentieth Infantry, June 23, 1864.

Klein, Peter—Age, 30 years; enlisted, June 3, 1861, at New York City, to serve three years; mustered in as private, Co. A, June 21, 1861; transferred to Seventy-third Infantry, July 23, 1861.

Koehler, Gustav—Age, 28 years. Enlisted, June 19, 1861, at New York City, to serve three years; mustered in as private, Co. A, June 21, 1861; died of disease, May 6, 1862, at General Hospital, near Yorktown, Va.

Koepler, Friedrich—Age, 39 years. Enlisted, June 1, 1861, at New York City, to serve three years; mustered in as private, Co. A, June 21, 1861; discharged for disability, May 31, 1862, at Budd's Ferry, Md.; also born as Koliler.

Kress, Andrew—Age, 32 years. Enlisted, May 27, 1861, at New York City, to serve three years; mustered in as private, Co. A, June 21, 1861; wounded in action, July 2, 1863, at Gettysburg, Pa.; transferred to One Hundred and Thirtieth Company, Second Battalion, Veteran Reserve Corps, December 28, 1863; also born as Kross.

Lamb, Richard—Age, 35 years. Enlisted at New York City, to serve three years, and mustered in as private, Co. A, December 4, 1861; captured, May 25, 1862; paroled, September 17, 1862; killed in action, May 3, 1863, at Chancellorsville, Va.

Laufer, Jacob—Age, 18 years. Enlisted, May 25, 1861, at New York City, to serve three years; mustered in as private, Co. A, June 21, 1861; promoted sergeant, December 6, 1863; re-enlisted as a veteran, December 24, 1863; promoted first sergeant, May 10, 1864; transferred to Co. B, One Hundred and Twentieth Infantry, June 23, 1864.

Lefz, Louis—Age, 20 years. Enlisted, May 28, 1861, at New York City, to serve three years; mustered in as private, Co. A, June 21, 1861; killed in action, May 5, 1862, at Williamsburg, Va.

Lind, Johannes—Age, 23 years. Enlisted, June 19, 1861, at New York City, to serve three years; mustered in as private, Co. A, June 21, 1861; re-enlisted as a veteran, December 24, 1863; promoted corporal, May 20, 1864; transferred to Co. B, One Hundred and Twentieth Infantry, June 23, 1864.

Lochbaum, William—Private, Co. D, Seventy-third Infantry; transferred to Co. A, this regiment, in July 1861; promoted corporal, November 5, 1861; wounded in action, place and date not stated; discharged for wounds, March 14, 1863, at New Haven, Conn.

Loderhose, George—Age, 22 years. Enlisted, May 27, 1861, at New York City, to serve three years; mustered in as private, Co. A, June 21, 1861; re-enlisted as a veteran and promoted corporal, December 24, 1863; promoted sergeant, May 12, 1864; transferred to Co. B, One Hundred and Twentieth Infantry, June 23, 1864.

Loewenthal, Adolph—Age, 18 years. Enlisted, May 25, 1861, at New York City, to serve three years; mustered in as private, Co. A, June 21, 1861; discharged for disability, September 26, 1862, near Alexandria, Va.

Lowe, Max—Age, 35 years. Enlisted, June 3, 1861, at New York City, to serve three years; mustered in as private, Co. A, June 21, 1861; died of disease, November 7, 1861, at Camp Baker, Md.

Maas, George—Age, 26 years. Enlisted, June 18, 1861, at New York City, to serve three years; mustered in as private, Co. A, June 21, 1861; deserted, January 26, 1863, at Camp Taylor, Falmouth, Va.

Mann, Peter—Age, 30 years. Enlisted, May 24, 1861, at New York City, to serve three years; mustered in as corporal, Co. A, June 21, 1861; promoted sergeant, August 4, 1862; returned to ranks, December 6, 1863; re-enlisted as a veteran, December 24, 1868; promoted sergeant, May 6, 1864; transferred to Co. B, One Hundred and Twentieth Infantry, June 20, 1864.

Mckenly, Thomas S.—Age, 24 years. Enlisted at New York City, to serve three years, and mustered in as private, Co. A, August 30, 1862; mustered out, May 31, 1865, at Frederick, Md.

Metz, Ludwig—Age, 19 years. Enlisted, May 25, 1861, at New York City, to serve three years; mustered in as private, Co. A, June 21, 1861; killed in action, July 1, 1862, at Malvern Hill, Va.

Meyer, Edward—Private, Co. D, Seventy-third Infantry; transferred to Co. A, this regiment, no date; mustered out, to date July 4, 1864, at New York City.

Meyer, John—Age, 32 years. Enlisted, June 3, 1861, at New York City, to serve three years; mustered in as private, Co. A, June 21, 1861; wounded in action, May 5, 1862, at Williamsburg, Va.; died of his wounds, May 20, 1862, at Mill Creek General Hospital.

Miler, Franz—Age, 26 years. Enlisted, May 27, 1861, at New York City, to serve three years; mustered in as corporal, Co. A, June 21, 1861; mustered out with company, June 20, 1864, near Petersburg, Va.

Miller, Andreas—Age, 36 years. Enlisted, June 3, 1861, at New York City, to serve three years; mustered in as private, Co. A, June 21, 1861; transferred to Seventy-third Infantry, July 23, 1861.

Miller, Jacob—Age, 20 years. Enlisted, June 17, 1861, at New York City, to serve three years; mustered in as private, Co. A, June 21, 1861; promoted corporal, August 4, 1862; wounded, no date or place; transferred to Co. I, Sixth Regiment, Veteran Reserve Corps, April 6, 1864, and discharged therefrom, June 23, 1864.

Miller, William—Age, 23 years. Enlisted, May 27, 1861, at New York City, to serve three years; mustered in as corporal, Co. A, June 21, 1861; returned to ranks, August 4, 1862; deserted, June 30, 1863, on the march to Gettysburg, Pa.

Mohr, Rudolph—Age, 20 years. Enlisted, May 27, 1861, at New York City, to serve three years; mustered in as private, Co. A, June 21, 1861; discharged for disability, June 23, 1862, at Washington, D.C.; also born as Moore.

Moller, Charles—Age, 28 years. Enlisted, June 3, 1861, at New York City, to serve three years; mustered in as private, Co. A, June 21, 1861; transferred to Seventy-third Infantry, July 23, 1861.

Motz, David—Private, Co. D, Seventy-third Infantry; transferred to Co. A, this regiment, no date; re-enlisted as a veteran, December 24, 1863; transferred to Co. B, One Hundred and Twentieth Infantry, June 23, 1864.

Motzer, Jacob—Age, 24 years. Enlisted, May 24, 1861, at New York City, to serve three years; mustered in as corporal, Co. A, June 21, 1861; promoted sergeant, November 1, 1862; deserted, January 22, 1863, at camp near Falmouth, Va.

Nahm, Christian—Age, 35 years. Enlisted, May 27, 1861, at New York City, to serve three years; mustered in as private, Co. A, June 21, 1861; no further record.

Ney, Balthaser—Age, 40 years. Enlisted, June 3, 1861, at New York City, to serve three years; mustered in as private, Co. A, June 21, 1861; transferred to Seventy-third Infantry, July 23, 1861.

Pauly, Peter—Age, 27 years. Enlisted, June 3, 1861, at New York City, to serve three years; mustered in as private, Co. A, June 21, 1861; transferred to Seventy-third Infantry, July 23, 1861.

Philipp, August—Age, 27 years. Enlisted, May 27, 1861, at New York City, to serve three years; mustered in as private, Co. A, June 21, 1861; discharged for disability, March 16, 1863, at New York City; also born as Fillipp.

Roberts, Henry—Age, 22 years. Enlisted, June 18, 1861, at New York City, to serve three years; mustered in as private, Co. A, June 21, 1861; discharged for disability, April 22, 1863, at Convalescent Camp, Va.

Roth, George—Age, 27 years. Enlisted, June 3, 1861, at New York City, to serve three years; mustered in as private, Co. A, June 21, 1861; transferred to Seventy-third Infantry, July 23, 1861.

Sarrsonn, Samuel—Age, 29 years. Enlisted at New York City, to serve three years, and mustered in as private, Co. A, June 21, 1861; died, no date.

Schiedecker, Franz—Private, Co. D, Seventy-third Infantry; transferred to Co. A, this regiment, July 1861; discharged for disability, no date.

Sciieferle, Henrich—Age, 26 years. Enlisted, June 3, 1861, at New York City, to serve three years; mustered in as private, Co. A, June 21, 1861; transferred to Seventy-third Infantry, July 23, 1861.

Schlegel, Johann—Age, 30 years. Enlisted, June 18, 1861, at New York City, to serve three years; mustered in as private, Co. A, June 21, 1861; discharged for disability, February 6, 1863, at Convalescent Camp, Va.

Schmidt, William—Private, Co. D, Seventy-third Infantry; transferred to Co. A, this regiment, July 1861; wounded in action, May 12, 1864, at Spotsylvania, Va.; mustered out with company, June 20, 1864, near Petersburg, Va.

Schneider, George—Age, 20 years. Enlisted, June 12, 1861, at New York City, to serve three years; mustered in as private, Co. A, June 21, 1861; died, November 27, 1863, at Mine Run, Va.

Schulz, Nigolaus—Age, 28 years. Enlisted, June 3, 1861, at New York City, to serve three years; mustered in as private, Co. A, June 21, 1861; transferred to Seventy-third Infantry, July 23, 1861.

Schwarzinyer, Michael—Age, 30 years. Enlisted, May 25, 1861, at New York City, to serve three years; mustered in as private, Co. A, June 21, 1861; deserted, no date.

Sebeck, Gottlob—Private, Co. D, Seventy-third Infantry; transferred to Co. A, this regiment, July 1861; captured, no date; died, September 1862, at Richmond, Va.

Sigglecove, John—Age, 40 years. Enlisted, September 8, 1862, at Dunkirk, to serve three years; mustered in as private, Co. A, September 20, 1862; discharged for disability, August 17, 1863, at Philadelphia, Pa.; born as John Sigglekove.

Simon, Samuel—Age, 33 years. Enlisted, May 29, 1861, at New York City, to serve three years; mustered in as wagoner, Co. A, June 21, 1861; sent to the ranks, April 5, 1862; died of disease, July 2, 1862, at Washington, D.C.

Stachlin, Charles—Age 21 years. Enlisted, May 25, 1861, at New York City, to serve three years; mustered in as sergeant, Co. A, June 21, 1861; discharged for disability, October 10, 1863, at Convalescent Camp, Va.

Teuscher, Jacob—Age, 33 years. Enlisted, May 25, 1861, at New York City, to serve three years; mustered in as private, Co. A, June 21, 1861; discharged for disability, December 15, 1862, at Philadelphia, Pa.

Tittsche, Mathias—Age, 38 years. Enlisted, June 3,

1861, at New York City, to serve three years; mustered in as private, Co. A, June 21, 1861; transferred to Seventy-third Infantry, July 23, 1861.

Wahl, Peter—Age, 42 years. Enlisted, May 27, 1861, at New York City, to serve three years; mustered in as corporal, Co. A, June 21, 1861; discharged for disability, May 21, 1863, at Philadelphia, Pa.

Walter, Wilhelm—Age, 26 years. Enlisted, May 27, 1861, at New York City, to serve three years; mustered in as private, Co. A, June 21, 1861; discharged for disability, January 5, 1863, at Point Lookout, Md.

Warster, Gottfried—Age, 30 years, Enlisted, May 27, 1861, at New York City, to serve three years; mustered in as private, Co. A, June 21, 1861; discharged for disability, March 15, 1862, at Camp Wool, Charles county, Md.; also born as Wurster.

Wild, Robert—Age, 19 years. Enlisted at New York City, to serve three years, and mustered in as private, Co. A, August 11, 1862; transferred to Veteran Reserve Corps, April 22, 1863.

Wilhelm, Sutzins—Age, 26 years. Enlisted, June 3, 1861, at New York City, to serve three years; mustered in as private, Co. A, June 21, 1861; transferred to Seventy-third Infantry, July 23, 1861.

Willeshauser, Jacob—Age, 30 years. Enlisted, June 12, 1861, at New York City, to serve three years; mustered in as private, Co. A, June 21, 1861; died of disease, March 8, 1864, near Annapolis, Md.

Wing, Charles—Age, 35 years. Enlisted, May 28, 1861, at New York City, to serve three years; mustered in as corporal, Co. A, June 21, 1861; returned to the ranks, December 26, 1861; deserted, July 1862, from Fair Oaks, Va.

Wittig, Moritz—Private, Co. D, Seventy-third Infantry; transferred to Co. A, this regiment, July 21, 1861; deserted from hospital, no date.

Wolf, Frederick—Age, 40 years. Enlisted at New York City, to serve three years, and mustered in as private, Co. A, September 8, 1862; wounded, no date or place; transferred to Co. B, One Hundred and Twentieth Infantry, June 23, 1864.

Zschan, Moritz—Age, 41 years. Enlisted, June 3, 1861, at New York City, to serve three years; mustered in as private, Co. A, June 21, 1861; transferred to Seventy-third Infantry, July 23, 1861.

Company B

Organized in Jamestown, N.Y., in May 1861. Mustered into the United States service, June 21, 1861.

Captains

James M. Brown, from June 20 to November 5, 1861.
Darwin Willard, from November 5, 1861, to May 5, 1862.
John P. Sandford, from May 5, 1862, to July 28, 1863.
Patrick Anderson, from August 17, 1863, to June 20, 1864.

First Lieutenants

Darwin Willard, from June 20 to November 5, 1861.
Alfred S. Mason, from November 5, 1861, to May 2, 1862.
Samuel Bailey, from May 2 to September 26, 1862.
William E. Wheeler, from September 26, 1862, to May 4, 1863.
Prentice Elijah Bishop, from May 4 to November 1, 1863.
Hennery C. Steward, from November 1, 1863, to June 20, 1864.

Second Lieutenants

Alfred S. Mason, from June 20 to November 5, 1861.
Samuel Bailey, from November 5, 1861, to May 2, 1862.
Rinaldo E. Jones, from May 2 to July 7, 1862.
Morris Soloman, from July 7 to October 11, 1862 (sentence of General Courts Martial).
Prentance Elijah Bishop, from October 11, 1862, to May 4, 1863.
Charles Ebersole, from May 5 to December 21, 1863.

Adams, Cyrus—Age, 24 years. Enlisted, May 28, 1861, at Jamestown, to serve three years; mustered in as private Co. B, June 20, 1861; killed in action, May 5, 1862, at Williamsburg, Va.

Allen, Marshall B.—Age, 21 years. Enlisted, May 28, 1861, at Jamestown, to serve three years; mustered in as private, Co. B, June 20, 1861; mustered out with company, June 20, 1864, near Petersburg, Va.

Annis, James Q.—Age, 22 years. Enlisted, May 28, 1861, at Jamestown, to serve three years; mustered in as private, Co. B, June 20, 1861; discharged for disability, July 15, 1863.

Arnold, Aaron—Age, 21 years. Enlisted, May 28, 1861, at Jamestown, to serve three years; mustered in as private, Co. B, June 20, 1861; discharged for disability, December 8, 1862, at Washington, D.C.

Arnold, Alexander W.—Age, 22 years. Enlisted, May 28, 1861, at Jamestown, to serve three years; mustered in as corporal, Co. B, June 20, 1861; discharged for disability, October 4, 1861, at Camp Caldwell, D.C.

Aummook, Leroy—Age, 18 years. Enlisted, May 28, 1861, at Jamestown, to serve three years; mustered in as private, Co. B, June 20, 1861; wounded in action, June 25, 1862, at Fair Oaks, Va.; discharged for his wounds, November 19, 1862, at New York City.

Ayrs, Alfred N.—Age, 26 years. Enlisted, May 28, 1861, at Jamestown, to serve three years; mustered in as corporal, Co. B, June 20, 1861; transferred to regimental band, July 24, 1861; retransferred to Co. B, July 22, 1862; re-enlisted as a veteran, December 24, 1863; transferred to Co. C, One Hundred and Twentieth Infantry, June 24, 1864.

Baker, Charles S.—Age, 18 years. Enlisted, May 28, 1861, at Jamestown, to serve three years; mustered in as private, Co. B, June 20, 1861; discharged for disability, September 6, 1862, at New York City.

Barber, Edmund B.—Age, 24 years. Enlisted, May 28, 1861, at Jamestown, to serve three years; mustered in as private, Co. B, June 20, 1861; reenlisted as a veteran, December 24, 1863; wounded in action, May 11, 1864, at Spotsylvania, Va.; transferred to Co. C, One Hundred and Twentieth Infantry, June 23, 1864.

Barber, Henry O.—Age, 21 years. Enlisted, October 13, 1861, at Jamestown, to serve three years; mustered in as private, Co. B, October 16, 1861; discharged for disability, January 31, 1862, at Camp Wool, Md.

Benz, Joseph—Age, 19 years. Enlisted, May 28, 1861, at Jamestown, to serve three years; mustered in as private, Co. B, June 20, 1861; wounded in action, July 1, 1862, at Malvern Hill, Va.; transferred to Forty-fourth Company, Second Battalion, Veteran Reserve Corps, November 1, 1863.

Bishop, Prentice Elijah—Age, 18 years. Enrolled, May 28, 1861, at Jamestown, to serve three years; mustered in as corporal, Co. B, June 20, 1861; promoted sergeant, November 1, 1861; first sergeant, August 5, 1862; mustered in as second lieutenant, October 11, 1862; as first lieutenant, May 4, 1863; wounded in action, July 2, 1863, at Gettysburg, Pa.; transferred to Co. F, November 1, 1863; discharged, December 26, 1863, at Brandy Station, Va. Commissioned second lieutenant, December 1, 1862, with rank from October 11, 1862, vice M. Solomon, dismissed; first lieutenant, August 7, 1863, with rank from May 4, 1863, vice W.E. Wheeler, promoted.

Bliss, Ephraim W.—Age, 18 years. Enlisted, May 28, 1861, at Jamestown, to serve three years; mustered in as private, Co. B, June 20, 1861; died of disease, January 7, 1862, at Camp Wool, Md.

Breton, John—Age, 42 years. Enlisted at Gerry, to serve three years, and mustered in as private, Co. B, December 28, 1863; transferred to Co. A, Twenty-fourth Regiment, Veteran Reserve Corps, no date, from which discharged for disability, May 13, 1865, at Washington, D.C.

Bristol, Solomon L.—Age, 21 years. Enlisted, May 28, 1861, at Jamestown, to serve three years; mustered in as private, Co. B, June 20, 1861; wounded in action, May 5, 1862, at Williamsburg, Va., promoted corporal, November 1, 1862; absent, sick, at Camp Convalescent, Alexandria, Va., at muster-out of company.

Brown, James M.—Age, 34 years. Enrolled, May 28, 1861, at Jamestown, to serve three years; mustered in as captain, Co. B, June 20, 1861; discharged, November 5, 1861; subsequent service in One Hundredth Infantry. Commissioned captain, October 9, 1861, with rank from June 20, 1861, original.

Brown, Lewis S.S.—Age, 19 years. Enlisted at Carroll, to serve three years, and mustered in as private, Co. B, January 29, 1864; transferred to Co. H, One Hundred and Twentieth Infantry, June 23, 1864.

Brunson, James—Age, 20 years. Enlisted, May 28, 1861, at Jamestown, to serve three years; mustered in as private, Co. B, June 20, 1861; wounded in action, August 27, 1862, at Bristoe Station, Va.; re-enlisted as a veteran, December 24, 1863; transferred to Co. C, One Hundred and Twentieth Infantry, June 23, 1864; also born as Bronson.

Butterfield, Joseph W.—Age, 18 years. Enlisted at Ashford, to serve three years, and mustered in as private, Co. B, February 4, 1864; transferred to Co. H, One Hundred and Twentieth Infantry, June 23, 1864.

Carroll, Charles—Age, 20 years. Enlisted, May 28, 1861, at Jamestown, to serve three years; mustered in as private, Co. B, June 20, 1861; died of disease, May 23, 1862, at Mount Pleasant Hospital, Washington, D.C.

Clark, Alexander M.—Age, 21 years. Enrolled, May 28, 1861, at Jamestown, to serve three years; mustered in as sergeant, Co. B, June 20, 1801; promoted first sergeant, May 4, 1862; sergeant-major, August 5, 1802; mustered in as second lieutenant, Co. K, September 8, 1862; transferred to Co. G, November 1, 1862; mustered in as first lieutenant, January 7, 1863; as adjutant, June 24, 1863; as captain, Co. D, January 1, 1864; mustered out with company, June 19, 1864, near Petersburg, Va. Commissioned second lieutenant, December 1, 1862, with rank from September 8, 1862, vice W. McGinnis, resigned; first lieutenant, June 13, 1863, with rank from January 7, 1863, vice W.H. Post, promoted; first lieutenant and adjutant, September 5, 1863, with rank from June 24, 1863, vice J.A. Smith, assigned to Co. G; captain, December 17, 1863, with rank from November 28, 1863, vice H.J. McDonough, killed in action.

Comstock, Albert M.—Age, 29 years. Enlisted, May 28, 1861, at Jamestown, to serve three years; mustered in as musician, Co. B, June 20, 1861; transferred to regimental band, July 24, 1861; re-transferred to Co. B, July 22, 1862; discharged for disability, July 30, 1862, at Harrison's Landing, Va.

Comstock, Butler—Age, 21 years. Enlisted, May 28, 1861, at Jamestown, to serve three years; mustered in as private, Co. B, June 20, 1801; wounded and captured in action, May 5, 1802, at Williamsburg, Va.; paroled, no date; discharged for his wounds, May 24, 1862, at Washington, D.C.

Conway, John—Age, 19 years. Enlisted, May 28, 1861, at Jamestown, to serve three years; mustered in as private, Co. B, June 20, 1861; promoted corporal, February 17, 1863; captured in action, May 3, 1863, at Chancellorsville, Va.; paroled, May 23, 1863, at City Point, Va.; mustered out with company, June 20, 1864, near Petersburg, Va.

Crane, Augustus—Age, 23 years. Enlisted, May 28, 1861, at Jamestown, to serve three years; mustered in as private, Co. B, June 20, 1861; promoted corporal, August 27, 1862; sergeant, January 7, 1863; re-enlisted as a veteran, December 24, 1863; transferred to Co. C, One Hundred and Twentieth Infantry, June 23, 1864.

Crouch, Eugene S.—Age, 18 years. Enlisted, May 28, 1861, at Jamestown, to serve three years; mustered in as private, Co. B, June 20, 1861; discharged for disability, September 19, 1862.

Crowe, William—Age, 18 years. Enlisted, July 30, 1862, at Jamestown, to serve three years; mustered in as private, Co. B, September 2, 1862; transferred to Co. C, One Hundred and Twentieth Infantry, June 23, 1864.

Damon, Dallas M.—Age, 18 years. Enlisted, May 28, 1861, at Jamestown, to serve three years; mustered in as private, Co. B, June 20, 1861; died of disease, November 12, 1862, at Alexandria, Va.

Davis, George W.—Age, 18 years. Enlisted, May 28, 1861, at Jamestown, to serve three years; mustered in as private, Co. B, June 20, 1861; wounded in action, May 5, 1862, at Williamsburg, Va.; discharged for his wounds, December 2, 1862, at Baltimore, Md.

Davis, John—Age, 19 years. Enlisted, May 28, 1861, at Jamestown, to serve three years; mustered in as private, Co. B, June 20, 1861; mustered out, June 1, 1864, at New York City.

Dowd, William E.—Age, 18 years. Enlisted, May 28, 1861, at Jamestown, to serve three years; mustered in as private, Co. B, June 20, 1861; mustered out with company, June 20, 1864, near Petersburg, Va.

Ekholm, Adolph F.—Age, 18 years. Enlisted at Carroll, to serve three years, and mustered in as private, Co. B, January 28, 1864; transferred to Co. C, One Hundred and Twentieth Infantry, June 23, 1864; also born as Eckholm.

Finch, John W.—Age, 30 years. Enlisted, May 28, 1861, at Jamestown, to serve three years; mustered in as private, Co. B, June 20, 1861; discharged for disability, January 19, 1863, near Alexandria, Va.

Fincke, Frederick M.—Age, 39 years. Enlisted, May 28, 1861, at Jamestown, to serve three years; mustered in as private, Co. B, June 20, 1861; promoted hospital steward to date, June 6, 1861; discharged for disability, October 17, 1862, at New York City.

Foley, Francis—Age, 18 years. Enlisted at Ellery, to serve three years, and mustered in as private, Co. B, February 8, 1864; transferred to Co. H, One Hundred and Twentieth Infantry, June 23, 1864.

Fuller, Duley B.—Age, 19 years. Enlisted, July 21, 1861, at Staten Island, to serve three years; mustered in as private, Co. B, July 24, 1861; promoted hospital steward, December 21, 1863; re-enlisted as a veteran, December 26, 1863; mustered out as supernumerary, September 1, 1864, near Petersburg, Va.

Griffith, Robert—Age, 25 years. Enlisted, July 17, 1861, at Westfield, to serve three years; mustered in as private, Co. G, July 23, 1861; transferred to Co. B, in July 1861; deserted, August 23, 1861, at Camp Caldwell, D.C.; surrendered himself, April 6, 1865; mustered out, May 15, 1865, at Elmira, N.Y., as Robert B. Griffith.

Hale, John W.—Age, 22 years. Enlisted, May 28, 1861, at Jamestown, to serve three years; mustered in as sergeant, Co. B, June 20, 1861; returned to ranks, December 21, 1861; wounded in action, May 5, 1862, at Williamsburg, Va.; discharged for wounds, September 3, 1862, at Baltimore, Md.

Hall, James—Age, 18 years. Enlisted, May 28, 1861, at Jamestown, to serve three years; mustered in as private, Co. B, June 20, 1861; promoted corporal, December 21, 1861; killed in action, July 1, 1862, at Malvern Hill, Va.

Hankin, George F.—Age, 21 years. Enlisted, May 28, 1861, at Jamestown, to serve three years; mustered in as private, Co. B, June 20, 1861; killed in action, July 2, 1863, at Gettysburg, Pa.

Harrington, Charles H.—Age, 25 years. Enlisted, May 28, 1861, at Jamestown, to serve three years; mustered in as first sergeant, Co. B, June 20, 1861; returned to ranks, October 26, 1861; discharged for disability, October 7, 1862, at New York City.

Hazeltine, Herbert W.—Age, 21 years. Enlisted, May 28, 1861, at Jamestown, to serve three years;

mustered in as corporal, Co. B, June 26, 1861; died of disease, May 27, 1862, at New York City.

Hibbard, William J.—Age, 24 years. Enlisted, May 28, 1861, at Jamestown, to serve three years; mustered in as corporal, Co. B, June 20, 1861; promoted sergeant, December 21, 1861; first sergeant, May 5, 1863; absent, sick in General Hospital at muster out of company.

Homer, Elliott A.—Age, 17 years. Enlisted, August 12, 1862, at Jamestown, to serve three years; mustered in as private, Co. B, September 2, 1862; wounded in action, July 2, 1863, at Gettysburg, Pa.; died of his wounds, July 23, 1863, at Jarvis Hospital, Baltimore, Md.

Homer, Eugene L.—Age, 20 years. Enlisted, July 1, 1861, at Staten Island, to serve three years; mustered in as private, Co. B, July 24, 1861; promoted corporal, May 28, 1862; re-enlisted as a veteran, December 24, 1863; transferred to Co. C, One Hundred and Twentieth Infantry, June 23, 1864.

Hosier, Elisha R.—Age, 20 years. Enlisted, May 28, 1861, at Jamestown, to serve three years; mustered in as private, Co. B, June 20, 1861; killed in action, May 5, 1862, at Williamsburg, Va.

Hosier, John B.—Age 18 years. Enlisted, May 28, 1861, at Jamestown, to serve three years; mustered in as private, Co. B, June 20, 1861; discharged for disability, October 25, 1862, at Philadelphia; Pa.

Hoskins, Everett C.—Age, 18 years. Enlisted at Ellington, to serve three years, and mustered in as private, Co. B, December 22, 1863; transferred to Co. H, One Hundred and Twentieth Infantry, June 23, 1864.

Howard, Luther—Age, 18 years. Enlisted, May 28, 1861, at Jamestown, to serve three years; mustered in as private, Co. B, June 20, 1861; wounded in action, May 5, 1862, at Williamsburg, Va.; mustered out with company, June 20, 1864, near Petersburg, Va.

Hubbard, Arthur P.—Age, 20 years. Enlisted, May 28, 1861, at Jamestown, to serve three years; mustered in as private, Co. B, June 20, 1861; died of disease, January 18, 1862, at Camp Wool, Md.

Hunt, Freeman J.—Age, 19 years. Enlisted, May 28, 1861, at Jamestown, to serve three years; mustered in as private, Co. B, June 20, 1861; mustered out with company, June 20, 1864, near Petersburg, Va.

James, Robert D.—Age, 18 years. Enlisted, May 28, 1861, at Jamestown, to serve three years; mustered in as private, Co. B, June 20, 1861; captured in action, August 29, 1862, at Bull Run, Va.; exchanged and returned to company, December 19, 1862; died of disease, August 19, 1863, at Mount Pleasant Hospital, D.C.

Jones, Rinaldo E.—Age, 18 years. Enrolled, May 28, 1861, at Jamestown, to serve three years; mustered in as sergeant, Co. B, June 20, 1861; promoted first sergeant, December 21, 1861; second lieutenant, May 2, 1862; first lieutenant, Co. H, July 7, 1862; dismissed, February 18, 1863, to date October 10, 1862. Commissioned second lieutenant, June 30, 1862, with rank from May 2, 1862, vice Samuel Bailey promoted; first lieutenant, July 21, 1862, with rank from July 7, 1862, vice Leopold Marcus resigned.

Landon, Lawrence J.—Age, 20 years. Enlisted, May 28, 1861, at Jamestown, to serve three years; mustered in as private, Co. B, June 20, 1861; wounded in action, May 5, 1862, at Williamsburg, Va.; died of his wounds in June 1862, at Fortress Monroe, Va.

Lawson, John—Age, 21 years. Enlisted, May 28, 1861, at Jamestown, to serve three years; mustered in as private, Co. B, June 20, 1861; discharged for disability, March 9, 1863, at camp, near Falmouth, Va.

Litchfield, Hiram—Age, 22 years. Enlisted, May 28, 1861, at Jamestown, to serve three years; mustered in as private, Co. B, June 20, 1861; transferred to Co. F, Ninth Regiment, Veteran Reserve Corps, September 26, 1863.

Lord, Samuel—Age, 23 years. Enlisted, May 28, 1861, at Jamestown, to serve three years; mustered in as private, Co. B, June 20, 1861; wounded in action, May 5, 1862, at Williamsburg, Va.; discharged for wounds, October 30, 1862, near Alexandria, Va.

Love, Marvin—Age, 23 years. Enlisted, May 28, 1861, at Jamestown, to serve three years; mustered in as private, Co. B, June 20, 1861; discharged for disability, February 9, 1863, at Fairfax Seminary, Va.

Lovell, William H.—Age, 22 years. Enlisted, May 28, 1861, at Jamestown, to serve three years; mustered in as private, Co. B, June 20, 1861; wounded in action, July 2, 1863, and died of his wounds, July 26, 1863, at Gettysburg, Pa.

Lyon, Chapin J.—Age, 20 years. Enlisted, May 28, 1861, at Jamestown, to serve three years; mustered in as private, Co. B, June 20, 1861; captured in action, May 5, 1862, at Williamsburg, Va.; exchanged and returned to company, December 10, 1862; wounded in action, July 2, 1863, at Gettysburg, Pa.; discharged for his wounds, May 23, 1864, at De Camp General Hospital, David's Island, New York Harbor.

Lyon, John Myron—Age, 22 years. Enlisted, May 28, 1861, at Jamestown, to serve three years; mustered in as corporal, Co. B, June 20, 1861; promoted sergeant, August 5, 1862; first sergeant, January 7, 1863; sergeant-major, December 20, 1803; re-enlisted as a veteran, December 26, 1863; wounded in action, May 1864, at the Wilderness, Va.; mustered out, September 1, 1864, rendered supernumerary by consolidation, near Petersburg, Va.

Mailer, James O.—Age, 18 years. Enlisted, May 28, 1861, at Jamestown, to serve three years; mustered in as private, Co. B, June 20, 1861; re-enlisted as a veteran, December 24, 1863; wounded in action, May 6, 1864, at Wilderness, Va.; transferred to Co. C, One Hundred and Twentieth Infantry, June 23, 1864.

Martin, William E.—Age, 21 years. Enlisted, May 28, 1861, at Jamestown, to serve three years; mustered in as private, Co. B, June 20, 1861; discharged for disability, February 5, 1863, at Third Corps Hospital, near Fort Lyon, Va.

Marvin, William R.—Age, 18 years. Enlisted, September 12, 1861, at Jamestown, to serve three years; mustered in as private, Co. B, October 16, 1861; discharged for disability, November 15, 1862.

Mason, Alfred S.—Age, 32 years. Enrolled, May 28, 1861, at Jamestown, to serve three years; mustered in as second lieutenant, Co. B, June 20, 1861; as first lieutenant, November 5, 1861; discharged, May 2, 1862. Not commissioned second lieutenant; commissioned first lieutenant, January 7, 1862, with rank from November 5, 1861, original.

McIntyre, Robert—Age, 42 years. Enlisted, August 12, 1862, at Jamestown, to serve three years; mustered in as private, Co. B, September 2, 1862; wounded in action, May 31, 1864, at Totopotomoy, Va.; died of his wounds, June 22, 1864, at Second Division United States General Hospital, Alexandria, Va.

Myers, Henry W.—Age, 22 years. Enlisted, May 28, 1861, at Jamestown, to serve three years; mustered in as private, Co. B, June 20, 1861; wounded in action, May 5, 1862, and died of his wounds, May 10, 1862, at Williamsburg, Va.

Nelson, Otto—Age, 22 years. Enlisted, May 28, 1861, at Jamestown, to serve three years; mustered in as private, Co. B, June 20, 1861; died of disease, December 16, 1861, at Camp Wool, Md.

O'Connell, Maurice—Age, 35 years. Enlisted, August 22, 1862, at Jamestown, to serve three years; mustered in as private, Co. B, September 2, 1862; transferred to Co. C, One Hundred and Twentieth Infantry, June 23, 1864.

O'Connell, Thomas—Age, 18 years. Enlisted, August 23, 1862, at Jamestown, to serve three years; mustered in as private, Co. B, September 2, 1862; wounded in action, July 2, 1863, at Gettysburg, Pa.; missing in action, May 6, 1864; transferred to Co. C, One Hundred and Twentieth Infantry, June 23, 1864.

Oliver, Albert—Age, 28 years. Enlisted, May 28, 1861, at Jamestown, to serve three years; mustered in as private, Co. B, June 20, 1861; killed in action, May 5, 1862, at Williamsburg, Va.

Ott, Philip—Age, 21 years. Enlisted, May 28, 1861, at Jamestown, to serve three years; mustered in as private, Co. B, June 20, 1861; re-enlisted as a veteran, December 21, 1863; wounded in action, May 6, 1864, at the Wilderness, Va.; transferred to Co. C, One Hundred and Twentieth Infantry, June 23, 1864.

Parker, Charles—Age, 21 years. Enlisted, May 28, 1861, at Jamestown, to serve three years; mustered in as private, Co. B, June 20, 1861; wounded in action, July 2, 1863, at Gettysburg, Pa.; mustered out with company, June 20, 1864, near Petersburg, Va.

Patchin, Jerome—Age, 28 years. Enlisted, May 28, 1861, at Jamestown, to serve three years; mustered in as wagoner, Co. B, June 20, 1861; died of disease, June 1, 1862, at White House, Va.

Patten, Esaus—Age, 29 years. Enlisted, May 28, 1861, at Jamestown, to serve three years; mustered in as private, Co. B, June 20, 1861; discharged for disability, July 23, 1862.

Peterson, John A.—Age, 24 years. Enlisted, May 28, 1861, at Jamestown, to serve three years; mustered in as private, Co. B, June 20, 1861; promoted corporal, December 21, 1861; wounded in action, May 5, 1862, and died of his wounds, May 10, 1862, at Williamsburg, Va.

Pickard, Charles G.—Age, 25 years. Enlisted, May 28, 1861, at Jamestown, to serve three years; mustered in as private, Co. B, June 20, 1861; promoted corporal, May 28, 1862; wounded in action, August 27, 1862, and died of his wounds, August 29, 1862, at Bristoe Station, Va.

Pickard, James H.—Age, 18 years. Enlisted, July 9, 1862, at Dunkirk, to serve three years; mustered in as private, Co. B, September 2, 1862; transferred to Co. C, One Hundred and Twentieth Infantry, June 23, 1864.

Pickard, Melvin E.—Age, 18 years. Enlisted, August 9, 1862, at Dunkirk, to serve three years; mustered in as private, Co. B, September 2, 1862; wounded in action, May 3, 1863, at Chancellorsville, Va.; promoted corporal, May 5, 1863; transferred to Co. C, One Hundred and Twentieth Infantry, June 23, 1864.

Platner, Dewitt M.—Age, 18 years. Enlisted at Ellington, to serve three years, and mustered in as private, Co. B, December 21, 1863; wounded in action, June 5, 1864, near Cold Harbor, Va.; transferred to Co. C, One Hundred and Twentieth Infantry, June 23, 1864.

Polder, Peter—Age, 20 years. Enlisted, May 28, 1861, at Jamestown, to serve three years; mustered in as private, Co. B, June 20, 1861; wounded in action,

June 25, 1862, near Fair Oaks, Va.; mustered out, June 24, 1864.

Porter, Edwin—Age, 27 years. Enlisted, May 28, 1861, at Jamestown, to serve three years; mustered in as private, Co. B, June 20, 1861; died of disease, December 21, 1861, at Camp Wool, Md.

Richarson, Franklin—Age, 24 years. Enlisted, May 28, 1861, at Jamestown, to serve three years: mustered in as private, Co. B, June 20, 1861: killed in action, May 5, 1862, at Williamsburg, Va.

Ross, Orville A.—Age, 18 years. Enlisted, May 28, 1861, at Jamestown, to serve three years; mustered in as private, Co. B, June 20, 1861; promoted corporal, December 21, 1861; sergeant, October 11, 1862; re-enlisted as a veteran, December 24, 1863; wounded in action, May 10, 1864, at Landrons Farm, Va.; transferred to Co. H, One Hundred and Twentieth Infantry, June 23, 1864.

Russell, Francis M.—Age, 27 years. Enlisted, May 28, 1861, at Jamestown, to serve three years; mustered in as private, Co. B, June 20, 1861; wounded in action, August 27, 1862, at Bristoe Station, Va.; discharged for wounds, November 18, 1862, at Alexandria, Va.

Sanford, Giles H.—Age, 23 years. Enlisted, May 23, 1861, at Jamestown, to serve three years; mustered in as private, Co. B, June 20, 1861; re-enlisted as a veteran, December 24, 1863; transferred to Co. C, One Hundred and Twentieth Infantry, June 23, 1864.

Schuyler, Francis—Age, 20 years. Enlisted, May 28, 1861, at Jamestown, to serve three years; mustered in as private, Co. B, June 20, 1861; discharged for disability, July 30, 1862, at Harrison's Landing, Va.

Schuyler, Thomas B.—Age, 18 years. Enlisted, May 28, 1861, at Jamestown, to serve three years; mustered in as private, Co. B, June 20, 1861; wounded in action, May 5, 1862, and died of his wounds, May 6, 1862, at Williamsburg, Va.

Simmons, Lewis—Age, 31 years. Enlisted, May 28, 1861, at Jamestown, to serve three years; mustered in as private, Co. B, June 20, 1861; re-enlisted as a veteran, December 24, 1863; transferred to Co. C, One Hundred and Twentieth Infantry, June 23, 1864.

Simmons, Obed—Age, 19 years. Enlisted, May 28, 1861, at Jamestown, to serve three years; mustered in as private, Co. B, June 20, 1861; discharged for disability, December 26, 1862, at Third Corps Hospital, near Fort Lyon, Va.

Slater, Bernard P.—Age, 18 years. Enlisted, May 28, 1861, at Jamestown, to serve three years; mustered in as private, Co. B, June 20, 1861; captured in action, May 5, 1862, at Williamsburg, Va.; exchanged December 19, 1862; wounded in action, July 23, 1863, at Wapping Heights, Va.; died of his wounds, July 81, 1863, at Mount Pleasant, D.C.

Smith, Edwin H.—Age, 18 years. Enlisted, May 28, 1861, at Jamestown, to serve three years; mustered in as private, Co. B, June 20, 1861; discharged for disability, January 8, 1863, at Georgetown, D.C.

Smith, Francis—Age, 18 years. Enlisted, August 16, 1862, at Jamestown, to serve three years; mustered in as private, Co. B, September 2, 1862; wounded in action, November 27, 1863, at Mine Run, Va.; discharged for disability, January 18, 1864, at Convalescent Camp, Va.

Southwick, David—Age, 18 years. Enlisted, August 12, 1862, at Jamestown, to serve three years; mustered in as private, Co. B, September 2, 1862; transferred to Co. C, One Hundred and Twentieth Infantry, June 23, 1864.

Southwick, Levi—Age, 26 years. Enlisted, August 12, 1862, at Jamestown, to serve three years; mustered in as private, Co. B, September 2, 1862; transferred to Co. C, One Hundred and Twentieth Infantry, June 23, 1864.

Standish, Amos—Age, 18 years. Enlisted, May 28, 1861, at Jamestown, to serve three years; mustered in as private, Co. B, June 20, 1861; died of disease, May 12, 1862, at Yorktown, Va.

Stoddard, Hiram D.—Age, 23 years. Enlisted, May 28, 1861, at Jamestown, to serve three years; mustered in as private, Co. B, June 20, 1861; promoted corporal, May 28, 1862; re-enlisted as a veteran, December 24, 1863; transferred to Co. C, One Hundred and Twentieth Infantry, June 23, 1864.

Story, Lewis M.—Age, 18 years. Enlisted at Ellington, to serve three years, and mustered in as private, Co. B, December 22, 1863; transferred to Co. H, One Hundred and Twentieth Infantry, June 23, 1864, from which discharged, May 26, 1865, from general hospital, Buffalo, N.Y.

Sutton, Robert—Age, 22 years. Enlisted, May 28, 1861, at Jamestown, to serve three years; mustered in as private, Co. B, June 20, 1861; transferred to One Hundred and Seventeenth Company, Second Battalion, Veteran Reserve Corps, January 16, 1864.

Swift, Gordon B.—Age, 18 years. Enlisted, May 28, 1861, at Jamestown, to serve three years; mustered in as private, Co. B, June 20, 1861; re-enlisted as a veteran, December 24, 1863; wounded in action, May 10, 1864, at the Wilderness, Va.; transferred to Co. C, One Hundred and Twentieth Infantry, June 28, 1864.

Taylor, George—Age, 30 years. Enlisted, May 28, 1861, at Jamestown, to serve three years; mustered in as private, Co. B, June 20, 1861; discharged for disability, June 27, 1862, at Annapolis, Md.

Taylor, Henry B.—Age, 22 years. Enlisted, May 28, 1861, at Jamestown, to serve three years; mustered in as private, Co. B, June 20, 1861; transferred to Co. B, Tenth Regiment, Veteran Reserve Corps, July 27, 1863, from which he deserted, January 28, 1865.

Thayer, Reuben E.—Age, 19 years. Enlisted at Ellicott, to serve three years, and mustered in as private, Co. B, February 3, 1864; transferred to Co. H, One Hundred and Twentieth Infantry, June 23, 1864.

Thomas, John W.—Age, 21 years. Enlisted, May 28, 1861, at Jamestown, to serve three years; mustered in as private, Co. B, June 20, 1861; wounded and captured in action, August 29, 1862, at Bull Run, Va.; paroled, no date; captured in action, July 2, 1863, at Gettysburg, Pa.; paroled, no date; mustered out, May 27, 1864, at New York City.

Todd, Edward—Age, 40 years. Enlisted at Villenova, to serve three years, and mustered in as private, Co. B, December 29, 1863; transferred to Co. H, One Hundred and Twentieth Infantry, June 23, 1864.

Tonnon, John—Age, 44 years. Enlisted at Chautauqua, to serve three years, and mustered in as private, Co. B, December 31, 1863; transferred to Co. C, One Hundred and Twentieth Infantry, June 23, 1864.

Torry, Edwin H.—Age, 25 years. Enlisted, May 28, 1861, at Jamestown, to serve three years; mustered in as private, Co. B, June 20, 1861; promoted corporal, December 21, 1861; re-enlisted as a veteran, December 24, 1863; transferred to Co. H, One Hundred and Twentieth Infantry, June 23, 1864.

Tounon, Frederick—Age, 35 years. Enlisted at Chautauqua, to serve three years, and mustered in as private, Co. B, December 31, 1863; wounded, May 10, 1864, at Spotsylvania, Va.; transferred to Co. H, One Hundred and Twentieth Infantry, June 23, 1864.

Towns, Arthur—Age, 24 years. Enlisted, May 28, 1861, at Jamestown, to serve three years; mustered in as corporal, Co. B, June 20, 1861; wounded in action, July 1, 1862, at Malvern Hill, Va.; captured, no date; exchanged, December 19, 1862; promoted sergeant, February 17, 1863; wounded in action, May 10, 1864, at Spotsylvania, Va.; absent in general hospital, Patterson Park, Baltimore, Md., at muster-out of company.

Trudell, Francis—Age, 44 years. Enlisted at Busti, to serve three years, and mustered in as private, Co. B, December 23, 1863; wounded in action, May 10, 1864, at Spotsylvania, Va.; died of his wounds, June 23, 1864, at Emory General Hospital, Washington, D.C.

Veasey, Charles—Age, 22 years. Enlisted at Elmira, to serve three years, and mustered in as private, Co. B, October 16, 1861; transferred to Co. C, One Hundred and Twentieth Infantry, June 23, 1864.

Waite, Delos—Age, 21 years. Enlisted, May 28, 1861, at Jamestown, to serve three years; mustered in as private, Co. B, June 20, 1861; captured in action, May 3, 1863, at Chancellorsville, Va.; paroled, no date; re-enlisted as a veteran, December 24, 1863; transferred to Co. C, One Hundred and Twentieth Infantry, June 23, 1864; also born as Lorenzo D.

Wheeler, Curtis—Age, 23 years. Enlisted, May 28, 1861, at Jamestown, to serve three years; mustered in as private, Co. B, June 20, 1861; died of disease, January 29, 1862, at Camp Wool, Charles County, Md.

Whitmore, Charles W.—Age, 20 years. Enlisted, May 28, 1861, at Jamestown, to serve three years; mustered in as private, Co. B, June 20, 1861; discharged for disability, July 30, 1862, at Harrison Landing, Va.; subsequent service in Co. L, Fifteenth Cavalry.

Willard, Darwin—Age, 34 years. Enrolled, May 28, 1861, at Jamestown, to serve three years; mustered in as first lieutenant, Co. B, June 20, 1861; as captain, November 5, 1861; killed in action, May 5, 1862, at Williamsburg, Va. Not commissioned first lieutenant; commissioned captain, January 7, 1862, with rank from November 5, 1861, vice J.M. Brown, resigned.

Yale, Edwin—Age, 31 years. Enlisted, May 28, 1861, at Jamestown, to serve three years; mustered in as sergeant, Co. B, June 20, 1861; promoted first sergeant, November 1, 1861; discharged for disability, February 17, 1863, near Falmouth, Va.

Yates, Henry Jones—Ago, 18 years. Enrolled, May 28, 1861, at Jamestown, to serve three years; mustered in as corporal, Co. B, June 20, 1861; promoted sergeant, May 4, 1862; first sergeant, October 11, 1862; mustered in as second lieutenant, Co. G, January 7, 1863; as first lieutenant, Co. D, May 10, 1863; re-transferred to Co. G, July 1, 1868; mustered in as adjutant, March 1, 1864; wounded in action at the Wilderness, Va., in 1864; absent sick at muster-out of regiment. Commissioned second lieutenant, June 13, 1863, with rank from January 7, 1863, vice A.M. Clark, promoted; first lieutenant, August 7, 1863, with rank from May 10, 1863, vice W.C. Brooks, killed in action.

Young, Albert P.—Age, 19 years. Enlisted, May 28, 1861, at Jamestown, to serve three years; mustered in as private, Co. B, June 20, 1861; discharged for disability, December 20, 1862, at Fairfax Seminary, Va.

Young, Robert H.—Age, 17 years. Enlisted, July 30, 1862, at Jamestown, to serve three years; mustered in as private, Co. B, September 2, 1862; transferred to Co. C, One Hundred and Twentieth Infantry, June 23, 1864.

Youngs, James M.—Age, 18 years. Enlisted, May 28, 1861, at Jamestown, to serve three years; mustered in as private, Co. B, June 20, 1861; captured in action, May 3, 1863, at Chancellorsville, Va.; paroled, no date; re-enlisted as a veteran, December 24, 1863; transferred to Co. C, One Hundred and Twentieth Infantry, June 23, 1864; awarded medal of honor for distinguished gallantry at the Wilderness, Va., May 6, 1864.

Zahn, Valentine A.—Age, 18 years. Enlisted, August 12, 1861, at New York City, to serve three years; mustered in as private, Co. B, August. 19, 1861; transferred to Co. C, One Hundred and Twentieth Infantry, June 23, 1864; also born as Valtine Yazen.

Zincke, Charles E.—Age, 17 years. Enlisted, August 12, 1861, at New York City, to serve three years; mustered in as musician, Co. B, August 19, 1861; wounded in action, June 9, 1864, at Cold Harbor, Va.; transferred to Co. H, One Hundred and Twentieth Infantry, June 23, 1864.

Company C

Organized in New York City in July 1861. Mustered into the United States service July 21, 1861.

Captains

Isaac Lynden Chadwick, from July 21, 1861, to January 16, 1863.
John S. Mann, from April 2, 1863, to June 1, 1864.
John W. Holmes, from June 1 to July 20, 1864.

First Lieutenants

Horatio B. Pennock, from September 1, 1861, to June 23, 1862.
Wakeman Holberton, from May 6, to June 13, 1862.
Berend Huttmann, from June 23 to November 1, 1862.
Charles H. Hydorn, from November 1, 1862, to May 3, 1863.
Thomas Clark, from January 16 to April 2, 1863.
Julius Kessler, from May 5 to June 25, 1863.
Robert H. Savage, from March 5 to July 20, 1864.

Second Lieutenants

Horatio B. Pennock, from July 21 to September 1, 1861.
Wakeman Holberton, from September 1, 1861, to May 6, 1862.
Thomas Clark, from June 2 to July 7, 1862.
William C. Brooks, from July 7 to November 1, 1862.
William McConnell, from October 31, 1862, to June 23, 1863.
Charles A. Foss, from May 5 to July 7, 1863.
Horatio S. Springer, from July 7, 1863, to February 23, 1864.

Abbott, William M.—Age, 25 years. Enlisted at Newton, to serve three years, and mustered in as private, Co. C, September 22, 1862; transferred to Co. K, One Hundred and Twentieth Infantry, July 23, 1864.

Ahrens, Lewis—Age, — years. Enlisted at New York City, to serve three years, and mustered in as private, Co. C, September 5, 1862; wounded in action, July 1863, at Gettysburg, Pa.; discharged for disability, December 6, 1864, at Alexandria, Va.; also born as Ohrens.

Amerman, George P.—Age, 21 years. Enlisted at New York City, to serve three years, and mustered in as private, Co. C, August 11, 1862; transferred to Company K, One Hundred and Twentieth Infantry, July 23, 1864.

Andrews, Stephen B.—Age, 27 years. Enlisted, June 8, 1861, at Newark, N.J., to serve three years; mustered in as private, Co. C, June 21, 1861; captured in action, May 5, 1862, at Williamsburg, Va.; paroled, no date; wounded in action, May 10, 1864, at Spotsylvania, Va.; discharged for disability, November 27, 1864, at Newark, N.J.

Arth, Daniel—Age, 43 years. Enlisted, April 28, 1861, at New York City, to serve three years; mustered in as private, Co. C, July 21, 1861; discharged for disability, March 17, 1862, at Camp Wool, Md.

Austin, William H.—Age, 41 years. Enlisted at New York City, to serve three years, and mustered in as private, Co. C, July 6, 1862; promoted corporal, December 11, 1862; discharged for disability, January 19, 1864, at Convalescent Camp, Va.

Ballard, Charles—Age, 30 years. Enlisted, July 17, 1861, at New York City, to serve three years; mustered in as private, Co. C, July 21, 1861; captured in action, May 5, 1862, at Williamsburg, Va.; paroled, not date; wounded in action, December 13, 1862, at Fredericksburg, Va.; absent, sick in General Hospital, at Alexandria, Va., at muster out of company; also born as John Ballard.

Barhyte, Charles A.—Age, 24 years. Enlisted at New York City, to serve three years, and mustered in as private, Co. C, August 12, 1862; transferred to Veteran Reserve Corps, June 16, 1864.

Barnes, John—Age, 36 years. Enlisted at New York City, to serve three years, and mustered in as private, Co. C, August 25, 1862; transferred to Co. K, One Hundred and Twentieth Infantry, July 23, 1864; also born as Barrens.

Bass, Abraham—Age, 24 years. Enlisted, July 8, 1861, at New York City, to serve three years; mustered in as private, Co. C, July 21, 1861; promoted corporal, July 29, 1861; wounded in action, May 5, 1862, at Williamsburg, Va.; dropped from rolls in October 1862, per General Order No. 92.

Benson, Nathan F.—Age, 21 years. Enlisted at New York City, to serve three years, and mustered in as private, Co. C, and transferred to Co. E, July 21, 1861; wounded, no date or place; mustered out with company, June 19, 1864.

Bloom, John A.—Age, 42 years. Enlisted, June 17, 1861, at Staten Island, to serve three years; mustered in as corporal, Co. C, July 21, 1861; returned to ranks, July 21, 1861, and again promoted corporal, August 12, 1861; discharged for disability, March 17, 1862, at Camp Wool, Md.

Breen, John—Age, 28 years. Enlisted, July 9, 1861, at New York City, to serve three years; mustered in as private, Co. C, July 21, 1861; discharged for disability, October 20, 1861, at Washington, D.C.

Brierly, Edward—Age, 30 years. Enlisted, June 25, 1861, at Newburg, to serve three years; mustered in as private, Co. O, July 21, 1861; discharged for disability, March 17, 1862, at Camp Wool, Md.; also born as Bryerly.

Brooks, Richard—Age, 29 years. Enlisted, July 7, 1861, at New York City, to serve three years; mustered in as private, Co. C, July 21, 1861; wounded in action, December 13, 1862, at Fredericksburg, Va.; transferred to Veteran Reserve.

Broom, James O.—Age, — years. Enlisted, June 22, 1861, at New York City, to serve three years; mustered in as private, Co. C, July 21, 1861; killed in action, May 5, 1862, at Williamsburg, Va.; Corps, June 5, 1864.

Broughton, William—Age, 33 years. Enlisted at New York City, to serve three years, and mustered in as private, Co. C, August 14, 1862; discharged for disability, February 12, 1863, at Camp Convalescent, Va.

Brower, Stephen H.—Age, 24 years. Enlisted, June 25, 1861, at Newburg, to serve three years; mustered in as private, Co. C, July 21, 1861; transferred to Co. K, January 28, 1862; wounded in action, May 5, 1862, at Williamsburg, Va.; deserted, June 25, 1862, from hospital at Washington, D.C.; also born as Brown.

Brown, Alexander—Age, 17 years. Enlisted, July 8, 1861, at New York City, to serve three years; mustered in as musician, Co. C, July 21, 1861; captured in action, no date or place; died of disease, June 25, 1864, while a prisoner of war, at Andersonville, Ga.

Brown, James—Age, 54. Enlisted at Delhi, to serve three years, and mustered in as private, Co. A, November 16, 1861; discharged for disability, March 15, 1862, at Camp Wool, Charles County, Md.

Burns, George—Age, 19 years. Enlisted, July 7, 1861, at New York City, to serve three years; mustered in as private, Co. C, July 21, 1861; discharged for disability, January 19, 1863, at Alexandria, Va.

Campbell, Nelson—Age, 17 years. Enlisted, June 7, 1861, at Hebron, Pa., to serve three years; mustered in as private, Co. C, July 21, 1861; killed in action, May 5, 1862, at Williamsburg, Va.

Carroll, Michael—Age, 18 years. Enlisted, July 17, 1861, at New York City, to serve three years; mustered in as private, Co. C, July 21. 1861; killed in action, May 5, 1862, at Williamsburg, Va.

Carson, Robert—Age, 34 years. Enlisted at New York City, to serve three years, and mustered in as private, Co. C, September 13, 1861; transferred to Co. K, One Hundred and Twentieth Infantry, July 23, 1864.

Chadwick, Isaac Lynden—Age, 27 years. Enrolled, April 28, 1861, at Staten Island, to serve three years; mastered in as captain, Co. C, July 21, 1861; discharged, January 16, 1863. Commissioned captain, January 7, 1862, with rank from July 21, 1861; original.

Chepelter, Charles—Age, 25 years. Enlisted at New York City, to serve three years, and mustered in as private, Co. C, May 15, 1861; deserted, July 21, 1861, at Camp Scott, Staten Island; also born as Chabsetler.

Clark, Leonard J.—Age, 25 years. Enlisted, April 28, 1861, at Hebron, Pa., to serve three years; mustered in as private, Co. C, July 21, 1861; re-enlisted as a veteran, December 22, 1863; promoted corporal, March 1, 1864; killed in action, May 10, 1864, at Spotsylvania, Va.

Coleman, John—Age, 26 years. Enlisted, July 17, 1861, at New York City, to serve three years; mustered in as private, Co. C, July 21, 1861; discharged for disability, October 9, 1862, near Alexandria, Va.

Collins, William D.—Age, 43 years. Enlisted at New York City, to serve three years, and mustered in as private, Co. C, October 7, 1861; discharged for disability, January 7, 1863, near Falmouth, Va.

Conway, Isaac—Age, 39 years. Enlisted at New York City, to serve three years, and mustered in as private, Co. C, August 19, 1862; wounded in action in July 1863, at Gettysburg, Pa.; transferred to Co. K, One Hundred and Twentieth Infantry, July 23, 1864.

Corr, Thomas—Age, 35 years. Enlisted, August 16, 1861, at New York City, to serve three years; mustered in as private, Co. C, August 19, 1861; transferred to Co. K, One Hundred and Twentieth Infantry, July 23, 1864; also born as Core.

Crator, Cornelius—Age, 19 years. Enlisted, April 28, 1861, at New York City, to serve three years; mustered in as private, Co. C, July 21, 1861; mustered out with company, July 20, 1864, near Petersburg, Va.; also born as Cretar, Creter, Creatore and Creteur.

Crossin, James—Age, 21 years. Enlisted, July 16, 1861, at Paterson, N.J., to serve three years; mustered in as private, Co. C, July 21, 1861; captured in action, May 5, 1862, at Williamsburg, Va.; paroled, no date; discharged, May 28, 1862, at Washington, D.C.

Crawford, David—Age, 23 years. Enlisted at New York City, to serve three years, and mustered in as private, Co. C, December 4, 1861; wounded in action, May 5, 1862, at Williamsburg, Va.; died of his wounds, May 29, 1862, at Baltimore, Md.

Cudberth, Thomas—Age, — years. Enlisted at New York City, to serve three years, and mustered in as private, Co. C, August 25, 1862; deserted, June 28, 1863, while on the march to Gettysburg, Pa.; also born as Catber.

Currey, Abner—Age, 28 years. Enlisted at New York city, to serve three years, and mustered in as private, Co. C, August 11, 1862; died of disease, January 31, 1864, at Cornwall, Orange County, N.Y.

Currey, Ebenezer—Age, 36 years. Enlisted at New York City, to serve three years, and mustered in as private, Co. C, August 8, 1862; transferred to Co. K, One Hundred and Twentieth Infantry, July 23, 1864.

Currey, Sylvanus—Age, — years. Enlisted at New York City, to serve three years, and mustered in as private, Co. C, August 11, 1862; deserted, January 18, 1863.

Curtis, Corydon—Age, 20 years. Enlisted at Staten Island, to serve three years, and mustered in as private, Co. C, July 21, 1861; transferred to regimental band, and appointed musician, same date; mustered out with band, July 22, 1862.

Curtis, Melville F.—Age, 23 years. Enlisted, May 28, 1861, at Jamestown, to serve three years; mustered in as musician, Co. B, June 20, 1861; transferred to regimental band, July 24, 1861; retransferred to Co. B, July 22, 1862; discharged for disability, December 24, 1862, at Convalescent Camp, Va.

Daley, John—Age, 20 years. Enlisted, July 16, 1861, at New York City, to serve three years; mustered in as private, Co. C, July 21, 1861; captured in action, May 5, 1862, at Williamsburg, Va.; paroled, May 11, 1862, at Richmond, Va.; discharged, August 18, 1862.

Dean, James—Age, 23 years. Enlisted at New York City, to serve three years, and mustered in as private, Co. C, August 22, 1862; promoted corporal, May 10, 1864; transferred to Co. K, One Hundred and Twentieth Infantry, July 23, 1864.

Dempsey, Edward—Age, 20 years. Enlisted, September 2, 1861, at New York City, to serve three years; mustered in as private, Co. C, September 4, 1861; wounded in action, July 2, 1862, at Malvern Hill, Va.; re-enlisted as a veteran, December 22, 1863; killed in action. May 6, 1864, at Brock Road, Va.

Deylin, William—Age, 22 years. Enlisted, September 19, 1861, at New York City, to serve three years; mustered in as private, Co. C, September 23, 1861; wounded in action, May 5, 1862, at Williamsburg, Va.; discharged for disability, July 16, 1862, at Harrison's Landing, Va.

Dill, Joseph—Age, 39 years. Enlisted at New York City, to serve three years, and mustered in as private, Co. C, September 13, 1861; captured in action, May 2, 1863, at Chancellorsville, Va.; paroled and transferred to Veteran Reserve Corps, no dates.

Dimin, David C.—Age, 18 years. Enlisted at New York City, to serve three years, and mustered in as private, Co. C; transferred to regimental band and appointed musician, July 21, 1861; mustered out with band, July 22, 1862.

Donnelly, Michael—Age, 32 years. Enlisted, July 7, 1861, at New York City, to serve three years; mustered in as private, Co. C, July 21, 1861; discharged for disability, September 15, 1862, near Fort Lyon, Va.

Duffey, Dennis—Age, 37 years. Enlisted, July 18, 1861, at New York City, to serve three years; mustered in as private, Co. C, July 21, 1861; wounded in action, May 5, 1862, at Williamsburg, Va.; died of his wounds, May 26, 1862, at Fortress Monroe, Va.

Dunn, Patrick—Age, 35 years. Enlisted at New York City, to serve three years, and mustered in as private, Co. C, September 11, 1862; discharged for disability, March 3, 1864, at Washington, D.C.

Dutcher, John—Age, 20 years. Enlisted, August 16, 1861, at New York City, to serve three years; mustered in as private, Co. C, August 10, 1861; captured in action, May 5, 1862, at Williamsburg, Va.; paroled same day; promoted corporal, December 21, 1862; re-enlisted as a veteran, December 22, 1863; transferred to Co. K, One Hundred and Twentieth Infantry, July 23, 1864.

Eagan, Matthew—Age, 29 years. Enlisted, July 15, 1861, at New York City, to serve three years; mustered in as private, Co. C, July 21, 1861; killed in action, May 5, 1862, at Williamsburg, Va.

Ebersold, Charles—Age, 20 years. Enrolled, August 12, 1861, at New York City, to serve three years; mustered in as sergeant, Co. C, August 19, 1861; wounded in action, May 5, 1862, at Williamsburg, Va.; promoted first sergeant, November 1, 1862; transferred to Co. B, no date; captured in action, May 3, 1863, at Chancellorsville, Va.; paroled, no date; promoted to second lieutenant, May 5, 1863; returned to ranks; transferred to Co. C, and promoted corporal, no dates; wounded in action, May 23, 1864, at North Anna, Va.; transferred to Co. K, One Hundred and Twentieth Infantry, July 23, 1864. Commissioned, not mustered, second lieutenant, August 7, 1863, with rank from May 4, 1863, vice P.E. Bishop, promoted.

Eldridge, James—Age, 24 years. Enlisted, July 18, 1861, at New York City, to serve three years; mustered in as wagoner, Co. C, July 21, 1861; sent to ranks in August 1861; deserted, August 4, 1861.

Emmons, David—Age, 42 years. Enlisted at New York City, to serve three years, and mustered in as private, Co. C, August 12, 1861; killed in action, May 5, 1862, at Williamsburg, Va.

Fallon, Henry—Age, 36 years. Enlisted, September 2, 1861, at New York City, to serve three years; mustered in as private, Co. C, September 4, 1861; captured in action, May 5, 1862, at Williamsburg, Va.; paroled, no date; discharged for disability, May 30, 1862, at Washington, D.C.

Farrell, David—Age, 25 years. Enlisted, April 28, 1861, at Patterson, N.J., to serve three years; mustered in as private, Co. C, July 21, 1861; wounded in action, July 2, 1862, at Malvern Hill, Va.; discharged for disability, October 7, 1862, at Providence, R.I.

Finch, Lorenzo D.—Age, 23 years. Enlisted at Staten Island, to serve three years; mustered in as private, Co. C; transferred to Co. E, July 21, 1861; mustered out with company, June 19, 1864, near Petersburg, Va.

Fitzgibbons, Patrick—Age, 37 years. Enlisted, July 16, 1861, at New York City, to serve three years; mustered in as private, Co. C, July 21, 1861; captured in action, May 5, 1862, at Williamsburg, Va.; paroled, May 11, 1862; captured in action, May 3, 1863, at Chancellorsville, Va.; paroled, May 15, 1863, at City Point, Va.; wounded in action, May 23, 1864, at North Anna River, Va.; transferred to Fourteenth Company, Second Battalion Veteran Reserve Corps, April 12, 1865.

Fitzsimmons, Thomas—Age, 42 years. Enlisted, July 18, 1861, at New York City, to serve three years; mustered in as private, Co. C, July 21, 1861; captured in action, May 5, 1862, at Williamsburg, Va.; paroled same date; re-enlisted as a veteran, December 23, 1863; transferred to Co. K, One Hundred and Twentieth Infantry, July 23, 1864.

Gardner, Anthony C.—Age, — years. Enlisted at Peekskill, to serve three years, and mustered in as private, Co. C, August 26, 1862; died of disease, February 16, 1863, at Regimental Hospital.

Gavitt, Sylvester—Age, 22 years. Enlisted at Staten Island, to serve three years, and mustered in as private, Co. C, and transferred to Co. H, Seventy-first Infantry, July 21, 1861.

Gillespie, James—Age, 23 years. Enlisted at Staten Island, to serve three years, and mustered in as private, Co. C, and transferred to Co. H, Seventy-first Infantry, July 21, 1861.

Golder, George W.—Age, 34 years. Enlisted, August 4, 1862, at New York City, to serve three years; mustered in as private, Co. C, August 21, 1862; transferred to Co. K, One Hundred and Twentieth Infantry, July 23, 1864.

Gore, William F.—Age, 17 years. Enlisted, July 15, 1861, at New York City, to serve three years; mustered in as musician, Co. C, July 21, 1861; re-enlisted as a veteran, December 22, 1863; transferred to Co. K, One Hundred and Twentieth Infantry, July 23, 1864.

Green, William H.—Age, 19 years. Enlisted at Staten Island, to serve three years; mustered in as private, Co. C and transferred to Co. E, July 21, 1861; discharged for disability, July 12, 1862, at Annapolis, Md.

Gregory, George—Age, 22 years. Enlisted at Staten Island, to serve three years; mustered in as private, Co. C and transferred to Co. H, Seventy-first Infantry, July 21, 1861.

Halley, Patrick—Age, 21 years. Enlisted at New York City, to serve three years, and mustered in as private, Co. C, November 7, 1862; transferred to Co. K, One Hundred and Twentieth Infantry, July 23, 1834.

Hallowell, John—Age, 21 years. Enlisted at New York City, to serve three years, and mustered in as private, Co. C, September 22, 1862; transferred to Co. K, One Hundred and Twentieth Infantry, July 23, 1864.

Hammond, William—Age, 41 years. Enlisted at New York City, to serve three years, and mustered in as corporal, Co. C, August 5, 1862; transferred to Co. K, One Hundred and Twentieth Infantry, July 23, 1864.

Hanna, George—Age, 39 years. Enlisted at New York City, to serve three years, and mustered in as private, Co. C, August 14, 1862; transferred to Co. K, One Hundred and Twentieth Infantry, July 23, 1864.

Hanner, James D.—Age, 20 years. Enlisted, July 8, 1861, at New York City, to serve three years; mustered in as private, Co. C, July 21, 1861; promoted corporal, September 7, 1862; sergeant, November 1, 1862; re-enlisted as a veteran, December 22, 1863; transferred to Co. K, One Hundred and Twentieth Infantry, July 23, 1864.

Head, Francis—Age, 30 years. Enlisted at New York City, to serve three years, and mustered in as private, Co. C, September 10, 1861; deserted, no date.

Heavey, James—Age, 18 years. Enlisted, April 28, 1861, at New York City, to serve three years; mustered in as private, Co. C, July 21, 1861; discharged for disability, February 15, 1863, at Harewood Hospital.

Hefferman, Cornelius F.—Age, 31 years. Enlisted at New York City, to serve three years, and mustered in as private, Co. C, October 7, 1861; captured in action, May 5, 1862, at Williamsburg, Va.; paroled, no date; discharged for disability, May 20, 1862, at Washington, D.C.

Henry, Mathew—Age, 20 years. Enlisted, July 17, 1861, at New York City, to serve three years; mustered in as private, Co. C, July 21, 1861; killed in action, May 5, 1862, at Williamsburg, Va.

Higley, John R.—Age, 21 years. Enlisted, July 17, 1861, at Hebron, Pa., to serve three years; mustered in as private, Co. C, July 21, 1861; re-enlisted as a veteran, December 22, 1863; transferred to Co. K, One Hundred and Twentieth Infantry, July 23, 1864.

Hilderbrand, William—Age, 32 years. Enlisted, July 15, 1861, at New York City, to serve three years; mustered in as private, Co. C, July 21, 1861; transferred to Co. A, September 28, 1861; discharged for disability, November 10, 1862, near Alexandria, Va.

Hoffman, Charles W.—Age, — years. Enlisted at New York City, to serve three years, and mustered in as private, Co. C, August 30, 1862; died of disease, January 14, 1863, in Division Hospital.

Holberton, Wakeman—Age, 22 years. Enrolled at New York, to serve three years, and mustered in as second lieutenant, Co. C, September 1, 1861; promoted first lieutenant, no date; discharged, June 13, 1862. Commissioned second lieutenant, January 7, 1862, with rank from September 1, 1861, original; first lieutenant, July 21, 1862, with rank from July 7, 1862, vice William Toomey, promoted; also born as Huffman.

Holland, John P.—Age, 34 years. Enlisted, July 9, 1861, at New York City, to serve three years; mustered in as private, Co. C, July 21, 1861; promoted corporal, February 1, 1862; sergeant, May 23, 1862; discharged for disability, September 30, 1862, near Alexandria, Va.

Holohan, Robert—Age, 30 years. Enlisted, August 16, 1861, at New York City, to serve three years; mustered in as private, Co. C, August 19, 1861; captured in action and paroled, May 5, 1862, at Williamsburg, Va.; re-enlisted as a veteran, December 22, 1863; transferred to Co. K, One Hundred and Twentieth Infantry, July 23, 1864; also born as Holihan.

Horton, John—Age, 30 years. Enlisted, September 2, 1861, at New York City, to serve three years; mustered in as private, Co. C, September 16, 1861; promoted corporal, no date; sergeant, May 6, 1862; first sergeant, July 6, 1862; discharged for disability, October 26, 1862, at Washington, D.C.; also born as Norton.

Howley, Patrick—Age, 21 years. Enlisted at New York City, to serve three years, and mustered in as private, Co. C, August 25, 1862; transferred to Co. K, One Hundred and Twentieth Infantry, July 23, 1864.

Hunt, Sylvester—Age, 23 years. Enlisted at Staten Island, to serve three years, and transferred to Co. H, Seventy-first Infantry, July 21, 1861.

Hydorn, Charles H.—Age, 22 years. Enrolled, April 28, 1861, at Hebron, Pa., to serve three years; mustered in as sergeant, Co. C, July 21, 1861; promoted sergeant-major, June 2, 1862; mustered in as second lieutenant, Co. H, June 19, 1862; as first lieutenant, Co. D, September 8, 1862; transferred to Co. C. November 1, 1862; killed in action, May 3, 1863, at Chancellorsville, Va. Commissioned second lieutenant, June 20, 1862, with rank from June 13, 1862, vice Daniel Loeb, promoted; first lieutenant, December 1, 1862, with rank from September 8, 1862, vice H. B. Pennock promoted.

Jes, Samuel J.—Age, — years. Enlisted at Brooklyn, to serve three years, and mustered in as private, Co. C, August 25, 1862; transferred to Co. H, Seventieth Infantry for promotion as second lieutenant, December 9, 1862.

Jamison, Samuel—Age, 36 years. Enlisted at New York City, to serve three years; mustered in as private, Co. C, August 16, 1862; transferred to Co. K, One Hundred and Twentieth Infantry, July 23, 1864.

Johnson, John—Age, 43 years. Enlisted at New York City, to serve three years, and mustered in as private, Co. C, September 3, 1862; discharged for disability, December 8, 1864, at Davids Island, New York Harbor.

Joseph, Lionel—Age, 21 years. Enlisted, July 15, 1861, at New York City, to serve three years; mustered in as private, Co. C, July 21, 1861; transferred to Co. K, January 28, 1862; killed in action, May 5, 1862, at Williamsburg, Va.; also born as Elionel Josephs.

Karcher, John—Age, 21 years. Enlisted, July 15, 1861, at New York City, to serve three years; mustered in as private, Co. C, July 21, 1861; transferred to Co. A, September 28, 1861; re-enlisted as a veteran, February 10, 1864; transferred to Co. B, One Hundred and Twentieth Infantry, June 23, 1864.

Keating, Thomas—Age, 39 years. Enlisted at New York City, to serve three years, and mustered in as private, Co. C, September 28, 1861; wounded in action, May 5, 1862, at Williamsburg, Va., and July 1863, at Gettysburg, Pa.; re-enlisted as a veteran, December 22, 1863; transferred to Co. K, One Hundred and Twentieth Infantry, July 23, 1864.

Kerns, Thomas—Age, 39 years. Enlisted, April 28, 1861, at New York City, to serve three years; mustered in as private, Co. C, July 21, 1861; discharged for disability, March 17, 1862, at Camp Wool, Md.

Kinch, Harvy—Age, 40 years. Enlisted at: New York City, to serve three years, and mustered in as private, Co. C, August 24, 1862; transferred to Co. K, One Hundred and Twentieth Infantry, July 23, 1864.

Lally, John—Age, 27 years. Enlisted at New York City, to serve three years, and mustered in as private, Co. C, August 12, 1861; promoted corporal, December 1, 1861; captured in action and paroled, May 5, 1862, at Williamsburg, Va.; transferred to Regular Army in December 1862.

Liney, Charles—Age, 19 years. Enlisted, July 15, 1861, at Newburg, to serve three years; mustered in as private, Co. C, July 21; 1861; missing in action, May 6, 1864, at Wilderness, Va.; no further record.

McCawley, Peter—Age, 37 years. Enlisted at New York City, to serve three years, and mustered in as private, Co. C, September 16, 1861; discharged for disability, September 26, 1862, near Alexandria, Va.

McChristol, Bernard—Age, 30 years. Enlisted at New York City, to serve three years, and mustered in as private, Co. C, January 22, 1862; wounded in action, May 5, 1862, at Williamsburg, Va.; discharged for disability, September 16, 1862, at New York City.

McConnell, Robert—Age, 28 years. Enlisted at New York City, to serve three years, and mustered in as private, Co. C, September 2, 1861; discharged for disability, July 28, 1862, at Washington, D.C.

McConnell, William—Age, 24 years. Enrolled, April 28, 1861, at Staten Island, to serve three years; mastered in as corporal, Co. C, July 21, 1861; promoted sergeant, December 1, 1861; first sergeant, May 23, 1862; mustered in as second lieutenant, Co. E, July 7, 1862; transferred to Co. C, October 31, 1862; mustered in as first lieutenant, Co. H, June 23, 1863; captain, Co. F, January 26, 1864; mustered out with company, June 20, 1864, near Petersburg, Va. Commissioned second lieutenant, July 21, 1862, with rank from July 7, 1862, vice G.W. Wallace, resigned; first lieutenant, June 13, 1863, with rank from December 23, 1862, vice J.A. Smith, promoted; captain, October 6, 1863, with rank from August 27, 1863, vice W.H. Post, resigned.

McDevitt, Patrick—Age, 23 years. Enlisted at Staten Island, to serve three years, and mustered in as private, Co. C, and transferred to Co. H, Seventy-first Infantry, July 21, 1861.

McDonald, John—Age, 22 years. Enlisted at Staten Island, to serve three years, and mustered in as private, Co. C, and transferred to Co. H, Seventy-first Infantry, July 21, 1861.

McDonald, John—Age, 23 years. Enlisted, July 8, 1861, at Paterson, N.J., to serve three years; mustered in as private, Co. C, July 21, 1861; captured in action, May 5, 1862, at Williamsburg, Va.; no further record.

McGrath, John H.—Enlisted at New York City, to serve three years, and mustered in as private, Co. C, August 22, 1862; captured in action, May 3, 1863, at Chancellorsville, Va.; paroled, May 14, 1863, at City Point, Va.; deserted in October 1863.

McGuire, John—Age, 40 years. Enlisted, August 8, 1862, at Dunkirk, to serve three years; mustered in as private, Co. H, September 2, 1862; died of disease, September 5, 1864, at David's Island Hospital, New York Harbor; also born as Maguire.

McGuire, Michael—Age, 26 years. Enlisted at New York City, to serve three years, and mustered in as private, Co. C, September 1, 1862; transferred to Co. K, One Hundred and Twentieth Infantry, July 23, 1864.

McKeon, Michael—Age, 32 years. Enlisted, July 16, 1861, at New York City, to serve three years; mustered in as private, Co. C, July 21, 1861; discharged for disability, January 31, 1862, at Camp Wool, Md.; also born as Keon.

McNulty, John—Age, 35 years. Enlisted, July 6, 1861, at New York City, to serve three years; mustered in as private, Co. C, July 21, 1861; re-enlisted as a veteran, December 22, 1863; deserted, on expiration of furlough, no date.

Meehan, John M.—Age, 24 years. Enlisted at New York City, to serve three years, and mustered in as private, Co. C, September 23, 1861; killed in action, May 5, 1862, at Williamsburg, Va.

Metz, James—Age, 43 years. Enlisted, April 28, 1861, at New York City, to serve three years; mustered in as private, Co. C, July 21, 1861; killed in action, May 5, 1862, at Williamsburg, Va.

Miller, Henry—Age, 28 years. Enlisted at New York City, to serve three years, and mustered in as private, Co. C, August 12, 1861; died of disease, August 15, 1862.

Miller, Henry—Age, 20 years. Enlisted at New York City, to serve three years, and mustered in as private, Co. C, August 7, 1862; transferred to Co. I,

November 24, 1862; to Co. A, One Hundred and Twentieth Infantry, June 20, 1864.

Miller, Michael—Age, 39 years. Enlisted at Staten Island, to serve three years, and mustered in as private, Co. C, July 10, 1861; transferred to Co. I, November 24, 1862; wounded in action, July 2, 1863, at Gettysburg, Pa.; discharged for wounds, May 12, 1864, at New York City.

Missell, John—Age, 40 years. Enlisted at New York City, to serve three years, and mustered in as private, Co. C, August 13, 1862; wounded in action, July 2, 1863, at Gettysburg, Pa.; transferred to Co. K, One Hundred and Twentieth Infantry, July 23, 1864; also born as Wissell.

Monroe, Monteville C.—Age, 15 years. Enlisted, June 7, 1861, at Hebron, Pa., to serve three years; mustered in as private, Co. C, July 21, 1861; wounded in action, May 5, 1862, at Williamsburg, Va.; died of his wounds, July 18, 1862, at David's Island, New York Harbor.

Mullett, Walter P.—Age, 19 years. Enlisted, August 13, 1862, at Dunkirk, to serve three years; mustered in as private, Co. D, September 2, 1862; transferred to Co. G, One Hundred and Twentieth Infantry, June 20, 1864.

Mulligan, Andrew F.—Age, 44 years. Enlisted, July 15, 1861, at New York City, to serve three years; mustered in as private, Co. C, July 21, 1861; discharged for disability, July 13, 1862, in the field, Virginia.

Muno, Henry—Age, 37 years. Enlisted, July 18, 1861, at New York City, to serve three years; mustered in as private, Co. C, July 21, 1861; wounded in action, May 5, 1862, at Williamsburg, Va.; discharged for disability, January 7, 1863, near Falmouth, Va.

Murphy, John—Age, 22 years. Enlisted at New York City, to serve three years, and mustered in as private, Co. C, January 20, 1862; wounded in action; May 5, 1862, at Williamsburg, Va.; promoted corporal, December 11, 1862; re-enlisted as a veteran, December 22, 1863; transferred to Co. K, One Hundred and Twentieth Infantry, July 23, 1864.

Murphy, Michael—Age, 28 years. Enlisted, July 5, 1861, at New York City, to serve three years; mustered in as private, Co. C, July 21, 1861; promoted corporal, December 11, 1862; wounded in action, May 3, 1863, at Chancellorsville, Va.; re-enlisted as a veteran, December 22, 1863; dishonorably discharged for desertion, to date March 3, 1864.

Murray, Thomas—Age, 18 years. Enlisted at New York City, to serve three years, and mustered in as private, Co. C, September 17, 1861; dishonorably discharged by general court martial, no date.

Myers, Charles—Age, 29 years. Enlisted at New York City, to serve three years, and mustered in as private, Co. C, September 30, 1861; killed in action, May 5, 1862, at Williamsburg, Va.

Nelson, William—Age, 29 years. Enlisted, July 15, 1861, at New York City, to serve three years; mustered in as private, Co. C, July 21, 1861; discharged for disability, October 18, 1861, at Washington, D.C.

Oakley, Edmund—Age, 19 years. Enlisted at Staten Island, to serve three years, and mustered in as private, Co. C, and transferred to Co. H, Seventy-first Infantry, July 21, 1861.

Oakley, Isaac S.—Enlisted at New York City, to serve three years, and mustered in as private, Co. C, August 23, 1862; captured in action, May 3, 1863, at Chancellorsville, Va.; paroled, no date; no further record.

Palmer, John—Age, 35 years. Enlisted at New York City, to serve three years, and mustered in as private, Co. C, July 21, 1862; transferred to Co. K, One Hundred and Twentieth Infantry, July 23, 1864.

Parkin, George E.H.—Age, 30 years. Enlisted, April 28, 1861, at Staten Island, to serve three years; mustered in as first sergeant, Co. C, July 21, 1861; killed in action, May 5, 1862, at Williamsburg, Va.

Parkinson, John—Age, 41 years. Enlisted, July 3, 1861, at Paterson, N.J., to serve three years; mustered in as private, Co. C, July 21, 1861; discharged for disability, September 13, 1862, at New York City.

Patton, Andrew—Age, 23 years. Enlisted, July 7, 1861, at Patterson, N.J., to serve three years; mustered in as private, Co. C, July 21, 1861; promoted corporal in May 1862; died, August 15, 1862, in New York City.

Paul, James D.—Age, 39 years. Enlisted, September 12, 1861, at New York City, to serve three years; mustered in as private, Co. C, October 31, 1861; wounded in action in July 1863, at Gettysburg, Pa.; transferred to Co. K, One Hundred and Twentieth Infantry, July 23, 1864.

Pennock, Horatio B.—Age, 30 years. Enrolled, April 28, 1861, at Staten Island, to serve three years; mustered in as second lieutenant, Co. C, July 21, 1861; promoted first lieutenant, September 1, 1861; captain, Co. A, June 23, 1862; died of disease, August 4, 1862, near Harrison's Landing, Va.; not commissioned second lieutenant. Commissioned first lieutenant, January 7, 1862, with rank from July 21, 1861, original; not commissioned captain.

Perkins, John—Age, 36 years. Enlisted, July 18, 1861, at New York City, to serve three years; mustered in as private, Co. C, July 21, 1861; wounded in action, May 5, 1862, at Williamsburg, Va.; promoted corporal, September 7, 1862; sergeant, December 21, 1862; re-enlisted as a veteran, December 22, 1863; returned to ranks, March 1, 1864; transferred to Co. K, One Hundred and Twentieth Infantry, July 23, 1864.

Perry, Joseph—Age, 19 years. Enlisted, July 16, 1861, at Paterson, N.J., to serve three years; mustered in as private, Co. C, July 21, 1861; captured, July 4, 1862, near Harrison's Landing, Va.; no further record.

Peters, Alexander G.—Age, 32 years. Enlisted at Staten Island, to serve three years, and mustered in as private, Co. C; appointed principal musician and transferred to regimental band, July 21, 1861; discharged, May 16, 1862, by order General Heitzelman.

Platts, George—Age, 20 years. Enlisted at Staten Island, to serve three years, mustered in as private, Co. C, and transferred to Co. H, Seventy-first Infantry, July 21, 1861.

Platts, John D.—Age, 18 years. Enlisted at Staten Island, to serve three years, mustered in as private, Co. C, and transferred to Co. H, Seventy-first Infantry, July 21, 1861.

Powers, James—Age, 21 years. Enlisted at New York City, to serve three years, and mustered in as private, Co. C, August 12, 1862; transferred to Co. I, November 24, 1862; captured in action, May 3, 1863, at Chancellorsville, Va.; paroled, May 14, 1863, at City Point, Va.; deserted, September 27, 1863.

Purcell, James—Age, 31 years. Enlisted at New York City, to serve three years, and mustered in as private, Co. C, September 6, 1861; no further record subsequent to November 21, 1861.

Quinn, Christy—Age, 23 years. Enlisted, July 5, 1861, at New York City, to serve three years; mustered in as private, Co. C, July 7, 1861; wounded in action, May 5, 1862, at Williamsburg, Va.; re-enlisted as a veteran, December 22, 1863; transferred to Co. K, One Hundred and Twentieth Infantry, July 23, 1864.

Rabey, James H.—Age, 27 years. Enlisted, July 11, 1861, at New York City, to serve three years; mustered in as private, Co. C, July 21, 1861; transferred to Co. K, January 28, 1862; captured in action, May 5, 1862, at Williamsburg, Va.; returned to company, December 19, 1863; transferred to Co. E, One Hundred and Twentieth Infantry, June 23, 1864.

Ray, William—Enlisted at New York City, to serve three years, and mustered in as private, Co. C, and transferred to Co. I, August 11, 1862; to Veteran Reserve Corps, February 15, 1864, from which discharged, June 17, 1865; also born as Rey.

Rice, George B.—Age, 39 years. Enlisted, April 28, 1861, at Staten Island, to serve three years; mustered in as corporal, Co. C, July 21, 1861; promoted sergeant, June 27, 1862; reenlisted as a veteran, December 22, 1863; transferred to Co. K, One Hundred and Twentieth Infantry, July 23, 1864.

Rice, William H.—Age, 28 years. Enlisted at New York City to serve three years, and mustered in as corporal, Co. C, August 12, 1862; promoted sergeant, June 15, 1863; re-enlisted as a veteran, December 22, 1863; transferred to Co. K, One Hundred and Twentieth Infantry, July 23, 1864.

Rierden, John—Age, 27 years. Enlisted, July 16, 1861, at New York City, to serve three years; mustered in as private, Co. C, July 21, 1861; wounded in action, July 2, 1862, at Malvern Hill, Va.; re-enlisted as a veteran, December 22, 1863; transferred to Co. K, One Hundred and Twentieth Infantry, July 23, 1864; also born as Riordan.

Robbins, John H.—Age, 19 years. Enlisted, April 28, 1861, at New York City, to serve three years; mustered in as private, Co. C, July 21, 1861; captured in action, June 30, 1862, at Glendale, Va.; paroled, no date; transferred to Seventy-eighth Company, Second Battalion, Veteran Reserve Corps, October 18, 1863.

Robinson, Charles—Age, 32 years. Enlisted, April 28, 1861, at New York City, to serve three years; mustered in as private, Co. C, July 21, 1861; promoted corporal, August 20, 1861; sergeant, August 1861; first sergeant, May 6, 1863; mustered out, July 20, 1863.

Robinson, John—Age, 25 years. Enrolled, June 4, 1861, at Delhi, to serve three years; mustered in as private, Co. I, June 21, 1861; promoted corporal, October 1861; sergeant, September 25, 1862; first sergeant, January 1863; mustered in as second lieutenant, Co. E, July 1, 1863; wounded in action, July 2, 1863, at Gettysburg, Pa.; transferred to Co. G, March 1, 1864; mustered out, July 23, 1864, near Petersburg, Va.; also born as Robertson. Commissioned second lieutenant, June 13, 1863, with rank from February 5, 1865, vice M. Cook, promoted.

Robinson, Joseph G.—Age, 45 years. Enlisted, July 15, 1861, at New York City, to serve three years; mustered in as private, Co. C, July 21, 1861; discharged for disability, October 8, 1861, at Washington, D.C.

Roper, Thomas—Enlisted at New York City, to serve three years, and mustered in as private, Co. C, September 16, 1862; deserted, January 18, 1863.

Russell, George W.—Enlisted at New York City, to serve three years, and mustered in as private, Co. C, September 15, 1862; deserted, January 20, 1863.

Searl, Milton—Age, 27 years. Enlisted at Staten Island, to serve three years, mustered in as private, Co. C, and transferred to Co. D, July 21, 1861; to Co. H, Seventy-first Infantry, March 1, 1862.

Shaver, Henry—Age, 23 years. Enlisted at Staten Island, to serve three years, mustered in as private, Co. C, and transferred to Co. H, Seventy-first Infantry, July 21, 1861.

Sherwood, Benjamin—Age, 25 years. Enlisted, June 1, 1861, at Staten Island, to serve three years; mustered in as sergeant, Co. C, July 21, 1861; returned to ranks, December 1, 1861; promoted corporal, March 1, 1862; discharged for disability, January 7, 1863, at Philadelphia, Pa.

Simpson, Thomas—Age, 39 years. Enlisted, July 7, 1861, at New York City, to serve three years; mustered in as private, Co. C, July 21, 1861; discharged for disability, October 14, 1861, at Washington, D.C.

Snyder, Andrew J.—Age, 26 years. Enlisted at New York City, to serve three years, and mustered in as private, Co. C, September 14, 1861; wounded in action, May 5, 1862, at Williamsburg, Va.; died of his wounds, May 16, 1862, at Fort Monroe, Va.

Starks, Lipman—Age, 21 years. Enlisted, July 6, 1861, at New York, to serve three years; mustered in as private, Co. C, July 21, 1861; transferred to Co. A, September 28, 1861; discharged for disability, November 16, 1862, at Baltimore, Md.; also born as Storks, Stocks.

Stevenson, Robert A.—Age, 18 years. Enlisted at New York City, to serve three years, and mustered in as private, Co. C, August 12, 1861; transferred to Co. K, One Hundred and Twentieth Infantry, July 23, 1861.

Sullivan, Florence—Age, 32 years. Enlisted, July 10, 1861, at New York City, to serve three years; mustered in as private, Co. C, July 21, 1861; discharged for disability, October 8, 1861, at Washington, D.C.

Talcott, Charles H.—Age, 25 years. Enlisted at Brooklyn, to serve three years, and mustered in as private, Co. C, August 30, 1862; transferred to Co. K, One Hundred and Twentieth Infantry, July 23, 1864.

Tallman, Samuel O.—Enlisted at New York City, to serve three years, and mustered in as private, Co. C, August 11, 1862; missing in action, May 3, 1863, at Chancellorsville, Va.; no further record.

Taylor, George—Age, 34 years. Enlisted at New York City, to serve three years, and mustered in as private, Co. C, August 20, 1862; wounded, no date or place; transferred to Co. K, One Hundred and Twentieth Infantry, July 23, 1864.

Thompson, Adam—Age, 20 years. Enlisted at New York City, to serve three years, and mustered in as private, Co. C, August 28, 1862; transferred to Co. I, November 24, 1862; discharged for disability, January 18, 1864, at Convalescent Camp, Va.

Torry, Edward—Age, 27 years. Enlisted, July 11, 1861, at Hebron, Pa., to serve three years; mustered in as private, Co. C, July 21, 1861; promoted corporal, August 12, 1861; killed in action, August 27, 1862, at Bristoe Station, Va.

Warren, Charles H.—Age, 30 years. Enlisted at Staten Island, to serve three years, and mustered in as private, Co. C, appointed musician, and transferred to regimental band, July 21, 1861; mustered out with band, July 22, 1862.

Webb, James—Age, 35 years. Enlisted at New York City, to serve three years, and mustered in as private, Co. C, October 11, 1861; wounded in action, July 2, 1863, at Gettysburg, Pa.; July 23, 1863, at Manassas Gap, Va.; discharged for wounds, January 29, 1864, at Washington, D.C.

Weith, George—Age, 42 years. Enlisted, April 28, 1861, at New York City, to serve three years; mustered in as private, Co. C, July 21, 1861; discharged for disability, May 6, 1862, at Budds Ferry, Md.

Welch, Michael—Age, 36 years. Enlisted at Staten Island, to serve three years, and mustered in as private, Co. C; transferred to Co. H, Seventy-first Infantry, July 21, 1861.

Wieburg, John A.—Age, 40 years. Enlisted, July 8, 1861, at New York City, to serve three years; mustered in as private, Co. C, July 21, 1861; died of disease, November 28, 1861, at New York City.

Willard, Henry Kirk—Age, 22 years. Enlisted at State Island, to serve three years, mustered in as private, Co. C, appointed musician and transferred to regimental band, July 21, 1861; died, November 11, 1861, at General Hospital, Good Hope, Md.

Williams, George—Age, 33 years. Enlisted at New York City, to serve three years, and mastered in as private, Co. C, August 11, 1862; promoted corporal, July 1863; transferred to Co. K, One Hundred and Twentieth Infantry, July 23, 1864.

Williams, James M.—Age, 33 years. Enlisted at New York City, to serve three years, and mustered in as wagoner, Co. C, September 3, 1861; discharged for disability, December 8, 1862, at New York City.

Williams, John H.—Age, 36 years. Enlisted at New York City, to serve three years, and mustered in as private, Co. C, September 19, 1861; transferred to Co. K, One Hundred and Twentieth Infantry, July 23, 1861.

Wilson, Edward—Age, 38 years. Enlisted at Staten Island, to serve three years; mustered in as private, Co. C, and transferred to Co. H, Seventy-first Infantry, July 21, 1861.

Wood, George W.—Age, 19 years. Enlisted, July 17,

1861, at New York City, to serve three years; mustered in as private, Co. C, July 21, 1861; wounded in action, May 5, 1862, at Williamsburg, Va.; discharged for wounds, January 27, 1863, at Camp Nelson Taylor, Va.

Wood, Stephen W.—Age, 43 years. Enlisted at New York City, to serve three years, and mustered in as private, Co. C, July 23, 1861; discharged for disability, September 15, 1862, near Falmouth, Va.

Company D

Organized in Dunkirk, N.Y., in May 1861. Mustered into the United States service June 20, 1861.

Captains
William O. Stevens, from June 21 to June 25, 1861.
Casper K. Abell, from June 25, 1861, to May 4, 1863.
William E. Wheeler, from May 4 to August 1863 (transferred to Co. G).
Henry J. McDonough, from October 28 to November 27, 1863.
Alexander M. Clark, from January 1 to June 19, 1864.

First Lieutenants
Casper K. Abell, from June 20 to July 25, 1861.
Hugh C. Hinman, from June 25, 1861, to July 8, 1862.
John H. Howard, from May 6 to September 8, 1862.
Charles H. Hydron, from September 8 to November 1, 1862.
John S. Mann, from November 1, 1862, to January 1, 1863.
William C. Brooks, from January 1 to May 3, 1863.
Henry Jones Yates, from May 10 to July 1, 1863.
James A. Smith, from June 24, 1863, to April 5, 1864.

Second Lieutenants
Hugh C. Hinman, from June 20 to June 25, 1861.
John H. Howard, from June 25, 1861, to May 6, 1862.
William H. Post, from May 10 to July 2, 1862.
Henry J. McDonough, from July 2 to October 25, 1862.
Julius Kessler, from October 25 to November 1, 1862.
Richard Leonard, from November 1862, to January 1, 1863.
Robert H. Savage, from January 17 to October 29, 1863.

Abell, Caspar K.—Age, 33 years. Enrolled, May 20, 1861, at Dunkirk, to serve three years; mustered in as first lieutenant, Co. D, June 20, 1861; as captain, June 25, 1861; as major, May 4, 1863; mustered out with regiment, June 19, 1864, near Petersburg, Va. Commissioned captain, January 7, 1862, with rank from June 25, 1861, original; major, August 7, 1863, with rank from May 4, 1863, vice J. Leonard, promoted; not commissioned first lieutenant.

Ames, Oscar—Age, 21 years. Enlisted, May 28, 1861, at Dunkirk, to serve three years; mustered in as private, Co. D, June 20, 1861; wounded in action, June 6, 1864, at Cold Harbor, Va.; discharged for his wounds, August 17, 1864, at DeCamp General Hospital, David's Island, New York Harbor.

Averill, Thomas J.—Age, 20 years. Enlisted, August 18, 1862, at Dunkirk, to serve three years; mustered in as private, Co. D, September 2, 1862; captured in action May 3, 1863, at Chancellorsville, Va.; paroled, no date; mustered out, June 1, 1865, at Annapolis, Md.

Averill, Webster—Age, 22 years. Enlisted, May 28, 1861, at Dunkirk, to serve three years; mustered in as private, Co. D, June 20, 1861; promoted corporal, May 6, 1862; killed in action, July 1, 1862, at Malvern Hill, Va.

Babcock, William—Age, 21 years. Enlisted, May 23, 1861, at Dunkirk, to serve three years; mustered in as private, Co. D, June 20, 1861; mustered out with company, June 19, 1864, near Petersburg, Va.

Bailey, Milo Y.—Age, 19 years. Enlisted, May 28, 1861, at Dunkirk, to serve three years; mustered in as private, Co. D, June 20, 1861; re-enlisted as a veteran, December 24, 1863; wounded in action, May 6, 1864, at Wilderness, Va.; transferred to Co. G, One Hundred and Twentieth Infantry, June 23, 1864.

Barrows, Frank—Age, 19 years. Enlisted, August 13, 1862, at Dunkirk, to serve three years; mustered in as private, Co. D, September 2, 1862; wounded in action, July 2, 1863, at Gettysburg, Pa.; transferred to One Hundred and Twenty-first Company, Second Battalion, Veteran Reserve Corps, December 22, 1863.

Barton, Thomas—Age, 19 years. Enlisted at Dunkirk, to serve three years, and mustered in as private, Co. D, June 20, 1861; promoted corporal, May 6, 1862; killed in action, August 27, 1862, at Bristoe Station, Va.

Bourne, John—Age, 23 years. Enlisted, August 11,

1862, at Dunkirk, to serve three years; mustered in as private, Co. D, September 2, 1862; transferred to Co. G, One Hundred and Twentieth Infantry, June 23, 1864.

Bouton, Joseph F.—Age, 22 years. Enlisted, May 23, 1861, at Dunkirk, to serve three years; mustered in as corporal, Co. D, June 20, 1861; returned to ranks in July 1861; deserted, July 15, 1861, from Camp Scott, Staten Island; subsequent service in Co. F, Thirty-ninth Infantry.

Bowen, James—Age, 21 years. Enlisted, May 20, 1861, at Dunkirk, to serve three years; mustered in as private, Co. D, June 20, 1861; promoted corporal, May 6, 1862; mustered out, June 20, 1864, at New York City.

Bowyer, Edward—Age, 20 years. Enlisted, August 23, 1862, at Dunkirk, to serve three years; mustered in as private, Co. D, September 2, 1862; transferred to Co. C, One Hundred and Twentieth Infantry, June 23, 1864.

Boyden, Martin—Age, 21 years. Enlisted, May 28, 1861, at Dunkirk, to serve three years; mustered in as private, Co. D, June 20, 1861; killed in action, May 5, 1862, at Williamsburg, Va.

Brevir, Henry—Age, 18 years. Enlisted, May 28, 1861, at Dunkirk, to serve three years; mustered in as musician, Co. D, June 20, 1861; promoted drum-major, September 20, 1862; transferred to Co. D, and returned to musician, April 1863; mustered out with company, June 19, 1864, near Petersburg, Va.; also born as Eerier.

Brooks, William C.—Age, 21 years. Enrolled, May 20, 1861, at Dunkirk, to serve three years; mustered in as sergeant, Co. D, June 20, 1861; promoted first sergeant, May 6, 1862; mustered in as second lieutenant, Co. C, July 7, 1862; first lieutenant, Co. F, November 1, 1862; transferred to Co. D, January 1, 1863; killed in action, May 3, 1863, at Chancellorsville, Va. Commissioned second lieutenant, July 21, 1862, with rank from July 7, 1862, vice Thomas Clark, promoted; again commissioned second lieutenant, December 1, 1862, with rank from July 7, 1862, vice; _____ first lieutenant, October 6, 1863, with rank from October 31, 1862, vice B. Huttman, promoted.

Brurtng, William—Age, 19 years. Enlisted, May 28, 1861, at Dunkirk, to serve three years; mustered in as private, Co. D, June 20, 1861; wounded in action, May 3, 1863, at Chancellorsville, Va.; discharged for disability, March 18, 1864, at Carver U.S. General Hospital, Washington, D.C.

Bugbee, Palmer—Age, 18 years. Enlisted at Ellington, to serve three years, and mustered in as private, Co. D, December 28, 1863; transferred to Co. G, One Hundred and Twentieth Infantry, June 23, 1864.

Chapman, Edwin—Age, 18 years. Enlisted, August 25, 1862, at Dunkirk, to serve three years; mustered in as private, Co. D, September 2, 1862; wounded in action, June 2, 1864, at Cold Harbor, Va.; transferred, to Co. G, One Hundred and Twentieth Infantry, June 23, 1864.

Chapman, William F.—Age, 19 years. Enlisted, May 20, 1861, at Dunkirk, to serve three years; mustered in as corporal, Co. D, June 20, 1861; promoted sergeant, June 21, 1861; discharged for disability, May 12, 1862, at U.S. General Hospital, Judiciary Square, Washington, D.C.

Clark, Noah D.—Age, 25 years. Enlisted, May 28, 1861, at Dunkirk, to serve three years; mustered in as private, Co. D, June 20, 1861; mustered out with company, June 19, 1864, near Petersburg, Va.

Cole, Charles P.—Age, 26 years. Enlisted, May 28, 1861, at Dunkirk, to serve three years; mustered in as private, Co. D, June 20, 1861; discharged for disability, October 2, 1862, at New York City.

Cox, Horace H.—Age, 23 years. Enlisted, May 23, 1861, at Dunkirk, to serve three years; mustered in as corporal, Co. D, June 20, 1861; returned to ranks, August 1, 1861; again promoted, September 8, 1862, and returned to ranks, no date; captured in action, May 3, 1863, at Chancellorsville, Va.; paroled no date; mustered out with company, June 19, 1864, near Petersburg, Va.

Crocker, Henry—Age, — years. Enlisted, August 11, 1862, at Dunkirk, to serve three years; mustered in as private, Co. D, September 2, 1862; captured in action, May 3, 1863, at Chancellorsville, Va.; paroled, May 14, 1863, at City Point, Va.; no record subsequent to July 24, 1863.

Davis, Villeroy—Age, 25 years. Enlisted, May 28, 1861, at Dunkirk, to serve three years; mustered in as private, Co. D, June 20, 1861; mustered out with company, June 19, 1864, near Petersburg, Va.

Doyle, John—Age, 21 years. Enlisted, August 11, 1862, at Dunkirk, to serve three years; mustered in as private, Co. D, September 2, 1862; deserted, April 22, 1863, on expiration of furlough, near Falmouth, Va.

Ebernan, William E.—Age, 22 years. Enlisted, August 11, 1862, at Dunkirk, to serve three years; mustered in as private, Co. D, September 2, 1862; captured in action, July 2, 1863, at Gettysburg, Pa.; paroled, no date; discharged for disability, January 11, 1864, at U.S. General Hospital, Division No. 1, Annapolis.

Eck, Andreas—Age, date, place of enlistment not stated; private, Co. D, Seventy-third Infantry; transferred to Co. A, this regiment, in July 1861; re-enlisted as a veteran, December 23, 1863; promoted corporal, May 12, 1864; transferred to Co. B, One Hundred and Twentieth Infantry, June 23, 1864.

Ellis, Harrison F.—Age, 24 years. Enrolled, May 28, 1861, at Dunkirk, to serve three years; mustered in as private, Co. D, June 20, 1861; promoted corporal, June 21, 1861; sergeant, May 6, 1862; first sergeant, July 7, 1862; mustered in as second lieutenant, Co. H, September 8, 1862; first lieutenant, Co. F, November 1, 1862; transferred to Co. K in January 1863; killed in action, May 3, 1863, at Chancellorsville, Va. Commissioned second lieutenant, December 1, 1862, with rank from September 18, 1862, vice B.B. Huttman, promoted; first lieutenant, June 13, 1863, with rank from January 16, 1863, vice T. Clark, promoted.

Farnsworth, Marvin J.—Age, 28 years. Enlisted, May 28, 1861, at Dunkirk, to serve three years; mustered in as corporal, Co. D, June 20, 1861; returned to ranks, May 6, 1862; discharged for disability, January 7, 1863, at camp near Falmouth, Va.

Ferry, Francis—Age, 18 years. Enlisted, May 28, 1861, at Dunkirk, to serve three years; mustered in as private, Co. D, June 20, 1861; deserted, January 21, 1863, near Falmouth, Va.

Flesher, George—Age, 10 years. Enlisted, August 23, 1862, at Dunkirk, to serve three years; mustered in as private, Co. D, September 2, 1862; captured in action, May 10, 1864, near Spotsylvania, Va.; transferred to Co. G, One Hundred and Twentieth Infantry, June 23, 1861, while prisoner of war.

Foss, Charles A.—Age, 22 years. Enrolled, May 23, 1861, at Dunkirk, to serve three years; mustered in as corporal, Co. D, June 20, 1861; promoted sergeant, June 25, 1861; first sergeant, September 8, 1862; second lieutenant, Co. C, May 5, 1863; wounded in action, July 2, 1863; died of his wounds, July 7, 1863, at Gettysburg, Pa. Commissioned second lieutenant, August 7, 1863, with rank from May 4, 1863, vice S. Howell, promoted.

Francis, Frederick J.—Age, 19 years. Enlisted, May 28, 1861, at Dunkirk, to serve three years; mustered in as private, Co. D, June 20, 1861; deserted, August 4, 1861, at Camp Marsh, Va.

Frazine, Charles E.—Age, 27 years. Enlisted, August 27, 1862, at Dunkirk, to serve three years; mustered in as private, Co. D, September 2, 1862; transferred to Co. G, One Hundred and Twentieth Infantry, June 23, 1864.

Gatchell, Orrin L.—Age, 31 years. Enlisted, August 12, 1862, at Dunkirk, to serve three years; mustered in as private, Co. D, September 2, 1862; transferred to Co. G, One Hundred and Twentieth Infantry, June 23, 1864.

Getz, Bernard—Age, 24 years. Enlisted, May 28, 1861, at Dunkirk, to serve three years; mustered in as private, Co. D, June 20, 1861; wounded in action, May 29, 1864, at Pamunkey River, Va., and June 8, 1864, at Cold Harbor, Va.; mustered out with company, June 19, 1864.

Gifford, Arthur L.—Age, 19 years. Enlisted, May 28, 1861, at Dunkirk, to serve three years; mustered in as private, Co. D, June 20, 1861; mustered out with company, June 19, 1861, near Petersburg, Va.

Gilbert, Hiram B.—Age, 23 years. Enlisted, May 28, 1861, at Dunkirk, to serve three years; mustered in as private, Co. D, June 20, 1861; mustered out with company, June 19, 1864, near Petersburg, Va.

Gillett, Alexander—Age, 19 years. Enlisted, May 28, 1861, at Dunkirk, to serve three years; mustered in as private, Co. D, June 20, 1861; mustered out with company, June 19, 1864, near Petersburg, Va.

Griswold, Onan—Age, 19 years. Enlisted, May 28, 1861, at Dunkirk, to serve three years; mustered in as private, Co. D, June 20, 1861; mustered out with company, June 19, 1864.

Halsey, Frank—Age, 18 years. Enlisted, May 28, 1861, at Dunkirk, to serve three years; mustered in as private, Co. D, June 20, 1861; killed in action, May 5, 1862, at Williamsburg, Va.

Hamilton, Almond B.—Age, 19 years. Enlisted, May 28, 1861, at Dunkirk, to serve three years; mustered in as private, Co. D, June 20, 1861; promoted corporal, May 1863; wounded in action, July 2, 1863, at Gettysburg, Pa.; discharged for wounds, June 22, 1864, at De Camp General Hospital, David's Island, New York Harbor.

Harris, Francis E.—Age, 33 years. Enlisted, August 23, 1862, at Dunkirk, to serve three years; mustered in as private, Co. D, September 2, 1862; transferred to Co. G, One Hundred and Twentieth Infantry, June 23, 1864.

Hayden, George W.—Age, 27 years. Enlisted, May 28, 1861, at Dunkirk, to serve three years; mustered in as private, Co. D, June 20, 1861; mustered out with company, June 19, 1864, near Petersburg, Va.

Hequenburg, Charles W.—Age, 10 years. Enlisted, August 20, 1862, at Dunkirk, to serve three years; mustered in as private, Co. D, September 2, 1862; transferred to Signal Corps, June 1, 1863.

Hinman, Hugh C.—Age, 29 years. Enrolled, May 20, 1861, at Dunkirk, to serve three years; mustered in as second lieutenant, Co. D, June 20, 1861; as first lieutenant and adjutant, July 8, 1862; discharged, December 26, 1862; not commissioned second lieutenant. Commissioned first lieutenant and adjutant, January 7, 1862, with rank from June 25, 1861, original.

Holt, Wiliam J.—Age, 22 years. Enlisted, August 18, 1862, at Dunkirk, to serve three years; mustered in as private, Co. D, September 2, 1862; wounded in action, May 6, 1864, at Wilderness, Va.; transferred to Co. G, One Hundred and Twentieth Infantry, June 23, 1864.

Horn, George—Age, 24 years. Enlisted, August 13, 1862, at Dunkirk, to serve three years; mustered in as private, Co. D, September 2, 1862; wounded in action, May 10, 1864, at Spotsylvania Court House, Va.; transferred to Co. G, One Hundred and Twentieth Infantry, June 23, 1864.

Howard, John H.—Age, 24 years. Enrolled, May 20, 1861, at Dunkirk, to serve three years; mustered in as first sergeant, Co. D, June 20, 1861; promoted second lieutenant, June 25, 1861; first lieutenant, May 6, 1862; captain, Co. F, September 8, 1862; discharged, January 7, 1863. Commissioned second lieutenant, January 7, 1862, with rank from June 25, 1861, original; first lieutenant, June 30, 1862, with rank from May 10, 1862, vice H.C. Hinman, appointed adjutant; captain, December 1, 1862, with rank from October 30, 1862, vice J. Leonard, promoted.

Howe, Ralph P.—Age, 21 years. Enlisted, August 27, 1862, at Dunkirk, to serve three years; mustered in as private, Co. D, September 2, 1862; transferred to Co. G, One Hundred and Twentieth Infantry, June 20, 1864.

Jewell, Alfred A.—Age, 22 years. Enlisted, May 23, 1861, at Dunkirk, to serve three years; mustered in as private, Co. D, June 20, 1861; killed in action, June 16, 1864, at Petersburg. Va.; also born as Augustus H. Jewell.

Johnson, George—Age, 25 years. Enlisted, August 25, 1862, at Dunkirk, to serve three years; mustered in as private, Co. D, September 2, 1862; transferred to Co. G, One Hundred and Twentieth Infantry, June 23, 1864.

Johnson, William P.—Age, 28 years. Enlisted, August 25, 1862, at Dunkirk, to serve three years; mustered in as private, Co. D, September 2, 1862; wounded in action, July 2, 1863, at Gettysburg, Pa.; transferred to Co. G, One Hundred and Twentieth Infantry, June 23, 1864.

Jones, Thomas C.—Age, 23 years. Enlisted, August 23, 1862, at Dunkirk, to serve three years; mustered in as private, Co. D, September 2, 1862; transferred to Co. G, One Hundred and Twentieth Infantry, June 23, 1864.

Kennedy, John—Age, 34 years. Enlisted, May 28, 1861, at Dunkirk, to serve three years; mustered in as private, Co. D, June 20, 1861; killed in action, May 3, 1863, at Chancellorsville, Va.

Kramer, Jacob—Age, 20 years. Enlisted, May 20, 1861, at Dunkirk, to serve three years; mustered in as private, Co. D, June 20, 1861; wounded in action, May 5, 1862, at Williamsburg, Va.; died of disease, February 25, 1863, in hospital at Chester, Pa.

Leroy, John—Age, 27 years. Enlisted, May 28, 1861, at Dunkirk, to serve three years; mustered in as private, Co. D, June 20, 1861; mustered out with company, June 19, 1864, near Petersburg, Va.

Lewis, Gilbert H.—Age, 25 years. Enlisted, May 28, 1861, at Dunkirk, to serve three years; mustered in as private, Co. D, June 20, 1861; mustered out with company, June 19, 1864, near Petersburg, Va.

Lewis, Ira L.—Age, 42 years. Enlisted, May 28, 1861, at Dunkirk, to serve three years; mustered in as wagoner, Co. D, June 20, 1861; sent to ranks, January 1, 1862; discharged for disability, August 15, 1863, at camp, near Fort Lyon, Va.

Light, Richard—Age, 21 years. Enlisted, August 25, 1862, at Dunkirk, to serve three years; mustered in as private, Co. D, September 2, 1862; killed in action, May 3, 1863, at Chancellorsville, Va.

Lines, Stephen H.—Age, 20 years. Enlisted, May 28, 1861, at Dunkirk, to serve three years; mustered in as private, Co. D, June 20, 1861; mustered out with company, June 19, 1864, near Petersburg, Va.

Lopez, Henry T.—Age, 23 years. Enlisted, May 20, 1861, at Dunkirk, to serve three years; mustered in as corporal, Co. D, June 20, 1861; promoted sergeant, June 21, 1861; returned to ranks and deserted in June 1862, from hospital at New York City.

Loughlin, Joseph—Age, 37 years. Enlisted, May 28, 1861, at Dunkirk, to serve three years; mustered in as private, Co. D, June 20, 1861; re-enlisted as a veteran, December 24, 1863; transferred to Co. G, One Hundred and Twentieth Infantry, June 23, 1864; also born as Laughlin.

Luce, Otis B.—Age, 33 years. Enlisted, May 28, 1861, at Dunkirk, to serve three years; mustered in as private, Co. D, June 20, 1861; promoted corporal, July 11, 1861; sergeant, May 6, 1862; first sergeant in May 1863; wounded in action, July 2, 1863, at Gettysburg, Pa.; mustered out with company, June 19, 1864, near Petersburg, Va.

Ludlow, Charles H.—Age, 19 years. Enlisted, May 20, 1861, at Dunkirk, to serve three years; mustered in as corporal, Co. D, June 20, 1861; promoted sergeant, July 7, 1862; mustered out with company, June 19, 1864, near Petersburg, Va.

Martin, Leroy—Age, 24 years. Enlisted, August 20, 1862, at Dunkirk, to serve three years; mustered in as private, Co. D, September 2, 1862; deserted, January 20, 1863, at Camp Nelson Taylor, Va.

McKinstry, Arthur—Age, 21 years. Enlisted, May 28, 1861, at Dunkirk, to serve three years; mustered in as private, Co. D, June 20, 1861; killed in action, May 5, 1862, at Williamsburg, Va.

Mewhiney, Joseph H.—Age, 30 years. Enlisted, August 25, 1862, at Dunkirk, to serve three years; mustered in as private, Co. D, September 2, 1862; discharged for disability, January 9, 1863, at Washington, D.C.; also born as Mawhinney.

Miller, Charles H.—Age, 18 years. Enlisted, May 28,

1861, at Dunkirk, to serve three years; mustered in as private, Co. D, June 20, 1861; killed in action, May 5, 1862, at Williamsburg, Va.

Moon, Percival R.—Age, 21 years. Enlisted, May 28, 1861, at Dunkirk, to serve three years; mustered in as private, Co. D, June 20, 1861; killed in action, May 5, 1862, at Williamsburg, Va.

Mount, James D.—Age, 23 years. Enlisted, May 28, 1861, at Dunkirk, to serve three years; mustered in as private, Co. D, June 20, 1861; deserted, January 29, 1862, at Camp Wool, Md.

Mullett, Walter P.—Age, 19 years. Enlisted, August 13, 1862, at Dunkirk, to serve three years; mustered in as private, Co. D, September 2, 1862; transferred to Co. G, One Hundred and Twentieth Infantry, June 20, 1864.

Neuberger, Ansel—Age, 16 years. Enlisted, June 3, 1861, at Camp Scott, to serve three years; mustered in as musician, Co. D, June 20, 1861; mustered out with company, June 19, 1864, near Petersburg, Va.; also born as Huslom Newberger.

Nuepling, John—Age, 26 years. Enlisted, May 28, 1861, at Dunkirk, to serve three years, mustered in as private, Co. D, June 20, 1861; killed in action, May 5, 1862, at Williamsburg, Va.; also born as Neapling.

O'Donoghay, Lee—Age, 25 years. Enlisted, May 28, 1861, at Dunkirk, to serve three years; mustered in as private, Co. D, June 20, 1861; promoted corporal, May 6, 1862; wounded in action, July 1, 1862, at Malvern Hill, Va.; discharged for wounds, December 13, 1862, at Carver Hospital, Washington, D.C.

O'Durrell, George—Age, 33 years. Enlisted, August 25, 1862, at Dunkirk, to serve three years; mustered in as private, Co. D, September 2, 1862; transferred to Co. G, One Hundred and Twentieth Infantry, June 20, 1864.

Page, Augustus A.—Age, 18 years. Enlisted, May 28, 1861, at Dunkirk, to serve three years; mustered in as private, Co. D, June 20, 1861; discharged for disability, November 6, 1863, at Carver General Hospital, Washington, D.C.

Palmer, James K.—Age, 27 years. Enlisted, May 28, 1861, at Dunkirk, to serve three years; mustered in as private, Co. D, June 20, 1861; promoted corporal in May 1863; captured in action, July 2, 1863, at Gettysburg, Pa.; paroled, no date; mustered out, June 23, 1864, at New York City; also born as Pulmer and as James Kavanagh.

Parker, David B.—Age, 19 years. Enrolled, May 28, 1861, at Dunkirk, to serve three years; mustered in as private, Co. D, June 20, 1861; as second lieutenant, Co. I, June 6, 1863; mustered out with company, June 20, 1864, near Petersburg, Va. Commissioned second lieutenant, August 21, 1863, with rank, from June 6, 1863, vice W.D. Hall, promoted.

Parker, George F.—Age, 40 years. Enlisted, May 28, 1861, at Dunkirk, to serve three years; mustered in as private, Co. D, June 20, 1861; wounded in action, May 5, 1862, at Williamsburg, Va.; transferred to Veteran Reserve Corps in July 1863.

Paxton, Thomas—Enlisted in August 1862, at Dunkirk, to serve three years; mustered in as private, Co. D, September 2, 1862; no further record.

Pennell, William—Age, 23 years. Enlisted, May 28, 1861, at Dunkirk, to serve three years; mustered in as private, Co. D, June 20, 1861; wounded in action, June 25, 1862, near Fair Oaks, Va.; discharged for wounds, November 24, 1862, at Detroit, Mich.; also born as Penwell.

Penugi, Charlie—Age, 37 years. Enlisted, May 28, 1861, at Dunkirk, to serve three years; mustered in as private, Co. D, June 20, 1861; wounded in action, May 29, 1864, at Pamunkey River, Va.; absent in hospital, Washington, D.C., at muster out of company; also born as Remige.

Pickard, Allen—Age, 21 years. Enlisted, May 28, 1861, at Dunkirk, to serve three years; mustered in as private, Co. D, June 20, 1861; wounded and captured in action, and paroled, May 5, 1862, at Williamsburg, Va.; discharged for wounds, August 20, 1862, at camp near Alexandria, Va.

Pickard, Franklin A.—Age, 18 years. Enlisted, May 28, 1861, at Dunkirk, to serve three years; mustered in as private, Co. D, June 20, 1861; wounded in action, July 2, 1863, at Gettysburg, Pa.; discharged for wounds, May 18, 1864.

Porter, Winson H.—Age, 27 years. Enlisted, May 28, 1861, at Dunkirk, to serve three years; mustered in as private, Co. D, June 20, 1861; wounded in action, July 2, 1863, at Gettysburg, Pa.; mustered out, June 19, 1864.

Post, William H.—Age, 22 years. Enrolled, May 20, 1861, at Dunkirk, to serve three years; mustered in as sergeant, Co. D, June 20, 1861; promoted second lieutenant, May 10, 1862; mustered in as first lieutenant, Co. G, July 2, 1862; as captain, Co. F, January 7, 1863; wounded in action, May 3, 1863, at Chancellorsville, Va.; discharged, August 26, 1863. Commissioned second lieutenant, June 30, 1862, with rank from May 10, 1862, vice J.H. Howard, promoted; first lieutenant, July 21, 1862, with rank from July 2, 1862, vice J.W. Holmes, promoted; captain, June 13, 1863, with rank from January 7, 1863, vice J.H. Howard, resigned.

Ransom, Richard—Age, 42 years. Enlisted, May 28, 1861, at Dunkirk, to serve three years; mustered in as private, Co. D, June 20, 1861; died of disease, June 9, 1862, at White House Landing, Va.

Ryther, Carmi L.—Age, 18 years. Enlisted, May 28, 1861, at Dunkirk, to serve three years; mustered in as private, Co. D, June 20, 1861; discharged for disability, September 6, 1862, at New York City.

Sanborn, Charles H.—Age, 21 years. Enlisted, May 20, 1861, at Dunkirk, to serve three years; mustered in as private, Co. D, June 20, 1861; wounded in action, May 10, 1864, at Spotsylvania, Va.; absent, in hospital, at muster-out of company.

Schlinder, William—Age, 42 years. Enlisted, May 28, 1861, at Dunkirk, to serve three years; mustered in as private, Co. D, June 20, 1861; discharged for disability, December 16, 1862, at Fort Monroe, Va.; also born as William Schindler.

Schluter, August—Age, 30 years. Enlisted, May 28, 1861, at Dunkirk, to serve three years; mustered in as private, Co. D, June 20, 1861; wounded in action, May 5, 1862, at Williamsburg, Va.; re-enlisted as a veteran, and transferred to Co. A, December 24, 1863; killed in action, May 12, 1864, at Spotsylvania, Va.

Schutt, Christopher—Age, 23 years. Enlisted, May 28, 1861, at Dunkirk, to serve three years; mustered in as private, Co. D, June 20, 1861; discharged for disability, January 13, 1863, at New York.

Shelly, George W.—Age, 34 years. Enlisted, May 23, 1861, at Dunkirk, to serve three years; mustered in as private, Co. D, June 20, 1861; died of disease, July 8, 1862, on board transport "Elm City."

Shelton, Otis W.—Age, 34 years. Enlisted, August 30, 1862, at Dunkirk, to serve three years; mustered in as private, Co. D, September 8, 1862; promoted commissary-sergeant, February 22, 1864; mustered out, September 1, 1864; rendered supernumerary by consolidation near Petersburg, Va.

Simpson, William H.—Age, 34 years. Enlisted, May 20, 1861, at Dunkirk, to serve three years; mustered in as corporal, Co. D, June 20, 1861; returned to the ranks, August 1, 1861; killed in action, May 5, 1862, at Williamsburg, Va.

Sisson, Charles F.—Age, 21 years. Enlisted, May 28, 1861, at Dunkirk, to serve three years; mustered in as private, Co. D, June 20, 1861; killed in action, May 5, 1862, at Williamsburg, Va.

Skidmore, Charles W.—Age, 20 years. Enlisted, August 13, 1862, at Dunkirk, to serve three years; mustered in as private, Co. D, September 2, 1862; transferred to Co. G, One Hundred and Twentieth Infantry, June 23, 1864.

Sprague, Jerome C.—Age, 18 years. Enlisted, May 28, 1861, at Dunkirk, to serve three years; mustered in as private, Co. D, June 20, 1861; killed in action, May 5, 1862, at Williamsburg, Va.

Staats, William H.—Age, 21 years. Enlisted, May 28, 1861, at Dunkirk, to serve three years; mustered in as private, Co. D, June 20, 1831; promoted corporal, July 7, 1862; mustered out with company, June 19, 1864, near Petersburg, Va.

Stafford, Rinaldo R.—Age, 23 years. Enlisted, May 28, 1861, at Dunkirk, to serve three years; mustered in as private, Co. D, June 20, 1861; wounded in action, May 5, 1862, at Williamsburg, Va.; discharged for wounds, October 27, 1862, at camp near Alexandria, Va.

Stevens, William O.—Age, 32 years. Enrolled, May 20, 1861, at Dunkirk, to serve three years; mustered in as captain, Co. D, June 21, 1861; promoted major, June 25, 1861; mustered in as colonel, September 8, 1862; killed in action, May 3, 1863, at Chancellorsville, Va.; not commissioned captain. Commissioned major, January 7, 1862, with rank from July 22, 1861, original; colonel, October 10, 1862, with rank from September 8, 1862, vice Nelson Taylor, promoted brigadier general.

Stillman, Charles A.—Age, 19 years. Enlisted, May 20, 1861, at Dunkirk, to serve three years; mustered in as private, Co. D, June 20, 1861; promoted corporal, September 26, 1862; mustered out with company, June 19, 1864, near Petersburg, Va.

Stillman, Henry C.—Age, 19 years. Enlisted, August 29, 1862, at Dunkirk, to serve three years; mustered in as private, Co. D, September 2, 1862; transferred to Co. G, One Hundred and Twentieth Infantry, June 23, 1864.

Tate, George—Age, 21 years. Enlisted, May 28, 1861, at Dunkirk, to serve three years; mustered in as private, Co. D, June 20, 1861; promoted corporal, August 1, 1861; wounded and captured in action, May 3, 1863, at Chancellorsville, Va.; paroled, no date; promoted sergeant, to date May 4, 1863; re-enlisted as a veteran, December 20, 1863; transferred to Co. G, One Hundred and Twentieth Infantry, June 20, 1864.

Taylor, Alfhonso T.—Age, 21 years. Enlisted, May 28, 1861, at Dunkirk, to serve three years; mustered in as private, Co. D, June 20, 1861; discharged for disability, October 28, 1862, at Providence, R.I.

Terrell, Daniel—Age, 37 years. Enlisted, May 28, 1861, at Dunkirk, to serve three years; mustered in as private, Co. D, June 20, 1861; discharged for disability, November 3, 1862, at Point Lookout, Md.; also born as Turrell.

Thompson, Francis T.—Age, 29 years. Enlisted, August 26, 1862, at Dunkirk, to serve three years; mustered in as private, Co. D, September 2, 1862; wounded in action, in July 1863, at Gettysburg, Pa.; mustered out, June 2, 1865, at Washington, D.C.

Tide, Frederick—Age, 25 years. Enlisted, May 28, 1861, at Dunkirk, to serve three years; mustered in as private, Co. D, June 20, 1861; wounded in action, May 5, 1862, and died of his wounds, May 7, 1862, at Williamsburg, Va.

Tiffany, Chapin—Age, 22 years. Enlisted, May 28, 1861, at Dunkirk, to serve three years; mustered in as private, Co. D, June 20, 1861; mustered out with company, June 19, 1864, near Petersburg, Va.

Trask, Henry—Age, 25 years. Enlisted, August 11, 1862, at Dunkirk, to serve three years; mustered in as private, Co. D, September 2, 1862; transferred to Co. G, One Hundred and Twentieth Infantry, June 23, 1864.

Vanhausen, Jacob—Age, 23 years. Enlisted, May 28, 1861, at Dunkirk, to serve three years; mustered in as private, Co. D, June 20, 1861; deserted, January 19, 1863, near Falmouth, Va.

Vanhautten, James H.—Age, 22 years. Enlisted, May 23, 1861, at Dunkirk, to serve three years; mustered in as private, Co. D, June 20, 1861; promoted corporal, June 21, 1861; killed in action, May 5, 1862, at Williamsburg, Va.

Van Wormer, Cornelius—Age, 18 years. Enlisted, May 28, 1861, at Dunkirk, to serve three years; mustered in as private, Co. D, June 20, 1861; wounded in action, May 23, 1864, at North Anna River, Va.; mustered out, June 19, 1864.

Walden, Theron D.—Age, 23 years. Enlisted, May 28, 1861, at Dunkirk, to serve three years; mustered in as private, Co. D, June 20, 1861; wounded, accidental, February 10, 1862; discharged for wounds, May 31, 1862, at Budd's Ferry, Md.

Warner, James G.B.—Age, 18 years. Enlisted, May 23, 1861, at Dunkirk, to serve three years; mustered in as private, Co. D, June 20, 1861; mustered out with company, June 19, 1864, near Petersburg, Va.

Weiler, Ferdinand—Age, 24 years. Enlisted, May 23, 1861, at Dunkirk, to serve three years; mustered in as private, Co. D, June 20, 1801; promoted hospital steward, November 24, 1862; discharged, December 11, 1863, to enlist as hospital steward in U.S.A.

Whitney, George—Age, 22 years. Enlisted, May 28, 1861, at Dunkirk, to serve three years; mustered in as private, Co. D, June 20, 1861; transferred to Sixth Battery, no date.

Whitney, John—Age, 19 years. Enlisted, May 28, 1861, at Dunkirk, to serve three years; mustered in as private, Co. D, June 20, 1861; mustered out with company, June 19, 1864, near Petersburg, Va.

Wilson, Charles—Age, 20 years. Enlisted, July 29, 1862, at Dunkirk, to serve three years; mustered in as private, Co. D, September 2, 1862; transferred to Co. G, One Hundred and Twentieth Infantry, June 23, 1864.

Wilson, Sidney—Age, 18 years. Enlisted, July 29, 1862, at Dunkirk, to serve three years; mustered in as private, Co. D, September 2, 1862; wounded in action, July 2, 1863, at Gettysburg, Pa.; discharged for wounds, May 31, 1865, at U.S.A. hospital, Rochester, N.Y.

Worth, Daniel W.—Age, 28 years. Enlisted, May 23, 1861, at Dunkirk, to serve three years; mustered in as private, Co. D, June 20, 1861; deserted, July 4, 1861, from Camp Scott, Staten Island.

Wriborg, Claus H.—Age, 28 years. Enlisted, May 23, 1861, at Dunkirk, to serve three years; mustered in as private, Co. D, June 20, 1861; wounded in action, May 5, 1862, and died of his wounds, May 7, 1862, at Williamsburg, Va.

Wright, Alonzo M.—Age, 21 years. Enlisted, May 28, 1861, at Dunkirk, to serve three years; mustered in as private, Co. D, June 20, 1861; wounded in action, May 5, 1862, at Williamsburg, Va.; discharged for wounds, September 15, 1862, at camp near Fort Lyon, Va.

Wright, Melvine—Age, 24 years. Enlisted, May 28, 1861, at Dunkirk, to serve three years; mustered in as private, Co. D, June 20, 1861; mustered out with company, June 19, 1864, near Petersburg, Va.

Youly, Charles—Age, 33 years. Enlisted, May 23, 1861, at Dunkirk, to serve three years; mustered in as private, Co. D, June 20, 1861; wounded in action, May 5, 1862, at Williamsburg, Va.; discharged for wounds, November 25, 1862, at Fifth Street Hospital, Philadelphia, Pa.

Company E

Organized in Dunkirk, N.Y., in May 1861. Mustered into United States service June 20, 1861.

Captains

Patrick Barrett, from June 20, 1861, to May 6, 1862.
William Toomey, from May 6, 1862, to June 19, 1864.

First Lieutenants

William J. O'Neill, from June 20 to November 1, 1861.
William Toomey, from November 1, 1861, to May 6, 1862.
Michael McDonald, from May 13 to June 25, 1862.

William J. O'Neill, from April 29 to July 7, 1862.
Patrick Anderson, from November 1, 1862, to June 7, 1863.
William D. Hall, from June 10, 1863, to February 21, 1864.
Thomas Harvey, from March 15 to June 19, 1864.

Second Lieutenants

William Toomey, from June 20 to November 1, 1861.
George W. Wallace, from November 1, 1861, to July 1, 1862.
William McConnell, from July 7 to October 31, 1862.
Michael Cooke, from October 31, 1862, to February 5, 1863.
John Robinson, from July 1, 1863, to March 1, 1864.
Horatio S. Springer, from February 23 to June 29, 1864.

Anderson, Patrick—Age, 22 years. Enrolled, May 23, 1861, at Dunkirk, to serve three years; mustered in as sergeant, Co. E, June 20, 1861; promoted, first sergeant, November 1, 1861; second lieutenant, Co. I, June 26, 1862; first lieutenant, Co. H, October 11, 1862; transferred to Co. E, November 1, 1862; mustered in as captain, Co. G, June 7, 1863; transferred to Co. B, August 17, 1863; mustered out with company, June 20, 1861, near Petersburg, Va.; not commissioned second lieutenant. Commissioned first lieutenant, December 1, 1862, with rank from October 11, 1862, vice W. Holberton, discharged; captain, August 21, 1863, with rank from June 6, 1863, vice H.J. Bliss, died of wounds received in action.

Bailey, George H.—Age, 24 years. Enlisted, May 28, 1861, at Dunkirk, to serve three years; mustered in as musician, Co. E, June 20, 1861; discharged by reason of enlistment as sergeant-major in Seventy-eighth U.S. Colored Troops, to date April 3, 1863.

Baker, Henry—Age, 22 years. Enlisted, May 28, 1861, at Dunkirk, to serve three years; mustered in as private, Co. E, June 20, 1861; re-enlisted as a veteran, December 25, 1863; transferred to Co. H, One Hundred and Twentieth Infantry, June 23, 1864.

Barrett, Patrick—Age, 20 years. Enlisted, May 28, 1861, at Dunkirk, to serve three years; mustered in as private, Co. E, June 20, 1861; discharged for disability, February 4, 1863, at Convalescent Camp, Va.

Barrett, Patrick—Age, 29 years. Enrolled, May 16, 1861, at Dunkirk, to serve three years; mustered in as captain, Co. E, June 20, 1861; wounded in action, May 5, 1862, and died of his wounds, May 6, 1862, at Williamsburg, Va. Commissioned captain, January 7, 1862, with rank from June 20, 1861, original.

Barry, John L.—Age, 25 years. Enlisted, May 16, 1861, at Dunkirk, to serve three years; mustered in as corporal, Co. E, June 20, 1861; killed in action, July 1, 1862, at Malvern Hill, Va.

Beck, Frederick—Age, 22 years. Enlisted, May 28, 1861, at Dunkirk, to serve three years; mustered in as private, Co. E, June 20, 1861; absent, wounded, and in General Hospital at muster-out of company.

Beers, John B.—Age, 25 years. Enlisted, May 28, 1861, at Dunkirk, to serve three years; mustered in as private, Co. E, June 20, 1861; discharged for disability, December 13, 1862, at Lovel Hospital, Portsmouth Grove, R.I.

Bourke, Daniel L.—Age, 27 years. Enlisted, May 16, 1861, at Dunkirk, to serve three years; mustered in as corporal, Co. E, June 20, 1861; promoted sergeant, in November 1861; killed in action, July 2, 1863, at Gettysburg, Pa.; also born as Burke.

Brooks, Alvin H.—Age, 19 years. Enlisted, May 16, 1861, at Dunkirk, to serve three years; mustered in as corporal, Co. E, June 20, 1861; returned to ranks in December 1861; wounded in action, August 27, 1862, at Bristoe Station, Va., and July 2, 1863, at Gettysburg, Pa.; discharged for his wounds, February 24, 1864, at Philadelphia, Pa.

Burns, John—Age, 35 years. Enlisted, May 16, 1861, at Dunkirk, to serve three years; mustered in as private, Co. E, June 20, 1861; mustered out with company, June 19, 1864, near Petersburg, Va.

Burr, Ovitt—Age, 21 years. Enlisted, May 28, 1861, at Dunkirk, to serve three years; mustered in as private, Co. E, June 20, 1861; promoted corporal in July 1862; wounded in action, August 27, 1862, at Kettle Run, Va.; mustered out with company, June 19, 1864, near Petersburg, Va.

Campbell, John—Age, 23 years. Enlisted, May 20, 1861, at Dunkirk, to serve three years; mustered in as private, Co. E, June 20, 1861; killed in action, July 1, 1862, at Malvern Hill, Va.

Carroll, Martin—Age, 28 years. Enlisted, May 16, 1861, at Dunkirk, to serve three years; mustered in as private, Co. E, June 20, 1861; missing in action, May 3, 1863, at Chancellorsville, Va.; no further record.

Carroll, Michael W.—Age, 22 years. Enlisted, May 26, 1861, at Dunkirk, to serve three years; mustered in as private, Co. E, June 20, 1861; wounded in action, July 1, 1862, at Malvern Hill, Va.; transferred to Co. B, Third Regiment Veteran Reserve Corps, July 1, 1863.

Cather, Thomas J.—Age, 21 years. Enlisted, August 25, 1862, at Dunkirk, to serve three years;

mustered in as private, Co. E, September 2, 1862; wounded in action, May 3, 1863, at Chancellorsville, Va.; died of his wounds, May 18, 1863.

Clark, Francis—Age, 21 years. Enlisted, May 28, 1861, at Dunkirk, to serve three years; mustered in as private, Co. E, June 20, 1861; deserted, July 22, 1861, at Staten Island.

Collins, Anthony—Age, 29 years. Enlisted, May 26, 1861, at Dunkirk, to serve three years; mustered in as private, Co. E, June 20, 1861; wounded in action, July 2, 1863, at Gettysburg, Pa.; mustered out with company, June 19, 1864, near Petersburg, Va.

Congdon, Thomas—Age, 23 years. Enlisted, May 10, 1861, at Dunkirk, to serve three years; mustered in as private, Co. E, June 20, 1861; mustered out with company, June 19, 1864, near Petersburg, Va.

Connell, Patrick—Age, 21 years. Enlisted, May 23, 1861, at Dunkirk, to serve three years; mustered in as private, Co. E, June 20, 1861; captured in action, May 5, 1862, at Williamsburg, Va.; paroled, May 13, 1862, at Newport News, Va.; injured by falling from a tree in which he was a lookout, July 1, 1862, and captured near Malvern Hill, Va.; paroled in November 1862; wounded in action, July 2, 1863, at Gettysburg, Pa., and again November 27, 1863, at Locust Grove, Va.; mustered out, to date May 23, 1864, at New York City.

Cook, Edward—Age, 22 years. Enlisted, May 23, 1861, at Dunkirk, to serve three years; mustered in as private, Co. E, June 20, 1861; wounded in action, August 27, 1862, at Kettle Run, Va.; transferred to Co. A, Third Regiment Veteran Reserve Corps, July 1, 1863.

Cook, Michael—Age, 30 years. Enrolled, May 26, 1861, at Dunkirk, to serve three years; mustered in as sergeant, Co. E, June 20, 1861; promoted first sergeant, June 23, 1862; mustered in as second lieutenant, Co. F, September 26, 1862; transferred to Co. E, October 31, 1862; mustered in as first lieutenant, Co. I, February 5, 1863; mustered out with company, June 20, 1864, near Petersburg, Va. Commissioned second lieutenant, December 1, 1862, with rank from September 26, 1862, vice W. McConnell, promoted; first lieutenant, June 13, 1863, with rank from February 5, 1863, vice J. Fogerty, resigned.

Cozier, William J.—Age, 30 years. Enlisted, June 15, 1861, at Dunkirk, to serve three years; mustered in as private, Co. E, June 20, 1861; discharged for disability, July 31, 1862, at Harrison's Landing, Va.

Cullenan, Thomas—Age, 30 years. Enlisted, May 16, 1861, at Dunkirk, to serve three years; mustered in as private, Co. E, June 20, 1861; promoted corporal, September 26, 1862; deserted in March 1863, at Dunkirk, N.Y., on expiration of furlough.

Daily, Michael—Age, 21 years. Enlisted, May 16, 1861, at Dunkirk, to serve three years; mustered in as sergeant, Co. E, June 20, 1861; died of wounds, November 24, 1861, at Union Hospital, Washington, D.C.

Desmond, Michael—Age, 20 years. Enlisted, June 15, 1861, at Dunkirk, to serve three years; mustered in as private, Co. E, June 20, 1861; deserted, July 24, 1861, at Staten Island, N.Y. Dilks, John W.—Age, 20 years. Enlisted, May 16, 1861, at Dunkirk, to serve three years; mustered in as private, Co. E, June 20, 1861; deserted, August 29, 1862, at Bull Run, Va.; subsequent service, Co. F, One Hundred and Forty-sixth Illinois Infantry.

Donaghoe, Daniel—Age, 35 years. Enlisted, May 16, 1861, at Dunkirk, to serve three years; mustered in as private, Co. E, June 20, 1861; discharged for his wounds, accidental bursting of shell, March 1, 1862, at Camp Wool, Md.

Downs, Patrick—Age, 19 years. Enlisted, August 23, 1862, at Dunkirk, to serve three years; mustered in as private, Co. E, September 2, 1862; captured in action, July 2, 1863, at Gettysburg, Pa.; paroled, no date; transferred to Co. H, One Hundred and Twentieth Infantry, June 23, 1864.

Edmonds, John L.—Age, 37 years. Enlisted, May 28, 1861, at Dunkirk, to serve three years; mustered in as private, Co. E, June 20, 1861; died of disease, August 27, 1862, at Warrenton Junction, Va.

Emery, Franklin—Age, 19 years. Enlisted, May 28, 1861, at Dunkirk, to serve three years; mustered in as private, Co. E, June 20, 1861; mustered out with company, June 19, 1864, near Petersburg, Pa.

Estes, Franklin—Age, 20 years. Enlisted, August 28, 1861, at Dunkirk, to serve three years; mustered in as private, Co. E, June 20, 1861; mustered out with company, June 19, 1864, near Petersburg, Va.

Fairbanks, Johny V.—Age, 16 years. Enlisted, December 2, 1861, at New York City, to serve three years; mustered in as musician, Co. E, December 31, 1861; re-enlisted as a veteran, February 16, 1864; transferred to Co. H, One Hundred and Twentieth Infantry, June 23, 1864.

Ferris, Samuel—Age, 30 years. Enlisted, May 28, 1861, at Dunkirk, to serve three years; mustered in as private, Co. E, June 10, 1861; re-enlisted as a veteran, December 25, 1863; transferred to Co. H, One Hundred and Twentieth Infantry, June 23, 1864.

Fieldrake, Daniel—Age, 35 years. Enlisted, June 15, 1861, at Dunkirk, to serve three years; mustered in as private, Co. E, June 20, 1861; mustered out with company, June 19, 1864, near Petersburg, Va.

Fitzgerald, Timothy—Age, 35 years. Enlisted, May 23, 1861, at Dunkirk, to serve three years; mustered in as private, Co. E, June 20, 1861; died of disease, November 15, 1862, at Washington, D.C.

Fleck, Joseph—Age, 25 years. Enlisted, May 28, 1861, at Dunkirk, to serve three years; mustered in as private, Co. E, June 20, 1861; transferred to One Hundred and Twenty-third Company, Second Battalion Veteran Reserve Corps, March 15, 1864.

Fleming, Thomas—Age, 20 years. Enlisted, May 28, 1861, at Dunkirk, to serve three years; mustered in as private, Co. E, June 20, 1861; transferred to Co. D, Twelfth Regiment Veteran Reserve Corps, July 16, 1863.

Flynn, Joseph—Age, 28 years. Enlisted, May 28, 1861, at Dunkirk, to serve three years; mustered in as private, Co. E, June 20, 1861; killed in action, July 1, 1862, at Malvern Hill, Va.

Foley, Patrick—Age, 20 years. Enlisted, August 25, 1862, at Dunkirk, to serve three years; mustered in as private, Co. E, September 2, 1862; wounded in action, July 2, 1863, at Gettysburg, Pa.; discharged for disability, January 2, 1864, at Convalescent Camp, Va.

Fontaine, Jeremiah—Age, 30 years. Enlisted, August 26, 1862, at Dunkirk, to serve three years; mustered in as private, Co. E, September 2, 1862; transferred to Co. H, One Hundred and Twentieth Infantry, June 23, 1864; also born as Fountain.

Gillis, Charles H.—Age, 20 years. Enlisted, May 28, 1861, at Dunkirk, to serve three years; mustered in as private, Co. E, June 20, 1861; wounded in action May 3, 1863, at Chancellorsville, Va.; died of his wounds May 18, 1863, at Potomac Creek, Va.

Golden, Michael J.—Age, 20 years. Enlisted, May 28, 1861, at Dunkirk, to serve three years; mustered in as private, Co. E, June 20, 1861; deserted, July 18, 1861, at Staten Island, N.Y.

Gordon, Ransom S.—Age, 23 years. Enlisted, May 16, 1861, at Dunkirk, to serve three years; mustered in as wagoner, Co. E, June 20, 1861; returned to ranks in December 1861; mustered out with company, June 19, 1864, near Petersburg, Va.

Gray, Henry B.—Age, 19 years. Enlisted, May 16, 1861, at Dunkirk, to serve three years; mustered in as corporal, Co. E, June 20, 1861; promoted sergeant, January 17, 1863; mustered out with company, June 19, 1864, near Petersburg, Va.

Hadley, Milton J.—Age, 21 years. Enlisted, May 28, 1861, at Dunkirk, to serve three years; mustered in as private, Co. E, June 20, 1861; discharged for disability, November 26, 1862, from general hospital.

Haight, George D.—Age, 19 years. Enlisted, May 28, 1861, at Dunkirk, to serve three years; mustered in as private, Co. E, June 20, 1861; killed in action, July 1, 1862, at Malvern Hill, Va.

Hall, Chauncey—Age, 20 years. Enlisted, May 28, 1861, at Dunkirk, to serve three years; mustered in as private, Co. E, June 20, 1861; transferred to Co. H, Sixth Regiment, U.S. Infantry.

Haryey, Thomas—Age, 20 years. Enrolled, May 16, 1861, at Dunkirk, to serve three years; mustered in as sergeant, Co. E, June 20, 1861; promoted first sergeant, September 26, 1862; second lieutenant, Co. H, January 17, 1863; wounded and captured in action, May 3, 1863, at Chancellorsville, Va.; paroled in June 1863; mustered in as first lieutenant, Co. E, March 15, 1864; mustered out with company, June 19, 1864, near Petersburg, Va.; also born as John T. Harvey. Commissioned second lieutenant, December 15, 1863, with rank from February 18, 1863, vice M. Solomon, dismissed; first lieutenant, December 17, 1863, with rank from November 28, 1863, vice R.H. Savage, promoted.

Henderson, James B.—Age, 22 years. Enlisted, May 28, 1861, at Dunkirk, to serve three years; mustered in as private, Co. E, June 20, 1861; died of disease, November 14, 1861, at Union Hospital, Georgetown, D.C.; also born as John P. Henderson.

Hickey, Thomas—Age, 21 years. Enlisted, May 28, 1861, at Dunkirk, to serve three years; mustered in as private, Co. E, June 20, 1861; wounded in action, July 2, 1863, at Gettysburg, Pa.; discharged for wounds, May 15, 1864, at U.S. General Hospital, Summit House, Philadelphia, Pa.

Holland, Thomas—Age, 27 years. Enlisted, August 25, 1862, at Dunkirk, to serve three years; mustered in as private, Co. E, September 2, 1862; wounded in action, July 2, 1863, at Gettysburg, Pa.; died of his wounds, July 6, 1863.

Hooker, Corydon—Age, 19 years. Enlisted, May 28, 1861, at Dunkirk, to serve three years; mustered in as private, Co. E, June 20, 1861; died of disease, May 13, 1862, on board the "Elm City." Horan, Thomas—Age, 22 years. Enlisted, May 28, 1861, at Dunkirk, to serve three years; mustered in as private, Co. E, June 20, 1861; promoted corporal, November 1861; sergeant, September 20, 1862; wounded and in hospital, at muster-out of company; awarded a medal of honor for distinguished gallantry in action at Gettysburg, Pa., July 2, 1863.

Horan, Thomas—Age, 22 years. Enlisted, May 28, 1861, at Dunkirk, to serve three years; mustered in as private, Co. E, June 20, 1861; promoted corporal, November 1861; sergeant, September 26, 1862; wounded and in hospital, at muster-out of company; awarded a medal of honor for distinguished gallantry in action at Gettysburg, Pa., July 2, 1863.

Howe, John—Age, 23 years. Enlisted, December 16, 1861, at Dunkirk, to serve three years; mustered in as private, Co. E, December 18, 1861; discharged for disability, January 24, 1863, at Philadelphia, Pa.

Hunt, James B.—Age, 22 years. Enlisted, May 28, 1861, at Dunkirk, to serve three years; mustered in as private, Co. E, June 20, 1861; mustered out with company, June 19, 1864, near Petersburg, Va.

Johnson, James B.—Age, 22 years. Enlisted, May 16, 1861, at Dunkirk, to serve three years; mustered in as private, Co. E, June 20, 1861; re-enlisted as a veteran, December 25, 1863; wounded, no date or place; transferred to Co. H, One Hundred and Twentieth Infantry, June 23, 1864.

Keene, Napoleon L.—Age, 34 years. Enlisted, July 25, 1861, at Dunkirk, to serve three years; mustered in as private, Co. E, August 8, 1861; deserted, July 10, 1863, at Middletown, Md.

Killian, James—Age, 23 years. Enlisted, May 16, 1861, at Dunkirk, to serve three years; mustered in as corporal, Co. E, June 20, 1861; promoted sergeant, June 23, 1862; discharged for disability, March 9, 1863, at camp, near Falmouth, Va.

Koffman, Michael—Age, 31 years. Enlisted, May 28, 1861, at Dunkirk, to serve three years; mustered in as private, Co. E, June 20, 1861; re-enlisted as a veteran, December 25, 1863; captured while on picket, in June 1864, near North Anna River, Va.; paroled, no date; transferred to Co. H, One Hundred and Twentieth Infantry, June 23, 1864.

Lawler, John—Age, 26 years. Enlisted, August 25, 1862, at Dunkirk, to serve three years; mustered in as private, Co. E, September 2, 1862; transferred to Co. H, One Hundred and Twentieth Infantry, June 23, 1864.

Lee, Jerome—Age, 24 years. Enlisted, May 28, 1861, at Dunkirk, to serve three years; mustered in as private, Co. E, June 20, 1861; deserted, September 8, 1862, from hospital, at Bedloe's Island, New York Harbor; mustered in as Joseph Lee.

Leonards, John—Age, 26 years. Enlisted, May 28, 1861, at Dunkirk, to serve three years; mustered in as private, Co. E, June 20, 1861; mustered out with company, June 19, 1864, near Petersburg, Va.; also born as Lynards.

Lindsley, Richard—Age, 23 years. Enlisted, May 28, 1861, at Dunkirk, to serve three years; mustered in as private, Co. E, June 20, 1861; transferred to Co. D, Sixth Veteran Reserve Corps, May 16, 1863.

Loftus, Anthony L.—Age, 20 years. Enlisted, May 16, 1861, at Dunkirk, to serve three years; mustered in as private, Co. E, June 20, 1861; promoted corporal in November 1861; wounded in action, July 1, 1862, at Malvern Hill, Va.; promoted sergeant, March 9, 1863; mustered out, June 19, 1864.

Lounin, Charles—Age, 23 years. Enlisted, May 28, 1861, at Dunkirk, to serve three years; mustered in as private, Co. E, June 20, 1861; deserted, July 8, 1861, at Staten Island, N.Y.

Lower, Amasa—Age, 19 years. Enlisted, May 28, 1861, at Dunkirk, to serve three years; mustered in as private, Co. E, June 20, 1861; discharged for disability, February 4, 1863, at Convalescent Camp, Va.

Lyons, John—Age, 21 years. Enlisted, May 16, 1861, at Dunkirk, to serve three years; mustered in as corporal, Co. E, June 20, 1861; promoted sergeant in November 1861; first sergeant, January 17, 1863; wounded in action, July 2, 1863, at Gettysburg, Pa.; discharged for wounds, May 6, 1864, at U.S. General Hospital, Newark, N.J.

Maloney, Cornelius—Age, 20 years. Enlisted, August 7, 1862, at Dunkirk, to serve three years; mustered in as private, Co. E, September 2, 1862; wounded in action, July 2, 1863, at Gettysburg, Pa.; transferred to Co. H, One Hundred and Twentieth Infantry, June 2.

Maloney, Patrick—Age, 23 years. Enlisted, August 27, 1862, at Dunkirk, to serve three years; mustered in as private, Co. E, September 2, 1862; promoted corporal, March 1, 1868; transferred to Co. H, One Hundred and Twentieth Infantry, June 23, 1864.

Mason, Reuben I.—Age, 19 years. Enlisted, May 16, 1861, at Dunkirk, to serve three years; mustered in as private, Co. E, June 20, 1861; discharged for disability, October 6, 1862, at camp, near Fort Lyon, Va.

Mathews, Franklin—Age, 22 years. Enlisted, May 28, 1861, at Dunkirk, to serve three years; mustered in as private, Co. E, June 20, 1861; died of disease, April 18, 1862, at Division Hospital, Budd's Ferry, Md.

Maysoner, Anton—Age, 26 years. Enlisted, May 28, 1861, at Dunkirk, to serve three years; mustered in as private, Co. E, June 20, 1861; wounded in October 1861, by the accidental explosion of a shell, near Budd's Ferry, Md.; mustered out with company, June 19, 1864, near Petersburg, Va.; also born as Masoner and Musoner.

McAleer, John—Age, 19 years. Enlisted, May 16, 1861, at Dunkirk, to serve three years; mustered in as private, Co. E, June 20, 1861; deserted July 8, 1861, at Staten Island, N.Y.

McLear, Charles—Age, 18 years. Enlisted, August 29, 1862, at Dunkirk, to serve three years; mustered in as private, Co. E, September 2, 1862; transferred to Co. H, One Hundred and Twentieth Infantry, June 23, 1864; also born as McAIleer.

McNemara, George—Age, 18 years. Enlisted, August 25, 1862, at Dunkirk, to serve three years; mustered in as private, Co. E, September 2, 1862; transferred to Co. H, One Hundred and Twentieth Infantry, June 23, 1864.

Mounce, Joseph—Age, 18 years. Enlisted, June 15, 1861, at Dunkirk, to serve three years; mustered in as private, Co. E, June 20, 1861; wounded, no date or place; mustered out, June 19, 1864.

Myres, Bartholomew F.—Age, 19 years. Enlisted, August 26, 1862, at Dunkirk, to serve three years;

mustered in as private, Co. E, September 2, 1862; promoted corporal, January 17, 1863; transferred to Co. H, One Hundred and Twentieth Infantry, June 23, 1864; also born as Myers.

Negus, James H.—Age, 26 years. Enlisted, May 16, 1861, at Dunkirk, to serve three years; mustered in as private, Co. E, June 20, 1861; killed in action, May 3, 1863, at Chancellorsville, Va.

O'Brien, Michael—Age, 23 years. Enlisted, May 16, 1861, at Dunkirk, to serve three years; mustered in as private, Co. E, June 20, 1861; wounded in action, May 5, 1862, at Williamsburg, Va.; discharged for wounds, October 6, 1862, near Port Lyon, Va.

O'Brien, Patrick—Age, 19 years. Enlisted, May 28, 1861, at Dunkirk, to serve three years; mustered in as private, Co. E, June 20, 1861; discharged for disability, June 9, 1862, at Budd's Ferry, Md.

O'Connor, James—Age, 20 years. Enlisted, May 16, 1861, at Dunkirk, to serve three years; mustered in as private, Co. E, June 20, 1861; wounded in action, July 1, 1862, at Malvern Hill, Va.; discharged for disability, November 26, 1862, at General Hospital, Convalescent Camp, Va.

O'Connor, Laurence—Age, 18 years. Enlisted, May 28, 1861, at Dunkirk, to serve three years; mustered in as private, Co. E, June 20, 1861; wounded in action, June 1, 1862, at Fair Oaks, Va.; discharged for wounds, October 6, 1862, near Fort Lyon, Va.

O'Connor, Thomas—Age, 25 years. Enlisted, June 15, 1861, at Dunkirk, to serve three years; mustered in as private, Co. E, June 20, 1861; discharged, March 16, 1862, at Camp Wool, Md.

O'Neill, William J.—Age, 32 years. Enrolled, May 16, 1861, at Dunkirk, to serve three years; mustered in as first lieutenant, Co. E, June 20, 1861; as adjutant, November 1, 1861; transferred to Co. E, April 29, 1862; discharged, July 7, 1862. Commissioned first lieutenant and adjutant, January 7, 1862, with rank from November 1, 1861, original; re-commissioned first lieutenant and adjutant, May 25, 1862, with rank from May 10, 1862, vice himself, resigned; captain, not mustered, June 30, 1862, with rank from May 6, 1862, vice Patrick Barrett, killed in action.

O'Shea, Laurence—Age, 28 years. Enlisted, August 28, 1862, at Dunkirk, to serve three years; mustered in as private, Co. E, September 2, 1862; deserted, January 21, 1863, at camp, near Falmouth, Va.

Patterson, Lee—Age, 22 years. Enlisted, May 23, 1861, at Dunkirk, to serve three years; mustered in as private, Co. E, June 20, 1861; mustered out, August 29, 1865, at Buffalo, N.Y.

Patton, Thomas D.—Age, 21 years. Enlisted, May 28, 1861, at Dunkirk, to serve three years; mustered in as private, Co. E, June 20, 1861; wounded in action, May 5, 1862, at Williamsburg, Va.; died of his wounds, May 20, 1862, at Hygeia General Hospital, Fortress Monroe, Va.

Perkins, Pisaro—Age, 20 years. Enlisted, May 28, 1861, at Dunkirk, to serve three years; mustered in as private, Co. E, June 20, 1861; re-enlisted as a veteran, December 25, 1863; transferred to Co. H, One Hundred and Twentieth Infantry, June 23, 1864.

Platte, Frederick—Age, 42 years. Enlisted, August 29, 1862, at Dunkirk, to serve three years; mustered in as private, Co. E, September 2, 1862; wounded in action, July 2, 1863, and died of his wounds, July 8, 1863, at Gettysburg, Pa.

Prudick, John—Age, 28 years. Enlisted, May 16, 1861, at Dunkirk, to serve three years; mustered in as private, Co. E, June 20, 1861; mustered out with company, June 19, 1864, near Petersburg, Va.

Reddenbery, William—Age, 27 years. Enlisted, August 18, 1862, at Dunkirk, to serve three years; mustered in as private, Co. E, September 2, 1862; transferred to Co. H, One Hundred and Twentieth Infantry, June 23, 1864.

Reeves, Delos—Age, 21 years. Enlisted, May 28, 1861, at Dunkirk, to serve three years; mustered in as private, Co. E, June 20, 1861; deserted, July 1, 1861, at Staten Island, N.Y.

Rouse, John W.—Age, 23 years. Enlisted, June 15, 1861, at Dunkirk, to serve three years; mustered in as private, Co. E, June 20, 1861; died from wounds, by accidental explosion of shell, October 23, 1861, near Budd's Ferry, Md.

Saunders, Edgar L.—Age, 21 years. Enlisted, May 28, 1861, at Dunkirk, to serve three years; mustered in as corporal, Co. E, June 20, 1861; captured in action, May 3, 1863, at Chancellorsville, Va.; paroled, no date; absent, sick in hospital, at New York City, at muster-out of company.

Scanlon, Richard—Age, 20 years. Enlisted, June 15, 1861, at Dunkirk, to serve three years; mustered in as private, Co. E, June 20, 1861; promoted corporal, June 23, 1862; sergeant, July 2, 1863, mustered out with company, June 19, 1861, near Petersburg, Va.

Schreiner, Frederick—Age, 28 years. Enlisted, August 23, 1862, at Dunkirk, to serve three years; mustered in as private, Co. E, September 2, 1862; wounded in action, July 2, 1863, and died of his wounds, July 4, 1863, at Gettysburg, Pa.; also born as Schwiemer.

Schrieder, Mathias—Age, 23 years. Enlisted, May 23, 1861, at Dunkirk, to serve three years; mustered in as private, Co. E, June 20, 1861; deserted, May 1862, at Yorktown, Va.; also born as Shrider.

Senfield, William—Age, 33 years. Enlisted, May 16,

1861, at Dunkirk, to serve three years; mustered in as private, Co. E, June 20, 1861; wounded in action, July 2, 1863, at Gettysburg, Pa.; discharged, May 16, 1864, at Portsmouth Grove, R.I.

Shields, Michael—Age, 23 years. Enlisted, May 16, 1861, at Dunkirk, to serve three years; mustered in as corporal, Co. E, June 20, 1861; wounded in action, July 1, 1862, at Malvern Hill, Va., and July 2, 1863, at Gettysburg, Pa.; discharged for wounds, December 11, 1863, at U.S. General Hospital, Newark, N.J.

Skinner, Ensign—Age, 25 years. Enlisted, May 28, 1861, at Dunkirk, to serve three years; mustered in as private, Co. E, June 20, 1861; discharged for disability, November 3, 1862, at Washington, D.C.

Smith, Ephraim B.—Age, 21 years. Enlisted, May 28, 1861, at Dunkirk, to serve three years; mustered in as private, Co. E, June 20, 1861; died of disease, November 15, 1861, at Camp Wool, Md.

Smith, George H.—Age, 30 years. Enlisted, May 28, 1861, at Dunkirk, to serve three years; mustered in as musician, Co. E, June 20, 1861; discharged, October 6, 1862, near Fort Lyon, Va.

Smith, William H.—Age, 19 years. Enlisted, May 28, 1861, at Dunkirk, to serve three years; mustered in as private, Co. E, June 20, 1861; died of disease, January 1, 1863, at Douglass Hospital, Washington, D.C.

Springer, Horatio S.—Age, 19 years. Enrolled, May 28, 1861, at Dunkirk, to serve three years; mustered in as private, Co. E, June 20, 1861; promoted second lieutenant, Co. C, January 19, 1863; returned to ranks, no date; promoted corporal, February 23, 1863; transferred to Co. E, February 23, 1864; discharged, June 29, 1864. Commissioned, not mustered, second lieutenant, March 12, 1863, with rank from January 19, 1863, vice W.J. Stanton, resigned.

Stafford, Austin—Age, 20 years. Enlisted, June 15, 1861, at Dunkirk, to serve three years; mustered in as private, Co. E, June 20, 1861; wounded and captured in action, May 5, 1862, at Williamsburg, Va.; paroled, no date; re-enlisted as a veteran, December 25, 1863; transferred to Co. H, One Hundred and Twentieth Infantry, June 23, 1864.

Thompson, Michael—Age, 38 years. Enlisted, May 28, 1861, at Dunkirk, to serve three years; mustered in as private, Co. E, June 20, 1861; wounded in action, July 1, 1862, at Malvern Hill, Va.; discharged for wounds, November 15, 1862, at General Hospital, Philadelphia, Pa.

Toomey, William—Age, 32 years. Enrolled, May 16, 1861, at Dunkirk, to serve three years; mustered in as second lieutenant, Co. E, June 20, 1861; as first lieutenant, November 1, 1861; as captain, May 6, 1862; mustered out with company, June 19, 1864, near Petersburg, Va.; also born as Tooney; not commissioned second lieutenant. Commissioned first lieutenant, January 7, 1862, with rank from November 1, 1861, original; captain, July 21, 1862, with rank from July 7, 1862, vice W.J. O'Neill, resigned.

Torrance, George S.—Age, 18 years. Enlisted, May 28, 1861, at Dunkirk, to serve three years; mustered in as private, Co. E, June 20, 1861; wounded in action, August 27, 1862, at Kettle Run, Va.; discharged for disability, July 30, 1863, at Government Insane Hospital, Washington, D.C.

Toulon, Patrick—Age, 19 years. Enlisted, August 12, 1862, at Dunkirk, to serve three years; mustered in as private, Co. E, September 2, 1862; discharged for disability, March 9, 1863, near Falmouth, Va.

Tracey, William, 1st—Age, 28 years. Enlisted, June 15, 1861, at Dunkirk, to serve three years; mustered in as private, Co. E, June 20, 1861; captured in action, May 3, 1863, at Chancellorsville, Va.; paroled, no date; mustered out, January 19, 1864, at New York City.

Tracey, William, 2d—Age, 22 years. Enlisted, May 28, 1861, at Dunkirk, to serve three years; mustered in as private, Co. E, June 20, 1861; died of disease, March 5, 1864, at Brandy Station, Va.

Tweedy, William—Age, 45 years. Enlisted, August 17, 1862, at Dunkirk, to serve three years; mustered in as private, Co. E, September 2, 1862; transferred to Co. C, Thirteenth Veteran Reserve Corps, August 1, 1863, from which discharged, July 1, 1865, at Boston, Mass.

Vanderweel, Leonard—Age, 39 years. Enlisted, August 29, 1862, at Dunkirk, to serve three years; mustered in as private, Co. E, September 2, 1862; wounded in action, July 2, 1863, at Gettysburg, Pa.; discharged for disability, October 14, 1863, at Camp Convalescent.

Walker, Jesse—Age, 19 years. Enlisted, May 28, 1861, at Dunkirk, to serve three years; mustered in as private, Co. E, June 20, 1861: promoted corporal, March 9, 1863; wounded in action, May 3, 1863, at Chancellorsville, Va.; mustered out with company, June 19, 1864, near Petersburg, Va.

Wallace, George W.—Age, 25 years. Enrolled, May 23, 1861, at Dunkirk, to serve three years; mustered in as first sergeant, Co. E, August 8, 1861; promoted second lieutenant, November 1, 1861; discharged, July 1, 1862. Commissioned second lieutenant, January 7, 1862, with rank from November 1, 1861, original.

Webster, James—Age, 19 years. Enlisted, May 16, 1861, at Dunkirk, to serve three years; mustered in as private, Co. E, June 20, 1861; wounded in action, July 1, 1862, at Malvern Hill, Va.; captured in action, May 3, 1863, at Chancellorsville, Va.;

paroled, no date; transferred to Co. G, February 12, 1864; re-enlisted as a veteran, February 13, 1864; transferred to Co. I, One Hundred and Twentieth Infantry, July 24, 1864; also born as William C. Webster and Clark Webster.

Wertner, Baldas—Age, 38 years. Enlisted, August 24, 1862, at Dunkirk, to serve three years; mustered in as private, Co. E. September 2, 1862; wounded in action, May 3, 1863, at Chancellorsville, Va.; transferred to Co. H, One Hundred and Twentieth Infantry, June 23, 1864.

Wertner, Martin—Age, 40 years. Enlisted, August 22, 1862, at Dunkirk, to serve three years; mustered in as private, Co. E, September 2, 1862; transferred to Co. H, One Hundred and Twentieth Infantry, June 23, 1864.

Wilbur, Charles I.—Age, 22 years. Enlisted, May 28, 1861, at Dunkirk, to serve three years; mustered in as private, Co. E, June 20, 1861; mustered out with company, June 19, 1864, near Petersburg, Va.

Wilbur, James—Age, 22 years. Enlisted, May 28, 1861, at Dunkirk, to serve three years; mustered in as private, Co. E, June 20, 1861; wounded in action, May 5, 1862, at Williamsburg, Va.; died of his wounds, June 4, 1862, at Fort Monroe, Va.

Wilcox, Enoch—Age, 25 years. Enlisted, May 28, 1861, at Dunkirk, to serve three years; mustered in as private, Co. E, June 20, 1861; mustered out with company, June 19, 1864, near Petersburg, Va.

Wilcox, Horace W.—Age, 37 years. Enlisted, September 16, 1862, at Dunkirk, to serve three years; mustered in as private, Co. E, September 20, 1862; captured in action, May 3, 1863, at Chancellorsville, Va.; deserted, June 22, 1863, at Camp Parole, Annapolis, Md.

Winter, Theodore—Age, 39 years. Enlisted, August 23, 1862, at Dunkirk, to serve three years; mustered in as private, Co. E, September 2, 1862; wounded in action, July 2, 1863, at Gettysburg, Pa.; transferred to Co. H, One Hundred and Twentieth Infantry, June 23, 1864.

Wycoff, James—Age, 30 years. Enlisted, June 15, 1861, at Dunkirk, to serve three years; mustered in as private, Co. E, June 20, 1861; died of disease, July 22, 1862, at Harrisons Landing, Va.; also born as Joseph Wyckoff.

Company F

Organized in Newark, New Jersey, in May 1861. Mustered into the United States service June 21, 1861.

Captains

John Leonard, from June 21, 1861, to September 8, 1862. John H. Howard, from September 8, 1862, to January 7, 1863. William McConnell, from January 26 to June 20, 1864.

First Lieutenants

Henry J. McConnell, from June 21, 1861, to January 2, 1862. John W. Holmes, from January 2 to July 2, 1862. William C. Brooks, from November 1, 1863, to May 3, 1863 (killed in action). John S. Mann, from January 1 to April 2, 1863. Henry C. Steward, from May 1 to November 1, 1863. Prentice Elijah Bishop, from November 1 to December 26, 1863.

Second Lieutenants

John W. Holmes, from June 21, 1861, to January 2, 1862. Berend Huttmann, from January 3 to June 23, 1862. William E. Wheeler, from June 23 to September 26, 1862. Michael Cooke, from September 26 to October 31, 1862. Richard Leonard, from January 1 to February 11, 1863. Horatio S. Springer, from January 19 to July 7, 1863. John B. Hare, from September 11 to November 1, 1863. Luke Healy, from November 1863, to June 20, 1864.

Anderson, James—Age, 21 years. Enlisted at Staten Island, to serve three years, and mustered in as private, Co. F, June 21, 1861; promoted corporal, no date; sergeant, May 20, 1863; wounded in action, November 27, 1863, at One-Mile Run, Va., and June 19, 1864, near Petersburg, Va.; absent, wounded at muster-out of company.

Bagley, Peter—Age, 23 years. Enlisted, May 27, 1861, at Newark, N.J., to serve three years; mustered in as private, Co. F, June 21, 1861; re-enlisted as a veteran, February 14, 1864; transferred to Co. F, One Hundred and Twentieth Infantry, June 23, 1864.

Barner, James—Age, 30 years. Enlisted, June 11, 1861, at Newark, N.J., to serve three years; mustered in as private, Co. F, June 21, 1861; wounded in action, July 1, 1862, at Malvern Hill, Va.; discharged for disability, September 25, 1862, at Philadelphia, Pa.

Bartlett, Jr., Daniel—Age, 24 years. Enlisted at Staten Island, to serve three years, and mustered in as private, Co. F, June 21, 1861; discharged for disability, August 7, 1862, at Fort McHenry, Md.

Bernhardt, Zachary—Age, 19 years. Enlisted at Oyster Bay, to serve three years, and mustered in as private, Co. F, August 20, 1862; deserted, January 18, 1863, at Falmouth, Va.; also born as Barnard.

Bowles, John—Age, 33 years. Enlisted at Staten Island, to serve three years, and mustered in as private, Co. F, June 21, 1861; deserted, July 10, 1861, from Camp Scott, Staten Island.

Boyne, John—Age, 24 years. Enlisted at Staten Island, to serve three years, and mustered in as private, Co. F, June 21, 1861; deserted, July 6, 1861, from Camp Scott, Staten Island.

Bradley, Philip—Age, 36 years. Enlisted, June 10, 1861, at Newark, N.J., to serve three years; mustered in as private, Co. F, June 21, 1861; discharged, September 26, 1861, at Camp Caldwell, Md.

Brown, Abraham—Age, 36 years. Enlisted, May 27, 1861, at Newark, N.J., to serve three years; mustered in as private, Co. F, June 21, 1861; discharged for disability, December 22, 1862, at Fairfax Seminary, Va.

Campbell, John—Age, 45 years. Enlisted at Staten Island, to serve three years, and mustered in as private, Co. F, June 21, 1861; deserted, July 10, 1861, at Camp Scott, Staten Island.

Carroll, James—Age, 21 years. Enlisted, June 3, 1861, at Newark, N.J., to serve three years; mustered in as private, Co. F, June 21, 1861; promoted corporal in May 1863; wounded in action, June 16, 1864, at Petersburg, Va.; absent in hospital at muster-out of company.

Clark, John—Age, 29 years. Enlisted at New York City, to serve three years, and mustered in as private, Co. F, September 10, 1861; wounded in action, May 23, 1864, at North Anna River, Va.; transferred to Co. F, One Hundred and Twentieth Infantry, June 23, 1864.

Clauson, William—Age, 21 years. Enlisted, June 3, 1861, at Newark, N.J., to serve three years; mustered in as private, Co. F, June 21, 1861; wounded in action, June 25, 1862, near Fair Oaks, Va.; discharged for his wounds, August 16, 1862, at Philadelphia, Pa.

Clements, Henry—Age, 38 years. Enlisted, May 8, 1861, at Newark, N.J., to serve three years; mustered in as private, Co. F, June 21, 1861; discharged for disability, October 13, 1862, at New York City.

Coe, Edward—Age, 27 years. Enlisted, June 19, 1861, at Newark, N.J., to serve three years; mustered in as private, Co. F, June 21, 1861; discharged for disability, May 2, 1864.

Cookerov, Peter—Age, 27 years. Enlisted, June 1, 1861, at Newark, N.J., to serve three years; mustered in as private, Co. F, June 21, 1861; captured in action, July 23, 1863, at Wapping Heights, Va.; died of disease while a prisoner of war, March 8, 1864, at Richmond, Va.; also born as Cookrean.

Costello, James—Age, 27 years. Enlisted, September 6, 1862, at New York City, to serve three years; mustered in as private, Co. F, September 21, 1862; wounded in action, May 6, 1864, at Wilderness, Va.; transferred to Co. F, One Hundred and Twentieth Infantry, June 23, 1864.

Coyle, James—Age, 33 years. Enlisted, August 28, 1862, at Dunkirk, to serve three years; mustered in as private, Co. F, October 2, 1862; wounded in action, July 2, 1863, at Gettysburg, Pa.; dishonorably discharged by general court martial, General Order No. 4, Second Division, Third Army Corp, January 25, 1864.

Daley, Thomas—Age, 23 years. Enlisted, January 7, 1862, at New York City, to serve three years; mustered in as private, Co. F, February 28, 1862; re-enlisted as a veteran, December 21, 1863; deserted, January 1, 1864.

Delisle, Daniel H.—Age, 42 years. Enlisted, November 18, 1861, at Sinclairville, to serve three years; mustered in as sergeant, Co. L, December 3, 1861; transferred to Co. A, February 25, 1862; to Co. F, First Regiment, Veteran Reserve Corps, February 6, 1864.

Donnelly, Patrick—Age, 27 years. Enlisted, April 17, 1861, at Newark, N.J., to serve three years;, mustered in as private, Co. F, June 21, 1861; discharged for disability, November 1, 1862; also born as Donely; subsequent service in Co. E, Eighteenth Cavalry, as Patrick Dunley.

Doremus, Thomas I.—Age, 36 years. Enlisted, June 19, 1861, at Newark, N.J., to serve three years; mustered in as private, Co. F, June 21, 1861; re-enlisted as a veteran, December 21, 1863; transferred to Co. F, One Hundred and Twentieth Infantry, June 23, 1864.

Dougherty, Daniel—Age, 22 years. Enlisted, June 8, 1861, at Newark, N.J., to serve three years; mustered in as corporal, Co. F, June 21, 1861; returned to ranks, in June 1861; killed in action, May 5, 1862, at Williamsburg, Va.

Doyle, John—Age, 34 years. Enlisted at New York City, to serve three years, and mustered in as private, Co. F, September 6, 1861; deserted, no date, from hospital, New York City; also born as John Boyle.

Duffie, John—Age, 37 years. Enlisted, May 27, 1861, at Newark, N.J., to serve three years; mustered in as private, Co. F, June 21, 1861; killed in action, May 5, 1862, at Williamsburg, Va.

Dunn, John—Age, 35 years. Enlisted, June 3, 1861, at Newark, N.J., to serve three years; mustered in as private, Co. F, June 21, 1861; wounded in action, May 5, 1862, at Williamsburg, Va.; transferred to Veteran Reserve Corps, September 30, 1863.

Dunphry, John—Age, 19 years. Enlisted, June 3,

1861, at Newark, N.J., to serve three years; mustered in as private, Co. F, June 21, 1861; wounded in action, July 1, 1862, at Malvern Hill, Va.; deserted in November 1862, from hospital at Newark, N.J.; also born as Humphrey.

Durie, James—Age, 27 years. Enlisted, May 23, 1861, at Newark, N.J., to serve three years; mustered in as private, Co. F, June 21, 1861; discharged for disability, May 3, 1864, at Alexandria, Va.; also born as Dwyer and Duire.

Everett, William—Age, 27 years. Enlisted at Staten Island, to serve three years, and mustered in as private, Co. F, June 21, 1861; deserted, June 23, 1861, from camp, at Staten Island, N.Y.

Farley, James—Age, 83 years. Enlisted, May 17, 1861, at Newark, N.J., to serve three years; mustered in as private, Co. F, June 21, 1861; wounded in action, July 1, 1862, at Malvern Hill, Va.; died of his wounds, September 21, 1862, at Bellevue Hospital, New York City.

Farrell, Philip—Age, 29 years. Enlisted, April 25, 1861, at Newark, N.J., to serve three years; mustered in as private, Co. F, June 21, 1861; re-enlisted as a veteran, December 10, 1863; transferred to Co. F, One Hundred and Twentieth Infantry, June 23, 1864; also born as Patrick Farrell.

Finegan, Thomas—Age, 40 years. Enlisted, May 23, 1861, at Newark, N.J., to serve three years; mustered in as private, Co. F, June 21, 1861; wounded in action, July 23, 1863, at Wapping Heights, Va.; discharged for disability, July 2, 1864, at New York City.

Fitzpatrick, Patrick—Age, 21 years. Enlisted at Staten Island, to serve three years; mustered in as corporal, Co. F, June 21, 1861; deserted, June 28, 1861, at Staten Island, N.Y.

Fox, John—Age, 28 years. Enlisted at New York City, to serve three years, and mustered in as private, Co. F, September 10, 1861; captured in action, May 5, 1862, at Williamsburg, Va.; paroled, no date; discharged, May 28, 1862, at Washington, D.C.

Fox, William—Age, 22 years. Enlisted, June 19, 1861, at Newark, N.J., to serve three years; mustered in as private, Co. F, June 21, 1861; discharged for disability, March 13, 1862, at Camp Wool, Md.

Gaffeney, Owen—Age, 20 years. Enlisted at Newark, N.J., to serve three years, and mustered in as private, Co. F, September 9, 1861; killed in action, June 19, 1864, at Petersburg, Va.

Gardner, Samuel—Age, 24 years. Enlisted, June 1, 1861, at Newark, N.J., to serve three years; mustered in as private, Co. F, June 21, 1861; promoted corporal, October 1, 1861; sergeant, May 12, 1862; wounded in action, July 1, 1862, at Malvern Hill, Va., and May 6, 1864, at Wilderness, Va.; mustered out, to date June 20, 1864, at New York City.

Garity, Daniel—Age, 36 years. Enlisted, April 18, 1861, at Newark, N.J., to serve three years; mustered in as private, Co. F, June 21, 1861; promoted corporal, November 1, 1861; sergeant, June 27, 1862; discharged for disability, January 26, 1863, at Convalescent Camp, Va.

Gorges, William—Age, 10 years. Enlisted, April 24, 1861, at Newark, N.J., to serve three years; mustered in as musician, Co. F, June 21, 1861; re-enlisted as a veteran, December 23, 1863; transferred to Co. F, One Hundred and Twentieth Infantry, June 23, 1864.

Hall, Benjamin—Age, — years. Enlisted at New York City, to serve three years, and mustered in as private, Co. F, August 16, 1862; died of disease, November 5, 1862, at Third Army Corps Hospital.

Hammell, Robert—Age, 28 years. Enlisted, April 23, 1861, at Newark, N.J., to serve three years; mustered in as corporal, Co. F, June 21, 1861; discharged for disability, March 18, 1862, at Camp Wool, Md.; also born as Hamill.

Havy, James—Age, 29 years. Enlisted at New York City, to serve three years, and mustered in as private, Co. F, November 25, 1861; promoted corporal, no date; sergeant, January 1863; transferred to Co. F, One Hundred and Twentieth Infantry, June 23, 1864; also born as Heavy.

Healy, Luke—Age, 20 years. Enrolled, April 22, 1861, at Newark, N.J., to serve three years; mustered in as private, Co. F, June 21, 1861; promoted corporal, August 1, 1861; sergeant, May 6, 1862; first sergeant, November 1, 1862; mustered in as second lieutenant, Co. G, May 10, 1863; transferred to Co. F, November 1863; mustered out with company, June 20, 1864, near Petersburg, Va. Commissioned second lieutenant, August 7, 1863, with rank from May 10, 1863, vice H.J. Yates, promoted.

Hereon, William H.—Age, 23 years. Enlisted at Staten Island, to serve three years, and mustered in as private, Co. F, June 21, 1861; deserted, July 13, 1861, from Camp Staten Island, N.Y.

Holmes, John H.—Age, 32 years. Enrolled, June 14, 1861, at Newark, N.J., to serve three years; mustered in as second lieutenant, Co. F, June 21, 1861; promoted first lieutenant, January 2, 1862; mustered in as captain, Co. H, July 2, 1862; wounded in action, May 3, 1863, at Chancellorsville, Va.; transferred to Co. C, June 1, 1864; mustered out with company, July 20, 1864, near Petersburg, Va. Commissioned second lieutenant, January 7, 1862, with rank from June 21, 1861, original; first lieutenant, January 17, 1862, with rank from January 2, 1862, vice H.J. McConnell, resigned; captain, July 21, 1862, with rank from July 2, 1862, vice Stephen M. Doyle, killed in action.

Hudson, Joseph—Age, 32 years. Enlisted, June 7, 1861, at Newark, N.J., to serve three years; mustered in as private, Co. F, June 21, 1861; captured in action, May 5, 1862, at Williamsburg, Va.; paroled, no date; died, no date, at Fort Hamilton, New York Harbor.

Jones, William H.—Age, 10 years. Enlisted, June 3, 1861, at Newark, N.J., to serve three years; mustered in as private, Co. F, June 21, 1861; mustered out with company, June 20, 1864, near Petersburg, Va.

Keller, John—Age, 29 years. Enlisted at Newark, N.J., to serve three years, and mustered in as private, Co. F, June 21, 1861; no record subsequent to June 30, 1861.

Kelley, Patrick—Age, 30 years. Enlisted, June 16, 1861, at Newark, N.J., to serve three years; mustered in as private, Co. F, June 21, 1861; wounded in action, June 16, 1864, at Petersburg, Va.; mustered out, to date June 30, 1864.

Kennedy, William—Age, 40 years. Enlisted at Staten Island, to serve three years, and mustered in as private, Co. F, June 21, 1861; deserted, July 16, 1861, from camp, at Staten Island, N.Y.

King, James—Age, 33 years. Enlisted, April 25, 1861, at Newark, N.J., to serve three years; mustered in as private, Co. F, June 21, 1861; mustered out with company, June 20, 1864, near Petersburg, Va.

Lacy, Bernard—Age, 21 years. Enlisted at Staten Island, to serve three years, and mustered in as private, Co. F, June 21, 1861; deserted, July 15, 1861, at Staten Island, N.Y.

Lavy, Patrick—Age, 28 years. Enlisted, June 17, 1861, at Newark, N.J., to serve three years; mustered in as private, Co. F, June 21, 1861; died, January 15, 1863, in camp near Falmouth, Va.

Leonard, John—Age, 28 years. Enrolled, April 15, 1861, at Newark, N.J., to serve three years; mustered in as captain, Co. F, June 21, 1861; as major, September 8, 1862; as lieutenant-colonel, May 4, 1863; mustered out with regiment, June 19, 1864, near Petersburg, Va. Commissioned captain, January 7, 1862, with rank from June 21, 1861, original; major, December 1, 1862, with rank from October 25, 1862, vice W.O. Stevens, promoted; lieutenant-colonel, August 7, 1863, with rank from May 4, 1863, vice J.S. Austin, promoted.

Leonard, Richard—Age, 22 years. Enrolled, April 24, 1861, at Newark, N.J., to serve three years; mustered in as corporal, Co. F, June 21, 1861; promoted sergeant, July 7, 1861; first sergeant, June 27, 1862; second lieutenant, Co. D, November 1, 1862; transferred to Co. F, January 1, 1863; discharged, February 11, 1863. Commissioned second lieutenant, October 6, 1863, with rank from October 31, 1862, vice W.C. Brooks, promoted.

Linc, Andrew—Age, 27 years. Enlisted at New York City, to serve three years, and mustered in as private, Co. F, August 18, 1862; wounded in action, May 3, 1863, at Chancellorsville, Va.; transferred to Co. F, One Hundred and Twentieth Infantry, June 23, 1864.

Lynch, Patrick—Age, 27 years. Enlisted, May 25, 1861, at Newark, N.J., to serve three years; mustered in as private, Co. F, June 21, 1861; wounded in action, May 5, 1862, at Williamsburg, Va.; transferred to Veteran Reserve Corps, January 27, 1864.

Mahony, John—Age, 28 years. Enlisted, September 8, 1862, at New York City, to serve three years; mustered in as private, Co. I, September 16, 1862; transferred to One Hundred and Second Company, Veteran Reserve Corps, December 14, 1863; died, January 1, 1864, at U.S. Hospital.

Mann, John S.—Age, 28 years. Enrolled, May 23, 1861, at Newark, N.J., to serve three years; mustered in as sergeant, Co. F, June 21, 1861; promoted first sergeant, December 7, 1861; sergeant-major, May 6, 1862; mustered in as second lieutenant, Co. A, May 17, 1862; as first lieutenant, August 5, 1862; transferred to Co. D, November 1, 1862; to Co. F, January 1, 1863; wounded in action, July 2, 1863, at Gettysburg, Pa.; mustered in as captain, Co. C, November 14, 1863; transferred to Co. H, June 1, 1864; mustered out with company, October 31, 1864, near Petersburg, Va. Commissioned second lieutenant, June 30, 1862, with rank from June 3, 1862, vice E.B. Harnett, promoted; first lieutenant, December 1, 1862, with rank from August 5, 1862, vice J.H. Howard, promoted; captain, September 5, 1863, with rank from April 2, 1863, vice T. Clark, discharged.

Marshall, James—Age, 25 years. Enlisted at New York City, to serve three years, and mustered in as private, Co. F, August 18, 1862; wounded in action, July 2, 1863, at Gettysburg, Pa.; transferred to Co. F, One Hundred and Twentieth Infantry, June 23, 1864, from which mustered out with detachment, June 28, 1865.

McCann, William—Age, 44 years. Enlisted, June 11, 1861, at Newark, N.J., to serve three years; mustered in as private, Co. F, June 21, 1861; killed in action, May 5, 1862, at Williamsburg, Va.

McCauley, James—Age, 36 years. Enlisted, July 24, 1861, at Staten Island, to serve three years; mustered in as private, Co. F, August 8, 1861; wounded in action, July 1, 1862, at Malvern Hill, Va.; no further record.

McConnell, Henry J.—Age, 31 years. Enrolled, April 19, 1861, at Newark, N.J., to serve three years; mustered in as first lieutenant, Co. F, June 21, 1861; discharged, January 2, 1862. Commissioned first lieutenant, January 7, 1862, with rank from June 21, 1861, original.

McCormick, John—Age, 29 years. Enlisted, May 21, 1861, at Newark, N.J., to serve three years; mustered in as private, Co. F, June 21, 1861; deserted, January 23, 1863, from camp, near Falmouth, Va.

McCormick, John T.—Age, 20 years. Enlisted, April 24, 1861, at Newark, N.J., to serve three years; mustered in as private, Co. F, June 21, 1861; killed in action, July 1, 1862, at Malvern Hill, Va.

McDonough, Henry J.—Age, 28 years. Enrolled, May 23, 1861, at Newark, N.J., to serve three years; mustered in as first sergeant, Co. F, June 21, 1861; promoted sergeant-major, June 23, 1862; mustered in as second lieutenant, Co. I, July 2, 1862; as first lieutenant, Co. I, October 25, 1862; transferred to Co. A in November 1862; mustered in as captain, Co. D, October 28, 1863; died of wounds, November 27, 1863, at Military Hospital, Brandy Station, Va. Commissioned second lieutenant, July 21, 1862, with rank from July 2, 1862, vice William H. Post, promoted; first lieutenant, December 1, 1862, with rank from October 30, 1862, vice J.A. Smith, appointed adjutant; captain, October 6, 1863, with rank from July 30, 1863, vice J.P. Sanford, resigned.

McEnroe, Nicholas—Age, 23 years. Enlisted, May 31, 1861, at Newark, N.J., to serve three years; mustered in as private, Co. F, June 21, 1861; captured in action, May 5, 1862, at Williamsburg, Va.; paroled, no date; re-enlisted as a veteran, December 21, 1863; wounded in action, May 6, 1864, at Wilderness, Va.; transferred to Co. F, One Hundred and Twentieth Infantry, June 23, 1864.

McGill, Daniel—Age, 33 years. Enlisted at Staten Island, to serve three years, and mustered in as private, Co. F, June 21, 1861; mustered out with company, June 20, 1864, near Petersburg, Va.

McGinity, Michael—Age, 40 years. Enlisted at Newark, N.J., to serve three years, and mustered in as private. Co. F, September 9, 1861; re-enlisted as a veteran, December 21, 1863; transferred to Co. F, One Hundred and Twentieth Infantry, June 23, 1864.

McRay, Nathan—Age, 32 years. Enlisted, May 26, 1861, at Newark, N.J., to serve three years; mustered in as private, Co. F, June 21, 1861; captured in action, May 10, 1864, at Landron's Farm, Va.; paroled, April 10, 1865; mustered out with detachment, July 6, 1865, at New York City; also born as McRae.

Megill, Williams C.—Age, 16 years. Enlisted, April 24, 1861, at Newark, N.J., to serve three years; mustered in as musician, Co. F, June 21, 1861; mustered out with company, June 20, 1864, near Petersburg, Va.; also born as Magill.

Moore, Edward—Age, 26 years. Enlisted, June 10, 1861, at Newark, N.J., to serve three years; mustered in as private, Co. F, June 21, 1861; wounded in action, July 1, 1862, at Malvern Hill, Va.; mustered out with company, June 20, 1864, near Petersburg, Va.

Murphy, John—Age, 43 years. Enlisted, April 23, 1861, at Newark, N.J., to serve three years; mustered in as private, Co. F, June 21, 1861; wounded in action, May 5, 1862, at Williamsburg, Va.; re-enlisted as a veteran, December 21, 1863; transferred to Co. F, One Hundred and Twentieth Infantry, June 23, 1864.

Murtha, John—Age, 40 years. Enlisted at Staten Island, to serve three years, and mustered in as private, Co. F, June 21, 1861; mustered out with company, June 20, 1864, near Petersburg, Va.

Myers, Cassy—Age, 36 years. Enlisted, May 20, 1861, at Newark, N.J., to serve three years; mustered in as private, Co. F, June 21, 1861; wounded in action, May 5, 1862, at Williamsburg, Va.; discharged for disability, February 12, 1863, at Fortress Monroe, Va.

Myers, Christian—Age, 38 years. Enlisted, May 26, 1861, at Newark, N.J., to serve three years; mustered in as private, Co. F, June 21, 1861; wounded in action, May 5, 1862, at Williamsburg, Va.; died, October 19, 1862, at Washington, D.C.

O'Brien, Patrick—Age, 23 years. Enlisted, April 13, 1861, at Newark, N.J., to serve three years; mustered in as sergeant, Co. F, June 21, 1861; discharged for disability, March 18, 1862, at Camp Wool, Md.

O'Grady, John—Age, 25 years. Enlisted, June 4, 1861, at Newark, N.J., to serve three years; mustered in as private, Co. F, June 21, 1861; deserted, January 18, 1863, at Camp Nelson Taylor, Va.

O'Meara, Patrick—Age, 27 years. Enlisted at Newark, N.J., to serve three years, and mustered in as private, Co. F, September 9, 1861; transferred to Co. F, One Hundred and Twentieth Infantry, June 23, 1864.

Parsons, Henry S.—Age, 29 years. Enlisted, August 12, 1862, at New York City, to serve three years; mustered in as private, Co. F, August 13, 1862; promoted corporal in May 1863; transferred to Co. F, One Hundred and Twentieth Infantry, June 23, 1864.

Powderly, Patrick—Age, 24 years. Enlisted at Staten Island, to serve three years, and mustered in as private, Co. F, June 21, 1861; deserted, July 2, 1861, at Staten Island, N.Y.

Powell, Thomas—Age, 50 years. Enlisted at New York City, to serve three years, and mustered in as private, Co. F, October 2, 1862; transferred to Veteran Reserve Corps, January 15, 1864, from which mustered out, July 22, 1865.

Quintin, Adolphus—Age, 34 years. Enlisted, June 3, 1861, at Newark, N.J., to serve three years; mustered in as private, Co. F, June 21, 1861; wounded in action, May 3, 1863, at Chancellorsville, Va.; mustered out with company, June 20, 1864, near Petersburg, Va.

Reitmiller, George—Age, 34 years. Enlisted, August 9, 1862, at New York City, to serve three years; mustered in as private, Co. F, August 12, 1862; wounded in action, July 2, 1863, at Gettysburg, Pa.; transferred to Co. F, One Hundred and Twentieth Infantry, June 23, 1864.

Renshoeler, Michael—Age, 21 years. Enlisted, April 25, 1861, at Newark, N.J., to serve three years; mustered in as private, Co. F, June 21, 1861; deserted, August 25, 1862, from hospital, Philadelphia, Pa.; also born as Ranseller.

Rudden, Henry—Age, 25 years. Enlisted at Staten Island, to serve three years, and mustered in as private, Co. F, June 21, 1861; deserted, July 1, 1861, from camp, Staten Island, N.Y.

Seaman, Philip—Age, 30 years. Enlisted, May 27, 1861, at Newark, N.J., to serve three years; mustered in as private, Co. F, June 21, 1861; promoted corporal, November 1, 1862; reported absent, sick in hospital, at muster-out of company.

Shaffery, Michael—Age, 20 years. Enlisted at Newark, N.J., to serve three years, and mustered in as private, Co. F, September 9, 1861; deserted, June 19, 1863, at Centreville, Va.

Shelley, John—Age, 21 years. Enlisted, May 27, 1861, at Newark, N.J., to serve three years; mustered in as private, Co. F, June 21, 1861; wounded in action, June 25, 1862, near Fair Oaks, and May 10, 1864, at Spotsylvania, Va.; absent, in hospital, at Washington, D.C., at muster-out of company.

Sheridan, John—Age, 25 years. Enlisted at New York City, to serve three years, and mustered in as private, Co. F, December 4, 1863; transferred to Co. F, One Hundred and Twentieth Infantry, June 23, 1864.

Skelley, Patrick—Age, 24 years. Enlisted at Newark, N.J., to serve three years, and mustered in as private, Co. F, June 21, 1861; no further record.

Sperbeck, Benjamin—Age, 22 years. Enlisted at New York City, to serve three years, and mustered in as private, Co. F, November 30, 1863; transferred to Co. F, One Hundred and Twentieth Infantry, June 23, 1864.

Stratton, Thomas—Age, 35 years. Enlisted, May 28, 1861, at Newark, N.J., to serve three years; mustered in as private, Co. F, June 21, 1861; killed in action, July 1, 1862, at Malvern Hill, Va.

Sutton, Wesley—Age, 21 years. Enlisted at Staten Island, to serve three years, and mustered in as private, Co. F, June 21, 1861; wounded in action, July 1, 1862, at Malvern Hill, Va.; August 27, 1862, at Bristoe Station, Va.; captured in action. May 6, 1864, at the Wilderness, Va.; paroled, April 29, 1865, at Jacksonville, Florida; mustered out, July 1, 1865, at New York City.

Taylor, Charles—Age, 37 years. Enlisted at Staten Island, to serve three years, and mustered in as private, Co. F, June 21, 1861; deserted, July 1, 1861, at Staten Island, N.Y.

Tormy, Patrick—Age, 22 years. Enlisted, April 15, 1861, at Newark, N.J., to serve three years; mustered in as sergeant, Co. F, June 21, 1861; deserted, July 5, 1861, from camp, Staten Island, New York.

Tormy, Walter—Age, 32 years. Enlisted, April 15, 1861, at Newark, N.J., to serve three years; mustered in as sergeant, Co. F, June 21, 1861; killed in action, May 5, 1862, at Williamsburg, Va.

Torpey, Thomas—Age, 22 years. Enlisted at Newark, N.J., to serve three years, and mustered in as private, Co. F, September 9, 1861; re-enlisted as a veteran, December 24, 1863; transferred to Co. F, One Hundred and Twentieth Infantry, June 23, 1864.

Tracy, James F.—Age, 21 years. Enlisted, May 21, 1861, at Newark, N.J., to serve three years; mustered in as wagoner, Co. F, June 21, 1861; mustered out with company, June 20, 1864, near Petersburg, Va.

Trimmer, Jacob—Age, 19 years. Enlisted, June 3, 1861, at Newark, N.J., to serve three years; mustered in as private, Co. F, June 21, 1861; wounded in action, June 25, 1862, near Fair Oaks, Va.; discharged for disability, September 27, 1862, at camp near Alexandria, Va.

Wade, Edward—Age, 22 years. Enlisted, May 21, 1861, at Newark, N.J., to serve three years; mustered in as private, Co. F, June 21, 1861; discharged for disability, August 29, 1862, at Fort McHenry, Md.

Wade, Samuel—Age, 27 years. Enlisted, July 24, 1861, at Staten Island, to serve three years; mustered in as private, Co. F, August 8, 1861; promoted corporal, August 10, 1861; discharged for disability, March 17, 1862, at Camp Wool, Md.

Walker, Charles W.—Enlisted at New York City, to serve three years, and mustered in as private, Co. F, September 17, 1862; deserted, November 2, 1862, on march, from Alexandria to Warrenton Junction, Va.

Walpole, Joseph S.—Age, 23 years. Enlisted, May 27, 1861, at Newark, N.J., to serve three years; mustered in as corporal, Co. F, June 21, 1861; promoted sergeant, March 1862; killed in action, May 5, 1862, at Williamsburg, Va.

Welch, Patrick—Age, 18 years. Enlisted, June 3, 1861, at Newark, N.J., to serve three years; mustered in as private, Co. F, June 21, 1861; wounded in action, May 19, 1864, at Petersburg, Va.; died of his wounds, October 24, 1864, at City Point, Va.; also born as Walsh.

Welsh, James S.—Age, 27 years. Enlisted, August 14, 1862, at New York City, to serve three years; mustered in as private, Co. F, August 15, 1862; promoted corporal, March 1, 1863; transferred to Co. F, One Hundred and Twentieth Infantry, June 23, 1864; also born as James S. Walsh.

Williams, Robert—Age, 32 years. Enlisted, June 8, 1861, at Staten Island, to serve three years; mustered in as corporal, Co. F, June 21, 1861; deserted, June 26, 1861, from camp, Staten Island, New York.

Williams, Samuel—Age, 22 years. Enlisted, April 17, 1861, at Newark, N.J., to serve three years; mustered in as private, Co. F, June 21, 1861; wounded in action, August 27, 1862, at Bristoe Station, Va.; discharged for disability, January 18, 1863, at Camp Nelson Taylor, Va.

Company G

Organized in Westfield, N.Y., in July 1861. Mustered into the United States service July 24, 1861.

Captains

Harmon J. Bliss, from July 23, 1861, to June 6, 1863.
Patrick Anderson, from June 7 to August 17, 1863.
William E. Wheeler, from August 1863 to August 23, 1864.

First Lieutenants

Collins Warren Bliss, from July 23, 1861, to May 17, 1862.
James Fogarty, from June 23 to November 1, 1862.
William H. Post, from July 2, 1862, to January 7, 1863.
Alexander M. Clark, from November 1862 to June 24, 1863.
Henry Jones Yates, from July 1, 1863, to March 1, 1864.

Second Lieutenants

James A. Smith, from July 23, 1861, to May 17, 1862.
William McGinnis, from June 2 to November 1, 1862.
Alexander M. Clark, from November to May 10, 1863.
Luke Healy, from May 10 to November 1863.
John B. Hare, from November 1, 1863, to January 13, 1864.
John Robinson, from March 1 to July 23, 1864.

Allen, Charles—Age, 23 years. Enlisted at Dunkirk, to serve three years, and mustered in as private, Co. G, August 25, 1862; promoted corporal, December 18, 1862; discharged for disability, April 26, 1864, at Brandy Station, Va.

Angwood, John—Age, 36 years. Enlisted at Silver Creek, to serve three years, and mustered in as private, Co. G, September 8, 1862; mustered out, May 27, 1865, at Washington, D.C.

Arnold, Daniele—Age, 21 years. Enlisted, May 28, 1861, at Westfield, to serve three years; mustered in as private, Co. G, July 23, 1861; wounded in action, May 5, 1862, at Williamsburg, Va.; discharged for disability, May 14, 1863, at Buffalo, N.Y.

Aular, George W.—Age, 28 years. Enlisted, August 30, 1862, at Dunkirk, to serve three years; mustered in as private, Co. G, September 8, 1862; transferred to Co. I, One Hundred and Twentieth Infantry, July 24, 1864.

Backus, William—Age, 19 years. Enlisted, July 17, 1861, at Westfield, to serve three years; mustered in as private, Co. G, July 23, 1861; wounded in action, May 5, 1862, at Williamsburg, Va.; discharged for his wounds, October 29, 1862, at Fort McHenry, Md.; also born as Bacus.

Bacon, Milton S.—Age, 22 years. Enlisted, July 17, 1861, at Westfield, to serve three years; mustered in as private, Co. G, July 23, 1861; promoted corporal, September 14, 1863; reenlisted as a veteran, December 21, 1863; killed in action, May 23, 1864, at North Anna River, Va.

Baker, James T.—Age, 20 years. Enlisted, July 17, 1861, at Westfield, to serve three years; mustered in as private, Co. G, July 23, 1861; transferred to Co. B in July 1861; wounded in action, July 1, 1862, at Malvern Hill, Va.; discharged for his wounds, August 25, 1862, at Philadelphia, Pa.

Baker, John Jr.,—Age, 22 years. Enlisted, July 17, 1861, at Westfield, to serve three years; mustered in as corporal, Co. G, July 23, 1861; returned to ranks, October 1, 1861; captured in action, May 5, 1862, at Williamsburg, Va.; paroled, no date; also May 3, 1863, at Chancellorsville, Va.; paroled, October 9, 1863: re-enlisted as a veteran, December 21, 1863; deserted, September 3, 1864, at Rochester, N.Y.

Barrows, Alvin E.—Age, 18 years. Enlisted, May 28, 1861, at Westfield, to serve three years; mustered in as private, Co. G, July 23, 1861; wounded in action, June 25, 1862, at Oak Grove, Va.; promoted corporal, July 23, 1862; captured in action, May 3, 1863, at Chancellorsville, Va.; returned, October 9, 1863; re-enlisted as a veteran, December 21, 1863; transferred to Co. I, One Hundred and Twentieth Infantry, July 23, 1864.

Barry, Dallas—Age, 18 years. Enlisted at Westfield, to serve three years, and mustered in as private, Co. G, August 7, 1862; wounded in action, May 3, 1863, at Chancellorsville, Va.; transferred to Co. I, One Hundred and Twentieth Infantry, July 24, 1864.

Bennett, Charles W.—Age, 18 years. Enlisted at Westfield, to serve three years, and mustered in as private, Co. G, August 7, 1861; died of disease, November 11, 1861, at Good Hope Hospital, Washington, D.C.

Benson, Clinton M.—Age, 34 years. Enlisted, September 11, 1862, at Dunkirk, to serve three years; mustered in as private, Co. G, September 20, 1862; transferred to Co. I, One Hundred and Twentieth Infantry, July 24, 1864.

Bliss, Collins Warren—Age, 23 years. Enrolled, May 28, 1861, at Westfield, to serve three years; mustered in as first lieutenant, Co. G, July 23, 1861; discharged, May 17, 1862. Commissioned first lieutenant, January 7, 1862, with rank from July 24, 1861, original.

Bliss, Franklin—Age, 18 years. Enlisted, August 3, 1861, at Westfield, to serve three years; mustered in as private, Co. G, August 7, 1861; appointed musician, September 1, 1861; discharged for disability, March 17, 1862, at Camp Wool, Md.

Bliss, Harmon J. Age, 30 years. Enrolled, May 28, 1861, at Westfield, to serve three years; mustered in as captain, Co. G, July 23, 1861; wounded in action, May 3, 1863, at Chancellorsville, Va.; died of his wounds, June 6, 1863. Commissioned captain, January 7, 1862, with rank from July 24, 1861, original, Wool, Md.

Bloomer, Samuel—Age, 18 years. Enlisted, July 17, 1861, at Westfield, to serve three years; mustered in as private, Co. G, July 23, 1861; wounded in action, May 5, 1862, at Williamsburg, Va.; re-enlisted as a veteran, December 21, 1863; transferred to Co. I, One Hundred and Twentieth Infantry, July 24, 1864.

Bond, James—Age, 18 years. Enlisted, May 28, 1861, at Westfield, to serve three years: mustered in as private, Co. G, July 23, 1861; discharged for disability, December 28, 1862, at Third Corps Hospital.

Bowdish, Walter A.—Age, 22 years. Enlisted, July 17, 1861, at Staten Island, to serve three years; mustered in as private, Co. G, August 8, 1861; wounded and missing in action, July 1, 1862, at Malvern Hill, Va.; no further record.

Boyle, Patrick—Age, 42 years. Enlisted, July 17, 1861, at Westfield, to serve three years; mustered in as private, Co. G, July 23, 1861; wounded in action, June 25, 1862, at Oak Grove, Va.; mustered out, July 16, 1864, at New York City.

Beightman, James W.—Age, 22 years. Enlisted, July 17, 1861, at Westfield, to serve three years; mustered in as private, Co. G, July 23, 1861; discharged for disability, September 23, 1862, at New York City.

Brockett, Jerry—Age, 36 years. Enlisted, August 3, 1861, at Westfield, to serve three years; mustered in as private, Co. G, August 7, 1861; re-enlisted as a veteran, December 21, 1863; transferred to Co. I, One Hundred and Twentieth Infantry, July 24, 1864; also born as Brackett.

Brooks, Giles—Age, 26 years. Enlisted at Westfield, to serve three years, and mustered in as private, Co. G, August 7, 1861; promoted corporal, May 6, 1862; sergeant, June 13, 1862; discharged for disability, January 1, 1863, at Georgetown, D.C.

Brooks, Uriah—Age, — years. Enlisted at Dunkirk, to serve three years, and mustered in as private, Co. G, August 7, 1861; wounded in action, July 3, 1863, at Gettysburg, Pa.; transferred to Veteran Reserve Corps, June 3, 1864, from which mustered out, August 19, 1865, from Hicks U.S.A. General Hospital, Baltimore, Md.

Brown, Henriele F.—Age, 19 years. Enlisted, July 17, 1861, at Westfield, to serve three years; mustered in as private, Co. G, July 23, 1861; transferred to Co. B in July 1861; promoted corporal, August 5, 1862; sergeant, May 5, 1863; re-enlisted as a veteran, December 24, 1863; transferred to Co. C, One Hundred and Twentieth Infantry, June 23, 1864; awarded medal of honor for most distinguished gallantry, May 6, 1864, at Wilderness, Va.

Brown, Perry—Age, 25 years. Enlisted, July 17, 1861, at Westfield, to serve three years; mustered in as private, Co. G, July 23, 1861; discharged for disability, September 24, 1861, at Camp Caldwell, D.C.

Burns, Rufus H.—Age, 21 years. Enlisted, July 17, 1861, at Westfield, to serve three years; mustered in as private, Co. G, July 23, 1861; transferred to Co. B in July 1861; wounded in action, August 27, 1862, at Bristoe Station, Va.; transferred to Co. C, One Hundred and Twentieth Infantry, June 23, 1864.

Bush, John—Age, 18 years. Enlisted at Westfield, to

serve three years, and mustered in as private, Co. G, July 17, 1861; deserted, May 5, 1862.

Callahan, Charles—Age, 39 years. Enlisted, July 17, 1861, at Westfield, to serve three years; mustered in as private, Co. G, July 23, 1861; transferred to Co. C in July 1861; killed in action, July 1, 1862, at Malvern Hill, Va.

Chadwick, Andrew—Age, 20 years. Enlisted, July 17, 1861, at Westfield, to serve three years; mustered in as private, Co. G, July 23, 1861; transferred to Co. F in July 1861; captured in action, May 5, 1862; paroled, no date; discharged May 28, 1862, at Washington, D.C., at Malvern Hill, Va.

Connell, William—Age, 21 years. Enlisted, July 17, 1861, at Westfield, to serve three years; mustered in as private, Co. G, July 23, 1861; transferred to Co. F in July 1861; promoted corporal, no date; sergeant, May 20, 1863; returned to ranks, no date; transferred to Co. F, One Hundred and Twentieth Infantry, June 23, 1864; also born as Conner and Connor.

Cook, Philander—Age, 25 years. Enlisted at Westfield, to serve three years, and mustered in as private, Co. G, September 6, 1861; promoted corporal, October 11, 1862; captured in action, May 3, 1863, at Chancellorsville, Va.; returned, October 9, 1863; re-enlisted as a veteran, December 21, 1863; transferred to Co. I, One Hundred and Twentieth Infantry, July 24, 1864.

Cottrell, Dwellyic—Age, 30 years. Enlisted, August 3, 1861, at Westfield, to serve three years; mustered in as private, Co. G, August 7, 1861; died of disease, May 25, 1862, at Yorktown, Va.

Cross, Ambrose—Age, 22 years. Enlisted, August 3, 1861, at Westfield, to serve three years; mustered in as private, Co. G, August 7, 1861; wounded in action, June 25, 1862, near Fair Oaks, Va.; discharged for disability, September 26, 1862, at camp near Alexandria, Va.

Culver, Thomas B.—Age, 21 years. Enlisted, August 3, 1861, at Westfield, to serve three years; mustered in as private, Co. G, August 7, 1861; wounded in action, May 5, 1862, at Williamsburg, Va.; discharged for his wounds, December 29, 1862, at Baltimore, Md.

Douglass, Richard—Enlisted at Dunkirk, to serve three years, and mustered in as private, Co. G, August 25, 1862; transferred to Co. G, Ninth Regiment, Veteran Reserve Corps, August 24, 1863.

Doyle, John—Enlisted at Jersey City, N.J., to serve three years, and mustered in as private, Co. G, October 30, 1861; wounded in action, May 5, 1862, at Williamsburg, Va.; deserted, August 29, 1862.

Dumphrey, Peter—Age, 20 years. Enlisted, July 17, 1861, at Westfield, to serve three years; mustered in as private, Co. G, July 23, 1861; transferred to Co. F, in July 1861; promoted corporal, November 1, 1861; sergeant, May 6, 1862; first sergeant, in May 1863; wounded in action, July 2, 1863, at Gettysburg, Pa.; transferred to Co. F, One Hundred and Twentieth Infantry, June 23, 1864.

Dunkan, Robert—Age, 21 years. Enlisted at Westfield, to serve three years, and mustered in as private, Co. G, August 7, 1861; discharged for disability, April 19, 1862, at Georgetown, D.C.; also born as Duncan.

Edwards, Henry—Age, 21 years. Enlisted at Westfield, to serve three years; mustered in as private, Co. G, August 7, 1861; killed in action, July 1, 1862, at Malvern Hill, Va.

Fox, Charles A.—Age, 20 years. Enlisted at Westfield, to serve three years, and mustered in as private, Co. G, August 7, 1861; wounded in action, July 2, 1863, at Gettysburg, Pa.; transferred to Co. I, One Hundred and Twentieth Infantry, July 24, 1864.

Fuller, Lyman—Age, 21 years. Enlisted at Dunkirk, to serve three years, and mustered in as private, Co. G, August 24, 1862; wounded in action, July 24, 1863, at Wapping Heights, Va.; transferred to Co. I, One Hundred and Twentieth Infantry, July 24, 1864.

Gagen, Henry—Age, 19 years. Enlisted at Stockton, to serve three years, and mustered in as private, Co. G, December 16, 1863; transferred to Co. I, One Hundred and Twentieth Infantry, July 24, 1864.

Galloway, Josiah—Age, 28 years. Enlisted, July 17, 1861, at Westfield, to serve three years; mustered in as private, Co. G, July 23, 1861; transferred to Co. C in July 1861; promoted corporal, July 10, 1862; sergeant, May 4, 1863; returned to ranks in June 1863; deserted, July 2, 1863.

Gerry, Daniel—Age, 18 years. Enlisted, July 17, 1861, at Westfield, to serve three years; mustered in as private, Co. G, July 23, 1861; wounded in action, December 13, 1862, at Fredericksburg, Va.; hanged by sentence of general court-martial, Order No. 194, July 15, 1864.

Gerry, Michael—Age, 18 years. Enlisted, July 17, 1861, at Westfield, to serve three years; mustered in as private, Co. G, July 23, 1861; appointed wagoner in November 1863; re-enlisted as a veteran, December 21, 1863; transferred to Co. I, One Hundred and Twentieth Infantry, July 24, 1864.

Gibson, Dewitt J.—Age, 18 years. Enlisted, July 17, 1861, at Westfield, to serve three years; mustered in as private, Co. G, July 28, 1861; wounded in action, December 13, 1862, at Fredericksburg, Va.; transferred to Co. I, One Hundred and Twentieth Infantry, July 24, 1864.

Gisler, William—Age, 25 years. Enlisted, July 17,

1861, at Westfield, to serve three years; mustered in as private, Co. G, July 23, 1861; wounded in action, May 3, 1863, at Chancellorsville, Va.; re-enlisted as a veteran, December 21, 1863; transferred to Co. I, One Hundred and Twentieth Infantry, July 24, 1864; also born as Grisler.

Gleason, Gifford C.—Age, 28 years. Enlisted, July 17, 1861, at Westfield, to serve three years; mustered in as private, Co. G, July 23, 1861; discharged by reason of re-enlistment in Battery D, First N.Y. Artillery, December 24, 1863.

Griffith, Robert—Age, 25 years. Enlisted, July 17, 1861, at Westfield, to serve three years; mustered in as private, Co. G, July 23, 1861; transferred to Co. B, in July 1861; deserted, August 23, 1861, at Camp Caldwell, D.C.; surrendered himself, April 6, 1865; mustered out, May 15, 1865, at Elmira, N.Y., as Robert B. Griffith.

Grimes, Thomas—Age, 16 years. Enlisted at New York City, to serve three years, and mustered in as musician, Co. G, November 21, 1861; re-enlisted as a veteran, December 21, 1863; transferred to Co. I, One Hundred and Twentieth Infantry, July 24, 1864.

Groat, Alfred T.—Age, 21 years. Enlisted, July 17, 1861, at Westfield, to serve three years; mustered in as private, Co. G, July 23, 1861; discharged for disability, November 21, 1862, at hospital of Third Corps.

Haight, John—Age, 22 years. Enlisted, July 17, 1861, at Westfield, to serve three years; mustered in as private Co. G, July 24, 1861; promoted corporal, September 1, 1861; wounded and captured in action and paroled, May 5, 1862, at Williamsburg, Va.; promoted sergeant, July 23, 1862; discharged for wounds March 1, 1863, at Camp Nelson, Taylor, Va.

Hall, Joseph H.—Age, 26 years. Enlisted, May 28, 1861, at Westfield, to serve three years; mustered in as first sergeant, Co. G, July 23, 1861; returned to the ranks, August 19, 1861; discharged for disability, September 21, 1861, at Camp Caldwell, Washington, D.C.

Hall, Willim D.—Age, 19 years. Enrolled, May 28, 1861, at Westfield, to serve three years; mustered in as sergeant, Co. G, July 23, 1861; wounded in action, June 25, 1862, at Fair Oaks, Va.; promoted first sergeant, October 11, 1862; mustered in as second lieutenant, Co. I, January 20, 1863; wounded and captured in action, May 3, 1863, at Chancellorsville, Va.; paroled, May 23, 1863, at City Point, Va.; mustered in as first lieutenant, Co. E, August 26, 1863; discharged, to accept appointment in Invalid Corps, February 21, 1864. Commissioned second lieutenant, June 18, 1863, with rank from January 11, 1863, vice W. McGinnis, resigned; first lieutenant, August 21, 1863, with rank from June 6, 1863, vice P. Anderson, promoted.

Hanghett, James H.—Age, 20 years. Enlisted, July 17, 1861, at Westfield, to serve three years; mustered in as private, Co. G, July 24, 1861; promoted corporal, January 11, 1863; captured in action, May 3, 1863, at Chancellorsville, Va.; paroled, no date; re-enlisted as a veteran, December 21, 1863; transferred to Co. I, One Hundred and Twentieth Infantry, July 24, 1864.

Harrison, Sprague—Age, 23 years. Enlisted, May 28, 1861, at Westfield, to serve three years; mustered in as private, Co. G, July 24, 1861; promoted corporal, October 4, 1861; sergeant, January 1, 1863; wounded in action, July 2, 1863, at Gettysburg, Pa.; mustered out, July 23, 1864, near Petersburg, Va.

Hay, Alexander—Age, 18 years. Enlisted at Ellery, to serve three years, and mustered in as private, Co. G, December 10, 1863; appointed musician, January 1864; transferred to Co. I, One Hundred and Twentieth Infantry, July 24, 1864. Hertenstine, Christopher, see Christitine Hepenstine.

Hibbard, Frederick M.—Age, 18 years. Enlisted, at Westfield, to serve three years, and mustered in as private, Co. G, August 7, 1861; discharged for disability, November 9, 1862, at hospital of Third Corps.

Hirschey, Morris—Age, 23 years. Enlisted at Westfield, to serve three years, and mustered in as private, Co. G, July 23, 1861; transferred to Co. C, July 1861; killed in action, May 5, 1862, at Williamsburg, Va.

Hopson, Jasper L.—Age, 28 years. Enlisted, July 17, 1861, at Westfield, to serve three years; mustered in as private, Co. G, July 24, 1861; transferred to Veteran Reserve Corps, September 20, 1863.

Horrigan, Thomas—Age, 21 years. Enlisted, July 17, 1861, at Westfield, to serve three years; mustered in as private, Co. G, July 23, 1861; transferred to Co. B, in July 1861; to Co. C, One Hundred and Twentieth Infantry, June 23, 1864.

Hosier, Abram B.—Age, 23 years. Enlisted at Westfield, to serve three years, and mustered in as private, Co. G, August 7, 1861; discharged for disability, September 24, 1861, at Camp Caldwell, Washington, D.C.

Houoh, John M.—Age, 22 years. Enlisted, May 28, 1861, at Westfield, to serve three years; mustered in as private, Co. G, July 24, 1861; re-enlisted as a veteran, December 21, 1863; promoted corporal, May 1864; transferred to Co. I, One Hundred and Twentieth Infantry, July 24, 1864.

Hunt, Alfred—Age, 18 years. Enlisted, July 17, 1861, at Westfield, to serve three years; mustered in as private, Co. G, July 24, 1861; wounded in action,

December 13, 1862, at Fredericksburg, Va.; died of disease, January 22, 1863, at Hammond General Hospital, Point Lookout, Md.

Hunt, Alvin—Age, 18 years. Enlisted, July 17, 1861, at Westfield, to serve three years; mustered in as private, Co. G, July 23, 1861; discharged for disability, September 24, 1861, at Camp Caldwell, Washington, D.C.

Hunt, Melvin E.—Age, 22 years. Enlisted, May 28, 1861, at Westfield, to serve three years; mustered in as corporal, Co. G, July 24, 1861; re-enlisted as a veteran and promoted first sergeant, February 13, 1864; returned to ranks, no date; transferred to Co. I, One Hundred and Twentieth Infantry, July 24, 1864.

Jameson, Walter—Age, 18 years. Enlisted, July 17, 1861, at Westfield, to serve three years; mustered in as private, Co. G, July 23, 1861; wounded in action, July 2, 1863, at Gettysburg, Pa.; discharged for his wounds, March 4, 1864, at Mower U.S.A. General Hospital, Philadelphia, Pa.

Jamieson, Robert—Age, 30 years. Enlisted, August 3, 1861, at Westfield, to serve three years; mustered in as private, Co. G, August 7, 1861; promoted corporal, January 7, 1862; killed in action, May 5, 1862, at Williamsburg, Va.

Jones, Charles N.—Age, 22 years. Enlisted at Westfield, to serve three years, and mustered in as private, Co. G, September 6, 1861; died of disease, January 8, 1862, at Camp Wool, Md.

Jones, Electcus W.—Age, — years. Enlisted at Westfield, to serve three years, and mustered in as private, Co. G, August 11, 1862; captured in action, May 3, 1863, at Chancellorsville, Va.; paroled, no date; died of disease, June 22, 1863, at Camp Convalescent, Va.; also born as Erastus Jones.

Jones, Miles—Age, 10 years. Enlisted, May 28, 1861, at Westfield, to serve three years; mustered in as corporal, Co. G, July 23, 1861; died of disease, January 5, 1862, at Camp Wool, Md.

Katline, John M.—Ago, 32 years. Enlisted, at Westfield, to serve three years, and mustered in as private, Co. G, July 23, 1861; transferred to Co. C, in July 1861; promoted corporal, July 29, 1861; discharged for disability, January 31, 1862, at Camp Caldwell, Md.; also born as Calton.

Kennish, Peter—Age, 26 years. Enlisted, July 17, 1861, at Westfield, to serve three years; mustered in as corporal, Co. G, July 23, 1861; killed in action, July 2, 1863, at Gettysburg, Pa.; also born as Cinnish.

Lacey, Samuel J.—Age, 20 years. Enlisted at Dunkirk, to serve three years, and mustered in as private, Co. G, August 25, 1862; transferred to Co. I, One Hundred and Twentieth Infantry, July 24, 1864; also born as Sherman Lacy.

Lauer, Charles—Age, 28 years. Enlisted, July 17, 1861, at Westfield, to serve three years; mustered in as private, Co. G, July 23, 1861; wounded in action, May 3, 1863, at Chancellorsville, Va.; transferred to Veteran Reserve Corps, in September 1863.

Lewis, Ezekiel—Age, 36 years. Enlisted, August 3, 1861, at Westfield, to serve three years; mustered in as private, Co. G, August 7, 1861; discharged for disability, February 17, 1864, at Rendezvous Distribution, Va.

Lilly, Frank G.—Age, 17 years. Enlisted, July 17, 1861, at Westfield, to serve three years; mustered in as musician, Co. G, August 31, 1861; discharged for disability, June 24, 1862, at Annapolis, Md.

Mahoney, Michael—Age, 20 years. Enlisted, May 28, 1861, at Westfield, to serve three years; mustered in as corporal, Co. G, July 23, 1861; wounded in action at Fair Oaks, Va., and died of his wounds in June 1862.

Manton, Henry—Age, 18 years. Enlisted, July 17, 1861, at Westfield, to serve three years; mustered in as private, Co. G, July 23, 1861; wounded in action, May 5, 1862, at Williamsburg, Va.; died of disease, September 14, 1862, at City Hospital, New York City.

Maples, Edward—Age, 32 years. Enlisted at Staten Island, to serve three years, and mustered in as private, Co. G, July 23, 1861; transferred to Co. C in July 1861; discharged for disability, July 13, 1862, in Field, Va.

Mason, Charles—Age, 18 years. Enlisted, August 3, 1861, at Westfield, to serve three years; mustered in as private, Co. G, August 7, 1861; wounded in action, June 25, 1862, near Fair Oaks, Va.; transferred to Co. I, One Hundred and Twentieth Infantry, July 24, 1864.

McCarthy, Daniel—Age, 24 years. Enlisted at Staten Island, to serve three years, and mustered in as private, Co. G, July 23, 1861; transferred to Co. F in July 1861; wounded in action, August 27, 1862, at Bristoe Station, Va.; died of wounds, September 4, 1862, at Washington, D.C.; also born as Samuel.

McCormick, Charles—Age, 42 years. Enlisted, May 18, 1861, at Westfield, to serve three years; mustered in as private, Co. G, July 23, 1861; discharged for disability, September 26, 1862, at Fortress Monroe, Va.

McGouger, Duncan—Age, 40 years. Enlisted, September 12, 1862, at Dunkirk, to serve three years; mustered in as private, Co. G, September 20, 1862; captured in action, May 3, 1863, at Chancellorsville, Va.; returned, October 9, 1863; transferred to Co. I, One Hundred and Twentieth Infantry, July 24, 1864; also born as McGregor.

McKernan, John—Age, 19 years. Enlisted at Staten Island, to serve three years, and mustered in as private, Co. G, July 23, 1861; transferred to Co. F in July 1861; wounded in action, November 27, 1863, at Locust Grove, Va.; discharged for wounds, May 24, 1864, at U.S.A. General Hospital, Newark, N.J.; also born as Samuel McKernan.

McMann, Patrick—Age, 40 years. Enlisted, July 17, 1861, at Westfield, to serve three years; mustered in as private, Co. G, July 23, 1861; captured in action, June 80, 1862, at Glendale, Va.; no further record; also born as McMahon.

McManus, Hugh—Age, 37 years. Enlisted, July 17, 1861, at Westfield, to serve three years; mustered in as private, Co. G, July 23, 1861; discharged for injuries received at Budd's Ferry, Md., October 10, 1862, at New York City.

McTague, Patrick—Age, 26 years. Enlisted at Staten Island, to serve three years, and mustered in as private, Co. G, July 23, 1861; transferred to Co. F, in July 1861; to Co. F, One Hundred and Twentieth Infantry, June 23, 1864; also born as McTigue and McTagen.

McWilliams, John—Age, 20 years. Enlisted at Staten Island, to serve three years, and mustered in as private, Co. G, July 23, 1861; died of disease, August 6, 1861, at General Hospital, Washington, D.C.

Meehan, William—Age, 35 years. Enlisted at Staten Island, to serve three years, and mustered in as private, Co. G, July 23, 1861; transferred to Co. C, July 24, 1861; discharged for disability, February 10, 1863, near Falmouth, Va.

Mitz, James B.—Age, 45 years. Enlisted at Staten Island, to serve three years, and mustered in as private, Co. G, July 23, 1861; deserted, July 24, 1861, from Camp Scott, Staten Island.

Morley, Hirad—Age, 24 years. Enlisted, August 3, 1861, at Westfield, to serve three years; mustered in as private, Co. G, August 7, 1861; transferred to Co. I, One Hundred and Twentieth Infantry, July 24, 1864.

Morrow, James B.—Age, 21 years. Enlisted at Staten Island, to serve three years, and mustered in as private, Co. G, July 23, 1861; transferred to Co. B, in July 1861; promoted corporal, January 7, 1863; captured in action, May 3, 1863, at Chancellorsville, Va.; paroled, no date; re-enlisted as a veteran, December 24, 1863; transferred to Co. H, One Hundred and Twentieth Infantry, June 23, 1864.

Murphy, John D.—Age, 29 years. Enlisted at Staten Island, to serve three years, and mustered in as private, Co. G, July 23, 1861; transferred to Co. F, in July 1861; promoted corporal, June 1, 1862; discharged for disability, May 2, 1863, at Washington, D.C.

Neff, Albert H.—Age, 18 years. Enlisted, July 17, 1861, at Westfield, to serve three years; mustered in as private, Co. G, July 23, 1861; deserted, July 2, 1862.

Nestle, William—Age, 33 years. Enlisted at Staten Island, to serve three years, and mustered in as private, Co. G, July 23, 1861; transferred to Co. C in July 1861; killed in action, May 5, 1862, at Williamsburg, Va.

Nichols, Clark—Age, 88 years. Enlisted, July 17, 1861, at Westfield, to serve three years; mustered in as private, Co. G, July 23, 1861; discharged for disability, December 24, 1861, at Camp Wool, Md.

Northrop, Austin—Age, 20 years. Enlisted, August 3, 1861, at Westfield, to serve three years; mustered in as private, Co. G, August 7, 1861; wounded in action, June 25, 1862, at Fair Oaks, Va.; transferred to Co. I, One Hundred and Twentieth Infantry, July 24, 1864.

Northrop, Calvin—Age, 23 years. Enlisted at Chautauqua, to serve three years, and mustered in as private, Co. G, January 23, 1864; missing in action, May 15, 1864; transferred to Co. I, One Hundred and Twentieth Infantry, July 24, 1864.

Ole, Ole—Age, 21 years. Enlisted at Staten Island, to serve three years, and mustered in as private, Co. G, July 23, 1861; wounded in action, May 5, 1862; died of his wounds, May 18, 1862, at Williamsburg, Va.

Ollmatzer, William—Age, 23 years. Enlisted, July 11, 1861, at Staten Island, to serve three years; mustered in as private, Co. G, July 23, 1861; transferred to Co. A, in July 1861; promoted corporal, September 19, 1861; died of disease, June 1, 1862, at White House Hospital, Va.

Osgood, Joshua—Age, 21 years. Enlisted, July 17, 1861, at Westfield, to serve three years; mustered in as private, Co. G, July 23, 1861; wounded in action, May 5, 1862, at Williamsburg, Va.; discharged, September 23, 1864, at Armory Square Hospital, Washington, D.C.

Palmer, James H.—Age, 22 years. Enlisted, July 17, 1861, at Westfield, to serve three years; mustered in as private, Co. G, July 23, 1861; wounded in action, November 27, 1863, at Mine Run, Va.; died of his wounds, November 28, 1863, at camp, near Brandy Station, Va.

Parr, James—Age, 20 years. Enlisted at Dunkirk, to serve three years, and mustered in as private, Co. G, August 15, 1862; transferred to Co. I, One Hundred and Twentieth Infantry, July 24, 1864.

Plumb, Arthur A.—Age, 25 years. Enlisted, May 28, 1861, at Westfield, to serve three years; mustered in as corporal, Co. G, July 23, 1861; wounded in action, August 29, 1862, at Bull Run, Va.; discharged for wounds, December 12, 1863, at Rochester, N.Y.

Purdy, Alonzo—Age, 18 years. Enlisted, July 17, 1861, at Westfield, to serve three years; mustered in as private, Co. G, July 23, 1861; killed on picket, June 21, 1862, near Fair Oaks, Va.; also born as Pardy.

Randall, Caleb F.—Age, 20 years. Enlisted, July 23, 1861, at Westfield, to serve three years: mustered in as private, Co. G, July 23, 1861; promoted to corporal, May 6, 1862; wounded in action December 13, 1862, at Fredericksburg, Va.; discharged for wounds, April 10, 1863, at Point Lookout, Md.

Rhinehart, George W.—Age, 21 years. Enlisted, August 3, 1861, at Westfield, to serve three years; mustered in as private, Co. G, August 7, 1861; died of disease, November 27, 1861, at Camp Wool, Md.

Rood, George W.—Age, 19 years. Enlisted at Dunkirk, to serve three years, and mustered in as private, Co. G, September 7, 1862; wounded in action, May 3, 1863, at Chancellorsville, Va.; discharged for wounds, August 8, 1864, at Buffalo, N.Y.; also born as Joseph W.

Rush, John—Age, 24 years. Enlisted, May 28, 1861, at Westfield, to serve three years; mustered in as private, Co. G, July 23, 1861; mustered out, June 8, 1864, at New York City.

Schrader, Charles—Age, 32 years. Enlisted at Staten Island, to serve three years, and mustered in as private, Co. G, July 24, 1861; wounded in action, July 2, 1863, at Gettysburg, Pa.; re-enlisted as a veteran, December 21, 1863; transferred to Co. I, One Hundred and Twentieth Infantry, July 24, 1864.

Schuyler, Charles—Age, 32 years. Enlisted at Staten Island, to serve three years, and mustered in as private, Co. G, July 23, 1861; no further record.

Servoss, Norman W.—Age, 22 years. Enlisted at Dunkirk, to serve three years, and mustered in as private, Co. G, August 25, 1862; transferred to Co. I, One Hundred and Twentieth Infantry, July 24, 1864.

Shafer, Jacob—Age, 23 years. Enlisted, May 28, 1861, at Westfield, to serve three years; mustered in as corporal, Co. G, July 24, 1861; returned to the ranks, September 1, 1861; discharged for disability, April 13, 1863, at Fort Monroe, Va.

Shaffner, Frederick—Age, 23 years. Enlisted, July 17, 1861, at Westfield, to serve three years; mustered in as private, Co. G, July 24, 1861; re-enlisted as a veteran, December 21, 1863; wounded in May 1864; transferred to Co. I, One Hundred and Twentieth Infantry, July 24, 1864; also born as Frederick S. Shaffner.

Shaffner, Philip L.—Age, 21 years. Enlisted at Westfield, to serve three years, and mustered in as private, Co. G, August 7, 1861; wounded in action, June 25, 1862, near Fair Oaks, Va.; deserted, August 27, 1863.

Shields, Patrick—Age, 26 years. Enlisted at Staten Island, to serve three years, and mustered in as private, Co. G, July 23, 1861; transferred to Co. F, and promoted corporal, July 1861; killed in action, May 5, 1862, at Williamsburg, Va.

Shufelt, Jeremiah—Age, 43 years. Enlisted at Westfield, to serve three years, and mustered in as private, Co. G, August 7, 1861; transferred to Veteran Reserve Corps, January 4, 1864.

Slattery, John—Age, 28 years. Enlisted at Staten Island, to serve three years, and mustered in as private, Co. G, July 23, 1861; transferred to Co. E, July 1861; to Co. C, Nineteenth Regiment, Veteran Reserve Corps, December 21, 1863.

Smith, James A.—Age, 23 years. Enrolled, May 28, 1861, at Westfield, to serve three years; mustered in as second lieutenant, Co. G, July 23, 1861; as first lieutenant, Co. K, May 17, 1862; transferred to Co. H, November 1, 1862; appointed adjutant, December 26, 1862; transferred to Co. G, June 24, 1863; to Co. D, December 1863; dismissed, April 5, 1864. Commissioned second lieutenant, January 7, 1862, with rank from July 24, 1861, original; first lieutenant, May 30, 1862, with rank from May 17, 1862, vice C. Grossinger, promoted; adjutant, June 13, 1863, with rank from December 28, 1862, vice H.C. Hinman, resigned.

Steward, Henry C.—Age, 20 years. Enrolled at Westfield, to serve three years, and mustered in as private, Co. G, August 7, 1861; promoted sergeant, August 19, 1861; first sergeant, July 23, 1862; second lieutenant, Co. I, October 11, 1862; transferred to Co. A, November 1, 1862; mustered in as first lieutenant, Co. F, May 1, 1863; wounded in action, July 3, 1863, at Gettysburg, Va.; transferred to Co. B, November 1, 1863; mustered out with company, June 20, 1864, near Petersburg, Va. Commissioned second lieutenant, December 1, 1862, with rank from October 11, 1862, vice J.S. Mann, promoted; first lieutenant, September 5, 1863, with rank from April 2, 1863, vice J.S. Mann, promoted.

Strain, Isaac C.—Age, 21 years. Enlisted at Westfield, to serve three years, and mustered in as private, Co. G, September 6, 1861; killed in action, July 2, 1863, at Gettysburg, Pa.

Sutton, Phinneas—Age, 21 years. Enlisted at Westfield, to serve three years, and mustered in as private, Co. G, September 6, 1861; discharged for disability, August 6, 1862, at Annapolis, Md.

Taylor, Joshua H.—Age, 23 years. Enlisted, July 17, 1861, at Westfield, to serve three years; mustered in as private, Co. G, July 23, 1861; mustered out, July 23, 1864, near Petersburg, Va.

Teale, John H.—Age, 21 years. Enlisted, July 17, 1861, at Westfield, to serve three years; mustered in as private, Co. G, July 23, 1861; died of disease, January 8, 1862, at Camp Wool, Md.

Thompson, Harrison—Age, 21 years. Enlisted at Westfield, to serve three years, and mustered in as private, Co. G, August 7, 1861; wounded in action, July 1, 1862, at Malvern Hill, Va.; discharged for wounds, October 22, 1862, at Philadelphia, Pa.

Thornton, Carey—Age, 21 years. Enlisted at Westfield, to serve three years, and mustered in as private, Co. G, August 7, 1861; died of disease, September 11, 1862, at McKinis General Hospital, Baltimore, Md.; also born as R. F. Thornton.

Tower, Mortimer F.—Age, 26 years. Enlisted at Staten Island, to serve three years, and mustered in as private, Co. G, July 23, 1861; appointed musician and transferred to the band in October 1861; mustered out with band, July 22, 1862.

Turner, Hugh—Age, 23 years. Enlisted, July 17, 1861, at Westfield, to serve three years; mustered in as private, Co. G, July 24, 1861; re-enlisted as a veteran, December 21, 1863; transferred to Co. I, One Hundred and Twentieth Infantry, June 24, 1864.

Van Dusen, Spencer—Age, 25 years. Enlisted, May 28, 1861, at Westfield, to serve three years; mustered in as sergeant, Co. G, July 23, 1861; promoted first sergeant, May 6, 1862; died of disease, July 20, 1862, Sixth and Market Streets Hospital, Philadelphia, Pa.

Varrin, Lewis—Age, 44 years. Enlisted at Staten Island, to serve three years, and mustered in as private Co. G, July 23, 1861; transferred to Co. F in July 1861; to Co. F, One Hundred and Twentieth Infantry, June 23, 1864; also born as Louis Verrin.

Volgstadt, Frank—Age, 32 years. Enlisted at Westfield, to serve three years, and mustered in as private, Co. G, December 4, 1863; transferred to Co. I, One Hundred and Twentieth Infantry, July 24, 1864; also born as Francis Volstead.

Walter, Frederick—Age, 38 years. Enlisted at Staten Island, to serve three years, and mustered in as private, Co. G, July 23, 1861; transferred to Co. C, July 1861; discharged for disability, October 8, 1861, at Washington, D.C.

Warren, Deforrest—Age, 21 years. Enlisted, May 28, 1861, at Westfield, to serve three years; mustered in as private, Co. G, July 24, 1861; died of disease, December 31, 1861, at Camp Wool, Md.

Watts, Oscar F.—Age, 26 years. Enlisted, July 17, 1861, at Westfield, to serve three years; mustered in as private, Co. G, July 24, 1861; wounded in action, May 5, 1862, at Williamsburg, Va.; promoted corporal, January 1, 1863; captured in action, May 3, 1863, at Chancellorsville, Va.; paroled, October 19, 1863; re-enlisted as a veteran, December 21, 1863; wounded in action, May 11, 1864, at Spotsylvania, Va.; died of his wounds, no date.

Wheeler, James B.—Age, 21 years. Enlisted, May 28, 1861, at Westfield, to serve three years; mustered in as private, Co. G, July 24, 1861; died of disease, December 31, 1861, at Camp Wool, Charles County, Md.

Wheeler, William E.—Age, 19 years. Enrolled, May 28, 1861, at Westfield, to serve three years; mustered in as sergeant, Co. G, July 23, 1861; promoted sergeant-major, June 13, 1862; second lieutenant, Co. F, June 23, 1862; mustered in as first lieutenant, Co. B, September 26, 1862; as captain, Co. D, May 4, 1863; transferred to Co. G in August 1863; mustered out, to date August 28, 1864, near Petersburg, Va. Not commissioned second lieutenant; commissioned first lieutenant, December 1, 1862, with rank from October 30, 1862, vice S. Bailey, promoted; captain, August 7, 1863, with rank from May 4, 1863, vice C.K. Abell, promoted.

Whittier, Joseph G.—Age, 22 years. Enlisted at Westfield, to serve three years, and mustered in as private, Co. G, September 6, 1861; re-enlisted as a veteran, February 13, 1864; transferred to Co. I, One Hundred and Twentieth Infantry, July 24, 1864.

Wilkins, Franklin—Age, 18 years. Enlisted at Staten Island, to serve three years, and mustered in as private, Co. G, July 23, 1861; deserted, August 8, 1861, while on the march.

Willing, John C.—Age, 18 years. Enlisted, August 3, 1861, at Westfield, to serve three years; mustered in as private, Co. G, August 7, 1861; promoted corporal, June 13, 1862; sergeant, March 6, 1863; transferred to Co. I, One Hundred and Twentieth Infantry, July 24, 1864.

Wilson, Robert B.—Age, 18 years. Enlisted, July 17, 1861, at Westfield, to serve three years; mustered in as private, Co. G, July 24, 1861; wounded in action, May 5, 1862, at Williamsburg, Va.; transferred to Veteran Reserve Corps, January 4, 1864.

Wilson, Wallace—Age, 21 years. Enlisted, May 28, 1861, at Westfield, to serve three years; mustered in as sergeant, Co. G, July 24, 1861; killed in action, May 5, 1862, at Williamsburg, Va.

Company H

Organized in Dunkirk, N.Y., in October 1861. Mustered into the United States service November 1, 1861.

Captains

Stephen N. Doyle, from November 1, 1861, to July 1, 1862.
John W. Holmes, from July 2, 1862, to June 1, 1864.
John S. Mann, from June 1 to October 31, 1864.

First Lieutenants

Leopold Marcus, from September 23, 1861, to July 7, 1862.
Rinaldo E. Jones, from July 7 to October 10, 1862.
Patrick Anderson, from October 11 to November 1, 1862.
James A. Smith, from November 1 to December 26, 1862.
Harrison F. Ellis, from November 1, 1862, to January 1863.
William McConnell, from June 23, 1863, to January 26, 1864.
William Chalmers, from November 23, 1863, to October 31, 1864.

Second Lieutenants

Daniel Loeb, from November 6, 1861, to June 19, 1862.
Charles H. Hydorn, from June 19 to September 8, 1862.
Harrison F. Ellis, from September 8 to November 1, 1862.
Warren J. Stanton, from November 1, 1862, to January 17, 1863.
Thomas Harvey, from February 18, 1863, to March 15, 1864.

Andrews, Robert—Age, 43 years. Enlisted at New York City, to serve three years, and mustered in as private, Co. H, November 7, 1861; deserted, December 8, 1861, at Camp Wool, Md.

Angus, Andrew—Age, 36 years. Enlisted at Dunkirk, to serve three years, and mustered in as private, Co. H, November 9, 1861; wounded in action, May 5, 1862, at Williamsburg, Va.; re-enlisted as a veteran, December 24, 1863; wounded in action, May 6, 1864, at Wilderness, Va.; transferred to Co. E, One Hundred and Twentieth Infantry, no date.

Arnold, Jacob—Age, 30 years. Enlisted at Dunkirk, to serve three years, and mustered in as private, Co. H, August 1, 1862; wounded in action, July 2, 1863, at Gettysburg, Pa.; transferred to Co. K, One Hundred and Twentieth Infantry, October 30, 1864.

Austria, Peter—Age, 21 years. Enlisted, August 23, 1862, at Dunkirk, to serve three years; mustered in as private, Co. H, September 2, 1862; wounded in action, May 6, 1864, at Wilderness, Va.; died of his wounds, June 1, 1864, at Stanton U.S.A. Hospital, Washington, D.C.; also born as Ostre.

Babcock, Isaac—Age, 25 years. Enlisted, September 25, 1861, at Dunkirk, to serve three years; mustered in as private, Co. H, October 31, 1861; captured in action at Locust Grove, Va., November 27, 1863; died while a prisoner of war, July 9, 1864, at Andersonville, Ga.

Babcock, Minard—Age, 25 years. Enlisted, August 22, 1862, at Dunkirk, to serve three years; mustered in as private, Co. H, September 2, 1862; captured in action, May 3, 1863, at Chancellorsville, Va.; paroled, no date; transferred to Co. K, One Hundred and Twentieth Infantry, October 30, 1864.

Barber, Philander—Age, 33 years. Enlisted, August 25, 1862, at Dunkirk, to serve three years; mustered in as private, Co. H, September 2, 1862; discharged for disability, September 20, 1863, at Convalescent Camp, Va.

Barron, George—Age, 36 years. Enlisted, August 23, 1862, at Dunkirk, to serve three years; mustered in as private, Co. H, September 2, 1862; discharged for disability, February 28, 1864, at Dunkirk, N.Y.

Bauer, Peter—Age, 32 years. Enlisted, September 23, 1861, at Dunkirk, to serve three years; mustered in as private, Co. H, October 31, 1861; captured in action, May 5, 1862, at Williamsburg, Va.; paroled and returned, December 20, 1863; mustered out with company, October 31, 1864, near Petersburg, Va.; also born as Bouer, Bowers and Brower.

Becker, George—Age, 22 years. Enlisted, October 14, 1861, at Dunkirk, to serve three years; mustered in as sergeant, Co. H, October 31, 1861; promoted first sergeant, July 3, 1862; wounded in action, August 27, 1862, at Bristoe Station, Va.; discharged, October 14, 1863, Special Order War Dept. No. 460.

Bertine, John—Age, 23 years. Enlisted, October 18, 1861, at Dunkirk, to serve three years; mustered in as private, Co. H, October 31, 1861; mustered out with company, October 31, 1864, near Petersburg, Va.

Bettinger, Nicholas—Age, 23 years. Enlisted, October 14, 1861, at Dunkirk, to serve three years; mustered in as private, Co. H, October 31, 1861; deserted, January 21, 1863, at camp near Falmouth, Va.

Boyle, John—Age, 43 years. Enlisted at New York City, to serve three years, and mustered in as private, Co. H, October 29, 1861; discharged for disability, no date, at Camp Wool, Md.

Brady, Thomas—Age, 20 years. Enlisted at New York City, to serve three years; mustered in as private, Co. H, October 16, 1861; discharged, March 15, 1862, at Camp Wool, Md.

Brennan, John—Age, 32 years. Enlisted, September 21, 1861, at Dunkirk, to serve three years; mustered in as private, Co. H, October 31, 1861; captured in action, May 3, 1863, at Chancellorsville, Va.; paroled, and returned to regiment, October 6, 1863; mustered out with company, October 31, 1864, near Petersburg, Va.; also born as Brannan.

Butchers, Richard—Age, 19 years. Enlisted, October 2, 1861, at Dunkirk, to serve three years; mustered in as private, Co. H, October 31, 1861; wounded in action at Fair Oaks, Va.; discharged for his wounds, October 8, 1864, at Third Division U.S. General Hospital, Alexandria, Va.

Carr, Francis—Age, 21 years. Enlisted, September 26, 1861, at Dunkirk, to serve three years; mustered in as private, Co. H, October 31, 1861; killed in action, May 5, 1862, at Williamsburg, Va.

Cassel, Michael—Age, 23 years. Enlisted, August 18, 1862, at Dunkirk, to serve three years; mustered in as private, Co. H, September 2, 1862; wounded in action, July 2, 1863, at Gettysburg, Pa.; transferred to One Hundred and Forty-third Company, Second Battalion Veteran Reserve Corps, February 29, 1864.

Coleman, Richard—Age, 33 years. Enlisted at Dunkirk, to serve three years, and mustered in as private, Co. H, October 23, 1861; wounded and captured in action, July 1, 1862, at Malvern Hill, Va.; paroled, no date; discharged for his wounds, February 14, 1863, at Convalescent Camp, Va.

Cooper, Elias—Age, 25 years. Enlisted, August 18, 1862, at Dunkirk, to serve three years; mustered in as private, Co. H, September 2, 1862; deserted, January 21, 1863, at camp near Falmouth, Va.

Cronin, Cornelius—Age, 28 years. Enlisted, October 5, 1861, at Dunkirk, to serve three years; mustered in as private, Co. H, October 31, 1861; wounded in action, May 5, 1862, at Williamsburg, Va.; discharged for his wounds, September 16, 1862, at camp near Fort Lyon, Va.

Cronin, Michael—Age, 27 years. Enlisted, October 14, 1861, at Dunkirk, to serve three years; mustered in as sergeant, Co. H, October 31, 1861; transferred to Veteran Reserve Corps, September 1, 1863.

Cunningham, Patrick—Age, 27 years. Enlisted, September 26, 1861, at Dunkirk, to serve three years; mustered in as private, Co. H, October 31, 1861; wounded in action, July 23, 1863, at Manassas Gap, Va.; re-enlisted as a veteran, December 24, 1863; transferred to Co. K, One Hundred and Twentieth Infantry, October 30, 1864.

Danaher, Michael—Age, 42 years. Enlisted, October 18, 1861, at Dunkirk, to serve three years; mustered in as private, Co. H, October 31, 1861; killed in action, July 1, 1862, at Malvern Hill, Va.; also born as Donohue.

Darragh, John—Age, 17 years. Enlisted at New York City, to serve three years, and mustered in as musician, Co. H, November 28, 1861; captured in action, December 14, 1862, at Fredericksburg, Va.; paroled and deserted, no dates.

Donovan, Eugene—Age, 23 years. Enlisted, October 18, 1861, at Dunkirk, to serve three years; mustered in as sergeant, Co. H, October 31, 1861; deserted in July 1862, from General Hospital, at Philadelphia, Pa.

Doty, Ralph A.—Age, 26 years. Enlisted, October 12, 1861, at Dunkirk, to serve three years; mustered in as corporal, Co. H, October 31, 1861; killed in action, May 5, 1862, at Williamsburg, Va.

Drake, Marius M.—Age, 27 years. Enlisted, August 20, 1862, at Dunkirk, to serve three years; mustered in as sergeant, Co. H, September 2, 1862; transferred to Co. D, One Hundred and Twentieth Infantry, October 30, 1864.

Dunn, William—Age, 20 years. Enlisted, October 4, 1861, at Dunkirk, to serve three years; mustered in as private, Co. H, October 31, 1861; wounded in action, July 2, 1863, at Gettysburg, Pa.; re-enlisted as a veteran, December 24, 1863; wounded in action, May 6, 1864, at the Wilderness, Va.; transferred to Co. G, One Hundred and Twentieth Infantry, October 30, 1864.

Ecker, Michael—Age, 40 years. Enlisted, October 16, 1861, at Dunkirk, to serve three years; mustered in as private, Co. H, October 31, 1861; died in insane asylum, Washington, D.C., no date; supposed to be identical with George Ecker.

Egert, John—Age, 17 years. Enlisted at Camp Baker, Md., to serve three years, and mustered in as private, Co. H, November 1, 1861; appointed musician in April 1863; re-enlisted as a veteran, December 24, 1863; deserted in May 1864, at Fredericksburg, Va.; also born as Egart.

Errion, Gotlieb—Age, 32 years. Enlisted, August 27, 1862, at Dunkirk, to serve three years; mustered in as private, Co. H, September 2, 1862; wounded in action, July 2, 1863, at Gettysburg, Pa.; also

May 6, 1864, at Wilderness, Va.; mustered out, June 5, 1865, at Washington, D.C.; also born as Gotlieb Freon.

Frank, Levi D.—Age, 27 years. Enlisted, August 24, 1862, at Dunkirk, to serve three years; mustered in as private, Co. H, September 2, 1862; wounded in action, July 2, 1863, at Gettysburg, Pa.; promoted corporal, April 11, 1864; wounded in action, May 6, 1864, at Wilderness, Va.; transferred to Co. F, One Hundred and Twentieth Infantry, October 30, 1864.

Fry, Joseph H.—Age, 22 years. Enlisted, August 27, 1862, at Dunkirk, to serve three years; mustered in as private, Co. H, September 2, 1862; transferred to Co. K, One Hundred and Twentieth Infantry, October 30, 1864.

Gibson, Allen—Age, 30 years. Enlisted at New York City, to serve three years, and mustered in as private, Co. H, October 27, 1861; killed in action, July 1, 1862, at Malvern Hill, Va.

Gudgesset, John—Age, 32 years. Enlisted, September 25, 1861, at Dunkirk, to serve three years; mustered in as private, Co. H, October 31, 1861; killed in action, May 5, 1862, at Williamsburg, Va.; also born as Gudgeset.

Gunn, Dennis—Age, 30 years. Enlisted, October 1, 1861, at Dunkirk, to serve three years; mustered in as private, Co. H, October 31, 1861; killed in action, May 5, 1862, at Williamsburg, Va.

Gunther, Charles—Age, 19 years. Enlisted at Dunkirk, to serve three years, and mustered in as private, Co. H, November 4, 1861; killed in action, May 5, 1862, at Williamsburg, Va.

Hare, John B.—Age, 30 years. Enrolled, October 14, 1861, at Dunkirk, to serve three years; mustered in as corporal, Co. H, October 31, 1861; promoted sergeant, July 3, 1862; mustered in as second lieutenant, Co. A, May 1, 1863; transferred to Co. F, September 1, 1863; to Co. G, November 1, 1863; dismissed, January 13, 1864. Commissioned second lieutenant, September 5, 1863, with rank from April 2, 1863, vice H.C. Steward, promoted.

Harrington, Joseph—Age, 27 years. Enlisted at New York City, to serve three years, and mustered in as private, Co. H, January 9, 1862; wounded in action, August 29, 1862, at Bull Run, Va.; discharged for disability, February 6, 1863, at Convalescent Camp, Va.

Harris, James—Age, 25 years. Enlisted, October 14, 1861, at Dunkirk, to serve three years; mustered in as corporal, Co. H, October 31, 1861; wounded in action, June 1, 1862, at Fair Oaks, Va.; discharged, to date August 1, 1862.

Hess, Henry—Age, 19 years. Enlisted, October 14, 1861, at Dunkirk, to serve three years; mustered in as private, Co. H, October 31, 1861; captured in action, May 5, 1862, at Williamsburg, Va.; paroled, May 11, 1862; discharged, May 23, 1862, at Washington, D.C.

Heyl, Frederick—Age, 20 years. Enlisted, August 25, 1862, at Dunkirk, to serve three years; mustered in as private, Co. H, September 2, 1862; promoted corporal, May 1, 1863; wounded in action, July 2, 1863, at Gettysburg, Pa.; discharged for his wounds, April 4, 1864, at Camp Stevens, near Brandy Station, Va.

Heyl, Henry—Age, 18 years. Enlisted, August 26, 1862, at Dunkirk, to serve three years; mustered in as private, Co. H, September 2, 1862; killed in action, May 3, 1863, at Chancellorsville, Va.

Higler, Godfred—Age, 18 years. Enlisted, August 27, 1862, at Dunkirk, to serve three years; mustered in as private, Co. H, September 2, 1862; wounded in action, May 3, 1863, at Chancellorsville, Va.; discharged for wounds, October 2, 1863, from U.S. General Hospital, Washington, D.C.; also born as Heighler.

Higler, John—Age, 42 years. Enlisted, August 27, 1862, at Dunkirk, to serve three years; mustered in as private, Co. H, September 2, 1862; killed in action, July 2, 1863, at Gettysburg, Pa.; born as Heiglar.

Hinman, Euratus E.—Age, 22 years. Enlisted, August 27, 1862, at Dunkirk, to serve three years; mustered in as private, Co. H, September 2, 1862; promoted corporal, May 1, 1863; wounded in action, July 2, 1863, at Gettysburg, Pa.; transferred to Veteran Reserve Corps, March 15, 1864.

Horth, Charles H.—Age, 24 years. Enlisted, October 17, 1861, at Dunkirk, to serve three years; mustered in as private, Co. H, October 31, 1861; wounded and captured in action, July 1, 1862, at Malvern Hill, Va.; paroled, no date; mustered out with company, October 31, 1864, near Petersburg, Va.

Joell, Isaac—Age, 24 years. Enlisted, October 12, 1861, at Dunkirk, to serve three years; mustered in as private, Co. H, October 31, 1861; promoted corporal, September 15, 1862; transferred to Veteran Reserve Corps, February 15, 1864.

Joell, Napoleon—Age, 25 years. Enlisted, October 14, 1861, at Dunkirk, to serve three years; mustered in as private, Co. H, October 31, 1861; mustered out with company, October 31, 1864, near Petersburg, Va.

Johansin, Christian—Age, 40 years. Enlisted, September 27, 1861, at Dunkirk, to serve three years; mustered in as private, Co. H, October 31, 1861; wounded in action, July 2, 1863, and deserted, July 27, 1863, at Gettysburg, Pa.

Johnson, Allen H.—Ago, 26 years. Enlisted, August 27, 1862, at Dunkirk, to serve three years; mustered in as private, Co. H, September 2, 1862; wounded in action, July 2, 1863, at Gettysburg, Pa., and again May 12, 1864, at Spotsylvania, Va.;

transferred to Co. H, One Hundred and Twentieth Infantry, October 30, 1864.

Jones, Lucius Jr., —Age, 18 years. Enlisted, October 2, 1861, at Dunkirk, to serve three years; mustered in as private, Co. H, October 33, 1861; promoted corporal, May 1, 1863; reenlisted as a veteran, December 24, 1863; transferred to Co. A, One Hundred and Twentieth Infantry, October 30, 1864.

Jones, William—Age, 32 years. Enlisted at Dunkirk, to serve three years, and mustered in as private, Co. H, November 2, 1861; wounded in action, May 5, 1862, at Williamsburg, Va.; promoted sergeant, July 3, 1862; discharged for disability, December 10, 1862, at camp, near Falmouth, Va.; also born as Ensign B. Jones.

Jones, William G.—Age, 43 years. Enlisted at New York City, to serve three years, and mustered in as private, Co. H, October 29, 1861; killed in action, May 5, 1862, at Williamsburg, Va.

Keoner, Nicholas—Age, 27 years. Enlisted, August 11, 1862, at Dunkirk, to serve three years; mustered in as private, Co. H, September 2, 1862; killed in action, May 6, 1864, at Wilderness, Va.; also born as Keiner.

Keopka, William—Age, 20 years. Enlisted, October 14, 1861, at Dunkirk, to serve three years; mustered in as private, Co. H, October 31, 1861; wounded in action, June 25, 1862, near Fair Oaks, Va.; discharged for wounds, September 15, 1862, at Philadelphia, Pa.

Kersh, Alexander—Age, 20 years. Enlisted, October 4, 1861, at Dunkirk, to serve three years; mustered in as private, Co. H, October 31, 1861; discharged for disability, February 7, 1863, at Convalescent Camp, Va.; also born as Alexander Kaist and Kerst.

King, Thomas W.—Age, 25 years. Enlisted, October 18, 1861, at Dunkirk, to serve three years; mustered in as wagoner, Co. H, October 31, 1861; discharged (for injury received at Fredericksburg, Va., December 13, 1862), May 8, 1863, at U.S. General Hospital, David's Island, New York Harbor.

Koch, Herman—Age, 19 years. Enlisted, October 11, 1861, at Dunkirk, to serve three years; mustered in as private, Co. H, October 31, 1861; re-enlisted as a veteran, December 24, 1863; wounded in action May 6, 1864, at the Wilderness, Va.; transferred to Co. K, One Hundred and Twentieth Infantry, October 30, 1864.

Krien, Mathias—Age, 21 years. Enlisted at Dunkirk, to serve three years, and mustered in as private, Co. H, November 6, 1861; captured in action, May 3, 1863, at Chancellorsville, Va.; paroled, no date; re-enlisted as a veteran, December 24, 1863; deserted in January 1864, on expiration of furlough.

Kruser, Edward—Age, 18 years. Enlisted, October 1, 1861, at Dunkirk, to serve three years; mustered in as private, Co. H, October 25, 1861; killed in action, May 5, 1862, at Williamsburg, Va.

Kugler, John—Age, 20 years. Enlisted, October 14, 1861, at Dunkirk, to serve three years; mustered in as private, Co. H, October 31, 1861; wounded in action, May 5, 1862, at Williamsburg, Va.; discharged for his wounds, October 18, 1862, at camp near Alexandria, Va.

Laporte, Benjamin—Age, 17 years. Enlisted at New York City, to serve three years, and mustered in as private, Co. H, October 23, 1861; wounded in action, May 5, 1862, at Williamsburg, Va.; killed in action, May 6, 1864, at the Wilderness, Va.

Lavigne, William—Age, 18 years. Enlisted, October 1, 1861, at Dunkirk, to serve three years; mustered in as private, Co. H, October 31, 1861; killed in action, May 5, 1862, at Williamsburg, Va.

Leimback, William—Age, 28 years. Enlisted, October 1, 1861, at Dunkirk, to serve three years; mustered in as private, Co. H, October 31, 1861; killed in action, May 5, 1862, at Williamsburg, Va.

Leinebach, Peter—Age, 28 years. Enlisted, October 1, 1861, at Dunkirk, to serve three years; mustered in as private, Co. H, October 31, 1861; wounded in action, August 27, 1862, at Bristoe Station, Va.; died of disease, February 24, 1863, at U.S. Hospital, Annapolis, Md.

Loeb, Daniel—Age, 31 years. Enrolled, October 23, 1861, at Dunkirk, to serve three years; mustered in as second lieutenant, Co. H, November 6, 1861; as first lieutenant, Co. I, June 19, 1862; captain, Co. K, October 25, 1862; discharged, November 1, 1862. Commissioned second lieutenant, January 7, 1862, with rank from September 23, 1861, original; first lieutenant, June 30, 1862, with rank from May 6, 1862, vice W.J. O'Neill, promoted; captain, October 25, 1862, with rank from same date, vice J.S. Austin, promoted.

Madell, Joseph—Age, 23 years. Enlisted, August 24, 1862, at Dunkirk, to serve three years; mustered in as private, Co. H, September 2, 1862; wounded in action, October 2, 1864, near Petersburg, Va.; transferred to Co. B, One Hundred and Twentieth Infantry, October 30, 1864; also born as Maidell.

Manch, John—Age, 24 years. Enlisted, August 29, 1862, at Sheridan, to serve three years; mustered in as private, Co. H, September 2, 1862; captured in action, May 3, 1863, at Chancellorsville, Va.; paroled, no date; promoted corporal in May 1864; transferred to One Hundred and Twentieth Infantry, October 30, 1864; also born as Mank.

Marcus, Leopold—Age, 30 years. Enrolled at Dunkirk, to serve three years, and mustered in as first lieutenant, Co. H, September 23, 1861; wounded in action, May 5, 1862, at Williamsburg, Va.; discharged, July 7, 1862. Commissioned first lieutenant, January 7, 1862, with rank from September 23, 1861, original.

Marks, Robert—Age, 19 years. Enlisted, August 30, 1862, at Dunkirk, to serve three years; mustered in as private, Co. H, September 2, 1862; died of disease, February 23, 1863, in General Hospital, Annapolis, Md.

Martins, Henry—Age, 32 years. Enlisted, August 24, 1862, at Dunkirk, to serve three years; mustered in as private, Co. H, September 2, 1862; deserted, November 1, 1862, at Alexandria, Va.

McGinnis, William—Age, 28 years. Enrolled, October 4, 1861, at Dunkirk, to serve three years; mustered in as first sergeant, Co. H, October 31, 1861; promoted sergeant, major, May 17, 1862; mustered in as second lieutenant, Co. G, June 2, 1862; transferred to Co. I, November 1, 1862; discharged, January 11, 1863. Commissioned second lieutenant, May 30, 1862, with rank from May 17, 1862, vice J.A. Smith, promoted.

McGuinn, Patrick—Age, 18 years. Enlisted, September 27, 1861, at Dunkirk, to serve three years; mustered in as private, Co. H, October 31, 1861; promoted corporal, December 11, 1862; sergeant, in November 1863; re-enlisted as a veteran, December 24, 1863; deserted in January 1864, on expiration of furlough; also born as McGinn and McGuire.

McGuire, John—Age, 40 years. Enlisted, August 8, 1862, at Dunkirk, to serve three years; mustered in as private, Co. H, September 2, 1862; died of disease, September 5, 1864, at David's Island Hospital, New York Harbor; also born as Maguire.

McGuire, Thomas—Age, 30 years. Enlisted, September 27, 1861, at Dunkirk, to serve three years; mustered in as private, Co. H, October 31, 1861; captured in action, May 8, 1863, at Chancellorsville, Va.; paroled, no date; transferred to Co. G, December 24, 1863; re-enlisted as a veteran, February 13, 1864; transferred to Co. I, One Hundred and Twentieth Infantry, July 24, 1864; also born as Maguire.

McMahon, John—Age, 30 years. Enlisted, October 5, 1861, at Dunkirk, to serve three years; mustered in as private, Co. H, October 81, 1861; promoted sergeant, July 3, 1862; discharged for disability, March 3, 1868, at Mount Pleasant Hospital, Washington, D.C.

McNamara, John—Age, 35 years. Enlisted, October 15, 1861, at Dunkirk, to serve three years; mustered in as private, Co. H, October 31, 1861; killed in action, May 5, 1862, at Williamsburg, Va.

Miller, Gottelyn—Age, 33 years. Enlisted, August 26, 1862, at Dunkirk, to serve three years; mustered in as private, Co. H, September 2, 1862; wounded in action, May 6, 1864, at the Wilderness, Va.; transferred to Co. H, One Hundred and Twentieth Infantry, October 30, 1864.

Moloch, John—Age, 21 years. Enlisted, October 1, 1861, at Dunkirk, to serve three years; mustered in as private, Co. H, October 31, 1861; wounded in action, July 2, 1863, at Gettysburg, Pa.; transferred to Veteran Reserve Corps, May 1, 1864; mustered out with detachment, September 9, 1864, at Philadelphia, Pa., veteran.

Morewood, Samuel H.—Age, 33 years. Enlisted, September 16, 1861, at Dunkirk, to serve three years; mustered in as corporal, Co. H, October 31, 1861; discharged for disability, June 23, 1862, at Annapolis, Md.

Murphy, Hamilton—Age, 30 years. Enlisted, September 17, 1861, at New York City, to serve three years; mustered in as private, Co. H, October 17, 1861; wounded in action, May 3, 1863, at Chancellorsville, Va.; discharged for disability, July 11, 1864, at Government Insane Asylum, Washington, D.C.

Nauohton, Francis—Age, 32 years. Enlisted at Dunkirk, to serve three years, and mustered in as private, Co. H, November 6, 1861; deserted, January 20, 1863, from Camp Nelson Taylor, Va.; also born as Patrick Naughton.

Paulius, Peter C.—Age, 32 years. Enlisted, August 23, 1862, at Dunkirk, to serve three years; mustered in as private, Co. H, September 2, 1862; captured in action, May 3, 1863, at Chancellorsville, Va.; paroled, no date; deserted in June 1863, at Camp Parole, Md.

Pipp, John—Age, 41 years. Enlisted, August 27, 1862, at Dunkirk, to serve three years; mustered in as private, Co. H, September 2, 1862; captured in action, May 3, 1863, at Chancellorsville, Va.; paroled, no date; wounded in action, May 6, 1864, at the Wilderness, Va.; transferred to Co. K, One Hundred and Twentieth Infantry, October 30, 1864.

Randall, Uriah S.—Age, 41 years. Enlisted, August 24, 1862, at Dunkirk, to serve three years; mustered in as private, Co. H, September 2, 1862; wounded in action, May 6, 1864, at the Wilderness, Va.; transferred to Co. H, One Hundred and Twentieth Infantry, October 30, 1864.

Reynolds, John G.—Age, 23 years. Enlisted, September 16, 1861, at New York City, to serve three years; mustered in as musician, Co. H, October 31, 1861; discharged for disability, January 13, 1863, at General Hospital, New Haven, Conn.

Robinson, Samuel—Age, 30 years. Enlisted, August 26, 1862, at Sheridan, to serve three years; mustered in as private, Co. H, September 2, 1862;

transferred to Co. K, One Hundred and Twentieth Infantry, October 30, 1864.

Rodenberg, Heinrich—Age, 23 years. Enlisted, May 27, 1861, at New York City, to serve three years; mustered in as private, Co. H, June 21, 1861; mustered out with company, June 20, 1864, near Petersburg, Va.

Rogers, Jerome—Age, 19 years. Enlisted, October 2, 1861, at Dunkirk, to serve three years; mustered in as private, Co. H, October 31, 1861; captured in action, June 1, 1862, at Fair Oaks, Va.; paroled, no date; no further record.

Ryan, Martin—Age, 26 years. Enlisted at Dunkirk, to serve three years, and mustered in as private, Co. H, November 2, 1861; wounded in action, between June 26 and July 2, 1862; captured in action, May 3, 1863, at Chancellorsville, Va.; paroled, no date; re-enlisted as a veteran, December 24, 1863; died of disease, October 3, 1864, in Field Hospital, Third Division, Second Corps.

Schneitter, John Charles—Age, 34 years. Enlisted, October 4, 1861, at Dunkirk, to serve three years; mustered in as private, Co. H, October 31, 1861; died of disease, January 7, 1862, at Regimental Hospital, Camp Wool, Md.

Schwornd, Charles—Age, 25 years. Enlisted, August 23, 1862, at Dunkirk, to serve three years; mustered in as private, Co. H, September 2, 1862; died of disease, March 1, 1864, at Regimental Hospital, Brandy Station, Va.; born as Charles Schwind.

Shay, James O.—Age, 35 years. Enlisted, October 11, 1861, at Dunkirk, to serve three years; mastered in as private, Co. H, October 31, 1861; discharged for disability, February 5, 1863, from General Hospital, Washington, D.C.; also born as O'Shay.

Shilling, John H.—Age 20 years. Enlisted, August 25, 1862, at Dunkirk, to serve three years; mustered in as private, Co. H, September 2, 1862; wounded in action, May 3, 1863, at Chancellorsville, Va.; transferred to Veteran Reserve Corps, August 1, 1863; discharged, July 1, 1865, at Boston, Mass.

Snowble, John F.—Age, 29 years. Enlisted, September 23, 1861, at Dunkirk, to serve three years; mustered in as corporal, Co. H, October 31, 1861; captured in action, May 5, 1862, at Williamsburg, Va.; paroled, no date; promoted sergeant, September 15, 1862; wounded in action, July 24, 1863, at Manassas Gap, Va.; discharged for wounds, July 26, 1864, at Judiciary Square Hospital, Washington, D.C.

Squibbs, Robert—Age, 35 years. Enlisted, August 27, 1862, at New York City, to serve three years; mustered in as private, Co. H, September 2, 1862; discharged for disability, January 5, 1863, at Washington, D.C.

Stanton, Warren J.—Age, 26 years. Enrolled, October 14, 1861, at Dunkirk, to serve three years; mustered in as sergeant, Co. H, October 31, 1861; promoted first sergeant, May 7, 1862; wounded in action, June 25, 1862, near Fair Oaks, Va.; promoted sergeant-major, July 2, 1862; second lieutenant, Co. A, August 5, 1862; transferred to Co. H, November 1, 1862; discharged for disability, January 17, 1863. Commissioned second lieutenant, December 1, 1862, with rank from August 5, 1862, vice C.H. Hydorn, promoted.

Streator, Harvey—Age, 21 years. Enlisted, August 28, 1862, at Dunkirk, to serve three years; mustered in as private, Co. H, September 2, 1862; transferred to One Hundred and Twentieth Infantry, October 30, 1864; born as Harry H. Stroator.

Strong, Gilbert—Age, 34 years. Enlisted, August 26, 1862, at Dunkirk, to serve three years; mustered in as private, Co. H, September 2, 1862; transferred to One Hundred and Twentieth Infantry, October 30, 1864.

Stroyer, George—Age, 28 years. Enlisted, August 27, 1862, at Dunkirk, to serve three years; mustered in as private, Co. H, September 2, 1862; wounded in action, July 2, 1863, at Gettysburg, Pa.; transferred to Co. B, One Hundred and Twentieth Infantry, October 30, 1864; born as John Stroyer.

Treptow, William—Age, 45 years. Enlisted, September 27, 1861, at Dunkirk, to serve three years; mustered in as private, Co. H, October 31, 1861; wounded, June 25, 1862, near Fair Oaks, Va.; discharged for disability, October 15, 1862, at Convalescent Hospital, Ellsworth, Va.; also born as Trepton and Tripton.

Warner, Hiram D.—Age, 24 years. Enlisted, August 23, 1862, at Dunkirk, to serve three years; mustered in as private, Co. H, September 2, 1862; discharged for disability, February 28, 1863, at U.S.A. General Hospital, Chestnut Hill, Philadelphia, Pa.

Werner, Phillip—Age, 23 years. Enlisted, September 25, 1861, at Dunkirk, to serve three years; mustered in as private, Co. H, October 31, 1861; promoted corporal, May 7, 1862; wounded in action, July 2, 1863, at Gettysburg, Pa.; discharged for wounds, December 22, 1863, at Philadelphia, Pa.; also born as Philip Warner.

Wild, Robert—Age, 33 years. Enlisted, October 19, 1861, at Dunkirk, to serve three years; mustered in as private, Co. H, October 31, 1861; died of disease, March 17, 1862, at Camp Wool, Md.

Williams, Daniel—Age, 19 years. Enlisted, June 1, 1861, at Flushing, to serve three years; mustered in as private, Co. H, August 8, 1861; transferred to Co. C, Seventy-fourth Infantry, January 1862.

Williams, Thomas L.—Age, 18 years. Enlisted, September 30, 1861, at Dunkirk, to serve three years; mustered in private, Co. H, October 31, 1861; discharged, to date, June 25, 1863.

Williams, William J.—Age, 18 years. Enlisted, September 30, 1861, at Dunkirk, to serve three years; mustered in as musician, Co. H, October 31, 1861; died of disease, December 9, 1861, in regimental hospital, at Camp Wool, Md.

Wiman, Lorenzo—Age, 23 years. Enlisted, September 25, 1861, at Dunkirk, to serve three years; mustered in as private, Co. H, October 31, 1861; wounded in action, August 29, 1862, at Bull Run, Va.; mustered out with company, October 31, 1864, near Petersburg, Va.; born as Weiman.

Wimmer, Carl T.—Age, 40 years. Enlisted at Dunkirk, to serve three years, and mustered in as private, Co. H, November 19, 1861; deserted, July 20, 1863, near Falmouth, Va.; born as Weimer.

Wolf, Charles H.R.—Age, 40 years. Enlisted, September 23, 1861, at Dunkirk, to serve three years; mustered in as private, Co. H, October 31, 1861; killed in action, May 5, 1862, at Williamsburg, Va.

Wyman, Alonzo—Age, 33 years. Enlisted, August 26, 1862, at Sheridan, to serve three years; mustered in as private, Co. H, September 2, 1862; wounded, no date or place; transferred to One Hundred and Twentieth Infantry, October 30, 1864.

Yerger, Mathew—Age, 32 years. Enlisted, August 26, 1862, at Dunkirk, to serve three years; mustered in as private, Co. H, September 2, 1862; transferred to Co. K, One Hundred and Twentieth Infantry, October 30, 1864.

Zahn, Jacob—Age, 22 years. Enlisted, October 9, 1861, at Dunkirk, to serve three years; mustered in as private, Co. H, October 31, 1861; died of disease, February 25, 1862, at Regimental Hospital.

Zimmer, Henry C.—Age, 22 years. Enlisted at New York City, to serve three years, and mustered in as private, Co. H, December 10, 1861; wounded, no date; died of his wounds, June 17, 1862, in general hospital, New York City.

Company I

Organized in Delhi, N.Y., in May 1861. Mustered into the United States service June 21, 1861.

Captains

Robert T. Johnson, from June 21, 1861, to September 26, 1862.
Samuel Bailey, from September 26, 1862, to June 20, 1864.

First Lieutenants

John P. Sandford, from June 21, 1861, to May 5, 1862.
Daniel Loeb, from June 19 to October 25, 1862.
Henry J. McDonough, from October 25 to November 1862.
James Fogarty, from November 1, 1862, to February 5, 1863.
Michael Cooke, from February 5, 1863, to June 20, 1864.

Second Lieutenants

Hugh J. Winters, from June 21, 1861, to April 17, 1862.
James Fogarty, from June 3 to June 23, 1862.
Patrick Anderson, from June 26 to October 11, 1862.
Henry C. Steward, from October 11 to November 1, 1862.
William McGinnis, from November 1, 1862, to January 11, 1863.
William D. Hall, from January 11 to June 10, 1863.
David B. Parker, from June 6, 1863, to June 20, 1864.

Bagley, Charles H.—Age, 21 years. Enlisted, June 4, 1861, at Staten Island, to serve three years; mustered in as private, Co. I, June 21, 1861; discharged for disability, March 15, 1862, at Camp Wool, Md.

Bailey, Oscar O.—Age, 16 years. Enlisted, January 16, 1864, at Delhi, to serve three years; mustered in as private, Co. I, January 26, 1864; transferred to Co. B, One Hundred and Twentieth Infantry, June 20, 1864.

Ballon, Charles—Age, 21 years. Enlisted, June 4, 1861, at Delhi, to serve three years; mustered in as private, Co. I, June 21, 1861; wounded in action, July 2, 1863, at Gettysburg, Pa.; mustered out with company, June 20, 1864, near Petersburg, Va.

Barber, Abraham J.—Age, 19 years. Enlisted, July 3, 1861, at Staten Island, to serve three years; mustered in as private, Co. I, July 10, 1861; died of disease, February 22, 1862, at Camp Wool, Md.

Bates, Benjamin G.—Age, 35 years. Enlisted, June 4, 1861, at Delhi, to serve three years; mustered in as private, Co. I, June 21, 1861; discharged for disability, July 28, 1862.

Bell, Douglas—Age, 20 years. Enlisted, June 4, 1861, at Delhi, to serve three years; mustered in as private, Co. I, June 21, 1861; wounded and captured in action, May 3, 1863, at Chancellorsville, Va.; paroled, May 14, 1863; discharged for disability, April 29, 1864.

Bell, Harvey W.—Age, 18 years. Enlisted, June 4, 1861, at Delhi, to serve three years; mustered in as private, Co. I, June 21, 1861; wounded in action, May 5, 1862, at Williamsburg, Va.; discharged for his wounds, April 28, 1863, at Albany, N.Y.

Bookhout, Talman C.—Age, 21 years. Enlisted, June 4, 1861, at Delhi, to serve three years; mustered in as private, Co. I, June 1861; mustered out with company, June 20, 1864, near Petersburg, Va.

Bostwick, George H.—Age, 21 years. Enlisted, June 4, 1861, at Delhi, to serve three years; mustered in as private, Co. I, June 21, 1861; mustered out with company, June 20, 1864, near Petersburg, Va.

Boyle, John—Age, 43 years. Enlisted at New Jersey, to serve three years, and mustered in as private, Co. L, October 30, 1861; transferred to Co. I, February 25, 1862; no further record.

Bryce, Peter—Age, 26 years. Enlisted, June 4, 1861, at Delhi, to serve three years; mustered in as private, Co. I, June 21, 1861; died of disease, December 5, 1861, at Camp Wool, Md.; also born as Brice.

Caskev, William J.—Age, 21 years. Enlisted, June 4, 1861, at Delhi, to serve three years; mustered in as private, Co. I, June 21, 1861; discharged for disability, August 1, 1862, at Harrison's Landing, Va.

Church, Delos—Age, 19 years. Enlisted, June 4, 1861, at Delhi, to serve three years; mustered in as private, Co. I, June 21, 1861; promoted corporal in May 1863; captured, October 13, 1863, at Greenwich, Va.; paroled, May 11, 1865; mustered out June 29, 1865, at New York City.

Clark, James W.—Age, 34 years. Enlisted, June 4, 1861, at Delhi, to serve three years; mustered in as private, Co. I, June 21, 1861; mustered out with company, June 20, 1864, near Petersburg, Va.

Clark, John—Age, 29 years. Enlisted, June 4, 1861, at Delhi, to serve three years; mustered in as sergeant, Co. I, June 21, 1861; discharged for disability, July 23, 1862, at Harrison's Bar, Va.

Conroy, William I.—Age, 18 years. Enlisted, July 24, 1861, at Staten Island, to serve three years; mustered in as private, Co. I, August 8, 1861; promoted quartermaster-sergeant in November 1862; mustered out, July 23, 1864, near Petersburg, Va.

Cormack, Francis—Age, 21 years. Enlisted, June 4, 1861, at Delhi, to serve three years; mustered in as corporal, Co. I, June 21, 1861; killed in action, May 5, 1862, at Williamsburg, Va.

Cowley, Charles V.—Age, 21 years. Enlisted, June 4, 1861, at Delhi, to serve three years; mustered in as private, Co. I, June 21, 1861; captured in action, May 3, 1863, at Chancellorsville, Va.; paroled, May 14, 1863, at City Point, Va.; wounded in action, May 10, 1864, at Spotsylvania, Va.; mustered out with company, June 20, 1864.

Cowley, Hector—Age, 24 years, Enlisted, June 4, 1861, at Delhi, to serve three years; mustered in as private, Co. I, June 21, 1861; killed in action, May 23, 1864, at North Anna River, Va.; also born as Crowley.

Crawford, Theodore W.—Age, 20 years. Enlisted, July 3, 1861, at Staten Island, to serve three years; mustered in as musician, Co. I, July 10, 1861; mustered out with company, June 20, 1864, near Petersburg, Va.

Davidson, George W.—Age, 25 years. Enlisted, June 4, 1861, at Delhi, to serve three years; mustered in as private, Co. I, June 21, 1861; mustered out with company, June 20, 1864, near Petersburg, Va.

Farrell, William—Age, 28 years. Enlisted, June 4, 1861, at Delhi, to serve three years; mustered in as private, Co. I, June 21, 1861; discharged for disability, August 1, 1862, at Harrison's Landing, Va.

Fisher, James P.—Age, 22 years. Enlisted, June 4, 1861, at Delhi, to serve three years; mustered in as private, Co. I, June 21, 1861; captured in action, May 3, 1863, at Chancellorsville, Va.; paroled, May 14, 1863, at City Point, Va.; discharged for disability, October 30, 1863, at Convalescent Camp, Va.

Fogerty, James—Age, 27 years. Enrolled, June 4, 1861, at Delhi, to serve three years; mustered in as sergeant, Co. I, June 21, 1861; promoted sergeant major, January 2, 1862; mustered in as second lieutenant, Co. I, June 3, 1862; first lieutenant, Co. G, June 23, 1862; transferred to Co. I, November 1, 1862; wounded in action, December 13, 1862; discharged, February 5, 1863. Commissioned second lieutenant, June 30, 1862, with rank from June 3, 1862, vice H.J. Winters, resigned; first lieutenant, December 1, 1862, with rank from June 23, 1862, vice E.B. Harnett, promoted.

Ford, Henry C.—Age, 20 years. Enlisted, June 4, 1861, at Delhi, to serve three years; mustered in as corporal, Co. I, June 21, 1861; promoted sergeant, September 25, 1862; wounded in action, no date or place; discharged for wounds, September 10, 1864, at McDougal General Hospital, Fort Schuyler, New York Harbor.

Foulks, Peter Y.—Age, 21 years. Enlisted, June 4, 1861, at Delhi, to serve three years; mustered in as private, Co. I, June 21, 1861; wounded, no date; mustered out with company, June 20, 1864, near Petersburg, Va.

Foulks, William S.—Age, 22 years. Enlisted, June 20, 1861, at Staten Island, to serve three years; mustered in as private, Co. I, July 10, 1861; discharged for disability, May 31, 1862, at Budds Farm, Md.;

subsequent service in Co. I, Eighteenth Cavalry.

French, John—Age, 24 years. Enlisted, June 4, 1861, at Delhi, to serve three years; mustered in as private, Co. I, June 21, 1861; killed in action, May 5, 1862, at Williamsburg, Va.

Garabant, Charles—Age, 19 years. Enlisted at New York City, to serve three years, and mustered in as corporal, Co. L, November 19, 1861; no record subsequent to December 31, 1861.

Goodrich, George H.—Age, 32 years. Enlisted, June 4, 1861, at Delhi, to serve three years; mustered in as corporal, Co. I, June 21, 1861; wounded and captured in action, July 2, 1862, at Malvern Hill, Va.; paroled, July 25, 1862, at City Point, Va.; mustered out with company, June 20, 1864.

Goodrich, Joseph W.—Age, 20 years. Enlisted, June 4, 1861, at Delhi, to serve three years; mustered in as musician, Co. I, June 21, 1861; sent to ranks in June 1861; killed in action, May 5, 1862, at Williamsburg, Va.

Gordon, James M.—Age, 27 years. Enlisted, June 4, 1861, at Delhi, to serve three years; mustered in as sergeant, Co. I, June 21, 1861; wounded in action, August 27, 1862, at Bristoe Station, Va.; discharged for wounds, May 9, 1863, at General Hospital, Alexandria, Va.; also born as John M. Gordon.

Gould, Charles W.—Age, 19 years. Enlisted, June 4, 1861, at Delhi, to serve three years; mustered in as private, Co. I, June 21, 1861; died of disease, February 22, 1862, at Camp Wool, Md.

Grady, John—Age, 35 years. Enlisted at New York City to serve three years, and mustered in as private, Co. I, August 12, 1862; transferred to Veteran Reserve Corps, February 15, 1864, from which mustered out July 20, 1865, at Washington, D.C.

Hager, Austin—Age, 21 years. Enlisted, June 4, 1861, at Delhi, to serve three years; mustered in as private, Co. I, June 21, 1861; re-enlisted as a veteran, March 15, 1864; transferred to Co. B, One Hundred and Twentieth Infantry, June 20, 1864.

Haynes, John J.—Age, 21 years. Enlisted, June 4, 1861, at Delhi, to serve three years; mustered in as private, Co. I, June 21, 1861; wounded in action, July 2, 1863, at Gettysburg, Pa.; discharged for wounds, May 23, 1864, at De Camp U.S. General Hospital, David's Island, New York Harbor.

Hogaboom, Levi L.—Age, 36 years. Enlisted, June 4, 1861, at Delhi, to serve three years; mustered in as private, Co. I, June 21, 1861; transferred to Co. B, Tenth Regiment, Veteran Reserve Corps, June 24, 1863.

Hogaboon, Henry—Age, 20 years. Enlisted, June 20, 1861, at Staten Island, to serve three years; mustered in as private, Co. I, August 8, 1861; died of disease, January 18, 1862.

Holibert, Charles H.—Age, 20 years. Enlisted, June 4, 1861, at Delhi, to serve three years; mustered in as private, Co. I, June 21, 1861; mustered out with company, June 20, 1864, near Petersburg, Va.; also born as Chas. W. Hulburt.

Horton, Herschel D.—Age, 20 years. Enlisted June 4, 1861, at Delhi, to serve three years; mustered in as corporal, Co. I, June 21, 1861; returned to ranks, September 1861; discharged for disability, July 20, 1862, at Harrison's Landing, Va.; also born as Norton.

Howard, Philip—Age, 25 years. Enlisted, June 4, 1861, at Delhi, to serve three years; mustered in as private, Co. I, June 21, 1861; killed in action, May 2, 1863, at Chancellorsville, Va.

Howell, Samuel—Age, 23 years. Enrolled, June 4, 1861, at Delhi, to serve three years; mustered in as corporal, Co. I, June 21, 1861; promoted sergeant, August 1, 1862; sergeant major, October 1862; second lieutenant, Co. C, December 26, 1862; mustered in as first lieutenant, Co. K, July 1, 1863; dismissed, May 9, 1864. Commissioned second lieutenant, August 7, 1863, with rank from December 26, 1862, vice W. McConnell, promoted; first lieutenant, August 7, 1863, with rank from May 4, 1863, vice H.F. Ellis, killed in action.

Hoyt, Lewis—Age, 21 years. Enlisted, June 4, 1861, at Delhi, to serve three years; mustered in as private, Co. I, June 21, 1861; transferred to Co. G, December 1863; re-enlisted as a veteran, December 21, 1863; transferred to Co. I, One Hundred and Twentieth Infantry, July 24, 1864.

Hughes, Daniel—Age, 20 years. Enlisted, September 18, 1861, at Delhi, to serve three years; mustered in as private, Co. I, September 20, 1861; wounded in action, May 5, 1862, at Williamsburg, Va.; promoted corporal, November 1, 1862; wounded in action, July 2, 1863, at Gettysburg, Pa.; discharged for wounds, August 17, 1864, from De Camp Hospital, David's Island, New York Harbor.

Husted, William H.—Age, 21 years. Enlisted, June 4, 1861, at Delhi, to serve three years; mustered in as private, Co. I, June 21, 1861; wounded in action, May 5, 1862, at Williamsburg, Va.; discharged for wounds, September 26, 1862, near Alexandria, Va.

Hyatt, Edgar S.—Age, 20 years. Enlisted, July 23, 1861, at Staten Island, to serve three years; mustered in as private, Co. I, August 8, 1861; promoted corporal, November 1, 1862; killed in action, May 2, 1863, at Chancellorsville, Va.

Ingraham, Gilbert—Age, 21 years. Enlisted at Delhi, to serve three years, and mustered in as private, Co. I, January 26, 1864; wounded in action at Spotsylvania, Va.; transferred to Co. A, One Hundred and Twentieth Infantry, June 20, 1864.

Johnson, George H.—Age, 19 years. Enlisted, June 4, 1861, at Delhi, to serve three years; mustered in as private, Co. I, June 21, 1861; mustered out with company, June 20, 1864, near Petersburg, Va.

Johnson, Robert T.—Age, 29 years. Enrolled, June 4, 1861, at Delhi, to serve three years; mustered in as captain, Co. I, June 21, 1861; wounded in action, May 5, 1862, at Williamsburg, Va.; discharged, September 26, 1862, for promotion to major, One Hundred and Forty-fourth Infantry. Commissioned captain, January 7, 1862, with rank from June 21, 1861, original.

Jones, Alvazi—Age, 23 years. Enlisted, July 23, 1861, at Staten Island, to serve three years; mustered in as private, Co. I, August 8, 1861; mustered out with company, June 20, 1864, near Petersburg, Va.

Jones, Stephen P.—Age, 21 years. Enlisted, June 4, 1861, at Delhi, to serve three years; mustered in as corporal, Co. I, June 21, 1861; returned to ranks, September 25, 1862; promoted corporal in March 1863, and returned to ranks in April 1864; mustered out with company, June 20, 1864, near Petersburg, Va.

Knight, Joseph S.—Age, 22 years. Enlisted, June 4, 1861, at Delhi, to serve three years; mustered in as private, Co. I, June 21, 1861; mustered out with company, June 20, 1864, near Petersburg, Va.

Kniskern, Matthew L.—Age, 22 years. Enlisted, June 4, 1861, at Delhi, to serve three years; mustered in as private, Co. I, June 21, 1861; captured in action, May 3, 1863, at Chancellorsville, Va.; paroled, May 14, 1863, at City Point, Va.; mustered out with company, June 20, 1864, near Petersburg, Va.

Lakin, Eugene B.—Age, 24 years. Enlisted, June 4, 1861, at Delhi, to serve three years; mustered in as private, Co. I, June 21, 1861; re-enlisted as a veteran, December 24, 1863; wounded in the Wilderness, Va.; transferred to Co. A, One Hundred and Twentieth Infantry, June 20, 1864, to Veteran Reserve Corps, no date; from which discharged, July 25, 1865.

Laon, James—Age, 21 years. Enlisted, June 4, 1861, at Delhi, to serve three years; mustered in as private, Co. I, June 21, 1861; wounded in action, August 27, 1862, at Bristoe Station, Va.; re-enlisted as a veteran, December 24, 1863; wounded at Petersburg, Va., no date; transferred to Co. A, One Hundred and Twentieth Infantry, June 20, 1864.

Lawrence, Thomas—Age, 19 years. Enlisted, June 4, 1861, at Delhi, to serve three years; mustered in as private, Co. I, June 21, 1861; died of disease, July 8, 1862, in hospital, at Fair Oaks, Va.

Loudon, Samuel B.—Age, 21 years. Enlisted, June 4, 1861, at Delhi, to serve three years; mustered in as private, Co. I, June 21, 1861; transferred to Co. G, December 1863; re-enlisted as a veteran, December 21, 1863; transferred to Co. I, One Hundred and Twentieth Infantry, July 24, 1864.

Mahony, John—Age, 28 years. Enlisted, September 8, 1862, at New York City, to serve three years; mustered in as private, Co. I, September 16, 1862; transferred to One Hundred and Second Company, Veteran Reserve Corps, December 14, 1863; died, January 1, 1864, at U.S. Hospital.

Mallon, Thomas—Age, 21 years. Enlisted, June 4, 1861, at Delhi, to serve three years; mustered in as wagoner, Co. I, June 21, 1861; re-enlisted as a veteran, December 24, 1863; transferred to Co. B, One Hundred and Twentieth Infantry, June 20, 1864.

Maxwell, Robert—Age, 21 years. Enlisted, June 4, 1861, at Delhi, to serve three years; mustered in as private, Co. I, June 21, 1861; died of disease, October 18, 1861, at Kalorama General Hospital, Washington, D.C.

McCall, Richard—Age, 20 years. Enlisted, June 4, 1861, at Delhi, to serve three years; mustered in as private, Co. I, June 21, 1861; mustered out with company, June 20, 1864, near Petersburg, Va.

McDonald, James—Age, 30 years. Enlisted, June 4, 1861, at Delhi, to serve three years; mustered in as private, Co. I, June 21, 1861; transferred to Veteran Reserve Corps in September 1863.

McFarland, Andrew—Age, 21 years. Enlisted, June 4, 1861, at Delhi, to serve three years; mustered in as private, Co. I, June 21, 1861; captured in action, October 14, 1863, at Bristoe Station, Va.; died while a prisoner of war, April 4, 1864, at Andersonville, Ga.

McLean, Daniel F.—Age, 21 years. Enlisted, June 4, 1861, at Delhi, to serve three years; mustered in as private, Co. I, June 21, 1861; wounded in action, June 25, 1862, near Fair Oaks, Va.; discharged for wounds, March 9, 1863, at Convalescent Camp, Va.

McNee, John A.—Age, 22 years. Enlisted, June 4, 1861, at Delhi, to serve three years; mustered in as private, Co. I, June 21, 1861; died of disease, January 2, 1862, at Camp Wool, Md.; also born as John M. McNee

Menger, Frederick—Age, 27 years. Enlisted, June 4, 1861, at Delhi, to serve three years; mustered in as private, Co. I, June 21, 1861; promoted corporal, September 25, 1862; re-enlisted as a veteran, December 24, 1863; transferred to Co. B, One Hundred and Twentieth Infantry, June 20, 1864.

Merrill, Emerson F.—Age, 19 years. Enlisted, July 23, 1861, at Staten Island, to serve three years; mustered in as private, Co. I, August 8, 1861; killed in action, May 3, 1863, at Chancellorsville, Va.

Mogel, Frederick—Age, 22 years. Enlisted, January 3, 1864, at Stuyvesant, to serve three years; mustered in as private, Co. I, January 4, 1864; transferred to Co. H, One Hundred and Twentieth Infantry, June 20, 1864.

Moscrip, Jehial—Age, 21 years. Enlisted, June 4, 1861, at Delhi, to serve three years; mustered in as private, Co. I, June 21, 1861; wounded in action, May 3, 1863, at Chancellorsville, Va.; re-enlisted as a veteran, December 24, 1863; promoted corporal, March 1, 1864; wounded, no date, at Petersburg, Va.; transferred to Co. A, One Hundred and Twentieth Infantry, June 20, 1864.

Newcomb, John—Age, 22 years. Enlisted, June 4, 1861, at Delhi, to serve three years; mustered in as private, Co. I, June 21, 1861; promoted corporal in September 1861; sergeant in March 1863; mustered out with company, June 20, 1864, near Petersburg, Va.

Northrop, Roswell B.—Age, 36 years. Enlisted, June 4, 1861, at Delhi, to serve three years; mustered in as private, Co. I, June 21, 1861; wounded in action, December 13, 1862, at Fredericksburg, Va.; discharged for disability, June 17, 1864, at Portsmouth Grove, R.I.

Ostrander, George—Age, 28 years. Enlisted, June 4, 1861, at Delhi, to serve three years; mustered in as private, Co. I, June 21, 1861; discharged for disability, January 22, 1863, at Third Corps Hospital, near Fort Lyon, Va.

Packard, Nathan A.—Age, 36 years. Enlisted, June 4, 1861, at Delhi, to serve three years; mustered in as first sergeant, Co. I, June 21, 1861; wounded in action, May 5, 1862, at Williamsburg, Va.; discharged for wounds, September 13, 1862, at New York City.

Patridge, James T.—Age, 19 years. Enlisted, June 4, 1861, at Delhi, to serve three years; mustered in as private, Co. I, June 21, 1861; killed in action, August 27, 1862, at Bristoe Station, Va.

Penny, Robert—Age, 22 years. Enlisted, June 4, 1861, at Delhi, to serve three years; mustered in as private, Co. I, June 21, 1861; died of disease, August 27, 1861, at Columbia Hospital, D.C.

Pierce, William D.—Age, 24 years. Enlisted, June 4, 1861, at Delhi, to serve three years; mustered in as private, Co. I, June 21, 1861; discharged for disability, September 10, 1862, at Philadelphia, Pa.

Potter, James W.—Age, 23 years. Enlisted at Staten Island, to serve three years, and mustered in as private, Co. I, July 3, 1861; discharged for disability, July 31, 1862, at Harrison's Landing, Va.

Robertson, George C.—Age, 23 years. Enlisted, June 4, 1861, at Delhi, to serve three years; mustered in as private, Co. I, June 21, 1861; promoted corporal, November 1, 1862; sergeant, January 1868; first sergeant, March 1863; wounded and captured in action, May 3, 1863, at Chancellorsville, Va.; paroled, May 14, 1863, at City Point, Va.; re-enlisted as a veteran, December 24, 1863; transferred to Co. A, One Hundred and Twentieth Infantry, June 20, 1864; also born as Robinson.

Robertson, Thomas—Age, 19 years. Enlisted, June 4, 1861, at Delhi, to serve three years; mustered in as private, Co. I, June 21, 1861; died of disease, December 21, 1861, at Camp Wool, Md.; also born as Robinson.

Robinson, John—Age, 25 years. Enrolled, June 4, 1861, at Delhi, to serve three years; mustered in as private, Co. I, June 21, 1861; promoted corporal, October 1861; sergeant, September 25, 1862; first sergeant, January 1863; mustered in as second lieutenant, Co. E, July 1, 1863; wounded in action, July 2, 1863, at Gettysburg, Pa.; transferred to Co. G, March 1, 1864; mustered out, July 23, 1864, near Petersburg, Va.; also born as Robertson. Commissioned second lieutenant, June 13, 1863, with rank from February 5, 1863, vice M. Cook, promoted.

Rosa, Eli—Age, 23 years. Enlisted, June 4, 1861, at Delhi, to serve three years; mustered in as private, Co. I, June 21, 1861; transferred to One Hundred and Thirtieth Company, Second Battalion, Veteran Reserve Corps, December 28, 1863.

Rose, Darwin M.—Age, 22 years. Enlisted, July 3, 1861, at Station Island, to serve three years; mustered in as private, Co. I, July 10, 1861; died of disease, June 1, 1862, at Yorktown, Va.

Russell, James H.—Age, 25 years. Enlisted, June 4, 1861, at Delhi, to serve three years; mustered in as private, Co. I, June 21, 1861; died, July 12, 1862.

Sands, Levi B.—Age, 18 years. Enlisted, June 4, 1861, at Delhi, to serve three years; mustered in as private, Co. I, June 21, 1861; died of disease, February 15, 1862, at Camp Wool, Md.

Sanford, John P.—Age, 35 years. Enrolled, June 4, 1861, at Delhi, to serve three years; mustered in as first lieutenant, Co. I, June 21, 1861; as captain, Co. B, May 5, 1862; wounded in action, August 27, 1862, at Bristoe Station, Va.; discharged, July 28, 1863. Commissioned first lieutenant, January 7, 1862, with rank from June 21, 1861, original; captain, June 30, 1862, with rank from May 5, 1862, vice Darwin Willard, killed in action.

Sewall, Milo C.—Age, 22 years. Enlisted, June 4, 1861, at Delhi, to serve three years; mustered in as private, Co. I, June 21, 1861; deserted, December 1, 1861, at Colchester, Delaware county, N.Y.; also born as Sewell.

Shafer, William B.—Age, 27 years. Enlisted, June 4, 1861, at Delhi, to serve three years; mustered in as sergeant, Co. I, June 21, 1861; promoted first sergeant, September 14, 1862; discharged for disability, January 31, 1863, at Baltimore, Md.

Signor, Elbridge—Age, 20 years. Enlisted, June 4, 1861, at Delhi, to serve three years; mustered in as private, Co. I, June 21, 1861; wounded in action, May 3, 1863, at Chancellorsville, Va.; discharged. for disability, December 11, 1863, at McDougall Hospital, Fort Schuyler, New York Harbor.

Sloat, George L.—Age, 26 years. Enlisted, June 4, 1861, at Delhi, to serve three years; mustered in as private, Co. I, June 21, 1861; transferred to Veteran Reserve Corps, February 15, 1861.

Smith, William—Age, 28 years. Enlisted, June 4, 1861, at Delhi, to serve three years; mustered in as private, Co. I, June 21, 1861; died of disease, February 5, 1862, at Camp Wool, Md.

Steele, Lewis E.—Age, 19 years. Enlisted, June 4, 1861, at Delhi, to serve three years; mustered in as musician, Co. I, June 21, 1861; discharged for disability, August 1, 1862, at Harrison Landing, Va.

Stevens, Ferris B.—Age, 26 years. Enlisted, June 4, 1861, at Delhi, to serve three years; mustered in as private, Co. I, June 21, 1861; discharged for disability, June 28, 1862, at Fort Monroe, Va.

Tate, Samuel—Age, 23 years. Enlisted at Delaware county, N.Y., to serve three years, and mustered in as private, Co. I, July 5, 1862; died of disease, January 1, 1864, at Kalorama Hospital, Washington, D.C.

Thompson, Michael—Age, 38 years. Enlisted, May 28, 1861, at Dunkirk, to serve three years; mustered in as private, Co. E, June 20, 1861; wounded in action, July 1, 1862, at Malvern Hill, Va.; discharged for wounds, November 15, 1862, at General Hospital, Philadelphia, Pa.

Thompson, William H.—Age, 24 years. Enlisted at Carroll, to serve three years, and mustered in as private, Co. I, December 29, 1863; transferred to Co. A or B, One Hundred and Twentieth Infantry, June 20, 1864.

Vanbradenburgh, Chester A.—Age, 21 years. Enlisted, June 4, 1861, at Delhi, to serve three years; mustered in as corporal, Co. I, June 21, 1861; promoted sergeant, January 2, 1862; discharged for disability, September 25, 1862, at Philadelphia, Pa.

Varnold, Charles—Age, 19 years. Enlisted, June 4, 1861, at Delhi, to serve three years; mustered in as private, Co. I, June 21, 1861; killed in action, August 27, 1862, at Bristoe Station, Va.; also born as Varnell.

Vonvradenburg, Harvey L.—Age, 29 years. Enlisted, July 23, 1861, at Staten Island, to serve three years; mustered in as private, Co. I, August 8, 1861; no further record.

Waldie, John L.—Age, 18 years. Enlisted, June 4, 1861, at Delhi, to serve three years; mustered in as private, Co. I, June 21, 1861; wounded in action, May 5, 1862, at Williamsburg, Va.; died, no date.

Wardell, Charles—Age, 25 years. Enlisted, June 23, 1861, at Staten Island, to serve three years; mustered in as wagoner, Co. I, August 8, 1861; transferred to Signal Corps, November 1861.

Warren, Timothy—Age, 23 years. Enlisted, June 4, 1861, at Delhi, to serve three years; mustered in as private, Co. I, June 21, 1861; wounded in action, May 5, 1862, and died of his wounds, May 15, 1862, at Williamsburg, Va.

Whitney, Truman W.—Age, 19 years. Enlisted, June 4, 1861, at Delhi, to serve three years; mustered in as private, Co. I, June 21, 1861; killed in action, May 3, 1863, at Chancellorsville, Va.

Whitney, William H.—Age, 17 years. Enlisted, September 1, 1861, at Delhi, to serve three years; mustered in as private, Co. I, September 4, 1861; died of disease, January 13, 1862, at Camp Wool, Md.

Wilcox, Stratford C.—Age, 31 years. Enlisted, June 4, 1861, at Delhi, to serve three years; mustered in as private, Co. I, June 21, 1861; mustered out with company, June 20, 1864, near Petersburg, Va.

Wilder, Lorey—Age, 18 years. Enlisted, July 23, 1861, at Staten Island, to serve three years; mustered in as private, Co. I, August 8, 1861; captured in action, May 3, 1863, at Chancellorsville, Va.; paroled, May 14, 1863, at City Point, Va.; mustered out, June 20, 1864, near Petersburg, Va.

Williams, Edgar S.—Age, 25 years. Enlisted, June 4, 1861, at Delhi, to serve three years; mustered in as private, Co. I, June 21, 1861; died of disease, December 23, 1862, at Camden Street Military Hospital, Baltimore, Md.

Winters, Hugh J.—Age, 23 years. Enrolled, June 4, 1861, at New York City, to serve three years; mustered in as second lieutenant, Co. I, June 21, 1861; promoted first lieutenant, Co. K, April 17, 1862; discharged, June 2, 1862. Commissioned second lieutenant, January 7, 1862, with rank from June 2, 1861, original; not commissioned first lieutenant.

Wood, James H.—Age, 19 years. Enlisted, June 4, 1861, at Delhi, to serve three years; mustered in as private, Co. I, June 21, 1861; promoted corporal, September 25, 1862; sergeant, January 1863; re-enlisted as a veteran, December 24, 1863; transferred to Co. B, One Hundred and Twentieth Infantry, June 20, 1864.

Company K

Organized in New York City in June 1861. Mustered into the United States service June 21, 1861.

Captains

John S. Austin, from June 21, 1861, to October 25, 1862.
Daniel Loeb, from October 25 to November 1, 1862.
Berend Huttmann, from November 1, 1862, to June 20, 1864.

First Lieutenants

William P. Holl, Jr. from June 21, 1861, to April 17, 1862.
Hugh J. Winters, from April 17 to June 2, 1862.
James A. Smith, from May 17 to November 1, 1862.
Thomas Clark, from October 31, 1862, to January 16, 1863.
Harrison F. Ellis, from January to May 3, 1863.
Samuel Howell, from July 1, 1863, to May 9, 1864.

Second Lieutenants

Michael McDonald, from June 21, 1861, to May 13, 1862.
Henry Bowers, from May 12 to September 15, 1862.
Alexander M. Clark, from September 8 to November 1, 1862
Julius Kessler, from November 1, 1862, to May 5, 1863.
John McKinley, from May 5 to November 2, 1863.

Acker, Martin—Age, 20 years. Enlisted, April 13, 1861, at New York City, to serve three years; mustered in as private, Co. K, June 21, 1861; wounded in action, August 29, 1862, at Bull Run, Va.; and July 2, 1863, at Gettysburg, Pa.; mustered out to date, June 20, 1864.

Alliston, Frank—Age, 23 years. Enlisted, April 13, 1861, at New York City, to serve three years; mustered in as private, Co. K, June 21, 1861; promoted corporal, July 1861; sergeant, April 20, 1862; mustered out with company, June 20, 1864, near Petersburg, Va.

Almark, William—Age, 44 years. Enlisted, April 15, 1861, at New York City, to serve three years; mustered in as private, Co. K, June 21, 1861, captured in action, May 5, 1862, at Williamsburg, Va.; paroled, May 11, 1862; deserted; no date or place.

Althiser, George C.—Age, 21 years. Enlisted, April 13, 1861, at New York City, to serve three years; mustered in as private, Co. K, June 21, 1861; transferred to Eighty-sixth Company, Second Battalion Veteran Reserve Corps, March 1, 1864.

Armstrong, James—Age, 25 years. Enlisted, April 13, 1861, at New York City, to serve three years; mustered in as private, Co. K, June 21, 1861; deserted, August 30, 1861, at Camp Caldwell, D.C.

Austin, John S.—Age, 44 years. Enrolled, May 15, 1861, at New York, to serve three years; mustered in as captain, Co. K, June 21, 1861; as lieutenant-colonel, October 25, 1862; as colonel, May 4, 1863; discharged for disability, June 27, 1864. Commissioned captain, January 7, 1862, with rank from June 21, 1861, original; lieutenant-colonel, December 1, 1862, with rank from October 25, 1862, vice I. Moses, resigned; colonel, August 7, 1863, with rank from May 4, 1863, vice W.O. Stevens, killed in action.

Austin, Samuel—Age, 35 years. Enlisted at New York City, to serve three years, and mustered in as private, Co. K, August 1, 1862; transferred to Co. E, One Hundred and Twentieth Infantry, June 23, 1864.

Baker, Samuel—Age, 43 years. Enlisted, April 13, 1861, at New York City, to serve three years; mustered in as private, Co. K, June 21, 1861; transferred to Co. C, Nineteenth Regiment Veteran Reserve Corps, December 23, 1863.

Beadle, Dewitt—Age, 38 years. Enlisted, April 13, 1861, at New York City, to serve three years; mustered in as private, Co. K, June 21, 1861; wounded in action, May 5, 1862, at Williamsburg, Va.; deserted, September 12, 1862, at Alexandria, Va.

Bell, William F.—Age, 19 years. Enlisted, April 13, 1861, at New York City, to serve three years; mustered in as private, Co. K, June 21, 1861; transferred to Co. C, July 16, 1861; wounded and captured in action, May 5, 1862, at Williamsburg, Va.; paroled, no date; deserted, no date; subsequent service in U.S. Navy.

Bendell, August—Age, 19 years. Enlisted, April 13, 1861, at New York City, to serve three years; mustered in as private, Co. K, June 21, 1861; killed in action, May 5, 1862, at Williamsburg, Va.

Bernard, Morris—Age, 21 years. Enlisted, April 13, 1861, at New York City, to serve three years; mustered in as corporal, Co. K, June 21, 1861; returned to ranks in August 1861; promoted corporal, August 13, 1863; re-enlisted as a veteran, December 21, 1863; transferred to Co. E, One Hundred and Twentieth Infantry, June 23, 1864; also born as Bernard Morris.

Berst, Lewis—Age, 21 years. Enlisted, April 13, 1861, at New York City, to serve three years; mustered in as private, Co. K, June 21, 1861; killed in action, May 5, 1862, at Williamsburg, Va.; also born as Borst.

Birmingham, James—Age, 28 years. Enlisted, April 13, 1861, at New York City, to serve three years; mustered in as private, Co. K, June 21, 1861; deserted August 30, 1861, at Camp Caldwell, D.C.

Brannigan, Thomas H.—Age, 21 years. Enlisted at New York City, to serve three years, and mustered in as private, Co. K, February 9, 1864; transferred to Co. E, One Hundred and Twentieth Infantry, June 23, 1864; prior service in Thirty-seventh New York Volunteers.

Burke, William—Age, 22 years. Enlisted, April 13, 1861, at Staten Island, to serve three years; mustered in as private, Co. K, June 21, 1861; wounded in action, July 1, 1862, at Malvern Hill, Va.; discharged for his wounds, January 13, 1863, at Convalescent Camp, Va.

Bushnell, John—Private, Co. K, Seventy-third Infantry; transferred to Co. K, this regiment, no date; deserted, September 6, 1862, at Alexandria, Va.; also born as Bushell.

Byrnes, Thomas—Age, 35 years. Enlisted, April 13, 1861, at New York City, to serve three years; mustered in as private, Co. K, June 21, 1861; deserted, August 30, 1861, at Camp Caldwell, D.C.

Caldwell, Owen—Private, Co. K, Seventy-third Infantry; transferred to Co. K, this regiment, no date; deserted, April 5, 1803, from McDougal Hospital, Fort Schuyler, N.Y.

Carroll, Thomas—Age, 30 years. Enlisted, April 13, 1861, at New York City, to serve three years; mustered in as private, Co. K, June 21, 1861; deserted, July 6, 1861, at Camp Scott, Staten Island.

Carry, Peter—Age, 25 years. Enlisted, April 13, 1861, at New York City, to serve three years; mustered in as private, Co. K, June 21, 1861; discharged for disability, October 17, 1861, at Camp Caldwell, D.C.

Celsing, Philip—Age, 24 years. Enlisted, April 13, 1861, at New York City, to serve three years; mustered in as private, Co. K, June 21, 1861; wounded in action, May 5, 1862, at Williamsburg, Va.; discharged for his wounds, October 14, 1862, near Alexandria, Va.; also born as Calsing.

Chalmers, William—Age, 26 years. Enrolled at New York City, to serve three years, and mustered in as private, Co. K, August 1, 1862; as first lieutenant, Co. H, to date November 23, 1863; mustered out with company, October 31, 1864, near Petersburg, Va. Commissioned first lieutenant, October 6, 1863, with rank from August 27, 1863, vice W.M. Connell, promoted.

Clark, Thomas—Age, 25 years. Enrolled, May 15, 1861, at New York, to serve three years; mustered in as sergeant, Co. K, June 21, 1861; promoted first sergeant in October 1861; sergeant-major, April 17, 1862; second lieutenant, Co. C, June 2, 1862; mustered in as first lieutenant, Co. E, July 7, 1862; wounded in action, August 29, 1862, at Bull Run, Va.; transferred to Co. K, October 31, 1862; to Co. C, January 16, 1863; discharged, April 1, 1863. Commissioned second lieutenant, June 30, 1862, with rank from June 13, 1862, vice W. Holberton, resigned; first lieutenant, July 21, 1862, with rank from July 7, 1802, vice W.P. Holl, Jr., resigned; captain, but revoked, June 13, 1863, with rank from January 16, 1863, vice J.R. Chadwick, resigned.

Clary, James—Age, 27 years. Enlisted, April 13, 1861, at New York City, to serve three years; mustered in as private, Co. K, June 21, 1861; captured in action, August 29, 1862, at Bull Run, Va.; paroled, September 2, 1862, at Centerville Va., and returned to regiment, November 18, 1862; mustered out with company, June 20, 1864, near Petersburg, Va.; subsequent service in Co. D, Third Regiment, Veteran Reserve Corps.

Clifford, John S.—Age, 30 years. Enlisted, April 13, 1861, at New York City, to serve three years; mustered in as sergeant, Co. K, June 21, 1861; returned to ranks, October 2, 1861; discharged for disability, February 12, 1862, at Camp Wool, Md.

Cloebsattle, Charles—Age, 19 years. Enlisted, April 13, 1861, at New York City, to serve three years; mustered in as private, Co. K, June 21, 1861; deserted, September 20, 1861, at Camp Caldwell, D.C.

Cobo, Charles—Age, 33 years. Enlisted, April 13, 1861, at New York City, to serve three years; mustered in as private, Co. K, June 21, 1861; deserted, September 1, 1862, at Centerville, Va.

Colyer, John—Private, Co. K, Seventy-third Infantry; transferred to Co. K, this regiment, no date; killed in action, July 2, 1863, at Gettysburg, Pa.

Comer, John—Age, 38 years. Enlisted, April 13, 1861, at New York City, to serve three years; mustered in as private, Co. K, June 21, 1861; mustered out with company, June 20, 1864, near Petersburg, Va.; also born as Conner and Connor.

Costello, William—Age, 35 years. Enlisted, April 13, 1861, at New York City, to serve three years; mustered in as private, Co. K, June 21, 1861; discharged for disability, August 11, 1862, at Harrison's Landing, Va.

Crosby, William—Age, 24 years. Enlisted, April 13, 1861, at New York City, to serve three years; mustered in as private, Co. K, June 21, 1861; deserted, August 20, 1861, at Camp Caldwell, D.C.

Crow, William—Age, 27 years. Enlisted, April 13, 1861, at New York City, to serve three years; mustered in as private, Co. K, June 21, 1861; killed in action, May 5, 1862, at Williamsburg, Va.

Danker, John—Age, 24 years. Enlisted, May 15, 1861, at New York City, to serve three years; mustered in as private, Co. K, June 21, 1861; missing in action, July 2, 1863, at Gettysburg, Pa; no further record.

Decatur, Edward—Age, 28 years. Enlisted, April 13, 1861, at New York City, to serve three years; mustered in as private, Co. K, June 21, 1861; discharged, April 28, 1863, at Government Hospital for the Insane at Washington, D.C.

Delany, James—Age, 19 years. Enlisted, April 15, 1861, at New York City, to serve three years; mustered in as private, Co. K, June 21, 1861; wounded in action, May 5, 1862, at Williamsburg, Va.; transferred to Seventeenth Company, Second Battalion, Veteran Reserve Corps, July 25, 1863.

Devaney, William—Age, 32 years. Enlisted, April 13, 1861, at New York City, to serve three years; mustered in as corporal, Co. K, June 21, 1861; returned to ranks in October 1861; mustered out with company, June 20, 1864, near Petersburg, Va.

Donnelly, James—Age, 23 years. Enlisted, April 13, 1861, at New York City, to serve three years; mustered in as corporal, Co. K, June 21, 1861; promoted sergeant, October 2, 1861; returned to ranks, March 3, 1862; captured in action, May 5, 1862, at Williamsburg, Va.; paroled, May 11, 1862; mustered out, June 20, 1864.

Driscold, Cornelius—Age, 34 years. Enlisted, April 13, 1861, at New York City, to serve three years; mustered in as private, Co. K, June 21, 1861; captured in action, May 5, 1862, at Williamsburg, Va.; paroled, no date; discharged, May 26, 1862, at Washington, D.C.

Dugan, Edward P.—Age, 20 years. Enlisted, April 13, 1861, at New York City, to serve three years; mustered in as corporal, Co. K, June 21, 1861; returned to ranks in August 1861; appointed wagoner in October 1861; mustered out with company, June 20, 1864, near Petersburg, Va.

Fisher, Humphrey—Age, 18 years. Enlisted, April 13, 1861, at New York City, to serve three years; mustered in as private, Co. K, June 21, 1861; deserted, July 6, 1861, at Camp Scott, Staten Island, N.Y.

Fitzgerald, John—Age, 22 years. Enlisted, May 15, 1861, at New York City, to serve three years; mustered in as private, Co. K, June 21, 1861; promoted corporal, July 1861; returned to ranks, March 3, 1862; promoted corporal, July 8, 1862; wounded in action, July 2, 1863, at Gettysburg, Pa.; transferred to Co. F, Twenty-fourth Regiment Veteran Reserve Corps, March 7, 1864.

Flynn, John—Age, 20 years. Enlisted, April 13, 1861, at New York City, to serve three years; mustered in as private, Co. K, June 21, 1861; captured in action, May 5, 1862, at Williamsburg, Va.; paroled, May 11, 1862; deserted from hospital, July 5, 1862.

Foghman, Frederick—Age, 36 years. Enlisted, April 13, 1861, at New York City, to serve three years; mustered in as private, Co. K, June 21, 1861; deserted, September 20, 1862, from hospital, at Alexandria, Va.; also born as Foughman and Foghtmann.

Follas, Richard—Age, 24 years. Enlisted, April 13, 1861, at New York City, to serve three years; mustered in as private, Co. K, June 21, 1861; wounded in action, May 5, 1862, at Williamsburg, Va.; discharged for wounds, August 8, 1862, at New York City.

Fox, Francis—Age, 19 years. Enlisted, April 13, 1861, at New York City, to serve three years; mustered in as private, Co. K, June 21, 1861; wounded in action, June 16, 1864, near Petersburg, Va.; absent, sick in hospital, at muster out of company.

Fox, John—Age, 19 years. Enlisted, May 15, 1861, at New York City, to serve three years; mustered in as private, Co. K, June 21, 1861; promoted corporal in October 1861; sergeant, July 8, 1862; wounded in action, May 3, 1863, at Chancellorsville, Va.; re-enlisted as a veteran, December 21, 1863; transferred to Co. E, One Hundred and Twentieth Infantry, June 23, 1864.

Fritman, Peter—Age, 39 years. Enlisted, April 13, 1861, at New York City to serve three years; mustered in as private, Co. K, June 21, 1861; discharged for disability, March 13, 1862, at Camp Wool, Md.; also born as Peter Friedman.

Garity, Thomas—Age, 26 years. Enlisted, May 28, 1861, at New York City, to serve three years; mustered in as private, Co. K, June 21, 1861; re-enlisted as a veteran, February 13, 1864; transferred to Co. E, One Hundred and Twentieth Infantry, June 23, 1864.

Ginther, Christian—Age, 24 years. Enlisted, April 13, 1861, at New York City, to serve three years; mustered in as private, Co. K, June 21, 1861; deserted, June 12, 1863, near Hartwood Church, Va.

Goss, Charles—Age, 18 years. Enlisted, May 15, 1861, at New York City, to serve three years; mustered in as private, Co. K, June 21, 1861; promoted corporal, March 10, 1862; wounded in action, July 23, 1863, at Manassas Gap, Va.; promoted sergeant, October 12, 1863; re-enlisted as a veteran, February 25, 1864; transferred to Co. E, One Hundred and Twentieth Infantry, June 23, 1864.

Gray, Joseph—Age, 37 years. Enlisted, April 13, 1861, at New York City, to serve three years; mustered in as private, Co. K, June 21, 1861; mustered out with company, June 20, 1864, near Petersburg, Va.

Grogan, Dennis—Age, 21 years. Enlisted, May 15,

1861, at New York City, to serve three years; mustered in as private, Co. K, June 20, 1861; promoted corporal in July 1861; sergeant, April 13, 1863; re-enlisted as a veteran, December 24, 1863; transferred to Co. E, One Hundred and Twentieth Infantry, June 23, 1864; also born as Groges.

Herman, Henry—Age, 40 years. Enlisted, April 13, 1861, at New York City, to serve three years; mustered in as private, Co. K, June 21, 1861; deserted, September 14, 1861, from Camp Caldwell, D.C.

Hickey, John—Ago, 20 years. Enlisted, May 15, 1861, at New York City, to serve three years; mustered in as private, Co. K, June 21, 1861; promoted corporal, November 1, 1862; transferred to Co. G, First Regiment, Veteran Reserve Corps, November 30, 1863.

Holl, Jr., William P.—Age, 24 years. Enrolled, May 15, 1861, at New York, to serve three years; mustered in as first lieutenant, Co. K, June 21, 1861; discharged, April 17, 1802; also born as Hall. Commissioned first lieutenant, January 7, 1862, with rank from June 21, 1861, original.

Howard, Francis—Age, 19 years. Enlisted, May 15, 1861, at New York City, to serve three years; mustered in as private, Co. K, June 21, 1861; promoted corporal, March 10, 1862; sergeant, July 4, 1863; re-enlisted as a veteran, February 14, 1864; transferred to Co. E, One Hundred and Twentieth Infantry, June 23, 1864.

Howell, John H.—Age, 36 years. Enlisted at Staten Island, to serve three years, and mustered in as private, Co. K, July 10, 1861; captured in action, August 29, 1862, at Bull Run, Va.; paroled, no date; died of disease, November 8, 1862, at General Hospital, Annapolis, Md.

Hunker, Philip—Age, 16 years. Enlisted, May 15, 1861, at New York City, to serve three years; mustered in as musician, Co. K, June 21, 1861; deserted, July 21, 1862, at Falmouth, Va.

Johnston, Allen—Age, 40 years. Enlisted, April 13, 1861, at New York City, to serve three years; mustered in as private, Co. K, June 21, 1861; discharged for disability, November 16, 1862, at Fortress Monroe, Va.

Jordan, Alfred—Age, 25 years. Enlisted at. New York City, to serve three years, and mustered in as private, Co. K, September 15, 1861; wounded in action July 2, 1863, at Gettysburg, Pa.; transferred to navy by special order No. 98, March, 1864.

Jordan, Charles—Age, 29 years. Enlisted, April 13, 1861, at New York City, to serve three years; mustered in as private, Co. K, June 21, 1861; discharged for disability, February 3, 1862.

Jost, Peter—Age, 22 years. Enlisted, April 13, 1861, at New York City, to serve three years; mustered in as private, Co. K, June 21, 1861; deserted, October 1, 1862, at Alexandria, Va.

Kelly, Joseph—Age, 19 years. Enlisted, April 13, 1861, at New York City, to serve three years; mustered in as private, Co. K, June 21, 1861; transferred to Co. C, July 16, 1861; no further record.

Kessler, Julius—Age, 28 years. Enrolled, May 15, 1861, at New York, to serve three years; mustered in as sergeant, Co. K, June 21, 1861; promoted first sergeant, July 8, 1862; mustered in as second lieutenant, Co. I, October 25, 1862; transferred to Co. K, November 1, 1862; promoted first lieutenant, Co. C, May 5, 1863; dismissed, June 25, 1863. Commissioned second lieutenant, October 25, 1862, with rank from same date, vice H. Bowers, discharged; first lieutenant, August 7, 1863, with rank from May 5, 1863, vice C.H. Hydorn, killed in action.

Killen, Peter—Age, 22 years. Enlisted, April 13, 1861, at New York City, to serve three years; mustered in as private, Co. K, June 21, 1861; deserted, January 25, 1863, from Armory Square Hospital, Washington, D.C.

Konigsdofer, Adolph—Age, 21 years. Enlisted, April 13, 1861, at New York City, to serve three years; mustered in as private, Co. K, June 21, 1861; re-enlisted as a veteran, December 24, 1863; transferred to Co. E, One Hundred and Twentieth Infantry, June 23, 1864.

Kossuth, Gottlieb—Age, 35 years. Enlisted, April 13, 1861, at New York City, to serve three years; mustered in as private, Co. K, June 21, 1861; promoted corporal in July, 1861; sergeant, November 1, 1862; wounded in action, July 2, 1863, at Gettysburg, Pa.; deserted, July 4,1863, near Gettysburg, Pa.

Krack, William—Age, 24 years. Enlisted, April 13, 1861, at New York City, to serve three years; mustered in as private, Co. K, June 21, 1861; deserted, August 30, 1861, at Camp Caldwell, D.C.

Larned, David—Age, 35 years. Enlisted, April 13, 1861, at New York City, to serve three years; mustered in as corporal, Co. K, June 21, 1861; deserted, July 24, 1861, at Staten Island, N.Y.

Lesner, Frederick—Age, 28 years. Enlisted, April 13, 1861, at New York City, to serve three years; mustered in as private, Co, K, July 21, 1861; absent, sick, in hospital, at Philadelphia, Pa., at muster-out of company.

Luciani, John—Age, 27 years. Enlisted, April 13, 1861, at New York City, to serve three years; mustered in as private, Co. K, June 21, 1861; deserted, May 25, 1862, at Alexandria, Va.

McCann, Henry—Age, 27 years. Enlisted, April 13, 1861, at New York City, to serve three years; mustered in as private, Co. K, June 21, 1861; killed in action, May 5, 1862, at Williamsburg, Va.

McCarthy, Jeremiah—Age, 21 years. Enlisted, April 13, 1861, at New York City, to serve three years; mustered in as private, Co. K, June 21, 1861; discharged for disability, June 14, 1864, from Insane Asylum, Washington, D.C.

McCarthy, John—Age, 20 years. Enlisted, April 13, 1861, at New York City, to serve three years; mustered in as private, Co. K, June 21, 1861; mustered out with company, June 20, 1864, near Petersburg, Va.

McCombs, Samuel—Age, 15 years. Enlisted, April 13, 1861, At New York City, to serve three years; mustered in as musician, Co. K, June 21, 1861; mustered out with company, June 20, 1864, near Petersburg, Va.

McCrosson, Hugh—Age, 24 years. Enlisted, April 13, 1861, at New York City, to serve three years; mustered in as private, Co. K, June 21, 1861; absent, sick, in hospital, at New York City, at muster-out of company.

McDonald, Michael—Age, 24 years. Enrolled, May 15, 1861, at New York, to serve three years; mustered in as second lieutenant, Co. K, June 21, 1861; as first lieutenant Co. E , May 13, 1862; discharged, June 25, 1862. Commissioned second lieutenant. January 7, 1862, with rank from June 21, 1861, original; first lieutenant, June 30, 1862, with rank from May 12, 1862, vice Warren Bliss, resigned.

Miller, John—Age, 44 years. Enlisted, April 13, 1861, at New York City, to serve three years; mustered in as private, Co. K, June 21, 1861; wounded in action, May 5, 1862, at Williamsburg, Va.; discharged for wounds, January 21, 1863, at Fortress Monroe, Va.

Miller, Michael—Age, 44 years. Enlisted, April 13, 1861, at New York City, to serve three years; mustered in as private, Co. K, June 21, 1861; wounded in action, July 1, 1862, at Malvern Hill, Va.; transferred to Co. C, Nineteenth Regiment, Veteran Reserve Corps, December 23, 1863; retransferred to Co. K, this regiment, and mustered out with company, June 20, 1864, near Petersburg, Va.

Miller, Michael—Age, 23 years. Enlisted, April 13, 1861, at New York City, to serve three years; mustered in as private, Co. K, June 21, 1861; discharged for disability, December 23, 1862, at Providence, R.I.; subsequent service in Seventeenth Veteran Infantry.

Monroe, John—Age, 23 years. Enlisted, April 13, 1861, at New York City, to serve three years; mustered in as private, Co. K, June 21, 1861; died of disease, May 5, 1862, at General Hospital near Yorktown, Va.

Myres, Ernest—Age, 21 years. Enlisted at New York City, to serve three years, and mustered in as private, Co. K, September 15, 1862; died of disease, December 15, 1863, at Finley Hospital, Washington, D.C.

Norton, Patrick—Age, 30 years. Enlisted, April 13, 1861, at New York City, to serve three years; mustered in as private, Co. K, June 21, 1861; wounded in action, July 1, 1862, at Malvern Hill, Va.; transferred to Co. A, First Regiment, Veteran Reserve Corps, July 16, 1863.

O'Keefe, James M.—Age, 19 years. Enlisted at New York City, to serve three years, and mustered in as private, Co. K, August 1, 1862; wounded in action, May 3, 1863, at Chancellorsville, Va.; discharged by S.O. No. 141, April 20, 1864.

O'Neil, Cornelius—Age, 21 years. Enlisted, April 13, 1861, at New York City, to serve three years; mustered in as private, Co. K, June 21, 1861; discharged for disability, August 17, 1863, at Convalescent Camp, Va.

O'Neil, Joseph—Age, 23 years. Enlisted, April 13, 1861, at New York City, to serve three years; mustered in as private, Co. K, June 21, 1861; re-enlisted as a veteran, December 24, 1863; transferred to Co. E, One Hundred and Twentieth Infantry, June 23, 1864.

Orswell, George S.—Age, 18 years. Enlisted, April 13, 1861, at New York City, to serve three years; mustered in as private, Co. K, June 21, 1861; re-enlisted as a veteran, December 24, 1863; transferred to Co. E, One Hundred and Twentieth Infantry, June 23, 1864.

Ostrander, Charles—Age, 21 years. Enlisted, April 13, 1861, at New York City, to serve three years; mustered in as corporal, Co. K, June 21, 1861; returned to ranks in August, 1861; discharged for disability, January 26, 1862, at Camp Wool, Md.

Philipson, William—Age, 22 years. Enlisted April 13, 1861, at New York City, to serve three years; mustered in as private, Co. K, June 21, 1861; captured in action, May 5, 1862, at Williamsburg, Va.; paroled, no date; discharged May 23, 1862 at Washington, D.C.

Rear, William H.—Age, 18 years. Enlisted, April 13, 1861, at New York City, to serve three years; mustered in as private, Co. K, June 21, 1861; discharged for disability, October 17, 1861, at Camp Caldwell, D.C.

Redman, Jerrett—Age, 39 years. Enlisted, April 13, 1861, at New York City, to serve three years; mustered in as private, Co. K, June 21, 1861; deserted, July 20, 1862, at Alexandria, Va.; also born as Redmond.

Remmen, Adam—Age, 23 years. Enlisted, April 13, 1861, at New York City, to serve three years; mustered in as private, Co. K, June 21, 1861; mustered out with company, June 20, 1864, near Petersburg, Va.; also born as Remner.

Rolland, Henry—Age, 22 years. Enlisted, April 13, 1861, at New York City, to serve three years; mustered in as private, Co. K, June 21, 1861; mustered out with company, June 20, 1864, near Petersburg, Va.; also born as Rowland.

Ryan, James—Private, Co. K, Seventy-third Infantry; transferred to Co. K, this regiment, no date; killed in action, May 5, 1862, at Williamsburg, Va.

Savage, Robert H.—Age, 22 years. Enrolled, May 15, 1861, at New York City, to serve three years; mustered in as first sergeant, Co. K, June 21, 1861; returned to sergeant, October, 1861; promoted first sergeant, October 15, 1862; mustered in as second lieutenant, Co. D, January 17, 1863; as first lieutenant, Co. A, October 29, 1863; appointed adjutant, January 1, 1864; transferred to Co. C, March 6, 1864; mustered out with company, July 20, 1864, near Petersburg, Va. Commissioned second lieutenant, June 13, 1863, with rank from January 16, 1863, vice H.F. Ellis, promoted; first lieutenant, October 6, 1863, with rank from July 30, 1863, vice H.J. McDonough, promoted; adjutant and first lieutenant, December 17, 1863, with rank from November 28, 1863, vice A.M. Clark, promoted.

Seible, John—Age, 22 years. Enlisted, May 15, 1861, at New York City, to serve three years; mustered in as private, Co. K, June 21, 1861; promoted corporal, July, 1861; deserted, August 24, 1862, at Alexandria, Va.

Slimner, Daniel—Age, 30 years. Enlisted, May 15, 1861, at New York City, to serve three years; mustered in as private, Co. K, June 21, 1861; promoted corporal, September, 1861; mustered out with company, June 20, 1864, near Petersburg, Va.

Smith, Peter—Age, 19 years. Enlisted, May 15, 1861, at New York City, to serve three years; mustered in as private, Co. K, June 21, 1861; re-enlisted as a veteran, February 13, 1864; transferred to Co. E, One Hundred and Twentieth Infantry, June 23, 1864.

Solomon, Morris—Age, 33 years. Enrolled, May 15, 1861, at New York, to serve three years; mustered in as sergeant, Co. K, June 21, 1861; promoted first sergeant, April 20, 1862; second lieutenant, Co. B, July 7, 1862; dismissed in October, 1862. Commissioned second lieutenant, July 21, 1862, with rank from July 7, 1862, vice R.E. Jones, promoted.

Statjb, Frederick—Age, 20 years. Enlisted, April 13, 1861, at New York City, to serve three years; mustered in as private, Co. K, June 21, 1861; re-enlisted as a veteran, December 24, 1863; transferred to Co. E, One Hundred and Twentieth Infantry, June 23, 1864.

Stevens, Frederick L.—Age, 21 years. Enlisted April 13, 1861, at New York City, to serve three years; mustered in as wagoner, Co. K, June 21, 1861; sent to the ranks, September, 1861; promoted corporal, November 1, 1862; first sergeant, January 16, 1863; re-enlisted as a veteran, December 24, 1863; transferred to Co. E, One Hundred and Twentieth Infantry, June 23, 1864.

Sumpter, Michael—Age, 35 years. Enlisted, May 15, 1861, at New York City, to serve three years; mustered in as corporal, Co. K, June 21, 1861; returned to the ranks, July, 1861; captured in action, May 3, 1863, at Chancellorsville, Va.; paroled, September 30, 1863; captured in action, May 12, 1864, at Spotsylvania, Va.; paroled, April 21, 1865; mustered out, July 8, 1865, at New York City.

Tilton, Remson—Age, 18 years. Enlisted, April 13, 1861, at New York City, to serve three years; mustered in as private, Co. K, June 21, 1861; promoted corporal, August 13, 1863; re-enlisted as a veteran, December 24, 1863; transferred to Co. E, One Hundred and Twentieth Infantry, June 23, 1864.

Vincent, Alfred—Age, 21 years. Enlisted, April 13, 1861, at New York City, to serve three years; mustered in as private, Co. K, June 21, 1861; discharged for disability, July 11, 1861, at Camp Scott, Staten Island, N.Y.

Walsh, John—Age, 27 years. Enlisted, May 15, 1861, at New York City, to serve three years; mustered in as private, Co. K, June 21, 1861; mustered out with company, June 20, 1864, near Petersburg, Va.

Walsh, Joseph—Age, 25 years. Enlisted, April 13, 1861, at New York City, to serve three years; mustered in as private, Co. K, June 21, 1861; wounded in action, June 25, 1862, at Fair Oaks, Va.; discharged for wounds, August 24, 1863, at Philadelphia, Pa.; also born as Welch.

Ward, John—Age, 24 years. Enlisted at New York City, to serve three years, and mustered in as private, Co. K, September 15, 1862; transferred to Co. E, One Hundred and Twentieth Infantry, June 23, 1864.

Watson, Benjamin—Age, 28 years. Enlisted at New York City, to serve three years, and mustered in as private, Co. K, August 1, 1862; discharged by sentence of court martial, September 24, 1863, at Culpeper, Va.

Whitford, William H.—Age, 23 years. Enlisted, May 15, 1861, at New York City, to serve three years; mustered in as private, Co. K, June 21, 1861; killed in action, May 5, 1862, at Williamsburg, Va.

Company L

Organized in New York City in October 1861. Mustered into the United States service October 1861. Disbanded, with members transferred to Companies A, I and K, February 25, 1862.

Captains

John D. Graham, from December 16, 1861, to February 7, 1862.

First Lieutenants

John D. Graham, from November 14 to December 15, 1861.

James Cormack, Jr., from November 14, 1861, to February 7, 1862.

Second Lieutenants

David B. Jones, from November 14, 1861, to February 7, 1862

Bailey, George W.—Age, 18 years. Enlisted, December 1, 1861, at Delhi, to serve three years; mustered in as private, Co. L, December 12, 1861; transferred to Co. A, February 25, 1862; discharged for disability, November 6, 1862, at Alexandria, Va.

Barling, Joseph—Age, 39 years. Enlisted, November 1, 1861, at New York City, to serve three years; mustered in as private, Co. L, November 18, 1861; transferred to Co. K, February 25, 1862; deserted, August 9, 1862, from Hammond General Hospital, Point Lookout, Md.; also born as Borling.

Birmingham, James—Age, 28 years. Enlisted, April 13, 1861, at New York City, to serve three years; mustered in as private, Co. K, June 21, 1861; deserted August 30, 1861, at Camp Caldwell, D.C.

Boggs, George A.—Age, 10 years. Enlisted, October 29, 1861, at Delhi, to serve three years; mustered in as private, Co. L, November 17, 1861; transferred to Co. I, February 25, 1862; wounded in action, July 1, 1862, at Malvern Hill, Va.; transferred to Co. H, One Hundred and Twentieth Infantry, June 20, 1864.

Boyle, John—Age, 43 years. Enlisted at New Jersey, to serve three years, and mustered in as private, Co. L, October 30, 1861; transferred to Co. I, February 25, 1862; no further record.

Brady, Philip—Age, 30 years. Enlisted, December 7, 1861, at Delhi, to serve three years; mustered in as private, Co. L, December 11, 1861; deserted, December 1861.

Brown, James—Age, 44 years. Enlisted at Delhi, to serve three years, and mustered in as private, Co. L, November 16, 1861; transferred to Co. I, February 25, 1862; discharged for disability, December 18, 1862.

Burke, John—Age, 36 years. Enlisted at New York City, to serve three years, and mustered in as private, Co. L, October 30, 1861; transferred to Co. H, February 25, 1862; to Co. A, February 28, 1862; re-enlisted as a veteran, December 23, 1863; promoted corporal, May 12, 1864; transferred to Co. B, One Hundred and Twentieth Infantry, June 23, 1864.

Butterfield, William R.—Age, 42 years. Enlisted, November 22, 1861, at Sinclairville, to serve three years; mustered in as private, Co. L, December 3, 1861; transferred to Co. A, February 25, 1862; discharged for disability, October 30, 1862, at Point Lookout, Md.

Cahil, John—Age, 43 years. Enlisted at New York City, to serve three years, and mustered in as private, Co. L, October 30, 1861; deserted, December 1861.

Callaghan, William—Age, 34 years. Enlisted, December 15, 1861, at Jersey City, to serve three years; mustered in as private, Co. L, December 10, 1861; transferred to Co. D, February 25, 1862; discharged for disability, March 10, 1862, at Camp Wool, Md.; also born as Calehan.

Campbell, George—Age, 34 years. Enlisted at New York City, to serve three years, and mustered in as private, Co. L, November 16, 1861; transferred to Co. D, February 25, 1862; discharged for disability, March 1862.

Cargo, John—Age, 38 years. Enlisted at New York City, to serve three years, and mustered in as wagoner, Co. L, October 28, 1861; transferred to Co. A, and sent to rank, February 25, 1862; discharged for disability, June 13, 1862, at Budd's Ferry, Md.; also appears in Co. H.

Clark, Richard W.—Age, 18 years. Enlisted at Dunkirk, to serve three years, and mustered in as private, Co. L, December 2, 1861; transferred to Co. H, February 25, 1862; promoted corporal, July 7, 1862; sergeant, December 11, 1862; re-enlisted as a veteran, December 24, 1863; promoted first sergeant, March 1, 1864; discharged, to accept commission in One Hundred and Twentieth Infantry, October 12, 1864.

Cormack, James, Jr.—Age, 31 years. Enrolled, October 23, 1861, at Delhi, to serve three years; mustered in as first lieutenant, Co. L, November 14,

1861; mustered out, February 7, 1862, at Camp Wool, Md.; not commissioned.

Cornelius, Charles B.—Age, 34 years. Enlisted, November 7, 1861, at Jersey City, N.J., to serve three years; mustered in as private, Co. L, November 9, 1861; transferred to Co. E, February 25, 1862; deserted, April 20, 1862, at Washington, D.C.; also appears in Co. H.

Cornog, George L.—Age, 32 years. Enlisted, December 5, 1861, at New York City, to serve three years; mustered in as private Co. L, December 7, 1861; transferred to Co. A, February 25, 1862; killed in action, November 28, 1863, at One Mile Run, Va.; also born as Canoc.

Cosgrove, William—Age, 20 years. Enlisted at New York City, to serve three years, and mustered in as private, Co. L, November 18, 1861; discharged in December 1861.

Crane, Henry C.—Age, 19 years. Enlisted at New York City, to serve three years, and mustered in as private, Co. L, November 4, 1861; transferred to Co. H, February 25, 1862; killed in action, May 5, 1862, at Williamsburg, Va.

Cronan, Michael—Age, 26 years. Enlisted, December 13, 1861, at New York City, to serve three years; mustered in as private, Co. L, December 14, 1861; deserted, December 1861.

Deeney, Edward—Age, 23 years. Enlisted at Newark, N.J., to serve three years, and mustered in as private, Co. L, December 13, 1861; transferred to Co. F, February 25, 1862; wounded in action, July 1, 1862, at Malvern Hill, Va.; also July 2, 1863, at Gettysburg, Pa.; re-enlisted as a veteran, December 21, 1863; wounded in action, May 10, 1864, at Spotsylvania, Va.; transferred to Co. F, One Hundred and Twentieth Infantry, June 23, 1864.

Delisle, Daniel H.—Age, 42 years. Enlisted, November 18, 1861, at Sinclairville, to serve three years; mustered in as sergeant, Co. L, December 3, 1861; transferred to Co. A, February 25, 1862; to Co. F, First Regiment, Veteran Reserve Corps, February 6, 1864.

Dennis, William—Age, 25 years. Enlisted at Jersey City, N.J., to serve three years, and mustered in as private, Co. L, December 7, 1861; transferred to Co. F, February 25, 1862; discharged for disability, March 13, 1862, at Camp Wool, Md.; also appears in Co. H.

Denslow, Mahlon—Age, 18 years. Enlisted, October 24, 1861, at Sinclairville, to serve three years; mustered in as private, Co. L, December 3, 1861; transferred to Co. F, February 25, 1862; deserted, August 15, 1862, while on march from Harrison's Landing to Yorktown, Va.

Devereaun, Thomas—Age, 20 years. Enlisted, December 6, 1861, at Plattsburg, to serve three years; mustered in as private, Co. L, December 11, 1861; transferred to Co. A, February 25, 1862; discharged for disability, October 16, 1862, at New York City.

Dougherty, James—Age, 35 years. Enlisted, November 1, 1861, at New York City, to serve three years; mustered in as private, Co. L, November 6, 1861; transferred to Co. H, February 25, 1862; killed in action, July 1, 1862, at Malvern Hill, Va.

Drenchfield, John—Age, 22 years. Enlisted at New York City, to serve three years, and mustered in as private, Co. L, October 27, 1861; deserted, December 1861.

Duffy, William—Age, 26 years. Enlisted, December 6, 1861, at New York City, to serve three years; mustered in as private, Co. L, December 9, 1861; no further records.

Duyer, Edmund—Age, 24 years. Enlisted, November 17, 1861, at New York City, to serve three years; mustered in as private, Co. L, November 18, 1861; transferred to Co. G, February 25, 1862; promoted corporal, June 13, 1862; sergeant, January 11, 1863; wounded in action, November 27, 1863, at Locust Grove, Va.; re-enlisted as a veteran, February 13, 1864; transferred to Co. K, Nineteenth Regiment Veteran Reserve Corps, August 9, 1864.

Edmunds, Albert J.—Age, 31 years. Enlisted at Topsfield, Mass., to serve three years; mustered in as corporal, Co. L, October 28, 1861; transferred to Co. H and returned to ranks, February 25, 1862; to Co. A, February 28, 1862; re-enlisted as a veteran, December 24, 1863; transferred to Co. B, One Hundred and Twentieth Infantry, June 23, 1864; also born as Albert G. Edmonds.

Engerman, Alonzo—Age, 19 years. Enlisted at New York City, to serve three years, and mustered in as private, Co. L, October 22, 1861; deserted, December 1861.

Fagan, Michael—Ago, 42 years. Enlisted at Jersey City, N.J., to serve three years; mustered in as private, Co. L, December 6, 1861; transferred to Co. G, February 25, 1862; wounded in action, May 5, 1862, at Williamsburg, Va.; died of his wounds, June 12, 1862, at Cook Hospital, New York City.

Farley, Bernard—Age, 19 years. Enlisted at Newark, N.J., to serve three years; mustered in as private, Co. L, December 10, 1861; deserted, December 1861.

Farrington, Thomas H.—Age, 30 years. Enlisted, October 29, 1861, at Delhi, to serve three years; mustered in as private, Co. L, November 17, 1861; transferred to Co. I, February 25, 1862; captured in action, May 3, 1863, at Chancellorsville, Va.; paroled, May 14, 1863, at City Point, Va.; mustered out, October 28, 1864, at New York City.

Finnegan, Simon—Age, 22 years. Enlisted at New York City, to serve three years; mustered in as private, Co. L, December 2, 1861; transferred to Co. G, February 25, 1862; wounded in action, May 5, 1862, at Williamsburg, Va.; no further record.

Geavon, Michael—Age, 26 years. Enlisted at New York City, to serve three years, and mustered in as private, Co. L, October 29, 1861; no record subsequent to December 31, 1861.

Giarrison, William H.—Age, 23 years. Enlisted at Hoboken, N.J., to serve three years, and mustered in as private, Co. L, December 17, 1861; transferred to Co. G, February 25, 1862; deserted, May 5, 1862.

Gore, Thomas—Age, 30 years. Enlisted, November 18, 1861, at New York City, to serve three years; mustered in as private, Co. L, November 20, 1861; no record subsequent to December 31, 1861.

Goslock, Enos—Age, 24 years. Enlisted, November 28, 1861, at Plattsburg, to serve three years; mustered in as private, Co. L, December 11, 1861; transferred to Co. A, February 25, 1862; discharged for disability, March 13, 1862, at Camp Wool, Md.

Graham, John D.—Age, 38 years. Enrolled, October 3, 1861, at New York, to serve three years; mustered in as first lieutenant, Co. L, November 14, 1861; promoted captain, December 15, 1861; mustered out, February 7, 1862, at Camp Wool, Md.

Hagen, Francis—Age, 35 years. Enlisted, at New York City, to serve three years; mustered in as private, Co. L, October 31, 1861; transferred to Co. G, February 25, 1862; captured in action, May 5, 1862, at Williamsburg, Va.; paroled, no date; mustered out October 30, 1864, at New York City; also appears in Co. H.

Hamman, Adam C.—Age, 19 years. Enlisted, December 1, 1861, at Delhi, to serve three years; mustered in as private, Co. L, December 11, 1861; deserted, December 1861.

Hamman, Ashel J.—Age, 21 years. Enlisted, November 18, 1861, at Delhi, to serve three years; mustered in as private, Co. L, December 10, 1861; transferred to Co. I, February 25, 1862; promoted corporal, November 1, 1862; killed in action, May 2, 1863, at Chancellorsville, Va.

Hammond, David D.—Age, 33 years. Enlisted, December 13, 1861, at Delhi, to serve three years; mustered in as private, Co. L, December 20, 1861; transferred to Co. I, February 25, 1862; to Co. B, One Hundred and Twentieth Infantry, June 20, 1864.

Hawkey, George W.—Age, 21 years. Enlisted, November 1, 1861, at New York City, to serve three years; mustered in as corporal, Co. L, November 5, 1861; transferred to Co. D, February 25, 1862; discharged for disability, March 16, 1862, from Camp Wool, Charles County, Md.

Heavey, James—Age, 18 years. Enlisted, April 28, 1861, at New York City, to serve three years; mustered in as private, Co. C, July 21, 1861; discharged for disability, February 15, 1863, at Harewood Hospital.

Hill, John D.—Age, 20 years. Enlisted, November 7, 1861, at Sinclairville, to serve three years; mustered in as private, Co. L, December 3, 1861; transferred to Co. H, February 25, 1862; wounded in action, July 1, 1862, at Fair Oaks, Va.; promoted corporal, September 15, 1862; wounded in action, July 2, 1863, at Gettysburg, Pa.; discharged for wounds, July 18, 1864, at West Philadelphia, Pa.

Hillock, Benjamin—Age, 29 years. Enlisted, November 23, 1861, at New York City, to serve three years; mustered in as private, Co. L, November 25, 1861; transferred to Co. G, February 25, 1862; wounded in accident at Seven Pines, no date; died of his wounds, June 25, 1862, at hospital, Davids Island, New York Harbor.

Holland, Philip—Age, 23 years. Enlisted, October 28, 1861, at New York City, to serve three years; mustered in as private, Co. L, October 29, 1861; transferred to Co. H, February 25, 1862; wounded in action, May 5, 1862, at Williamsburg, Va.; died of his wounds, June 1862, at hospital, Fort Monroe, Va.

Hutchinson, John—Age, 41 years. Enlisted, November 28, 1861, at Jersey City, N.J., to serve three years; mustered in as private, Co. L, November 29, 1861; transferred to Co. G, February 25, 1862; discharged for disability, March 13, 1862, at Camp Wool, Md.

Ingraham, William—Age, 18 years. Enlisted, December 1, 1861, at Delhi, to serve three years; mustered in as private, Co. L, December 10, 1861; transferred to Co. A, February 25, 1862; re-enlisted as a veteran, December 24, 1863; wounded, no date or place; transferred to Co. B, One Hundred and Twentieth Infantry, June 23, 1864.

Jackson, William R.—Age, 30 years. Enlisted at New York City, to serve three years; mustered in as private, Co. L, December 7, 1861; transferred to Co. G, February 25, 1862; discharged for disability, March 13, 1862, at Camp Wool, Md.; also appears in Co. H.

Jagoe, Thomas—Age, 19 years. Enlisted at New York City, to serve three years; mustered in as private, Co. L, December 4, 1861; transferred to Co. G, February 25, 1862; wounded in action, July 1, 1862, at Malvern Hill, Va.; captured in action, July 2, 1803, at Gettysburg, Pa.; paroled in May 1864; transferred to Co. I, One Hundred and Twentieth Infantry, July 24, 1864; subsequent service in Co. I, One Hundred and Twelfth Infantry.

Johnson, Frank—Age, 24 years. Enlisted, December 3, 1861, at Jersey City, N.J., to serve three years; mustered in as private Co. L, December 4, 1861; transferred to Co. H, February 25, 1862; wounded in action May 5, 1862, at Williamsburg, Va.; discharged for disability, September 16, 1862, at Camp near Fort Lyon, Va.

Jones, David B.—Age, 34 years. Enrolled, October 9, 1861, at Berlin, Mass., to serve three years; mustered in as second lieutenant, Co. L, November 14, 1861; mustered out February 7, 1862, at Camp Wool, Md.

Jones, Edward—Age, 44 years. Enlisted, October 16, 1861, at Jersey City, N.J., to serve three years; mustered in as private, Co. L, October 26, 1861; transferred to Co. G, February 25, 1862; discharged for disability, March 13, 1862, at Camp Wool, Md.

Kerr, Matthew W.—Age, 28 years. Enlisted, November 2, 1861, at New York City, to serve three years; mustered in as private, Co. L, November 6, 1861; deserted in December 1861; also appears in Co. H.

King, Edmund—Age, 18 years. Enlisted at New York City, to serve three years, and mustered in as private, Co. L, November 23, 1861; deserted in December 1861.

Knox, James P.—Age, 19 years. Enlisted, November 25, 1861, at New York City, to serve three years; mustered in as private, Co. L, November 29, 1861; transferred to Co. H, February 25, 1862; re-enlisted as a veteran, December 24, 1863; promoted sergeant in January 1864; transferred to Co. D, One Hundred and Twentieth Infantry, October 30, 1864.

Larah, Robert J.—Age, 28 years. Enlisted, October 28, 1861, at Jersey City, N.J., to serve three years; mustered in as private, Co. L, October 29, 1861; transferred to Co. H, February 25, 1862; wounded in action, June 30, 1862, at White Oak Swamp, Va.; discharged for his wounds, December 23, 1862, at New York City; also born as Laroh.

Lascell, Richard—Age, 41 years. Enlisted, December 1, 1861, at Sinclairville, to serve three years; mustered in as sergeant, Co. L, December 3, 1861; transferred to Co. A, February 25, 1862; promoted corporal, February 1, 1863; transferred to Veteran Reserve Corps, December 19, 1863.

Leguire, William R.—Age, 19 years. Enlisted, December 13, 1861, at Hohokus, N.J., to serve three years; mustered in as private, Co. L, December 18, 1861; transferred to Co. H, February 25, 1862; discharged for disability, June 9, 1862, at Budd's Ferry, Md.

Lyon, Francis E.—Age, 27 years. Enlisted, October 3, 1861, at New York City, to serve three years; mustered in as corporal, Co. L, November 1, 1861; transferred to Co. H and returned to ranks, February 25, 1862; to Co. G, February 28, 1862; discharged for disability, December 24, 1862, at Point Lookout, Md.

Macey, Francis—Age, 18 years. Enlisted, November 28, 1861, at Plattsburg, to serve three years; mustered in as private, Co. L, December 11, 1861; transferred to Co. A, February 25, 1862; discharged for disability, November 26, 1862, at Washington, D.C.

Madden, James—Age, 41 years. Enlisted, December 8, 1861, at New York City, to serve three years; mustered in as private, Co. L, December D, 1861; transferred to Co. H, February 25, 1862; discharged for disability, June 26, 1862, at Annapolis, Md.

Matchett, John—Age, 31 years. Enlisted at New York City, to serve three years, and mustered in as private, Co. L, December 7, 1861; deserted in December 1861.

McCarthy, Michael—Age, 31 years. Enlisted, November 28, 1861, at New York City, to serve three years; mustered in as private, Co. L, December 2, 1861; transferred to Co. H, February 20, 1862; wounded in action, August 27, 1862, at Bristoe Station, Va., and again, July 2, 1863, at Gettysburg, Pa.; transferred to Co. H, One Hundred and Twentieth Infantry, October 31, 1864, from which mustered out, to date December 31, 1864, at New York City.

McDermott, Owen—Age, 40 years. Enlisted, December 11, 1861, at New York City, to serve three years; mustered in as private, Co. L, December 16, 1861; transferred to Co. A, February 25, 1862; killed in action, May 5, 1862, at Williamsburg, Va.

McGarry, Patrick—Age, 30 years. Enlisted at New York City, to serve three years, and mastered in as private, Co. L, December 11, 1861; no record subsequent to December 31, 1861.

McGee, Joseph—Age, 31 years. Enlisted, December 6, 1861, at New York City, to serve three years; mustered in as private, Co. L, December 9, 1861; transferred to Co. F, February 25, 1862; deserted, August 25, 1862, at Alexandria, Va.

McGuire, Francis—Age, 23 years. Enlisted at New York City, to serve three years, and mustered in as private, Co. L, October 31, 1861; deserted in December 1861.

McKernan, Hugh—Age, 20 years. Enlisted at New York City, to serve three years, and mustered in as private, Co. L, November 25, 1861; transferred to Co. H, February 25, 1862; wounded in action, May 5, 1862, at Williamsburg, Va.; discharged for wounds, October 8, 1862, at Alexandria, Va.

McMahon, Patrick—Age, 22 years. Enlisted at New

York City, to serve three years, and mustered in as private, Co. L, December 7, 1861; no record subsequent to December 81, 1861.

Moran, James—Age, 38 years. Enlisted at New York City, to serve three years, and mustered in as private, Co. L, November 4, 1861; transferred to Co. H, February 25, 1862; discharged for disability, March 15, 1862, at Camp Wool, Md.

Nolan, Thomas—Age, 40 years. Enlisted, December 2, 1861, at New York City, to serve three years; mustered in as private, Co. L, December 4, 1861; transferred to Co. H, February 25, 1862; to Co. K, One Hundred and Twentieth Infantry, October 30, 1864.

O'Brien, John—Age, 40 years. Enlisted at New York City, to serve three years, and mustered in as private, Co. L, November 21, 1861; transferred to Co. E, February 25, 1862; no further record.

Osborn, William—Age, 40 years. Enlisted at New York City, to serve three years, and mustered in as private, Co. L, December 10, 1861; transferred to Co. A, February 25, 1862; discharged for disability, June 3, 1864, at Deport Camp, D.C.

Ott, John—Age, 35 years. Enlisted at Hackensack, N.J., to serve three years, and mustered in as private, Co. L, December 10, 1861; deserted in December 1861.

Phipps, Gordon S.—Age, 23 years. Enlisted, October 11, 1861, at New York City, to serve three years; mustered in as sergeant, Co. L, October 31, 1861; transferred to Co. K, and returned to ranks, February 25, 1862; promoted sergeant, March 10, 1862; wounded in action, August 27, 1862, at Bristoe Station, Va.; died of his wounds, September 10, 1862, at Washington, D.C.; also appears in Co. H.

Purdy, William H.—Age, 30 years. Enlisted, December 1, 1861, at Delhi, to serve three years; mustered in as private, Co. L, December 11, 1861; transferred to Co. H, February 25, 1862; discharged for disability, March 15, 1862; also appears in Co. L.

Rieley, Thomas—Age, 42 years. Enlisted, November 6, 1861, at New York City, to serve three years; mustered in as private, Co. L, November 16, 1861; transferred to Co. H, February 25, 1862; discharged for disability, March 15, 1862, at Camp Wool, Md.

Rose, Alexander—Age, 30 years. Enlisted, November 18, 1861, at Sinclairville, to serve three years; mustered in as private, Co. L, December 3, 1861; transferred to Co. H, February 25, 1862; wounded in action, August 27, 1862, at Bristoe Station, Va.; discharged for disability, October 3, 1862, at Columbus, Ohio.

Ryan, Michael—Age, 27 years. Enlisted at New York City, to serve three years, and mustered in as private, Co. L, October 25, 1861; transferred to Co. H, February 25, 1862; wounded in action, July 1, 1862, at Malvern Hill, Va.; deserted in March 1863, at expiration of furlough.

Schwarzinyer, Michael—Age, 30 years. Enlisted, May 25, 1861, at New York City, to serve three years; mustered in as private, Co. A, June 21, 1861; deserted, no date.

Scudder, George—Age, 21 years. Enlisted at New York City, to serve three years, and mustered in as private, Co. L, October 17, 1861; transferred to Co. H, February 25, 1862; wounded in action, May 5, 1862, at Williamsburg, Va.; discharged to date, June 13, 1862.

Sears, George W.—Age, 19 years. Enlisted at New York City, to serve three years, and mustered in as private, Co. L, November 22, 1861; transferred to Co. H, February 25, 1862; wounded in action, June 1, 1862, at Fair Oaks, Va.; transferred to Co. E, Tenth Regiment, Veteran Reserve Corps, July 1, 1863; mustered out, November 16, 1865, at Washington, D.C.

Smith, Amasa J.—Age, 31 years. Enlisted, October 29, 1861, at Delhi, to serve three years; mustered in as private, Co. L, December 10, 1861; transferred to Co. I, February 25, 1862; promoted to corporal, May 1862; sergeant, September 25, 1862; wounded in action, July 2, 1863, at Gettysburg, Pa.; discharged for wounds, July 9, 1864, at Baltimore, Md.

Smith, Patrick—Age, 25 years. Enlisted, December 10, 1861, at Newark, N.J., to serve three years; mustered in as private, Co. L, December 11, 1861; deserted, December 1861.

Stilson, Albert—Age, 44 years. Enlisted, December 1, 1861, at Delhi, to serve three years; mustered in as private, Co. L, December 12, 1861; transferred to Co. H, February 25, 1862; discharged for disability, September 14, 1862, at Fort Monroe, Va.

Twomey, David—Age, 20 years. Enlisted, November 9, 1861, at New York City, to serve three years; mustered in as private, Co. L, November 11, 1861; transferred to Co. K, February 25, 1862; wounded in action, June 25, 1862, near Fair Oaks, Va.; July 1, 1862, at Malvern Hill, Va.; transferred to Co. E, One Hundred and Twentieth Infantry, June 23, 1864; also appears in Co. H.

Vause, Lewis N.—Age, 38 years. Enlisted, November 24, 1861, at New York City, to serve three years; mustered in as private, Co. L, December 2, 1861; no further record.

Ward, James—Age, 18 years. Enlisted at Chautauqua, to serve three years, and mustered in as private, unassigned, January 22, 1864; no further record.

Webber, John R.—Age, 39 years. Enlisted, October 21, 1861, at Poughkeepsie, to serve three years;

mustered in as private, Co. L, October 29, 1861; transferred to Co. C, February 25, 1862; died of disease, February 1, 1863, in hospital, New York City.

Whalen, Daniel—Age, 27 years. Enlisted at New York City, to serve three years, and mustered in as private, Co. L, November 14, 1861; transferred to Co. K, February 25, 1862; died of disease, April 16, 1863, near Falmouth, Va.

Whycoff, Charles—Age, 19 years. Enlisted, December 13, 1861, at Delhi, to serve three years; mustered in as private, Co. L, December 20, 1861; transferred to Co. I, February 25, 1862; discharged for disability, March 16, 1862, at Camp Wool, Charles County, Md.

Williams, Frederick—Age, 19 years. Enlisted, October 13, 1861, at New York City, to serve three years; mustered in as private, Co. L, November 1, 1861; transferred to Co. K, February 25, 1862; captured in action, May 5, 1862, at Williamsburg, Va.; paroled, May 11, 1862; deserted, July 20, 1862, at Alexandria, Va.

Williams, James A.—Age, 34 years. Enlisted at New York City, to serve three years, and mustered in as private, Co. L, October 29, 1861; transferred to Co. H, February 25, 1862, to Co. K, February 28, 1862; re-enlisted as a veteran, December 24, 1863; transferred to Co. E, One Hundred and Twentieth Infantry, June 23, 1864; also born as James A. Williamson.

Field and Staff

Bailey, Samuel—Age, 22 years. Enrolled, July 23, 1861, at Staten Island to serve three years; mustered in as sergeant-major, July 24, 1861; as second lieutenant, Co. B, November 5, 1861; as first lieutenant, May 2, 1862; wounded in action, May 5, 1862, at Williamsburg, Va.; mustered in as captain Co. I, September 26, 1862; mustered out with company, June 20, 1864, near Petersburg, Va. Commissioned second lieutenant, January 7, 1862, with rank from November 5, 1861, original; first lieutenant, June 30, 1862, with rank from May 2, 1862, vice A. S. Mason, resigned; captain, December 1, 1862, with rank from October 30, 1862, vice R.T. Johnson, discharged.

Brooks, Isaac A.—Age, 45 years. Enlisted at Staten Island, to serve three years, and mustered in as commissary sergeant, July 23, 1861; discharged, February 24, 1864.

Crawford, M.H.—Age, 24 years. Date, place of enlistment and muster in as quartermaster-sergeant not stated; died of wounds, August 24, 1864, at hospital, Frederick, Md.

Eastman, William R.—Age, 27 years. Enrolled near Falmouth, Va., to serve three years, and mustered in as chaplain, January 1, 1863; mustered out with regiment, June 19, 1864, near Petersburg, Va. Commissioned chaplain, April 24, 1863, with rank from January 1, 1863, vice L.W. Norton, resigned.

Fry, Thomas W.G.—Age, 28 years. Enrolled at Staten Island, to serve three years, and mustered in as first lieutenant and quartermaster, July 23, 1861; discharged, to accept appointment as captain and commissary of subsistence, U.S. Volunteers, April 2, 1863. Commissioned first lieutenant and quartermaster, January 7, 1862, with rank from June 21, 1861, original.

Grant, John McNeil—Age, 23 years. Enrolled, July 23, 1861, at Staten Island, to serve three years; mustered in as quartermaster-sergeant, July 24, 1861; as first lieutenant and quartermaster, November 22, 1862; mustered out with regiment, June 19, 1864, near Petersburg, Va. Commissioned first lieutenant and quartermaster, December 13, 1862, with rank from November 22, 1862, T.W.S. Fry, appointed commissary, United States Volunteers.

Irwin, Charles K.—Age, 36 years. Enrolled, July 23, 1861, at Staten Island, to serve three years; mustered in as surgeon, July 24, 1861; mustered out with regiment, June 10, 1864, near Petersburg, Va. Commissioned surgeon, January 7, 1862, with rank from June 21, 1861.

Jones, William M.—Age, 49 years. Enrolled at Albany, to serve three years, and mustered in as assistant surgeon, November 3, 1862; discharged for disability, July 29, 1863. Commissioned assistant surgeon, October 31, 1862, with rank from October 27, 1862; original.

Leighton, Nathaniel W.—Age, 28 years. Enrolled at Staten Island, to serve three years, and mustered in as assistant surgeon, July 23, 1861; discharged, October 3, 1862. Commissioned assistant surgeon, December 1, 1862, with rank from June 30, 1861, original.

Moses, Israel—Age, 38 years. Enrolled at Staten Island, to serve three years, and mustered in as lieutenant-colonel, June 3, 1861; mustered out, October 20, 1862, at Washington, D.C., to accept appointment as surgeon, U.S. Volunteers. Commissioned lieutenant-colonel, January 7, 1862, with rank from July 23, 1861; original.

Norton, Levi W.—Age, 41 years. Enrolled, July 23,

1861, at Staten Island, to serve three years; mastered in as chaplain, July 24, 1861; discharged, April 20, 1862. Commissioned chaplain, January 7, 1862, with rank from July 17, 1861; original.

Perkins, Edward D.—Age, 35 years. Enrolled at Washington, to serve three years, and mustered in as assistant surgeon, October 17, 1862; discharged, May 13, 1863, for promotion to surgeon, Seventy-first Infantry. Commissioned assistant surgeon, October 14, 1862, with rank from October 11, 1862, vice N.W. Leighton, resigned.

Taylor, Nelson—Age, 40 years. Enrolled at Staten Island, to serve three years, and mustered in as colonel, July 23, 1861; discharged, September 9, 1862, for promotion to brigadier general. Commissioned colonel, January 7, 1862, with rank from July 23, 1861, original.

Townsend, George D.—Enrollment, place and muster-in as assistant surgeon not stated; appointed assistant surgeon, October 21, 1862; missing since October 1863. Not commissioned.

Chapter Notes

Chapter 1

1. David B. Parker, *A Chautauqua Boy in '61 and Afterward: Reminiscences by David B. Parker, Second Lieutenant, Seventy-Second New York; Introduction by Albert Bushnell Hart* (Boston: Small, Maynard, 1912), 3.
2. "Departure of the Volunteers," *The Fredonia Censor*, June 5, 1861, excerpted from *Dunkirk Journal*.
3. Ibid.
4. Francis T. Lynch and Samuel C. Sandoli, *Come Cry with Me: The Letter of Emerson F. Merrell, Native of the Town of Coventry in Chenango County, New York, Who Served in Company I, 72nd Regiment, New York Infantry, New York Excelsior Brigade, Army of the Potomac 1861–1863* (self-published by the authors, 2001), 2–3.
5. W.A. Swanberg, *Sickles the Incredible* (Gettysburg: Stan Clark Military Books, 1956), 53–55.
6. Ibid., 72–76.
7. Ibid., 115.
8. Ibid., 116.
9. Ibid., 116–17.
10. Ibid., 117.
11. For more information regarding specific composition of the Excelsior Brigade, reference Fredrick H. Dyer's "70th–74th New York Infantry" found in *A Compendium of the War of the Rebellion* (Indiana: Guild, 1997). Additional information can be found in Col. W.F. Fox's work *Regimental Losses in the American Civil War, 1861–1865: A Treatise on the Extent and Nature of the Mortuary Losses in the Union Regiments, with Full and Extensive Statistics Compiled from the Official Records on file in the State Military Bureaus and at Washington* (Albany, NY: Albany, 1889).
12. Henri LeFevre-Brown, *History of the Third Regiment Excelsior Brigade 72nd New York Volunteer Infantry 1861–1865* (Jamestown, NY: Journal, 1902), 7.
13. W.A. Swanberg, ibid., 117–18.
14. Ibid., 119.
15. Ibid., 120.
16. Ibid., 120–21.
17. As quoted by W.A. Swanberg, *Sickles the Incredible*, referencing the *Journal of the Military Service Institution of the United States*, 121.
18. Swanberg, *Sickles the Incredible*, 118–22.
19. Ibid.
20. "Departure of the First Company of Volunteers from Delaware County, 1861," transcribed from the *Bloomville Mirror* (date of article unknown) by Linda Robinson, April 17, 2002, New York Genealogy and History Site http://www.dcnyhistory.org/milvol1861.html, date of access December 9, 2012.
21. LeFevre-Brown, *History of the Third Regiment*, 8–9.
22. Ibid., insert between pages 37 and 38.
23. "A Letter from Camp Scott, June 24, 1861," *The Fredonia Censor*, July 3, 1861.
24. Arthur McKinstry, "A Letter from the Camp, June 18th, 1861," *The Fredonia Censor*, June 19, 1861.
25. David B. Parker, ibid., 4.
26. McKinstry, "Letter from the Camp, June 18th, 1861."
27. Henri LeFevre-Brown, ibid., 9.
28. Ibid., 9–12.
29. David B. Parker, ibid., 4–5.
30. Henri LeFevre-Brown, ibid., 10.
31. "Departure of the Volunteers," *The Fredonia Censor*, June 5, 1861, excerpted from *Dunkirk Journal*.
32. Stephen Beszedits, "Some Lesser Hungarians of the American Civil War," http://www.sk-szeged.hu/statikus_html/vasvary/newsletter/05jun/civil_war.htm, accessed November 11, 2009, and December 9, 2012.
33. LeFevre-Brown, *History of the Third Regiment*, 9.
34. Pendergast Library, "The Man the Jamestown GAR Honored," http://www.prendergastlibrary.org/?page_id=4201, accessed November 11, 2009, and December 9, 2012.
35. Henri LeFevre-Brown, ibid., 125.
36. Ibid., 11.
37. Charles W. Gould, "The Captain's Tent, June 9th, 1861," compilation by Robert F. Harris in *Civil War Times Illustrated: The Battleground of Virtue* (October 2001), pp. 26, 68.
38. Ibid.
39. "Indignation in Westfield," *The Fredonia Censor*, July 31, 1861, reprinted from an article in the *Westfield Republican*.
40. LeFevre-Brown, *History of the Third Regiment*, 12.
41. David B. Parker, ibid., 5.
42. LeFevre-Brown, *History of the Third Regiment*, 13.
43. Ibid., 13–14
44. Swanberg, *Sickles the Incredible*, 123–24.

Chapter 2

1. Henri LeFevre-Brown, *History of the Third Regiment Excelsior Brigade 72nd New York Volunteer Infantry 1861–1865* (Jamestown, NY: Journal, 1902), 15.
2. Ibid., 17–18.

3. W.A. Swanberg, *Sickles the Incredible*. (Gettysburg: Stan Clark Military Books, 1956), referencing the *Journal of the Military Service Institution of the United States*, 145.
4. Arthur McKinstry, "Camp Correspondence July 6th 1861," *The Fredonia Censor*, July 24, 1861.
5. The Mount Sinai Hospital, "The Unexpected, 1860–1869," 1852–2002 Sesquicentennial Pamphlet, 5.
6. LeFevre-Brown, *History of the Third Regiment*, 63 ½.
7. Ibid., 81½.
8. Peter Messent and Steve Courtney, eds., *The Civil War Letters of Joseph Hopkins Twichell: A Chaplain's Story* (Athens, Georgia: University of Georgia Press), 47.
9. "Departure from Camp Scott, July 28th, 1861," *The Fredonia Censor*, August 7, 1861.
10. Messent and Courtney, *Civil War Letters*, 47.
11. Gettysburg Foundation, "Feeding the Troops," www.gettysburgfoundation.org/media/assets/FeedingtheTroops.pdf, accessed March 13, 2013.
12. Messent and Courtney, *Civil War Letters*, 48.
13. LeFevre-Brown, *History of the Third Regiment*, 17.
14. Francis T. Lynch and Samuel C. Sandoli, *Come Cry with Me: The Letter of Emerson F. Merrell, Native of the Town of Coventry in Chenango County, New York, Who Served in Company I, 72nd Regiment, New York Infantry, New York Excelsior Brigade, Army of the Potomac 1861–1863* (self-published by the authors, 2001), 4.
15. Hiram Stoddard, "Camp Nelson Taylor, March 27th, 1863," in *Wartime Letters of Hiram Stoddard, Company I, 72nd NYSV*, Gowanda Area Historical Society.
16. Charles W. Gould, "Washington D.C., August 7th, 1861," in compilation by Robert F. Harris, *Civil War Times Illustrated: The Battleground of Virtue*, October 2001, 68.
17. Fr. Joseph O'Hagan, "Woodstock Letters VIII, 1879," *Civil War History, VI* (Maryland: Woodstock College Press, 1879), 173–83.
18. "Departure from Camp Scott, July 28th, 1861," *The Fredonia Censor*, August 7, 1861.
19. LeFevre-Brown, *History of the Third Regiment*, 17–18.
20. Ibid., 18.
21. *The War of the Rebellion: A Compilation of the Official Records of the Union and Confederate Armies* (Washington, D.C.: U.S. Government Printing Office, 1880–1901), vol. 107, 438. Hereafter cited as "O.R." for "Official Records."
22. Ibid., 19–20.
23. Swanberg, *Sickles the Incredible*, 128.
24. H.B. Taylor, "From the Third Regiment, Camp Caldwell, September 1861," *The Fredonia Censor*, September 11, 1861.
25. Swanberg, *Sickles the Incredible*, citing *New York World*, June 30, 1869, 125.
26. Lynch and Sandoli, *Come Cry with Me*, 5.
27. "From the Third Regiment, August 11th, 1861," *The Fredonia Censor*, August 21, 1861.
28. LeFevre-Brown, *History of the Third Regiment*, 20.
29. "From the Third Regiment, August 11th, 1861," *The Fredonia Censor*, August 21, 1861.
30. Ibid.
31. Lynch and Sandoli, *Come Cry with Me*, 32.
32. 72nd N.Y. Volunteer Infantry, Civil War Newspaper Clippings, Unit History Project, New York State Military Museum.
33. David B. Parker, *A Chautauqua Boy in '61 and Afterward: Reminiscences by David B. Parker, Second Lieutenant, Seventy-Second New York; Introduction by Albert Bushnell Hart* (Boston: Small, Maynard, 1912), 6.
34. "From the Third Regiment, August 26, 1861," *The Fredonia Censor*, September 4, 1861.
35. Ibid.
36. Ibid.
37. "August 3, 1861," 73rd N.Y. Volunteer Infantry, Civil War Newspaper Clippings, Unit History Project, New York State Military Museum.
38. *New York Times*, "Local Military Movements, August 23, 1861."
39. "August 24, 1861," 73rd N.Y. Volunteer Infantry, Civil War Newspaper Clippings, Unit History Project, New York State Military Museum.
40. Ibid., "October 14, 1861."
41. LeFevre-Brown, *History of the Third Regiment*, 20.
42. "From the Third Regiment, Camp Caldwell, October 17th, 1861," *The Fredonia Censor*, October 23, 1861.
43. Ibid.
44. Ibid.
45. LeFevre-Brown, *History of the Third Regiment*, 20.
46. "From the Third Regiment, Camp Caldwell, September 14th, 1861," *The Fredonia Censor*, September 25, 1861.
47. Ibid.
48. Ibid.
49. Ibid.
50. "Reconnaissance of the Excelsior Brigade in Southern Maryland," *The New York Times*, October 3, 1861.
51. Ibid.
52. "From the Third Regiment, Camp Caldwell, September 14th, 1861," *The Fredonia Censor*, September 25, 1861.
53. *New York Times*, "Local Military Movements, August 23, 1861."

Chapter 3

1. Francis T. Lynch and Samuel C. Sandoli, *Come Cry with Me: The Letter of Emerson F. Merrell, Native of the Town of Coventry in Chenango County, New York, Who Served in Company I, 72nd Regiment, New York Infantry, New York Excelsior Brigade, Army of the Potomac 1861–1863* (self-published by the authors, 2001), 24–25.
2. Henri LeFevre-Brown, *History of the Third Regiment Excelsior Brigade 72nd New York Volunteer Infantry 1861–1865* (Jamestown, NY: Journal, 1902), 22.
3. Walter H. Hebert, *Fighting Joe Hooker* (Lincoln: University of Nebraska Press, 1999), 50.
4. Ibid., 51–52.
5. Ibid., 54.
6. W.A. Swanberg, *Sickles the Incredible* (Gettysburg: Stan Clark Military Books, 1956), 132.
7. H.B. Taylor, "From the Third Regiment, October 23rd, 1861," *The Fredonia Censor*, November 6, 1861.
8. Peter Messent and Steve Courtney, eds., *The Civil War Letters of Joseph Hopkins Twichell: A Chaplain's Story* (Athens, Georgia: University of Georgia Press), 76.
9. Hebert, *Fighting Joe Hooker*, 66.
10. Ibid.
11. "Adjutant S.M. Doyle," *The Fredonia Censor*, October 9, 1861.
12. Lucius Jones, Jr., *In the War of the Rebellion from 1861 to 1865* (New York: Fredonia, 1913), 2.

13. Ibid.
14. "From the Third Regiment, October 1861," *The Fredonia Censor*, October 30, 1861.
15. H.B. Taylor, "From the Third Regiment, October 23rd, 1861," *The Fredonia Censor*, November 6, 1861.
16. "Dear Uncles, October 1861," *The Fredonia Censor*, October 30, 1861.
17. O.R., vol. 5, 372.
18. LeFevre-Brown, *History of the Third Regiment*, 22–24.
19. "From the Third Regiment, November 17th, 1861," *The Fredonia Censor*, November 27, 1861.
20. LeFevre-Brown, *History of the Third Regiment*, 22–23.
21. H.B. Taylor, "From the Third Regiment, October 23rd, 1861," *The Fredonia Censor*, November 6, 1861.
22. LeFevre-Brown, *History of the Third Regiment*, 24.
23. Hebert, *Fighting Joe Hooker*, 58.
24. LeFevre-Brown, *History of the Third Regiment*, 24.
25. "From the Third Regiment, November 17, 1861," *The Fredonia Censor*, November 27, 1861.
26. Ibid.
27. Lynch and Sandoli, *Come Cry with Me*, 32.
28. Sandy Point, "From the Third Regiment, March 9th, 1862," *The Fredonia Censor*, March 19, 1862.
29. Ibid.
30. G.W. Shelley, "From the Third Regiment, A Private Letter, December 12th, 1861," *The Fredonia Censor*, December 25, 1861.
31. Hebert, *Fighting Joe Hooker*, 60.
32. David B. Parker, *A Chautauqua Boy in '61 and Afterward: Reminiscences by David B. Parker, Second Lieutenant, Seventy-Second New York; Introduction by Albert Bushnell Hart* (Boston: Small, Maynard, 1912), 6.
33. Hebert, *Fighting Joe Hooker*, 60–61.
34. Swanberg, *Sickles the Incredible*, 133.
35. G.W. Shelley, "Extract from a Private Letter from the Third Regiment, December 7th, 1861," December 18, 1861.
36. Hebert, *Fighting Joe Hooker*, 60.
37. "From the Third Regiment, November 17th, 1861," *The Fredonia Censor*, November 27, 1861.
38. Hebert, *Fighting Joe Hooker*, 61.
39. "From the Third Regiment, March 30th, 1862," *The Fredonia Censor*, April 9, 1862.
40. Hebert, *Fighting Joe Hooker*, 62.
41. "From the Third Regiment, December 9th, 1861," *The Fredonia Censor*, December 18, 1861.
42. Swanberg, *Sickles the Incredible*, 138.
43. "From the Third Regiment, Camp Wool, March 15th, 1862," *The Fredonia Censor*, March 26, 1862.
44. Ibid.
45. James F. Rusling, *Men and Things I Saw in Civil War Days* (New York: Eaton and Mains, 1899), 61–62.
46. Hebert, *Fighting Joe Hooker*, 63–64.
47. "From the Third Regiment, Camp Caldwell, September 14th, 1861," *The Fredonia Censor*, September 25, 1861.
48. Charles W. Gould, "The Captain's Tent, June 10th, 1861," *The Battleground of Virtue: Civil War Times Illustrated*, October 2001, 71.
49. "From the Third Regiment, Camp Wool, December 22nd, 1861," *The Fredonia Censor*, January 1, 1862.
50. Owen Street, *The Young Patriot: A Memorial of James Hall, 1862* (Massachusetts: Sabbath School Society, 1862), 147–148.
51. Lynch and Sandoli, *Come Cry with Me*, 40.
52. Daniel Edgar Sickles, *Address Delivered in Boston Before the Hooker Association of Massachusetts* (Norwood, Massachusetts: Norwood, 1910), 2.
53. Hebert, *Fighting Joe Hooker*, 67.
54. "From the Third Regiment, Headquarters, Company D on Picket, Sandy Point, February 28th, 1862," *The Fredonia Censor*, March 12, 1862.
55. Ibid.
56. Swanberg, *Sickles the Incredible*, 135.
57. Hebert, *Fighting Joe Hooker*, 66.
58. "From the Third Regiment, November 23rd, 1861," *The Fredonia Censor*, December 4, 1861.
59. "From the Third Regiment, December 3rd, 1861," *The Fredonia Censor*, December 11, 1861.
60. "From the Third Regiment, December 9th, 1861," *The Fredonia Censor*, December 18, 1861.
61. "From the Third Regiment, Camp Wool, December 22nd, 1861," *The Fredonia Censor*, January 1, 1862.
62. "From the Third Regiment, Camp Wool, December 30th, 1861," *The Fredonia Censor*, January 15, 1862.
63. "From the Third Regiment, Camp Wool, January 2nd, 1862," *The Fredonia Censor*, January 22, 1862.
64. Ibid.
65. Ibid.
66. Ibid.
67. "From the Third Regiment, Camp Wool, January 14th, 1862," *The Fredonia Censor*, January 29, 1862.
68. Owen Street, *The Young Patriot: A Memorial of James Hall, 1862* (Massachusetts: Sabbath School Society, 1862), 148–50.
69. Ibid., 157–59.
70. "From the Third Regiment, Camp Wool, January 21st, 1862," *The Fredonia Censor*, January 29, 1862.
71. Ibid.
72. Ibid.
73. Ibid.
74. Ibid.
75. Ibid.
76. Ibid.
77. Gould, "The Captain's Tent," 74–75.
78. G.W. Shelley, "Extract from a Private Letter from the Third Regiment, December 7th, 1861," *The Fredonia Censor*, December 18, 1861.
79. Hebert, *Fighting Joe Hooker*, 68–69.
80. Gould, "The Captain's Tent," 74–75.
81. Hebert, *Fighting Joe Hooker*, 71.
82. Lynch and Sandoli, *Come Cry with Me*, 53.
83. Ibid.
84. Street, *Young Patriot*, 152–153.
85. LeFevre-Brown, *History of the Third Regiment*, 22.
86. Lynch and Sandoli, *Come Cry with Me*, 54.
87. "From the Third Regiment, Camp Wool, March 30th, 1862," *The Fredonia Censor*, April 9, 1862.
88. LeFevre-Brown, *History of the Third Regiment*, 25.
89. Ibid.
90. Talman C. Bookout, "Camp Wool, Maryland, April 5th, 1862," *The Bloomville Mirror*, April 22, 1862.
91. Ibid.
92. Ibid.
93. Ibid.
94. LeFevre-Brown, *History of the Third Regiment*, 25.
95. Daniel Sickles, "General Sickles Farewell to His Soldiers, 1862," *The New York Times*, April 10, 1862.
96. Talman C. Bookout, "Camp Wool, Maryland, April 5th, 1862," *The Bloomville Mirror*, April 22, 1862.

Chapter 4

1. "From the Third Regiment, April 11th, 1862," *The Fredonia Censor*, April 23, 1862.
2. Ibid.
3. Walter H. Hebert, *Fighting Joe Hooker* (Lincoln: University of Nebraska Press, 1999), 76.
4. "From the Third Regiment," *The Fredonia Censor*, April 14, 1862.
5. David Hastings and Earl C. Hastings, Jr., *A Pitiless Rain: The Battle of Williamsburg, 1862* (Shippensburg: White Mane, 1997), 10–19.
6. David B. Parker, *A Chautauqua Boy in '61 and Afterward: Reminiscences by David B. Parker, Second Lieutenant, Seventy-Second New York; Introduction by Albert Bushnell Hart* (Boston: Small, Maynard, 1912), 12.
7. Owen Street, *The Young Patriot: A Memorial of James Hall* (Massachusetts: Massachusetts Sabbath School Society, 1862), 162.
8. Christopher Ryan Oates, *Fighting for Home: The Story of Alfred K. Oates and the Fifth Regiment, Excelsior Brigade* (Cornelius, NC: Warren, 2006), 44.
9. "Camp Scott Near Yorktown, April 22nd, 1862," *The Bloomville Mirror*, May 6 1862.
10. Parker, *Chautauqua Boy,* 15.
11. Ibid.
12. Ibid., 15–16.
13. E.J. Warner, *Generals in Blue: Lives of the Union Commanders* (Baton Rouge: Louisiana State University Press, 1964), 227–28.
14. A.H. Guernsey and H.M. Alden, *Harper's Pictoral History of the Civil War* (New York: Fairfax, 1866), 336.
15. "General Sickles," *The Fredonia Censor*, April 30, 1962, 1.
16. Ibid.
17. Emerson F. Merrell, "Letter to His Brother Henry, April 4th, 1862, sent from Camp Winfield Scott," in Francis T. Lynch and Samuel C. Sandoli, *Come Cry with Me: The Letter of Emerson F. Merrell, Native of the Town of Coventry in Chenango County, New York, Who Served in Company I, 72nd Regiment, New York Infantry, New York Excelsior Brigade, Army of the Potomac 1861–1863* (self-published by the authors, 2001), 58.
18. "From the Third Regiment, Camp Wilfred Scott, April 29th, 1862," *The Fredonia Censor*, May 14, 1862.
19. Street, *Young Patriot,* 164–65.
20. Warner, *Generals in Blue,* 193–94.
21. Ibid., 362–63.
22. R.L. Murray, *Excelsior Brigade at Williamsburg in the Army of the Potomac Journal* (Wolcot: Benedum, 2005), 3.
23. Ibid.
24. Ibid., 4–5.
25. Ibid., 4.
26. Murray, *Excelsior Brigade,* 9.
27. Lucius Jones, Jr., *In the War of the Rebellion from 1861 to 1865* (New York: Fredonia, 1913), 7.
28. Hastings and Hastings, *Pitiless Rain,* 36–38.
29. O.R., vol. 11, part 1, 465.
30. R.L. Murray, ibid., "Hartwell Dickinson Letter, May 8, 1862," 8.
31. Ibid.
32. O.R., vol. 11, part 1, 484.
33. Murray, *Excelsior Brigade,* 8.
34. Ibid., 9.
35. Ibid., 9–11.
36. O.R., vol. 11, part 1, 467.
37. Hebert, *Fighting Joe Hooker* 85.
38. O.R., vol. 11, part 1, 8.
39. "J.F.'s Letter to the Editor Camp Near Williamsburg, Virginia, May 7, 1862," *The Fredonia Censor*, May 21, 1862.
40. Ibid.
41. Alan H. Archambault, *A Sketchbook of the Union Infantryman* (Gettysburg: Thomas, 1999), 86–87.
42. Parker, *Chautauqua Boy,* 16.
43. O.R., vol. 11, part 1, 480.
44. "Report of Lt. Col. Charles H. Burtis, 74th N.Y. Infantry, May 5, 1862," O.R., series 1, vol. 11, part 1, 486.
45. Murray, *Excelsior Brigade,* "Henry Ford Letter, May 8, 1862," 23.
46. Ibid.
47. Henri LeFevre-Brown, *History of the Third Regiment Excelsior Brigade 72nd New York Volunteer Infantry 1861–1865* (Jamestown, NY: Journal, 1902), 142–43.
48. O.R., vol. 11, part 1, 482.
49. Ibid., 482–83.
50. Paul Mathless, *Voices of the Civil War: The Peninsula* (Alexandria: Time-Life, 1998), 42.
51. Murray, *Excelsior Brigade,* "A Lieutenant in Sickles Brigade," 27.
52. O.R., vol. 11, part 1, 480.
53. Hastings and Hastings, *Pitiless Rain,* 98–111.
54. Paul Mathless, *Voices of the Civil War: The Peninsula,* 42.
55. Emerson F. Merrell, "Letter to His Parents, May 6th, 1862, sent from Camp Winfield Scott," in Lynch and Sandoli, *Come Cry with Me,* 62.
56. "A Letter for the Third Regiment," *The Fredonia Censor*, May 21, 1862.
57. Hastings and Hastings, *Pitiless Rain,* 115–18.
58. Parker, *Chautauqua Boy,* 16–17.
59. O.R., vol. 11, part 1, 450.
60. Ibid., 533–43.
61. Ibid., 450.
62. Ibid., 459.
63. Ibid., 468.

Chapter 5

1. O.R., vol. 11, part 1, 465.
2. Martin A. Haynes, *A History of the Second Regiment, New Hampshire Volunteer Infantry in the War of the Rebellion* (Lakeport, NH: n.p., 1896), 74.
3. Peter Messent and Steve Courtney, eds., *The Civil War Letters of Joseph Hopkins Twichell: A Chaplain's Story* (Athens, GA: University of Georgia Press), 124–125.
4. Walter H. Hebert, *Fighting Joe Hooker* (Lincoln: University of Nebraska Press, 1999), 117.
5. Ibid.
6. James F. Rusling, *Men and Things I Saw in Civil War Days* (New York: Eaton and Mains, 1899), 63.
7. Paul Mathless, *Voices of the Civil War: The Seven Days* (Alexandria, VA: Lifetime Books, 1998), 113.
8. David B. Parker, *A Chautauqua Boy in '61 and Afterward: Reminiscences by David B. Parker, Second Lieutenant, Seventy-Second New York; Introduction by Albert Bushnell Hart* (Boston: Small, Maynard, 1912), 17–18.
9. O.R., vol. 11, part 3, 166.
10. Christopher Ryan Oates, *Fighting for Home: The

Story of Alfred K. Oates and the Fifth Regiment, Excelsior Brigade (Cornelius, NC: Warren, 2006), 60–61.

11. Henri LeFevre-Brown, *History of the Third Regiment Excelsior Brigade 72nd New York Volunteer Infantry 1861–1865* (Jamestown, NY: Journal, 1902), 151–58.

12. "The Killed and Wounded," *The Fredonia Censor*, May 14, 1862.

13. "The Battle of Williamsburgh," *The Fredonia Censor*, May 14, 1862.

14. "The Honored Dead," *The Fredonia Censor*, May 21, 1862.

15. Ibid.

16. "The Victims of the Williamsburgh Fight, by J.P.," *The Fredonia Censor*, May 21, 1862.

17. Hebert, *Fighting Joe Hooker*, 95.

18. Emerson F. Merrell, "Letter to His Brother Henry, April 4th, 1862, Sent from Camp Winfield Scott," in Francis T. Lynch and Samuel C. Sandoli, *Come Cry with Me: The Letter of Emerson F. Merrell, Native of the Town of Coventry in Chenango County, New York, Who Served in Company I, 72nd Regiment, New York Infantry, New York Excelsior Brigade, Army of the Potomac 1861–1863* (self-published by the authors, 2001), 58.

19. Hebert, *Fighting Joe Hooker*, 95.

20. "Return of Sickles to His Brigade," *The New York Times*, May 24, 1862.

21. Ibid.

22. Hebert, *Fighting Joe Hooker*, 95.

23. Ibid., 95–96.

24. Ibid., 96.

25. Mathless, *Voices of the Civil War: The Seven Days*, 114.

26. Ibid.

27. "Taylor's Report," May 31–June 4, 1862, O.R., series 1, vol. 11, part 1, 830.

28. Mathless, *Voices of the Civil War: The Seven Days*, 116.

29. "Taylor's Report," 830.

30. Mathless, *Voices of the Civil War: The Seven Days*, 116.

31. Hebert, *Fighting Joe Hooker*, 97.

32. "Taylor's Report," 17.

33. Ibid., 830.

34. O.R., ibid., "Sickles Report of Fair Oaks," 822.

35. Ibid, 822.

36. Mathless, *Voices of the Civil War: The Seven Days*, "Walter Donaldson Letter," 147.

37. O.R., ibid., "Sickles Report of Fair Oaks," 822.

38. "Hall Report of Fair Oaks, May 31–June 1, 1862, O.R., series 1, vol. 11, part 1, 826.

39. Mathless, *Voices of the Civil War: The Seven Days*, "Walter Donaldson Letter," 147.

40. Ibid.

41. O.R., vol. 11, part 1, 822.

42. Ibid., 830.

43. Ibid.

44. Mathless, *Voices of the Civil War: The Seven Days*, 116.

45. Hebert, *Fighting Joe Hooker*, 98.

46. "Conduct of the War Report by Joint Committee in 1863," Part I, 578.

47. O.R., vol. 11, part 1, 830.

48. Lucius Jones, Jr., *In the War of the Rebellion from 1861 to 1865* (New York: Fredonia, 1913), 8.

49. Parker, *Chautauqua Boy*, 19.

50. Ibid.

51. Ibid.

52. LeFevre-Brown, *History of the Third Regiment*, 40.

53. O.R., vol. 11, part 1, 830–31.

54. Hebert, *Fighting Joe Hooker*, 98–99.

55. O.R., vol. 11, part 1, 826.

56. Owen Street, *The Young Patriot: A Memorial of James Hall* (Massachusetts: Massachusetts Sabbath School Society, 1862), 174–75.

57. Mathless, *Voices of the Civil War: The Seven Days*, 127–28.

58. O.R., vol. 11, part 1, 831.

59. Ibid.

60. Lynch and Sandoli, *Come Cry with Me*, 64.

61. Martin A. Haynes, *A History of the 2nd Regiment, New Hampshire Volunteer Infantry, in the War of the Rebellion* (Lake Port, NH: n.p.), 1896, 91.

62. Gustavus B. Hutchinson, *A Narrative of the Formation and Services of the Eleventh Massachusetts Volunteers* (Boston, MA: Alfred Mudge, 1893), 26.

63. Parker, *Chautauqua Boy*, 20.

64. Hebert, *Fighting Joe Hooker*, 98.

Chapter 6

1. Peter Messent and Steve Courtney, eds., *The Civil War Letters of Joseph Hopkins Twichell: A Chaplain's Story* (Athens, Georgia: University of Georgia Press), 139–140.

2. Walter H. Hebert, *Fighting Joe Hooker* (Lincoln: University of Nebraska Press, 1999), 99.

3. Francis T. Lynch and Samuel C. Sandoli, *Come Cry with Me: The Letter of Emerson F. Merrell, Native of the Town of Coventry in Chenango County, New York, Who Served in Company I, 72nd Regiment, New York Infantry, New York Excelsior Brigade, Army of the Potomac 1861–1863* (self-published by the authors, 2001), 66.

4. Paul Mathless, *Voices of the Civil War: The Seven Days* (Alexandria, VA: Lifetime, 1998), 9–11.

5. Messent and Courtney, *Civil War Letters*, 146.

6. Hebert, *Fighting Joe Hooker*, 101–02.

7. O.R., vol. 11, part 2, 108.

8. Ibid.

9. Ibid.

10. Ibid., 134–35.

11. Ibid.

12. Ibid, 108.

13. Messent and Courtney, *Civil War Letters*, 146.

14. *The New York Times*, July 9, 1862.

15. O.R., vol. 11, part 2, 109.

16. Ibid., 136.

17. Ibid.

18. Ibid., 109.

19. Ibid., 136.

20. Henri LeFevre-Brown, *History of the Third Regiment Excelsior Brigade 72nd New York Volunteer Infantry 1861–1865* (Jamestown, NY: Journal, 1902), 51.

21. O.R., vol. 11, part 2, 137.

22. Ibid.

23. Lucius Jones, Jr., *In the War of the Rebellion from 1861 to 1865* (New York: Fredonia, 1913), 9.

24. O.R., vol. 11, part 2, 137.

25. Ibid.

26. Ibid.

27. Ibid., 138.

28. Mathless, *Voices of the Civil War: The Seven Days*, 88.

29. Messent and Courtney, *Civil War Letters*, 155.
30. O.R., vol. 11, part 2, 138.
31. Ibid.
32. Ibid.
33. Ibid., 123.
34. Ibid., 138.
35. Ibid.
36. Ibid., 123.
37. Ibid., 138.
38. Ibid.
39. Hebert, *Fighting Joe Hooker*, 110.
40. O.R., vol. 11, part 2, 139.
41. Ibid.
42. Ibid.
43. Ibid.
44. Hebert, *Fighting Joe Hooker*, 111.
45. O.R., vol. 11, part 2, 140.
46. Ibid.
47. Ibid.
48. Jones, *War of the Rebellion*, 10.
49. O.R., vol. 11, part 2, 145.
50. Ibid.
51. Jones, *War of the Rebellion*, 10.
52. Owen Street, *The Young Patriot: A Memorial of James Hall* (Massachusetts: Massachusetts Sabbath School Society, 1862), 179–80.
53. O.R., vol. 11, part 2, 146.
54. Ibid.
55. "Taylor's Report of Malvern Hill," O.R., series 1, vol. 11, part 2, 146.
56. Ibid.
57. Ibid.
58. Issac L. Chadwick, 72nd New York, "Affidavit to Origin of Disability, January 1893," United States National Archives and Records.
59. "Taylor's Report of Malvern Hill," O.R., series 1, vol. 11, part 2, 146.
60. Charles F. Bryan and Nelson D. Lankford, *Eye of the Storm: A Civil War Odyssey Written and Illustrated by Private Robert Knox Sneden* (New York: Free Press, 2000), 96–97.
61. "Taylor's Report of Malvern Hill," O.R., series 1, vol. 11, part 2, 146.
62. American Civil War Research Database, "Various Analysis of Regimental Enrollment and Casualties, 72nd New York Volunteer Infantry" (Kingston, MA: American Civil War Research Database).
63. O.R., vol. 11, part 2, 142.
64. Ibid., 116.
65. Street, *Young Patriot,* 65.
66. Ibid., 181–82.
67. Hebert, *Fighting Joe Hooker*, 112.
68. Warren H. Cudworth, *History of the First Regiment Massachusetts Infantry* (Boston, MA: Walker, Fuller, 1866), 241–49.
69. Hebert, *Fighting Joe Hooker*, 112.
70. Ibid., 114.
71. Ibid., 115.
72. O.R., vol. 11, part 2, 951–52.
73. Lynch and Sandoli, *Come Cry with Me*, 71.
74. D.H. Donald, *Gone for a Soldier: The Civil War Memoirs of Private Alfred Bellard* (Boston: Little, Brown, 1975), 113.
75. Hebert, *Fighting Joe Hooker*, 116.
76. O.R, vol. 11, part 2, 952.
77. Hebert, *Fighting Joe Hooker*, 117.
78. Ibid.
79. Lynch and Sandoli, *Come Cry with Me*, 67.
80. LeFevre-Brown, *History of the Third Regiment*, 149–158.
81. Messent and Courtney, *Civil War Letters*, 159.

Chapter 7

1. Francis T. Lynch and Samuel C. Sandoli, *Come Cry with Me: The Letter of Emerson F. Merrell, Native of the Town of Coventry in Chenango County, New York, Who Served in Company I, 72nd Regiment, New York Infantry, New York Excelsior Brigade, Army of the Potomac 1861–1863* (self-published by the authors, 2001), 71.
2. Henri LeFevre-Brown, *History of the Third Regiment Excelsior Brigade 72nd New York Volunteer Infantry 1861–1865* (Jamestown, NY: Journal, 1902), 152–58.
3. Ibid.
4. W.A. Swanberg, *Sickles the Incredible* (Gettysburg: Stan Clark Military Books, 1956), 157.
5. Charles F. Bryan and Nelson D. Lankford, *Eye of the Storm: A Civil War Odyssey Written and Illustrated by Private Robert Knox Sneden* (New York: Free Press, 2000), 113.
6. Peter Messent and Steve Courtney, eds., *The Civil War Letters of Joseph Hopkins Twichell: A Chaplain's Story* (Athens, Georgia: University of Georgia Press), 172.
7. LeFevre-Brown, *History of the Third Regiment*, 64.
8. O.R., vol. 16, 450.
9. Ibid.
10. Ibid.
11. Ibid.
12. Ibid., 451.
13. Ibid.
14. Ibid.
15. Ibid.
16. O.R., vol. 12, part 2, 437–38.
17. Ibid., 454.
18. Ibid.
19. D.H. Donald, *Gone for a Soldier: The Civil War Memoirs of Private Alfred Bellard* (Boston: Little, Brown, 1975), 129–30.
20. "Carr's Report," O.R., vol. 12, part 2, 454.
21. Ibid.
22. "Taylor's Report," 454.
23. Ibid., 444.
24. "Young's Report," O.R., series 1, vol. 12, part 2, 447.
25. Ibid., 447.
26. Messent and Courtney, *Civil War Letters*, 173.
27. J. Hayward, *Give It to Them, Jersey Blues! A History of the 7th Regiment, New Jersey Veteran Volunteers in the Civil War* (Hightstown: Longstreet House, 1998), 61.
28. "Taylor's Report," 444.
29. Ibid.
30. "Young's Report," 447.
31. Ibid.
32. Hayward, *Give It to Them*, 61.
33. "Young's Report," 447.
34. Ibid.
35. "Taylor's Report," 444.
36. R.C. Cheeks, *Ewell's Flawless Performance at Kettle Run in America's Civil War* (Leesburg: Premedia, 2000), 55.
37. E.J. Stackpole, *From Cedar Mountain to Antietam:*

August–September, 1862 (Harrisburg: Stackpole, 1959), 161–162.

38. "Grover's Report," O.R., series 1, vol. 12, part 2, 439.
39. Ibid.
40. "Taylor's Report," 445.
41. "Young's Report," 447.
42. "Taylor's Report," 445.
43. "Johnson's Report," O.R., series 1, vol. 12, part 2, 665.
44. Ibid., 666.
45. "Bliss Report," O.R., series 1, vol. 12, part 2, 452.
46. Ibid.
47. Christopher Ryan Oates, *Fighting for Home: The Story of Alfred K. Oates and the Fifth Regiment, Excelsior Brigade* (Cornelius, NC: Warren, 2006), 92–93.
48. Paul Mathless, *Voices of the Civil War: Second Manassas* (Alexandria, VA: Lifetime, 1998), 114.
49. Ibid.
50. "Taylor's Report," 445.
51. "Bliss Report," 452.
52. Mathless, *Voices of the Civil War: Second Manassas*, 114.
53. Ibid.
54. American Civil War Research Database, Kingston, MA, various sources, http://www.civilwardata.com, accessed June 1, 2013.
55. "Bliss Report," 452.
56. Lynch and Sandoli, *Come Cry with Me*, 75.
57. "Hooker," O.R., series 1, vol. 12, part 2, 437.

Chapter 8

1. Francis T. Lynch and Samuel C. Sandoli, *Come Cry with Me: The Letter of Emerson F. Merrell, Native of the Town of Coventry in Chenango County, New York, Who Served in Company I, 72nd Regiment, New York Infantry, New York Excelsior Brigade, Army of the Potomac 1861–1863* (self-published by the authors, 2001), 75.
2. O.R., vol. 12, part 2, 443.
3. Ibid.
4. A.H. Guernsey and H.M. Alden, *Harper's Pictoral History of the Civil War* (New York: Fairfax, 1866), 390.
5. "Taylor Report," May 31–June 4, 1862, Kettle Run, Groveton, Bull Run, O.R., Series 1, vol. 12, part 2, 445–446.
6. Henri LeFevre-Brown, *History of the Third Regiment Excelsior Brigade 72nd New York Volunteer Infantry 1861–1865* (Jamestown, NY: Journal, 1902), 75.
7. W.A. Swanberg, *Sickles the Incredible* (Gettysburg: Stan Clark Military Books, 1956), 158.
8. Ibid., 159.
9. Daniel Sickles, "Uncited Military Movements in the City, August 7th, 1862," *New York Times*.
10. Swanberg, *Sickles the Incredible*, 158.
11. F.H. Dyer, "70th–74th New York Infantry," *A Compendium of the War of the Rebellion* (Des Moines, IA: Dyer, 1908), part 1, 296.
12. LeFevre-Brown, *History of the Third Regiment*, 75.
13. American Civil War Research Database, Kingston, MA, various sources, http://www.civilwardata.com, accessed June 1, 2013.
14. James Dean Letters, Documents, and Memorials, courtesy of the Dean family, unpublished, rights to publish excerpts by generosity of the Dean family. Henceforth referred to as the "Dean Family Collection."
15. C. Van Santvoord, *The One Hundred and Twentieth Regiment NYS Volunteers in the Civil War* (Saugerties: Hope Farm, 1997), 9–13, 27.
16. LeFevre-Brown, *History of the Third Regiment*, 75.
17. Dyer, "70th–74th New York Infantry," part 1, 294.
18. "Letter to Parents, October 13th, 1862," Dean Family Collection.
19. Ibid.
20. "Letter to Parents, October 25, 1862," Dean Family Collection.
21. LeFevre-Brown, *History of the Third Regiment*, 79.
22. "Letter to Parents, October 25, 1862," Dean Family Collection.
23. LeFevre-Brown, *History of the Third Regiment*, 80.
24. Lynch and Sandoli, *Come Cry with Me*, 87.
25. J. Hayward, *Give It to Them, Jersey Blues! A History of the 7th Regiment, New Jersey Veteran Volunteers in the Civil War* (Hightstown: Longstreet House, 1998), 73.
26. "Sickles Report, November 19th, 1862," O.R., series 1, vol. 19, part 2, 562.
27. Peter Messent and Steve Courtney, eds., *The Civil War Letters of Joseph Hopkins Twichell: A Chaplain's Story* (Athens, Georgia: University of Georgia Press), 187.
28. Ibid., 188.
29. D.H. Donald, *Gone for a Soldier: The Civil War Memoirs of Private Alfred Bellard* (Boston: Little, Brown, 1975), 169.
30. Ibid., 171.
31. "Letter to Parents, November 13th, 1862," Dean Family Collection.
32. "Sickles Report," 166.
33. "Letter to Parents, November 13th, 1862," Dean Family Collection.
34. Lynch and Sandoli, *Come Cry with Me*, 89.
35. Ibid.
36. Ibid.
37. Paul Mathless, *Voices of the Civil War: Fredericksburg* (Alexandria, VA: Lifetime, 1998), 10.
38. A.H. Guernsey and H.M. Alden, *Harper's Pictoral History of the Civil War* (New York: Fairfax, 1866), 407.
39. Lynch and Sandoli, *Come Cry with Me*, 89.
40. Ibid.
41. Mathless, *Voices of the Civil War: Fredericksburg*, 11.
42. Ibid., 12.
43. "Letter to Parents, December 8th, 1862," Dean Family Collection.
44. Lynch and Sandoli, *Come Cry with Me*, 77.
45. Messent and Courtney, *Civil War Letters*, 191.
46. Lynch and Sandoli, *Come Cry with Me*, 92.
47. George Bailey, "Letter to Brother, December 7th, 1862," unpublished, War Time Letters of George Bailey, Company H, 72nd NYSV, courtesy of the Gwanda Area Historical Society.
48. C.W. Gould, "The Battleground of Virtue," *Civil War Times Illustrated* (Leesburg, VA: Weider History Group, 2001), "Letter to Brother Marvin, December 14th, 1861," 75.
49. Dyer, "70th–74th New York Infantry," part 1, 296–97.
50. Messent and Courtney, *Civil War Letters*, 195.
51. Mathless, *Voices of the Civil War: Fredericksburg*, 14.
52. Ibid.
53. Ibid., 33–34.
54. Ibid., 54.

55. Ibid., 56.
56. Ibid.
57. O.R, vol. 26, part 1, 668.
58. Mathless, *Voices of the Civil War: Fredericksburg*, 54.
59. "Report of Colonel George B. Hall," O.R., series I, vol. 21, 384.
60. Ibid., 385.
61. Ibid.
62. "Letter to Parents, December 18th, 1862," Dean Family Collection.
63. Ibid.
64. Ibid.
65. Ibid.
66. Messent and Courtney, *Civil War Letters*, 195.
67. "Letter to Parents, November 13th, 1862," Dean Family Collection.
68. Mathless, *Voices of the Civil War: Fredericksburg*, 131.
69. Van Santvoord, *One Hundred and Twentieth*, 34.
70. "Report of Colonel George B. Hall," 385.
71. "Report of Brigade General Daniel E. Sickles," O.R., series 1, vol. 21, part 1, 381.
72. Ibid.
73. LeFevre-Brown, *History of the Third Regiment*, 82.
74. "Letter to Parents, December 18th, 1862," Dean Family Collection.
75. Mathless, *Voices of the Civil War: Fredericksburg*, 131.
76. Ibid., 132.
77. Ibid.
78. Ibid., 133.
79. Lynch and Sandoli, *Come Cry with Me*, 93.

Chapter 9

1. Hiram Stoddard, "Letter to Parents, December 28th, 1862," Wartime Letters of Hiram Stoddard, Company I, 72nd NYSV, unpublished, courtesy of Gowanda Area Historical Society, New York.
2. Ibid.
3. Francis T. Lynch and Samuel C. Sandoli, *Come Cry with Me: The Letters of Emerson F. Merrell, Native of the Town of Coventry in Chenango County, New York, Who Served in Company I, 72nd Regiment, New York Infantry, New York Excelsior Brigade, Army of the Potomac 1861–1863* (self-published by the authors, 2001), 97.
4. Lynch and Sandoli, *Come Cry with Me*, "Letter to Sister Mary, Camp 3rd Regiment near Falmouth, Virginia, February 21st, 1863," 104.
5. Stoddard, *Wartime Letters*, "Letter to Parents, December 28th, 1862."
6. Peter Messent and Steve Courtney, eds., *The Civil War Letters of Joseph Hopkins Twichell: A Chaplain's Story* (Athens, Georgia: University of Georgia Press), 206.
7. E.J. Warner, *Generals in Blue: Lives of the Union Commanders* (Baton Rouge: Louisiana State University Press, 1964), 395–96.
8. Messent and Courtney, *Civil War Letters*, 208.
9. Lynch and Sandoli, *Come Cry with Me*, 98.
10. Henri LeFevre-Brown, *History of the Third Regiment Excelsior Brigade 72nd New York Volunteer Infantry 1861–1865* (Jamestown, NY: Journal, 1902), 83.
11. Ibid.
12. Lynch and Sandoli, *Come Cry with Me*, 101.

13. *Annual Report of Adjutant-General of the State of New York for the Year 1901* (Albany, NY: J.B. Lyon, 1902), 872, 874.
14. "Letter from Dr. C. K. Irwin, January 15th, 1863," Compiled Military Service File: Issac L. Chadwick, Company C, 72nd New York, National Archives.
15. *Annual Report of Adjutant-General*, 808, 841, 866, and 886.
16. "Letter to Parents, January 13th, 1863," Compiled Military Service File: John S. Austin, New York National Archives.
17. David B. Parker, *A Chautauqua Boy in '61 and Afterward: Reminiscences by David B. Parker, Second Lieutenant, Seventy-Second New York; Introduction by Albert Bushnell Hart* (Boston: Small, Maynard, 1912), 23–24.
18. Walter H. Hebert, *Fighting Joe Hooker* (Lincoln: University of Nebraska Press, 1999), 166, citing "Extracts from the Journal of Henry W. Raymond, January 1880," in *Scribner's Monthly*, vol. 19, ed. Henry W. Raymond, C.J. Holland, (New York: Scribner's), n.p.
19. Hebert, *Fighting Joe Hooker*, "Lincoln Letter to Hooker, January 26th, 1863," 12.
20. Stoddard, *Wartime Letters*, "Letter to Mother, January 11th, 1863."
21. James Dean Letters, Documents, and Memorials, courtesy of the Dean family, unpublished, rights to publish excerpts by generosity of the Dean family (henceforth referred to as the "Dean Family Collection"), "Letter to Parents, Camp Near Falmouth, Virginia, January 7th, 1863."
22. "Letter to Parents, Camp Near Falmouth, Virginia, February 27th, 1863," Dean Family Collection.
23. "Letter to Parents, Camp Nelson Taylor, January 19th, 1863," Dean Family Collection.
24. Lynch and Sandoli, *Come Cry with Me*, 101.
25. LeFevre-Brown, *History of the Third Regiment*, 85.
26. "Letter to Parents, Camp near Falmouth, Virginia, February 27th, 1863," Dean Family Collection.
27. Messent and Courtney, *Civil War Letters*, 212–14.
28. Lynch and Sandoli, *Come Cry with Me*, 103.
29. George Bailey, "Letter to Franklin Bates, February 7th, 1863," War Time Letters of George Bailey, Company H, 72nd NYSV, unpublished, courtesy of the Gwanda Area Historical Society.
30. Ibid.
31. Ibid.
32. Francis T. Lynch and Samuel C. Sandoli, ibid., "Letter to Sister, 3rd Regiment Camp near Falmouth, Virginia, March 6th, 1863, 105."
33. Ibid.
34. O.R., series 1, vol. 40, part 1, 152.
35. "Letter to Parents, May 26th, 1863," Dean Family Collection.
36. "Letter to Brother and Sister, Camp Nelson Taylor, March 11th, 1863," Dean Family Collection.
37. Lynch and Sandoli, *Come Cry with Me*, 106–07.
38. "Letter to Parents, May 30th, 1863," Dean Family Collection.
39. O.R., series I, vol. 25, part I, 466.
40. Ibid.
41. Stoddard, *Wartime Letters*, "Letter to Parents, Camp near Falmouth, Virginia, May 7th, 1863."
42. William K. Goolrick, *The Civil War, Rebels Resurgent, Fredericksburg to Chancellorsville* (Alexandria, VA: Time Life, 1985), 125.
43. Stephen Sears, *Chancellorsville* (New York: Houghton Mifflin, 1996), 212.

44. "Letter to Parents, Camp Nelson Taylor, May 9th, 1863," Dean Family Collection.
45. Ibid.
46. O.R., series I, vol. 25, part I, 386.
47. Warner, *Generals in Blue*, 31–32.
48. F.H. Dyer, "70th–74th New York Infantry," *A Compendium of the War of the Rebellion* (Des Moines, IA: Dyer, 1908), part 1, 297.
49. "Camp Nelson Taylor, May 9th, 1863," Dean Family Collection.
50. "Report of John Leonard, May 8th, 1863," O.R., series 1, vol. 25, part 1, 466.
51. "Report of Brigade General Joseph W. Revere, May 3rd, 1863," O.R., series 1, vol. 25, part 1, 461.
52. "Letter to Parents, Camp Nelson Taylor, May 9th, 1863," Dean Family Collection.
53. Ibid.
54. Ibid.
55. O.R., series I, vol. 25, part I, 471.
56. Ibid., 461.
57. "Sickles Report," 388–90.
58. "Revere Report," O.R., Series 1, vol. 25, part 1, 461.
59. LeFevre-Brown, *History of the Third Regiment*, 88–89.
60. Stoddard, *Wartime Letters*, "Letter to Parents, Camp near Falmouth, Virginia," May 7th, 1863."
61. Ibid., "Letter to Parents, Camp Nelson Taylor, May 9th, 1863."
62. O.R., ibid., "Report of Captain Francis E. Taylor, 74th N.Y., May 7th, 1863," 469.
63. Ibid.
64. Sears, *Chancellorsville*, 321.
65. "Report of Captain John Poland, May 13th, 1863," O.R., Series 1, vol. 25, part 1, 450.
66. Ibid.
67. "Sickles Report," 391.
68. Ibid., "Tyler Report," 470.
69. "Revere Report," 462.
70. "The Roll of Honor, Colonel William O. Stevens, May 29th, 1863," *Jamestown Journal*.
71. LeFevre-Brown, *History of the Third Regiment*, 89.
72. Ibid.
73. *Annual Report of Adjutant-General*, 729.
74. LeFevre-Brown, *History of the Third Regiment*, 89–90.
75. Stoddard, *Wartime Letters*, "Letter to Parents, Camp near Falmouth, Virginia May 7th, 1863."
76. Lucius Jones, Jr., *In the War of the Rebellion from 1861 to 1865* (New York: Fredonia, 1913), 14.
77. Ibid., 15.
78. Ibid.
79. Ibid.
80. "Letter to Parents, May 9th, 1863," Dean Family Collection.
81. "Report of Brigade General Joseph B. Carr, May 13th, 1863," O.R., series 1, vol. 25, part 1, 445.
82. "Revere Report," 462.
83. Ibid.
84. "Sickles Report," 392.
85. "Report of Lieutenant Colonel Cornelius Westbrook, May 7th, 1863," O.R., series 1, vol. 25, part 1, 472.
86. "Revere Report," 462–63.
87. "Carr Report," O.R., series 1, vol., 25, part 1, 445–46.
88. Paul Mathless, *Voices of the Civil War: Chancellorsville* (Alexandria, Virginia: Lifetime Books Press, 1998), 100.
89. "Revere Report," 462.
90. "Sickles Report," 392.
91. "Report of Colonel J. Egbert Farnum, May 7th, 1863," O.R., series 1, vol., 25, part 1, 464.
92. LeFevre-Brown, *History of the Third Regiment*, 89.
93. "Letter to Parents, May 9th 1963," Dean Family Collection.
94. Ibid.
95. "Leonard Report," O.R., series 1, vol., 25, part 1, 467.
96. John S. Austin, Colonel Commander 3rd Regiment Excelsior Brigade, "Death of Captain Harmon J. Bliss, Company G. 3rd Excelsior," 72nd N.Y. Volunteer Infantry Civil War Newspaper Clippings, Unit History Project, New York State Military Museum.
97. Lynch and Sandoli, *Come Cry with Me*, 123.
98. LeFevre-Brown, *History of the Third Regiment*, 93–94.
99. W.F. Fox, *Regimental Losses in the American Civil War, 1861–1866: A Treatise on the Extent and Nature of the Mortuary Losses in the Union Regiments, with Full and Extensive Statistics Compiled from the Official Records on File in the State Military Bureaus and at Washington* (New York: Albany, 1889), various entries throughout.
100. Hebert, *Fighting Joe Hooker*, 231–32.
101. Joseph W. Revere, "A Statement of the Case of Brigadier-General Joseph W. Revere," published in defense of Joseph W. Revere's court-martial (New York: C. A. Alvord, 1863).
102. LeFevre-Brown, *History of the Third Regiment*, 96–97.
103. "The Roll of Honor, Colonel William O. Stevens, May 29th, 1863," *Jamestown Journal*, 72nd N.Y. Volunteer Infantry Civil War Newspaper Clippings, Unit History Project, New York State Military Museum.
104. LeFevre-Brown, *History of the Third Regiment*, 98.
105. Ibid., 98–99.
106. Austin, "Death of Captain Harmon J. Bliss."
107. William Swinton, "Campaigns of the Army of the Potomac" (New York: Scribner's, 1882), 275.

Chapter 10

1. Christopher Ryan Oates, *Fighting for Home: The Story of Alfred K. Oates and the Fifth Regiment, Excelsior Brigade* (Cornelius, NC: Warren, 2006), 123–24.
2. *Annual Report of Adjutant-General of the State of New York for the Year 1901* (Albany, New York: J. B. Lyon, 1902), various entries for 72nd New York.
3. "72nd New York Volunteers," Grand Army of the Republic Records, New York State Library Preservation Unit.
4. A.H. Guernsey and H.M. Alden, *Harper's Pictoral History of the Civil War* (New York: Fairfax, 1866), 500.
5. James Dean Letters, Documents, and Memorials, courtesy of the Dean family, unpublished, rights to publish excerpts by generosity of the Dean family (henceforth referred to as the "Dean Family Collection"), "Letter to Parents, May 17th, 1863."
6. Oates, *Fighting for Home*, 123–24.

7. "Letter to Parents, May 17th, 1863," Dean Family Collection.
8. Walter H. Hebert, *Fighting Joe Hooker* (Lincoln: University of Nebraska Press, 1999), 199, citing John Bigelow, Jr., *The Campaign of Chancellorsville* (New Haven: Yale University Press, 1910).
9. O.R., series 1, vol. 25, part 1, 171.
10. Hebert, *Fighting Joe Hooker*, 221.
11. Larry Tagg, *The Generals of Gettysburg: The Leaders of America's Greatest Battle* (Cambridge: Da Capo, 2003), 77–78.
12. Ibid.
13. Ibid., 73–74.
14. "Letter to Parents, May 26th, 1863," Dean Family Collection.
15. Ibid.
16. Hebert, *Fighting Joe Hooker*, 232–34.
17. W.A. Swanberg, *Sickles the Incredible* (Gettysburg: Stan Clark Military Books, 1956), 192–93.
18. O.R., vol. 27, part 3, 3.
19. "Letter to Brother David, Camp Nelson Taylor, June 9th, 1863," Dean Family Collection.
20. Peter Messent and Steve Courtney, eds., *The Civil War Letters of Joseph Hopkins Twichell: A Chaplain's Story* (Athens, Georgia: University of Georgia Press), 237.
21. *Annual Report of Adjutant-General*, various entries for 72nd New York.
22. "Receipt for Flag Dated June 3, 1863," Third Excelsior Association Historical Collection.
23. "Letter to Rick Barram from Donald Cody and Richard Landwehrle, June 28th, 2009," Austin Family History.
24. American Civil War Research Database, "Company K, 72nd New York Infantry" (Kingston, MA: American Civil War Research Database).
25. "General Order # 50, June 7th, 1863, Headquarters 2nd Division, 3rd Corps, Camp Near Falmouth, Virginia," Compiled Military Service File: John S. Austin, Company K, 72nd New York National Archives.
26. Henri LeFevre-Brown, *History of the Third Regiment Excelsior Brigade 72nd New York Volunteer Infantry 1861–1865* (Jamestown, NY: Journal, 1902), 100.
27. Messent and Courtney, *Civil War Letters*, 240.
28. Ibid.
29. Ibid., 243.
30. Ibid.
31. LeFevre-Brown, *History of the Third Regiment*, 100.
32. Ibid., 100–01.
33. Messent and Courtney, *Civil War Letters*, 247.
34. LeFevre-Brown, *History of the Third Regiment*, 103–04.
35. Oates, *Fighting for Home*, 129.
36. Messent and Courtney, *Civil War Letters*, 246.
37. O.R., vol. 27, part 1, 530.
38. Ibid., 531.
39. Ibid.
40. LeFevre-Brown, *History of the Third Regiment*, 104.
41. O.R., vol. 27, part 1, 531.
42. Swanberg, *Sickles the Incredible*, 209, citing Capt. C.A. Stevens, *Berdan's U.S. Sharpshooter* (St. Paul: Price-McGill, 1892), 303–04.
43. Swanberg, *Sickles the Incredible*, 208.
44. James A. Hessler, *Sickles at Gettysburg* (New York: Savas Beaties, 2009), 109.
45. O.R., series 1, vol. 27, part 1, 482.
46. Ibid., 482–83.
47. Ibid., 483.
48. Ibid., 532.
49. Ibid., 531.
50. Ibid., 558.
51. Ibid., 532.
52. H.W. Pfanz, *Gettysburg: The Second Day* (Chapel Hill: University of North Carolina Press, 1987), 144, citing George G. Meade, Jr., *With Meade at Gettysburg* (Philadelphia: John C. Winton, 1930), 114.
53. Pfanz, *Gettysburg*, 144.
54. Pfanz, *Gettysburg*, citing Henry H. Humphreys, *Andrew Atkinson Humphries: A Bibliography* (Philadelphia: John C. Winston, 1924), 193–94.
55. Pfanz, *Gettysburg*, 313–17.
56. Ibid., 145, citing "Pennsylvania at Gettysburg," citation 75.
57. Ibid., 145, citing "New York at Gettysburg," citation 76.
58. O.R., series 1, vol. 27, part 1, 532.
59. Ibid.
60. Ibid., 558.
61. Ibid., 483.
62. "Letter to Parents, Camp Near Gettysburg, July 6th, 1863," Dean Family Collection.
63. Oates, *Fighting for Home*, 134.
64. O.R., series 1, vol. 27, part 1, 533.
65. LeFevre-Brown, *History of the Third Regiment*, 105.
66. O.R., series 1, vol. 27, part 1, 483, 533.
67. "Letter to Parents, Camp Near Gettysburg, July 6th, 1863," Dean Family Collection.
68. O.R., series 1, vol. 27, part 1, 559.
69. Ibid., 490.
70. Pfanz, *Gettysburg*, 347–48.
71. C. Van Santvoord, *The One Hundred and Twentieth Regiment NYS Volunteers in the Civil War* (Saugerties: Hope Farm, 1997), 74.
72. Pfanz, *Gettysburg*, 349.
73. O.R., series 1, vol. 27, part 1, 568.
74. Van Santvoord, *One Hundred and Twentieth*, 74.
75. Pfanz, *Gettysburg*, 349.
76. O.R., series 1, vol. 27, part 1, 543.
77. Ibid., 533.
78. Ibid.
79. W.F. Fox, *New York at Gettysburg* (Albany: J.B. Lyon, 1900), 606
80. O.R., series 1, vol. 27, part 1, 490.
81. "Letter to Parents, Camp Near Gettysburg, July 6th, 1863," Dean Family Collection.
82. Ibid.
83. O.R., ibid., "Report of Col. Austin," 566.
84. Ibid., 533.
85. Ibid.
86. "Letter to Parents, Camp Near Gettysburg, July 6th, 1863," Dean Family Collection.
87. O.R., series 1, vol. 27, part 1, 543.
88. Ibid., 559.
89. "Letter to Parents, Camp Near Gettysburg, July 6th, 1863," Dean Family Collection.
90. LeFevre-Brown, *History of the Third Regiment*, 143.
91. Ibid., 105.
92. Ibid.
93. "Letter to Parents, Camp Near Gettysburg, July 6th, 1863," Dean Family Collection.
94. Ibid.

95. Swanberg, *Sickles the Incredible*, 220.
96. "Letter to Parents, Camp Near Gettysburg, July 6th, 1863," Dean Family Collection.
97. O.R., series 1, vol. 27, part 1, 559.
98. Ibid.
99. Ibid., 560.
100. W.F. Fox, *Regimental Losses in the American Civil War, 1861-186: A Treatise on the Extent and Nature of the Mortuary Losses in the Union Regiments, with Full and Extensive Statistics Compiled from the Official Records on File in the State Military Bureaus and at Washington* (New York: Albany Publishing, 1889), 607.
101. Ibid., 822.
102. Ibid., 593.
103. Ibid., 594.
104. O.R., series 1, vol. 27, part 1, 565.
105. O.R., series 1, vol. 27, part 1, 490.

Chapter 11

1. W.A. Swanberg, *Sickles the Incredible* (Gettysburg: Stan Clark Military Books, 1956), 222-23.
2. Paul Mathless, *Voices of the Civil War: Gettysburg* (Alexandria, VA: Lifetime, 1998), 145.
3. Jeffry Wert, *The Sword of Lincoln* (New York: Simon & Schuster, 2005), 305-09.
4. O.R., series 1, vol. 27, part 1, 78.
5. Don Edward and Virginia Fehrenbacher, eds., *Recollected Words of Abraham Lincoln* (Stanford, CA: Stanford University Press, 1996), 166.
6. Wert, *The Sword of Lincoln*, 305.
7. Ibid., 305-06.
8. American Civil War Research Database, Kingston M.A. "Company K, 72ND New York Infantry," various entries (Kingston, MA: American Civil War Research Database).
9. Wert, *The Sword of Lincoln*, 307.
10. E.J. Werner, *Generals in Blue: Lives of the Union Commanders* (Baton Rouge: Louisiana State University Press, 1964), 162.
11. Ibid., 386-87.
12. Ibid., 467.
13. Henri LeFevre-Brown, *History of the Third Regiment Excelsior Brigade 72nd New York Volunteer Infantry 1861-1865* (Jamestown, NY: Journal, 1902), 115.
14. James Dean Letters, Documents, and Memorials, courtesy of the Dean family, unpublished, rights to publish excerpts by generosity of the Dean family (henceforth referred to as the "Dean Family Collection"), "Letter to Sister, July 12th, 1863."
15. Ibid.
16. Shelby Foote, *The Civil War, A Narrative: Fredericksburg to Meridian* (New York: Vintage, 1986), 592.
17. A.H. Guernsey and H.M. Alden, *Harper's Pictoral History of the Civil War* (New York: Fairfax, 1866), 516.
18. Ibid.
19. Wert, *The Sword of Lincoln*, 310-11.
20. "Report of Henry Prince," O.R., series 1, vol. 27, part 1, 538.
21. Hiram Stoddard, *Wartime Letters of Hiram Stoddard, Company I, 72nd NYSV* (unpublished; courtesy of Gowanda Area Historical Society, New York), "Letter to Parents, Camp near Westmount, Virginia, July 27th, 1863."
22. "Report of French," O.R., series 1, vol. 27, part 1, 489.
23. Ibid.
24. "Reports of Brewster, Farnum," O.R., series 1, vol. 27, part 1, 560-61.
25. "Report of Captain Lovell Purdy," O.R., series 1, vol. 27, part 1, #107, 205.
26. "Report of French," O.R., series 1, vol. 27, part 1, #43, 489.
27. Ibid., 490.
28. Ibid.
29. "Report of C. H. Andrews," O.R., series 1, vol. 27, part 2, #44, 626.
30. "Report of French," 490.
31. "Report of Henry Prince," 538.
32. "Report of C. H. Andrews," 626.
33. Ibid.
34. Lucius Jones, Jr., *In the War of the Rebellion from 1861 to 1865* (New York: Fredonia, 1913), 18.
35. "Report of French," 490.
36. Ibid.
37. "Report of Captain Lovell Purdy," 205.
38. "Letter to Parents, July 28th, 1863," Dean Family Collection.
39. Ibid.
40. "Letter to Parents, August 10th, 1863," Dean Family Collection.
41. "Letter to Parents, July 28th, 1863," Dean Family Collection.
42. "Report of Colonel John S. Austin," O.R., vol. 27, part 1, #47, 567.
43. "Letter to Parents, July 28th, 1863," Dean Family Collection.
44. "Report of Andrews," O.R., series 1, vol. 27, part 2, #44, 626-27.
45. Ibid.
46. "Letter to Parents, July 28th, 1863," Dean Family Collection.
47. "Prince Report," O.R., series 1, vol. 27, part 1, 539.
48. "Report of R.E. Rodes," O.R., series 1, vol. 27, part 2, #44, 560-61.
49. "Report of William R. Brewster," O.R., vol. 27, part 1, #43, 562.
50. "Report of Colonel Austin," O.R., series 1, vol. 27, part 2, 567.
51. "Prince Report," 538.
52. Ibid.
53. "Report of Colonel Farnum," O.R., vol. 27, part 1, #43, 561.
54. "Letter to Parents, July 28th, 1863," Dean Family Collection.
55. Ibid.
56. Ibid.
57. "Report of Prince," O.R., series 1, vol. 27, part 1, 539.
58. Ibid.
59. "Report of R.E. Rodes," 561.
60. "Report of Major William H. Hugo," O.R, series 1, vol. 27, part 1, #43, 564.
61. Guernsey and Alden, *Harper's Pictoral History*, 518.
62. "Report of Farnum," O.R., series 1, vol. 27, part 1, 561.
63. Stoddard, *Wartime Letters*, "Letter to Parents, Camp near Warrenton, Virginia, July 27th, 1863."
64. "Report of Brewster," O.R., series 1, vol. 27, part 1, 562.

65. Stoddard, *Wartime Letters*.
66. Ibid.
67. "Report of Captain Lovell Purdy," 206.
68. *Annual Report of Adjutant-General of the State of New York for the Year 1901* (Albany, New York: J. B. Lyon, 1902), 831.
69. *Annual Report of Adjutant-General*, multiple entries cited: 741, 802, 865, 796, and 805.
70. Stoddard, *Wartime Letters*, "Letter to Parents, Camp near Warrenton, Virginia, August 12th, 1863."
71. Stoddard, *Wartime Letters*, "Letter to Parents, Camp near Warrenton, Virginia, July 27th, 1863."
72. Ibid.
73. "Letter to Parents, August 10th, 1863," Dean Family Collection.
74. Peter Messent and Steve Courtney, eds., *The Civil War Letters of Joseph Hopkins Twichell: A Chaplain's Story* (Athens, Georgia: University of Georgia Press), 237–59.
75. Stoddard, *Wartime Letters*.
76. Christopher Ryan Oates, *Fighting for Home: The Story of Alfred K. Oates and the Fifth Regiment, Excelsior Brigade* (Cornelius, NC: Warren, 2006), 145–146.
77. "Letter to Parents, September 9th, 1863," Dean Family Collection.
78. Gregory Jaynes, *Time-Life: The Civil War Series*, vol. 1, "The Killing Ground: Wilderness to Cold Harbor" (New York: Time Life Education, 1986), 28.
79. Messent and Courtney, *Civil War Letters*, 262.
80. Ibid.
81. Stoddard, *Wartime Letters*, "Letter to Parents, Camp Near Beverly Ford," September 14th, 1863.
82. Stoddard, *Wartime Letters*, "Letter to Parents, Camp Near Culpepper," Virginia, September 26th, 1863.
83. Oates, *Fighting for Home*, 142–43.
84. Messent and Courtney, *Civil War Letters*, 264.
85. "Letter to Parents, September 22nd, 1863," Dean Family Collection.
86. Jaynes, *Time-Life: The Civil War Series*, 28.
87. Shelby Foote, *Civil War: Fredericksburg to Meridian*, 786.
88. Ibid., 786–84, 789.
89. LeFevre-Brown, *History of the Third Regiment*, 119.
90. Messent and Courtney, *Civil War Letters*, 267.
91. Ibid.
92. Ibid.
93. Ibid., 267–68.
94. Wert, *The Sword of Lincoln*, 310–11.
95. Messent and Courtney, *Civil War Letters*, 267.
96. Ibid.
97. LeFevre-Brown, *History of the Third Regiment*, 119.
98. Shelby Foote, *Civil War: Fredericksburg to Meridian*, 787.
99. Messent and Courtney, *Civil War Letters*, 267–68.
100. LeFevre-Brown, *History of the Third Regiment*, 120.
101. Shelby Foote, *Civil War: Fredericksburg to Meridian*, 795.
102. Messent and Courtney, *Civil War Letters*, 270.
103. *Committee of the Conduct of the War* (1865), vol. 1, 304.
104. "Bristoe Station," www.mycivilwar.com, accessed March 14, 2013.
105. LeFevre-Brown, *History of the Third Regiment*, 120.
106. "Letter to Parents, October 27th, 1863," Dean Family Collection.
107. Ibid.
108. Ibid.
109. Foote, *Civil War: Fredericksburg to Meridian*, 800.
110. *Annual Report of Adjutant-General*, 839–40.
111. LeFevre-Brown, *History of the Third Regiment*, 120.
112. Guernsey and Alden, *Harper's Pictoral History*, 521.
113. Messent and Courtney, *Civil War Letters*, 276.
114. Foote, *Civil War: Fredericksburg to Meridian*, 801.
115. Messent and Courtney, *Civil War Letters*, 277.
116. Ibid.
117. Foote, *Civil War: Fredericksburg to Meridian*, 801–02.
118. Guernsey and Alden, *Harper's Pictoral History*, 521.
119. Ibid.
120. Messent and Courtney, *Civil War Letters*, 278.
121. "Letter to Brother, Camp near Brandy Station November 22nd, 1863," Dean Family Collection.
122. Ibid.
123. National Park Service, "Battle of Mine Run," brochure, www.nps.gov/frsp/mine.htm, accessed February 8, 2013.
124. Ibid.
125. Ibid.
126. "Prince Report," O.R., series I, vol. 29, #48, 761.
127. "French Report," O.R., series 1, vol. 29, part 1, 737.
128. Ibid., 737–38.
129. "Prince Report," O.R., series 1, vol. 29, part 1, 761.
130. Ibid.
131. Ibid., 761–62.
132. Messent and Courtney, *Civil War Letters*, 280.
133. "Prince Report," 761–62.
134. National Park Service, "Battle of Mine Run."
135. "Prince Report," 762.
136. Ibid.
137. Ibid., 763.
138. Ibid.
139. Ibid.
140. Ibid.
141. "Report of Colonel Robert McAllister," O.R., series 1, vol. 29, part 1, 768.
142. "Prince Report," 763.
143. "Report of Lieutenant Colonel John Leonard," O.R., series 1, vol. 29, part 1, 772.
144. National Park Service, "Battle of Mine Run."
145. "Letter to Parents, Camp near Brandy Station, December 5th, 1863," Dean Family Collection.
146. Messent and Courtney, *Civil War Letters*, 280.
147. Ibid.
148. "Report of Colonel John Leonard," O.R., series 1, vol. 29, part 1, 772.
149. "Letter to Parents, Camp near Brandy Station, December 5th, 1863," Dean Family Collection.
150. "Report of Colonel John Leonard," O.R., series 1, vol. 29, part 1, 772.
151. "Letter to Parents, Camp near Brandy Station, December 5th, 1863," Dean Family Collection.
152. O.R., series 1, vol. 29, part 1, 772.

153. Ibid.
154. "Report of Prince," O.R., series 1, vol. 29, part 1, 763–64.
155. Ibid., 764.
156. Ibid.
157. Ibid., 763.
158. National Park Service, "Battle of Mine Run."
159. "Letter to Parents, Camp near Brandy Station, December 5th, 1863," Dean Family Collection.
160. Ibid.
161. Ibid.
162. Ibid.
163. Ibid.
164. Messent and Courtney, *Civil War Letters*, 282.
165. "Report of Major General Jubal A. Early," O.R., series 1, vol. 29, part 1, 833.
166. National Park Service, "Battle of Mine Run."
167. Messent and Courtney, *Civil War Letters*, 282.
168. Ibid., 282–83.
169. "Report of Prince," 764.
170. Guernsey and Alden, *Harper's Pictoral History*, 523.
171. "Reports of William H. French," O.R., series 1, vol. 29, part 1, 740.
172. Messent and Courtney, *Civil War Letters*, 283.
173. Guernsey and Alden, *Harper's Pictoral History*, 523.
174. Messent and Courtney, *Civil War Letters*, 284.
175. "Report of French," 740.
176. "Report of Prince," 764.
177. LeFevre-Brown, *History of the Third Regiment*, 121.
178. "Letter from A. A. Humphries, Chief of Staff, to French, December 3rd, 1863," O.R., series 1, vol. 29, part 1, 746.
179. Ibid.
180. "Letter from French, December 14th, 1863," O.R., series 1, vol. 29, part 1, 743.
181. Ibid.
182. "Letter to Parents, Camp Near Brandy Station, December 14th, 1863," Dean Family Collection.
183. Ibid.

Chapter 12

1. James Dean Letters, Documents, and Memorials, courtesy of the Dean family, unpublished, rights to publish excerpts by generosity of the Dean family (henceforth referred to as the "Dean Family Collection"), "Letter to Parents, Camp near Brandy Station December 13th, 163."
2. B. Catton, *The Army of the Potomac: A Stillness at Appomattox* (Garden City: Doubleday, 1953), 1–2.
3. Ibid., 33–34.
4. Ibid., 34.
5. *New York Times*, "Re-Enlistment of Troops—An Important Movement in the Army," November 9, 1863.
6. Christopher Ryan Oates, *Fighting for Home: The Story of Alfred K. Oates and the Fifth Regiment, Excelsior Brigade* (Cornelius, NC: Warren, 2006), 145–46.
7. "Letter to Parents, November 1863, Camp Near Brandy Station," Dean Family Collection.
8. "Letter to Brother, November 22nd, 1863, Camp Near Brandy Station," Dean Family Collection.
9. Lucius Jones, Jr., *In the War of the Rebellion from 1861 to 1865* (New York: Fredonia, 1913), 21.
10. Paul Mathless, *Voices of the Civil War: The Wilderness* (Alexandria, VA: Lifetime, 1998), 11.
11. W.F. Fox, *New York at Gettysburg* (Albany: J.B. Lyon, 1900), "Oration of Lieutenant Colonel John N. Cayne of the First Excelsior," 595.
12. Henri LeFevre-Brown, *History of the Third Regiment Excelsior Brigade 72nd New York Volunteer Infantry 1861–1865* (Jamestown, NY: Journal, 1902), 137–38.
13. Fox, *New York at Gettysburg*, 595.
14. G.C. Rhea, *The Battle of the Wilderness: May 5–6, 1864* (Baton Rouge: Louisiana State University Press, 2002), 1–4.
15. Ibid., 3–6.
16. Christopher Ryan Oates, *Fighting for Home: The Story of Alfred K. Oates and the Fifth Regiment, Excelsior Brigade* (Cornelius, NC: Warren, 2006), 149–50.
17. *Compiled Military Service File: John S. Austin, Company K, 72nd New York National Archives*, "General Courts Martial, General Order # 13, February 11th–16th, 1864."
18. "Letter to Brigade Head Quarters from John S. Austin, January 29th, 1864," Compiled Military Service File: John Leonard, Company F, 72nd New York National Archives.
19. Ibid.
20. *Compiled Military Service File: John Leonard, Company F, 72nd New York National Archives*, "Letter to Brigade Head Quarters from John S. Austin, January 30th, 1864."
21. "Letter to Honorable Hugh Hastings, from Henri Le-Fevre Brown, February 22nd, 1898," Veteran's Association Notes from Henri Le-Fevre Brown, 1898–1899, Grand Army of the Republic Records, 72nd New York Volunteers, New York State Library Preservation Unit.
22. "General Courts Martial General Order #13, February 11th–16th, 1864," Compiled Military Service File: John S. Austin, Company K, 72nd New York National Archives.
23. A.H. Guernsey and H.M. Alden, *Harper's Pictoral History of the Civil War* (New York: Fairfax, 1866), 624.
24. Ibid.
25. G.C. Rhea, *The Battles for Spotsylvania Court House and the Road to Yellow Tavern: May 7–12, 1864* (Baton Rouge: Louisiana State University Press, 1997), 11.
26. Ibid., 10–11.
27. LeFevre-Brown, *History of the Third Regiment*, 123.
28. Ibid.
29. Ibid.
30. "Letter to Parents, April 4th, 1864, Camp Stevens," Dean Family Collection.
31. "Correspondence of the Journal. Letter from the 3d Excelsior, Camp of the 3d Excelsior, near Brandy Station, Virginia., March 26, 1864," 72nd Regiment New York Volunteer Infantry, Civil War Newspaper Clippings, New York State Military Museum.
32. Gregory Jaynes, *Time-Life: The Civil War Series*, vol. 1, "The Killing Ground: Wilderness to Cold Harbor" (New York: Time Life Education, 1986), 37.
33. "Letter to Parents, April 4th, 1864, Camp Stevens," Dean Family Collection.
34. "Correspondence of the Journal. Letter from the 3d Excelsior, Camp of the 3d Excelsior, near Brandy Station, Virginia., March 26, 1864," 72nd Regiment New York Volunteer Infantry, Civil War Newspaper Clippings, New York State Military Museum.

35. Stoddard, *Wartime Letters*, "Letter to Parents, April 19th, 1864, Camp Stevens, Near Brandy Station."
36. Ibid.
37. LeFevre-Brown, *History of the Third Regiment*, 123.
38. Peter Messent and Steve Courtney, eds., *The Civil War Letters of Joseph Hopkins Twichell: A Chaplain's Story* (Athens, Georgia: University of Georgia Press), 298.
39. LeFevre-Brown, *History of the Third Regiment*, 125.
40. Mathless, *Voices of the Civil War: The Wilderness*, 23.
41. F.H. Dyer, "70th–74th New York Infantry," *A Compendium of the War of the Rebellion* (Des Moines, IA: Dyer, 1908), part 1, 293.
42. E.J. Werner, *Generals in Blue: Lives of the Union Commanders* (Baton Rouge: Louisiana State University Press, 1964), 333–38.
43. LeFevre-Brown, *History of the Third Regiment*, 125.
44. Mathless, *Voices of the Civil War: The Wilderness*, 23–24.
45. Ibid.
46. Ibid., 24–25.
47. LeFevre-Brown, *History of the Third Regiment*, 125.
48. Jones, *War of the Rebellion*, 22.
49. Mathless, *Voices of the Civil War: The Wilderness*, 60–61.
50. LeFevre-Brown, *History of the Third Regiment*, 126.
51. Ibid.
52. LeFevre-Brown, *History of the Third Regiment*, 126–27.
53. "Report of Lieutenant Colonel Michael Burns," O.R., series 1, vol. 36, part 1, 503.
54. LeFevre-Brown, *History of the Third Regiment*, 143.
55. "Report of Lieutenant Colonel Michael Burns," O.R., series 1, vol. 36, part 1, 503.
56. LeFevre-Brown, *History of the Third Regiment*, 126–27.
57. Ibid., 143.
58. Mathless, *Voices of the Civil War: The Wilderness*, 65.
59. Jeffry Wert, *The Sword of Lincoln* (New York: Simon & Schuster, 2005), 343.
60. LeFevre-Brown, *History of the Third Regiment*, 127.
61. Wert, *The Sword of Lincoln*, 345.
62. Rhea, *Battle of the Wilderness*, 89–91.
63. Ibid., 124.
64. LeFevre-Brown, *History of the Third Regiment*, 127–28.
65. Ibid., 128.
66. Rhea, *Battle of the Wilderness*, 165.
67. Ibid., 167–68.
68. Ibid., 165–68.
69. Ibid., 169–75.
70. Messent and Courtney, *Civil War Letters*, 302.
71. LeFevre-Brown, *History of the Third Regiment*, 128.
72. Rhea, *Battle of the Wilderness*, 215–21.
73. LeFevre-Brown, *History of the Third Regiment*, 128–29.
74. Mathless, *Voices of the Civil War: The Wilderness*, 86–87.
75. LeFevre-Brown, *History of the Third Regiment*, 129.
76. Rhea, *Battle of the Wilderness*, 292.
77. Ibid., 308.
78. Congressional Medal of Honor List, "Medal of Honor Recipients," *The Third Excelsior Association*, http://www.72ndnewyork.org/MEDALOFHONOR.htm.
79. Mathless, *Voices of the Civil War: The Wilderness*, 124.
80. Ibid., 87.
81. LeFevre-Brown, *History of the Third Regiment*, 129–30.
82. James Dean, ibid., "Letter to Parents, North of Richmond, Virginia, Chickahominy Swamp, [September], 1864."
83. Rhea, *Battle of the Wilderness*, 302–07.
84. Ibid., 324–27.
85. "Burney's Orders, May 13th, 1864," O.R., series 1, vol. 32, part 68, 711–12.
86. Jaynes, *Time-Life: The Civil War Series*, 125.
87. "Letter to Parents, North of Richmond, Virginia, Chickahominy Swamp, [September], 1864," Dean Family Collection.
88. Ibid.
89. Stoddard, *Wartime Letters*, "Letter to Parents, in the Rifle Pits, May 16th, 1864."
90. Mathless, *Voices of the Civil War: The Wilderness*, 151.
91. LeFevre-Brown, *History of the Third Regiment*, 131.
92. C.G. Rhea, *To the North Anna River: Grant and Lee, May 13–24, 1864* (Baton Rouge: Louisiana State University Press, 2000), 139–49.
93. Ibid., 159.
94. LeFevre-Brown, *History of the Third Regiment*, 131.
95. C.G. Rhea, ibid.
96. Ibid., 160.
97. LeFevre-Brown, *History of the Third Regiment*, 132.
98. Mathless, *Voices of the Civil War: The Wilderness*, 151.
99. C.G. Rhea, ibid., 167–168.
100. Ibid., 171–75.
101. Ibid., 181–85.
102. LeFevre-Brown, *History of the Third Regiment*, 131.
103. Ibid., 132.
104. Rhea, *North Anna River*, 261, 279.
105. "Grant to Meade," O.R., series 1, vol. 36, part 3, 81–82.
106. Rhea, *North Anna River*, 289–88.
107. Ibid., 294, 300–01.
108. LeFevre-Brown, *History of the Third Regiment*, 132.
109. *Annual Report of Adjutant-General of the State of New York for the Year 1901* (Albany, New York: J. B. Lyon, 1902), 731.
110. "Letter to Parents, North of Richmond, Virginia, Chickahominy Swamp, [September], 1864," Dean Family Collection.
111. LeFevre-Brown, *History of the Third Regiment*, 132–33.
112. Rhea, *North Anna River*, 302–03.
113. LeFevre-Brown, *History of the Third Regiment*, 132–33.

114. Stoddard, *Wartime Letters*, "Letter to Brother, In Line of Battle Near Hanover, Virginia, May 29th, 1864,"
115. Shelby Foote, *The Civil War, A Narrative: Fredericksburg to Meridian* (New York: Vintage), 267–68.
116. Rhea, *North Anna River*, 304–15.
117. Ibid., 320–23.
118. Ibid.
119. Ibid., 330, 337–41.
120. Ibid., 331–33.
121. LeFevre-Brown, *History of the Third Regiment*, 133.
122. Rhea, *North Anna River*, 344–46.
123. LeFevre-Brown, *History of the Third Regiment*, 133.
124. Rhea, *North Anna River*, 352.
125. LeFevre-Brown, *History of the Third Regiment*, 133.
126. C. Van Santvoord, *The One Hundred and Twentieth Regiment NYS Volunteers in the Civil War* (Saugerties: Hope Farm, 1997), account of the battle by a "Member of the Regiment," 130.
127. Rhea, *North Anna River*, 353.
128. Ibid., 360–62, 367.
129. LeFevre-Brown, *History of the Third Regiment*, 133–34.
130. C.G. Rhea, *Cold Harbor: Grant and Lee, May 26–June 3, 1864* (Baton Rouge: Louisiana State University Press, 2000), 22–23.
131. Stoddard, *Wartime Letters*, "In line of Battle, Near Hanover, Virginia, May 29th, 1864."
132. LeFevre-Brown, *History of the Third Regiment*, 133.
133. Ibid., 133–34.
134. Rhea, *Cold Harbor*, 189–90.
135. Ibid., 263–64.
136. LeFevre-Brown, *History of the Third Regiment*, 134.e
137. Foote, *Civil War: Fredericksburg to Meridian*, 288.
138. Ibid.
139. LeFevre-Brown, *History of the Third Regiment*, 134.
140. Jaynes, *Time-Life: The Civil War Series*, 156–58.
141. Foote, *Civil War: Fredericksburg to Meridian*, 291.
142. Ibid.
143. Jaynes, *Time-Life: The Civil War Series*, 165.
144. Foote, *Civil War: Fredericksburg to Meridian*, 292.
145. Ibid., 295–96.
146. Ibid.
147. LeFevre-Brown, *History of the Third Regiment*, 134.
148. Stoddard, *Wartime Letters*, "Letter to Parents, in Line of Battle, 8 Miles from Richmond, Virginia, June 8th, 1864."
149. Ibid.
150. Ibid.
151. Ibid.
152. Ibid.
153. Foote, *Civil War: Fredericksburg to Meridian*, 299–300.
154. Ibid., 300.
155. LeFevre-Brown, *History of the Third Regiment*, 134.
156. Foote, *Civil War: Fredericksburg to Meridian*, 427–29.
157. Messent and Courtney, *Civil War Letters*, 305.
158. Ibid.
159. Jones, *War of the Rebellion*, 24.
160. LeFevre-Brown, *History of the Third Regiment*, 136.
161. Jones, *War of the Rebellion*, 24.
162. LeFevre-Brown, *History of the Third Regiment*, 136–37.
163. Ibid., 136.
164. Ibid.
165. Ibid.
166. Ibid., 136–37.
167. Ibid., 137.
168. Jones, *War of the Rebellion*, 25.
169. Foote, *Civil War: Fredericksburg to Meridian*, 431.
170. Stoddard, *Wartime Letters*, "In Line of Battle Near Petersburg, June 19th, 1864."
171. LeFevre-Brown, *History of the Third Regiment*, 137.
172. Ibid.
173. Jones, *War of the Rebellion*, 25.

Chapter 13

1. Lucius Jones, Jr., *In the War of the Rebellion from 1861 to 1865* (New York: Fredonia, 1913), 28.
2. Henri LeFevre-Brown, *History of the Third Regiment Excelsior Brigade 72nd New York Volunteer Infantry 1861–1865* (Jamestown, NY: Journal, 1902), 138.
3. "Return of the 72nd Regiment," 72nd Regiment New York Volunteer Infantry, Civil War Newspaper Clippings, New York State Military Museum.
4. New York Genealogy and History, "Letter about return of Delhi 3rd Excelsior Regiment, Sickles Brigade Survivors to Delaware County, July 1864 Delhi, July 9th 1864," transcribed from the Bloomville Mirror (date of article unknown) by Linda Robinson, April 17, 2002, http://www.dcnyhistory.org/milvol1861.html, accessed December 9, 2012.
5. "120th New York Infantry Regiment (Ulster Reiment and Washington Guard)," http://www.civilwarintheeast.com/USA/NY/NY120.php, accessed June 2, 2013.
6. "Roster of Surviving Members of the 72nd N.Y., 1899," Grand Army of the Republic Records, 72nd New York Volunteers, New York State Library Preservation Unit.
7. "Report of the Annual Re-Union, Third Regiment, Excelsior Brigade, 1900," *Grand Army of the Republic Records* (Albany, NY: J.B. Lyon, State Printers). 72nd New York Volunteers, New York State Library Preservation Unit.
8. Various reports and *New York Times* obituary, Compiled Military Service File: John S. Austin, Company K, 72nd New York National Archives.
9. The Mount Sinai Hospital, 1852–2002 sesquicentennial pamphlet, "The Unexpected, 1860–1869," 5.
10. Compiled Pension File: John S. Mann, Co. C, 72nd New York, National Archives.
11. Colusa Cemetery Dedication Program, September 2010, information packet on John C. Willing compiled by Preservation Committee Chairman David Resh, Third Excelsior Historical Collection.
12. Stoddard, *Wartime Letters*, "Letter to Father, July 20th, 1864."

13. Stoddard, *Wartime Letters*, "Forward, August 9th, 1976."

14. James Dean Letters, Documents, and Memorials, courtesy of the Dean family, unpublished, rights to publish excerpts by generosity of the Dean family (henceforth referred to as the "Dean Family Collection"), "Obituary of James Dean," date and publication unknown.

15. Jones, *War of the Rebellion*, 37–39.

16. David B. Parker, *A Chautauqua Boy in '61 and Afterward: Reminiscences by David B. Parker, Second Lieutenant, Seventy-Second New York; Introduction by Albert Bushnell Hart* (Boston: Small, Maynard, 1912), xix–xxi.

17. *Reports of Committees of the Senate of the United States for the First Session of the Forty-Eighth Congress, 1883–84, Report No. 641*. Washington, D.C.: Government Printing Office, 1884.

18. Ibid.

19. Francis T. Lynch and Samuel C. Sandoli, *Come Cry with Me: The Letter of Emerson F. Merrell, Native of the Town of Coventry in Chenango County, New York, Who Served in Company I, 72nd Regiment, New York Infantry, New York Excelsior Brigade, Army of the Potomac 1861–1863* (self-published by the authors, 2001), 123.

20. Various documents, Compiled Military Service and Pension Files: Issac L. Chadwick, Company C, 72nd New York, National Archives.

21. E.J. Werner, *Generals in Blue: Lives of the Union Commanders* (Baton Rouge: Louisiana State University Press, 1964), 495–96.

22. "Report of the Annual Re-Union, Third Regiment, Excelsior Brigade, 1900," Grand Army of the Republic Records, New York State Library Preservation Unit.

23. W.A. Swanberg, *Sickles the Incredible* (Gettysburg: Stan Clark Military Books, 1956), chapters 21–36.

Bibliography

Articles and Books

Annual Report of the Adjutant-General of the State of New York for the Year 1901. Albany: J.B. Lyon, State Printers, 1902.

Archambault, A.H. *A Sketchbook of the Union Infantryman.* Gettysburg: Thomas, 1999.

Bauer, K.J., ed. *Soldiering: The Civil War Diary of Rice C. Bull.* Novato: Presidio, 1977.

Billings, W.R. *Hardtack and Coffee.* Originally published in 1887. Old Saybrook, CT: Konecky & Konecky, 1995.

Brown, Henri LeFevre. *History of the Third Regiment Excelsior Brigade 72nd New York Volunteer Infantry 1861–1865.* Jamestown, NY: Journal, 1902.

Bryan, C.F., and N.D. Lankford, eds. *Eye of the Storm: A Civil War Odyssey, Written and Illustrated by Private Robert Knox Sneden.* New York: Free Press, 2000.

Catton, Bruce. *The American Heritage Picture History of the Civil War.* New York: American Heritage/Bonanza, 1960.

_____. *The Army of the Potomac: Glory Road.* Garden City: Doubleday, 1952.

_____. *The Army of the Potomac: Mr. Lincoln's Army.* Garden City: Doubleday, 1951, 1962.

_____. *The Army of the Potomac: A Stillness at Appomattox.* Garden City: Doubleday, 1953.

Cheeks, R.C. "Ewell's Flawless Performance at Kettle Run." In *America's Civil War,* Vol. 13, No. 5. Leesburg: Primedia, Nov. 2000, 50–55.

Cowles, C.D., ed. *The Official Military Atlas of the Civil War.* New York: Barnes and Noble, 2003.

Cudworth, Warren H. *History of the First Regiment Massachusetts Infantry.* Boston, MA: Walker, Fuller, 1866.

Donald, D.H., ed. *Gone for a Soldier: The Civil War Memoirs of Private Alfred Bellard.* Boston: Little, Brown, 1975.

Drury, I., and T. Gibbons. *The Civil War Military Machine: Weapons and Tactics of the Union and Confederate Armed Forces.* New York: Smithmark, 1993.

Dyer, F.H. *A Compendium of the War of the Rebellion.* New York: T. Yoseloff, 1959.

Fehrenbacher, Don Edward, and Virginia, eds. *Recollected Words of Abraham Lincoln.* Stanford, CA: Stanford University Press, 1996.

Foote, Shelby. *The Civil War, A Narrative: Fredericksburg to Meridian.* New York: Vintage, 1986.

_____. *The Civil War, A Narrative: Red River to Appomattox.* New York: Vintage, 1986.

Fox, W.F. *New York at Gettysburg.* 1900. Albany: J.B. Lyon, 1898.

_____. *Regimental Losses in the American Civil War, 1861–1865: A Treatise on the Extent and Nature of the Mortuary Losses in the Union Regiments, with Full and Extensive Statistics Compiled from the Official Records on File in the State Military Bureaus and at Washington.* Albany: Albany Publishing, 1889.

Goolrick, William K. *Rebels Resurgent: Fredericksburg to Chancellorsville.* The Civil War Series. Alexandria, VA: Time Life, 1985.

Gould, C.W. "The Battleground of Virtue." *Civil War Times Illustrated* 40:5 (Oct 2001): 26, 68, 71, 74, 76 and 79.

Guernsey, A.H., and H.M. Alden. *Harper's Pictorial History of the Civil War.* Originally published in 1866. New York: Fairfax, 1977.

Hastings, E.C., Jr., and D. Hastings. *A Pitiless Rain: The Battle of Williamsburg, 1862.* Shippensburg, PA: White Mane, 1997.

Hebert, W.H. *Fighting Joe Hooker.* Originally published in 1944. Lincoln: University of Nebraska Press, 1999.

Hayward, J. *Give It to Them, Jersey Blues! A History of the 7th Regiment, New Jersey Veteran Volunteers in the Civil War.* Hightstown: Longstreet, 1998.

Hessler, James A. *Sickles at Gettysburg.* New York: Savas Beatie, 2009.

Hunt, R.D. *Colonels in Blue: Union Army Colonels of the Civil War: New York.* Atglen, PA: Schiffer Military History, 2003.

Humphreys, Henry H. *Andrew Atkinson Humphries: A Bibliography.* Philedelphia: John C. Winston, 1924.

Hutchinson, Gustavus B. *A Narrative of the Formation and Services of the Eleventh Massachusetts Volunteers.* Boston: Alfred Mudge, 1893.

Johnson, C., and M. McLaughlin. *Civil War Battles.* Originally published in 1977. New York: Fairfax, 1981.

Johnson, Robert Underwood, and Clarence Clough Buel. *Battles and Leaders of the Civil War.* Vols. 1–4. Originally published in 1887. New York: Castle, 1982.

Jones, Lucius Jr. *In the War of the Rebellion from 1861 to 1865.* Fredonia, NY: n.p., 1913.

Katcher, P. *The Civil War Source Book.* New York: Facts on File, 1982.

Keneally, T. *American Scoundrel: The Life of the Notorious Civil War General Dan Sickles.* New York: Nan A. Talese, 2002.

Kostyal, K.M. *Field of Battle: The Civil War Letters of Major Thomas J. Halsey.* Washington, D.C.: National Geographic, 1996.

Lord, F.A. *They Fought for the Union.* New York: Bonanza, 1960.

Lynch, F.T., and S.C. Sandoli, compilers. *Come Cry with Me: The Letter of Emerson F. Merrell, Native of the Town of Coventry in Chenango County, New York, Who Served in Company I. 72nd. Regiment, New York Infantry, New York Excelsior Brigade, Army of the Potomac 1861–1863*. Self published, 2001.

Mathless, Paul. *Voices of the Civil War: Chancellorsville*. Alexandria, VA: Time-Life, 1998.

_____. *Voices of the Civil War: Fredericksburg*. Alexandria, VA: Time-Life, 1998.

_____. *Voices of the Civil War: Gettysburg*. Alexandria, VA: Time-Life, 1998.

_____. *Voices of the Civil War: The Peninsula*. Alexandria, VA: Time-Life, 1998.

_____. *Voices of the Civil War: Second Manassas*. Alexandria, VA: Time-Life, 1998.

_____. *Voices of the Civil War: The Seven Days*. Alexandria, VA: Time-Life, 1998.

_____. *Voices of the Civil War: The Wilderness*. Alexandria, VA: Time-Life, 1998.

McMahon, Thomas L. "Hooker's First Fight." In *America's Civil War*, Vol. 12, No. 2. Leesburg: Primedia, May 2003, 22–28.

Meade, George G., Jr. *With Meade at Gettysburg*. Philadelphia: John C. Winton, 1930.

Messent, Peter, and S. Courtney, eds. *The Civil War Letters of Joseph Hopkins Twichell*. Athens: University of Georgia Press, 2006.

Murray, R.L. "Excelsior Brigade at Williamsburg." In *Army of the Potomac Journal*. Wolcot: Benedum, 2005.

Oates, Christopher Ryan. *Fighting for Home: The Story of Alfred K. Oates and the Fifth Regiment, Excelsior Brigade*. Cornelius, NC: Warren, 2006.

Parker, David B. *A Chautauqua Boy in '61 and Afterward: Reminiscences by David B. Parker, Second Lieutenant, Seventy-second New York*. Introduction by Albert Bushnell Hart. Boston: Small, Maynard, 1912.

Pfanz, H.W. *Gettysburg: The Second Day*. Chapel Hill: University of North Carolina Press, 1987.

Price, W.H. *Civil War Handbook*. Fairfax, VA: Prince Lithograph, 1961.

Raymond, Henry W., and C.J. Holland, eds. *Scribner's Monthly*, vol. 19. New York: Scribner's, 1879.

Reports of Committees of the Senate of the United States for the First Session of the Forty-Eighth Congress 1883-'84, Report No. 641. Washington, D.C.: Government Printing Office, 1884.

Revere, Joseph W. *A Statement of the Case of Brigadier-General Joseph W. Revere, 1863. Published in Defense of Joseph W. Revere's Court Marshal*. New York: C.A. Alvord.

Rhea, G.C. *The Battle of the Wilderness: May 5–6, 1864*. Baton Rouge: Louisiana State University Press, 1994.

_____. *The Battles for Spotsylvania Court House and the Road to Yellow Tavern: May 7–12, 1864*. Baton Rouge: Louisiana State University Press, 1997.

_____. *Cold Harbor: Grant and Lee, May 26–June 3, 1864*. Baton Rouge: Louisiana State University Press, 2002.

_____. *To the North Anna River: Grant and Lee, May 13–25, 1864*. Baton Rouge: Louisiana State University Press, 2000.

Rice, Gary R. "Devil Dan Sickles' Deadly Salients." In *America's Civil War*, Vol. 11, No. 5. Leesburg: Primedia, Nov. 1998, 38–45.

Rusling, James F. *Men and Things I Saw in Civil War Days*. New York: Eaton and Mains, 1899.

Sassaman, R. "The Washington Tragedy." *American History*, Oct. 1998, 44–52.

Sears, Stephen. *Chancellorsville*. New York: Houghton Mifflin, 1996.

Sickles, Daniel Edgar. *Address Delivered in Boston Before the Hooker Association of Massachusetts*. Norwood, MA: Norwood, 1910.

Sifakis, S. *Who Was Who in the Civil War*. New York: Facts on File, 1988.

Stackpole, E.J. *From Cedar Mountain to Antietam: August–September, 1862*. Harrisburg: Stackpole, 1959.

Stevens, Captain C.A. *Berdan's U.S. Sharpshooter*. St. Paul: Pric-McGill, 1892.

Street, Owen. *The Young Patriot: A Memorial of James Hall*. Massachusetts Sabbath School Society, 1862.

Swanberg, W.A. *Sickles the Incredible*. Gettysburg, PA: Stan Clark, 1956.

Swinton, William. *Campaigns of the Army of the Potomac*. New York: Scribner's, 1882.

Tagg, L. *The Generals of Gettysburg: The Leaders of America's Greatest Battle*. Cambridge: Da Capo, 2003.

Tocin, Kerry R. "To Hell and Back: Companies D, E, and H; 72nd New York Volunteers Dunkirk, New York (1861–1864)." In *Niagara Frontier*, Winter 1974, 80–95.

Twichell, J.H., chaplain of the Second Excelsior. "Oration at Dedication of Excelsior Brigade Monument at Gettysburg, July 2, 1888." In *New York at Gettysburg*. Albany, NY: J.B. Lyon, 1900.

Van Santvoord, C. *The One Hundred and Twentieth Regiment NYS Volunteers in the Civil War*. Originally published in 1894. Saugerties, NY: Hope Farm, 1997.

The War of the Rebellion: A Compilation of the Official Records of the Union and Confederate Armies. Washington, DC: U.S. Government Printing Office, 1880–1901.

Warner, E.J. *Generals in Blue: Lives of the Union Commanders*. Baton Rouge: Louisiana State University Press, 1964.

Wert, Jeffry D. *The Sword of Lincoln*. New York: Simon & Schuster, 2005.

Wiley, B.I. *The Life of Billy Yank*. Baton Rouge: Louisiana State University Press, 1952.

Web Sites

The American Civil War. www.mycivilwar.com.

American Civil War Research Database, 72nd New York Volunteer Infantry. http://www.civilwardata.com.

Biographical Directory of the United States Congress. http://bioguide.congress.gov.

Civil War in the East. http://www.civilwarintheeast.com.

Civil War Preservation Trust. *Battlefields: Chantilly*. http://www.civilwar.org/battlefields/chantilly.html.

Delaware County: New York Genealogy and History Site. http://www.dcnyhistory.org/milindexlindar.html.

Morss, Robert. *Hooker's Brigade*. 2009. http://genealogy.morssweb.com/.

National Park Service. www.nps.gov/frsp/mine.htm.

New York State Military Museum and Veterans Research Center. http://dmna.ny.gov/historic/mil-hist.htm.

Seventy-second Regiment N.Y. Vol. Inf., Civil War Newspaper Clippings, Unit History Project, New York State Military Museum. http://dmna.ny.gov/historic/reghist/civil/infantry/72ndInf/72ndInfCWN.htm.

"Some Lesser Known Hungarians of the American Civil

War." *Vasvary Collection Newsletter.* http://www.sk-szeged.hu/statikus_html/vasvary/newsletter/05jun/civil_war.html.

The Third Excelsior Association. http://www.72ndnewyork.org.

Letters and Other Collections

Bailey, George. War Time Letters of George Bailey, Company H, 72nd NYSV. Unpublished. Courtesy of the Gowanda Area Historical Society.

Dean, James. War Time Letters of James Dean, Company C, 72nd NYSV. Unpublished. Courtesy of Diana Firth.

Cody, Donald, and Richard Landwehrle. "John S. Austin in Pre-War New York." Letter to Rick Barram of Austin family history.

Compiled Military Service File: Issac L. Chadwick, Company C, 72nd New York. National Archives.

Compiled Military Service File: John Leonard, Company F, 72nd New York. National Archives.

Compiled Military Service File: John S. Austin, Company K, 72nd New York. National Archives.

Compiled Military Service File: John S. Mann, Company C, 72nd New York. National Archives.

Compiled Military Service File: Nathan McCrea, Company F, 72nd New York. National Archives.

Compiled Military Service File: Nelson Taylor, 72nd New York. National Archives.

Compiled Military Service File: William O. Steven, Company D, 72nd New York. National Archives.

Grand Army of the Republic records, 70th NYV. New York State Library, Preservation Unit.

Grand Army of the Republic records, 72nd NYV. New York State Library, Preservation Unit.

Historical Data Systems, Kingston, MA. Various analyses of regimental enrollment and casualties.

Mount Sinai Hospital. *1852–2002 Sesquicentennial Pamphlet.*

O'Hagan, Fr. Joseph. "Woodstock Letters VIII, 1879." In *Civil War History*, vol. 6, ed. James I. Robertson, 402–409. Iowa City: University of Iowa Press, 1960.

Ostre, Peter. HCWRTColl-GACColl (Enlisted man's letters, October 30, 1862–June 1, 1864). Military History Institute, Carlisle, PA.

Stoddard, Hiram. War Time Letters of Hiram Stoddard, Company I, 72nd NYSV. Unpublished. Courtesy of the Gowanda Area Historical Society.

The Third Excelsior Association Historical Collection: Colusa Cemetery Dedication Program, September 2010. Included in a packet on John C. Willing presented to the Third Excelsior Association. Compiled by Preservation Committee chairman David Resh.

Twichell, Joseph Hopkins. Joseph Hopkins Twichell Papers. Yale Collection of American Literature, Beinecke Rare Book and Manuscript Library, Yale University, New Haven, Connecticut.

Newspapers

The Bloomville Mirror
The Fredonia Censor
The Jamestown Journal
The New York Times

Index

Abell, Caspar 12, 14, 24, 26, 42, 123, 130–131, 135, 207–208, 231, 257
Abercrombie, John J. 65–67, 81
Alabama Regiments 133
Alexandria, Va. 21, 88–89, 101–102, 104, 105, 113, 132
Anderson, James 126, 190, 244
Anderson, Patrick 135, 215, 238, 250, 253, 258, 264
Anderson, Richard H. 68–69, 147
Andrews, C.H. 155–158
Appomattox River, Va. 198
Aquia Creek, Va. 46, 88
Auldridge, Thomas 126, 222

Bacon, Milton S. 190, 194, 250
Bailey, George 106, 117–118, 238, 276
Bailey, Samuel 126, 190, 202, 215, 218, 257, 264, 281
Baker, Fort 24, 26
Baltimore, Md. 17, 32, 35, 152, 159, 175
Barksdale, William 144, 146
Barlow, Fancis 195
Barrett, Patrick 4, 12, 62, 66, 200
Bates, Van Buren 78
Bermuda Hundred, Va. 176, 197
Berry, Hiram G. 122, 125, 127, 131
Beverly Ford, Va. 159
Big Bethel 50
Birney, David 109, 120, 139, 140, 142–144, 146–147, 172, 186–189, 191–193, 195–196
Black Horse Tavern 138
Bliss, Collins 13, 15, 66
Bliss, Harmon 13, 15, 53, 66, 70, 80–82, 84, 88, 90–91, 93–98, 100–101, 126, 129, 130, 135, 238, 250–251
The Bloomville Mirror 9
Blue Ridge Mountains 88, 153, 154, 162
Bookhout, Talmon 47, 48, 265
Bottom's Bridge, Va. 67–68, 70, 73
Bourke, Dan 158, 238

Bowen, James 79, 232
Boyden, Martin 3, 4, 15, 17, 32–33, 53, 62, 232
Boydton Plank Road, Va. 201
Brackett's Ford, Va. 78
Brandy Station, Va. 134, 166–167, 172, 174, 178, 198, 199
Brewster, William R. 23, 59, 130, 132, 140, 142, 146–148, 150, 152, 157–159, 161, 168–170, 174–177, 179, 181, 186
Bristoe Station, Va. 88–92, 94–95, 104, 163, 164, 166
Broad Run, Va. 88, 94
Brooks, William 82, 129, 221–222, 231, 232, 244, 247
Brown, Henri Le Fevre 14, 34, 46, 144, 148, 158, 160, 164, 178, 181–182, 187, 194–195, 197–198, 200, 202, 208, 252
Brown, James 3, 12, 18, 37, 73, 215–216, 221
Budd's Ferry, Md. 28–30, 33, 36, 45
Bull Run, Va. 88, 95, 98; Battle of First 14–16, 18, 20, 24, 29, 50, 95, 132; Battle of Second 87, 95, 100, 103, 111, 132, 136, 161, 163
Burling, George C. 138–139, 142, 157
Burns, Michael 181–182
Burns, William 94
Burnside, Ambrose 105–110, 114–115, 117, 134, 181, 186, 194
Burr, Ovett 194–195, 238
Burtis, Charles 47–48, 59
Butler, Benjamin 175–176, 197

Caldwell, John C. 139–140
Camden, N.J. 17
Camp Caldwell 20, 23, 28, 35, 36
Camp Marsh 18, 20
Camp Scott 8–11, 13, 15, 22
Carr, Joseph 76, 80, 92–94, 96, 107–109, 122–123, 125, 127, 135, 140, 142–143, 147–148, 150–151, 157, 186, 169
Carroll, Thomas 40, 271
Casey, Silas 69–70, 73

Catlett's Station, Va. 87–88, 90–91, 165
Cedarville, Md. 25
Centerville, Va. 95, 98–100, 103, 136, 163, 165
Chadwick, Issac 13, 15, 41, 43, 49–50, 67, 70, 76–78, 81, 83, 85, 101–102, 106, 114, 205, 222–223
Chancellorsville, Va. 1, 39, 117, 119, 128–135, 139–140, 144, 152–153, 179–180, 204–205
Chantilly, Va. 100
Charles City Court House, Va. 197
Charles County, Md. 28
Chautauqua County, N.Y. 52, 61, 66, 90, 123, 117, 178, 200, 210, 204
Chenango County, N.Y. 4, 38
Chesterfield Bridge, Va. (Battle of N. Anna River) 189, 191–194
Chickahominy River, Va. 67–68, 194, 197
Chopawamsic Creek, Md. 33
City Point, Va. 200
Clark, Thomas 66, 208, 222, 232–233, 247, 270–271
Cold Harbor, Va. 195–197
Companies of 72nd New York: A 11–12, 62, 85, 95, 117, 210, 214; B 12, 14, 20, 24, 29, 37–38, 46, 58–59, 73, 81, 85, 94, 113, 144, 148, 156, 158, 165, 170, 173, 178–179, 181, 186, 196, 202, 208; C 11, 13–14, 41, 49, 85, 102, 106, 114, 116, 118, 125, 131, 135, 137, 144, 147, 152, 165, 196, 205, 222; D 11, 15–16, 24, 26, 36, 42–44, 52, 59, 82, 123, 128, 131, 135, 152, 231; E 12, 32–33, 39, 62, 66, 72, 79, 82, 84, 118, 148, 159, 194, 204, 237; F 12, 78, 115, 131, 153, 165, 190, 203, 244; G 13, 60, 80, 88, 131, 135, 190, 203, 250; H 13, 30, 32, 72, 77, 81–82, 85, 106, 126, 175, 180, 197, 204, 258; I 12, 15, 19, 38, 42, 45–47, 51, 53, 59, 75, 98, 100, 114, 190, 201, 264; K 40,

303

41, 66, 102, 126, 131, 135, 139, 270; L 36, 45, 276
Connell, Patrick 79, 239
Cormack, James 36, 276
Couch, Darius N. 73, 80–81
Coyne, John 60
Culpepper Court House, Va. 160, 163

Daly, Michael (also Daily) 32, 239
Davis, Jefferson 38, 40
Dean, James 102–104, 106, 109, 116, 118–120, 122–125, 127, 129, 131, 133–135, 138, 143–144, 146–149, 151, 153–160, 163–167, 169–170, 173–175, 178, 186–187, 190–191, 199, 203–205, 224
Delaware County, N.Y. 9, 18, 42
Delhi, N.Y. 4, 9, 11–12, 47, 61, 201, 264
Dickenson, Hartwell 56, 209
Doles, George 184
Donaldson, Walter A. 71
Dowdall's Tavern, Va. 128
Doyle, Steven M. 30, 32, 43, 81–82, 200, 207, 246, 258
Dunkirk, N.Y. 3–4, 11–12, 14, 17, 30, 32, 61–62, 66–67, 115, 129–130, 152, 200, 208, 231
Dunkirk Journal 30
Duyrea, Joseph T. Rev. 179
Dwight, Charles 96–97
Dwight, William 58, 60, 62

Early, Jubal 60, 168
Egan, Thomas 189
XVIII Corps, U.S. 197–198
Ellery Center, N.Y. 3
Ellis, Harrison 129, 231, 258, 266, 270
Elm City, Steamer 47–51
Ely Ford, Va. 179
Emmitsburg, Md. 137–138
Emmitsburg Road (Gettysburg) 138–140, 142–143, 146, 148–149, 159
Erie, Lake 1, 16, 49
Ewell, Richard 90–91, 93–94, 149, 155, 158, 162, 164–165, 167, 179–180, 184, 186, 188–189
Excelsior Brigade (also Sickles' Brigade) 1–2, 4, 7–11, 13–16, 18–20, 23–24, 26, 28, 30, 34, 36, 40, 43, 47–49, 51, 53, 60, 62–65, 71, 75–77, 79–80, 83–84, 86, 90, 92, 96, 99, 101–104, 107–110, 114, 119, 123–124, 129–132, 138, 140, 143, 146–150, 152, 155–156, 158, 160–161, 164, 172, 174, 176, 179, 181–183, 185, 189, 197, 207

Fair Oaks Station, Va. 70
Fairfax Station, Va. 105, 163–164
Fairman, James 22–23
Falmouth, Va. 105–107, 113–115, 130–131, 133–135, 154, 176
Farnum, Egbert 128, 157–158, 161, 169
Fenton, Reuben 21–22
V Corps, U.S. 78–80, 105, 108, 119–120, 132, 142, 149, 152, 154, 161, 167–168, 180, 183–184, 189, 191–192
I Corps, C.S.A. 88, 95, 106, 142, 181
I Corps, U.S. 102, 105, 108, 118, 136, 138, 167, 177, 205
Fisher, Humphrey 40, 272
Florida, 8th Regiment 148, 159
Fogarty (also Forgerty), James 66, 250, 264, 266
Forbes, David 4, 11, 13
Ford, Henry 59, 265
Fort Baker 24, 26
Fort Lyon 101, 103
Fort Magruder 57–58, 60–61, 63, 87
Fort Wagner 24, 26
Fortress Monroe 49, 50, 200
Foss, Charles 131–136–137, 147, 150, 152, 222, 233
IV Corps, U.S. 57, 68–69, 77
Fox, William 1, 143, 206
Franklin, William 78, 105, 108, 114
Frayser's Farm, Va. 79
Fredericksburg, Va. 16, 88, 100, 105–109, 111, 113–115, 119, 122, 131–132, 134, 152, 172, 175, 203, 205
Fredonia Censor 10, 30, 53, 66–67
Freeman's Ford, Va. 163
Freestone Point, Md. 33
French, William 152, 154–156, 163, 167–172, 177–178
Front Royal, Va. 154–155, 158
Fry, Thomas 59, 208, 281

Gainesville, Va. 91, 163
Gardner, Anthony 118, 225
Georgia Regiments: 3rd 155–156; 22nd 155; 48th 155; 60th 95
Germanna Ford, Va. 167, 179
Germantown, Va. 100
Girardey, Victor 156
Glendale, Va. 78–79, 83–84
Good Hope Heights, Md. 20–21
Good Hope Tavern, Md. 24, 26
Gould, Charles 12, 19, 38, 44–45, 107, 266
Graham, Charles 35–36, 48, 65, 68, 140, 142, 144, 146, 150
Graham, John 26, 45, 276, 278
Grand Army of the Republic (GAR) 201, 203
Grant, Ulysses S. 12, 29, 177–179, 181–189, 191–197, 204
Grecheneck, George 11–12, 51, 85, 210–211

Grossinger, Charles 11–12, 85, 21–211, 256
Grover, Curvier 56–58, 63, 68, 76, 78–80, 92–94, 96, 100
Groveton, Va. 95

Haight, John 60, 208, 253
Hall, George B. 30, 41, 71, 76, 102, 107–110, 113
Hall, James 38, 43, 50, 54, 73, 81–82, 208, 217
Hamilton, Charles S. 53
Hancock, Winfield S. 60–62, 64, 143–144, 147–148, 178–181, 183, 185, 187–189, 191–195, 198
Hankin, George 159, 217
Hanovertown, Va. 194
Harpers Ferry 22, 152, 154
Harrison's Landing, Va. 78–79, 83–88, 101
Hatcher's Run, Va. 201
Hazel Grove, Va. 128–140
Healy, Luke 131, 136, 244, 246, 250
Heintzelman, Samuel P. 52–53, 58, 62, 64, 68, 70–76, 78, 82–83, 87–88, 96, 99, 102–103
Henagan, John 189, 191, 194
Heyl, Henry 180, 260
Higler, John 159, 260
Hill, A.P. 78, 123, 147, 162–163, 179, 181
Hill, D.H. 68
Hinman, Hugh 12, 44, 90, 207, 231, 233–234, 256
Hoffman, Charles 117, 226
Holburton, Wakeman (also Holberton) 84, 222, 226, 238, 271
Holl, William 66, 270–271, 273
Holmes, John W. (also John H.) 12, 82, 126, 222, 236, 244, 258
Holt, Thomas 128, 143
Homer, Elliott 159, 218
Hooker, Joseph 28–30, 33–38, 40–41, 45–48, 52–53, 56–60, 62–68, 70, 72–73, 75–80, 82–84, 86–100, 102, 105, 108, 113, 115–116, 118–120, 122, 128–135, 137, 152, 178, 204
Horan, Thomas 148, 159, 208, 241
Howard, John 115, 231, 234, 236, 244, 248
Howard, Luther 58–59, 148, 218
Howard, Oliver O. 119–120, 138, 140, 164
Huger, Benjamin 69
Humphreys, Andrew A. 132, 138–140, 142–144, 146–150, 152
Huttmann, Berend 85, 102, 212, 222, 244, 270
Hydorn, Charles 125, 129, 222, 258, 263

Indiana Regiments 37, 95; 3rd Cavalry 29

Index

Irwin, Charles Dr. 17, 65, 73, 129, 208

Jacob's Ford, Va. 167
James River, Va. 78–79, 83, 197–198, 200
Jamestown, N.Y. 3, 10, 12, 17, 21, 61–62, 66, 73, 130, 215
Jamestown Journal 126, 130, 178, 202
Johnson, Bradley T. 96
Johnson, Robert 4, 9, 12–13, 15, 45–46, 201, 264, 267
Johnston, Joseph 56–58, 63, 65–70, 74
Jones, Ensign 202, 261
Jones, Lucius 32, 72, 77, 126, 175, 179, 197–200, 204, 261

Kay, William J. 94
Kearney, Philip 58, 60, 72, 76–77, 79–80, 87, 91–92, 97, 100–101, 164, 178
Kershaw, Joseph 142–143
Kettle Run, Va. 88, 90–93, 94, 99, 126, 136, 165
Key, Phillip Barton 5
Keyes, Erasmus D. 68
Kilpatrick, Judson 162
King, Rufus 95
Klingle, Daniel 142–143, 150

Lee, Robert E. 74, 80, 82–85, 88, 91, 98, 101–102, 105–107, 114, 119–120, 123, 130, 134–135, 138, 149, 151–155, 158–168, 170, 172–173, 176–180, 182–189, 191–197, 201
Leonard, John 12, 70, 78, 102, 119, 122, 126–127, 129–131, 133, 135, 146–148, 152–158, 161–165, 169–170, 176–177, 181, 183, 185–187, 189, 193–195, 197–198, 205, 207, 231, 234, 244, 247
Lincoln, Abraham 3–5, 7–8, 12, 18, 20, 37, 44–46, 51, 53, 65, 68, 86, 101, 103, 105–106, 110, 115, 117–118, 129, 133–134, 137, 151, 153, 159, 162, 165, 174
Lindsey (also Lindsley), Richard 118, 241
Liverpool Point, Md. 34, 43, 45–47
Lockwood, Abram 146
Loeb, Daniel 4, 32, 212, 258, 262, 264, 270
Longstreet, James 58, 64, 68–70, 78, 88, 91, 95–96, 98, 106, 142, 181, 206
Louisiana troops 92–93
Lovell, William H. 158–159, 218
Lowe, Thaddeus 36
Lyon, Fort 101, 103
Lyon, John M. 181, 218

Magruder, John 51, 78
Magruder, Fort 57–58, 60–61, 63, 87
Malvern Hill, Va. 79–80, 82–85, 101, 106, 205
Manassas Gap, Va. 154–155, 158, 173
Manassas Junction, Va. 88–89, 91, 94–95, 103–104, 136, 162–163, 165
Mann, John S. 66, 135, 137, 139, 143, 147, 203, 210, 222, 231, 244, 247
Maryland troops 125, 170
Mason, Alfred 12, 14, 66, 215, 219
Massachusetts troops 7, 18, 38, 104; 1st 29, 79, 122, 123; 11th 29, 58, 73, 79, 122, 179; 16th 79, 122, 143
Mathias Point, Md. 26, 35
Mattawoman Creek, Md. 36
Maxwell, Robert 38, 267
McAllister, Robert 169, 185
McCall, George 79
McClellan, George 29–30, 34–38, 45–46, 49–51, 53, 56–57, 61–69, 72–75, 77–79, 82–86, 88, 101, 105–106, 115, 117, 132, 134, 197, 201
McConnell, William 12, 165, 222, 227, 238–239, 244, 258, 266
McDonald, Michael 72, 84, 238, 270
McDonough, Henry J. 165, 170–171, 210, 217, 231, 248
McDowell, Irwin 65, 68, 86
McGinnes (McGinnis?), William 67, 115, 250, 253, 262, 264
McKinley, John 131, 248, 270
McKinstry, Arthur 10, 16–17, 19–22, 24, 26, 32, 34, 36–38, 40–42, 44, 46, 49–50, 53, 59, 66–67, 235
McLaws, Lafayette 143
Meade, George 108, 137–140, 142, 149, 151–155, 158–160, 162–168, 170–172, 176–177, 179, 204, 206
Meehan, Dennis 7
Merrell (also Merrill), Emerson 4, 15, 18, 20–21, 28, 34, 38, 45, 53, 61, 63, 67, 70, 73, 75, 78, 81, 83–85, 95–96, 99–100, 103–106, 111, 113–117, 125, 129, 204, 205, 268
USS *Merrimac* 50–51
Mine Run, Va. 170–172, 177
Minnesota, 1st Regiment 148
USS *Monitor* 50–51
Monocacy River 136
Morgan, Gov. Edwin 7, 8, 36–37, 46, 50
Moriarity, John 23
Morris, William 176
Moses, Israel 17, 24, 47, 54–59, 65, 84, 88, 102, 139, 202, 207, 270, 281
Mott, Gersham 64, 122–123, 127, 161, 179, 181, 183–186
Mule Shoe (Battle of Spotsylvania) 183–188
Mulholland, St. Clair A. 143

Nagle, James 96
New Jersey troops: 2nd Artillery 80; 5th 64, 70, 73, 92; 6th 70, 73, 92; 7th 76, 92, 94, 114, 127; 8th 36, 58, 92–93; Jersey Blues 36, 62, 58, 63, 96, 103, 107, 122, 140, 179
New York City, N.Y. 1, 5, 7, 8, 11–13, 16, 18, 36, 41, 49, 54, 60–61, 72, 76, 101–102, 126, 132, 135, 139, 178–179, 200, 205, 210, 222, 270
New York Herald 18
New York Naval Yard 18
New York Regiments: 2nd 92–93; 40th 175; 50th N.Y. Engineers 107; 68th 4, 11–12, 67; 69th Militia 20; 70th (First Excelsior Regiment) 15, 36, 41, 48, 58–60, 62, 65, 67–68, 71, 78, 80–81, 93–94, 96–97, 104, 123, 128, 143, 148, 150, 157–158, 161, 163, 169, 175, 185; 71st (Second Excelsior Regiment) 41, 57, 63, 71, 73, 77, 79, 96–98, 102, 104, 107, 113, 118, 123, 140, 143, 146, 169–170, 175, 189; 73rd (Fourth Excelsior Regiment, Second Fire Zouaves) 18, 22–23, 47, 55–60, 71, 80, 94, 96, 102, 104, 122–123, 126–127, 130, 132, 142–144, 150, 152, 175, 179, 181, 185, 201, 204, 74th (Fifth Excelsior Regiment) 9, 19, 22, 35–36, 47, 58–59, 67, 71, 82, 97, 104, 118, 123, 125, 143, 150, 156, 158, 175; 120th 102, 104, 108, 110, 123, 143, 146–147, 150, 155, 158, 162, 175, 179, 193, 199–201, 203–204; 163rd 175
New York Times 23, 26, 67, 174
IX Corps, U.S. 105, 108, 119
North Anna River, Va. 188–189, 191–194, 198
North Carolina, 23rd Regiment 167
Norton, Levi Chaplain 17, 66, 208, 281–282

O'Hagan, Joseph Father 18–19, 118
Old Wilderness Church 128
O'Neill, William 12, 238, 242–243, 262
Orange and Alexandria Railroad 87–88, 103, 105, 136, 162–165
Orange-Fredericksburg Turnpike 180–181

Orange Plank Road 122, 167, 181
Orange Turnpike 168, 170
Ox Ford, Va. 193

Pamunkey River, Va. 194
Parker, David 3–4, 14–18, 21, 32, 34–35, 52–53, 59, 61–62, 65, 74, 84, 115, 204, 235, 264
Patterson, Francis 56, 58, 68, 84, 103–104, 114
Peach Orchard (Gettysburg) 140, 144
Pender, William 123, 125
Pennock, Horatio 85, 210, 222, 228
Pennsylvania troops: 26th 29, 58, 122–123, 168; 31st 81; 84th 169, 179; 115th 122, 125; 116th 143
Penny, Robert 38, 268
Pickett, George 149
Pierce, Byron 189–190
Piscataway, Md. 26, 30, 41
Platte, Frederick 159, 242
Pleasonton, Alfred 134
Pope, John 85–91, 94–96, 98–101, 106, 136, 161–162, 165
Poplar Hill, Va. 68
Port Royal, Va. 49
Port Tobacco, Md. 26, 49
Porter, Fitz John 53, 80
Posey, Timothy and family 33–34, 38
Post, William 43, 212, 216, 227, 231, 235, 248, 250
Potomac Flotilla 34–35, 46
Potomac River 20, 24, 26–30, 32–33, 36, 44–45, 49, 88, 136, 152–154
Potter, H.L. 24–26, 33, 41, 143, 150
Prince, Henry 152, 156–158, 160–162, 166, 168–173, 178
Purdy, Lovell 156, 158

Quantico Creek, Md. 33

Raccoon Ford Road, Va. 168
Ramsey, John 73, 183–185
Rapidan River 88, 91, 161–162, 166–167, 172, 174, 176, 178–179
Rappahannock River 104–105, 107–108, 110, 114, 116, 119, 134, 158–160, 162–166
Rappahannock Station 135
Revere, Joseph Warren 107, 109, 113–114, 122–123, 125, 127–132
Reynolds, John 98, 138
Richmond, Va. 13, 49–51, 63, 65, 67–68, 70, 72–75, 77–78, 83–84, 86, 88, 105, 115, 119, 134, 176, 178, 188, 191, 193–195, 197–198
Robertson's Tavern, Va. 167–168, 170–172
Rodes, Robert 155, 157–158, 168

Roper, Thomas 102, 114, 229
Rouse, John 32, 242
Russell, George W. 102, 114, 230

Sanford (also Sandford), John 12–13, 45, 85, 94, 130, 211, 215, 248, 264, 269
Satellite (gunboat) 46
Savage Station, Va. 78
Scott, Winfield 29, 34
II Corps, C.S. 88, 95, 98, 122, 167, 180, 186, 188
II Corps, U.S. 70–71, 78, 105, 108, 118–119, 123, 127, 139–140, 142–144, 147–149, 152, 154, 163, 168, 171, 176–181, 183, 185–189, 192, 195, 197–198
Second Fire Zouaves *see* 73rd N.Y., Fourth Excelsior Regiment
Secretary (locomotive) 89
Sedgwick, John 79, 82, 84, 131, 152, 171–172, 176, 178, 180, 183
Seven Pines, Va. 68, 70–72, 74–75, 77
72nd N.Y.S.V. Veteran's Association
Shelly, George 53, 42, 44, 236
Sickles, Daniel 1, 4–5, 7–11, 13–20, 22–24, 26–27, 30, 33, 35, 36–37, 40–41, 45–48, 50, 53, 65–68, 70–73, 76–81, 83–86, 88, 94, 101–104, 107–110, 113–115, 118, 120, 122–123, 125, 127–129, 131–132, 134, 137–137, 140, 142–144, 146, 149, 151–152, 164, 200, 206
Sickles, Teresa 5
Sickles' Brigade *see* Excelsior Brigade
Sigel, Franz 95–96
Sinfield, Sarah 204
Sinfield (also Senfield), William 204, 243
VI Corps, U.S. 78, 80, 105, 108, 131, 167, 171, 177, 179–180, 183
Slater, Bernard P. 159, 220
Smith, Gustavus W. 70
Smith, Martin 191
Smith, T.C.H. 91
Smith, William 57–58, 60
Sneden, Robert Knox 82, 86
Spinola, Fancis B. 152, 156–158
Spotsylvania Court House 182–183, 185, 187–189, 191, 193
Stafford Court House 47
Stanton, Edwin 5, 103, 132, 137
Stanton, Warren 115, 210, 243, 258, 263
Starke, William E. 97
Staten Island, N.Y. 8–10, 12, 14–16, 19, 51, 62, 85, 117, 152, 190, 204
Stevens, Frank G. 23, 209
Stevens, William O. 3, 4, 11, 14–15, 17–18, 24, 32, 58–59, 62, 73, 79–80, 88, 102–105, 109, 116–

118, 120, 122–123, 125–126, 128–131, 139, 152, 200, 205, 207, 231, 236, 247, 270
Stoddard, Hiram 19, 70, 72, 83–84, 87, 96, 98, 100, 113, 115, 116, 120, 124–126, 143, 154, 158–161, 164, 166, 179, 187, 191–192, 194, 196, 198, 203, 220
Stoneman, George 56–57, 102, 110
Street, Owen 43
Stuart, Jeb 90, 134, 162
Sumner, Edwin 57–58, 60, 62, 70, 78–79, 82, 105–107, 119,
Sykes, George 168

Tate, George 128, 236
Taylor, Henry B. 24, 221
Taylor, Nelson 9–17, 19, 21–22, 24, 30, 32, 32–34, 36, 40–43, 46–51, 53, 55, 57–60, 62, 63, 65–66, 68, 71–73, 76–77, 79–82, 84–86, 88, 90–97, 102, 130, 139, 205, 207, 282
III Corps, C.S. 147, 167, 181
III Corps, U.S. 2, 52–53, 62, 64, 68–69, 73, 75–78, 80, 86–89, 91, 96, 99–102, 107–108, 118–120, 123, 129, 131–132, 137–140, 142–144, 146, 148–149, 151–152, 154–156, 158, 160, 163–164, 166–168, 170–172, 176–179, 203, 206
Toomey, William 12, 226, 237–238, 243
Totopotomoy Creek, Va. 194–195
Tremain, Henry 96–97, 146
Trostle Farm 142–144
Twichell, Joseph 17, 30, 63, 75, 77, 84, 86, 93, 103–104, 106–107, 109, 113–114, 118, 135–137, 160, 162–164, 166, 169–170, 172, 179, 184, 206

Union Mills, Va. 163
United States Ford, Va. 119, 129
United States Regiments: 1st Artillery 29; 1st Sharpshooters 139–140; 4th Artillery 169; 10th Infantry 56
Upper Marlborough, Md. 25
Upton, Emory 184–186

Vanderbilt (steamer) 87–88
Vermont, 13th Regiment 148
CSS *Virginia* 50
Virginia Central Railroad 191
Virginia Regiments: 21st 97; 42nd 96; 56th 185

Wagner, Fort 24, 26
Walker, E.J. 155
Wallace, George W. 84, 227, 238, 244
Wapping Heights 155–156, 158, 170

Index

Warrenton Junction, Va. 88, 90–91, 95, 103–105, 166
Warwick River, Va. 50
Washington D.C. 5, 7, 14–21, 23–24, 26–30, 32–33, 35, 38, 41, 43, 46–49, 65, 83–84, 86, 88–89, 100–102, 105–106, 114–115, 118, 133–134, 136–137, 149, 151, 153, 160, 162–164, 176–178, 188, 200–201, 203–204
Weldon Railroad 199
Westbrook, Cornelius 123
Westfield, N.Y. 61, 250
Wheeler, William E. 131, 135, 215–216, 231, 244, 250, 257

Whipple, Amiel 122, 127, 131
White Oak Swamp, Va. 78
Whiting, W.H.C. 68–70
Wilcox Landing, Va. 197
Wilder, Lorey 4, 15, 20, 53, 61, 269
The Wilderness 179–180, 182, 186, 193, 202
Wiley, William 5, 7, 14, 20
Willard, Darwin 12, 37, 43, 46, 59, 62, 66, 215, 221, 269
Williamsburg, Va. 1, 11, 54, 56, 58, 60–68, 83, 85–87, 115, 132
Williamson, R.S. 28, 33
Williamsport, Pa. 152–154

Willing, John C. 203, 258
Winters, Hugh J. 12, 84, 264, 266, 270
Worsham, John 97
Wriborg, Claus 52, 59, 61–62, 237

Yates, Henry 126, 202, 207, 221, 231, 247, 250
Yorktown, Va. 50–54, 56–57, 63, 65, 75, 86–88, 100, 102
Young, Charles 93–94, 96
Young, James 181–182, 208, 222

Zouave 18, 22–24, 26, 47, 60, 67, 179

www.ingramcontent.com/pod-product-compliance
Lightning Source LLC
Chambersburg PA
CBHW081540300426
44116CB00015B/2697